WORLD POLICE
ENCYCLOPEDIA

BOARD OF EDITORS & ASSOCIATE EDITORS

Samuel Bwana
Senior Research and Information Manager
Kenya Anti-Corruption Commission
Kenya National Police
Nairobi, Kenya

Mark Ming-Chwang Chen
Professor
Department of Border Police
Central Police University
Kwei-Shan, Taiwan

Lucia Dammert
Researcher
Editor
Police Practice and Research: An International Journal
Latin American Faculty of Social Science (FLACSO)
Santiago, Chile

Mintie Das
WPE Project Assistant to the Editor-in-Chief
International Police Executive Symposium (IPES)
South Burlington, Vermont, USA

Ramesh Deosaran
Professor of Criminology
and Social Psychology, and Director
Centre for Criminology and Criminal Justice
Faculty of Social Sciences
The University of the West Indies
St. Augustine, Trinidad and Tobago

Robert F. J. Harnischmacher
Editor-in-Chief Polizeiforum
Lecturer, Department of Criminology
Criminal Politics and Police Sciences
Faculty of Law
Ruhr-University
Bochum, Germany

Peter Hobbing
Associate Fellow
Centre for European Policy Studies (CEPS)
Brussels, Belgium

Peter Johnstone
Associate Dean
College of Human Ecology
East Carolina University
Greenville, North Carolina, USA

Želimir Kešetović
Associate Professor of Crisis Management
Faculty of Civil Defense
University of Belgrade, Serbia

Marke Leong
University of New England
Armidale, NSW, Australia

Colleen Lewis
Associate Professor of Criminal Justice and Criminology
Faculty of Arts, and Co-Director of the Parliamentary Studies Unit
Monash University
Melbourne, Australia

Paulo R. Lino
Guest Lecturer
Lutheran University of Brazil
Consultant to the Organization of American States
Director
International Police Executive Symposium (IPES)
Rio Grande, Brazil

Agbonkhese Shaka Moses
Department of Sociology
Ambrose Alli University
Ekpoma, Nigeria
Editor
Police Practice and Research: An International Journal
Ekpoma, Nigeria

William Mubanga
Former Lieutenant
Zambia Police Department
Lusaka, Zambia

Tonita Murray
Former Head of Canadian Police College
Police and Gender Advisor
Afghan Ministry of the Interior
Kabul, Afghanistan

John P. Mutonyi
Police Superintendent, Kenya
Department of Criminology
University of Leicester
Leicester, United Kingdom

Mike Rowe
Lecturer in Policing and Public Order Studies
Department of Criminology
University of Leicester
Leicester, United Kingdom

John Scott
Lecturer
School of Social Science
University of New England
Armidale, NSW, Australia

Jakkrit Singhsilarak
Police Colonel
Thai National Police
Bangkok, Thailand

Mark Ungar
Associate Professor
Brooklyn College
City University of New York
New York, New York, USA

Ernesto Lopez Portillo Vargas
President
Institute for Security and Democracy
Mexico City, Mexico

Arvind Verma
Associate Director of India Studies
Department of Criminal Justice
Indiana University
Bloomington, Indiana, USA

WORLD POLICE ENCYCLOPEDIA

Volume 2
L-Z
INDEX

Dilip K. Das

EDITOR

Michael J. Palmiotto

Managing Editor

Routledge
Taylor & Francis Group
New York   London

Published in 2006 by
Routledge
Taylor & Francis Group
270 Madison Avenue
New York, NY 10016

Published in Great Britain by
Routledge
Taylor & Francis Group
2 Park Square
Milton Park, Abingdon
Oxon OX14 4RN

Printed in the United States of America on acid-free paper
10 9 8 7 6 5 4 3 2 1

International Standard Book Number-10: 0-415-94250-0 (Hardcover)
International Standard Book Number-13: 978-0-415-94250-8 (Hardcover)
Library of Congress Card Number 2005044342

Library of Congress Cataloging-in-Publication Data

World police encyclopedia / Dilip K. Das, editor in chief, Michael J. Palmiotto, managing editor.
    p. cm.
    Includes bibliographical references and index.
    ISBN 0-415-94250-0 (set : alk. paper) -- ISBN 0-415-94251-9 (v. 1 : alk. paper) -- ISBN 0-415-94252-7 (v. 2. : alk. paper)
    1. Police--Encyclopedias. 2. Criminal justice, Administration of--Encyclopedias. 1. Das, Dilip K., 1941- II. Palmiotto, Michael.

HV7901.W64 2005
363.2'03--dc22
    2005044342

Taylor & Francis Group is the Academic Division of T&F Informa plc.

Visit the Taylor & Francis Web site at
http://www.taylorandfrancis.com

and the Routledge Web site at
http://www.routledge-ny.com

TABLE OF CONTENTS

INTRODUCTION

Policing is both a local and global activity, a practice within nations and a responsibility shared between them. It is thus the aim of the *World Police Encyclopedia* to present in one publication a comprehensive survey of policing around the world, providing the reader with rounded descriptions and keen analyses of national policing systems while placing each national system within an international policing perspective.

The *Encyclopedia* recognizes that every nation has a police system and no two police systems are the same. Every country polices its own territory with distinct methods and judicial procedures, with varying penalties and prison standards, and within unique cultural and historical contexts that apply specific pressures and pose specific challenges. Thus, the encyclopedia contains articles on each of the member nations of the United Nations as well as the non-member nation of Taiwan, covering the globe in two comprehensive volumes.

To enable the work to function systematically as a cross-cultural, global reference work, each article is also executed with a uniform design. Where possible, articles share the same structure and contain the same kinds of information, enabling readers to compare historical contexts; policing institutions; cultural, ethnic, and religious forces; and other demographic variables that contribute to the formation, shape, and dynamic of policing systems. Readers can research how various nations educate and train police, how they finance and administer police systems, what political oversight they exercise, and how they legitimize or ban practices such as the death penalty, life imprisonment, or public surveillance.

Critical to any reference work, especially one that seeks to offer a great diversity of information within a comparable format, a thorough analytical index is included. The index guides the reader to topics of interest wherever discussed within the work. It also encourages exploration of the contents so readers may discover new information and easily see connections that they otherwise may have overlooked.

A reference work of this kind also recognizes the changes in policing systems around the world and the growing need to understand them because local practices are taking on more and more global significance. With the accelerated expansion of communications, trade, and transnational political organizations, issues such as judicial, penal, and policing protocols, while locally administered, are increasingly subject to international review, praise, and critique. This encyclopedia will contribute to the reader's ability to evaluate these practices, where they have arisen, and the direction they are evolving.

With the globalization of organized criminal activities, the drug trade, illicit arms deals, prostitution, and terrorism, the need for countries to cooperate and coordinate their policing efforts has increased dramatically into the twenty-first century—a theme throughout the book. Indeed, international criminal activities have made international policing efforts a priority. Imperative and expensive, these efforts have entered the business of our daily lives as never before. However, the context and history of such efforts also demand our understanding. Hopefully, this encyclopedia will aid readers to an informed and balanced understanding of accomplishments and challenges involved in any policing effort.

Organization of the Book

There are 193 entries in *World Police Encyclopedia*. Given the range and scope of these entries, the following tools have been employed to ensure easy navigation of the volume and access to essential information:

- An alphabetical list of all entries;
- A comprehensive index; and
- A template format, applied to each entry.

Every entry in *World Police Encyclopedia* includes the following sub-headings, summarizing as much relevant information as is available for the particular nation in question:

Background Material
Each entry begins with a brief overview of that nation's history and current statistical information,

including population, ethnic composition of the population, and GDP per capita.

Contextual Features

In this section, the political structure of the government of the nation in question is discussed. Other information relevant to an understanding of the police of any given nation is also included in this section, including information on crime, the criminal justice system, and penal codes and prisons.

The primary section of each entry is titled **Police Profile**. This section is broken down further, under the following subheadings:

Background covers the history and development of the police system.

Demographics provides statistical information on the police force, including total number of members and the gender and ethnic composition of the police force.

Organizational Description describes who controls the police, ranks and hierarchy structure, special response units, and support services (as applicable).

Functions provides an overview of police powers in regard to various police functions, discussing administrative duties as well as criminal justice matters.

Training covers the requirements for joining the police force, including any special schooling.

Police Public Projects may cover crime prevention, traffic control, or school-based police outreach programs, if any such programs exist in the nation in question.

Police Use of Firearms describes laws and regulations relating to police firearm use and ownership.

Complaints and Discipline provides an overview of police accountability regarding citizen complaints, as well as police respect for human rights.

Terrorism describes any terrorist organizations that are active in the nation in question and police efforts to combat terrorism.

International Cooperation enumerates international assistance being provided to the police of the nation in question, exchange of officers among nations, if any, and any international policing efforts to which the police have contributed.

When applicable, entries also include a section on **Police Education, Research, and Publications**. This section provides an overview of:

- Institutions of higher education for the police;
- Leading researchers, authors, reporters, and columnists, with affiliations;
- The extent and sources of funding for police research, and areas of recent research;
- Leading police journals, magazines, and newsletters;
- Major police publications (books or reports);
- Police-related websites.

Each entry concludes with a **Bibliography** of relevant cited sources, as well as suggestions for further reading.

A Note on Coverage

Every attempt has been made to provide comprehensive coverage of policing practices in every nation. However, a number of factors have prevented equal coverage of all countries. Accessibility to reliable information varies widely from country to country, for a variety of reasons. Some nations do not make public statistical or demographic information regarding their national security forces. In the case of numerous countries, primarily several located in Africa, data relating to the police and policing activities is simply not consistently recorded. The editors of the *World Police Encyclopedia* have relied on 125 contributors and 25 associate editors, the vast majority of whom are either criminal justice scholars or working professionals in each of the countries or geographical regions addressed, to make every reasonable attempt to procure as much reliable and detailed information as possible. It is unfortunately the case that, in general, far more statistical data and information is available for Western nations, as opposed to less developed and developing nations. It is the editors' hope that any perceived lack of data in the *Encyclopedia* will inspire further archival work and research among scholars and police professionals to ensure access to police-related information for every interested party in every nation.

LIST OF CONTRIBUTORS

Felipe Abbott. University of Chile, Santiago, Chile.

Pavel Abraham. Professor, President, Romanian Antidrug Agency, Bucharest, Romania.

Marcelo F. Aebi. University of Lausanne, Lausanne, Switzerland; Autonomous University of Barcelona, Barcelona, Spain.

Biko Agozino. Assistant Professor, Department of Social and Behavioural Sciences, Cheyney University of Pennsylvania, Cheyney, Pennsylvania, USA.

Maria Pia Scarfo Allocca. Specialist in Central America, New York, New York, USA.

Oyesoji Aremu. Department of Guidance and Counselling, University of Ibadan, Ibadan, Nigeria.

Ahmet Hamdi Aydin. Lecturer, Kahramanmaras S. University, Kahramanmaras, Turkey.

David Baker. Head of Criminal Justice and Criminology, Monash University, Melbourne, Australia.

Oleg Balan. Director of Public Administration Department, Academy of Public Administration, Chisinau, Moldova.

Adrian Beck. Senior Lecturer, Scarman Centre, University of Leicester, Leicester, United Kingdom.

G.Q. Billings. Central Missouri State University, Missouri State Highway Patrol, Warrensburg, Missouri, USA.

Christopher Birkbeck. Professor of Criminology, University of Los Andes, Merida, Venezuela.

Ivor Blake. Divisional Commander, Royal Saint Christopher & Nevis Police Force, Basseterre, Nevis.

József Boda. Director of Ministry of Interior International Training Centre, Budapest, Hungary.

Margaret Brignell. Team Leader, Collections Management, Canadian Police College Library, Ottawa, Canada.

Christopher Brooks. School of World Studies and African American Studies, Virginia Commonwealth University, Richmond, Virginia, USA.

Antanas Bukauskas. Lecturer, Department of Public Administration, Mykolas Romeris University, Lithuania.

Michele Caianiello. Professor, International Criminal Justice, University of Bologna and University of Camerino, Italy.

Irena Cajner-Mraovic. Assistant Professor and Head of the Department of Criminology, Police College, Zagreb, Croatia.

Henry F. Carey. Assistant Professor, Department of Political Science, Georgia State University, Atlanta, Georgia, USA.

Cathy Casey. Program Leader, Crime and Justice, Auckland University of Technology, Auckland, New Zealand.

Jacqueline Azzopardi Cauchi. Professor, Department of Sociology, University of Malta, Malta.

Adam Chapman. Postdoctoral Fellow, Centre for Cross Cultural Research, Australian National University, Canberra, Australia.

Wisootrujira Chatsiri. Border Patrol, Royal Thai Police, Bangkok, Thailand.

Mark Ming-Chwang Chen. Professor, Department of Border Police, Central Police University, Kwei-Shan, Taiwan.

Pavel Cincar. Police Presidium of the Czech Republic, Deputy Head, International Police Co-Operation Division, Prague, The Czech Republic.

Gonzalo Jar Couselo. Brigadier General of Guardia Civil, Madrid, Spain.

Marcos Josegrei da Silva. Professor, Criminal Law, Law School, Tuiuti University, Parana, Brazil.

Mintie Das. WPE Project Assistant to the President, International Police Executive Symposium (IPES), South Burlington, Vermont, USA.

Carmen Rosa de León-Escribano. Author and Researcher, Guatemala City, Guatemala.

Monica den Boer. Dean of Studies, Police Academy of The Netherlands and Police Academy Professor, Free University Amsterdam, Amsterdam, The Netherlands.

Osman Dolu. Kent State University, Kent, Ohio, USA.

Bruno Domingo. Center for Police Study and Research, (CERP), Toulouse, France.

Fiona Donson. NGO Worker, Phnom Penh, Cambodia.

Vejnović Duško. Director of the Center for Geostrategic Studies, University of Banja Luka, Banja Luka, Bosnia and Herzegovina.

Maximilian Edelbacher. Senior Advisor, Federal Police, Vienna, Austria.

Andreas Egeryd. Senior Administrative Officer, Division for Police Issues, Stockholm, Sweden.

Jean-Etienne Elion. Colonel, Department of Police and Security, Brazzaville, Republic of Congo.

Theodora Ene. School of Sociology and Social Work, University of Bucharest, Bucharest, Romania.

Eduardo E. Estevez. Coordinator, Public Security, Ministry of Interior, Buenos Aires, Argentina.

Charles Fields. Professor of Criminal Justice, College of Justice and Safety, Eastern Kentucky University, Richmond, Kentucky, USA.

Daniel Fontanaud. National Expert to the European Commission, Paris, France.

Javier Galarza. Police Captain, Ecuador National Police, Quito, Ecuador.

Victor Manuel Garcia. Visiting Police Executive, Central Police University, Kwei-Shan, Taiwan.

Farid Gardashbayov. Public Finance Monitoring Center, Baku, Azerbaijan.

Gilbert Geis. Professor (Emeritus), Department of Criminology, Law, and Society, University of California-Irvine, Irvine, California, USA.

Roland Genson. Councellor for Justice and Home Affairs, Permanent Representation of the Grand-Duchy of Luxembourg to the European Union, Brussels, Belgium.

Ruth Geva. Chief Superintendent, Israel Police (retired), Consultant, Community Safety and Crime Prevention, Jerusalem, Israel.

Rune Glomseth. Assistant Professor, National Police Academy, Oslo, Norway.

Georgi Glonti. Institute of State and Law, Tbilisi, Georgia.

Paulo Gomes. Portuguese Ministry of the Interior, Lisbon, Portugal.

Recep Gultekin. Head of Foreign Relations Department, Turkish National Police, Ankara, Turkey.

Ismail Dincer Gunes. Department of Sociology, University of North Texas, Denton, Texas, USA.

Nelson Armando Vaquerano Gutiérrez. Professor, Human Rights and International Law, University of El Salvador, Salvador, El Salvador.

Robert F.J. Harnischmacher. Editor-in-Chief, *Police Forum*, Lecturer, Department of Criminology, Criminal Politics and Police Sciences, Faculty of Law, Ruhr-University, Bochum, Germany.

Michele Harrigan. Ph.D. Candidate, Transnational Police Co-operation, Institute of Social Psychology, Department of Sociology, London School of Economics & Political Science, London, United Kingdom.

Anthony Harriott. Senior Lecturer, Department of Government, University of the West Indies (Mona Campus), Mona, Jamaica.

William Harry. Commissioner of Police, Royal St. Vincent and the Grenadines Police Force, Kingstown, St. Vincent.

Abdul Qadir Haye. Inspector General of Police (retired), Rawalpindi, Pakistan.

Haruhiko Higuchi. Police Policy Research Center, National Police Agency, Tokyo, Japan.

Brunon Hoyst. Faculty of Law and Administration, University of Łódź, Lódź, Poland.

Paul Ibbetson. Ph.D. Candidate, Wichita State University, Wichita, Kansas, USA.

LIST OF CONTRIBUTORS

Analida Ivankovich. Police Researcher, John Jay College of Criminal Justice, Managing Editor, *Police Practice and Research: An International Journal*, New York, New York, USA.

Andrew Jackson. Assistant Director, European Asylum Policy Unit, Asylum and Appeals Policy Directorate, Brussels, Belgium.

Yateendra Singh Jafa. Member of Indian Police Service (retired), and Fellow, Jawaharlal Nehru University, New Delhi, India.

Mark Jones. Professor, East Carolina University, Greenville, North Carolina, USA.

Arunas Juska. Assistant Professor, East Carolina University, Greenville, North Carolina, USA.

Andreas Kapardis. Author and Researcher, University of Cyprus, Nicosia, Cyprus.

Zoran Keković. Assistant Professor, Faculty of Civil Defense, Police College, Serbia and Montenegro, Belgrade, Serbia.

Karin Keller. Canton Police Executive, Zurich, Switzerland.

Želimir Kešetović. Associate Professor, Crisis Management, Faculty of Civil Defence, University of Belgrade, Belgrade, Serbia.

Ranjan Koirala. Senior Superintendent, Armed Police Headquarters, Kathmandu, Nepal.

Betsy Wright Kreisel. Associate Professor, Criminal Justice Department, Central Missouri State University, Warrensburg, Missouri, USA.

Peter Kruize. Faculty of Law, University of Copenhagen, Copenhagen, Denmark.

Hamid R. Kusha. Associate Professor, Criminal Justice, Department of Social Sciences, Texas A&M International University, Laredo, Texas, USA.

Ahti Laitinen. Professor, Criminology and Sociology of Law, University of Turku, Turku, Finland.

Velibor Lalić. Associate Researcher, Center for Geostrategic Studies, University of Banja Luka, Bosnia and Herzegovina.

Uwe Langenbahn. Deputy Chief, National Police of Liechtenstein, Verwaltungsgebaude, Liechtenstein.

Musa Bockarie Lappia. Sierra Leone Police Headquarters, Loidu, Sierra Leone.

Marke Leong. University of New England, Armidale, NSW, Australia.

Colleen Lewis. Associate Professor of Criminal Justice and Criminology, Faculty of Arts, and Co-director of the Parliamentary Studies Unit, Monash University, Melbourne, Australia.

Meruert Makhmutova. Director, Public Policy Research Center, Almaty, Kazakhstan.

Mary Fran Malone. Lecturer, Department of Political Science, University of New Hampshire, Durham, New Hampshire, USA.

Francesco Marelli. Consultant, United Nations Interregional Crime and Justice Research Institute (UNICRI), Turin, Italy.

Joan R. Mars. Assistant Professor, Department of Sociology, Anthropology & Criminal Justice, University of Michigan-Flint, Flint, Michigan, USA.

Noel McGuirk. University of Ulster, Ulster, Northern Ireland.

Kenethia L. McIntosh. Department of Criminal Justice, University of Maryland-Eastern Shore, Eastern Shore, Maryland, USA.

Erica McKim. Policy Analyst, National Security Policy and Planning Section, Criminal Intelligence Directorate, Royal Canadian Mounted Police, Nepean, Ontario, Canada.

Cindy McNair. Department of Criminal Justice, Indiana University, Bloomington, Indiana, USA.

Jean-Louis Messing. Commissioner of Police, Yacuande, Cameroon.

J. Mitchell Miller. Director of Graduate Studies in Drug and Addictions and Associate Professor, Department of Criminology & Criminal Justice, University of South Carolina, Columbia, South Carolina, USA.

Ruth Montgomery. Editor, Canadian Association of Chiefs of Police (CACP) Publications, Ontario, Canada.

Agbonkhese Shaka Moses. Department of Sociology, Ambrose Alli University, Ede State, Nigeria.

Thomas Mosley. Department of Criminal Justice, University of Maryland-Eastern Shore, Eastern Shore, Maryland, USA.

Aogán Mulcahy. Department of Sociology, University College Dublin, Dublin, Ireland.

Tonita Murray. Police and Gender Advisor, Afghan Ministry of the Interior, Kabul, Afghanistan.

Yem Xuan Nguyen. Deputy Director of Standing Office on Drug Control, Da Nang, Vietnam.

Gilbert Norden. Institute of Sociology, University of Vienna, Vienna, Austria.

Evaristus Obinyan. Fort Valley State University, Fort Valley, Georgia, USA.

Jonathan C. Odo. Department of Criminal Justice, University of Maryland-Eastern Shore, Eastern Shore, Maryland, USA.

Ihekwoaba D. Onwudiwe. Associate Professor, Department of Criminal Justice, University of Maryland-Eastern Shore, Eastern Shore, Maryland, USA.

Michael O'Shea. Asia Centre, University of New England, Armidale, Australia.

Milan Pagon. Dean, College of Police and Security Studies, Ljubljana, Slovenia.

Michael J. Palmiotto. Professor of Criminal Justice, Wichita State University, Wichita, Kansas, USA.

Nancy Park. Library Manager, Canadian Police College, Ottawa, Canada.

Vassiliki Petoussi. Lecturer, Sociology of Law and Deviance, Department of Sociology, University of Crete, Crete, Greece.

João José Ramalhete Marques Pires. Cabinet of External Affairs and Cooperation, National Directorate of Public Security Police, Lisbon, Portugal.

Nii-K Plange. Professor, Sociology, School of Social and Economic Development, The University of the South Pacific, Suva, Fiji.

A. R. Ramsaran. Law Department, Faculty of Law and Management, University of Mauritius, Reduit, Mauritius.

Husnija Redžepagiæ. Principal, High School of Internal Affairs, Serbia and Montenegro, Belgrade, Serbia.

Michael Reid. Press Office, Belize Police Department, Belize City, Belize.

Aigi Resetnikova. Researcher, Institute of Law, University of Tartu, Tartu, Estonia.

Fiorella Espinosa Ribeiro. National Police of Uruguay, Montevideo, Uruguay.

Annette Robertson. Scarman Centre, University of Leicester, Leicester, United Kingdom.

Walter Rombaut. Police Advisor, Belgian Federal Police, Brussels, Belgium.

Mike Rowe. Lecturer, Department of Criminology, University of Leicester, Leicester, United Kingdom.

Daniel Linares Ruestra. Financial Investigation Unit, National Police, Lima, Peru.

Mohammad Salahuddin. Department of Criminal Justice. Indiana University, Bloomington, Indiana, USA.

Juan Carlos Valenzuela Sanchez. Visiting Police Executive, Central Police University, Kwei-Shan, Taiwan.

Kim Yong Sang. International Program Coordinator, National 119 Rescue Services, Seoul, Korea.

Martijn Schilstra. Policy Advisor, Amsterdam City Hall, Department of Public Order and Safety, Amsterdam, The Netherlands.

Eric Schultz. Senior Assessment Coordinator, Criminal Justice Training Assessment, Excelsior College, Albany, New York, USA.

John Scott. School of Social Sciences, University of New England, Armidale, Australia.

Sankar Sen. Indian Police Service (retired) and Senior Fellow, Institute of Social Sciences, New Delhi, India.

Amanda Marie Sharp. Department of Criminal Justice, East Carolina University, Greenville, North Carolina, USA.

Hasan Shkembi. Police Academy, Tirana, Albania.

Martin Sitalsing. Deputy Chief Constable, Regional Police Force, Friesland, Amsterdam, The Netherlands.

Nils-Henrik Sjölinder. Administrator, Ministry of Justice, Division for Police Issues, Public Order and Safety, Stockholm, Sweden.

Nelly Sonderling. Communication Research, South African Police, Pretoria, South Africa.

Trpe Stojanovski. Senior Executive, Ministry of the Interior, Republic of Macedonia, Skopje, Macedonia.

Kathleen Sweet. CEO and President, Risk Management Security Group, Assistant Professor, Purdue University, West Lafayette, Indiana, USA.

Ian Taylor. School of International Relations, University of St. Andrews, St. Andrews, Scotland.

Samih Teymur. Department of Information Sciences, University of North Texas, Denton, Texas, USA.

Mark Ungar. Associate Professor, Brooklyn College, City University of New York, New York, USA.

Endang Usman. Corruption Crime Department, Jakarta Metropolitan Police, Jakarta, Indonesia.

L.N. Uusiku. Office of the Inspector-General, Namibian Police, Windhoek, Namibia.

Ernesto Lopez Portillo Vargas. President, Institute for Security and Democracy, Mexico City, Mexico.

Nicole Vartanian. Senior Research Associate, Institute of Education Sciences, Washington, DC, USA.

Bryan Vila. National Institute of Justice, U.S. Department of Justice, Washington, DC, USA.

S. George Vincentnathan. Professor and Chair, Department of Criminal Justice, University of Texas-Pan American, Edinburg, Texas, USA.

Anwar Yehya. Director of Training, Internal Security Forces, Beirut, Lebanon.

Lola Gulomova Zarifovna. The Paul H. Nitze School of Advanced International Studies (SAIS), Johns Hopkins University, Baltimore, Maryland, USA.

Sitora Gulomova Zarifovna. Female Lawyers League, and Tax & Law Institute, Dushanbe, Tajikistan.

LIST OF ENTRIES A-Z

Kazakhstan	Qatar
Kenya	Romania
Kiribati	Russia
Korea, North	Rwanda
Korea, South	St. Kitts and Nevis
Kuwait	Saint Lucia
Kyrgyzstan	Saint Vincent and the Grenadines
Laos	Samoa
Latvia	San Marino
Lebanon	São Tomé and Príncipe
Lesotho	Saudi Arabia
Liberia	Senegal
Libya	Serbia
Liechtenstein	Seychelles
Lithuania	Sierra Leone
Luxembourg	Singapore
Macedonia	Slovakia
Madagascar	Slovenia
Malawi	Solomon Islands
Malaysia	Somalia
Maldives	South Africa
Mali	Spain
Malta	Sri Lanka
Marshall Islands	Sudan
Mauritania	Suriname
Mauritius	Swaziland
Mexico	Sweden
Micronesia	Switzerland
Moldova	Syria
Monaco	Taiwan, Republic of China (ROC)
Mongolia	Tajikistan
Montenegro	Tanzania
Morocco	Thailand
Mozambique	Togo
Myanmar	Tonga
Namibia	Trinidad and Tobago
Nauru	Tunisia
Nepal	Turkey
Netherlands, The	Turkmenistan
New Zealand	Tuvalu
Nicaragua	Uganda
Niger	Ukraine
Nigeria	United Arab Emirates
Norway	United Kingdom
Oman	United States
Pakistan	Uruguay
Palau	Uzbekistan
Panama	Vanuatu
Papua New Guinea	Venezuela
Paraguay	Vietnam
Peru	Yemen
Philippines	Zambia
Poland	Zimbabwe
Portugal	

L

LAOS

Background Material

The Lao People's Democratic Republic (Lao PDR) was established on December 2, 1975. Its predecessor, the Kingdom of Laos, was a constitutional monarchy that had governed since Laos gained independence from France in 1953. The French had governed Laos since 1887, first as a protectorate and later in 1899 incorporating it into the colony of French Indochina.

Before the arrival of Europeans, the territory of modern-day Laos was ruled by a succession of Lao, Siamese, and Vietnamese kingdoms. The largest of these was the Lao Kingdom of Lan Xang (1 million elephants), founded in 1353 by Fa Ngum, which endured until the early eighteenth century when it split into three smaller kingdoms: Louang Phabang, Vientiane, and Champasak. By 1779, these kingdoms had all been reduced to tributary states of Siam, the new centre of power in the region. French exploration of Indochina began in the first half of the nineteenth century, and resulted in the creation of the colony of French Indochina consisting of modern-day Vietnam, Cambodia, and Laos.

Since the creation of the Lao PDR in 1975, the Lao People's Revolutionary Party (LPRP) has been the sole legal and governing party. The communists' ascendancy to power was the final result of a thirty-year-long civil war against the Royal Lao government (RLG). The Lao civil war was part of the broader conflict fought across Indochina between the early 1950s and 1975, which not only pitted the Lao royalists and communists against one another but also saw extensive, undeclared American and Vietnamese involvement.

In 1976, the Lao government began a brief but disastrous experiment with socialist economic planning. Its failure led to the implementation of economic reforms in 1986 that encouraged a market economy and allowed the state begin to ease some of its central controls. The twin effects of war and economic hardship brought on by the early socialist economic policies caused an exodus of the country's population; an estimated 10% of the population of over 3 million had fled by 1980, most settling as refugees in the United States, Canada, France, and Australia.

In 2002, the country's population was estimated to be slightly over 5 million inhabitants, of whom 62% were born after 1975. Slightly more than 50% of the total population belongs to the politically and economically dominant lowland Lao ethnic group. The population is ethnically diverse, consisting of four major ethno-linguistic groups: Tai, Mon-Khmer, Tibeto-Burman, and Hmong-Yao. Until the early 1990s, the population was officially classified via three ethnic categories: Lao Loum (the lowland Lao groups speaking Tai languages); Lao Theung (upland Lao groups speaking Mon-Khmer languages); and Lao Sung (highland Lao groups speaking Tibeto-Burman and Hmong-Yao languages). Although these terms retain some currency in Laos, they no longer appear in official documents having been replaced by group-specific autonyms of the more than forty-seven ethnic groups (such as Hmong, Khmu, and so on). The 1991 constitution provides for equal rights and citizenship for all minority people born in Laos, a status not enjoyed by ethnic minority groups in neighbouring Thailand.

The state religion, Theravada Buddhism, is mainly practiced by the dominant ethnic Lao group. Freedom of religious expression is guaranteed under the 1991 constitution. However, the government exercises direct control over Buddhism through the Lao Buddhist Union and, during the early years of its rule, attempted to suppress "superstitions," such as the animistic beliefs and ancestor worship still widely practiced among the non-Tai groups and some of the smaller Tai groups. There is a small Christian population that has been persecuted by provincial governments throughout the 1990s and early 2000s.

In 2002, the per capita income for Lao citizens was $310. A 2002 survey revealed that remittances from overseas relatives are an integral part of household incomes in towns along the Mekong River, accounting for 29% of their total income. The economy is largely agricultural with very little industry outside of Vientiane. Timber and hydroelectricity are its two major exports with gypsum, tin, and gold and gem mining also contributing. There is a growing textile and garment industry, and tourism is rapidly expanding.

The Lao PDR is among the world's least-developed nations, and is highly dependent upon official foreign aid. Economic reforms toward a market-oriented economy open to foreign investment have slowed since 1997, as the government has balked at relinquishing control. Laos's greatest challenges revolve around building and strengthening its capacity in the following areas: poverty reduction and meeting basic human needs; political/civil institutions and administration; human resources; human/children's rights; gender, ethnic, and regional disparities; and social infrastructure in health and education. All of these have been targeted by the United Nations Development Programme (UNDP) and other official aid programs.

Contextual Features

The Lao PDR is governed by the Lao People's Revolutionary Party (LPRP). Although the socialist economic policies and totalitarian control that characterised the early years of the Lao PDR are long abandoned, the LPRP remains the sole political party and shows little sign of permitting liberal democratic reform in the nation's political system. Theoretically, the National Assembly is the peak legislative body, but it does little more than implement the policies and directives set down by the LPRP central committee and politburo. National Assembly elections are held every four years, for which all candidates must be approved by the LPRP, although the vast majority of them are already party members. The state president commands the armed forces, appoints provincial governors and the prime minister, and has the right to preside over meetings of the government. The government is headed by the prime minister and the council of ministers. Originally, the state president was largely a ceremonial position, but since 1991 the position has been held concurrently with the leadership of the LPRP making it the most powerful political position in Laos.

The Lao government has two primary divisions: the ministries and the party organisation. The policies set down by these two organisations are implemented through the party's civil organisations such as the Lao Front for National Reconstruction, the Lao Women's Union, and the Federation of Lao Trade Unions.

For administrative purposes, the country is divided into seventeen provinces (*khwaeng*): Phongsali, Louang Namtha, Bokèo, Oudômxai, Phôngsali, Louang Phabang, Houaphan, Xiang Khouang, Xaignabouli, Vientiane, Bôlikhamxai, Khammouan, Savannakhét, Salavan, Champasak, Xe-kong, and Attapu. The capital Vientiane is administered as a separate municipality, and there is the special zone of Xaisomboun straddling the border of Vientiane and Xiang Khouang provinces. Each province is divided into district (*muang*), which are further divided into villages (*ban*). The Xaisomboun special zone was established during the 1990s in order to control pockets of unrest in the area. The Lao government blames these disturbances on "bandits," but it is widely believed that the government has been fighting several small groups of Hmong who are the remnants/descendants of the Hmong forces that fought against the communists during the civil war. In mid-2003, these groups attracted world attention when several Western journalists ventured into the jungle to record their stories.

The Lao judicial system has three levels, mirroring the hierarchical system of government. At the national level is the People's Supreme Court, which has jurisdiction over the provincial, district, and military courts. There are eighteen provincial courts and the Vientiane municipality court, below which are approximately 126 district courts. All courts are administered and controlled through the Ministry of Justice. All Lao courts operate with panels of three judges that act on the decisions of a majority within the panel. The LPRP-dominated National Assembly Standing Committee (NASC) has the power to remove judges and is the final arbiter of the law. Consequently, the judges do not have the power to make law through their judgments. Laos also lacks a juvenile justice code as well as courts and correctional facilities specifically dedicated to juveniles.

The 1991 constitution formally established the judiciary that had evolved through a series of prime ministerial decrees in the 1970s and 1980s. A separate Office of the Public Prosecutor (OPP) was established at the same time. Economic laws were also set in place by the 1991 constitution as a means to attract badly needed foreign investment. Laws for the criminal/penal code and procedure and some civil laws were promulgated in 1989. In economic cases, the judiciary is seen to be impartial but in politically contentious cases, it remains subservient to the party-dominated NASC. Two high-profile criminal cases involving Westerners in 2001 and 2003 highlighted the arbitrary and politicised nature of the Lao criminal justice system.

The Lao legal system is gradually moving away from arbitrary use of power toward the rule of law. Between 2000 and 2002, the UNDP ran a series of projects entitled Strengthening the Institutional Foundations for the Rule of Law that aimed to strengthen the OPP and the judiciary as well as improve the drafting, implementation, and dissemination of laws. Lawyers are trained at the Institute of Law and Administration, but few practice privately and are not allowed to promote themselves as attorneys at law. In theory, the government provides counsel to defendants in criminal cases but more often than not defendants are responsible for their own defence. As with the courts, there are public prosecution institutes at each level of government whose task is to control the observance of laws by all ministries, organisations, state employees, and citizens. They prosecute under the guidance of the public prosecutor gen-

eral, who appoints and removes deputy public prosecutors at all levels.

The penal code expressly forbids any "destabilising subversive activities," which include any criticism of the LPRP or its right to govern. This law has been used on several occasions to convict dissidents from within and outside the LPRP and sentence them to lengthy terms in gaol.

Police Profile

Background

The current civilian police force replaced military led law enforcement in Laos in the late 1970s. The RLG police force was disbanded along with almost every civil and military institution in December 1975 following the establishment of the Lao PDR (see Dueve 1998 for a history of the RLG police force). The present police force is influenced by French and Vietnamese police structures, and was established with the assistance of the Vietnamese, a staunch ally and partner of the Lao government. A village-level volunteer paramilitary force exists in Laos that assists the police in keeping the peace and in surveillance.

Organizational Description and Functions

Reliable and accurate information on the Lao police force is not available. The Lao Ministry of Security, formerly the Ministry of the Interior, does not release any information detailing police numbers, gender and ethnic makeup of the Lao police force, nor its organisational structure. Indeed, the Lao government tends to treat these details as a state secret. The ministry also refrains from publishing any crime rate statistics, so it remains impossible to assess the effectiveness of the Lao police force. As a consequence, the information presented here can only outline the major functions and known divisions of the police organisation.

The Lao police force is divided into discrete departments, the precise number of which is unknown but does include a traffic department; a department for criminal police; an immigration, foreigners and aliens protection department; a judicial police who have powers of arrest; and a secret police department. The force is headed by a director general who oversees the Directorate of National Police that governs the provincial and municipal divisions of the force which oversee the work of the district police forces. Provincial branch heads report to the provincial government and to the director general. Provincial police commissioners also participate in their provincial government administration. The extent and nature of the links between the LPRP and the Lao police force are unknown; however, it is certain that membership of the LPRP is a prerequisite for those aspiring to the senior ranks of the police force.

No reliable information is available on the number and names of the various ranks within the Lao police force. The ranks may be loosely based upon the French colonial system or may reflect current usage in neighbouring Vietnam from whom Laos receives assistance on internal security and national defence issues.

Training

Training is undertaken at the Lao National Police Training Centre located at Ban Don Nuon in east Vientiane. This building also served as the police academy for the RLG police force as well. There are four main training categories: recruit training, cadet officer training, courses for senior staff and noncommissioned officers, and specialist training in areas such as fingerprinting and telecommunications. In 1998, the International Committee of the Red Cross (ICRC) provided government officials, including police officers, with training on human rights law. In 2003, the Australian government funded the publication of a handbook for human rights for law enforcement officials and also convened a workshop on international law and human rights. Inquiries into allegations of human rights violations are the responsibility of the Human Rights Unit of the Department of International Treaties and Legal Affairs within the Ministry of Foreign Affairs. However, this unit does not appear to respond to individual cases nor to complaints originating from Lao citizens.

Complaints and Discipline

The U.S. State Department's yearly human rights reports of 2001 and 2002 were highly critical of Laos. These reports noted that conditions in Lao prisons were extremely harsh, and that political prisoners were often mistreated. They also noted the Lao police "used arbitrary arrest, detention, and surveillance," and that there were problems with lengthy pre-trial and incommunicado detention. The Lao judiciary was also criticised for being corrupt, subject to executive influence and failing to ensure due process for Lao citizens and foreigners.

Terrorism

It is unknown whether transnational terrorist groups like Jemaah Islamiah and al-Qaeda have established themselves in Laos. In 2000 and 2001, a series of bomb blasts occurred in the capital Vientiane, some arrests were made but the Lao government has never made its investigations public. Responsibility for the explosions has been attributed to the dissident Hmong groups mentioned above and to dissatisfied elements within the government and party, but these observations are based on speculation rather than fact.

Police Education, Research, and Publications

Because the Ministry of Security publishes no material for dissemination outside the Lao government it is impossible to assess the current state of education, research and publications concerning policing in the Lao PDR. However, given the close cooperation between the Lao and Vietnamese governments over national security issues, there is certain to be an ongoing exchange of ideas, training, and expertise between the police forces of these two countries. The United Nations Development Programme (UNDP) also runs programs on governance that may eventually result in information becoming available in the future. It is unlikely that the Ministry of Security will become more open on matters concerning internal security and policing in the foreseeable future.

ADAM CHAPMAN

Bibliography

Deuve, Jean. *Histoire de la police nationale du Laos*. Paris: L'Harmattan, 1998.

Evans, Grant. *A Short History of Laos: The Land in Between*. Sydney: Allen and Unwin, 2002.

Lao National Assembly. *The Constitution of the Lao People's Democratic Republic*. Vientiane: Lao National Assembly, 1991.

Phongsavath, Boupha. *The Evolution of the Lao State*. New Delhi: Konark, 2002.

Stuart-Fox, Martin. "Socialist Construction and National Security in Laos." *Bulletin of Concerned Asian Scholars* 13, no. 1 (1981): 61–71.

Stuart-Fox, Martin. "The Constitution of the Lao People's Democratic Republic." *Review of Socialist Law* 17 (1991): 299–317.

U.S. Department of State. *Country Reports on Human Rights Practices: Laos*. Washington, DC: U.S. Department of State, Bureau of Democracy, Human Rights and Labor, 2001.

LATVIA

Background Material

On November 18, 1918 the independent Republic of Latvia was proclaimed. After a brief period of independence, Latvia was annexed by the Soviet Union in 1940 under the Molotov-Ribbentrop Pact. It reestablished its independence on August 21, 1991 following the breakup of the Soviet Union. A significant percentage of the population is made up of noncitizens (22% in 2003). Russians make up two-thirds of this group, and Belorussians and Ukrainians together comprise about 20%. In the 1990s, Latvia started the transition to a market economy. Unemployment (13% to 14%) remains a concern, especially as it does not significantly decrease, in spite of strong economic growth. Latvia joined both NATO and the European Union in spring 2004.

The population of Latvia is 2,319,203 (2004 estimate). The ethnic composition is as follows: 60.3% Latvians, 28.4% Russians, 3.6% Byelorussians, 2.3% Poles, 2.2% Ukrainians, 1.3% Lithuanians, and 1.9% other ethnicities (2003 estimate).

The official language is Latvian; other widely used languages are Lithuanian and Russian. Religions followed include the Lutheran, Roman Catholic, and Russian Orthodox branches of Christianity.

The GDP per capita is US$4,881 (2003 estimate). The main sector contributing to GDP is services with 70%, followed by industry 19%, construction 6%, and agriculture, forestry, and fisheries with 5% (2001). Other main contributors to economic activity are wholesale and retail trade (19%), food processing (5%), wood products (3%), and textiles (2%).

Contextual Features

The Latvian legal system is based on civil law. The basic legal document is the constitution. Latvia is a parliamentary democracy in which the highest executive power lies with the cabinet of ministers.

Shortly after restoration of independence in 1991, major modifications and amendments were introduced into the Criminal Code and Criminal Procedure Code of the Latvian Republic. These changes reflected legal aspects of continuing socio-economic, political, and crime trends. Since then, further amendments have been introduced in both codes. In 1992, the overall crime rate in Latvia had grown by 47.6%, whereas homicides had increased by 37.6%. Homicides accounted for 0.5% of all recorded crimes in 1992. In 2003, the total number of crimes recorded by the police was 51,773 (2,221 crimes per capita). The number of homicides recorded by the police was 220, which made up 9.4 homicides per capita, and constituted 0.4% of all recorded crimes.

In compliance with the Law of Judicial Powers, a three-level court system exists in Latvia: District (or City) Courts, Regional Courts, and Supreme Court. District Courts form the first level of the court system, and are established in accordance with the administrative territorial division of the Republic of Latvia. There are thirty-five District Courts in Latvia. Five Regional Courts established according to historical and existing regions form the second level of the court system. Each Regional Court covers a particular number of District Courts. District and Regional Courts are courts of first instance and their competence is determined by relevant criminal procedure and civil procedure laws. The Supreme Court forms the highest level of the court system and the judgments thereof are final. The Constitutional Court exists as a separate court in Latvia, and it reviews matters concerning compliance of the laws with the Constitution within its jurisdiction as provided for by law, as well as other matters, regarding which jurisdiction is conferred on it by law.

The Prison Administration is subordinated to the Ministry of Justice. Latvia's prison system consists of a staff training center and fifteen prisons, of which three are investigative pre-trial detention centers, and there are also pre-trial units in five other prisons. There are three types of prison regime: closed, semi-closed, and open. Of the fifteen prisons, seven are closed, three semi-closed, and two open. One of the facilities is a re-education institution for juveniles and two are remand houses. Also, there are six small remand units in the closed and semi-closed prisons (in accordance with the regional principle). The level and type of prison can be changed during the prisoner's sentence.

According to 2001 data, the prison population in Latvia was 8,831, or about one per 370 citizens. However, a significant number of all prisoners (43% in 2003) were pre-trial detainees and those awaiting the result of an appeal against sentence. Since prisoners have the right to make more than one appeal against their sentences, the process of sentencing is time consuming. For all crimes, the court process often takes a long time before the sentence is finally confirmed. According to the new legislation, juveniles should be in pre-trial for no more than six months and adults eighteen months.

Police Profile

Background

On June 4, 1991 the Republic of Latvia Supreme Soviet passed the Law on Police that charged the Ministry of Interior with the task of reorganizing militia institutions by July 1, 1992. The Ministry of the Interior Police Department Training Center was established in 1991. Its task was, within a short time, to train police officers who would carry out the duties of maintaining public order. The need for a quick change from the former militia-style training system to a new approach resulted because of the need to train native applicants in Latvian language with the new mentality of policing. The militia, being under the control of military, had the military mind-set, was trained in Russia and most of the force spoke Russian.

Demographics

In 2000, the number of sworn police officers was 9,829; women accounted for 17.1% (1,651). The number of employees in the police service was 11,211, whereas the total number of women was 1,938, making up 17.3% of the all personnel. Since then, the number of sworn police staff has diminished to 7,927 members (2003 data), equivalent to one officer per 340 citizens.

Organizational Description

The police are an armed, militarized state or local government authority whose duty is to protect from criminal and other illegal threats against life, property, and the interests of society and the state. The police encompass the State Police, Security Police, and local government (or municipal) police. The State Police act in accordance with regulations approved by the Ministry of the Interior. The Security Police operates according to the National Security Law, Law on Police, Law on State Security Institutions, and statutes approved by the cabinet. It is a state administrative institution subordinated to the Ministry of the Interior, having the status of a state security institution. The local government police are incorporated in the relevant local government and operate under its control. Model regulations for local government police are approved by the Ministry of the Interior.

The State Police consist of central headquarters and subordinate organizational units. The head of the police is called the chief of police. The country has been divided into twenty-eight city and regional police districts. The central authority of the State Police organizes and coordinates activities of its structural units. The central authority includes the Administrative Department, Complaints and Discipline Branch, Personnel and Recruitment Board, Secret Regime Guarantee Unit, Special Correspondence Unit, and Planning and Finance Board. The Main Criminal Police Department, Main Public Order Police Department, Railroad Police Board, Pre-trial Investigation Board, Forensic Center of the State Police, Police School of the State Police, and territorial police boards of the cities and regions are subordinate structural units. The Civil Police consist of the State Police Central Civil Police administration, Traffic Police and the association Apsardze services subject to its control, and territorial, transport, and immigration institution civil police subordinated units, as well as the police precincts. Their function is to guarantee public order, combat crime, and to guard specific objects. The Criminal Police consist of the State Police Central Criminal Police administration, and the territorial and other police institution criminal police. Functions of the Criminal Police include prevention and disclosure of criminal offenses; search for missing people, as well as those who are evading inquiry, investigation, and the court, or serving of a sentence; and ensuring the participation of criminalistic experts in investigatory activities.

One of the State Police's special units is the Quick Reaction Unit, which falls under the subordination of the Central Criminal Police. There is also an Economic Police Department, with responsibilities that include planning, coordinating, controlling, and accomplishing measures with the aim of preventing and detecting criminal offenses committed in the economic sphere in the areas of competence of the State Police. Additionally, the Organized Crime Enforcement Department examines and neutralizes positions and actions of organized crime groups, organizes and implements preventive measures to prevent and detect such crimes. A unit specialized in combating computer crime was set up in 2001. Also, the Financial Police of the Tax Revenue Service accept complaints, and detect and investigate developments that point to possible criminal activity, investigating each situation in accordance with Latvia's criminal procedure laws.

The Latvian police adhere to an equal opportunity policy. No minimum or maximum quotas have been set for the number of women in the police. State Police officers and Security Police officers are appointed to office and removed from office by procedures prescribed in regulatory enactments. The regulations for a higher rank/position in the police service are included in the Law on Police Article 21, annex "On Conferment of Subsequent Rank" to the Regulation No. 317 by the cabinet of ministers. Before local government police are appointed to office, their eligibility for a given office is verified in accordance with procedures prescribed by the Ministry of the Interior. Such persons must complete the professional training course and pass relevant examinations. The local government police may consist of a chief, her or his deputies, senior inspectors, and inspectors and junior inspectors, as well as senior civil officers, civil officers, and junior civil officers. The chiefs of the State Police and the Security Police are appointed to and removed from office by the cabinet pursuant to the recommendation of the Ministry of the Interior. They are selected from among senior commanding personnel in the police, with higher legal education and not less than five years police service in management positions. The chief and deputy chiefs of the local government police are appointed to office by the relevant city council, district council, or parish council only after consent from the Ministry of the Interior has been received for the approval of the relevant candidate. The chief or deputy chiefs of local government police are removed from office by the relevant city council, district council or parish council on their own initiative or pursuant to an order of the Ministry of the Interior, which the council must examine within seven days. The Ministry of the Interior has the right, up to the day that a council removes from office the local government police chief or the deputy chief, to suspend respective officials from performing their duties.

Functions

The legal basis for the operations of the police is the constitution, international agreements, Law on Police, other laws and regulatory enactments of the Republic of Latvia, and decisions of local governments, if they are not contrary to national laws. The operations of the police are under the control of the cabinet, the Ministry of the Interior, and local government institutions, within the scope of their competence. Supervision regarding observance of the law in police operations is carried out by the Prosecutor General of the Republic of Latvia and prosecutors subordinate to her or him. The Ombudsman ensures oversight of Latvian police institutions.

The tasks of the police are to guarantee the safety of persons and society; prevent criminal offenses and the violations of law; disclose criminal offenses and search for persons who have committed criminal offenses; provide assistance in accordance with procedures prescribed by law to persons, institutions, undertakings, and organizations in the protection of their rights and the carrying out of tasks prescribed by law; and implement, within the scope of competence, administrative sanctions and criminal sentences.

Training

Currently, State Police training is delivered by two institutions: the Police School of the State Police, which delivers vocational training to junior officers; and the Police Academy of Latvia, which delivers professional tertiary-level education to specialists and senior officers. Usually the police service employs people who have completed educational institutions of the Ministry of the Interior or the Police Academy of Latvia. The elementary training, re-training, and raising qualifications of police officers may also be done on a contractual basis in the police educational institutions of other states.

Police Public Projects

The Nordic-Baltic campaign on trafficking in women, carried out during 2002 in all Baltic states, was coordinated by nongovernmental organizations and financed by the Nordic Council of Ministers. The Latvian campaign included a TV program about human trafficking and youth going to work abroad, production of small calendars with information about what to be aware of before signing employment contracts abroad, and a radio program by and for students. The campaign also included seminars on trafficking in human beings for government officials and students.

Police Use of Firearms

The police in Latvia are routinely armed. Local government police officers have the right to receive, keep, and carry firearms, and to use them in accordance with procedures specified and in the cases provided in the Law on Police.

Complaints and Discipline

The Latvian National Human Rights Office (LNHRO) has been set up to review residents' complaints regarding possible violations of their human rights, including complaints having to do with such violations at the hands of employees of the police department. LNHRO complaints having to do with the State Police usually contain information on inhumane treatment at the moment of arrest, and physical aggression or moral aggression during the questioning process. In cases where the complaint contains specific information regarding police violence resulting in bodily harm to the individual, the complaint is usually sent for verification purposes to a competent institution. Complaints regarding illegal activities by the State Police employees are examined by the State Police Personnel Inspection and the Ministry of Internal Affairs Chief Inspection.

Police training has not included training for human rights. A training strategy for the period from 2005 until 2011 is being worked out in cooperation with the Police Academy of Latvia and the Police School of the State Police. The goal of the project is to improve police training by introducing several new training courses, including human rights.

Terrorism

The Security Police scope of activities in the field of state security provision includes reconnaissance and counterespionage measures aimed at doing away with terrorism, as well as distribution of chemical and radioactive substances, firearms, and other types of weapons, and the unauthorized circulation of explosives.

International Cooperation

Agreements on police cooperation have been signed with Belgium, the Netherlands, Sweden, Georgia, the Russian Federation and Slovakia. An intergovernmental cooperation agreement to combat terrorism, organized crime, and drug trafficking was signed with Uzbekistan and Kazakhstan. Foreign liaison officers posted in Latvia are from France, Germany, and the Nordic police liaison officer is housed in the Swedish Embassy to Latvia. The State Police have had close cooperation in human trafficking issues with German and Danish police authorities. Experts in the PHARE 2003 National Program Project "Police Training" from Northern Ireland began working in Latvia in spring 2004. Also, Scottish police officers are training the State Police in measures to combat organized crime.

Police Education, Research, and Publications

The main task of the Police School of the State Police is the implementation of professional basic education for police officers by carrying out the necessary legal and professional preparation for police service. The basic functions of the school are to ensure professional education and qualification of officers, as well as education in general knowledge and skills. Two educational programs offered, which include both theoretical studies and practical experience. The first program lasts one year. After completing these studies, students receive either a qualification certificate or a diploma of professional secondary education. The professional education that is granted is a "constable," the second level of professional qualification. The duration of the second program is two years. The professional qualification granted is "junior officer," which is the third level of professional qualification.

The objective of the activity of the Police Academy of Latvia is ensuring professionally oriented curricula and of academic studies in science of law, carrying out scientific research for the Ministry of the Interior and other institutions, and improvement of professional skills of the officers of these institutions by implementation of supplementary development courses. The Police Academy provides higher education. The first-level professional higher education is provided by the Police College of the Police Academy of Latvia, the qualification received corresponds to the fourth level of qualification. The qualification of the second-level higher education corresponds to the fifth level of qualification.

Leading Researchers

I. Bulgakova, Reader, Chair of Criminal Law, Police Academy of Latvia

A. Kavalieris, Head of Department, Professor, Chair of Criminalistics, Police Academy of Latvia

S. Kazaka, Reader, Chair of Criminal Law, Police Academy of Latvia

A. Lieljuksis, Associate Professor, Chair of Criminalistics, Police Academy of Latvia

A. Loskutovs, Head of Corruption Analysis and Countermeasures Methodology Division, Corruption Prevention and Combating Bureau

A. Meikalisa, Rector, Professor, Police Academy of Latvia

D. Mežulis, Head of Department, Associate Professor, Chair of Criminal Law, Police Academy of Latvia

K. Strada-Rozenberga, Vice Dean, Associate Professor, Faculty of Law, University of Latvia

A. Vilks, Director, Criminological Research Centre

Leading Police Journals

Latvijas Vestnesis "Jurista Vard" (The Latvian Herald "Lawyer's Word"). D. Gailite (Ed.), Bruņinieku 36, Riga, LV-1011, Latvia (Latvian).

Administrativa un Kriminala Justicija (Administrative and Criminal Justice). Police Academy of Latvia, Ezermalas 8, Riga, LV — 1014, Latvia (Latvian).

Likums un Tiesibas (Law and Justice). D. Iļjanova (Ed.), Raiņa bulvāris 19, Riga, LV-1586, Latvia (Latvian).

Police and Related Websites

The State Police. Available at: *www.vp.gov.lv/*
Ministry of the Interior. Available at: *www.iem.gov.lv/*
Ministry of Justice: Available at: *www.tm.gov.lv/*

Police Academy of Latvia: Available at: *www.polak.edu.lv/*
Public policy site: Available at: *www.policy.lv/*

AIGI RESETNIKOVA

Bibliography

Barclay, G., and Tavares, C. *International Comparison of Criminal Justice Statistics 2001*. Issue 12/03. London: Research Development & Statistics Directorate, October 24, 2003.

Central Intelligence Agency. *The World Factbook*. 2004. Available at: www.cia.gov/cia/publications/factbook/geos/lg.html. Accessed December 12, 2004.

Interpol. European Police and Justice Systems–Latvia. Available at: www.interpol.int/public/Region/Europe/pjsystems/Latvia.asp. Accessed September 29, 2004.

Kangaspunta, K., ed. *Profiles of Criminal Justice Systems in Europe and North America*. HEUNI Publication Series, 26, 1995.

Kangaspunta, K., Joutsen, M., Ollus, N., and Nevala, S., eds. *Profiles of Criminal Justice Systems in Europe and North America 1990–1994*. HEUNI Publication Series, 33, 1999.

Latvia, Republic of. Law on Police. 1991. Available at: www.legislationline.org/view.php?document=59672&ref=true. Accessed September 29, 2004.

Meibergs, A. *The New Approach to Police Training in Latvia After Political Changes in 1991*. Ljubljana, Slovenia: College of Police and Security Studies, 1996.

Van de Beek, F., ed. *Facts, Figures & General Information 2000*. Amersfoort, The Netherlands: European Network of Policewomen, September 2000.

LEBANON

Background Material

Lebanese history goes back thousands of years. Lebanon played a major role in trade and politics of the Middle East and beyond due to its strategic location in the center of the old world. It is named in the Bible as the source of the wood used to build the Temple of King Solomon. Its coastal cities were home to many civilizations.

Lebanon, a small country with an area of 10,452 square kilometers, lies on the eastern side of the Mediterranean Sea. It is bordered by Syria at the east and north, the Mediterranean Sea at the west, and Israel to the south.

Before World War I, Lebanon was occupied by the Ottoman Empire. With the defeat of Turkey in 1918, France controlled Lebanese politics through a mandate that lasted until 1943. The French system of internal security forces was copied in Lebanon, and this constituted the first real organization of police. In 1926, Lebanon became a republic and declared Beirut as its capital. Its first constitution was drafted and implemented in what was known as Great Lebanon. In 1943, Lebanon gained its independence from the French mandate, and the final withdrawal of foreign troops took place on December 31, 1946.

In the mid-1970s, a civil war erupted in Lebanon. This war was provoked and financed by foreign countries. It ended in 1990 when all Lebanese powers agreed in Taif (Saudi Arabia) to put an end to the fighting.

Currently, more than 4 million Lebanese live in Lebanon, and Lebanon hosts around 400,000 Palestinian refuges in temporary camps. Because Lebanon has been a democratic and free republic, many minorities choose to settle there, such as Armenians and Kurds. Lebanon has eighteen recognized religious sects, with Islam and Christianity being the main religions.

Lebanese citizens speak Arabic as the official language, but French and English are spoken and taught at schools as second tongues. French, American, English, Italian, and German schools and universities are established in Lebanon. The American University of Beirut was founded in 1866, and Saint Joseph University (USJ) in 1912.

Major economic activities include tourism, industry, and trade (open transit). Tourists from all the Arab states, especially from the Gulf region, comprise around 90% of the tourism in Lebanon. They come to enjoy the pleasant weather, tourist attractions, and security. However, the country's major threat continues to be occasional instability on its southern border with Israel.

Contextual Features

Lebanese citizens elect 128 members to the parliament, which constitutes the legislative system. The parliament enacts laws and elects the president of the Republic. Parliamentary terms are four year. The parliament supervises the government and endorses its activities. The Parliament approves the budget prepared by the cabinet and can impose amendments.

The president of the Republic, who is elected by the Parliament, appoints the prime minister after an obligatory discussion with the Parliament members. Then the prime minister chooses his cabinet in cooperation with the speaker of the Parliament and the president. About twenty ministers represent the various, religions, and territories in Lebanon form the cabinet. The cabinet rules the country with consent of the Parliament. There is no set time span for the term of the government; it is bound to the constitution and the laws. The cabinet appoints public servants and proposes laws to the Parliament, which issues the laws.

The judicial authority issues appropriate sanctions for violations of the law. The government appoints judges proposed by the High Judiciary Commission. Lebanon has three levels of courts. First instance courts may be comprised of a single judge or a judge with two assistant counselors. The Appeal Courts are comprised of three judges and stationed in the center of the Mohaffaza (district). There are six main Mohafazzas in Lebanon: Beirut, Beqaa, North, South, Mountain of Lebanon, and Nabatieh. In every district court, a general prosecutor, with the assistance of other judges, ensures implementation of the law and the right follow-up on judicial matters. Also, there is a magistrate judge who carries out initial investigations on crimes with potential sanctions exceeding ten years (felonies and misdemeanors). The sentence of the appeal court may reach capital punishment. There are seven courts located in Beirut in the judicial palace. Some sentences issued by the appeal courts could be re-judged in front of the cassation courts. In addition to the judicial courts, there are the administrative courts that look after the pleas and suits raised against municipalities, government services, and public utilities. Also, the military court, composed of military and civilian judges, looks after crimes done by the army or police in active service. This court was established to improve supervision of duties carried out by militia members and police. The Supreme Court ensures that the laws are in harmony with the constitution. The Parliament and cabinet elect its members, who are retired judges or highly qualified lawyers.

The criminal code, issued as Law 340 dated January 3, 1994, is amended periodically to deal with new types of crime materialized in the new millennium such as money laundering, terrorism, human being trafficking, violation of intellectual property rights, and cyber crime.

The most common crimes in Lebanon are theft, burglary, financial crimes, terrorism, credit and bank card fraud, and homicide. The police arrest suspects and execute the warrants and sentences issued by judges. Correction centers are under the supervision of the judicial system, but their security is under the police authority. A major corrections center is in Roumyeh, which houses around 5,000 inmates. The police are aided by social assistants to help juveniles and women offenders build productive lives upon release.

Police Profile

Background

Lebanon adopted a police system during the rule of Emir-Fakhredine II (1589–1635), the founder of the modern Lebanon. Changes took place on June 9, 1861 when a protocol was set by France, United

Kingdom, Prussia (Germany), Russia, and Ostreich, and determined the creation of the Lebanese gendarmerie with the ratio of seven members for every 1,000 inhabitants (Article 14 of the protocol). The force started with 1,500 members supported by the Turkish army (Drakons) who ruled the territory of "Mutasrifiat" Jabal Lobnan (police of Mount Lebanon). Their mission included guarding prisons, investigations, and escorting VIPs. All citizens were Ottomans until 1920 when General Gorou, the French high commissioner, established Great Lebanon with an area of 10,452 square kilometers. A French commissioner was sent to Beirut to reorganize the police force, and to build up the force by recruiting new members at the police academy.

The police served in the cities and the gendarmerie in the rural areas, similar to the French system of policing. The director of police stationed in Beirut commanded all police forces in Beirut, Tripoli, Saida, Zahle, and Baalbeck. All detectives and general security officers were commanders of the gendarmerie. They ran all the forces, implemented security operations outside the cities, and supported the police force when needed. The French forces were the effective commanders of both the police and gendarmerie until 1943 when Lebanon was liberated and became independent. During the French era (1920–1943), horses were used frequently to patrol the rural areas. Later, motorcycles and cars were introduced gradually.

Demographics

The police force in Lebanon is comprised of approximately 14,000 men and only two women, who are commissioned officers in the computer division. The force also employs approximately 300 civilians of both genders, most of whom work in administrative services.

Organizational Description

The police and gendarmerie worked separately until 1959, when both were united under the Directorate General of the Internal Security Force (ISF) that consisted of the gendarmerie, Beirut police, judicial police (detectives), and the Institute.

Each unit is headed by a senior commander; duties are carried out under the supervision of judges. A general inspection department was enacted to check all police stations to improve the service. The Internal Security Forces are accountable to the Ministry of the Interior.

In 1967, Law No. 54 was enacted to reorganize the four units that constituted the internal security forces. This new law enforced new administrative

sanctions and granted more authority to the commanders to improve service. It was implemented until 1990, when the civil war ended in Lebanon. In that year, a new policing service organization was regulated through Law No. 17. This law is still in effect, and has created new units within the directorate, and set the rules for promotions and ranking, use of firearms, accountability regulations, and many other principles.

The territorial gendarmerie is headed by a general. This unit looks after security outside Beirut, the capital, and accounts for about 65% of all internal security forces.

The territorial gendarmerie keeps order through patrols (by car, boat, and on foot). Ninety-five percent of these officers wear the uniform, and the rest use the informal ISF dress. Gendarmerie officers are selected from the internal security forces, and share the same criteria for selection, promotion, and sanctions as all other forces.

The judiciary police (detectives) comprise a specialized unit focusing on felonies and misdemeanors. It is headed by a senior officer who works under the commandant of the director general and under the supervision of the state prosecutor. This force is constituted of a general criminal investigations division and three bureaus focused on drugs, gambling, and moral protection. Each bureau has specialized sergeants and officers, and they enforce the law according to their duties within the entire country. These bureaus, especially the one responsible for combating drug trafficking, are considered very effective.

The special criminal investigation division focuses on financial crimes and terrorism. It is composed of bureaus specialized in finance and money laundering offenses; terrorism prevention; and international theft prevention. These bureaus carry out their duties under the direction and supervision of the financial prosecutor.

The scientific police division is the internal security force's forensic science laboratory. It includes the identification bureau and criminalistics laboratories.

The criminal records division is the archive of the various forces' documents and records.

The central criminal investigation division is under the direct supervision of the state prosecutor, and exercises initial investigations at the judge's request.

The territorial criminal Investigations Division is comprised of fourteen judiciary territorial brigades spread across Lebanon. Their duties are to prosecute each crime (homicide, theft, rape, and forgery), and carry out missions to collect evidence and arrest the perpetrators.

The judiciary identifies and the Explosive Division carries out missions using dogs and people (explosive detectors) and the crises squad to identify victims and offenders.

The Tourist Division carries out its duties in cooperation with the Ministry of Tourism to enforce laws and ensure the security of tourists.

The mobile gendarmerie is the reserve unit of the ISF. It has specialized divisions focused on issues and situations relating to public order, peace maintenance, escorts, demonstrations, hostage crises, and snipers.

Functions

The main missions of the ISF follow:

To keep order and maintain security in Lebanese territory

To protect life and property

To protect liberties under the law

To enforce the law and implement orders of the judicial system, fight crime (preventive and reactive), and guard diplomatic missions and prisons (corrections)

Members of the police force work as administrators when assisting government public servants, and if they detect a crime they act as assistants for the judge and preserve the crime scene. Searching for evidence, keeping the perpetrator under control, helping the victim are typical duties; sometimes the prosecutor asks the police to go on with their investigation actions and carry out the same authority as the judge.

Training

ISF requirements include Lebanese citizenship, passing physical and mental health exams, and passing an extensive training program.

The ISF Institute is the police academy. Promotion to a higher rank requires the successful completion and passing of the training exam at the Institute. Training for special types of service requires appropriate session training.

Police Use of Firearms

The police force cannot use firearms except when all other options have already been exhausted, as in the following cases:

- Execution of an assignment from administrative authority while establishing security
- Legitimate self defense
- Prevent loss of firearms or seizure of equipment

- Defend their stations and the places they are assigned to guard
- Preserve the persons of or ensure the safety of individuals they are assigned to guard
- Arrest suspects who try to escape and do not comply to a clear warning
- Stopping vehicles that cross the check points despite warnings

Complaints and Discipline

Lebanon, as a free democratic country, complies with the Charter of Human Rights and has joined most of the international pacts in this field. The ISF has the authority to check and investigate all allegations lodged against police officers at the request of the victim or the Ministry of the Interior.

There are programs run by the directorate and in cooperation with the United Nations to train police officers how to carry out respectful investigation and collecting evidence, voluntary confessions, and using modern information technology to handle the offender. Lebanon's criminal procedure code specifies the human rights of suspects, including the right to remain silent, the right to request an attorney, the right to medical treatment as necessary, and the right to a translator.

Lebanese police take part in international seminars in Europe, America, Asia, and Australia on trafficking in human beings, terrorism, money laundering, drug trafficking, and cyber crime that are organized by Interpol and IPES (International Police Executive Symposium).

Terrorism

In Lebanon, the police sometimes find themselves in direct confrontations with perpetrators who are backed by foreign powers. In 2004, a terrorist group supported by Zarkawi was responsible for political crimes committed in defense of their creeds and beliefs.

The judicial police unit includes the terrorism prevention bureau, whose members are trained to deal with terrorist threats in conjunction with the intelligence services of the Lebanese army. This bureau is headed by a senior officer who is subject to continuous training.

International Cooperation

Lebanon cooperates with the international community through the IPSG, the Interpol command center in Lyons, France, through which the Lebanese National Central Bureau (NCB) cooperated with other Interpol administrations, especially in matters relating to drug trafficking, car theft, money laundering, the financing of terrorist organizations, illegal immigration, and trafficking in human beings.

Lebanon also works with Europol, the Australian federal police, and the U.S. Federal Bureau of Investigation (FBI). Many Lebanese police officers have graduated from FBI training programs. Lebanon also sends officers to complete the ten-week training program offered by the United Kingdom police academy, Bramshill.

Police Education, Research, and Publications

Lebanese police attend the following:

Commissioned Officer College (CO): This college prepares the recruit who joins the force with the bachelor degree in law, training for one year. Upon successful completion, the graduate is a commissioned officer. In addition, the CO trains people who finish training in the Lebanese army's military school for three years. These graduates receive six months of police training in order to start as a sworn CO. The program consists of theoretical and practical training and research.

Noncommissioned Officers School: This school welcomes the successful civilian recruit who passes medicine, physical fitness, and culture exams, and nine months of training in theoretical and practical studies.

Common School: Here officers are trained to deal with issues relating to drug trafficking, terrorism, money laundering, and forgery. In this school, academics and skilled COs teach the junior officers special training in public order and penal code procedures that assist the police in better performing their duties.

Relevant publications are listed below:

- *Al Amen* (Security): Monthly publication that covers important operational tasks carried out by the force, provides guidance for officers and reflects the daily lives of officers, and serves as an advocate for retired officers
- *The Security Research Publication*: Seasonal publication consisting of essays related to police subjects written by police officers or civilians.

ANWAR YEHYA

Websites
Internal Security Force: *www.isf.gov.lb*
Lebanese Army: *www.lebarmy.gov.lb*
Crime Stoppers International: *www.c-s-i.org*

LESOTHO

Background Material

Basutoland was renamed the Kingdom of Lesotho upon independence from the United Kingdom in 1966. King Moshoeshoe was exiled in 1990. Constitutional government was restored in 1993 after twenty-three years of military rule. In 1998, violent protests and a military mutiny following a contentious election prompted a brief but bloody South African military intervention. Constitutional reforms have since restored political stability; peaceful parliamentary elections were held in 2002.

More than 99% of Lesotho's population is ethnically Basotho; other ethnic groups include Europeans and Asians. The country's population is 80% Christian, the majority of whom are Roman Catholic. Other religions are Islam, Hindu, and indigenous beliefs. Sesotho and English are official languages, and other languages spoken in-clude Zulu and Xhosa.

Small, landlocked, and mountainous, Lesotho relies on remittances from miners employed in South Africa and customs duties from the Southern Africa Customs Union for the majority of government revenue, but the government has strengthened its tax system to reduce dependency on customs duties. Completion of a major hydropower facility in January 1998 now permits the sale of water to South Africa, also generating royalties for Lesotho. As the number of mineworkers has declined steadily over the past several years, a small manufacturing base has developed based on farm products that support the milling, canning, leather, and jute industries, and a rapidly growing apparel assembly sector. The economy is still primarily based on subsistence agriculture, especially livestock, although drought has decreased agricultural activity. The extreme inequality in the distribution of income remains a major drawback. Lesotho has signed an Interim Poverty Reduction and Growth Facility with the International Monetary Fund.

Contextual Features

Lesotho is a constitutional monarchy, based on English common law and Roman-Dutch law, with King Letsie III as head of state. Under the 1993 constitution, the king fills a ceremonial role, has no executive authority, and is proscribed from actively taking part in political initiatives. Prime Minister Pakalitha Mosisili, the leader of the Lesotho Congress for Democracy (LCD) party, took office in June 1998 and is the head of government.

The Lesotho Congress for Democracy (LCD) controls a majority in the National Assembly (the lower house of parliament), with the Basotho National Party (BNP), Lesotho People's Congress, and the National Independent Party among the nine opposition parties represented. The upper house of parliament, called the Senate, is composed of twenty-two principal chiefs whose membership is hereditary, and eleven appointees of the king, acting on the advice of the prime minister.

The constitution provides for an independent judicial system. The judiciary is made up of the Court of Appeal, the High Court, Magistrate's Courts, and traditional courts that exist predominately in rural areas. All but one of the Justices on the Court of Appeal are South African jurists. There is no trial by jury; rather, judges make rulings alone, or, in the case of criminal trials, with two other judges as observers. Judicial review of legislative acts takes place in High Court and Court of Appeals. The constitution also protects basic civil liberties, including freedom of speech, association, and the press; freedom of peaceful assembly; and freedom of religion.

In the past, magistrates appeared to be subject at times to government and chieftainship influence. Opposition parties alleged that the High Court was biased against them in relation to cases they filed following the May 1998 elections; however, court officials indicated that the opposition cases failed to succeed due to a lack of evidence to support their claims.

The High Court also provides procedural and substantive advice and guidance on matters of law and procedure to military tribunals; however, it does not participate in arriving at judgments. Military tribunals operating under the 1996 Defense Act have jurisdiction only over military cases, such as the trial of alleged army mutineers. Decisions by military tribunals can be appealed only to a special court-martial appeal court, which is composed of two judges from the High Court, one retired military officer with a legal background, and the registrar of the High Court.

Persons detained or arrested in criminal cases and defendants in civil cases have the right to legal counsel; however, there is no system to provide public defenders. The Ministry of Justice and the nongovernmental organization community maintain a few legal aid clinics. The authorities generally respect court decisions and rulings. There is no trial by jury. Criminal trials normally are adjudicated by a single High Court judge who presides, with two assessors serving in an advisory capacity. In civil cases, judges normally hear cases alone. The 1981 Criminal Procedures and Evidence Act, as amended in 1984, makes provision for granting bail. Bail is granted regularly and generally fairly. There is a large case backlog, which leads to lengthy delays in trials. In September 1998, a Molotov cocktail attack on the High Court destroyed case files and other important documents and further hampered the operations of the courts.

In civil courts, women and men are accorded equal rights; however, in traditional and customary courts, certain rights and privileges accorded to men are denied to women. When traditional law and custom are invoked in a court case, a male plaintiff can opt for customary judgments by a principal chief rather than a civil court, and the judgment is binding legally. This system is greatly disadvantageous to women. For administrative purposes, Lesotho is divided into ten districts, each headed by a district secretary.

Prison conditions are poor. Prison facilities are overcrowded and in disrepair, but conditions do not threaten the health or lives of inmates. Amnesty International representatives visited the LDF soldiers accused of mutiny being held in the maximum security prison in Maseru, and reported that cells were infested with insects, and there was a lack of ventilation, light, proper bedding, and adequate sanitation facilities. In January 1999, the Judge Advocate ordered prison officials to improve conditions in the cells in which the soldiers accused of mutiny were being held. As a result, the soldiers received cots and better food. Women are housed separately from men, and juveniles are housed separately from adults. Rape in prison reportedly is not a problem.

Police Profile

The security forces consist of the Lesotho Defense Force (LDF), the Lesotho Police Service (LPS—previously known as the Royal Lesotho Mounted Police—[RLMP]), and the National Security Service (NSS). The prime minister is the minister of defense, with direct authority over the LDF and the NSS. The police force is under the authority of the Ministry of Home Affairs. In 1996 and 1997, the Parliament passed the Lesotho Defense Act (1996) and Regulations for Military Justice (1997), and amended the Royal Lesotho Mounted Police Force Act. This legislation was designed to bring these services under direct civilian control. However, the politicized armed services have a history of intervening in the country's politics and government. The LDF ruled the country with two successive military regimes from 1985–1990, and 1990–1993. In September 1998, a South African Development Community (SADC) task force put down an army rebellion, arrested LDF rebels, and disarmed the remaining soldiers. Fifty army personnel were accused of fomenting mutiny in September 1998, and charged in December 1998 with the capital offense of mutiny and high treason: They were brought before court-martial hearings in January. This is the first instance in which a courtmartial prosecuted LDF soldiers for infractions against the Defense Act. The LDF continues to be the subject of a national debate on the structure, size, and role of the military. The NSS and the LPS also are undergoing comprehensive restructuring. There were allegations that the members of the security forces on occasion committed human rights abuses.

The government generally respects many of the human rights of its citizens; however, there continue to be problems in some areas. There were unconfirmed allegations of torture by security forces, and credible reports that the police, at times, used excessive force against detainees. Prison conditions are poor, and lengthy pretrial detention is a problem. There are long delays in trials; the RLMP members charged with treason in a February 1997 police mutiny have remained in the maximum security prison for eighteen months without significant progress toward finishing the trials in their cases. Discipline within the security services was undermined severely during the 1998 crisis. Clashes with SADC forces initiated by armed opposition supporters and army mutineers in September 1998 resulted in the death of nine members of the South African National Defense Force, sixty LDF soldiers, and more than forty citizens allied with the opposition. A total of thirty-three members of the RLMP face sedition and high treason charges following their involvement in the February 1997 police mutiny, which reflected entrenched mistrust and political competition between the government and some elements within the police force, and an uneasy institutional rivalry between elements of the police and the army. The LDF ultimately quelled the police mutiny. This step away from active partisan engagement in politics to a more professional civil/military relationship was reversed by the junior officer mutiny in 1998, which undermined the integrity of the security forces.

Authorities infringe on citizens' privacy rights. Although search warrants are required under normal circumstances, the 1984 Internal Security Act (ISA) provides police with wide powers to stop and search persons and vehicles and to enter homes and other places without a warrant. There are no prohibitions against monitoring telephone conversations. The security services are believed to monitor routinely telephone conversations of Basothos and foreigners, ostensibly on national security grounds.

MINTIE DAS

Bibliography

Central Intelligence Agency. *The World Factbook*. 2005. Available at: www.cia.gov/cia/publications/factbook.

Library of Congress. "Country Reports." 1987. Available at: www.lcweb2.loc.gov/rfd/cs.

U.S. Department of Justice. 2005. "Background Note." Available at: www.travel.state.gov/travel.

LIBERIA

Background Material

The Republic of Liberia, located on the west cost of Africa, is Africa's oldest nation-state. It comprises an area of 111,370 square kilometers, and has a population of 3,390,635 (July 2004 estimate).

Liberia, which means "land of the free," was founded by freed slaves from the United States in 1820. Its capital, Monrovia, is named after the fifth president of the United States, James Monroe. Those freed slaves were members of the American Colonization Society. On July 26, 1847, the Liberian Declaration of Independence was adopted and signed. Britain was one of the early nations to recognize the Republic of Liberia. Although the U.S. government nurtured the idea of settling slaves in Africa, it did not recognize Liberia as a sovereign nation until the American Civil War. In 1919, Liberia became one of the first countries in the world to sign the League of Nations covenant.

William V.S. Tubman was voted to the first of seven terms as Liberian president in 1944. As a result of Tubman's death in 1971, William R. Tolbert, Jr. was elected to that office after concluding Tubman's unfinished tenure. Until 1980, when indigenous Liberian Master Sergeant Samuel K. Doe, from the Krahn ethnic group, seized power in a coup d'etat, Liberia was, largely, a stable nation. This event of April 12, 1980 ended the 133-year reign of Americo-Liberian political domination in Liberia. President Doe's power lasted until 1989 when Charles Taylor, an Americo-Liberian, and his associates took over power. The demise of Doe led to a civil war in Liberia, which culminated in various ethnic groups fighting for political control.

Some observers have argued that Liberia became a "failed state" because of increased armed conflict in the country, which led to the deterioration of all of its state structures and violations of human rights with utter impunity. With the aid of the international community, Charles Gyude Bryant was elected to the office of the executive president on October 14, 2003. Taylor moved into exile in Nigeria, which some believe may improve the quality of life of the Liberian people.

Liberia is still recuperating from the ravages of war. Its public affairs are in tatters. Its educational institutions are in glaring disarray. The most elementary security needs of individual citizens have not been met, as violence during Doe's and Taylor's administrations became the norm inside and outside of government. The economy was very badly damaged. Relationships with neighboring ethnic groups have resulted in major setbacks. Liberia's civil war created difficulties with neighboring Sierra Leone, Guinea, and Cote d'Ivoire by forcing violent situations in those countries. Under Taylor, the government of Liberia did little to improve the lives of the Liberian people.

The Armed Forces of Liberia (AFL), the government army under the Doe government, remains one of the major challenges to continued peace and stability in Liberia. The AFL has a history of ethnic and political persecutions and serious human rights violations in Liberia during the Doe administration. Doe's, Taylor's, and Johnson's troops used the army to kidnap foreign expatriates in Liberia, which was tantamount to acts of state terrorism. The AFL also was responsible for extensive killings of Liberian citizens, particularly, members of the Gio and Mano ethnic groups, not to mention the wanton destruction and looting of properties. Because of these acts, members of the Economic Community of West African States (ECOWAS) decided to establish a framework for peace by creating an interim government. This was accomplished with the support of a regional peacekeeping force known as ECOMOG, that is, the ECOWAS Monitoring Group. Although ECOMOG, a predominantly Nigerian military force, failed to prevent the execution and gruesome torture of Doe on September 10, 1990, it still represented the only deployed military force that provided assistance in Liberia during that period.

The people of Liberia can be categorized into various ethnic groups, with Kpelle representing 20% of the population, Bassa 16%, Gio 8%, Kru 7%, and about 49% of the people representing over twelve other ethnic groups. These sixteen ethnic groups may be classified into three indigenous ethno-linguistic groups: Mande, Kwa, and Mel. According to the 2003 population estimate, together they account for the total population of 3,317,176 people.

Like many other West African countries that experienced the residual effects of colonialism, the official language of Liberia is English. However, there are also about twenty other ethnic group languages, some of which can be written and may be used in conducting business and official matters. About 40% of the people are Christians. Those with indigenous beliefs make up about 40%, while about 20% are Muslim. The Kpelle ethnic group alone constitutes the largest number of Christians, with the Basa being the next largest. The Mande peoples in the northwest region of the country are primarily Muslim.

In terms of economic activities, Liberia is richly endowed in water, mineral resources, forests, and a climate conducive to agriculture. Since 1951, Liberia has been a leading producer of iron ore in Africa, and it is one of the primary nations that exports iron ore to the world. In addition, it also produces other minerals, such as diamonds, gold, lead, manganese, graphite, cyanite, and barite. It has offshore oil reserves. Liberia also has the capacity to develop hydroelectric power. It has rich rubber plantations. As an agrarian economy, farming is the most essential economic activity for the majority of the people.

Liberian farmers grow and produce rice, cassava, sugarcane, palm oil, bananas, potatoes, and other crops for the general population. But the civil war, along with mismanagement, has contributed to the deterioration of the Liberian economy, particularly its infrastructure in Monrovia and the surrounding areas. In addition, many indigenous business entrepreneurs have deserted the country, leaving the economy in ruins. Perhaps, with the new administration, peaceful coexistence in the nation, and the support and encouragement of foreign investment, the economy will grow again. The average per capita income was estimated in 2002 at less than $170. The country has an unemployment rate of at least 70%, with a literacy rate of only 30%.

Contextual Features

Due to the Liberian civil war, which was one of Africa's bloodiest, more than 200,000 Liberians were killed, and about a million others were displaced and fled into refugee camps in neighboring African countries. In the northwest section of the country, government troops and pro-government militias and police were responsible for killing, torturing, and abusing civilians, raping women and girls, and abducting civilians for forced labor and combat. In such a disorganized era of the society, the police were corrupt and were used at the pleasure of the authorities for their own selfish motives.

Individual rights were violated without any regard for the rule of law. Police used unnecessary force to achieve their violent goals. The government security apparatus targeted members of civil society groups, legitimate political opposition, and the independent media, including the police. As reported by the Human Rights Watch (1997), Henry Cooper, chairman of Bong County, the Unity Party's opposition group, was taken into police custody and later found dead. Eyewitness accounts indicated that he was deliberately shot several times. Several newspaper editors and executives were also detained and tortured. The most horrible act of the police was the abduction and torture of Hassan Bility, the editor of the *Analyst*, one of Liberia's premier independent newspapers. According to some published reports, he was arrested with three other Mandingo men. Suffering from malaria, he was locked in a filled sewage tank. He was reportedly accused of engaging in acts of terrorism against the state.

All these violations happened without regard for the Liberian Constitution. According to Chapter 111, Article 21 of the constitution, no person charged, arrested, restricted, detained, or held in custody shall be subjected to torture or inhumane treatment. The constitution also prohibits placing innocent citizens together with convicted prisoners or treating those citizens as convicts without due process of the law.

Indeed, the constitution empowers the legislature to make it a criminal offense and provides for proportionate sanctions against any police or security officer, including prosecutors, who violate the provisions of the constitution, described as the final law of the land. In addition, the constitution directed that any person arrested or detained should have the right to appear in court of law within forty-eight hours of such arrests. Both the Doe and Taylor regimes abandoned these fundamental principles of the constitution in their treatment of political opponents accused of terrorist activities.

In mid-1980s, the state of Israel, aptly recognized for its intelligence and security alertness, provided special training for the Liberian government, leading to the establishment of an elite unit called Special Anti-Terrorist Unit (SATU). Also, in 1992, the Guinean government, with ECOWAS's consent, trained a special division referred to as the Black Berets. This division, together with ECO-MOG troops, battled against Liberian National Police Force rebels during operation OCTOPUS in 1992 and 1993.

The regular security forces in Liberia consist of the following: Armed Forces of Liberia (AFL), a Liberian military with the responsibility to defend the homeland against external aggressors; Liberia National Police (LPN), which have the primary responsibility for maintaining internal security; Antiterrorist Unit (ATU), with members from foreign nationals such as Burkina Faso, Gambia, and Sierra Leone who make up an elite special forces group; and the Special Security Service (SSS), composed of a heavily armed executive protection force. In addition, there are a number of other irregular security services involved with cardinal ministries and parastatal corporations without clear responsibilities. In 2002, it was reported that the security forces committed many unlawful killings, accused of the disappearances of many people, especially ethnic Mandigos suspected of antigovernment activities. Security forces also frequently tortured citizens, violated citizens' privacy rights, restricted freedom of movement of the people, harassed human rights monitors, detained and intimated journalists, and continued to use capricious arrests in the country.

Politically, the country's government structure is patterned like that of the United States. The constitutions for both nations provide for three branches of government—executive, legislature, and judiciary. Liberia's centralized republic is dominated by a strong executive presidency. The president is both the chief of state and head of government, elected by popular vote for a six-year term. President Gyude Bryant assumed office as chairman of the National Transitional Government on October 14, 2003 after a U.N.- brokered cease-fire agreement among various ethnic factions. The bicameral national legislature consists of twenty-six senators and sixty-four representatives. Senators serve nine-year terms, while house members serve for six years.

According to the constitution, the judicial branch is headed by a Supreme Court consisting of a chief justice and four associate justices. Inferior courts may be established as deemed necessary by legislative acts. All judges in the country are appointed by the president with the consent and advice of the Senate.

Under the control of the executive branch, the judicial system is functional. The new administration has insisted that it will allow a strong and independent judiciary. The newly reconstituted Supreme Court has sworn in Gloria Scott as the chief justice. She has pledged to maintain the honor of the Court and to be autonomous of the executive branch of government. Basically, a five-judge Supreme Court that supervises other lower courts such as criminal courts, appeals court, and magistrate's courts heads the Liberian justice system. In addition to its statutory legal system, the country recognizes the essential role of traditional courts and other lay courts in the various counties. Trial by ordeal is also practiced in some parts of the country.

The constitution provides that the bicameral legislature has the power to establish inferior courts whenever it is needed. Currently, Liberia does not have a judicial council or corresponding body. However, the Supreme Court of Liberia developed a Judicial Reform Commission. According to the commission's recommendations, in order to maintain the judicial integrity and competence of lawyers seeking judicial positions, the president of Liberia must appoint a Judicial Service Commission with the power and authority to review credentials, records, the backgrounds of lawyers, and to make recommendations to the president. It is similar to the role the American Bar Association plays when presidents make judicial appointments in the United States.

The government is highly centralized. The local government structure is represented in the formations of town chiefs, county superintendents, and district commissioners, all of whom are appointed by the president. Furthermore, there are clan chiefs and paramount chiefs. Public schools, hospitals, roads, and police are controlled by the central government. While mayors are elected in Liberia, superintendents appointed by the executive president administer the fifteen counties. These counties face an increase in the numbers of armed robberies, which have escalated due to the destruction of the country's economy and infrastructure, coupled with factional acts of violence and a lack of a broad spectrum of peaceful prospects.

Liberia's Ministry of Justice is responsible for the corrections system. The prisons operated by the Ministry of Justice have the basic function of holding individuals who are either charged or convicted of crimes. Prisons in Liberia have, historically, been overcrowded. However, during the Doe administration, the Armed Forces of Liberia managed military prisons. Police cells were used to confine persons without charging them and their keepers often subjected suspects to violence. There were three main prisons during Doe's term in office, including the Monrovia Central Prison, the Post Stockade Military Prison (in Monrovia), and the Belle, Yalla, Maximum-Security Prison Camp, located in Lofa County.

The Liberian Central Prison is now in operation under the new administration. Generally, prisons in Liberia are poorly managed, but the new government is determined to see that prisoners are treated with dignity under the rule of law. In 2002, prison conditions remained harsh and sometimes life-threatening. Lengthy pretrial detention is still common in Liberia.

Police Profile

Background

The Liberian Ministry of Justice has the ultimate responsibility of promoting the rule of law in Liberia. In addition, it is also entrusted with the power for the administration of the judiciary, the Bureau of Rehabilitation, and National Police Force.

The Doe administration utilized the police force as a means of providing employment to his political clientele. Despite the fact that a high school certificate was a requirement for recruitment into the police force, the majority of the police under Doe were illiterate. Prior to the civil unrest that wrecked the Liberian economy, the police force numbered approximately 2,000. Indeed, the role of the police during the war was limited to traffic control and the protection of civilians from common crime in the capital city of Monrovia.

Preceding the development of the Liberian National Police Force in 1924, law enforcement functions and internal security of the country were the responsibility of the Liberian Frontier Force or the Liberian Regular Military. During the mid-1950s when the criminal investigation division of the police force was established, the security apparatus of the country was reorganized to include the Special Security Service, National Bureau of Investigation, Executive Action Bureau, and National Intelligence and Security Service. Moreover, President Tubman also established a network of informants known as public relations officers (PROS), which reported directly to his office. The National Bureau of Investigation worked closely with the police in criminal matters and criminal investigations. One of the functions of the Executive Action Bureau was to control subversive activities against the president. Another organization, the Liberian Joint Security Commission, serves as a strategic institute responsible for coordinating the police and armed forces of Liberia.

Demographics

It is important to assert that the Liberian National Security Agency, which has similar functions like the American Central Intelligence Agency (CIA), had about forty-three trained professional agents in 1994. That number is not inclusive of other agency personnel, such as essential employees who were involved in divergent assignments across the country. It has also been reported that former President Taylor established another security arm of the government known as the Ministry of National Security (MNS) during the 1998–1999 period.

It has been estimated that the Liberian National Police Force maintained about 2,300 members in 1994. Promotion in the force during this tumultuous era was based, not on merit, but on a political patronage system. Although there were more police officers than patrolmen to carry out their law enforcement missions, generally, the police were highly dedicated professionals.

Organizational Description and Functions

The Liberian National Police is both local and national in its representation. Police stations are established throughout the country. Members of the police force are recruited on a voluntary basis from all areas of the counties. The Mende ethnic group makes up the largest staff of the police. The police headquarters are located in the capital city of Monrovia, under the supervision of the Attorney General of the republic. The president appoints the director general of the police, who holds the rank of colonel. Other top police bureaucrats hold honorary military ranks.

The Central Police Headquarters consists of two major components, namely, the Operations Office and the Technical and Administrative Services. The Operations Office is responsible for the active police forces, and is under the leadership of a senior inspector who is the third most senior police executive next to the director and deputy director of police. This office maintains centralized control of all police units in the nation. The Operations Office consists of four main areas: the Criminal Records and Identification Division, Traffic Division, Patrol Division, and Criminal Investigation Department (CID). Together, their functions respectively range from gathering and maintaining the repository of all identification and crime data;

directing traffic; supervision of patrol officers in all regions; and providing detective services and investigation of crimes. The Technical and Administrative Services unit is responsible for the Liberian Police Academy. Under the auspices of an Inspector General, this arm of the police is in charge of all administrative duties of the local and national police headquarters.

There are also two principal field components of the Liberian Police Force. They are the Monrovia Police and the County and Provincial Police. The Monrovia police supervise all police operations within the capital. A deputy inspector of police heads it. An inspector charged with the authority to govern all regional police posts controls the County and Provincial Police. Because of its centralized nature, rural and local police units have autonomous powers from the centralized police command in Monrovia due, primarily, to a lack of proper supervision from Monrovia. Although such a scenario may exist, the bureaucratic structure of the national police is clearly delineated by a chain of command.

Like their American counterparts, the Liberian Police Force rank and grade structures follow a military style. With the exception of the director and the deputy director, the police ranks in Liberia begin from patrol officers to senior inspectors of police. Patrol officers can advance in their career by attaining the rank of sergeant, lieutenant, captain, and inspector. Steps on the salary scale are established in each position classification. New recruits usually start at the bottom of the salary scale. Each regional police post in Liberia has at least a lieutenant, patrol officers, and more than two sergeants that carry out police missions.

The missions of the police are to maintain order, ensure conformity of the regulation and laws of the region that they have authority to police, and provide for the security of all persons and their property within the state. This is accomplished with fairness according to the utmost professional law enforcement values, with paramount respect for human rights and dignity, with the objective of gaining and building public assurance and trust. While these missions are bold and reasonable, police functions also should include the apprehension of criminals based on democratic principles.

Police Use of Firearms

It has also been reported that former President Taylor established another security arm of the government known as the Ministry of National Security (MNS) during the 1998–1999 period. President Taylor's agency employed about 350 national police officers as well as members of the AFL. It was during this period of instability that rifles were introduced as part of the police arsenal in Liberia. The continued use of rifles by the police has been rejected and abandoned by the officials of the International Police Service (IPS), which is now training a new reconstituted national police.

While patrol officers are only allowed to carry nightsticks and whistles, the Liberian police were originally armed with revolvers. As observed by the Human Rights Watch Report of 1997, Liberian police officers were not allowed to carry arms, but were allowed access to batons and backup radios to enable them to seek armed assistance when in trouble. In 2004, Commissioner Mark A. Kroeker, appointed by the United Nations to reform the police in Liberia, indicated that the police should only be permitted to carry sidearms during the transition period.

Complaints and Discipline

Prior to the new executive government in 2003, the Liberian police have been responsible for arbitrary and capricious arrests, detention without trial, and corruption and brutality. Prior to the war, the police force numbered approximately 2,000 personnel, as the warring factions utilized the police force employment as a means to reward their political supporters.

Terrorism

Prior to the al-Qaeda network's havoc against the people of the United States and the world on September 11, 2001, Taylor was involved in trading diamonds with some terrorist organizations. The U.N. Special Court on Sierra Leone asserted that Taylor was harboring terrorists from the Middle East. Liberia may not be alone, because Africa in general may become a breeding ground for international terrorist organizations (Brooks 2003). The Liberian National Police Force, coupled with its intelligence apparatus, may be trained to combat terrorism, provide intelligence that will aid in alleviating the penetration of international terrorist cells in Liberia.

International Cooperation

It is abundantly clear that the new administration has an urgent need to restructure the police and to determine the appropriate size for the Liberian police force. The Security Council established the United Nations mission in Liberia (UNMIL) in 2003. A relevant mandate of the UNMIL was to provide support for security reform. Indeed, its goal was to support the transitional government of Liberia in examining and restructuring the police force of Liberia, consistent with democratic policing. It is also charged with the mandate of developing a civilian police education curriculum, and to assist in the training of civilian police, in collaboration with ECOWAS.

As a result, Commissioner Mark A. Kroeker, a U.S. citizen, has been appointed by the United Nations to run and supervise the International Police Service, the Civilian Police Operation of the United Nations in Liberia. Currently, he has seventy-two personnel in his office that represents about twenty countries. There are also 240 armed police officers in two police posts, one from Jordan and the other from Nepal. According to Commissioner Kroeker, the police unit from Jordan is positioned at the Police Academy, and the Nepalese are located at the Liberia National Police Headquarters. The functions of these police posts are to help to develop the parameters of the rule of law and to establish suitable police capability in all regions of the country.

Meanwhile, Commissioner Kroeker's office has implemented a rigorous crime prevention strategy designed to involve the community as co-producers of justice in the crime prevention programs of the IPS. The program enumerates what the community needs to do in order to combat robberies, how to report crimes to the police, and how the police can be involved equally in crime prevention.

The IPS is also involved in a process called co-locating, which assigns police officers in various levels of the organization, such as consulting, technology transfer, sharing of information, and methods of providing assistance. In the area of responses to crime, the IPS has developed and introduced the 911 system with the support of the Lone Star Company. The 911 system will enable the police in emergency situations to locate the geographic position of the caller and provide immediate assistance. The IPS has also introduced procedures that will encourage people to report crimes, and has embarked on the process of crime analysis.

Most importantly, the IPS is also devoting valuable time to the problem of the custodial conditions involving prisoners and detainees, as well as addressing the problem of prison overcrowding. Currently, the police headquarters jail is over-crowded with inmates because of inadequate facilities to house convicted offenders. The International Committee of the Red Cross is another international agency that is helping to alleviate the problem of prison overcrowding so that convicted prisoners can be placed in total institutions separate from police stations.

In the fundamental area of police training and accountability, the Civil Police (CIVPOL) Operations have a mandated role to the members of the National Police Force. Components of the training sessions include the following: rule of law, tactical situation, reporting crimes, managing crowds, democratic policing principles, and human rights requirements for policing citizens in a democratic society. In addition, the IPS has an obligation to help to equip the police adequately enough to carry out important functions of law enforcement. Police training must emphasize, as the IPS has noted, the need that the law must govern police actions under democratic rule. The rule of law, not the vigilante tactics of mob governance, prevails in all democratic societies. In a democracy, the police must use deadly or punitive force only when necessary.

Police Education, Research, and Publications

In Liberia, police training and education are essentially performed by the Police Academy. Established in 1961, the Police Academy is also used today by the IPS to provide training and education to the Liberian National Police Force. The office also prepares various police strategies that employ members of the public in its crime prevention efforts. Currently, IPS is training about 4,000 interim police officers at the police academy facilities. All of the rookies entering the academy are expected to leave the academy with a professional understanding of police work in a democratic society. The academy buildings have independent classrooms where a group of twenty-five interim police officers, who have been carefully screened and psychologically evaluated, participate in the training. The hope is that they will continue to be become members of the police workforce after training. Basically, the IPS provides twelve days of training to police officers, with particular emphasis on policing citizens as dictated by the rule of law.

The literature on research and publications regarding the National Police Force of Liberia is, currently, very scanty. However, the UNMIL has been mandated by the United Nations to assist Liberia in its efforts to retrain and restructure its civilian police. ECOWAS has also played a pivotal role in training and reforming the police in Liberia.

Finally, the regular security forces in Liberia consist of the following: Armed Forces of Liberia (AFL), which have the responsibility of defending the homeland against external aggressors; Liberian National Police, which has the primary responsibility of maintaining internal security; Antiterrorist Unit (ATU), with members from Burkina Faso, Gambia, and Sierra Leone, among other countries, who make up an elite special forces group; and the Special Security Service (SSS), composed of a heavily armed executive protection force.

In addition, there are a number of other irregular security services involved with ministries and parastatal corporations without clear responsibilities. In 2002, it was reported that the security forces committed many unlawful killings, and were blamed for the disappearances of many people, especially ethnic Mandigos suspected of antigovernment activities. Security forces also frequently tortured citizens, violated citizens' privacy rights, restricted freedom of movement of the people, harassed human rights monitors, detained and intimidated journalists, and continued to use capricious arrests in the country.

IHEKWOABA D. ONWUDIWE

Bibliography

Brooks, Peter. "Liberating Liberia." 2003. Available at: www.townhall.com/columnists/peterbrookes/pb20030722.shtml. Accessed 22 April 2003.

Henry, Fenwick Reeve. The Black Republic: Liberia; Its Political and Social Conditions To-Day. New York: Negro Universities Press, 1969.

Human Rights Watch. "Human Rights Reports: Liberia—Rebuilding State Institutions." 1997. Available at: www.hrw.org/reports/1997/liberia/liberia-04.htm. Accessed 26 April 2004.

International Legal Assistance Consortium. "Assessment of the Liberian Judicial System." Stockholm, Sweden, 2003. Available at: www.ilacinternational.org. Accessed 25 April 2004.

Jessup, A. Frank. Manpower Analysis of the Liberian National Police: Report to the Secretary of State by the U.S. Survey Mission to Liberia, Dated April 11, 1966. Washington, DC: Office of Public Safety, Agency for International Development, 1966.

Kurian, George Thomas. World Encyclopedia of Police Forces and Penal Systems. New York: Facts on File, 1989.

Liebenow, Gus. Liberia. Bloomington: Indiana University Press, 1987.

Ramsay, F. Jeffress. Global Studies: Africa. An Annual Edition's Publications. Guilford, CT: Dushkin Publishing Group, 1993.

Samukai, Brownie. "Disarmament and Demobilization Towards a Civic Oriented Mission." 2003. Available at: www.theperspective.org. Accessed 27 April 2004.

Sawyer, Amos. The Emergence of Autocracy in Liberia: Tragedy and Challenge. San Francisco: ICS Press, 1992.

U.S. Agency for International Development. "Liberia: Annual Report." Washington, DC, 2003. Available at: www.dec.org. Accessed 21 April 2004.

U.N. Mission in Liberia. "Liberia: Press Briefing by Acting SRSG Souren Seraydarian, Acting Force Commander Maj. Gen. Joseph Owonibi, and Police Commissioner Mark A. Kroeker." 2004. Available at: www.un.org. Accessed 27 April 2004.

LIBYA

Background Material

Since he took power in a 1969 military coup, Col. Muammar Abu Minyar al-Qadhafi has espoused his own political system—a combination of socialism and Islam—which he calls the "third international theory." Viewing himself as a revolutionary leader, he used oil funds during the 1970s and 1980s to promote his ideology outside Libya, even supporting subversives and terrorists abroad to hasten the end of Marxism and capitalism. Libyan military adventures failed; for instance, the prolonged foray of Libyan troops into the Aozou Strip in northern Chad was finally repulsed in 1987. Libyan support for terrorism decreased after UN sanctions were imposed in 1992. Those sanctions were suspended in April 1999.

Qadhafi's confrontational foreign policies and use of terrorism, as well as Libya's growing friendship with the Soviet Union, led to increased tensions with the West in the 1980s. Following a terrorist bombing at a discotheque in West Berlin frequented by American military personnel, in 1986 the U.S. retaliated militarily against targets in Libya, and imposed broad unilateral economic sanctions.

After Libya was implicated in the 1988 bombing of Pan Am flight 103 over Lockerbie, Scotland, UN sanctions were imposed in 1992. UN Security Council resolutions (UNSCRs) passed in 1992 and 1993 obliged Libya to fulfill requirements related to the Pan Am 103 bombing before sanctions could be lifted. Qadhafi initially refused to comply with these requirements, leading to Libya's political and economic isolation for most of the 1990s.

In 1999, Libya fulfilled one of the UNSCR requirements by surrendering two Libyans suspected in connection with the bombing for trial before a Scottish court in The Netherlands. One of these suspects, Abdel Basset al-Megrahi, was found guilty; the other was acquitted. Al-Megrahi's conviction was upheld on appeal in 2002. In August 2003, Libya fulfilled the remaining UNSCR requirements, including acceptance of responsibility for the actions of its officials and payment of appropriate compensation to the victims' families. UN sanctions were lifted on September 12, 2003.

On December 19, 2003, Libya announced its intention to rid itself of weapons of mass destruction and missile technology control regime (MTCR)-class missile programs. Since that time, it has cooperated with the United States, United Kingdom, International Atomic Energy Agency, and the Organization for the Prohibition of Chemical Weapons toward these objectives. Libya has also signed the IAEA Additional Protocol and has become a state party to the Chemical Weapons Convention.

Libya has a small population in a large land area. Population density is about fifty people per square kilometer in the two northern regions of Tripolitania and Cyrenaica, but falls to less than one person per square kilometer elsewhere. Total population estimates are approximately 5,499,074. Ninety percent of the people live in less than 10% of the area, primarily along the coast. More than half the population is urban, mostly concentrated in the two largest cities, Tripoli and Benghazi. Fifty percent of the population is estimated to be under age fifteen.

Native Libyans are primarily a mixture of Arabs and Berbers. Small Tebou and Touareg tribal groups in southern Libya are nomadic or seminomadic. Among foreign residents, the largest groups are citizens of other African nations, including North Africans (primarily Egyptians and Tunisians), West Africans and Sub-Saharan Africans. Approximately 97% of the people are Sunni Muslim. Arabic, English, and Italian are widely understood in the major cities.

The socialist-oriented economy depends primarily on revenues from the oil sector, which contribute practically all export earnings and about one quarter of GDP. These oil revenues and a small population give Libya one of the highest per capita GDPs in Africa, but little of this income flows down to the lower levels of society. Import restrictions and inefficient resource allocations have led to periodic shortages of basic goods and foodstuffs. The non-oil manufacturing and construction sectors, which account for about 20% of GDP, have expanded from processing mostly agricultural products to include the production of petrochemicals, iron, steel, and aluminum. Climatic conditions and poor soils severely limit agricultural output, and Libya imports about 75% of its food. Higher oil prices in recent years led to an increase in export revenues, which has improved macroeconomic indicators, but has done little to stimulate broad-based economic growth. Libya is making slow progress toward economic liberalization and the upgrading of economic infrastructure, but truly market-based reforms will be slow in coming.

On September 20, 2004, President George W. Bush signed an Executive Order ending economic sanctions imposed under the authority of the International Emergency Economic Powers Act (IEEPA). U.S. persons are no longer prohibited from working in Libya, and many American companies are actively seeking investment opportunities in Libya. The government has announced ambitious plans to increase foreign investment in the oil and gas sectors to significantly boost production capacity. The government is also pursuing a number of infrastructure projects such as highways, railways, telecommunications backbones, and irrigation.

Contextual Features

Libya professes to have a government in which the people rule directly. The highest official organ is the General People's Congress, consisting of representatives from local peoples' committees. In practice, Libya is a military regime, with power vested in the revolutionary leader, Muammar al-Qaddafi, who holds no official title but is the de facto chief of state. The head of government is the secretary of the general people's committee.

Libya's political system is theoretically based on the political philosophy in Qadhafi's Green Book, which combines socialist and Islamic theories and rejects parliamentary democracy and political parties. In reality, Qadhafi exercises near total control over the government. For the first seven years following the revolution, Qadhafi and twelve fellow army officers, the Revolutionary Command Council, began a complete overhaul of Libya's political system, society, and economy. In 1973, he announced the start of a "cultural revolution" in schools, businesses, industries, and public institutions to oversee administration of those organizations in the public interest. On March 3, 1977, Qadhafi convened a General People's Congress (GPC) to proclaim the establishment of "people's power," change the country's name to the Socialist People's Libyan Arab Jamahiriya, and to vest, theoretically, primary authority in the GPC.

The GPC is the legislative forum that interacts with the General People's Committee, whose members are secretaries of Libyan ministries. It serves as the intermediary between the masses and the leadership, and is composed of the secretariats of some six hundred local "basic popular congresses." The GPC secretariat and the cabinet secretaries are appointed by the GPC secretary general and confirmed by the annual GPC congress. These cabinet secretaries are responsible for the routine operation of their ministries, but Qadhafi exercises real authority directly or through manipulation of the people's and revolutionary committees.

Qadhafi remained the de facto chief of state and secretary general of the GPC until 1980, when he gave up his office. Although he holds no formal office, Qadhafi exercises absolute power with the assistance of a small group of trusted advisers, who include relatives from his home base in the Sirte region, which lies between the rival provinces of Tripolitania and Cyrenaica.

The Libyan court system consists of three levels: the courts of first instance; the courts of appeals, and the Supreme Court, which is the final appellate level. The GPC appoints justices to the Supreme Court. Special "revolutionary courts" and military courts operate outside the court system to try political offenses and crimes against the state. Libya's justice system is nominally based on Sharia law, the sacred law of Islam.

The Libyan system of criminal justice has been heavily influenced by Islamic law, particularly since Qadhafi's proclamation of the Popular Revolution on April 15, 1973. On that date, the Libyan leader announced that all existing laws formulated by the monarchy were to be replaced by the Sharia. Some amendments to bring the criminal code into conformity with Islam had been made before this proclamation. In October 1972, the government enacted a law providing for the amputation of the right hands of convicted thieves. (As a modern note to this traditional Islamic punishment, the government gave assurances that amputation would be performed at a hospital under sanitary conditions with an anesthetic.) In practice, this penalty has not been commonly imposed.

Qadhafi's proclamation involved a reorientation of Libya's entire criminal code, because, according to the 1954 code, no act was a crime unless defined as such by law. Yet the code also specified that nothing in the criminal code affected the individual rights provided for in Islamic Sharia. The two provisions were basically incompatible because the 1954 code identified crimes in decreasing order of seriousness as felonies, misdemeanors, and contraventions, assigning maximum sentences to each, whereas under the Sharia an act could be—depending on the circumstances—mandatory, commendable, permissible, reprehensible, or forbidden.

Efforts to align the criminal code's three categories of offense with the five classifications embodied in the Sharia involved Libyan legal and religious scholars in an extensive and slow-moving process to minimize the obvious contradictions in the two systems. Changes in the code's provisions were announced from time to time, but the basic philosophical issues had not been completely resolved by 1973.

Amendments to the criminal code after 1973 addressed both moral issues related to Islamic beliefs and purely secular matters, notably those concerning state security. In official legal announcements in 1973 and 1974, lashings and imprisonment of adulterers, imprisonment of homosexuals for up to five years, and floggings for those transgressing the fast of Ramadan were issued as laws "in line with positive Islamic legislation." Another law provided forty lashes for any Muslim who drank or served alcoholic beverages. For alcoholic-related offenses, non-Muslims could receive fines or imprisonment, and fines and jail terms were set for possession of or trafficking in liquor.

In August 1975, following a major coup attempt, the criminal code was further revised to strengthen state security. Such actions as "scheming" with foreigners to harm Libya's military or political position, facilitating war against the state, revealing state or defense secrets, infiltration into military reservations, and possession of means of espionage were made subject to harsh penalties, including life imprisonment and hanging. Punishments for public servants were stiffer than for ordinary citizens.

An increasing number of acts have brought the threat of execution. A 1975 law provided that membership in a political party opposing the principles of the 1969 revolution could result in death. In 1977 economic crimes, such as damaging oil installations or stockpiles of basic commodities, were added. Qadhafi's repeated calls for abolition of the death sentence have not been translated into legislative action.

The Libyan criminal justice system under the Qadhafi-led government has been characterized by many repressive features. Victims reported torture and beatings during interrogation as a matter of practice, and long jail sentences for political nonconformity. Other irregularities included bypassing the regular court system by special tribunals and holding show trials. The international human rights organization, Amnesty International, has repeatedly reported evidence of grave violations of civil rights and of Libyan law. Most of Amnesty International's inquiries and appeals to Libya to free political prisoners, to abandon torture to extract confessions, and to commute death penalties have gone unanswered.

The Qadhafi regime has regarded crime as an anomaly in conflict with its revolutionary goals, inasmuch as all Libyans are expected to contribute to the common good of society and its social, political, and economic advancement. During an earlier phase of his rule, Qadhafi deplored a pattern of increasingly unlawful behavior that included an unacceptable incidence of theft, violence, and traffic accidents. He had hoped to follow the British model of police officers enforcing public order with "a notebook, a pencil or a map to guide people, but not a gun or a stick." Instead, he lamented, he was obliged to depend on an armed police force because "the Third World will need another 500 years to understand that a policeman, even unarmed, must be respected."

Because meaningful data had not been available for many years, no up-to-date assessment of the extent and nature of criminal activity has been made. When last reported, statistics showed a high incidence of property theft and relatively fewer violent crimes, such as rape, manslaughter, and murder. A significant number of convictions were under the category of "crimes against freedom, honor, and the public," which could range from public drunkenness to student demonstrations and more serious political offenses. To judge from reports in the official press in the mid-1980s, the nation's

economic strains were reflected in a growing number of cases of smuggling, illegal deposit of money abroad, bribery, and misappropriation of funds by public officials.

Corruption in government has been an abiding concern. In 1975, a tough new law made the acceptance of a bribe by a public official punishable by up to ten years in prison plus fines set at twice the amount of the bribe. A person proffering a bribe could receive up to five years in prison plus fines of up to LD500. According to press reports, verdicts handed down by people's courts involved relatively moderate jail sentences of one to two years but harsh fines of LD50,000 and more. An official found guilty of paying unearned overtime salaries to relatives and friends, however, was condemned to a ten-year prison term.

Police Profile

Throughout its prerevolutionary history, the mission and operating concepts underlying the Libyan police system were the same as those in many other Muslim societies. The traditional concept of police or *shurtah* was a broad one. Because the *shurtah* were used from time to time by the government in power to undertake new conquests, security force commanders often had full-sized armies at their disposal. Domestically, however, the *shurtah* were primarily responsible for suppressing dissidence and insurrections as well as performing other internal security duties. The latter duties typically embraced the kinds of administrative and judicial functions often required of urban and rural police, such as the prevention of crime, investigation and arrest of criminals, and maintenance of public order. Some of these concepts have survived in present-day Libya; others have been altered in response to the changing needs of the society.

Shortly after the 1969 coup, military officers were temporarily integrated into key police positions to guard against a countercoup. A complete reorganization of the police followed over the next three years. An early step in the process of stripping the police of paramilitary status was the consolidation of the regional police forces into a unified organization under the Ministry of Interior. In 1971, new separate agencies to handle civil defense and fire protection were provided for by law. Ministerial decrees established other units, such as the Central Traffic Department, the Central Department for Criminal Investigation, the Arab International Criminal Police Bureau, the Ports Security Department, the Identity Investigation, and the Police Training Department. A special police law promulgated by the Revolutionary Command Council in January 1972 spelled out the new functions of the police force, which was formally redesignated the Police at the Service of the People and the Revolution. The police were specifically charged with responsibility for "the administration of prisons, civil defense activities, passport and nationality affairs, identity card affairs, and other functions set forth by laws and bills."

Individual police units were under the jurisdiction of regional security directorates throughout the country, with primary responsibility for enforcing the laws and administering the police falling under the minister of interior and his deputy. A special police affairs council—composed of the deputy minister as chairman, the directors of the central police department, the regional chiefs, and a legal adviser—was empowered to coordinate activities of various police branches and to issue decrees on police matters.

Police ranks followed closely those of the armed forces. An officer candidate had to be a Libyan citizen at least twenty years of age, of good conduct and behavior, in good physical condition, and not married to a foreigner. He also had to be a graduate of the police academy. Police work was considered a prestigious occupation, and its attractive working conditions and benefits reportedly produced well-qualified applicants who underwent stiff competition for vacancies. However, standards may have deteriorated as more lucrative opportunities in the oil industry and in government became available for those with sufficient education.

In a counterpart to the media attacks on the professional military in 1983, the official Libyan press targeted the police as lacking revolutionary zeal. The press demanded greater direct responsibility for the masses in protecting the people's security. Articles recalled that the police were descended from the mobile forces of the Idris regime, headed by "fascist, bourgeois officers" who had suppressed all manifestations of discontent with the royalist system. Police officials were accused of engaging in licentious behavior, drinking liquor, and carrying on illegal businesses. They were charged with being "feudalistic" in their behavior, of being ill-educated because many lacked a high school diploma, and often unfit for duty because of advancing age.

Declaring that "security is the responsibility of the people as a whole in the same way as the defense of the homeland is," Qadhafi announced in 1985 that the police would henceforward be known as the People's Security Force. Whether this name change accomplished much seemed doubtful; the official press complained that all that had happened was that signs over the police stations now read "People's Security Station."

Internal security mechanisms reach into every corner of Libyan society, and fears of harsh retribution have successfully prevented antipathy to Qadhafi's actions from reaching a stage of public demonstrations or open questioning. As many as 50,000 Libyans—mostly from the more prosperous classes—have taken up residence abroad, but the opposition groups that have sprung up among the exiles have not presented a convincing threat to the regime.

Numerous attempts have been launched to overturn Qadhafi's rule. In most instances, these attempts have originated among military officers who have access to weapons and the necessary communications and organizational networks. In no case, however, did they appear to come close to achieving their goal. The effectiveness of the internal security apparatus and the infiltration of officers loyal to Qadhafi have frustrated most plots before they could develop sufficiently to have a chance of success.

The system installed in the early 1970s with Egyptian help was modeled on its Egyptian counterpart, and was once described as "composed of several overlapping but autonomously directed intelligence machines." Libya maintains an extensive security apparatus, consisting of several elite military units, including Qadhafi's personal bodyguards, local Revolutionary Committees, and People's Committees, as well as the "Purification" Committees, which were formed in 1996. The result is a multilayered, pervasive surveillance system that monitors and controls the activities of individuals. The secret service and, at a lower level, the police were constantly on the alert for suspicious conduct, as were the revolutionary committees and the Basic People's Congresses. The committees constituted an effective informer network and may also act independently of other security agencies when authorized and encouraged by Qadhafi. This multilayered complex assured tight control over the activity of individuals in virtually every community.

The various security forces committed numerous serious human rights abuses. Security personnel reportedly torture prisoners during interrogations or for punishment. Government agents reportedly periodically detain and torture foreign workers, particularly those from sub-Saharan Africa. Reports of torture have been difficult to corroborate because many prisoners are held incommunicado. Methods of torture reportedly include chaining to a wall for hours, clubbing, applying electric shock, applying corkscrews to the back, pouring lemon juice in open wounds, breaking fingers and allowing the joints to heal without medical care, suffocating with plastic bags, deprivation of food and water, and beatings on the soles of the feet. The law calls for fines against any official using excessive force; however, there are no known cases of prosecution for torture or abuse.

Prison conditions reportedly are poor. While there is insufficient information to make a clear determination on overall prison conditions, a mutiny in July 1996 at the Abu Salim prison was caused by inmates protesting poor conditions. The prisoners went on a hunger strike and captured guards to protest the lack of medical care, overcrowding, and inadequate hygiene and diet provided at the facility. Security units were dispatched to suppress the uprising; as many as 100 persons were killed by security forces. The government does not permit prison visits by human rights monitors.

Security forces arbitrarily arrest and detain citizens. By law, the government may hold detainees incommunicado for unlimited periods. It holds many political detainees incommunicado in unofficial detention centers controlled by members of the Revolutionary Committees. Hundreds of political detainees, many associated with banned Islamic groups, reportedly are held in prisons throughout the country (but mainly in the Abu Salim prison in Tripoli); many are held for years without charge. Hundreds of other detainees may have been held for periods too brief (three to four months) to permit confirmation by outside observers.

MINTIE DAS

Bibliography

Central Intelligence Agency. *The World Factbook*. 2005. Available at: www.cia.gov/cia/publications/factbook.

Library of Congress. "Country Reports." 1987. Available at: www.lcweb2.loc.gov/rfd/cs.

U.S. State Department. "Background Note." 2005. Available at: www.travel.state.gov.

LIECHTENSTEIN

Background Material

The inhabitants of Liechtenstein are descendants of the Germanic tribe of the Alemans who settled the region after the year 500. During the Middle Ages, Liechtenstein was governed by various noble families. In 1719, it was raised to the imperial principality of Liechtenstein, which, after the downfall of the Roman Empire of German Nations and subsequent admission to the Confederation of the Rhine, became an independent state. In 1862, Liechtenstein obtained its first constitution.

Close ties with Switzerland—both countries are linked by a customs union since 1924 and a monetary union since 1980—are of major importance. They also led to the mutual abolition of border controls. The common external customs border with Austria on Liechtenstein territory is protected by the Swiss border guard.

The official currency is the Swiss franc.

By December 31, 2000, the population was 32,863, of whom 11,320 (34.4%) did not have Liechtenstein citizenship. Of the foreigners, 5,300 (46.8%) originated from the European Economic Area (EEA) and 3,805 (33.6%) were Swiss citizens.

The official language is German, spoken in an Alemannic dialect. Seventy-seven percent of the inhabitants are Roman Catholic, 7% Protestant, and 3.6% Islamic.

Liechtenstein has a thriving economy and counts, with a purchasing power parity GDP of US$825 million and per capita GDP of US$ 25,000 (1999), as one of the richest states in the world. The unemployment rate is extremely low (1.2%). A total of 53.5% of the 25,343 jobs (9,741 are commuters) are jobs in the service sector, 45.2% concern trade and industry, and 1.3% forestry. The main export markets are Europe, the United States, and the Far East.

Contextual Features

The Principality of Liechtenstein is a constitutional hereditary monarchy on a democratic and parliamentary basis. The state authority is founded on the prince and the people.

Liechtenstein has its own law system, derived from Roman law and roughly corresponding to that of neighboring countries. The independency and irremovability of the judge is guaranteed by the constitution. The procedure in criminal matters is governed by the principle of accusation.

Various fundamental rights and liberties are guaranteed by the constitution. Liechtenstein is also a party to the European Human Rights Convention and respects the rights therein contained.

About 83% of the crimes reported to national police in 2001 concern crimes against property in the sense of the penal code. About one-fourth of them are economic crimes. Ten percent of the 2001 statistics concern crimes of violence. Capital crimes are nevertheless practically at zero.

Competence in civil and criminal matters lies with the Princely Court of Justice (Landgericht). In administrative matters, the government authorities are generally competent in the first instance; in the second instance, it is the appeal authority (court). In the case of alleged violations of fundamental and human rights, the state court (Staatsgerichtshof) is competent. All courts are seated in Vaduz.

The state prosecutor is obliged to prosecute all punishable offenses of which he is informed (generally through a police report). During a pre-trial procedure, it is verified whether the elements of suspicion are sufficient to file an accusation. Where fundamental rights of the defendant are invoked, an independent examining judge has to rule. In urgent cases, also national police may carry out certain infringements of fundamental rights with out a judicial warrant such as provisional arrests or house searches.

In case of accusation, the Princely Court of Justice is competent in the first instance, whereby, according to the type of offense, the case may be treated by either an individual judge (misdemeanor, minor offenses), the court of lay assessors (Schöffengericht, with professional judges and jurors, for all other offenses), or the criminal court (Kriminalgericht, equally with professional judges and jurors, for crimes). Procedures against juveniles are covered by the juvenile court.

Instances of appeal are the Superior Court (second instance) and Supreme Court (third and last instance). Judgments may be taken only after the completion of an oral and generally public trial, except for minor offenses and misdemeanors that may be sanctioned with a summary sentence. Such sentences only allow for fines. The Prince possesses the right of abolition, that is, to pardon, mitigate, or transform punishments in force or to dismiss ongoing investigations.

Liechtenstein has only one penal institution. The state prison (Landesgefängnis) in its present form has existed since 1991. Originally created as a mere pre-trial prison, it now also serves to execute prison sentences up to a maximum of two years. Longer sentences are served in Austrian prisons on the basis of treaty concluded with this country in 1982. The state prison has nineteen cells with a total of twenty-two places. Work arrangements exist for all inmates (simple manual work, mainly assembly of electronic appliances); prisoners sentenced are obliged to work whereas those awaiting trial participate at a voluntary level. The wages earned are credited to a blocked account of the inmate.

Police Profile

Background

Until 1932, the main responsibility for public security rested with the municipalities. From 1871, the country provided two and later three Landweibel (state law enforcement officers) as security forces, according to the Swiss model. This structure eventually became insufficient. A new police statute reorganized the police in 1932, creating the Princely Liechtenstein Security Corps as today's National Police was then called, with a force of initially eight policemen. In 1937, an auxiliary police force with nineteen members was added. After a further reorganization in 1964, creating the three departments Department for Administrative Laws, Investigative (or Criminal) and Traffic Police, the new national police law entered into force in 1989, which is still valid today. It covers the tasks and organization, as well as rights and duties of the National Police.

In 1994, the first two female officers entered the police service. A new reorganization took place in 1998, due to the increase in duties. In the framework of the extensive measures to ensure the integrity of Liechtenstein as a financial center, the National Police also underwent a strategic reorientation in

2000 leading to a continuous reinforcement of staff up to the year 2007.

Demographics and Organizational Description

Because of the abovementioned high degree of municipal independence, municipalities still cover the field of local policing under the supervision of the state. This mainly concerns the issue of orders to prevent infringements of law and order. The head of municipality (mayor) acts as the local police authority, and may, for the exercise of this function, make use of a separate municipal police force. The National Police has nevertheless to support the municipalities in the fulfillment of these tasks.

The headquarters of the National Police are situated in Vaduz. Due to the small size of the country, there are no regional subdivisions. By December 31, 2002, there were 102 persons employed (6 female and 69 male police officers, as well as 27 civilian employees). Out of the 75 police officers, 70 were Liechtenstein nationals whereas the remaining were from other central European countries (four from Austria and one from Germany; the recruitment of non-nationals is possible in justified cases with the previous consent of Parliament). Forty-one officers exercised service in uniform at the date given.

The National Police are supplemented by an on-call police with an authorized strength of forty members. These are persons who, as a side job but vested with police authority, support the national police by providing auxiliary services. This mainly concerns the maintenance of order and traffic control. Liechtenstein has a police density of 435 inhabitants per police officer. The National Police are responsible to the national government. If someone feels treated unjustly by the police, he/she may address a supervision complaint to the government.

The Chief of Police presides over the National Police. Under him/her, three further officers head the departments criminal police, traffic and mobile police, and command services (logistic and administration). Under the heads of departments, group commanders head various command groups with up to twelve persons each.

The uniformed Traffic and Rapid Response Police coordinate the training and operational tasks of the intervention unit SWAT, which is based on a militia system. The members of this special force are recruited from all departments.

This police force, with its forty-one officers, is generally responsible for maintaining law and order and taking urgent measures in case of immediate danger. It provides assistance in case of accidents and disasters and carries out searches for missing persons. In addition, it supervises and regulates road traffic, and investigates infringements of administrative provisions. Its duties also comprise patrol service and the establishment of initial reports on criminal offences in the sense of the penal code.

The criminal police have a staff of twenty-five persons. Their duties include the investigation of criminal offenses in the sense of the penal code, the drug-related law, and the law on residence and establishment. They are also responsible for state security and investigation in this field. They include a Crime Scene Investigations service that is supported, in case of more important incidents, by the corresponding departments of Swiss police. Due to the importance of Liechtenstein as a financial market, there is now a Special Force for White Collar Crime and Organized Crime.

The department of command services with its thirty-six officers as well as the majority of civil employees provides support to the two other departments through the fulfillment of logistic and administrative tasks (procurement, information technology, and so on), as well as the operation of the statewide emergency call system and the state prison. It also operates the National Central Bureau of Icpo-Interpol.

In principle, police officers, after completion of police school, are deployed to the Traffic and Rapid Response Police. After several years of service in this department and completion of relevant training courses, they may be transferred to special services or other departments.

Functions

The National Police may, in case of immediate danger (that is, when, according to the situation, an immediate reaction is indispensable, and it is not possible to obtain a judicial order), provisionally arrest a suspected person. Within forty-eight hours, this person must either be dismissed or handed over to the examining judge. The national police may also take persons into custody when this is urgently necessary in view of their own protection, and no other legitimate coercive means achieve this objective.

The national police may also, under certain conditions, search objects and vehicles. Persons may be stopped and asked for identity documents. Coercive measures against female persons may only be carried out by female officers.

There are specific services covering the financial sector, such as the Finance Intelligence Unit.

Liechtenstein reorganized the supervision of financial services and ratified eleven of the twelve relevant UN resolutions.

As regards human rights, the recent creation of the national chapter of Amnesty International should be mentioned.

The national police conduct traffic education in school and kindergarten. There are presentations in secondary schools on the dangers of narcotics as well as general public information campaigns in the area of crime prevention.

Training

There is no police school in Liechtenstein. The basic training takes place in Switzerland with the special Liechtenstein features being taught subsequently after the return of the trainees. Further training and upgrade events are conducted either in the country or by attending courses with cooperating police administrations. Human rights, in particular the European Human Rights Convention, represent an important part of any basic or continuous police training to ensure their respect in day-to-day police practice.

Use of Firearms

Police officers on duty are armed with a pistol. There may be additional special weapons according to the specific operation. The use of firearms is regulated by the law. It is legitimate when the officer or a third person are attacked or threatened by with attack; and when persons who have committed a crime or are suspected for having done so, try to avoid arrest by escape. There are further cases such as the liberation of hostages or preventing an imminent crime that implies a particular danger to the general public.

During the past few years, there was no need for police to make use of firearms.

The law requires a license for the acquisition of handguns. Long weapons—except for submachine guns and similar arms that require a special license—may be acquired freely. So-called pump guns are prohibited. The carrying of arms in public requires an additional license that is issued only when evidence of a special need has been provided. The issue of these documents is handled in a very restrictive manner.

Disciplinary matters of the police (as well as those of all other public authorities) are handled by the government. Procedures may be opened following a report or complaint by a citizen or ex officio. The officer concerned is immediately informed of the charge and entitled to a fair hearing and defense. In case of minor charges, the police chief may impose certain sanctions on his own, but has to inform the government thereof. In the case of major charges, the officer concerned may be suspended from his duty until the complete clarification of all charges. The officer concerned may lodge a complaint against the disciplinary measures taken.

There have never been any formal charges against the national police because of alleged human rights violations. As a party to the European Human Rights Convention (ECHR), Liechtenstein recognizes the competence of the European Court of Human Rights to examine individual complaints because of the violation of rights guaranteed by the ECHR. Decisions by the court are legally binding for Liechtenstein. As a contracting party to all six core UN instruments in the field of human rights, Liechtenstein delivers regular reports on the respect of relevant rights.

Terrorism

Due to its high degree of social control, Liechtenstein is neither a base for terrorist networks nor do such organizations based elsewhere operate on its soil. In view of the highly developed financial marketplace, counterterrorist activities concentrate on the financing of terrorism. A specific penal provision against terrorism is under development.

International Cooperation

In practice, the most important cooperation takes place with neighboring Switzerland and Austria, based on a police cooperation treaty in force since 2001. This instrument facilitates mutual assistance and allows for joint patrols in border regions, cross-border observations, and controlled deliveries as well as hot pursuit.

Liechtenstein became a member of Interpol in 1960. Due to globalization and other developments, the tasks of Interpol Vaduz are rapidly increasing.

The Lake Constance Conference, composed of the police presidents of the neighboring countries Germany, Austria, Switzerland, and Liechtenstein, organizes joint staff training courses. There is a particularly close cooperation in training matters with Swiss police. Staff exchanges take place particularly with Swiss and Austrian police.

Police Education, Research, and Publications

Due to the absence of it own police schools, specific police research and police publications in Liechtenstein do not exist.

As of 2003, the National Police website, was under preparation. Provisionally police-related information may be obtained from the government's website, at *www.llv.li*.

BRUNO GSTÖHL

Bibliography

Funk, Bernd-Christian. "Das liechtensteinische Polizeigesetz und das österreichische Sicherheitspolizeigesetz. Zwei Regelwerke im Vergleich ihrer rechtlichen Grundsätze und Systembedingungen" (Comparison of police laws in Liechtenstein and Austria). In *Kleinstaat und Menschenrechte*. Festgabe für Gerard Batliner zum 65. Basel/Frankfurt aM: Geburtstag, 1993.

Stotter, Heinz Josef. *Die neue liechtensteinische Strafprozessordnung (StPO)*. (The new law on penal procedure of Liechtenstein). Vaduz, 1988.

LITHUANIA

Background Material

The Republic of Lithuania is situated between Western and Eastern Europe on a direct route from Germany to Russia. It borders the countries of Central and Eastern Europe, specifically Latvia, Belarus, Poland, and the Kaliningrad region of the Russian Federation. Lithuania is also one of the nine Baltic Sea countries. Lithuania is a former Soviet Union republic that regained its independence on March 11, 1990, and since then has been an independent and democratic state. The major challenges facing the country are accession to the North Atlantic Treaty Organization and the European Union, and negotiations over transit conditions between the Kaliningrad region and Russia. More than 200,000 citizens, especially young people, have left Lithuania in search for jobs in foreign countries because of a high level of unemployment.

Lithuania was first mentioned in historical records in 1009. A state, the Grand-Duchy of Lithuania, was established in the middle of thirteenth century that existed until the end of eighteenth century, when it was annexed by Russia. In 1918, Lithuania reemerged as the independent Republic of Lithuania. The Soviet Union occupied Lithuania in 1940. During World War II, Lithuania was occupied by Nazi Germany in 1941, and again by the USSR in 1944. The latter occupation was to last over four decades until freedom was regained in 1990. During the 1941–1951 period, the country lost about 30% of its population, who had been deported to Siberia and other remote Soviet areas, or had been killed during the fights, repatriated, or emigrated to other countries.

Latvia has an area of 653,000 square kilometers, and a population of 3.5 million (2001 estimate). The capital is Vilnius.

The GDP per capita is US$4180 (2002 estimate). Major industries include agriculture, wood and wood processing, food industry processing, electronics, chemicals, pharmaceuticals, oil refining, manufacture of machinery, metal processing, and textiles. As much as 80% of the economy is located in the private sector.

Sixty percent to 80% of Lithuania's inhabitants consider themselves Roman Catholic.

Contextual Features

Lithuania adheres to a continental law system. The Constitution has the supreme legal power. There are Civil and Civil Procedure Codes, Criminal and Criminal Procedure Codes, the Code of Administrative Offenses, Labor Code, Customs Code, and other codes.

The Constitution of the Republic of Lithuania, approved in 1992, defines the nation's political, economic, and legal systems. The powers of the state are exercised by the Seimas (parliament), the president, the government, and the judiciary. The Seimas consists of 141 members, who are elected for a four-year term on the basis of universal, equal, and direct suffrage by secret ballot. The president is the head of state, elected for a five-year term by direct popular vote. The government of the Republic of Lithuania is the highest executive body. It is made up of the prime minister and thirteen ministers. The Constitutional Court and the following general jurisdiction courts operate in Lithuania: the Supreme Court, the Court of Appeal, and county, district, and administrative courts.

About 80% of all reported crimes are property crimes (thefts, burglaries, fraud, and so on); the remaining 20% are violent crimes. During the last five years an increase in smuggling, drug-related crimes, tax evasion, forgery, and human trafficking has been observed. In the last few years, crime has tended to decline. In 2002, 72,646 crimes were registered, which is 8.4% less than in 2001.

The Department of Prisons is established under the Ministry of Justice. In 2002, the number of convicts per 10,000 inhabitants was 33.

Police Profile

Background

Since 1990, the Lithuanian Police has been reformed from repressive, paramilitary policing to the existing decentralized, deconcentrated, community-based police organization. The reform was oriented toward EU standards and implemented according to the Guidelines of the Lithuanian Police Reform, envisaged by the government of the Republic of Lithuania in 1997. The new Criminal and Criminal Procedure Codes, and Correctional Code went into effect on May 1, 2003, which brought changes in pre-trial investigation.

In 1795, when Lithuania was brought into the Russian Empire, the gendarmerie was the main institution for the maintenance of public order. The first police institutions were formed at the beginning of the nineteenth century by order of the Tsar of Russia, establishing the Department of Police under the Ministry of Internal Affairs. The Department carried out repressive functions, and acted as an implementer of national oppression policy.

In the years of independence, 1918 to 1940, the militia was renamed the "police" (up to 1924, the word "militia" was used instead of "police"). During the first Soviet occupation (1940–1941), the police were transformed into a militia again. German occupation lasted from 1941 to 1944. In 1944–1945, when the Soviet Union occupied Lithuania again, the militia was directed by the Ministry of the Interior of the Soviet Union (MVD), and was supervised by the Soviet Ministry of the Interior. That was a paramilitary organization, the activity of which at all levels was influenced by the Communist Party.

In 1990, after the reestablishment of the Lithuanian independence, the Law on Police was adopted, on the basis of which the militia was reformed to the present police. The Department of Police of the Ministry of Interior was established. In 1994, the Border Police Department was established under the Ministry of the Interior; in 1997, the Tax Police Department and Special Investigation Service (aimed at fighting corruption) were formed. In recent years, the police system has become narrower in scope. In 2000, the Special Investigation Service has become an autonomous institution; in 2001, the Border Police Department was reorganized into the State Border Control Service; and in 2002, the Tax Police was organized into Financial Crime Investigation Service. The latest step in the development of the Lithuanian police is related to the adoption of the new Law on the Police Activities in 2000.

Organizational Description

In 1990, the number of the militia personnel was 7,400. According to 2003 data, 12,706 police officers and 3,268 civil staff members worked in the police force. There are about 365 police officers per 10,000 inhabitants. The average age of the staff is between thirty and thirty-six. Women make up about 20% of the total staff.

Parliamentary control over the police is carried out by the Committee on Legal Affairs, as well as by the Ombudsmen that is subordinate to the Seimas. The interior minister is a state politician setting major trends of police strategy when implementing the government program. The police commissioner general heads the Police Department. At the proposal of the interior minister and on the recommendation of the government, the police commissioner general is appointed for a five-year term of office and dismissed by the president of the republic. He is directly subordinate to the interior minister and accountable to the president.

Territorial police bodies are police commissariats that consist of police headquarters of a higher level and police units of a lower level. Police headquarters at a higher level are established in centers, and ensure implementation of police tasks throughout the entire country. There are ten higher-level police headquarters, and forty-nine lower-level police commissariats in the municipalities. Territorial police units in the neighborhoods can establish police stations. A total of 115 police stations acting on a territorial principle are functioning in towns and districts. The local inspector serves the territory where the population reaches 3,000 on average. Specialized police bodies are police divisions established on a nonterritorial principle, including Criminal Police Bureau, Public Police Bureau, Police Information Center, Police Material Supply Center, and Quick Response Team ARAS, among others.

Police ranks follow: policeman probationer, policeman, senior policeman, first sergeant, junior inspector, senior inspector, commissioner inspector, commissioner, senior commissioner, chief commissioner, and commissioner general. The police ranks are granted to police officers when they are appointed to corresponding posts and after they pass a qualification examination. Police institutions' reserves are comprised of retired police officers.

Functions

The police both handle criminal law and fulfill administrative functions. The Criminal Police performs the following functions: prevent and investigate murders, burglaries, thefts, illegal circulation of weapons and drugs, and other criminal offences and violations of law. Officers participate in a number of task forces to prevent crime and organized crime, including operations at the international level. The Interrogation Service belongs to the structure of the Criminal Police. The major function of this service is to carry out the interrogation (primary investigation) in criminal cases.

The Public Police ensure public order and peace, protect civil rights and freedoms, analyze the crime, and envisage preventive measures.

Training

Sworn police officers of all ranks are educated and receive training at the faculty of Police of the Law University of Lithuania, Klaipeda High Police School, and Police Training Center at the Police Department. Foreign police experts and law enforcement institutions carry out special training courses. The main requirements to join the police force aside from schooling follow: Lithuanian citizenship, secondary education, good health and physical condition, and emotional balance.

Police Public Projects

The police cooperate with other state institutions, local authorities, public organizations, and residents when implementing crime control and prevention programs. The public organization "Stop the Crime" cooperates with the police on public security issues. The Center for Crime Prevention in Lithuania was established in 1997 as a public nonprofit agency to contribute to the realization of police public project.

Police Use of Firearms

A police officer has the right to use coercion when it is necessary to prevent violations of law, and to apprehend the persons who have committed said violations, as well as in other cases when protecting and defending lawful interests of an individual, society, and the state. When other coercive measures are ineffective, the police officer has the right to use a firearm as an extraordinary measure. Without posing a threat to human life, the police officer has the right to use explosives, to destroy explosive devices, and to enter the place where hostages are being kept or where other criminal acts posing a threat to human life or health.

Complaints and Discipline

The public prosecutor is responsible for the investigation of criminal allegations against police. Citizens are expected to file complaints directly at the police station concerned, or to send in the written complaint to the Police Department. The General Inspectorate of the Ministry of the Interior is authorized to initiate and carry out quality checks of the performance of various police duties. The Police Department includes the Internal Investigation Service. It also looks into all public complaints about improper police conduct. Opinion polls show that the traffic police are considered one of the most corrupt institutions.

The police are trained to respect internationally recognized human rights. There are no violations as such, although standard requirements for treatment of the suspended are not fully met.

Terrorism

The Department of State Security is responsible for fighting terrorism. The Quick Response Team ARAS, which belongs to the structure of police, implements special antiterrorist operations. No terrorist organization has been registered in Lithuania.

International Cooperation

International cooperation in the fields of combating organized crime, cross-border crime, and police training is under way with Canadian, Finnish, German, British, Dutch, Swedish, U.S., and other foreign police structures. Lithuania has entered into cooperation with Europol. Since 1996, police officers have participated in peacekeeping missions. At present, Lithuania has forty-eight specially trained police officers. Nine of them have been sent to Kosovo, Croatia, Bosnia, and Herzegovina.

Police Education, Research, and Publications

Police officers are trained at the Faculty of Police of the Law University of Lithuania. There are undergraduate (bachelor) degree studies and postgraduate (master) degree studies.

Leading researchers at the Law University of Lithuania include Dr. Assoc. Prof. A. Sakocius, head of the Department of Police Law; Dr. R. Kalesnykas, lecturer; Dr. A. Laurinavicius, head of the Department of Customs Activities; A. Bukauskas, lecturer at the Department of Public Administration; D. Zilinskas, deputy director of the Department of Law of the Ministry of the Interior; and A. Sviklas, project coordinator of the Center for Crime Prevention in Lithuania.

Sources of funding for police research are the following: EU programs for scientific research, Open Society Foundation, Research and Study Foundation of Lithuania, and Law University of Lithuania. Areas of recent research include police law, police and human rights, community policing, police reform, and police administration. A number of doctoral theses cover the topics of police activities in the implementation of the environmental protection, statutory police, and police regulation issues, the fight against organized crime, and privatization processes in law enforcement. Applied research topics include police and violence in Lithuania, community policing, and use of firearms.

Leading police journals include a quarterly scientific journal, *Jurisprudencija*, Law University of Lithuania, Ateities g. 20, LT-2057 Vilnius, Lithuania; quarterly *Information Bulletin*, Center for Crime Prevention in Lithuania, Gyneju g. 6, Vilnius; and Lithuanian police newspaper *Sargyba* (The Guard), Police Department of Lithuania, Didzioji g. 7, LT-2001 Vilnius.

Major publications include R. Kalesnykas, *Cooperation of Police and Other Institutions Providing Social Services for Citizens*, 2000 (Lithua-

nian), A. Sakocius, and N. Uildriks, "Police and Violence in Lithuania," School of Human Rights Research, Utrecht University, Netherlands, and Law University of Lithuania, COLPI (English), 2002; A. Laurinavicius, *Police and Human Rights*, 2003 (Lithuanian).

ANTANAS BUKAUSKAS

Websites

Center for Crime Prevention in Lithuania. Available at: *www.nplc.lt/english/index.html*

Law University of Lithuania. Available at: *www.ltu.lt/ padaliniai/english/index.html*

Police Department, Ministry of Internal Affairs. Available at: *www.policija.lt*

Bibliography

Bukauskas, Antanas. "Guidelines of the Lithuanian Police Reform." In *Policing in Central and Eastern Europe: Organizational, Managerial, and Human Resource Aspects*, edited by Milan Pagon, 377–384. Ljubljana: College of Police and Security Studies, 1998.

Katuoka, Saulius. *Policija ir Zmogaus teises* (Police and Human Rights). Vilnius: Council of Europe Center for Information and Documentation, 1998.

Kuconis, Pranas, and Vytautas Nekrosius. *Teisesaugos institucijos.* (Law enforcement institutions). Vilnius: Justitia, 2001.

Lithuania, Department of Police. "The Lithuanian Police." Information Booklet. Vilnius: Department of Police, Ministry of the Internal Affairs, 2002.

Lithuania, Republic of. *Constitution of the Republic of Lithuania*. Vilnius: Publishing House of the Seimas, 1993.

Lithuania, Republic of. *Crime and the Law Enforcement Activity 2001*. Vilnius: Department of Statistics, Government of the Republic of Lithuania, 2002.

Lithuania, Republic of. Law on Police Activities. 17 October 2000 No. VIII-2048, Vilnius (as amended by 12 December 2000 No. IX-74).

Lithuanian Public Police Bureau Prevention Service, and Center for Crime Prevention in Lithuania. *Information Bulletin*, no. 6 (2002).

Sakocius, Alvydas, and Niels Uildriks. "Police and Violence in Lithuania." Research Report. School of Human Rights Research, Faculty of Law, Utrecht University (The Netherlands) Faculty of Police, Law University of Lithuania, COLPI, 2002.

Sesickas, Linas. "Judicial Capacity in Lithuania." In *Monitoring the EU Accession Process: Judicial Capacity*, 137–151. Budapest: Open Society Institute, 2002.

Svedas, Gintaras. *Lithuania: Criminal Justice Systems in Europe and North America*. Helsinki: HEUNI, 2000.

Valionis, Arvydas, ed. *Lithuania. An Outline*. Vilnius: Artlora, 2002.

LUXEMBOURG

Background Material

In 963, the Constitution of the Earldom of Luxembourg was established. At the 1815 Vienna Congress, the Grand-Duchy of Luxembourg was created.

From 1914 to 1918, during World War I, Luxembourg was occupied by Germany. This occurred again during World War II, from 1940 to 1944. In 1948, Luxembourg joined the North Atlantic Treaty Organization (NATO) as a founding member. The nation was a founding member of the CECA (European Coal and Steel Community) in 1951, and of the EEC (European Economic Community) in 1957.

Luxembourg has a surface area of 2,586 square kilometers, and a population of 439,500, comprised of 277,200 Luxembourgers and 162,300 (36.9%) foreigners, 85% of whom come from European Union nations.

The national language is Luxembourgish, and the administrative languages are French, German, and Luxembourgish. Catholicism is the major religion.

The per capita gross domestic product in purchasing power parity is 44,460 euros. Major economic activities include financial services and business-related activities, communications, and transport.

Contextual Features

Luxembourg is a constitutional monarchy, and a member-state of the European Union, with one Chamber of Deputies elected every five years. The head of state is the grand-duke. The head of government is the prime minister. Luxembourg has a civil law system based on the Constitutional Court, judicial jurisdiction, and administrative jurisdiction. The judicial jurisdiction consists of the Supreme Court, two District Courts, and three Justices of the Peace, responsible in civil, commercial, and criminal matters, respectively. Under the authority of the Prosecutor General, in each district a public prosecutor's office is competent for prosecution of criminal cases. A judicial enquiry has to be opened for serious offenses where special investigation techniques or compulsory measures are necessary; it is carried out under the authority of an examining magistrate (*juge d'instruction*).

Criminal law divides penal offenses into three main categories punishable by financial penalties ("contraventions"); eight days to five years imprisonment ("délits"); and five years to life imprisonment ("crimes").

In 1979, the death penalty was abolished. In 2001, 74% of all criminal offenses were directed against property, 10.5% against persons, and 5% were drug-related cases. Since 1994, police statistics have been decreasing (in all 22% over eight years).

Police Profile

Background

Until 2000, there were two police forces in Luxembourg: the Gendarmerie Grand-Ducale and the Police. Up to the twentieth century, the "Police" were comprised of a few local, independent units. At the beginning of the thirteenth century, several cities had obtained the right of self-administration and policing. During the French revolutionary period, first texts conferred attributions to local municipalities confirming the obligation to guarantee public peace, health, and security.

First indications concerning the Gendarmerie can be found in 1732 under Austrian rule when a Maréchaussée was established. In 1795, the former Duchy of Luxembourg was integrated into France as the Département des Forêts (Forest Department). The Gendarmerie Nationale was introduced and organized in accordance with the law of 28 Germinal An VI (April 17, 1798).

In 1813, Luxembourg became part of the Middle-Rhine Province, governed by Prussia. In 1814, the Gendarmerie was replaced by a governmental militia (Milice gouvernementale).

In 1815, Luxembourg, Belgium, and Holland formed the Kingdom of The Netherlands. The decree of 1814, creating a Corps de Maréchaussée in Belgium based on the French Gendarmerie model, was extended to Luxembourg.

After the Belgian revolution in October 1830, Luxembourg was divided into two parts, the larger one becoming the Belgian province of Luxembourg, and the other, the Grand-Duchy of Luxembourg, which remained linked to The Netherlands.

In 1839, the London Treaty restored the independence of the Grand-Duchy; the creation of a national police force became necessary. In January 1840, the Maréchaussée royale grand-ducale was set up, perpetuating the structure of the French Gendarmerie model, and was renamed "Gendarmerie" in December 1840.

In 1842, the Gendarmerie lost its autonomy through integration into the military Contingent fédéral, with its name changing to Königliche Grossherzogliche Gendarmerie Kompagnie by 1863. In 1843, the law on the organization of the municipalities and districts provided the college of the mayor and his deputies with legislative law enforcement capacities, but without real changes for the few local police units.

The London Treaty of 1867 imposed neutrality on Luxembourg. After a first military reorganization in 1868, the Gendarmerie regained autonomy in 1877. But the 1881 military law integrated the company of the Gendarmerie into the Force Armée (Armed Forces).

At the beginning of the twentieth century, new municipal police stations were set up under political pressure in the south of the country. In 1903, a criminal investigation brigade was established within the Gendarmerie to assist the judicial authorities.

The Force Armée of the Grand-Duchy remained intact during World War I, despite permanent occupation of the territory. In 1930, a first step was undertaken to change the local police forces into a state Police force. The state became responsible for all organizational matters related to the new Police Locale Etatisée; a second national police force was born. In 1940, the Gendarmerie and the centralized police structures were dissolved. Under the arms, the members of the Gendarmerie had to follow a retraining and to collectively take the oath of allegiance to the Reich. Integrated into German police forces, they were transferred to occupied countries at the Eastern front. Many gendarmes became victims of deportation and died in concentration camps.

After World War II, the Gendarmerie and police were completely reorganized and restructured. In 1945, a common Gendarmerie-Police school was created. The 1952 military law placed the Force Publique (Public Force), composed of Gendarmerie, Police (both with military status), and Army personnel under the administrative authority of the Force Publique Ministry. Interior and justice ministers shared competences for public order and criminal investigation matters.

In 1968, major financial charges of the police were transferred from the municipalities to the state. In 1980 and 1989, the Police obtained general territorial competences for public order, respectively criminal investigation matters.

The results of an independent audit of all police services induced the government in 1993 to reorganize and merge the Gendarmerie and Police. The law

establishing the new Police Grand-Ducale (May 31, 1999) entered into force on January 1, 2000.

Organizational Description

In 2000, with some 1,350 police personnel (police/citizen ratio, 1:340), the Grand-Ducal Police became the only police force with general competences for administrative police missions and criminal investigation tasks.

The Police, with a military status, is actually under the authority of the Ministry of Interior except for criminal investigation matters falling under the responsibility of the judicial authorities (public prosecutor or examining magistrate), or missions under the competence of the Ministry of Justice (legislation on foreigners, gambling control, and so on).

The Police are controlled and monitored by an independent Inspectorate General, reporting directly to the Minister of Interior and having permanent audit and general inspection rights, as well as investigative powers with regard to offenses committed by police staff. Reorganization of police forces occurred within the framework of the administrative reform as undertaken by the government and committed to the aims of better public service and improved objective and subjective safety. The new police had to correspond to four major objectives:

- Ensuring an optimum territorial coverage for rapid emergency interventions
- Offering a qualified proximity policing adapted to social environment
- Optimizing police work by simplification of internal procedures and by regrouping of missions at regional and national levels
- Allowing continuous development and evolution of structures, working methods, and procedures according to the evolution of society and criminality

To comply with these requirements, local units became regrouped under six regional police districts responsible for emergency response, neighborhood policing and preventive action. Each regional district operates one to three Emergency Centers set up following the criteria: coverage of the national territory, year-round twenty-four-hour/day availability, and high-speed and high-quality interventions.

Their number and localization were determined according to geographical and social aspects to ensure a comparable emergency service all over the country. Activities at these centers are coordinated at regional level. Per region, approximately 50% of the police staff are assigned to Emergency Centers with the task of responding to emergency calls and carrying out prevention and safety patrols. Emergency Centers are permanently open to people needing advice, assistance, or wanting to lodge a complaint.

Proximity policing, inspired by Anglo-Saxon community policing, falls within the competence of about fifty Proximity Police Stations. Discharged from intervention tasks, they undertake primarily prevention and security activities in close contact with the population. They are established locally according to demographic density and criminal activity location. Operational hours are flexible to respond to public needs and requests. Police staff deployed to these stations should have at least six to ten years of practical experience (depending on basic qualifications). More than 25% of regional manpower is dedicated to proximity policing.

Administrative and operational services of the regional districts are in charge of the day-to-day management of all territorial units. Moreover, the implementation of police services with specific competences on regional level makes it possible to have specialized agents all over the country, while their distribution at local level would have required disproportionate investments in staff and equipment. To reach an optimization of resources, regionalization accompanied by a certain amount of functional autonomy were considered the most appropriated steps to release a maximum of synergies.

Thus, each regional district includes a regional crime squad, charged with investigations of small and medium criminality, including preventive and repressive action in the fight against drug abuse; services to survey commercial activities, bankruptcies, clandestine work, and environmental protection; and a traffic control unit.

The dialogue with all actors involved in the field of public security is also organized at the regional level. Municipalities play an essential role in this respect, and cooperation takes place in the framework of institutionalized prevention committees that deal with a wide range of current security questions.

Regional police forces are supported by central services according to the subsidiary principle. National services are only competent for tasks going beyond the regional framework by their nature, technical characteristics, and national or international specificity.

National operational units include:

National Crime Investigation Department, competent for serious crime at the national or international level

Special response units of the Police, for particularly dangerous situations requiring sensitive action techniques

Mobile reserve and guard unit, assuming public order missions, person and property protection, and the security of the Grand-Ducal residences

National traffic control unit competent for the survey of motorways, security of convoys and dangerous transports, technical support for regional districts, and the escort of the Grand-Duke

Security and control services at the international airport of Luxembourg

Police school

Police management cannot ignore that phenomena related to society, safety, and criminality are of an evolutionary nature, always generating new risks. Mechanisms must in place for necessary flexibility of organizational development. Static structures have to give way to dynamic bodies, characterized by genuine quality management. Policies, concepts, and management tools have to be designed in a way that police action meets in the most appropriate manner the internal security objectives set by the government, as well as expectations of the citizens and local representatives. To respond to these requirements, the central Directorate General of the Police has following management departments:

- Organization, management, and methods
- Police operations and prevention
- Human resources
- Data processing
- Budget and logistics

Public relations and international police cooperation fall under the direct authority of the director general. The 1999 reorganization should also be considered in a more general framework of modernization of police forces in a number of EU member-states. Especially through the Schengen agreements and the Maastricht Treaty, European institutions have expressed their interest in matters of freedom of movement, security, and justice. Thus, questions related to internal security take a different dimension, as the security of a country is more and more dependent on policies developed on the multilateral level and their applications. In a geographical area without internal borders, each state and its police forces have to assume their part of responsibility to guarantee the necessary security of all partners.

Functions

The administrative police missions are defined by the 1999 police law, whereas police powers in the framework of criminal investigations are ruled by the Criminal Procedure Code. Except in *flagrante delicto* cases, arrest, search, and seizure can only be carried out on the basis of a warrant issued by an examining magistrate. A judicial warrant is always necessary to make use of special surveillance techniques (e.g., interceptions) in serious cases.

Police Public Projects

The Police are a permanent partner in prevention campaigns in the fields of drug abuse, juvenile violence, road traffic accidents, and runs a number of security awareness programs.

Staff, Recruitment, Training

There are three different career tracks:

Brigadiers (police sergeants), 15% of police strength, recruited in the Army (24 months military service)
Inspecteurs (police inspectors)
Cadre supérieur (senior management, police superintendents)

Candidates for the brigadier and inspecteur careers must have secondary education of at least three and five years, respectively; take an entrance examination and follow a twelve- and twenty-four-month curriculum, respectively, at the national police school; and take an admission examination, including human rights and police deontology. After six years, members of both career tracks have to take another examination to access their upper ranks.

All members of the cadre supérieur (5%), who are responsible for police management, have a master's degree (in law, criminology, economy, or related discipline) from a European Union university, and have completed superior police training in Belgium and/or France. A number of seminars and specialization cycles abroad are foreseen over an entire career. The director general of the Police is chosen within the cadre supérieur.

Women have had access to police careers since 1980; today they represent 7% of police personnel.

Police Use of Firearms

Without prejudice to legitimate defense rights, police officers can also make use of service firearms when violence is directed against them, which include the following scenarios:

- Attack by unarmed persons, or being threatened by armed persons.
- When required to lend assistance to attacked persons whose life, physical integrity, or property are exposed to a considerable and present danger.

It is the only way to defend posts, buildings, premises, or persons under their protection.

- It is the only possibility to stop persons or vehicles from fleeing the scene

Use of firearms in transborder operations falls under provisions of the 1990 Schengen convention and is limited to legitimate defense.

Complaints and Discipline

Discipline is supervised at regional and national levels of the police structure. The Inspectorate General investigates all complaints, including cases of human rights violations. The latter remain quite rare and there is no general criticism concerning police methods; nevertheless, police authorities have to keep the awareness with regard to proportionality of police reactions. Human rights training is based on the Council of Europe Human Rights Convention and related police deontology standards

Terrorism

The State Intelligence Service and the Police have regulations regarding terrorism. All law enforcement aspects are coordinated by the public prosecutor's office. To date, no terrorist attacks have been committed in Luxembourg.

International Cooperation

A particularly close cooperation exists under the European Union instruments (for instance, Schengen agreements, European police office Europol, and so on) and the Benelux treaties. The Schengen Convention (1990, Schengen, Luxembourg) establishes the free movement of persons by abolishing controls at internal borders between the Schengen states and introduces compensatory police cooperation measures: transborder observation and hot pursuit, information exchange, and the Schengen Information System (a common database of various categories of wanted persons and objects).

In 1946, Luxembourg joined the ICPO-Interpol. Luxembourg has bilateral police cooperation agreements with Belgium, France, and Germany.

Police Education, Research, and Publication

Due to its size, Luxembourg has no institution for higher police education. However, Luxembourg is founding member of the Europäische Rechtsakademie (ERA, Academy of European Law), in Trier, Germany, which has a department for public European law including law enforcement issues (www. era.int). Moreover, the Police are members of the European Police College (CEPOL, www.pfa.nrw. de/CEPOL) and has links with:

Ecole Fédérale pour Officiers, Brussels, Belgium
Polizei Führungs Akademie (PFA), Münster, Germany (www.pfa.nrw.de)
Institut des Hautes Etudes de la Sécurité Intérieure (IHESI), Paris, France (www.ihesi. interieur.gouv.fr)

ROLAND GENSON

Website

Luxembourg Police: *www.police.lu.*

Bibliography

Fröhling, Fernand. *Berittene Gendarmerie in Luxembourg* (Mounted gendarmerie in Luxembourg), Vol. I: 963–1815. Luxembourg: Association de Secours Mutuels du Corps de la Gendarmerie Grand-Ducale, 1990.

Fröhling, Fernand. *Berittene Gendarmerie in Luxembourg, Teil II: 1815–1945.* Luxembourg: Association de Se-cours Mutuels du Corps de la Gendarmerie Grand-Ducale, 1991.

Fröhling, Fernand. *Centenaire de l'Association de Secours Mutuels du Corps de la Gendarmerie Grand-Ducale* (Centenary of gendermarie). Luxembourg: Association de Secours Mutuels du Corps de la Gendarmerie Grand-Ducale, 1990.

Gendarmerie Grand-Ducale Luxembourg, ed. *Die Gendarmerie in Luxembourg 1797–1997 (The Gendarmerie in Luxembourg 1797–1997).* Luxembourg: Imprimerie Saint-Paul, 1997.

Genson, Roland. "The Schengen Agreements—Police Cooperation and Security Aspects." In *Crime sans frontières: International and European Legal Approaches,* Hume Papers on Public Policy, Vol. 6, edited by Peter J Cullen and William C. Gilmore, 133-140. Edinburgh: Edinburgh University Press, 1998.

Gerges, Martin, ed. *Mémorial 1989: La société luxembourgeoise de 1839 à 1989* (Luxembourg society from 1839 to 1989, with extensive explanation of the role of the security forces). Luxembourg: Les publications mosellanes, 1989.

Majerus, Pierre. *L'Etat luxembourgeois. Manuel de droit constitutionnel et de droit administratif* (The Luxembourg State. Handbook of constitutional and administrative law), 6th ed., rev. compl. mise à jour by Marcel Majerus, Esch/Alzette, 1990.

Reuland, Pierre. "La police à Luxembourg ville" (The police in Luxembourg City)." *Ons Stad* no. 34 (1990): 10–12.

Simon, Arthur. *Die Polizei in Staat und Gemeinde einst und jetzt* (State and municipal police now and in the past). Luxembourg, 1961.

Spielmann, Alphonse, and Spielmann, Dean. *Droit pénal général luxembourgeois (General criminal law of Luxembourg).* Bruxelles: Bruylant, 2002.

Trausch, Gilbert. *Le Luxembourg. Emergence d'un Etat et d'une Nation.* (Emergence of a state and a nation, with extensive coverage of police role). Anvers: Fonds Mercator, 1989.

Vogel, Gaston. *Lexique de procédure pénale de droit luxembourgeois (Dictionary of criminal procedure and law of Luxembourg).* Brussel: Larcier, 2001.

M

MACEDONIA

Background Material

The Republic of Macedonia gained its independence by separating from the former Yugoslav federation in late 1991. The Republic of Macedonia is situated in the central part of the Balkan Peninsula, with no outlet to the sea. It has a total area of 25,713 sq km, 80% of which are hills and mountains.

The Republic of Macedonia has a population of approximately two million, nearly a third of which are ethnic minorities, including ethnic Albanians, Turks, Romanies, Serbs, and Vlachs. The bulk of the population are ethnic Macedonians. Some 80% of the population are concentrated in urban areas. The largest concentration is in Macedonia's capital, Skopje.

Major religions are Orthodox Christianity and the Muslim religion. Macedonian is the official language, and Albanian is also used officially under specific conditions.

About 36% of the Gross National Product (GNP) is generated by industry, which employs approximately 40% of the population. Some 22% of the GNP is generated by agriculture and fishing, and 20% by commerce. The remaining GNP percentages are generated by general services. The highest unemployment rate was 32%, recorded in 2001 and 2002.

Contextual Features

The Assembly of the Republic of Macedonia is a representative body of its citizens, and the legislative power of the Republic is vested in it. The President of the Republic of Macedonia represents the Republic. The President of the Republic is Commander-in-Chief of the Armed Forces. Executive power is vested in the Government of the Republic of Macedonia.

The criminal justice system is civil. After gaining independence, Macedonia enacted new laws. The police has the dominant role in pre-trial procedure, but the judicial procedure is dominated by a very active role of the judge.

Judiciary power is exercised by courts. Courts are autonomous and independent. Courts decide on the basis of the Constitution and laws as well as international agreements ratified in accordance with the Constitution. The judiciary is organized as a single system, and emergency courts are prohibited.

The Constitutional Court is a body that protects the country's constitutionality and legality.

The Public Prosecutor's Office is an autonomous state body.

In the period from 1995–2002, the most common crimes were those against property (30%) and offenses against traffic safety (17%).

Institutions responsible for carrying out the sentence of deprivation of liberty are founded and abolished through decrees of the Government at the proposal of the Justice Minister.

Closed-type institutions are responsible for carrying out prison sentences exceeding two years, the sentence of life imprisonment, and the sentence of imprisonment for repeated crimes, regardless of sentence length.

Half-closed institutions are responsible for carrying out prison sentences of up to two years.

Open-type institutions are responsible for carrying out prison sentences for crimes committed out of negligence, as well as prison sentences of up to five years for other crimes if there is a reasonable expectation that the goal of punishment will be achieved by confining a person in an institution of this type.

There are special departments or sections within the existing institutions intended for specific categories of convicted persons. As far as juveniles are concerned, Macedonia has one prison for juveniles, one house of education and correction, and several educational institutions.

Police Profile

Background and Organizational Description

The Bureau of Public Security is responsible for the maintenance of public security, through uniformed and criminal police.

The Ministry of the Interior (MoI) is organized on three levels: central (seat), regional, and local sub-districts.

The Bureau of Public Security has two departments: Uniformed Police Department and Criminal Police Department.

The Uniformed Police Department is responsible for maintenance of public order, road traffic regulation and control, control of state border crossings, lake safety, and other duties determined by the Internal Affairs Act.

The current Uniformed Police Department consists of the MoI Duty Operational Centre, the Public Order Sector, the Road Traffic Safety Sector, the Border Crossings Centre, the Special Unit Sector, and the Special Task Unit.

The Criminal Police Department carries out the following tasks: prevention of crimes, discovery and apprehension of crime perpetrators, forensic technical work, control of the residence and movement of aliens, inspection and surveillance of and protection from fires and explosions, and other activities determined by law.

The Criminal Police Department is composed of the Common Crime Sector, the INTERPOL National Central Bureau, the Sector for Trafficking in Drugs, the Unit for Trafficking in Weapons, the Organized Crime Sector, and the Forensic Science Sector.

The Crime Sector takes measures and carries out activities and actions concerning the prevention of common crime, the discovery and apprehension of crime perpetrators, and their registration and transfer to courts.

The Sector carries out its duties based on the subordination and territorial principles, involving deployed linear inspectors throughout the country within the framework of the Sectors and Department of Internal Affairs.

Demographics

Following European standards in police organization and national characteristics, the Macedonian Police Department has accepted the ratio of 1.300 (one police officer per 300 citizens).

In 2002, the Ministry of the Interior carried out its duties with more than 10,000 employees. The highest percentage of employees are 31 to 35 years old. As far as ethnic affiliation (background) is concerned, the number of ethnic Macedonians tends to decrease, while the number of members of ethnic minority communities, particularly ethnic Albanians, is on the rise.

Regarding gender representation, the percentage of women in 2002 was 15.7%. As a comparison, in 1998, women composed 15.1% of the police.

The number of law enforcement officers employed in the MoI with an ethnic background other than Macedonian is steadily increasing, reflecting the general policy of the government.

Functions

According to the Internal Affairs Act, the Ministry of the Interior (MoI) is authorized to perform the following duties: protection of life, personal safety, and property of the citizens; prevention of crimes; discovery and apprehension of crime per-

Structure of MoI employees according to status

	1992	1998	2002
Law enforcement officers	72.9%	74.4%	81.7%
Others*	27.1%	25.6%	18.3%

*In 2002, the group Others consisted of 6.2% of Ministry employees with a civil servant status, 7.2% of firemen, and 4.9% of the administrative-technical staff

Ethnic background of MoI employees

	Macedonians	Albanians	Turks	Serbs	Romanies	Others
1992	92.6%	2.7%	0.4%	2.0%	0.5%	1.8%
1998	92.3%	3.0%	0.3%	2.1%	0.5%	1.8%
2002	89.6%	5.9%	0.4%	1.9%	0.7%	1.5%

petrators and their delivery to the competent authorities; protection of liberties and human rights; prevention of violent destruction of democratic institutions established by the Constitution; maintenance of public order; prevention of ethnic, racial, and religious hatred and intolerance; provision of security for specific individuals; road traffic regulation and control; control of state border crossing movement and movement of persons in border areas; residence and movement of aliens; verification and resolution of border incidents; placement, control, and maintenance of signs for demarcation of the border; protection from fires and explosions; control of conditions related to the production, trade, supply, possession, and carrying of weapons and ammunition; production, trade, storage, transportation, and protection of explosives and other dangerous materials; storage and protection of flammable liquids and gases; control of citizens' registration of and departure from dwellings and places of residence; passport control at state border crossings; assistance in the elimination of consequences caused by natural disasters and outbreaks that could endanger the life and health of citizens and their property; research and development in areas of its responsibility, and other duties determined by law.

Police Use of Firearms

In performing official assignments, police officers have the right to use the harshest means of force possible: firearms.

Legal bases for the use of firearms, under the Internal Affairs Act, are fulfilled in cases when it is necessary:

(1) To protect human lives;
(2) To resist an illegal direct attack endangering the police officer's life;
(3) To resist an attack on a protected person or object;
(4) To avert the flight of a person who:
- has been caught while perpetrating a crime punishable by a prison sentence of five years or more;
- has performed another criminal act, but

there are grounds of suspicion that he/she may use firearms;
- has been arrested, or there is an arrest warrant on grounds of suspicion that he/she has committed some of the aforementioned crimes.

The Constitution, the Internal Affairs Act, the Criminal Code, and various other documents stipulate the rights, obligations, and responsibilities of police employees in detail, providing legal guarantees for maintaining such a balance.

In 2000, the police in Macedonia used firearms on four occasions, causing two injuries and one death. In 2001, one death was caused by use of a firearm. During that year, however, because of the armed conflict and frequent use of firearms, it was impossible to keep accurate statistics. In 2002, police used firearms on seven occasions, causing three injuries and three deaths. All cases were within the law.

Complaints and Discipline

Horizontal control is performed by immediate superior officers and administrators, through different forms of monitoring the work of each police officer, usually through inspection of official documents, conversations with clients who have objections to the work of individual police officers, through immediate inspection, or through control of the police officer's workplace.

Vertical control is performed by senior officers from the MoI as well as by a special section active within the Ministry. This is the Unit for Professional Standards, whose objective is the investigation of all cases of violation of human rights and freedoms, abuse of official position, or conduct that is not in line with the professional and moral principles defined by the ethical code of the police.

Citizens can submit a request for investigation to this unit as parties who have suffered a loss, but very frequently this is done by immediate superior officers who have been informed of such demands.

The Unit for Professional Standards follows an objective and impartial procedure, and its findings are given to superior administrators. Depending on the findings, they can take specific measures against

Ethnic background of uniformed police employees

	Macedonians	Albanians	Turks	Serbs	Romanies	Others
1992	92.5%	2.7%	0.4%	2.0%	0.5%	1.9%
1998	91.7%	3.2%	0.3%	2.3%	0.5%	2.0%
2002	88.2%	6.6%	0.4%	2.1%	0.9%	1.8%

any breaches of professional, disciplinary, material, or criminal responsibility.

The Judiciary and Public Prosecution Unit has a special place in the vertical control. It is authorized, as an independent branch of power, to request data and information concerning events in the MoI that may involve abuse of regulations, overstepping of authority, or any violation of human rights and freedoms.

International Cooperation

As a signatory to the European Convention of Human Rights and Freedoms, the Republic of Macedonia is open to all international organizations that monitor the protection and respect of human rights and freedoms. For example, the Committee for the Prevention of Torture visited several institutions in the country in 1998, 2001, and 2002. The Committee members' objective was to perform immediate inspection and control of the legal standards for treatment of individuals during police and judicial procedures and imprisonment.

The reports of this organization have had considerable effect on the measures taken and activities carried out by all appropriate institutions in improving conditions and raising the standards of practical protection of human rights and freedoms.

To help the police come even closer to internationally accepted professional standards and build measures for strengthening the confidence of the population, the Ohrid Framework Agreement (2001) aims to promote a police service that reflects the ethnic composition of the population of the Republic of Macedonia. This Agreement also seeks to create a police organization in which all citizens, regardless of ethnic background, will have confidence, and whose officers act fairly and without prejudice in all circumstances.

In accordance with the Framework Agreement, by 2004 the police generally reflected the ethnic composition of the population of Republic of Macedonia. Five hundred police officers from minority communities were trained by July, 2002 and deployed in those communities. By July, 2003, a further 500 police officers were trained and deployed. The purpose of this process is to achieve ethnic balance and equal representation of the members of all of Macedonia's ethnic communities within the police force.

In carrying out police reforms, the issue of developing acceptable, transparent, and fair selection and recruitment procedures for future police officers is of particular significance.

Under the Internal Affairs Act and the Collective Agreement of the MoI, a person can be hired, by either public notice or without public notice, for a job in the MoI, for a job involving special duties and competencies, for students receiving scholarships from the MoI, and for graduates working in the MoI educational institution.

The MoI cooperates on a bilateral basis with other police organizations, having signed cooperation agreements in the area of security. Such agreements have already been signed or are to be signed shortly with all neighboring countries.

The Ministry's chief cooperation partners include the police organizations of the United States, Germany, France, Turkey, Canada, the Netherlands, Denmark, Switzerland, Russia, Italy, Sweden, and Norway. Main areas of cooperation include education, study visits, and joint projects.

The Macedonian MoI has so far sent a liaison officer only to the SECI Centre. Bearing in mind the experiences of other countries and the sophisticated nature of some new crimes, the exchange of officers between countries and appropriate organizations is seen as a strategic orientation of the Ministry.

Police Education, Research, and Publications

The commitment of the Republic of Macedonia to develop a rule of law on democratic principles (i.e., maintain the lawfulness of procedure in all state institutions) requires that the police staff receive appropriate training during the course of regular education, and acquire additional knowledge and skills during their work.

In the early 1970s, the Republic of Macedonia had one of the best systems for police education in the region. In 1995, however, a decision was made to close down the Faculty of Security, which is to cease its activity by September 30, 2003. In addition, the Secondary Police School had to stop enrolling new students in 1997. All this has had a negative impact on the competence of the staff the MoI needs.

Currently, the education of newly recruited police officers is organized through the office of the OSCE in Skopje. The basic training course lasts three months and includes human rights education.

Since 2001, the MoI participates in all programs organized by AEPC (Association of European Police Colleges) for the Southeast European countries.

In 2002 and 2003, the Government accepted the proposal for the establishment of a Police Academy, and the draft of the new law is currently in parliamentary procedure. A Police Academy will be established as a special state institution responsible for providing university-level education in the areas of police science, criminology, intelligence, and counterintelligence.

Leading Researchers/Authors with Affiliations

- Prof. Ljupčo Arnaudovski, Ph.D., member of AMCJC (Association of Macedonian Criminal Justice and Criminology);
- Prof. Trpe Stojanovski, Ph.D., member of IPES (International Police Executive Symposium) and AMCJC;
- Prof. Zvonimir Jankuloski, Ph.D.;
- Assistant Professor Gordan Kalajdžiev, LLM, member of AMCJC;
- Prof. Oliver Bacanovik, Ph.D., member of AMCJC;
- Pavel Manev, MA.
- Jovan Jovcevski, MA.
- Voislav Zafirovski.

Sources of Funding for Police Research

- Ministry of Education & Science;
- Fulbright Scholar Program;
- FRESTA – Denmark Centre for Human Rights;
- European Commission.

Examples of recent research on police and justice are the following projects:

- *Police and human rights*, by Gordan Kalajdgiev, Trpe Stojanovski, Zvonimir Jankuloski, and Voislav Zafirovski;
- *Police, Public Prosecutor's office and Courts in pre-trial criminal procedure*, by Pavel Manev, Ljupco Arnaudovski, and Gordan Kalajdgiev;
- *Policing in the multiethnic community: challenge, necessity or unavoidability*, by Ljupco Arnaudovski, Trpe Stojanovski, Dijana Tafčievska, and General Risto Galevski.

Leading Journals

- *Bezbednost (Security,)* a journal published by the MoI (publication currently suspended), Ministry of Interior, 1000 Skopje, Republic of Macedonia;

- *Review of Criminology and Criminal Law*, Association for Criminal Justice and Criminology, Editor: Nikola Matovski, Ph.D.; address: Faculty of Law, 1000 Skopje, Republic of Macedonia;
- *Annual Edition for the School of Security*, Principal editor Oliver Bacanovik Ph.D.; address: Faculty of Security, 1000 Skopje, Republic of Macedonia.

Review of Major Police Publications

- *The Police in a Democratic Society*, T. Stojanovski, 1997, 2 AvgustS, Skopje.
- *Police and Human Rights, Collection of International Instruments*, Helsinki Committee for Human Rights of Macedonia, 2002, Skopje.
- *Police and Human Rights, Manual*, Z. Jankuloski, T. Stojanovski, G. Kalajdžiev, V. Zafirovski, Helsinki Committee for Human Rights of Macedonia, 2002, Skopje.
- *Policing in a Multiethnic Community*, Lj. Arnaudovski, T. Stojanovski, D. Tafčievska, Gen. R. Galevski, COC — Center for Open Communication, 2002, Skopje.

TRPE STOJANOVSKI AND GORDAN KALAJDŽIEV

Websites

www.gov.mk
www.scramble.ul/mk.htm
www.izbori98.gov.mk/html/politickisistem.htm
www.smultimedia.com Encyclopaedia Macedonica

Bibliography

Arnaudovski, Ljupco, Trpe Stojanovski, Dijana Tafčievska, and General Risto Galevski. *Policing in a Multiethnic Community*. COC (Center for Open Communication). Skopje, 2003.

Joint European Project. *Advanced Training for Fight Against Organized Crime – Final Observations*. Skopje: Faculty of Security, February 2003.

Ministry of Interior. *Annual Report*. Skopje, Republic of Macedonia.

MADAGASCAR

Background Material

Madagascar's population is predominantly of mixed Asian and African origin. There are small groups of Comorians, French, Indians, and Chinese. The population is almost 17 million in the first decade of the twenty-first century. The average population growth runs about 3% annually.

The Malagasy language is of Malayo-Polynesian origin and is spoken throughout the island. Since Madagascar is a former colony of the French, the educated population speaks French. The majority of the people of Madagascar observe the traditional religion of the island; the next largest group observes the Christian religion, equally divided between Catholics and Protestants.

In the seventh century, the written history was initiated when the Arabs established trading post on the northwest coast. In the 1500s, the Portuguese began contact with the island. The French, in the late 1700s, established trading posts on the east coast, and the British gave financial and military assistance. In 1885, Madagascar became a protectorate of the French government, with the British accepting French control. In 1958, the Malagasy Republic was proclaimed as an autonomous state within the French community. Full independence was obtained in 1960.

Natural resources in Madagascar include graphite, chrome, bauxite, nickel, gold, tar sand, semiprecious stones, and hardwoods. Agriculture products include rice, livestock, seafood, coffee, vanilla, sugar, cloves, cotton, peanuts, and tobacco. Industry includes clothing, textiles, mining, paper, glassware, refined petroleum products, soap, cement, and tanning. The GDP for the country is $5.5 billion . Other information relating to economy is not available.

Contextual Features

Madagascar has been an independent republic since 1960. Its constitution became effective in 1998. There are three branches of government: executive, legislative, and judicial. The executive branch consists of a president, prime minister, and cabinet. The legislative branch consists of a National Assembly and a Senate. The Judicial branch consists of a Supreme Court, High Court of Justice, and Constitutional High Court.

The criminal justice process involves policing, prisons, and the judiciary. The Constitution of 1998 provides for an autonomous judiciary. The judiciary consists of three levels: local courts for civil and criminal cases carrying limited fines and sentences; the Court of Appeals, which hears cases with a sentence of five years or more; and a Supreme Court. There are special courts that handle theft of cattle. The High Supreme Court is autonomous and does technical reviews of laws, decrees, and ordinances, and it certifies election results.

The Penal Code of Madagascar primarily has been based on the French penal codes and procedures but has been influenced by Malagasy customs. Trials are public, and defendants have a right to a lawyer, to confront witnesses, and to present evidence. The most severe punishments are deaths and forced labor.

Madagascar has a nationwide prison system. Each province has a main prison for prisoners who serving a sentence of less than five years. Also, each province has several prisons for terms of less than two years and for prisoners awaiting trial. Local courts maintain jails for offenders serving a sentence of up to six months.

Prisons in Madagascar are harsh. Prisoners receive little food, and some may go for days without food. Medical care is inadequate, and prisoners suffer from malnutrition, infections, malaria, and tuberculosis. At times, prisoners are used for forced labor.

Generally, the treatment of women and children in prison is poor. The separation of genders in prison does not always occur, and rapes by other prisoners are reported.

Police Profile

The Ministry of Interior for Public Security and the national police who are under the State Secretary have the responsibility for maintaining public safety in urban areas. The gendarmerie have primary responsibility for security, except in major urban areas, and they are assisted in some areas by the regular army against bandit gangs and cattle thieves. At the local level, traditional laws known as "*dina*" are enforced by village-level law enforcement, specifically in the areas where the government's presence is weak.

The national police force is commanded by a police commissioner and organized according to the British organizational model. The national police have 500 members with a sixty-member paramilitary unit. Generally, the national police are unarmed, but mobile unit personnel are armed with modern weapons. The national police are divided into the Central Police Division, which consists of the capital; the South Division; and the Praslin/La Digue Police Division. Each division has 17 police stations. The organization of the national police includes Headquarters, Criminal Investigation Division (CID), Special Force (Police Mobile Unit), General Duties, and Special Branch. The police training school has a commander. The course is 15 weeks long, and there are also refresher courses for recruits, two-week supervisory officers' courses, two-week promotion courses, and a four-week basic course. Each district has field training for recruits.

The Madagascar Constitution supports human rights, although there appear to be violations of human rights. Violations are reported to include politically motivated disappearances, failure to separate prisoners according to gender, and inadequate food and medical care for prisoners, to name a few.

PAUL IBBETSON AND MICHAEL J. PALMIOTTO

Bibliography

Country Reports on Human Rights Practices, 2000: Madagascar. www.terrorismcentral.com/Library/government/US/ State Department/DemocracyHuman Rig... 1/18/2005.

"History of Madagascar." *Wikipedia, the free encyclopedic.* http://en.wikipedia.org/wiki/History_of_Madagascar 1/18/2005.
Human Rights. www.state.gov/g/dr/rls/hrrpt/2003.27736.
"Madagascar." The *World Factbook. www.odci.gov/cia/ publications/factbook/geos/ma.html 1/18/05.*
"Madagascar." *AllRefer.com Reference.* http://reference.all-refer.com.
Madagascar. U.S. Department of State. www.state.gov/r/ pa/ei/bgn/5460.htm. 1/18/2005.

MALAWI

Background

Malawi has an area of 45,747 sq mi and is bordered by Mozambique, Tanzania, and Zambia. Lake Nyasa (Lake Malawi), which lies north to south along the Tanzania/Mozambique/Malawi border, is the third largest of the East African Rift Valley lakes. From north to south, the lake is approximately 363 miles long, and it ranges in width from 10 to 50 miles. Lake Nyasa, containing a great variety of fish (including Chambo, a fresh water perch), is traditionally a major food source for Malawians. In addition, Malawians and tourists utilize the lake for recreation, including canoeing, swimming, caving, and hiking.

In 1998, the National Statistical Office (NSO) reported the Malawi population at 9.9 million (4.9 million males and 5.0 million females). Of the 9.9 million persons, 5.7 million are under the age of 20. The Southern region is the most densely populated (47%), followed by the Central Region (41%), and finally the Northern region (12%). Most Malawians live in rural areas (86%). The most densely populated districts are Rumphi, Likoma, Blantyre, and Chiradzulu. There are 11 ethnic groups represented in the area: Chewa, Nyanja, Tumbuka, Yao, Lomwe, Sena, Tonga, Ngoni, Ngonde, Asian, and European. In addition, 55% are Protestant; 20% are Roman Catholic; 20% are Muslim; 3% have indigenous beliefs, and 2% are categorized as "other" (U.S. Census Bureau, est. 2004).

The census results show that 5.7 million, or 57% of Malawians, use Chichewa as their first language. Other commonly used languages are Chinyanja (13%), Chiyao (10%), and Chitumbuka (9%). The official languages of Malawi are English and Chichewa; however, the census result does not include a percentage of English speakers.

The literacy rate among persons over the age of five is 58%. This is a 38% increase from the 1987 census. Literacy rates among males and female are 64% and 51%, respectively. Approximately 2.7 million persons, or 33%, over the age of five have never attended school. During the census month (August, 1998), 2.4 million persons, over the age of five, attended primary, secondary, or university schools.

The main agricultural products cultivated in Malawi are cassava, cattle, cotton, goats, groundnuts, macadamia nuts, maize, potatoes, sorghum, sugar cane, tea, and tobacco. The NSO 1998 census report states that 4.5 million persons over the age of 10 are economically active. Of this group, 78% are subsistence farmers, while 13% are employees.

Approximately 55% (2003 est., U.S. Census Bureau) of Malawians live below the poverty line. According to the NSO, 27% of the people have access to boreholes for their main water source, while the rest draw water from unprotected sources or communal standpipes. In addition, sanitary toilet facilities are lacking; 73% have access to pit latrines, and 22% do not have access to toilet facilities. For cooking, 94% of Malawians use firewood as their main energy source. Only 2% have access to electricity for cooking, and 5% have electricity for lighting purposes.

In 2004, the U.S. Census Bureau estimated the Malawi population at 11.9 million, 90% of whom live in rural areas. The estimated distribution of age is as follows: 0–14 (46.8%), 15–64 (50.5%), and over 65 (2.8%). The median estimated age is 16.4 years old. The overall estimated population growth rate is 2.14%. The 2001 estimated HIV/AIDS prevalence rate is 15%. Finally, the NSO projects a population of 16 million by the year 2013.

In 1859, David Livingstone, a Scottish missionary, along with several British missionaries, visited Lake Nyasa. They discovered and brought to the attention of Europeans the extent of the slave trade in the region. Over the next 20 years, missionaries settled the region of Nyasaland, which includes most of present-day Malawi, in hopes of reducing the slave trade network. By 1883, the British sent a consul to the area and declared itself Protectorate of the region. In 1890, British forces ended the slave trade. Subsequently, in 1891, the British Central African Protectorate was formally established. As was common of British colonial governments, traditional rulers retained status as administrative leaders. Colonial rule, however, greatly influenced and controlled the traditional rulers.

By the early 1930s, native associations formed to confront colonial rule. Initially, the native associations acted as intermediaries between the traditional rulers and the colonial government. By 1944, the regional associations had organized to form the Nyasaland African Congress, or the NAC. This organization was determined to end colonial rule. However, leadership of the NAC was weak and unorganized. In 1959, the NAC dissolved and was reformed under the leadership of Hastings Kamuzu Banda as the Malawi Congress Party, or MCP. Banda led successful protests against colonial rule, which resulted in the independence of Malawi on July 6, 1964. Under a new constitution, Banda became the first president of Malawi in 1966. In 1971, the MCP named Banda president for life.

Political turmoil and charges of human rights abuses forced the MCP to reevaluate Banda's life term. In 1993, Malawians, with support from the United Nations and other international organizations, voted to end one-party rule. Subsequently, in addition to the MCP, two other parties formed: the Alliance for Democracy (AFORD), and the United Democratic Front (UDF). During a free election in 1994, Elson Bakili Muluzi (UDF) replaced Banda as president of Malawi for two terms. Then, in May 2004, during free elections, Bingu wa Mutharika (UDF) replaced Muluzi as president.

Contextual Features

The constitution, adopted on May 18, 1994, patterns the Malawian governmental structure after that of the U.S. government. Every five years, Malawi holds Presidential elections by popular vote. The elected President is the Chief of State and the Head of Government. As of June 2004, President Mutharika has appointed 12 ministers and nine deputy ministers to the cabinet. Past cabinets consisted of 46 members.

As of September 2004, the legislative branch (Malawi National Assembly) consists of 185 seats, representing 28 districts, including: Balaka, Blantyre, Chikwawa, Chiradzulu, Chitipa, Dedza, Dowa, Karonga, Kasungu, Likoma, Lilongwe, Machinga, Mangochi, Mchinji, Mulanje, Mwanze, Mzimba, Neno, Nkhatabay, Nkhotakota, Nsanje, Ntchisi, Phalombe, Rumphi, Salima, Thyolo, and Zomba. The parties represented include the following: UDF (51%), MCP (31%), Independent (21%), Mgwirizano Coalition (13%), NDA (4%), and AFORD (3%). The constitution also provides for a Senate, which to date has not been formed.

The judicial branch, based on the English model, consists of the High Court (the Chief Justice is appointed by the President), the Supreme Court of Appeals, and Magistrate Courts. Traditional courts, while abolished under Banda, do still exist, but have limited power. Malawi has not accepted the International Court of Justice (ICJ).

The 1994 constitution established a Human Rights Commission, a Law Commission, a Judicial Services Commission, an Ombudsman, and the National Compensation Tribunals, which hear claims against the government.

Police Profile

Background

By 1896, the British Protectorate had removed the military police and established a civil police force. It is estimated that the civil police initially employed 418 men. Each district was responsible for training and determining the extent of police duties and terms of service. The duties of civil police were varied but mostly provided for cash escorts, serving writs, and making arrests. It is suggested that the early civil police were ill disciplined, often making demands for food and women from the local population. To curb officers' illicit behavior, the British Protectorate established the Civil Police Ordinance of 1909. This ordinance instituted punishments for police misconduct, which included imprisonment, fines, whipping or flogging, and dismissal.

Early records indicate that the Town Council of Blantyre employed two African Constables as town police. Records note that uniforms were issued in 1900. In addition, it is noted that these Constables were responsible for supervising road laborers and maintaining order in the markets.

From 1913 to 1923, Sir George Smith, K.C.M.G. acted as Governor and Commander in Chief of Nyasaland. In 1920, he established the Nyasaland Police Force under the direction of Major F.T. Stephens, O.B.E., M.C., who was appointed the first Chief Commissioner of Police on July 22, 1920. Under Major Stephens, police districts were reorganized; Zomba, Blantyre, Mlanje, and Fort Johnston were placed under the direct control of the Chief Commissioner and District Superintendent, W.B. Bithrey. The remaining districts continued under civil administration under the control of the district commissioners: R.J. Paul, W.L. Ozanne, Lt. Colonel H.B. Stephens, B.G. Pearson, and J. Green. African ranks consisted of 20 sergeants, 23 corporals, 34 lance corporals, 24 buglers, 344 constables, and six detectives.

It is noted that Major Stephens was successful in getting approval to create a criminal investigations department; however, limited funds prevented its formation. Major Stephens and Mr. W.B. Bithrey were trained as fingerprint experts, and they conducted criminal investigations on their own until 1922, when Mr. V.C. Churnock was appointed by the Governor to organize the department. In the formation of this department, eight detectives were employed. By 1923, the Criminal Investigations Department consisted of the Fingerprint Bureau, Criminal Records and Statistics, Police Circulars, and Censorship and Deportation.

There was limited funding for police administrative offices and stations. In Blantyre and Fort Johnson, the administrative offices were located in the superintendent's home. In Zomba, the police station was located in the Agricultural Department offices. The Police Training Depot was located in Zomba until 1924, when it closed due to a depletion of Protectorate funding. The training depot provided instruction in drill, police duties, and elementary law. Africans were taught to read and write in their native languages. After 1924, training was remanded to district officials. Later, in 1937, the Red Cross provided first aid training. It is recorded that police principally acted as tax collectors, messengers, and orderlies.

Between October 1921 and October 1922, records indicate the following crime statistics:Of the 1619 cases reported to police, 1136 court cases resulted. There were 1026 convictions; serious offenses included: murder (17), housebreaking or burglary (32), larceny (629).

In 1923, the Nyasaland Police force was reorganized to include the districts of Cholo, Chiradzulu, Lilongwe, Nsanje (Port Herald), Neno, Dedza, Chinteche, Nkhotakota, and Karonga. The force employed 13 Europeans and 457 Africans. They were equipped with .303 Rifles, which replaced single-shot M.E. Rifles.

Major Stephens established a Dog Branch in 1924. However, by 1925 the branch was dissolved, due to the death of the dogmaster and the subsequent deaths of the dogs. Limited funds prevented continuation of the Dog Branch.

Major Stephens was also responsible for establishing a Traffic Branch in Blantyre in 1936, which flourished due to increased motor vehicle activity in the major district centers. By 1938, he also increased the police force territory to include the Northern Provinces. With this reorganization, the Police (Amendment) Ordinance of 1938 changed the following official titles: the Chief Commissioner became the Commissioner of Police, and the Deputy Commissioner became the Assistant Commissioner. These changes brought Nyasaland Police Force administrative titles in line with the East African Police Force titles.

From 1939–1943, Superintendent W.B. Bithrey was appointed Commissioner of Police. He was also appointed the Principal Immigration Officer, Chief Inspector of Prisons and Lunatic Asylums, Chairman of the Language Board, Registrar of Firearms and Pedal-bicycles, Registrar of Motor Vehicles, and Director of the Passport Office.

In 1940, in an attempt to boost police morale and public perceptions of the police, Bithrey established a Police Band. Instruments were donated, and money for a three-year salary for a bandmaster (Shansher Signh Khawas, from Nepal) was donated by officers of the force. The first band performance was conducted at a Governor's house dinner on July 31, 1940. In addition to the Police Band, a morale boost resulted from the Nyasaland Police force winning five East and West African Shooting Cups as of 1946.

Prior to 1940, no effort was made to collect and record political intelligence. The Governor, during World War II, decided to create a Political Intelligence Bureau that would be administered separate from the government police force by one superintendent and six detectives in Blantyre. Subsequently, a secret service was authorized, but only until the end of the war when its necessity would be reviewed. At the outbreak of the war, the Commissioner of Police was appointed Director of Intelligence and Security. All German Nationals, Italian Nationals, and other enemy aliens were interned. To accommodate this added stress, a special force of 40 African police officers was established in Chileka.

In 1944, the Nyasaland police force underwent further reorganization. The territory was divided in three divisions: Northern Division, Central Division, and Southern Division. Administration remained organized under the Commissioner of Police and the District Commissioners.

The 1950s signaled a time of police expansion. A special Constabulary was formed, and the Commissioner of Police was replaced by Superintendent P. Long. The force consisted of 799 Europeans, 156 Asians, and 106 Africans. Communication was improved by the introduction of motor vehicle radio equipment and special communications stations. In addition, a Mobile Police Force was established to supplement district policing when needed. By 1954, 30 motor vehicles and 15 motorcycles were utilized.

By 1960, due to the return of President Banda and political disruption, the governor declared a state of emergency. Police from Tanganyika, Northern Rhodesia, and the British South African Police retained control of Nyasaland. During this period, many police buildings were upgraded, and over 700 recruits were added. Over 40 experienced officers from the United Kingdom strengthened the force. The total number of officers reached 225, and junior rank officers numbered 2604.

On July 6, 1964, Malawi gained independence. The Nyasaland Police Force was replaced by the Malawi Police Force. The transition from colonial policing to local policing occurred slowly. Africans were trained to take over the upper ranks in police college courses in the United Kingdom. In addition, a Dog Section was re-established in 1966, with six dogs and handlers, which increased to 23 working dogs and six puppies in 1969. Relative peace ensued for the duration of the transition from colonial rule to Banda's rule.

On September 27, 1970, Mr. Mc. J. Kamwana became the first Malawian Deputy Commissioner of Police. By 1971, only 26 European police officers remained. The strength of the African force numbered 2,986. According to the Annual Report of the Malawian Police Force, 1967–1972, no major police issues were experienced. Crime statistics indicate that the total felony and statutory offenses for 1971 and 1972 reached 71,528 and 72,524, respectively. Total murders in 1970 and 1971 reached 150 and 141, respectively.

From the mid-1970s, government reporting of crime statistics and information regarding the police organization are extremely limited. Independent organizations have attempted to ascertain crime data. A 1996 report commissioned by the Public Affairs Committee, Centre for Human Rights and Rehabilitation, and The Norwegian Initiative on Small Arms Transfer suggests crime statistics as seen in the table (below). This report notes that the data are incomplete, suggesting serious crime rates actually reached 30,000 cases from January 1996 to July 1996.

Complaints and Discipline

The results of a study commissioned by the British High Commission in 1999 on the public's perception of the Malawian Police force are dismal. The major findings of this report suggest that the police are "remote and unfamiliar to the people." People are dissatisfied with police response. This study suggests that the police have inadequate transportation, personnel, and remuneration. Victims report having to provide transportation for the police or that they actually apprehended the criminal and subsequently transported him/her to the police station themselves.

A 2001 report published by the Human Rights Commission, Lilongwe, Malawi, states that the conditions of police stations are very inadequate. The report states that the police station in Karonga has two cells to house 20 people. However, one of the cells cannot be used, due to a leaky pipe flooding the area. Stations at Iponga and Songwe are dilapidated and have no communication equipment, uni-

Crime statistics as reported by victims January 1996–July 1996 (Phiri, 1999)

General thefts	6,675
Burglaries	3,084
Robberies	689
Assaults	1,211
Complaint against police	35
Murder	399
Theft of vehicle	374
Sexual cases	154
Total	12,826

forms, vehicles, or female officers to handle female offenders. Tha Nkhata Bay police station has two cells with a capacity of seven people each. There are toilet facilities, but no showers. Chintheche and Mzimba have two cells each, all in poor repair. Mzuzu has four cells that can hold 10 people each.

Another report by the International Organization Development, Ltd. (2001) states that Blantyre, with approximately 400,000 residents, has one police station with one vehicle, 28 police officers, and limited communication equipment. This contributes to the current public opinion of the Malawian Police Force as inadequate.

CINDY MCNAIR

Bibliography

Benson, Todd. *An Atlas of Social Statistics.* Washington, D.C.: International Food Policy Institute and National Statistics Office, 2002.
Chanock, M. *Law, Custom and Social Order: the colonial experience in Malawi and Zambia.* Cambridge: University Press, 1987.
CIA World Fact Book. www.cia.gov/cia/publications/factbook/geos/mi.html. Accessed December 2004.
Commission, The. *A Report on visits made to Northern Region Prisons and Police Stations, Malawi Human Rights Commission.* Lilongwe, Malawi: The Commission, 2001.
Commonwealth Human Rights Initiative. *Concern for Small Arms Trade: Over a Barrel Light Weapons Trade in the Commonwealth.* A report by non-governmental Commonwealth Human Rights Advisory Board. London, 1999.
Country Watch. *Malawi Country Review.* Houston: Commercial Data International. www.countrywatch.com, 2004.
International Organization Development Ltd. *Final Report on Primary Systems, Malawi.* A report prepared for the Government of Malawi. Final report and Annexes. IOD Project No: 292, May 1999.
Malawian Government. *Annual Report of the Malawian Police Force 1967–1972.* Zomba, Malawi. The Government Printer, 1967–1972.
Malawian Government Web Page. www.malawi.gov.mw/ accessed December 2004.
Malawian Prison Service Web Page. http://chambo.sdnp.org.mw/ruleoflaw/prisons/index.html. Accessed December 2004.
Marlow, Cyril. *A History of the Malawi Police Force.* Malawi: Government Printer, 1971.
McCraken, John. "Coercion and Control in Nyasaland: Aspects of the History of a Colonial Police Force." *Journal of African History,* 27(1), (1986) 124–147.
National Statistics Office: Malawi. http://nso.malawi.net. Accessed December 2004.
Phiri, Robert. *National Crime Statistics and the Proliferation of Small Arms in Malawi: A Preliminary Study.* Commissioned by the Public Affairs Committee, Centre for Human Rights and Rehabilitation and the Norwegian Initiative on Small Arms Transfer for a roundtable conference. Oslo, Norway, July 1999.
Thomas-Konyani, S.E. *Malawi Police Public Perceptions Study.* Zomba, Malawi: Centre for Social Research, 1999.

MALAYSIA

Background Material

During the late eighteenth and nineteenth centuries, Great Britain established colonies and protectorates in present-day Malaysia. These colonies were occupied by Japan from 1942 to 1945. In 1948, the British-ruled territories formed the Federation of Malaya, which became independent in 1957. Malaysia was formed in 1963, when the former British colonies of Singapore and the East Malaysian states of Sabah and Sarawak on the northern coast of Borneo joined the Federation. The first several years of the country's history were marred by Indonesian efforts to control Malaysia, by Philippine claims to Sabah, and by Singapore's secession from the Federation in 1965.

Malaysia is located in southeastern Asia. It has a total area of 329,750 sq km and a total population of 23,522,482 (July 2004 est.). The ethnic composition of the population is: Malay and other indigenous (58%), Chinese (24%), Indian (8%), and others (10%). Islam, Buddhism, Taoism, Hinduism, Christianity, and Sikhims are all practiced in Malaysia. Shamanism is practiced in East Malaysia. Bahasa Melayu is the official language, although English, Chinese dialects, Tamil, Telugu, Malayalam, Panjabi, and Thai are spoken. In East Malaysia, several indigenous languages are spoken.

The GDP per capita in Malaysia is $9,000 (2003 est.).

Contextual Features

Malaysia is a constitutional monarchy.

The legal system is based on English common law; it allows judicial review of legislative acts in the Supreme Court at the request of the Supreme Head of the Federation. Malaysia has not accepted compulsory ICJ jurisdiction.

The legal system in Malaysia is based on both written and unwritten laws. The Federal Constitution, the individual constitutions of the thirteen states, and legislation passed by the Parliament comprise the major written laws. Unwritten law includes those aspects of British common law that were adopted. Islamic law is an important law source for the Muslim population.

Malaysia is headed by a Paramount Ruler and a bicameral Parliament, consisting of an appointed upper house and an elected lower house. The Paramount Ruler is the chief of state, while the Prime Minister is the head of the government. The members of the Cabinet are appointed by the Prime Minister from among the members of Parliament, with the consent of the Paramount Ruler.

The bicameral Parliament, or Parlimen, consists of the Senate, or Dewan Negara (70 seats; 44 appointed by the Paramount Ruler, 26 appointed by the state legislatures) and the House of Representatives, or Dewan Rakyat (219 seats; members elected by popular vote to serve five-year terms).

Malaysia has two high courts (the Court of Malaya and the High Court of Borneo) and a system of inferior courts. The Federal Court is the supreme court in the country. The subordinate courts include juvenile, magistrate, and session courts.

Police Profile

The police force is headed by an Inspector General of Police, who has a deputy and four directors beneath him. There is one director for each department: the Criminal Investigation department, the Special Branch, Security and Public Order, and Management. The Inspector General of Police answers to the Minister of Home Affairs.

The police force is charged with the basic duties of crime prevention, including the protection of the general welfare and safety of the citizenry, as well as investigating crime, identifying and apprehending offenders, and prosecuting criminals. The force also works to investigate and put a stop to the trafficking of drugs and arms.

A commission inquiry was set up to investigate charges of corruption and brutality made against the police. The full report of the commission was made public in February 2005. The report is entitled *Police Abuse in Malaysia (1992 to Dec 31, 2004)—A General Overview*, and it charges the police with corruption, rape, and inefficiency.

Bibliography

"Malaysia." *CIA World Fact Book*. www.cia.gov/cia/pub lications/factbook/geos/my.html.

"Malaysia Police Brutal, Corrupt." *BBC News*. August 10, 2004.http://news.bbc.co.uk/2/hi/asia-pacific/3550552. stm.

"Some Background on the Criminal Justice System of Malaysia." *The 'Lectric Law Library Stacks*. www.lect law.com/files/int15.htm.

MALDIVES

Background

The Republic of Maldives is situated in the Indian Ocean, southwest of India and Sri Lanka. It consists of an archipelago of more than 1,000 coral islands, 192 of which are inhabited. The islands form a land mass of 300 sq km. Except for coconut palms, vegetation on the islands is sparse, and there are few minerals or energy resources.

The Maldive population, currently 300,000, forms a single ethnic identity, speaking a distinct language, *Dhivehi,* derived from the same unknown root language as Sri Lankan *Sinhala*. English is now widely spoken, especially among younger Maldivians. The adult *Dhivehi* literacy rate is over 96% for both men and women.

Historical evidence suggests that Maldives began converting to Islam during the twelfth century, when Muslims from Persia and Yemen married into Buddhist Maldive families on the Meedhoo Island in the Addu atoll. Today, Maldives is exclusively Sunni Islamic, with secular authorities expressing open hostility to religious diversification. Despite this, remnants of beliefs in a variety of island deities and spirits persist, and the government licenses the practice of *fanditha*, an indigenous mixture of magic rituals and Koranic chants and texts. Maldivians use *fanditha* to influence football and other competitions, personal relationships, and important decisions.

Maldives has undergone profound economic development during the second half of the twentieth century. Based on GDP statistics for the period from 1998–2001, the country has the highest per capita income in the South Asia region, over US$2,000. This figure climbs to US$4,000 when adjusted for purchasing power parity, but there is a significant income differential between Malé and the atolls. In 1998, Malé's per capita income was 75% higher than atoll income. Life expectancy is also much higher in Malé—77 years, compared to 68 years for atoll dwellers.

Nevertheless, the UNDP's report into Human Development in Maldives cautions against reading too much into common economic indicators for the country, and claims that statistics "fail to capture the true vulnerability of people, the insecurity of the population, and the extraordinary challenges for ensuring sustainable human development." Thirty percent of the Maldive population live beneath the poverty line, and over 40% of the children below the age of five are undernourished.

During 2000, tourism earned 70% of Maldives' foreign exchange and generated a third of the country's GDP, but local worker participation rate in the resort industry is low. The first serious reduction in the Maldive tourist industry occurred in 2001, as the world economy faltered and further deteriorated after the al-Qaeda terrorist attacks in September. Maldive tourism is dependent on the health of the EU and Japanese economies, and on public perceptions of South Asian security issues.

Fishing accounts for 10% of the GDP and employs 20% of the total workforce. Over 1,000 boats are involved in the industry, which is the major employer of the local population outside Malé, the islands' capital. Other large employment sectors are bureaucracy, manufacturing, and transport and distribution. Significant income is also earned from rents in Malé. These rents are paid by foreign workers and Maldivians from other islands who live in the capital for employment and education. Many Malé families are using rent income to live overseas. Work participation rates for women, 19% in 1998, are among the lowest in the world.

Foreign aid is also an important part of the national income; it finances capital expenditures on infrastructure, planning, and education. Maldives has received economic assistance from the UN Development Program, the Asian Development Bank, the World Bank, the Islamic Development Bank, and the Kuwaiti Fund. Major country donors are Japan, India, Australia, and European and Arab nations.

Contextual Features

Maldives has two legal systems—Islamic Sharia, and the 1968 Maldive Penal Code, which closely resembles British colonial emergency law. On the atolls, local magistrates deal with neighborhood disputes, theft, debt, slander, and illegal sexual activity. In recent times, the courts have seen an increase in cases of pedophilia and the illegal use of drugs, including alcohol. Politically sensitive and serious charges are heard at the criminal court and high court in Malé.

The President's Office rules the country's bureaucracy, and it also controls the courts and legal administration. Court penalties range from fines (often paid to the complainant), house arrest, whipping, imprisonment, and exile to an island in a distant atoll. Drug offenders have the option of rehabilitation treatment in an under-resourced facility on an island north of Malé. Major prisons are located in Dhoonidhoo, Gamaadhoo, and Maafushi islands on the Malé atoll. Conditions in the Gamaadhoo and Maafushi prisons are overcrowded and brutal, and torture is routine. The facilities at Dhoonidhoo are better, in comparison to other prisons.

In Maldives, there has traditionally been no real distinction between the military and the police. A government copper plate, dated 1194 AD, notes the existence in the islands of a Commander-in-Chief and a Chief Justice. One hundred and fifty years later, a Moroccan traveller, Ibn Battuta, arrived on Maldives and became Chief Judge. He mentions a Commander of the Army and Minister of Police. The association of the militia with policing functions has been a consistant feature of Maldive history, with the militia having an active role in political struggles and governance throughout Maldives.

By the nineteenth century, the militia had become a distinct class, having established a close relationship with the monarchy. Maldives was compelled to become a British Protectorate in 1887, after Malé was threatened with naval bombardment, but the United Kingdom never established a colonial administration in Maldives.

King Ibrahim Nooruddheen (1888–1892) taught martial arts to selected younger members of the Maldive elite. The training ground was at the King's private residence, and instruction took place under the direct supervision of the monarch. Ismail Didi, who had learned foot drill at an English school in Galle in Sri Lanka, was ordered to train the elite young men in the Western military style. Light arms were issued to this special squad, who were known by the Turkish name *sifain*. Later, commoners were permitted to join.

During the reign of King Shamsuddheen (1903–1933), the militia successfully defended Malé from several armed mercenary attacks led by exiled Maldivians. Government accounts for 1917–1922 show that the cost of "chiefs and militia" was half of total government expenditures. In 1944, Mohamed Ameen became the ruler of Maldives. He was proud to wear a military uniform and had a close relationship with the British. The militia's uniform had been Turkish hats, white coats, white trousers, and white shoes. Ameen changed this to a white shirt with a black strip collar. The Maldive sarong became the soldiers' off-duty wear, and on formal occasions the army wore coats, trousers, shoes, and an angled hat.

In 1968, Prime Minister Nasir became the President, and two years later the *sifain* was renamed in English as the National Security Service, or NSS. Recruitment was open to any eligible male with a height of at least 165 cm. President Nasir ordered the arbitrary imprisonment and torture of his opponents. The two main prisons were on Vilingili island off Malé's western shore, and in the capital's Henveiru ward.

Large increases in the Maldive "defense" budget and other areas of government expenditure occurred during the rule of the incumbent President Maumoon Gayyoom, first elected in 1978. Spending rose sharply after an attempted coup by seaborne mercenaries in 1988. NSS armed infantry forces were doubled to 2,000; intelligence services formed, and six British vessels were added to the Maldive coast guard, which expanded to 400 personnel.

The Ministry of Defense and National Security has a variety of functions:

(a) Protecting the state and the government from internal and external threats;
(b) Maintaining law and order;
(c) Enforcing judicial and executive decisions;
(d) Maintaining airport security;
(e) Guarding the exclusive economic zone and territorial waters;
(f) Responding to all types of emergency situations;
(g) Enforcing the country's immigration policies.

The President is the Minister of Defence and National Security, and also the Commander-in-Chief of the NSS. The President is directly involved in the day-to-day decisions at the ministry. Officers undergo military training in many countries, including India, the United States, and Libya; and foreign combat experts and advisors visit Maldives regularly. Maldive vessels take part in joint naval exercises organized by India and the United States to maintain "sea lanes of communication" and "energy security" in the Arabian Sea and Indian Ocean. The cadet corps is actively promoted in Maldive high schools, and potential paramilitary forces are optimistically estimated at over 40,000. Ministry staff receive special housing and health benefits.

The National Security Service is administered by the Chief of Staff, and its operational units are: the three Quick Reaction Forces, a Special Protection Group (also known as Delta Force) that looks after the President's security and visiting VIPs; and the Coast Guard and Fire Service. NSS support services include engineering, transport, medical, catering, construction and maintenance, training, uniform, and three armories.

Police Profile

Organizational Description and Functions

Police Headquarters is run by the Deputy of Chief of Staff, who is the Commissioner of Police. This section has responsibility for all criminal and civil cases, including matters such as debt collection. The Airport Security Unit is also controlled by the Commissioner. Most police resources are spent on collecting intelligence and investigating matters relating to political issues, including the prevention of freedom of speech, the prevention of lawful assembly, and freedom to practice religions other than Islam. Police officers are NSS personnel.

Training

All police officers undergo a three-month military training course conducted by the NSS training section. They do not undergo a formal police training course. However, there are small numbers of personnel trained in India, Sri Lanka, Pakistan, and Singapore. Previously, officers had been sent to the United Kingdom for advanced police training.

The Ministry administers the Department of Immigration and Emigration. This was previously a function of the Ministry of Foreign Affairs. The change was adopted to make it easier to collect intelligence, carry out surveillance, and control movements of people.

Complaints and Discipline

International human rights organizations allege serious civil rights abuses and torture by NSS officers. These allegations are denied by the government and banned from public discussion in Maldives, but the evidence is overwhelming that arbitrary arrest, imprisonment, and torture are routine and brutal, and that the security forces regularly act with impunity at the command of the President's Office and specific government ministers. The Maldive reality is that there is no separation of executive and legal power. The Maldive government arrests and imprisons Islamic and secular activists who are openly critical of the regime and its policies. There is evidence that important legal judgments are influenced by the executive. Defense lawyers are usually not allowed in Maldive courts, and most important trials and sentences are unreported by the Maldive press. Unofficially, the situation is justified as a cultural tradition, necessary to maintain respect for authority and public order in Maldive society. Acting on behalf of their political masters, regardless of justice or legality, is seen by many Maldivians as a traditional and necessary part of police and other administrative work. The President is the constitutional head of the state, law, and Islamic religion in Maldives, and the President's Office and the NSS together control the bureaucracy, courts, and civil life, just as for centuries the royal court and the militia controlled the Maldive kingdom.

Changes in December 2002, to criminal procedure law, have provided accused people the right to legal aid lawyers, but the power of those lawyers to act on behalf of their clients is restricted. Meetings between a lawyer and client must be witnessed by the investigating officer, and lawyers can be dismissed or charged in relation to those discussions.

Major security operations in the last decade have included the quelling of civil unrest in Fua Mulaku in late 1995 and 1996, and on Naifaru island in 2001. Naifaru is adjacent to the large NSS training island at Madivaru island on the Lhaviyani atoll.

MICHAEL O'SHEA

Websites

Amnesty International: www.amnesty.org
Indian Armed Forces: www.indianarmedforces.com
Institute of Peace and Conflict Studies: www.ipcs.org/
Maldives Culture: www.maldivesculture.com
US Department of State: www.state.gov/g/drl/rls/hrrpt/2000/sa/698.html

Bibliography

Books and articles

Asian Development Bank. *Key Indicators of Developing Asian and Pacific Countries, Maldives.*

Bell, H.C.P., and W. L. de Silva. *The Maldive Islands, Monograph on the History, Archaeology and Epigraphy* (Maldives, Malé, Novelty Press, 1986. Facsimile reprint of the edition originally published in Ceylon Sri Lanka, Colombo Government Printer, 1940.

Committee of Maldivian History and Culture. *Dhivehi Thaareekhu.* Maldives, Malé, National Centre of Linguistics and Historical Research, 1981.

Fulhu, Buraara Mohamed, transcribed by Ibn Ismail Feeboa, Al-Hajj Ibrahim. *The Story of Bodu Thakurufaan.* Maldives, Malé, Department of Education 1958–1970.

Ibn Battuta, translation and commentary by Mahdi Husain. *The Rehla of Ibn Battuta.* India, Baroda, Oriental Institute, 1976.

Maldives Ministry of Planning and Development, and the United Nations Development Program. *Maldives Human Development Report, Challenges and Responses.* Maldives, Ministry of Planning and National Development and United Nations Development Programme, 2000.

Manik, Abdul Hakeem Hussein. *Yesterday.* Maldives, Novelty Press, 1997.

Maniku, Hassan A., and G.D. Wijayawardhana. *Isdhoo Loamaafaanu.* Colombo, Royal Asiatic Society of Sri Lanka, 1986.

Pyrard, Francois, (1570–1621), translated by Albert Grey assisted by H.C.P. Bell. *The Voyage of Francois Pyrard de Laval to the East Indies, the Maldives, the Moluccas, and Brazil.* New York, Burt Franklin, 1888, 1937.

United Nations Development Programme. *Human Development Report, 2001.*

United Nations Development Programme. *Asian Development Outlook, 2002.*

World Bank Group. *Country Profile Table, 2002.*

Young, Lieutenant J. A., and W. Christopher. "Memoir of the inhabitants of the Maldiva Islands." *Transactions of the Bombay Geographical Society from 1836 to 1838,* 54–86.

MALI

Background Material

The present République de Mali in West Africa was a French colony from the 1890s until 1960, when the Sudanese Republic and Senegal formed an independent federation. That union lasted only a few months; thereafter, what had been the Sudanese Republic became Mali. Modibo Keita created a socialist government that, near its end, saw the establishment of a 3,000-person youth-dominated Popular Militia, akin to the Red Guard in China. The regime was ousted by a military coup in November 1968 that put in place a dictatorship under Moussa Traoré that lasted until 1991. Mali's first democratic election took place the following year. Alpha Oumar Konaré was chosen as president for a five-year period, and he was re-elected in 1997. He stepped down when he reached the two-term constitutional limit in 2002. His elected replacement was retired General Amadou Toumani Touré, who had led the 1991 "democratic coup."

The country covers 478,775 square miles, making it slightly less than twice the size of Texas, and it shares borders with seven other countries. Mali is landlocked, with its population concentrated in sites along the Niger River, which flows inside Mali for 1,010 miles, one third of the river's total length. Eighty percent of the people are engaged in farming, herding, and fishing. The country is among the poorest in the world, with 65% of its land area desert and semi-desert, and almost two thirds of its population living below the poverty line. It suffers from the highest illiteracy rate and the highest rate of infant mortality on the African continent.

Mali's population was estimated in July 2004 as 11,956,788 people, with 47% under 14 years of age, and only 3% 65 or over. Life expectancy at birth is 45.3 years, and at least 100,000 people are infected with AIDS. More than 90% of the population is Muslim, and Mali stands as the Islamic world's strongest democracy. About half of the country's people are members of the Mande ethnic group. The remainder are divided among some 20 groups, each with its own language. French is the official language, though the overwhelming majority of persons do not speak it. It is not uncommon to conduct criminal trials in French using an interpreter, even though the judge, the attorneys, and the defendant are all conversant in Bamanankan, the language of the Bambara ethnic group, and the *lingua franca* of the country.

Contextual Features

Mali enjoys a constitutional parliamentary democracy. French legal codes prevail, but customary law often will be invoked by the courts when it appears to be more appropriate. The death penalty can be imposed, but no one has been executed in more than a decade. Criminal statistics, based on irregular reports to Interpol and the United Nations, are far from reliable, in part because crimes often are dealt with outside the official justice system. People may rely on local leaders to settle grievances, including criminal matters. Illustrative is a case in which a woman killed her husband on the day of the "naming ceremony" for his second wife's child. It was decided to banish the offender from the village; no one proposed turning her over to the police. There also is a fatalistic element in the culture that bears upon the reporting of crime: "People have learned to live with disaster and with the feeling that there are many situations they cannot control," Saskia Brand writes. "The ultimate solution for many is therefore to accept things as they come."

A 1998 census of Mali's 48 prisons showed an inmate total of 3,135 persons as well as 755 persons incarcerated on remand without having been tried. An inspection team found a civil servant who had been imprisoned for nine years in Kayes without being brought to trial and a man who had been detained for five years in the prison at Koulikoro. Prison wardens appear to have a very high turnover rate; those interviewed by a Ghana reporter typically had been at the job only a short time. Prison wardens now are civil servants, having replaced the former military supervisors. Prisoners are almost exclusively male. The few women incarcerated (only 2% of the total, compared to more than 6% in the United States) typically are held for infanticide and abortion. Abortions, though illegal, can be secured at the hospitals in Bamako for a particularly high price and an uncertain result. Traditional abortifacients are more commonly employed.

MALI

In 1999, detained minors were moved to the Bollé Observation and Rehabilitation Center in Bamako, which also houses women, separating them for the first time from adults. The majority of women incarcerated in Bollé are domestic servants from rural areas who had come to the city to obtain enough money to finance their weddings. Many were sexually assaulted by males in the household where they worked and resorted to abortions or infanticide to terminate pregnancies. Foreigners in Mali prisons most usually have been convicted of counterfeiting or drug smuggling.

Inmates in Mali prisons, which are under the direction of the Nationale l'Administration Penitentiare et de l'Education Surveillée, commonly complain about the quality and the quantity of the food. Medical treatment is generally regarded as deplorable and protection against mosquitoes unsatisfactory. The lack of soap is noted; inmates are likely to get a bar of soap once a month.

Police Profile

Reliable and accurate information on the police in Mali is extremely difficult to access. The limited available information is presented below.

Background

During the colonial period, French commandants, who reported directly to the governor in the capital, had broad authority and could order the arrest of Africans without trial, even for petty offenses. This action was usually taken in regard to nonpayment of taxes, refusal to work on labor gangs, and disrespect to colonial officials.

For administrative purposes, Mali was subdivided into eight official regions and what in time became more than 50 *cercles*, which in turn were made up of almost 300 *arrondissements*. The police were headquartered in the larger villages or towns in the *cercles* and answered to delegates of the central government and, until 1968, local party leaders.

Demographics

There are 33 police chiefs (*commissaires*) and approximately 3,000 police officers in the country, spread thinly throughout the urban areas.

Organizational Description

Policing in Mali is divided between the gendarmerie (*brigade territoriale de gendarmarie*), who are responsible for the areas surrounding the cities; and the police, who patrol the urban areas and handle traffic. Both are paramilitary forces, though not all are armed. The police are posted in Bamako and eight other cities: Kayes, Koulikoro, Segou, Sikasso, Mopti, Gao, Timbuktu, and Kida. Policing elsewhere is a community affair in accord with the government's current decentralization emphasis. Except for the jurisdictional distinction, there is little difference between the gendarmerie and the police, though the gendarmerie are unpopular with some segments of the Mali public because they remind people of the period of French domination of the country. None of the policing forces, nor Mali life itself, is beset by deep ethnic conflict; the minority groups (except for the Tuareg) generally place their Mali identity ahead of their ethnic partisanship.

The police operate under the supervision of the Minister of Internal Security and Civil Protection.

Functions

In Kayes, besides their regular duties, the police are responsible for oversight of the country's major train, which operates between Bamako and Dakar in Senegal. Common railroad offenses involve pickpocketing at train stations and failure to pay the fare. There also is a thriving black market in the sale of train tickets.

The gendarmerie also serve as "judicial police," charged with collecting evidence on behalf of prosecutors and magistrates before a case is forwarded to the courts. The technical backup for both the police and the gendarmerie is inadequate.

According to the police, they deal primarily with the crimes of theft, assault, and varieties of fraud (abuses of confidence). In Bamako, for instance, a man was arrested for a three-month spree of impersonating a tax collector and garnering "taxes" from people gullible enough to pay him. Cases of fraud and other financial disputes may be resolved following an arrest if the accused party offers payment at the police precinct station; the police will keep a portion of the settlement money.

Organized gangs are not uncommon. Between January and May of 2004, six armed robbers caused 11 deaths, mostly in the town of Sikasso. The Home Security Minister was taken aback by the gall of the gangsters: "We cannot understand how criminals get away with attacks carried out only yards from a police station or security post," he lamented. The outbreak prompted the authorities to establish special crime brigades to target such activity.

In 2000, the level of banditry in northern Mali led the U.S. Department of State to issue a tourist warning, noting that there had been incidents of carjacking involving American citizens, and that three Dutch tourists had been murdered while traveling by car in the Kidal region of Mali.

Training

Training for law enforcement takes place at the national *Ecole de Police*, with advanced instruction in Algiers and France. In one precinct in Bamako, Mali's capital, 62 officers monitor a population of 167,000 persons. Pay is low; in 2000, the police union called a strike, demanding higher wages. The officers went off the job again right before Mali was to host the prestigious CAN2002 (or African Cup of Nations) pan-African soccer tournament. In mid-2003, the government added 700 police officers to the force and 500 gendarmes, and also supplied 300 additional camels for transport.

Complaints and Discipline

The pervasiveness of police corruption in Mali at the time is reflected in the 1999 survey by *Afrobarometer*, conducted under the auspices of Michigan State University. Only 43% of the respondents in Mali indicated that they believed the police were not corrupt. The courts also fared badly, with only 50% of the people indicating trust in their operation. Yet, 92% of those surveyed said they did not feel threatened by street crime, and 75% responded that they felt safe against house burglary. Notably striking were the 91% (15% higher than the average in other African countries surveyed) who believed that they enjoyed freedom of speech, and the 92% (16% higher) who felt the same way about freedom of association.

In Mopti, a city of about 115,000 persons, the police average five complaints a day, most having to do with stealing, some with assault. Crime tends to decrease during the harvest season but escalates thereafter when unemployed workers drift into urban areas. The police are allowed by law to detain persons for 48 hours. With the prosecutor's permission, that time can be extended an additional 24 hours, but there is compelling evidence that the rule is occasionally ignored.

The facility operated by the gendarmerie in Mopti to detain arrested persons has only one cell. Families of detainees are responsible for bringing them food. If no relation is available, the police are expected to feed the prisoner.

Terrorism and International Cooperation

The U.S. Army 10th Special Forces unit has been assigned the task of training Malians to deal with arms smuggling, drug traffickers, and terrorists. Sixteen anti-government Arab militants and pro-government members of the Kounta ethnic group had escaped from prison in the north Mali desert town of Gao in the fall of 2004. The United States sees the Arabs as potential al-Qaeda recruits, and the Mali government has pledged to increase police monitoring in the region.

In October 2004, the United States inaugurated the Pan-Sahel Initiative, which sought to tighten up the porous border crossings in countries in the Sahara desert region. The program involves 60 days of training and the supply of Toyota Land Cruisers, uniforms, and other equipment to Malian border patrols.

Human rights groups tend to focus reform efforts directed at Mali on the trafficking, mostly to the Ivory Coast, of thousands of young girls who are sold into forced labor on coffee, cotton, rice, and cocoa farms and as domestic servants. Other matters for which remedies are sought include the genital mutilation of females, a near-universal practice, and polygamy.

In addition, there is a thriving smuggling business involving valuable artifacts stolen from archeological sites. The United States forbids the import of such materials from Mali, and in 1998 French president Jacques Chirac returned to Mali a stolen clay ram statuette that he said he had been given as a gift.

GILBERT GEIS

Bibliography

Bingen, R. James, David Robinson, and John M. Stolz. *Democracy and Development in Mali*. East Lansing, MI: Michigan State University Press, 2000.

Brand, Saskia. *Mediating Means and Fate: A Socio-Political Analysis of Fertility and Demographic Change in Bamako, Mali*. Leiden, The Netherlands: Brill, 2001.

Bratton, Michael, Robert Mattes, and Emmanuel Gyimah-Boadi. *Public Opinion, Democracy, and Market Reform in Africa*. Capetown, South Africa: Cambridge University Press, 2005.

Dankwa, Emmanuel Victor Oware. *Mali Prisons Revisited: Report on a Visit 27 November - 8 December 1998*. Bajul, Gambia: African Commission on Human and People's Rights, 1998.

Imperato, Pascal James. *Historical Dictionary of Mali*. 3d ed. Lanham, MD: Scarecrow Press, 1996.

———. *Mali: A Search for Direction*. Boulder, CO: Westview, 1989.

Lipman, Hal, and Barbara Lewis. *Democratic Decentralization in Mali: A Work in Progress*. Impact Evaluation No.

2. Arlington, VA: U.S. Agency for International Development, 1998.

Nagel, Mechthild. "Gender, Incarceration and Peacemaking in Mali." Cortland, NY: Department of Philosophy, State University of New York, 2004.

Sacko, Kaba. *La Criminalité Organisée dans le District de Bamako*. Bamko, Mali: Le Centre Djobila, 1989.

Stamm, Andrea L., Dawn Bastian, and Robert A. Meyers. *Mali*. [World Bibliograhical Series Volume 27]. Santa Barbara, CA: CLIO Press, 1998.

MALTA

Background Material

The Maltese archipelago has passed from one foreign rule to another, including the Phoenicians, Romans, Arabs, Knights of St. John, and the British. The Malta police force was founded in 1814 under British colonial government, making it one of the oldest police forces in Europe. However, this does not mean that some form of police did not exist before then. Attard (1994) explains how even under Arab rule (870 AD) public order was maintained by a police force called "*Sahib el-Xurta*." Under the Aragonese (1283 AD) public order was safeguarded by a police force consisting of "Guards to the Captain of Justice," "*Della Verga*," and "*Tal-Balliju*" (mainly responsible for prisons, customs, and for controlling gambling). Later on, the "*Dejma*" corps was established. Although military in nature (it was intended to defend the islands from foreign invasion), the "*Dejma*" corps conducted work frequently associated with policing. During the reign of the Knights of St. John, police work fell under the command of the "*Gran Visconte*." During this period, the Knights and the Inquisitor co-existed and had their own law courts. The Inquisitor's guards were called "*Cursores*." They arraigned people before the Inquisitor. However, it was not until the year 1814 that the Maltese police started its evolution toward its current structure. Malta remained officially a British colony until September 21, 1964, when it was finally granted independence. The last British troops left Malta on March 31, 1979.

Frendo (1991) argues that making independence work in Malta was "never easy," due to a combination of factors, including its small size, limited material resources, and lack of experience in self-government. Before 1971, Malta had a conservative government headed by Dr. George Borg Olivier. Frendo (1991) maintains that, while Dom Mintoff's Malta Labour Party was animated by his charisma, Borg Olivier's Nationalist Party was kept alive by "traditional allegiances and networks, the electorate's presumed common sense, and distrust or fear of Mintoff." The Nationalists represented traditional values. Their relationship with the working class was almost nonexistent, even to the extent that they did not use the same language (Frendo 1991). In turn, the working class regarded the Nationalists as elitists and as Catholic bigots.

Malta has a population of 396,851 (2004 est.).

Contextual Features

In 1971, the Labour Party won the general elections, and Mintoff became Prime Minister. Malta's government leaned heavily to the left, influenced by Soviet socialism (Azzopardi Cauchi, 2004; Borg, 2001). Between 1971 and 1987 (under Labour governments), Maltese society became increasingly polarized. Extremists from both parties clashed, transforming Maltese roads into battlefields (Darmanin, 1996). The late 1970s and the 1980s were characterized by disorder, violence, frame-ups, and torture (Borg, 2001; Darmanin, 1996). Maltese society began to tear itself apart. There were oppressors and victims, with some naïve bystanders. The litany of conflict was both ugly and damaging (Azzopardi Cauchi, 2004).

Azzopardi Cauchi's research (2004) suggests that most Maltese police officers consider victims of crime as bystanders in the criminal justice system. They are aware that, in Malta, victims of crime are not satisfied with the feedback they receive from the police. However, on the positive side, the data recovered by Azzopardi Cauchi

(2004) suggest that the vast majority of Maltese police officers acknowledge that crime victims deserve better treatment and, consequently, they should always be kept informed about their cases. Respondents seemed to blame their poor relationship with victims on their lack of training in dealing with them. Clearly, dealing with victims of crime needs to be thoroughly covered in future police training programs.

Police officers are not the only ones to blame for the bystander status of crime victims in Malta. Unfortunately, a crime-victimization survey has only been conducted once in Malta (in 1997). There is a void when it comes to determining the real picture of crime in Malta, forcing scholars to mainly depend on statistics provided by police records. For example (see tables below), police statistics show that in 2004 the following crimes were the most common (in order of decreasing frequency): theft, damage to property, attempted offenses, and bodily harm. Generally (in order of decreasing frequency) the following forms of theft were committed: from vehicles, from bars/hotels, and theft of vehicles. The same trend was also recorded during the previous four years (2000–2004).

Police trainers also give considerable attention to the law, since it is the system of law that makes and regulates the police force. The steady flow of colonizers who laid anchor in Malta left an impact, not only on Maltese culture, traditions, folklore, and language, but also on its system of law.

A cursory view of the Maltese criminal system may give the impression that it is very similar to the British one. However, a closer look would put in evidence the fact that the influence of the Inquisitorial system is almost as strong in Malta as it is in its closest neighbour, Italy. The existence of the inquiring magistrate echoes the Inquisitorial system, which also strongly reverberates in the Italian system of law. Another very important component of the Maltese system is the Attorney General's Office, composed of "the chief law enforcement officers ... lawyers for the government ... defend[ing] the interests of the state and the community" Karmen (1990).

The most common crimes	Reported in 2004
Theft	11,333
Damage to property	3,593
Attempted offences	1,252
Bodily harm	1,055

The most common forms of theft	Reported in 2004
Theft of vehicle	796
Theft from vehicle	3,401
Theft from bars/hotels, etc.	803

Source: Unpublished police statistics from the Malta police statistics office

Police Profile

Background

The Maltese constable's image as protector of the weak faded and was replaced by that of a gangster—or agent—at the service of the state. The respect once enjoyed by the Malta police has transformed into fear and distrust. Although it is difficult to find a politically neutral account of policing, it is undeniable that a Police Commissioner was once sentenced for having contributed to the violent death of a suspect, while the latter was in custody, when it was his precise duty to prevent such an abuse from happening (In-Nazzjon Taghna 1993). At the time, police culture in Malta was seen to be heavily predicated on malign neglect (at best) or active political hooliganism (at worst).

One could say that Mintoff's government had imported Soviet-style policing (Borg, 2001), rendering the Malta police force "a militarized body suppressing political opposition" (Shelley in Mawby, 1999). Falzon (in Borg, 2001) claims that during the 1980s, the Maltese lived in fear, and were deprived of liberty and democracy. Borg (2001) explains how this period was characterised by violence, political murders, and abuse of power by a group of police officers, giving a detailed account of the cases of police malpractice. This decade left an indelible scar on policing in Malta. Shelley (in Mawby, 1999) claims that "All the former socialist states are left with a common legacy: demoralized and corrupted police forces with little or no respect for citizens' rights."

In 1987, the leaders of the Nationalist party, now in government, thought the time was ripe for reconciliation, not retaliation. Malta started its healing process. Safeguarding human rights became a priority, and there was a powerful drive to instill a new-found respect in the Malta police force. The police academy was set up, and the Institute of Forensic studies was established within the University of Malta. Corrupt, abusive elements were weeded out; recruit-selection processes started being done professionally, and newly admitted recruits were vigorously trained. A 1998 survey, commissioned by the Malta police

Superior Courts		
For crimes punishable by a maximum of 10 years, imprisonment and over.	Courts of Criminal Appeal Criminal Court (Trial by Jury)	Final court in all criminal matters. Tries serious offenses as a court of first instance.

Inferior Courts		
For crimes punishable by a maximum of 6 months' imprisonment.	Courts of Magistrate Dual jurisdiction	(a) Inquiring Magistrate. At the pre-trial stage as a court of criminal inquiry. (b) Trial of summary offenses and as a court of criminal judicature.

Small Claims Tribunal
For victims of crime who have a claim of less than 100 Maltese liri (240 euros), the adjudicator may be a lawyer with at least one year of experience.

Tried by either the Superior or the Inferior Courts—Crimes punishable by a sentence of 6 years to 10 years' imprisonment.

force, concluded that: "Following a period in the eighties where the public image was somewhat negative, there has been a conscious effort on the part of the Police to improve their image and to gain the trust of the public." In her research, Azzopardi Cauchi (2004) uncovered aspects of police culture in Malta that bodes well for the future. These include apolitical policing, officers' liberalism, focus on victims, and an increasing acceptance of women. Such attitudes could very well exorcise the modern Maltese police force from the spectre of the 1980s.

Demographics and Organizational Description

The Malta police force comprises about 1,600 officers who occupy the lower ranks (constables, sergeants, sergeant majors) and more than 100 officers who occupy the higher ranks (inspectors, superintendents, assistant commissioners, the deputy commissioner, and the commissioner of police). Police officers are deployed either in districts (managing police stations or in the general headquarters), doing administrative duties, or working within the different specialized squads. The police headquarters houses the following units: vice squad (which deals with sex crimes, prostitution, domestic violence, victims, usury), drug squad (which deals with narcotics), criminal investigations department (which investigates serious crimes), forensics (which conducts scene-of-crime investigations), the traffic section, administrative law enforcement (which deals with environmental crime), public complaints (monitored by a board composed of outside, male and female

experts), human resources/internal affairs, Interpol (which manages links with foreign police forces), and the European Union office (which manages links with European Union institutions). The special assignment group, the mounted police, and the canine section are housed in more adequate structures.

Training

Recruits are not automatically accepted into the police force; they must first undergo a rigorous training program within the police academy. This is headed by the Police Commandant (usually a police veteran) and monitored/counselled by a board composed of experts from policing, education, and criminology. The new Police Act (2004) also made provisions for the employment of a Director of Studies. However, so far, this post has remained vacant.

The Police Academy provides the folowing: four-month courses for recruits, regular in-service training (varies in duration), and a one-year, full-time intensive Certificate in Policing course, held at the University of Malta for officer cadets (prospective

The lower ranks (2004)

Lower Ranks	Females	Males	Number of police officers
Constables	176	1,146	1,322
Sergeants	27	296	323
Sergeant Majors	0	2	2
Total	203	1,444	1,647

The higher ranks (2004)

Higher Ranks	Females	Males	Number of police officers
Inspector	15	67	82
Superintendent	0	22	22
Assistant Commissioner	0	5	5
Deputy Commissioner	0	1	1
Commissioner of Police	0	1	1
Total	15	96	111

Police Inspectors). The Police Academy provides prospective police inspectors with the following training: unarmed combat, target practice, crowd control, traffic control, and mock trials. At university, officer cadets study academic subjects, including law. The curricula of these courses emphasise: human rights, gender equality, domestic violence, racism, law, and victims of crime.

Police Education, Research, and Publications

This brief summary of the state of policing in Malta is a cursory view of the events that have shaped the Malta police force, a police force that has suffered the harsh realities of pestilence, poverty, war, and political strife. Studies and publications such as those written by Attard (1994), Darmanin (1996), Azzopardi Cauchi (2004), Borg (2001), and Zammit (2004) could generate the knowledge needed to harness the energy of Maltese police officers and to provide the foundations for adequate training, leading to an improved police force in Malta.

JACQUELINE AZZOPARDI CAUCHI

Bibliography

Attard, E. Il-Korp tal-Pulizija ta' Malta. Malta: Palprint Press, 1994.

Azzopardi Cauchi, J. Police Culture in Malta. Unpublished PhD thesis, University of Leicester, Leicester, UK, 2004.

Borg, D. Liberta' mhedda: Ksur ta' drittijiet fundamentali tal-bniedem fi stat polizjesk 1980-1987. Malta: Pin Publications, 2001.

Chan, J. B. L. Changing police culture: Policing in a multicultural society. Cambridge: Cambridge University Press, 1997.

Darmanin, P. Imatra li diga' nsejt: Eku tal-mar il-lejl socjalista. Malta: Pin Publications, 1996.

Frendo, H. Party politics in a fortress colony: The Maltese experience. Malta: Midsea Books Limited, 1991.

Il-qorti tikkundanna lil Lawrence Pullicino 15 il-sena abs. Pullicino jappella mis-sentenza tal-qorti. (1993, March 10th). In-Nazzjon Taghna, p. 3.

Karmen, A. Crime victims: An introduction to victimology (2nd ed.). USA: Wadsworth Publishing Company, 1990.

Mawby, R.I. Policing Across the World: Issues for the Twenty-first Century. London: UCL Press, 1999.

Zammit, R. Meta Jibki L-Korp. Malta: Palprint Press, 2004.

MARSHALL ISLANDS

Background Material

Dates as to when the Marshall Islands were first settled are unclear, but archaeological findings suggest that it may be as long ago as 2000 BC. A British Naval Captain, William John Marshall, named the islands in 1788, when he sailed through them while transporting convicts to New South Wales in Australia. The first significant commercial development was initiated in 1869 by Germans who were interested in trade. This led to Germany acquiring the Marshall Islands for $4.5 million in 1885. In 1914, Japan captured the islands and maintained control over them until 1944, when they were occupied by the United States of America (USA). In 1946, the United States began a nuclear testing program in the area. It evacuated the Bikini Atoll site for its first test and later expanded its program to include the Enewetak Atoll.

In 1947, the Marshall Islands became part of the United Nations Establishing Trust Territory of the Pacific Islands, and the United States became the trustee. In 1979, the government of the Marshall Island was established. The country became self-governing in 1986 and joined the United Nations in 1991. The Republic of the Marshall

Islands (RMI) remains closely dependent on the United States for defense and economic assistance.

The Marshall Islands have a parliamentary system of government. Legislative authority is vested in the thirty-three member Parliament (*Nitijela*), which is elected every four years. The President selects the eight-member Cabinet. The council of *Iroij,* a twelve-member council of Chiefs, advises the President on issues to do with land and custom.

The challenges facing the Marshall Islands are similar to those experienced by other small Pacific Island states. They include a small population, isolation, lack of natural resources, and global climate change. The "Compact of Free Association," a critical treaty governing US-RMI relations, expired in 2003. The outcome of negotiations between the United States of America and the Marshall Islands could have a significant impact on the country.

Preventing international organized crime gangs from using small Pacific Island states such as the Marshall Islands for drug trafficking and people smuggling poses particular challenges. The Marshall Islands is one of 35 jurisdictions named by the OECD as harmful tax havens and has been put on notice to agree to tax reforms scheduled to be implemented by December 2005. The OECD also placed the Islands on a list of 15 jurisdictions that have been accused of having tax laws that in effect allow them to ignore the laundering of profits from international crime activities. In March 2002, the Islands refused to comply with OECD requirements.

Currently, firearm-related crime is a problem, and legislation is in force to prohibit the importation of any firearms into the Marshall Islands.

As of July 2001, the population was 70,822. The Islands have the youngest population in the world, with almost 50% below the age of 15.

English is the universal language, with Marshallese dialects and Japanese also spoken. The primary religion is Christianity, mainly the Protestant denomination. The GDP per capita is US$1670 (1998 est.).

The Marshall Islands have a very small economy that is largely aid dependent. The major industries include copra, fish, tourism, and craft items from shell, wood, and pearls. The Islands are also developing as a financial centre.

Contextual Features

The Marshallese Constitution is the supreme law of the land, and both common law and customary law are recognized by the Constitution. The Marshel-

lese Parliament (the *Nitijela*) enacts laws from time to time.

Prior to 2002, there do not appear to be any official crime statistics from the local or national police forces. In 2002, the most common crimes recorded by the national and local government police on Majuro, the capital, were: 989 for drunken disorderly conduct, 694 for drunk disturbing the peace, 192 for malicious mischief, 76 for grand larceny, and 73 for burglary. Homicide is rare, occurring approximately once in five years.

In 2001, the Marshall Islands were listed by the Financial Action Task Force on Money Laundering as among the "least cooperative jurisdictions" (FATF, 2001).

The Supreme Court of the Marshall Islands is the highest court in the land. It hears appeals from the High Court and has the discretionary power to hear appeals in relation to final decisions of other courts.

The High Court is a Trial Court that has original jurisdiction. It also acts as an Appellate Court for cases from Subordinate Courts. The High Court may pass on to the Supreme Court any matter involving the interpretation or effect of the Constitution.

The District Court has original jurisdiction concurrently with the High Court in civil matters where the property in question does not exceed $5,000. It also hears criminal cases, including matters where the maximum penalty does not exceed a fine of $2,000, or imprisonment for a term of three years, or both. The District Court exercises appellate jurisdiction over decisions of Community Courts.

The Community Courts hear cases where the value of the property or amount claimed does not exceed $100. It deals with less serious criminal cases where the maximum penalty does not exceed a fine of $200 or imprisonment for six months, or both.

Questions relating to customary titles, land rights, and other legal interests which depend wholly or in part on customary law or traditional practice, are heard by the Traditional Rights Court. Its jurisdiction is supplementary to proceedings in the other courts and may be invoked "as of right" by a party to a pending proceeding, but only if the court hearing the case certifies that a "substantial question has arisen within the jurisdiction of the Traditional Rights Court." A High Court judge can appoint one or more Traditional Rights Court assessors to advise the High Court on customary law or traditional practice, but the assessors are excluded from participating in the determination of the case.

The Marshall Islands prison can only house 24 prisoners. Conditions have been described by the U.S. State Department as "spartan," but they meet international minimum standards, and independent inspections are permitted.

Police Profile

Background

The Department of Public Safety, which is responsible for the policing function in the Marshall Islands, was established in 1952. It is a quasi-military organization and at present falls under the Ministry of Justice.

Demographics

The number of persons in the National Police Force at the end of 2002 was 133, compared to 294 police personnel under the control of local governments (excluding the Sea Patrol). The breakdown was: National Majuro, 106; National Ebeye, 21; National Jabwor, 6; Local Majuro, 96; Local Ebeye, 43; Other Atolls, 133.

Organizational Description

The Department of Public Safety is one component of the Ministry of Justice. It is headed by the Minister of Justice and is the only law enforcement branch of the National Government (Republic of the Marshall Islands). The most senior rank in the police force is the Police Commissioner, followed by Police Majors, Captains, Lieutenants, Sergeants, and Police Officers I, II, III. The head of the Criminal Investigation Division (CID) holds the rank of Captain, and he is assisted by a Lieutenant, Sergeant, and Detectives.

The CID only investigates criminal complaints. The Department of Public Safety has its own special response unit of specifically trained police officers. All civil matters are referred to government agencies involved in civil matters. Local governments have their own police agencies that enforce their own local legislation.

Functions

The main functions of the Department of Public Safety of the Republic of the Marshall Islands are to protect lives and property, and to preserve the peace as outlined in the *Public Safety Act*.

Training

The majority of Marshall Islands police officers have graduated from overseas police academies, for example, the Alaska State Troopers Academy; the Micronesian Public Safety Academy, and the FBI National Academy. Each academy runs a three-month basic and advanced police course. Upon completion, police officers are given a certificate and 15 college credit hours. Instructors are selected from U.S. Law Schools and Expert on Law Enforcement Studies. Police also receive firearm training.

The Marshall Islands also conduct in-service police training, where instructors from the United States, Australia, and New Zealand conduct a variety of courses.

All police officers take a three-month course in human rights, and the existing program on human rights awareness is run by the Ministry of Health and Environment. Police officers are trained to understand that everyone should be treated equally, and that they should not discriminate when they are performing their daily duties. Police officers have never been criticized for human rights violations.

Police Public Projects

Police officers visit schools and address public meetings in relation to police issues. As part of the youth crime prevention program, police help to coordinate youth sporting activities, such as baseball and basketball. There is also a 30-minute radio program on crime prevention.

Police Use of Firearms

Marshall Islands police officers are authorized to use firearms in operational matters.

Complaints and Discipline

An Internal Investigation Unit investigates all complaints against police officers.

Terrorism

The Department of Public Safety has responsibility for investigating and preventing terrorism, but there have been no terrorist incidents or known terrorist activities in the Marshall Islands.

International Cooperation

The Honiara Declaration is the basis for law enforcement cooperation in the Pacific.

The Marshall Islands have mutual law enforcement agreements with countries such as the United States and also belong to Interpol, the Pacific Islands Forum's Regional Law Enforcement Capacity Development and Cooperation Program, and the South Pacific Islands Central Intelligence Network.

At a meeting of seven police services in the Pacific region in 1970, the South Pacific Chiefs of Police Conference was founded. The forum is designed to foster cooperation and the sharing of information to help combat crime and provide formal liaison among police in the South Pacific. In 2003, delegates to the annual conference finalized a four-year strategic plan, which establishes key law enforcement priorities for the region.

Police Education, Research, and Publication

Institutions

The University of the South Pacific and the College of the Marshall Islands have been approached to formulate a curriculum for Marshallese police officers. This project is still under consideration by the college and the university. The two institutions have the capacity to conduct research on police studies in the Marshall Islands. Educational institutions include:

Researchers College of the Marshall Islands, www.cmiedu.net/
University of Hawaii, www.hawaii.edu/
University of the South Pacific, www.usp.ac.fj/ (Institute of Justice and Applied Legal Studies (IJALS), Laucala Campus, Fiji)

Researchers

Newton, T. (1998). *An introduction to policing in the South Pacific region.*
University of the South Pacific School of Law Working Papers.

Leading Journals

Journal of South Pacific Law, *http://easol. vanuatu.usp.ac.fj/jspl/current.*

Major Police Publications

There is currently no police publication in the Marshall Islands, but if there were to be one, the government would bear the cost of the publication.

Police-Related Websites

Prison data: www.kcl.ac.uk/depsta/rel/icps/ worldbrief/oceania_records.php?code=8
Marshall Islands Crime Statistics: www.spc.int/ prism/country/mh/stats/Social/Crime/offses. htm
Republic of the Marshall Islands: www. rmiembassyus.org/

COLLEN LEWIS

Bibliography

Australian Federal Police, South Pacific Chiefs of Police Conference www.afp.gov.au/page.asp?ref=/news/events/ spcpc.xml.
Economic Policy, Planning and Statistics Office, Office of the President, Republic of Marshall Islands, www.spc. int/prism/country/mh/stats/Index.htm.
Economic Policy, Planning and Statistics Office, Office of the President, Republic of Marshall Islands, *RMI Statistical Yearbook,* 2002. www.spc.int/prism/country/mh/ stats/Index.htm.
Identifying Non-Cooperative Countries and Territories. FATF, Paris: 2001. www1.oecd.org/fatf/fatdocs_en.htm.
SBS World Guide. www.theworldnews.com.au/Worldguide/ index.php3?country=128&header=6.

MAURITANIA

Background Material

The Islamic Republic of Mauritania is situated in northwestern Africa. It is bordered by the Atlantic Ocean, Western Sahara, Algeria, Mali, and Senegal, and it covers an area of 398,000 sq mil. The capital is Nouakchott.

The climate is predominantly hot and dry, predisposing the country to occasional severe droughts.

The geography ranges from Saharan sand dunes (with an occasional oasis) to the rich alluvial soil of the Senegal River Valley.

The population of Mauritania was estimated at 2,998,563 in 2004. It is composed of a number of ethnic groups, including Maurs or Moors; Arabs; Berbers; and a black minority of Peul, Soninke, Wolof, Fulbe, Toucouleur, and Bambara tribal groups. Forty percent of the population is mixed

Maur and Black, 30% Maur, and 30% Black. The official language is Arabic, but French, Pular, Soninke, and Wolof are also spoken. Ninety-nine percent of the population is Sunni Muslim, but there is a Christian, mainly Roman Catholic, element (0.4%) and a small number who practice Judaism.

The country was dominated by Berber tribes from about 100 AD and converted to Islam during the eleventh century. It became a French protectorate in 1903, a colony in 1920, gained independence from France on November 28, 1960, and became a predominantly one-party state in 1964.

In 1976, there were border conflicts over the Western Sahara. A military coup in 1978 was followed by racial tensions between black Mauritanians and Moors. Unrest among black Mauritanians in the same time period led to civil disturbances and their removal from the Army, Gendarmerie, and National Guard as well as other high government offices. Also, large numbers of the black community were expelled from Mauritania during these crises. This was followed by three years of border friction with Senegal, starting in the late 1980s. The introduction of Islamic law was accelerated in 1986 to counteract growing internal unrest and to stress the Islamic character of Mauritanian culture. In 1996, there were serious refugee problems with Senegal and Mali, primarily because Mauritania was unwilling to take back the black population that had escaped to those countries during internal conflicts. As a result of all the warfare, there are reports of unexploded land mines still within Mauritania.

Mauritania is a developing country. Its main economic activities are agriculture, fishing, and mining. It also produces cement, industrial gas, paints, and textiles, and it exports iron ore and processed fish. In 2000, per capita income averaged $1,630 international dollars a year. The country relies heavily on international financial aid. Compulsory primary school education for both sexes was introduced in 2001. During the 1990s, over 80% of all children received primary school education, but only 19% of males and 10% of females received secondary school education. In 2001, primary education became compulsory for all children.

Contextual Features

Challenges facing Mauritania include political instability, border issues, racial division, human rights abuses, slavery, and poor economic development.

Mauritania is a republic with a strong executive president. The country was formerly governed by a military *junta* but now has elections. Politics are subject to tribal and ethnic pressures centering on language and land tenure. It is reported that political repression increased in 2002, and opposition party members have been subject to torture and arbitrary arrest.

The government is composed of traditional ministries, special agencies, and government-controlled companies. It is modeled on the French system of local administration. Under this system, Mauritania is divided into 13 regions (*wilayas*) and one district (Nouakchott). Control is tightly centralized. Political parties reflect social division along ancestral lines.

The executive branch consists of the President, who must be Muslim. The legislative branch consists of a directly elected lower house of 81 members, and an upper house of 56 members, chosen indirectly by municipal councilors. Among the ministries responsible for government administration are the Prime Minister, Minister of the Interior, Post and Telecommunications, Minister of Justice, and Secretary of State for Women's Affairs.

In 1991, a new constitution accorded extensive powers to the President of the Republic, and Arabic was designated as the sole official language. The legal system is a combination of Islamic or Shari'a law and French civil law. Shari'a has been the official legal code since 1980. Among the provisions of the Mauritanian constitution is the explicit duty to know the law. Persons violating Mauritanian law, even unknowingly, may be expelled, arrested, or imprisoned.

Also in 1980, slavery was formally abolished in Mauritania, but it still persists. Anyone escaping slavery has no legal protection. Anti-slavery activists and other human rights defenders work under constant threat of arrest and imprisonment.

Crime has been rising in Mauritania since 2001. Most incidents involve petty crime, such as pickpocketing, and crimes of opportunity. Residential burglaries, robberies, and assaults also occur. Penalties for possession, use, or trafficking in illegal drugs in Mauritania are strict, and convicted offenders can expect jail sentences and heavy fines. Consumption of alcohol is prohibited. This means expulsion for foreign nationals and 40 lashes in public for Mauritanian violators. All forms of prostitution are forbidden. Sexual acts with an infant, incest, sodomy, and indecency are crimes under the Penal Code. Homosexuality is punishable by death. Mauritanian legislation does not prevent child pornography, although it is forbidden under Islam.

The highest tribunal is the Supreme Court. Courts of first instance are situated in major towns. The Appeal Court and Supreme Court are

Crime (Source Interpol)	1999	1997	1996
Murder	19	33	27
Sex Offenses (including rape)	72	72	52
Rape	22	46	36
Serious assault	674	808	989
Theft	1,057	1,414	857
Aggravated theft	48	783	542
Robbery and violent theft		411	347
Breaking and entering	182	372	195
Theft of motor cars	62	426	177
Other thefts		205	138
Fraud	185	117	33
Counterfeit currency offenses	4	2	1
Drug offenses	60	57	81
Total number of offenses	2,385	4,746	3,475

in the capital. These courts are subject to control of the executive branch; judicial decisions are rendered mainly on the basis of Shari'a law for social and family matters and on a western-style legal code for commercial and some criminal cases.

The correctional system comes under the Ministry of Justice. The department for prison administration and penal affairs is responsible for the supervision of the health and safety of prisons, their budget, the preliminary examination of requests for conditional release, the petitions for mercy and questions related to amnesty, the holding of central judicial cases, and the re-education and social reintegration of minor delinquents. In 2002, the prison population numbered 1,354, or 48 per 100,000. population. There are 16–18 lock-ups and two intermediary centers. The official capacity of prisons is approximately 900, which mean they are roughly 50% over capacity.

Police Profile

Background

The Mauritanian police services were developed under the French colonial system, so their structure is similar to the French model of policing. The government maintains order with regular armed forces, the Gendarmerie, the National Guard, and the National Police. They are deployed in the Nouakchott District and 12 regions. The regions are subdivided into 44 departments.

The Gendarmerie falls under the Ministry of Defense. Its mission is internal security, and it enforces both civilian and military law. It is organized on a national basis with a military command and is equipped with military weapons. It is deployed in both rural and urban areas of the nation and is responsible for maintaining civil order throughout. Originally, the Gendarmerie was part of the Army, but it became a separate entity in 1987 while remaining responsible to the armed forces chief of staff. At that time, the Gendarmerie was divided into six regional companies and numbered 2,500 men. In 2002, the ranks of the Gendarmerie included lieutenant colonel, commandant, chief adjutant, and gendarme fourth, second, and first class. The ranks of new recruits include chief adjutant, sergeant, and corporal first and second class.

The National Guard is responsible for working with other police forces and security agencies, and maintaining and restoring public order in administrative districts under the direction of the minister. The Presidential Guard is a subdivision of the National Guard and is responsible for protecting the President and his home.

Demographics

In 2001, the strength of the Gendarmerie was 3,000 and the National Guard 2,000. There was no gender representation reported in either force in 1978. The 2001 Country Reports on Human Rights Practices for Mauritania indicated the percentage of minorities in government or politics, as a whole, did not correspond to their percentage of the population.

Organizational Description and Functions

The National Police and the National Guard are under the authority of the Ministry of the Interior, Post and Telecommunications. The Ministry is responsible for general policing, maintaining and re-establishing public order, public security, and civil protection in the territories. Prefects and town mayors have some authority and discretion in using the police under their jurisdiction, but the Ministry exercises ultimate control through the governors of the 13 regions.

The organization of the National Police is fixed by statutory order. It is tasked with maintaining public order, preparing routine reports on legal infractions, providing security intelligence, frontier surveillance, control of arms and munitions, and enforcing rules concerning meetings and public gatherings. In the name of keeping order, police can ban demonstrations and meetings or force them to disperse if order is threatened. The police can also suspend individual liberties if the president declares a state of emergency.

The National Police is organized hierarchically in three main ranks of agent, inspector, and commissioner. The promotion structure can be politically influenced. In 1986, as part of a large-scale repression of black Mauritanians and the Toucouleur community in particular, the administration purged itself of all its Toucouleur governors, prefects, and deputy prefects serving in the south. Among those who lost their positions was the Minister of Interior, Information and Telecommunications.

In addition to the organizational separation of the police, there is a functional separation between the administrative and judicial police. The main distinction between the two is the preventive role of the administrative police and the repressive role of the judicial police. The administrative police function also cuts across other ministries that have regulatory functions such as Fisheries, Agriculture, and Finance.

There are judicial police in both the Gendarmerie and the National Police. In the judicial role they are empowered and directed by the Code of Criminal Procedure. Under the Code of Criminal Procedure, officers of the judicial police are responsible for investigating infractions of the penal code, gathering evidence, and searching for the perpetrators. They come under the authority of the Minister of Justice and directly under the authority of the Public Prosecutor. They are auxiliaries to *juges d'instruction*, or examining magistrates, who delegate to them by rogatory commission the power to examine or to investigate suspects. They also receive complaints and charges and with the instruction of the attorney general can hold preliminary inquiries.

Training

The Military Inter-Service School trains both the Gendarmerie and National Guard. There is a police training school in Nouakchott for the National Police, which also appears to function as a detention centre. The officer cadre also may be trained in France. External groups, such as the International Committee of the Red Cross (ICRC), have organized training seminars for the police. One such seminar in 1999 on humanitarian law and human rights was attended by instructional officers from the National Guard, the Police, the Army, and the Gendarmerie.

Complaints and Discipline

Within the National Police there are various methods of handling misconduct. In 1993, the government passed legislation that granted an unconditional amnesty for all military and security personnel convicted for the deaths of black Mauritanians between April 1991 and April 1992. In 1996 an investigation into drug trafficking in Mauritania resulted in the imprisonment of seven high-ranking police officers and four magistrates. The most visible police complaints procedure is legal action against the government and its representatives by concerned foreign agencies.

International Cooperation

As a member of the Economic Community of West African States (ECOWAS), Mauritania cooperates with other members in dealing with international crimes and fugitives. It announced a three-year moratorium on the importation, export and manufacture of light weapons involving member states. Mauritania has ratified the 1999 *African Charter on Human and Peoples' Rights*. As a signatory, the government is bound to guarantee the independence of the judiciary, equality before the law, the right to recourse procedure and fair trial, and the right to an appeal to a higher court.

In 2001, the U.S. Department of State reported that Mauritania's human rights record remained generally poor, and the UN International Convention on the Elimination of all Forms of Racial Discrimination stated that some groups are still suffering from various forms of exclusion and discrimination. Some local police regularly beat and detain returnees who attempt to visit their former plots of land.

Mauritania is also a signatory of three conventions regarding the safety of aviation, and has signed the Law of the Sea and Nuclear Test Ban international agreements, but not ratified it. It has also ratified the Chemical Weapon convention (1998) and the Nations Supporting a Global Ban on Anti-Personnel Mines (2000). It has not, however, signed the Biological and Toxic Weapons Convention.

Mauritania has been a member of Interpol since 1962 in the Africa Sub-Directorate. As a member of the U.N. North African Sub-Regional Development Centre (NA-SRDC), Mauritania participates in the promotion of regional cooperation and details on trade indicators. In 1996, Mauritania, Mali, and Senegal agreed to increase joint patrols and other measures to improve security along their borders and to prevent the movement of terrorists, rebels, arms, drugs, and refugees. Mauritania is fighting terrorism and condemned the terrorist acts perpetrated on September 11, 2001. It has received international assistance in training from France and the International Committee of the Red Cross, and has participated as a military observer in the Cooperative Osprey command-post exercise training session conducted by the Lester B. Pearson Peacekeeping Centre in Canada.

MARGARET BRIGNELL

Bibliography

Africa: South of the Sahara. London: Europa Publications Limited, 1997.

Amnesty International."Mauritania: a future free from slavery," 2002. www.amnesty.org/library/(March 3, 2003).

Atlapedia Online: Countries A to Z. "Islamic Republic of Mauritania," 1993-2003. www.atlapedia.com/online/countries/mauritan.htm. (January 3, 2003).

Canada, Immigration and Refugee Board. "Mauritania," REFINFO, 2002, www.cisr.gc.ca/cgi-bin/foliocgi.exe/refinfo_e/query=mauritania/doc/{@1740} (January 7, 2003).

Central Intelligence Agency. The World Factbook 2004, "Mauritania," 2004. www.odci.gov/cia/publica tions/factbook/geos/mr.html. (November 11, 2004).

Economist Intelligence Unit. Country profile: Mauritania, 2002. www.eiu.com. (December 2, 2002).

Government of Mauritania. Le Ministre de l'Intérieur, des Postes et Télécommunications, 2002. www.mauritania.mr/fr/admin/gov/minist.asp (April 2, 2003).

Government of Mauritania. "Mauritanie-Forces Armées," Ministère de la Défence Nationale, December 25, 2002. www.mauritania.mr/fr/mainframeset.asp (March 5, 2003).

Institut international de droit d'expression et s'inspiration françaises. *La direction de la police judiciare et son contrôle par les autorités judiciaires en Mauritanie*, Juriscope – 1999. (November 11, 2004). http://juriscope.org/publications/etudes/police.htm.

Interpol. "International Crime Statistics: Mauritania," 1999, 1997, 1996. www.interpol.int/Public/Statistics/ICS/downloadList.asp. (October 15, 2002).

Library of Congress. "Country Studies: Mauritania," 1988. lcweb2.loc.gov/frd/cs/mrtoc.html. (October 15, 2002).

U.S. Department of State. "Country Reports on Human Rights Practices: 2001," March 4, 2002. www.state.gov/g/drl/rls/hrrpt/2001/af/8392.htm. (July 31, 2002).

MAURITIUS

Background Material

The Republic of Mauritius is a volcanic island, situated in the southwest region of the Indian Ocean, approximately 110 km east of Madagascar and 2400 km from the African coast. The Mauritian territory consists of the main island of Mauritius, which is situated on latitude 20 South and longitude 57 East, and the outer islands of Agalega, St. Brandon, and Rodrigues.

Human settlement in Mauritius dates back to the seventeenth century AD. The island was first discovered by the Portuguese, and was subsequently colonized by the Dutch, the French (1721–1810). and the British (1810–1968). Mauritius became an independent state in 1968, and in 1992 it became a Republic.

The population of Mauritius is multi-ethnic, multi-cultural, multi-linguistic, and multi-religious, the inevitable remnants of its colonial heritage. Permanent settlement during the French and early British period was characterized by the exploitation of a mass of black slave workers, mostly from Madagascar and Africa, by a wealthy bourgeoisie of white colonists. The abolition of slavery in 1835 brought an influx of Indian immigrants and a small group of Chinese to form the new working class proletariat.

Mauritius has four main ethnic groups: Hindus, Muslims, Chinese, and the general population (with a distinct Hindu majority), which can be further subdivided into subgroups and strata. The major religions reflecting the ethnic composition of the island include various forms of Hindi, Islam, Buddhism, and Christianity.

The national language is English; French is also widely taught and practiced, although Mauritian Creole is spoken throughout the republic. In addition, Oriental languages such as Bhojpuri, Hindi, Marathi, Tamil, Telegu, Gujrathi, Urdu, and Arabic are popular among the Indians and Muslims; while Cantonese, Hakka, Mandarin, and Chinese are prevalent within the Chinese community.

Mauritius has shifted from a concentration on a single-crop agricultural economy in 1968, to one where other major sectors (mainly industry, tourism, and services) provide a substantial contribution. Sugar cultivation and exports were the backbone of the economy during the 1960s and 1970s, accounting for over 25% of the GDP. After

1982, growth prospects were boosted through political change, which provided the required impetus for the development of export-oriented industries (mainly textiles) and tourism. The sector of financial services, including off-shore banking and information technology, is also emerging.

Mauritius has joined the group of upper-middle income countries. The per capita domestic product GDP for 2000 was 102,447 Mauritian rupees.

Contextual Features

Mauritius is a parliamentary democracy based on the Westminster model, practicing separation of powers between the three main branches of the government: the legislative, the Executive, and the Judiciary. A one-chamber parliament, consisting of a National Assembly, is supreme in law making. Executive authority is vested in the President of the Republic. However, all major government policies and decisions are made by the Cabinet, a committee of senior government Ministers; while executive power resides with the Prime Minister. As for the Judiciary, Mauritian law provides a peculiar combination derived from French and English laws. The substantive civil and criminal law is largely of French origin, while the remaining laws and the legal system are of British inspiration.

The political structure is based on a multi-party system. The main parties have a policy of election for the party leader and are structured into front-bench and back-bench members. Parliament consists of the government, elected by a simple majority vote; the opposition, the second largest party in the House; and other minority parties.

Mauritius has inherited an accusatorial system of law from the British, guaranteeing the principle of presumption of innocence and affording reasonable protection to the accused. The legal provisions of criminal procedure are scattered in various legislations (the *Police Act*, *Criminal Procedure Act*, *Courts Act*, and *Criminal Appeal Act*), and in case of legislative vacuum, the *Common Law of England*, which prevailed throughout the United Kingdom prior to 1946, still applies. Indeed, Mauritius has legalized and constitutionalized many Common Law principles, provisions, and administrative directions, from the Judge's Rule in the UK. In addition, equity laws also prevail, to the extent that the Supreme Court is empowered to exercise equitable jurisdictions in those cases where the law falls short of providing a remedy.

Crime figures in Mauritius are mainly computed from official statistics of the police. No victim survey has yet been carried out in the island.

The following table provides a brief picture of the most common crimes committed.

Mauritius has followed a hierarchical structure of courts, following the English model for the organization of courts. At the top is the Judicial Committee of the Privy Council, a British court of appeal for some Commonwealth countries with residual powers for a limited jurisdiction in the United Kingdom. Further down the hierarchy, the Supreme Court has unlimited jurisdiction in civil and criminal matters. It acts as a court of First Instance (hearing civil and criminal cases for the first time) and a Court of Appeal for cases from lower courts.

The Intermediate Court is a court of record; its criminal jurisdiction includes serious offenses heard by the Court of Assizes of the Supreme Court, and minor offenses heard by the District Court. It also hears civil cases where the claims do not exceed Rs 500,000.

The Industrial Court has exclusive civil and criminal jurisdiction for cases pertaining to labor and industrial relations.

The District Court is the lowest court, and it hears minor offenses (misdemeanors and contraventions) and civil cases where the claims do not exceed Rs. 50,000. The District Magistrate also acts as a mediator and conciliator for problems met by people living in the district, and can also refer a matter to arbitration.

In addition to the courts, there are also several specialized tribunals:

- The Tax Appeal Tribunal, which hears appeals against decisions made by Revenue Commissions under the Income Tax Act;
- The Permanent Arbitration Tribunal, which handles industrial disputes between employers and employees;
- The Industrial Relations Commission, a conciliatory body in industrial disputes;
- The Rent Tribunal, which deals with urgent problems pertaining to rent.

The Mauritian correction system is also a remnant of its colonial heritage, modeled on the British pattern, both in its philosophy and practice. The law under which the system functions dates back as far as 1881 to the *Revised Laws of Mauritius*, subsequently updated by the *Reform Institutions Act* of 1988; and the system is geared toward crime prevention and reform/rehabilitation of offenders.

	1998	1999	2000
Total recorded crimes	37,562	38,049	35,943
Intentional homicides, completed	31	23	26
Intentional homicides, attempted	13	12	17
Non-intentional homicides	5	5	2
Major assaults	116	109	199
Assaults	12,663	11,422	10,784
Rapes	42	29	27
Robberies	980	1,145	1,166
Major thefts	384	611	487
Thefts	9,998	10,994	9,532
Burglaries	1,235	1,628	1,584
Frauds	914	932	914
Embezzlements	495	495	535
Drug offences	2,118	1,963	2,473
Bribery crimes	13	17	7

Source: World Bank

The penal system, directly controlled by a Commissioner and a Deputy Commissioner of Prisons, includes five prisons for male adults (two maximum-security prisons, a high-security prison, a medium-security prison, and an open prison), one for females, three for juveniles (consisting of a Correctional Youth Centre and two male/female Rehabilitation Youth Centres), and one for Rodrigues.

A Probation and Aftercare Service was created as far back as 1947, and it was remodeled in 1988 (as per the *Reform Institutions Act*) to conduct social inquiries and to supervise people placed on probation, as well as to provide follow-up and aftercare to inmates of the juvenile penal institutions and to prisoners released on parole.

A Community Service Order is expected on the agenda of the Correction System.

Police Profile

Background

The formal institutionalization of the police began in 1768, under the French Royal Government of Louis XVI. Prior to this, public services, under the French East India Company, were not functioning effectively.

In 1767, a contingent of the French National Troupe (*Légion de Garde*) reached the island. This body of armed people (*Maréchaussée*) also controlled a repressive judiciary. Indeed, the first Commissioner of the island appointed in December 1767 simultaneously acted as a "Supreme Court Judge," holding the position of "*Juge du Conseil Supérieur*" (Paul, 1997); he directly controlled the capital, while local military commanders policed the country districts.

In 1796, a "*Corps de Gendarmerie*" was installed to replace the *Maréchaussée,* following the institution of the "*Gendarmerie Nationale*" in France in 1791; the Gendarmerie was suppressed in 1797 and legalized again in 1808, when it was organized into four brigades. By then, the police force, as a whole, was structured into the "*Police Générale*" and "*Police Particulière,*" established in 1803 (Paul, 1997). The CID had been created in 1794, while the Police Headquarters was formed in 1803.

Under British rule, from 1810, no immediate change was introduced in the police organization. A Commission of Enquiry, set up in 1859, gave the Police organization its formal structure, whereby the municipalities were relieved of their policing functions, and the *Police Ordinance 16*, 1893 (remodeled as the *Police Act* 1974), still prevails, having been subject to minor adjustments over the years.

Under the Police Act, the police organization received its title of Mauritius Police Force (MPF), and the term "police officer" means "a person who holds an office or is appointed to serve in the Mauritius Police Force."

Demographics

The MPF numbered 10,576 employees in 2002 (10,045 men and 531 women officers). Its total strength, all ranks included, is about 10,763. The ethnic composition of the MPF, being a sensitive issue, is not publicized, although the general perception is that the MPF reflects the same characteristics as that of the population, and is therefore largely Hindu-dominated.

Of the total number of officers employed during 2002, around 2,876 do not wear uniforms. Additionally, some 780 civilian personnel have been admitted, employed mainly for administrative duties and organized as follows:

- Support staff: 110;
- Prime Minister's Office: 9;
- Manual workers: 663.

Organizational Description

The MPF is under the direct command of the Commissioner of Police, who is accountable to the Prime Minister, or to any other minister to whom responsibility for the MPF is assigned. The ratio of citizens to police is about 19:1.

The ranks (in hierarchical order) of the MPF are designated as follows:

- The Commissioner of Police, acting under the authority of the Prime Minister, directs and controls the whole system of police in Mauritius and its dependencies.

- Deputy Commissioners/Women Deputy Commissioners have the same prerogatives and powers as the Commissioner in the temporary absence of the latter, or when acting on his behalf.
- The Principal Police Medical Officer is responsible to the Commissioner for the state of health generally and for hygiene of the Force and is assisted by Police Medical Officers.
- Assistant Commissioners/Women Assistant Commissioners direct and control Police Divisions or Branches.
- Superintendents/Women Superintendents have general charge under Assistant Commissioners of all matters pertaining to their division or branch.
- Assistant Superintendents/Women Assistant Superintendents have general charge under Superintendents of all matters pertaining to their subdivision or branch.
- Deputy Assistant Superintendents constitute the link between the Gazetted Ranks and the Inspectorate.
- Chief Inspectors/Women Chief Inspector of Police;
- Inspectors/Women Inspector;
- Sergeants/Women Police Sergeants;
- Constables/Women Police Constables.

Promotional exams are held for promotion from the rank of

(a) Constables (who have completed five years of service) to that of Sergeant;
(b) Sergeants (who have completed two years of service) to Inspectors.

Successful candidates are then required to follow a Sergeants' / Inspectors' Cadre Course, following which they are considered for promotion on a substantive capacity.

Subsequent promotions above the rank of Inspectors follow seniority and/or specialist qualifications.

The Police Headquarters houses the office of the Commissioner of Police and Deputy Commisioner of Police (DCPs), as well as the Police Information and Operations Room (PIOR), which directly controls the MPF. The MPF itself is organized under various divisions, specialized Departments, and Support Units.

For administrative purposes and operational efficiency, the island has been divided into six territorial boundaries of Police Divisions: the Metropolitan (City of Port-Louis), Northern, Eastern, Western, Central, and Southern Divisions. Each can be further subdivided into smaller police station areas. Each division is headed by a Divisional Commander of the rank of Assistant Commissioner, responsible for developing local policing plans in consultation with his community. The Commander is supported by two SPs, write out one in charge of operations and the other of prosecutions; and supported by ASPs, who are entrusted with the responsibility for the supervision of inquiries, prosecutions, and the general organization of police stations. Police station divisional areas are in turn headed either by Chief Inspectors or Inspectors, depending upon the importance of the workload.

The Departments:

- The Traffic Branch:

  - Traffic Police Headquarters, responsible for the issuance and control of driving licenses, and maintenance of record of convictions for offences under the Road Traffic Act, and
  - Mobile Field Division, which consists of mobile patrols in each of the six Divisions. They monitor traffic, especially during peak hours, and enforce laws relating to parking, drunken driving and speeding.
  - The Central Criminal Investigative Department (CCID).

The CCID deals with sensitive cases involving larger public interest, and consists of the following:

- Fraud Squad, which investigates frauds that relate to immovable property.
- Major Crime Investigation Team, which investigates cases of homicides and sexual assault.
- Technical Support Unit, responsible for preserving evidence in a scene of crime and made up of Draftsmen, Photographers, and Scene-of-Crime Officers (SOCO).
- Anti-Drug and Smuggling Unit (ADSU). As its name implies, the ADSU is responsible for the legal repression of drugs. This unit enforces provisions instituted under the Dangerous Drugs Act, Psychotropic Substances Act, and the Customs and Excise Laws. It has attracted public attention in the fight against prostitution, gambling, smuggling, and other such forms of contrabands.
- Passport and Immigrations Office (PIO). This is the sole authority responsible for the processing and issuance of passports, travel

documents, and certificates of identity. The office is also responsible for controlling and regulating entry, exit, and duration of stay of non-citizens in the island. The PIO usually works in collaboration with the police, to track down any form of illegal stay, and it regulates immigrant prostitution in the island.

- Outer islands police—the Rodrigues Police.
- Helicopter Squadron. The squadron assists the regular police by conducting specific operations, such as "Search and Rescue" and Casualty Evacuation, Maritime Surveillance and Reconnaissance Missions, operations to combat *Gandia* cultivation, tracking of criminals, and traffic patrols and security escort of convoys.
- National Coast Guard (NCG). This is a specialized unit of the MPF responsible for the detection, prevention, and suppression of illegal activities within the maritime zone.
- Special Supporting Unit (SSU). The SSU, also known as the Anti-Riot Police, mainly assists the regular police in controlling extreme cases of civil unrest. The SSU is mainly involved in functions such as crowd control, the location of missing persons, tracking criminals, and escorting dangerous prisoners.
- Special Mobile Force (SMF). The SMF is a paramilitary force mainly responsible for the internal and external security of the country, but also involved in search and rescue operations, bomb disposal, route clearance, detecting and destroying *gandia,* and illicit distillation. It also asists in the opening of roads after cyclones.
- The National Security Service (NSS). The NSS has been established to obtain, correlate, and evaluate intelligence pertaining to national security and security of the Prime Minister, and other such persons as directed by the Prime Minister.

The Support Units:

- Emergency Response Services (ERS). The ERS is a mobile unit launched in 1998 to provide prompt and effective response to the community's call for assistance in case of victimization or any emergency, and to ensure visible police presence so as to enhance the quality of life of citizens in terms of safety and security. They have been very active as a front-line intervention force, in drug enforcement, salesmen protection, tourist policing, breath test exercises (alcotest), and aggressive patrols.

- Road Safety Unit (RSU). The RSU carries out control measures such as speed checks, alcohol testing, vehicle checks, preventive patrols, and wheelclamping (to discourage illegal parking), and is also responsible for sensitizing the population on road safety issues.
- Crime Prevention Unit (CPU). The CPU has been created to promote a sense of awareness of preventive issues in the community, to secure the community's involvement in the fight against crime, to instill basic concepts of good citizenship and law-abiding principles among the younger generation, to reduce fear of crime, thereby improving the quality of life of citizens, and to enhance the police-public relationship.
- Family Protection Unit (FPU). The FPU provides an expedient response to requests for assistance by children, women, and men who are subject to abuse and violence. As such, it is largely concerned with protecting the welfare of the family.
- Anti-Piracy Unit. The Anti-Piracy Unit was established in 2001 to enforce the provisions of the Copyrights Act of 1997.
- Airport and Port Police. Consisting of the Airport Police, Harbor Police, and the Bulk Sugar Terminal Police, this department is responsible for the prevention and detection of offenses in the port and airport areas, and for regulating access to and security in these areas.
- Police Medical and Scientific Unit. This unit consists of a pathology branch (carries out autopsies and gives evidence in court) and a clinical branch (examines victims and suspects in cases of sexual assault and homicides).

Functions

The police not only handle criminal law, they also carry out duties of an administrative nature. The specific duties of the Mauritius Police Force, prescribed under Section 9 of the *Police Act of 1974*, consist of the following:

(a) Preserving the public peace;
(b) Preventing and detection of offences;
(c) Apprehending persons who have committed, or who are reasonably suspected of having committed offences;
(d) Regulating processions and gatherings on public roads and in public places, or places of public resort;
(e) Regulating traffic and preventing or removing obstructions from public roads;

(f) Preserving order in public places and places of public resort, at public gatherings, and assemblies for public amusement;

(g) Assisting and implementing health, quarantine, customs, and excise laws;

(h) Assisting and preserving order in ports, harbours, and airports;

(i) Executing process issued by a court;

(j) Swearing information and conducting prosecutions;

(k) Performed such other functions as may be conferred on police officers under any other enactment.

In addition, Subsection 2 of the said Section of the Act clearly stipulates that:

> Every police officer shall perform such para-military duties as he may be required to do and for that purpose may serve in any specialised unit of the Police Force.

Consequently, the police are entrusted with the power to arrest and contravene, and may use such force as is necessary for that purpose. The officer is also empowered to "stop and search," "enter and search," and seize any illegal article.

The basic requirements for joining the MPF are:

- Good physical fitness;
- Normal eyesight (the applicant should not be wearing spectacles);
- Minimum height of 5 ft 7 in;
- Chest measurement of 84 cm;
- Cambridge School Certificate or its equivalent, the General Certificate of Education "Ordinary" level;
- No criminal record.

Training

Recruits, at their inception in the MPF, are posted to the Police Training School for a six-month period, where they receive instruction in

- Physical training;
- Squad, arms, and riots drill;
- Small arms training;
- Police orders and administration;
- Laws and evidence relating to police duties;
- Police duties;
- First aid;
- Local and general knowledge;
- Self-defense;
- Customer care.

During the last two months, they are detailed for on-the-job training in police stations.

Further training is also offered in-house, as per requirement, such as

- Conversion courses for Police Constables;
- Development courses for Sergeants and Inspectors;
- Prosecutor course;
- Refresher course for in-service personnel in specific fields of intervention;
- Investigation course;
- Information technology;
- Continuous in-service training on a rotational basis.

Additionally, selected police officers have the opportunity to take courses in specialized fields in friendly countries. Foreign instructors—short-term training teams—from friendly countries also deliver training in specific issues.

A degree course—BSc (Honours)—in Police Studies has been institutionalized since 1999, and as of 2002, some 225 selected officers have been channeled to follow the course.

Police Public Projects

Police Public projects include roads policing and educating the public in critical areas requiring police intervention. These have focused on:

- Interventions of the RSU to educate the road user through:

  - Publicity: daily info-route, TV interventions, programs and video clips, magazine publications, exhibitions, manuals, police traffic diversion schemes (to guide the road user at different sites where possibilities of road accidents exist), pictorial boards, posters.
  - Targeting children: regular lectures are given to children of pre-primary, primary, and secondary schools, as well as to teachers to enable them to organize road safety activities in the school compound. In addition, 10 traffic playgrounds have been set up in various localities to better reach out to children.
  - Talks and seminars to adults.

- Crime Prevention:

  - The neighborhood watch scheme has been set up in critical areas in an attempt to increase regional control within the community and to improve detection.
  - Safety campaigns involve the local families and tourists.

- FPU:
  - Proactive policing is designed to promote an awareness of domestic violence and child abuse issues in community resource centres, rehabilitation centres, factories, and parent-teacher associations, mainly through talks and seminars.
  - To assist victims of domestic violence in courts regarding protection/occupation/tenancy orders.

Police Use of Firearms

The *Police Act* (1974) prescribes that police officers be provided with the staves, arms, ammunition, and other equipment necessary for the effective discharge of their duties. Accordingly, revolvers and ammunition are issued to all police stations and other specialized branches, while rifles and ammunition are provided at the SSU and division level.

Complaints and Discipline

Complaints against the police are investigated by the Complaints Investigation Bureau (CIB), which works in close collaboration with the National Human Rights Commission (NHRC), established under Section 3 of the Protection of Human Rights Act 1998. The Commissioner of Police exercises administrative control over the CIB.

Any member of the public who feels aggrieved by the conduct of a police officer may make a complaint in writing to either the Chairman of the NHRC, the Commissioner of Police, the CIB, the Divisional Commander, or by calling at any police station and registering a complaint.

Complaints are investigated by the CIB, under the supervision of a police officer at least of the rank of an Assistant Superintendent, and after completion will be submitted to the NHRC, which will, if satisfied, issue a certificate to that respect.

The NHRC will submit cases requiring police disciplinary action to the Disciplined Forces Service Commission. In other cases, the matter will be referred to the Director of Public Prosecutions for advice. If there is a recommendation for prosecution, the complainant will be called upon to give evidence before the court. Even at a hearing in a disciplinary case, which is generally held in private, the complainant has a right to attend and will normally be expected to give evidence. Further, in cases where there is remedy at Civil Law and a complainant wishes to bring civil action, the investigation of the complainant will not as a rule begin until completion of civil proceedings.

The police are not officially trained in the internationally recognized field of human rights, but officers are cognizant of the *Protection of Human Rights Act* (1998), and those earmarked for further education in policing have an academic insight of human rights issues. Otherwise, policy measures regarding human rights have not really been acknowledged, whether within the MPF or nationally.

Terrorism

Terrorism is controlled under the *Prevention of Terrorism Act* (2002). No organization or individual has, as of 2003, been arrested or convicted under this Act.

A police officer not below the rank of Superintendent may apply to a District Magistrate for the issue of a warrant for a terrorist investigation, and thereafter any police officer can

- Enter the premises specified in the warrant;
- Search the premises and any person found therein;
- Seize and retain any relevant material found therein; and
- Arrest and detain any person whom he reasonably suspects of having committed or of being about to commit a terrorist offense.

International Cooperation

Mauritius has been a member state of Interpol since 1969; Interpol's National Central Bureau (NCB) in the island has been formally headed by the Commissioner of Police since 1995. Mauritius has also adhered to Interpol's regionally based international police cooperation network operating throughout the Southern African Development Community (SADC) and the Southern African Regional Police Chiefs Cooperation Organisation (SARPCCO), established at the Interpol African Regional Conference (1995). The other countries involved in SARPCCO are Angola, Botswana, Lesotho, Malawi, Mozambique, Namibia, South Africa, Swaziland, Tanzania, Zambia, and Zimbabwe.

Police Education, Research, and Publications

Major institutions for higher education:

- The University of Mauritius;
- British University of Portsmouth.

Leading police magazine:

- Mauritius Police Magazine, Police Press Office, Police Headquarters, line barracks, Port-Louis.

There has been a dearth of police research and publications in Mauritius, essentially because of the relatively low tertiary education level of officers and lack of sources of funding. This discrepancy has been partially remedied with the inception of the degree course in policing; as of 2004, however, no research in the field has been published.

Police-Related Website:

- http://ncb.intnet.mu/pmo/police/index.html

A. R. RAMSARAN

Bibliography

Interpol SRB - Harare, *Report to 3rd SARPCCO AGM 27-30 July 1998*, Harare: SARPCCO Secretariat,1998.

Mauritius Police Force (n.d), *ICPO - Interpol: Mauritius National Central Bureau*, Port-Louis, Mauritius: MPF.

Mauritius Police Force, *Mauritius - Country Report*, Report to the 3rd SARPCCO AGM, Gaborone, Botswana, Port-Louis: MPF, 1998.

Mauritius Police Force, *SARPCCO: Background brief*, Port-Louis, Mauritius: MPF, 2001.

Paul, L.J., *Deux Siècles d'histoire de la Police à L'Ile Maurice* (Two centuries of History of the Police in the Island of Mauritius) (1768-1968), Paris: L'Harmattan, 1997.

SARPCCO PCC, *Report Presented to the 5th SARPCCO Annual General Meeting Blantyre, Malawi by outgoing Chairman of SARPCCO Mr. E. E. Hilary*, Harare: SARPCCO Secretariat, 2000b.

SARPCCO PCC, *Report to 5th SARPCCO AGM 30th July - 4th August 2000*, Harare: SARPCCO Secretariat, 2000.

MEXICO

Background Material

The United Mexican States (*Estados Unidos Mexicanos*), commonly referred to as Mexico, has a territorial surface of 1,964,375 sq km. The population is 104,959,594 (2004 est.). The ethnic composition of the population is 60% *Mestizo* (of mixed racial ancestry, primarily European and indigenous); 30% Amerindian; 9% European; 1% others. Spanish is the official language, although 66 Amerindian languages are also spoken. The population is 89.7% Catholic; 4.9% Protestant; 0.1% Jewish; 2.1% others; and 3.2% non-religious.

Mexico's natural resources include petroleum, silver, copper, gold, lead, zinc, natural gas, and wood. The GDP per capita is $9,000 (2003 est.).

Mexico was the place of settlement of some of the most ancient and highly developed civilizations in the western hemisphere. The Aztec group was the foremost power in central and southern Mexico around the fifteenth century. In 1521, Hernán Cortés conquered the Aztec capital. In 1535, New Spain was instituted under a colonial form of government with the appointment of the first Spanish viceroy, Antonio de Mendoza. The Mexican Independence War began on September 16, 1810. The last viceroy of New Spain was Juan O'Donojú, who, upon his arrival to Mexico in July of 1821, accepted the Córdoba Treaty, thus acknowledging the sovereignty of Mexico.

For decades thereafter, the conflict between centralists (conservatives) and federalists (liberals) continued. From among the latter group arose the leadership of Benito Juárez; and a federal system of government, freedom of expression, and other liberties were instituted in Mexico, through its Constitution of 1857. France imposed a conservative government from 1864 to 1867, when Juárez rose to power. Porfirio Díaz was President of Mexico from 1877 to 1911. After Díaz was reelected in 1910, Francisco I. Madero initiated the Mexican Revolution. Díaz was forced to resign in 1911 and, immediately thereafter, left Mexico permanently.

Madero was elected President. A new wave of armed resistance movements began, and Venustiano Carranza seized power. A new Constitution was promulgated in 1917, giving way to the creation of a labor policy, outlawing presidential reelection, expropriating clergy property, and restoring communal territory to indigenous groups. In 1934,

Lázaro Cárdenas was elected President. In 1936, the expropriation law was approved, allowing the government to expropriate private property, provided that said expropriation was necessary and in benefit of public and social well-being. During 1968, the Mexican government was faced with massive student uprisings. On October 2, 1968, the government attempted to appease the social discontent expressed in a protest march held in Tlatelolco Plaza, located in the capital's historic center or downtown area. As a result of the repressive measures taken, a great number of students and citizens from other social sectors who supported the movement perished, while many more were incarcerated and forcefully "disappeared." In 1970, Luis Echeverría Álvarez took office as President and adopted measures aimed to reduce foreign influence in areas of national economy, as well as to increase exports. José López Portillo was elected President in 1976, and toward the end of his term, he imposed currency control and the nationalization of the bank system. In 1989, Carlos Salinas de Gortari's administration accelerated the privatization of state-run corporations and modified restrictive commerce and investment policies in order to stimulate foreign investment, allowing for majority interest control of corporations on behalf of foreign investors. In October of that same year, Salinas and then-U.S. President George Bush signed the North American Free Trade Agreement (NAFTA). In August 1994, Ernesto Zedillo Ponce de León won the presidential race and was faced with one of the worst financial crises in Mexican history. A national rescue program was designed under the coordination of then-U.S. President, Bill Clinton, and Zedillo announced austerity measures and the privatization of State property. After an electoral reform that took three decades to secure, the National Action Party's (PAN: *Partido Acción Nacional*) candidate took office as President, thereby putting an end to the hegemonic party regime.

Contextual Features

Mexico is divided into 32 federal entities or states, each of which is in turn subdivided into municipalities, the sum of which is 2,443. The country has a Federal District, which is divided into 16 local political districts (*delegaciones políticas*). The Executive branch of the Federal Government is represented by the President of the Republic. The President is elected via a direct voting system, serves a six-year term, and is not eligible for reelection. The Legislative branch of the Federal Government is composed of two chambers or houses: deputies or representatives (*diputados*), and senators. There are 128 senate members and 500 representatives, none of whom are eligible for reelection. The highest tribunal of the Judicial branch of the Federal Government is the National Supreme Court of Justice, composed of 11 justices, each of whom serves a 15-year term. The President of the Supreme Court is elected every four years. Each state follows, in its own government, the same checks and balances system. The General Constitution of the United Mexican States (*Constitución General de los Estados Unidos Mexicanos*) establishes three areas of jurisdiction for penal law: federal, state, and military. The Mexican judicial system is based on Germanic-Roman tradition and codified through general and abstract laws.

In Mexico, the institution titled the *Ministerio Público* (MP) or the Public Prosecutor, subject to the Executive branch of government, is in charge of criminal investigation processes. The phase under its command is called *Averiguación Previa* (Initial Inquiry). Law enforcement agencies are directly subject to this institution. Once an individual is arrested, the Public Prosecutor (MP) has 48 hours—96 in cases of organized crime—to release the individual or to bring the case before a judge. The judge then has 72 hours to determine whether or not the individual being accused by the Public Prosecutor (MP) will be subject to due process. The penal procedure then passes on to the examination phase, whereupon evidence is presented before the judge. This is followed by first instance sentencing; and, if appealed, the case goes on to the second instance, whereupon a new penal procedure is initiated and which, in turn, reaches its end with second instance sentencing as issued by the appeals judge. During the development of the penal process, the subject of said process may be confined to preventive prison. There are federal, state, and municipal prisons.

The following table illustrates the makeup of the penitentiary population of Mexico.

Police Profile

Background

In Mexico, public access to information regarding the internal workings of law enforcement is an exception, not the rule. There are no public information sources designed to explain the characteristics of the thousands of federal, state, and municipal law enforcement agencies. In order to generate this

Penitentiary situation in January, 2004

Correctional Facility	Capacity	Population	Over Population	
			Absolute	Relative
State prisons (includes the Federal District)	138,912	178,801	39,889	28.72%
Municipal prisons	3,288	3,368	80	2.43%
Federal prisons	5,672	2,552	−3,120	−55.01%
Total	147,872	184,721	36,849	24.92%

Source: National Public Safety System (Sistema Nacional de Seguridad Pública)

text, data were collected from documentary sources and interviews with public officials. There is not enough information for broad or precise descriptions. In order to illustrate the basic characteristics of the Mexican law enforcement model, some examples regarding specific law enforcement agencies were gathered.

Demographics

Throughout the country, there are slightly over 325,000 law enforcement officers. Preventive law enforcement officers comprise 87% of the total number of officers in the country. Slightly more than 286,000 uniformed individuals are distributed among the 31 states, the Federal District, and the 2,430 municipalities. Three percent of the total national police force is composed of 5,470 federal thoroughfare patrol officers and 4,400 military officers, both bodies of which are part of the Federal Preventive Police Force (PFP: *Policía Federal Preventiva*). The judicial or ministerial police force comprises the remaining 10% of the country's police force.

Almost nine out of 10 law enforcement officers in the country are male, and 10.8% are female. The average age among both is 35. The average number of years of formal schooling is 8.8 years. The highest average of formal schooling is 11.1 years, achieved by officers in the Federal District. Female officers possess higher levels of formal schooling than male officers. Slightly less than 21% of female law enforcement officers possess some form of higher education, and these form part of the police forces that are subject to the Public Prosecutor (MP).

Organizational Description

Mexico is a Federal Republic; for this reason, law enforcement agencies are divided into three jurisdictional entities: federal, state, and municipal. Agencies are also divided in terms of their roles, which are two: preventive and investigative. Preventive law enforcement operates within all three jurisdictional entities, while investigative law enforcement (*policía judicial*: "judicial law enforcement officers," or *policía ministerial*: "ministerial law en- forcement officers") operates only on federal and state levels and is intended as an auxiliary branch of the Public Prosecutor (MP). In general terms, preventive state law enforcement bodies are governed by general statutes included in the public safety laws of the states and their corresponding regulations, while municipal law enforcement bodies are governed by local administrative statutes. Judicial law enforcement bodies are governed by the organic laws of the state offices of the Attorney General and their statutes, as well as by procedural penal legislation. Mexico has a Federal Penal Code and one for each state of the Republic. Over 90% of reported crimes fall under state jurisdiction.

At the head of the Federal Preventive Police Force (PFP) is the Commissioner. The following fall under his jurisdiction: the Presidential Guard, four Departments, the Learning Institute, Technical Services, Air Transport, Social Development, the Liaison and Communication Unit, Legal Affairs, and the Internal Comptroller. The Presidential Guard is subdivided into five sections (Personal, Information, Operations, Logistics, Planning) and one General Supervision Division. The Departments are: Intelligence for Prevention (which is in turn sectioned into seven divisions: traffic and smuggling, analysis, tactical support, airports and borders, abduction and theft, information and networks, terrorism); Federal Support Forces (which is in turn sectioned into three divisions: immediate response and alert, special operations, and strategic installations); Regional Security (subdivided into the federal thoroughfare security district, the ports and borders district, the

Federal jurisdiction

Processed	Sentenced	Total	Total
14,599	32,502	47,101	178,801
153	57	210	3,368
362	1,137	1,499	2,552
15,114	33,696	48,810	184,721

federal zones district, and 32 regional headquarters); and Administration and Services (with four divisions: human resources, material resources and warehousing, financial resources, and infrastructure and services). Finally, the Learning Institute is sectioned into three general divisions: a Training Center, a Learning Center, and a Higher Law Enforcement Studies Center.

The Federal Support Forces Department (*Coordinación de Fuerzas Federales de Apoyo*) stands out due to the fact that 4,400 military officers belonging to the Ministry of Defense were integrated. In June of 2002, the press reported that another 826 members of the armed forces were integrated, which brings the total of the Federal Support Forces to over 5,000 military personnel operating as civil law enforcement officers, and it has been reported that 1,500 more are to be added to this group.

Another unit is that of the Regional Security Department (*Coordinación de Seguridad Regional*), consisting of the areas of Federal Thoroughfare, Ports and Borders, and Federal Zone Security. In this unit, 5,500 members of the institution previously titled the *Policía Federal de Caminos* (Federal Thoroughfare Patrol), which already performed these services prior to the creation of the Federal Preventive Police Force (PFP), are in operation. As per the table above, in actuality, the PFP now consists of nearly 15,000 officers.

The Federal Agency of Investigation (AFI) is sectioned into six substantive areas and three support areas. The substantive areas are: AFI Management, Law Enforcement Investigation, Regional Law Enforcement Deployment, Special Operations, Law Enforcement Planning, and the General Department Central Headquarters Interpol Mexico. The support areas are: Technical Services, Judicial Matters, and Administration and Services.

For advancement in a law enforcement career within the Federal Investigations Agency (AFI), the officer must ascend several ranks, serve for a certain number of years, and comply with specialization programs. This career begins with basic training (Investigator C, Investigator B), followed by progressive levels of operation (Investigator A); subsequently, the officer moves on to advanced training (Official Investigator, Chief Investigator), and from there, to Supervision and Control levels (General Investigator); the following stage is that of management training, involving upper management training courses, as well as political context, media, and general knowledge courses (Supervisor, Chief Supervisor); from there, the officer may pass on to the highest rank as First Chief of Police.

The Preventive Police Force of Mexico City (*Policía Preventiva de la Ciudad de México*) is the largest force in the country. Following is its organizational structure: the sectional police force (divided into 70 territorial divisions); the metropolitan police force (including transportation patrol, female patrol, horseback patrol, tourism patrol, special rescue and emergency units, and grenadier units); special forces (the Special Unit, helicopters, task force, and Alpha Group); and Road Safety and Internal Affairs (*Marte* Unit and *Homero* Unit).

There are four main hierarchies (each with its respective levels) in the Law Enforcement Career System of Mexico City: Law Enforcement Officer (private or non-ranking, third, second and first); Law Enforcement Official (Sub-official, Second Official and first Official); Inspector (Sub-inspector, Second Inspector and First Inspector); and Superintendent (First and Second).

Functions

In federal jurisdiction, the Federal Preventive Police Force (PFP: *Policía Federal Preventiva*) was created in December of 1998. The Federal Preventive Police Force (PFP) is immediately subject to the Ministry of Public Safety (*Secretaría de Seguridad Pública*). On November 1, 2001, the Federal Agency of Investigation (AFI: *Agencia Federal de Investigación*), a body immediately subject to the State Attorney General (*Procuraduría General de la República*), was also created. The Federal Preventive Police Force (PFP) is designed to provide the following services: prevent federal crimes and infringements; assist other authorities; keep public peace and order in federal zones, resources, and spaces; assist in crime investigation and persecution; perform arrests in cases of *flagrante delicto*; collaborate with state and municipal authorities; participate in conjoint operations with other law enforcement agencies; carry out crime prevention intelligence efforts; monitor the main arteries of transportation, airports, maritime ports and customs; and collaborate with civil protection authorities.

Training

On July 18, 1996, as part of the National Public Safety Program 1995–2000 (PNSP: *Programa Nacional de Seguridad Pública*), a diagnosis of national law enforcement was published in the *Official Federal Journal*. To date, this diagnosis has not been followed up by any type of public evaluation on a national scale. In 1996, it was stated that almost half of the law enforcement training institutions in the country initiated their undertakings over the last two decades. The national average length of a basic training course was of four and a half months. From the 58 academies that were in existence, only 17 required minimum schooling from their candidates for enrollment in the basic training course, which is to say that, up until 1996, two thirds of law enforcement training institutions did not require any type of minimum schooling from trainees. The program reported on the lack of any center whatsoever aimed toward specialization of law enforcement instructors.

Up until 1996, 56% of the total police force (255,533 officers) either did not possess any formal schooling whatsoever, had not completed an elementary education, or had completed only an elementary education; 24% (99,450 officers) had either not completed or had only completed a junior high school education, and 13% had either not completed or had only completed a high school education. Less than 1% of law enforcement officers had attended teachers' training schools in a complete or incomplete manner. The cited document reported on the lack of technically valid and reliable performance evaluation instruments, as well as on insufficient technological support for training programs.

On January 14, 2003, the National Public Safety Program (PNSP) (1995–2000) was created; it states the following: "there is diversity in terms of the training ... of law enforcement bodies, which hinders the suitable performance of the companies that integrate them.... The training level is deficient and in many cases non-existent. There are no efficient improvement programs ... the majority of officers are trained (sic), without having even satisfied the minimum academic requirements of basic education and, in some cases, with some type of addiction or criminal record."

The Chief of Police of preventive law enforcement of the Federal District, which is the largest in the country, reported that "More than 90% of law enforcement officers have not received any additional training after having entered the force" (*Testimony of Mr. Marcelo Ebrard Casaubón, Minister of Public Safety*, Legislative Assembly of the Federal District, 2nd Legislature, April 1, 2003. Unpublished version). The statement provoked the signing of agreements with the National Autonomous University of Mexico (*Universidad Nacional Autónoma de México*) and with the National Polytechnic Institute (*Instituto Politécnico Nacional*). In the former case, 19,000 law enforcement officers are to attend 60 hours of class on substantive and procedural law, criminology, ethics, and human rights,

while in the latter case, the teaching will focus on transportation engineering, languages, and computer knowledge. In the case of judicial law enforcement officers of the Federal District, the tendency is to include personnel with Bachelor's Degrees in law.

The National Public Safety Program (PNSP) created a National Evaluation and Certification Program that "consists of the application of physical, psychometric and general knowledge exams, to public safety personnel." Between 1998 and 2002, 173,305 individuals were evaluated.

The Technical Institute of Law Enforcement Training offers a six-month Basic Law Enforcement Training Course. This course consists of two parts: the Academic and Active Training. In the former, subjects taught are: Law Enforcement Documentation, Law Enforcement Legislation, Civic Justice, Human Rights, Road and Traffic Regulations, Citizen Assistance, Public Safety and Prevention, Armament and Gunfire, Law Enforcement Discipline and Training, Law Enforcement Defense I, Physical Training I, Knowledge of Mechanics and Handling of Motor Vehicles, Sports, and Individual Studies. In the Active Training stage, the subjects taught are: Law Enforcement Ethics, Body Spirit, Citizen Attention and Treatment, Service Area, Armament and Gunfire II, Law Enforcement Training, Law Enforcement Defense II, Physical Training II, Law Enforcement Techniques and Tactics, Community Service, Sports, and Individual Studies.

Complaints and Discipline

Article 21 of the Political Constitution of the United Mexican States (*Constitución Política de los Estados Unidos Mexicanos*) establishes, since 1994, four principles of operation with regard to the exercise of law enforcement: legality, efficiency, professionalism, and honesty. The available information, both national and foreign, allows for the assertion that the average performance level of law enforcement officers throughout the country does not satisfy said principles. Two specific factors are most noticeable: first, the continuous reports of systematic human rights violations and infringement of constitutional rights; and, second, the information issued by law enforcement agencies themselves, which shows the lack of an efficient system of accountability.

When the aforementioned principles were introduced, a constitutional base was also granted to the National Public Safety System (SNSP: *Sistema Nacional de Seguridad Pública*), the law for which was published one year later. It is a coordination mechanism, the superior body of which is the National Public Safety Council (*Consejo Nacional de Seguridad Pública*), headed by the Minister of Federal Public Safety (*Secretario de Seguridad Pública Federal*), who represents the President of the Republic. All state governors and the Head of Government of the Federal District participate in this council.

ERNESTO LOPEZ PORTILLO VARGAS

MICRONESIA

Background Material

The Federated States of Micronesia (FSM) is a group of 607 islands spread across 3 million sq mi in the North Pacific Ocean. The islands occupy a land area of 702 sq km, over half of which is taken up by the island of Pohnpei. FSM consists of four states, which from east to west include Kosrea, Pohnpei, Chuuk, and Yap. The capital of FSM is Palikir.

The ancestors of the present-day Micronesians began to settle in the islands about 4,000 years ago. The Spanish established sovereignty over what was then known as the Caroline Islands during the sixteenth century. The Carolines then passed to German (1899) and Japanese (1914) control. In 1947, under United Nations auspices, the islands became a U.S. Trust Territory. On 10 May 1979, the country became unified and independent, following ratification of a new constitution by Four Trust Territory Districts to form the Federated States of Micronesia. The neighboring districts of Palau, the Marshal Islands, and Mariana Islands chose not to participate in the process, and thus they continued as autonomous states. Guam remains part of the United States. On 3 November 1986, FSM attained independence under a Compact of Free Association with the United States. The Compact of Free Association recognizes the sovereignty of FSM and allows for a continued provision of U.S. economic and technical assistance. The United States is also responsible for military protection of the islands. FSM became a UN member in 1991.

The FSM currency is the U.S. dollar. Economic activities in FSM are weak and reliant on foreign aid. Economic activity consists primarily of subsistence farming and fishing. The following contribute to the GDP: services (77%); agriculture (19%); industry (4%). Over half of all workers are government employees. The GDP per capita purchasing parity power is $2,000 (2002 est.). The value of real wages and benefits declined 1.7% during 2002 and 2003, and approximately a quarter of the population live below the poverty line. The average life expectancy at birth is 69.44 years. The literacy rate of the total population is about 89%. Economic difficulties facing FSM are evident in the country's dependence on the U.S. whose aid equals two thirds of the GDP, amounting to about $100 million annually. The large amount of assistance to FSM allows it to run a substantial trade deficit. During 2000, exports totaled $22 million, with imports totaling $149 million. Attempts to promote the economy have focused on tourism, fishing, and building the country's small industrial sector. Geographical isolation, poorly developed infrastructure, lack of marketable mineral deposits, slow growth of the private sector, and a reduction in U.S. assistance are immediate impediments to future economic prosperity.

In July 2004, the population of FSM was estimated at 108,155 people, composed of nine ethnic Micronesian and Polynesian groups. While English is the official and common language, native dialects include Trukese, Pohnpeian, Yapese, Kosrean, Ulithian, Woleaian, and Kapingamarangi. The main religions of FSM are Roman Catholic (40%) and Protestant (47%).

Contextual Features

Although traditional customs and values dominate cultural life throughout FSM, within each state traditional laws, practices, and customs vary. American and Christian values have mixed with traditional values to produce the distinct cultural amalgam that is the present-day FSM.

The political institutions of FSM are built upon U.S. models.

FSM is a constitutional government in free association with the United States. The 1979 constitution guarantees human rights and freedoms, including "traditional" rights, and establishes a separation of governmental powers. Equal protection is provided under the law, disallowing discrimination on the basis of sex, race, ancestry, national origin, language, or social status. The National Government consists of the legislature (Congress, elected by popular vote), the executive, and judiciary, each with separate powers. Many major governmental functions are carried out by state governments. Each of FSM's four states has its own constitution, elected legislature, and governor. The unicameral Congress has 14 seats elected by popular vote. One senator is elected from each state to serve a four-year term. The remaining 10 senators, representing districts based on population, serve two-year terms. The President and Vice President are elected by Congress from among the four state-based senators; they serve four-year terms.

The legal system is based on Trust Territory laws; acts of legislature; and municipal, common, and customary laws. The judicial branch of the National Government is the FSM Supreme Court, which is divided into trial and appellate divisions. The President appoints judges for life, with the advice and consent of the Congress. Laws relating to arrest, warrants, access to counsel, and bail are patterned on U.S. models. The Constitution provides for public trials. Juveniles are entitled to closed hearings. The Supreme Court is the highest court in the nation. It has exclusive jurisdiction in cases involving disputes between states, foreign officials, admiralty and maritime cases, FSM constitution, national laws or treaties, and other domestic laws. The State Courts also have trial and appellate divisions. States may also provide for a Court in each municipality. Local courts are presided over by judges whose knowledge of local custom encourages the mediation of

minor disputes before they go to State Courts. The functioning of the criminal justice system has been hampered by under funding, delays in judicial appointments, and unavailability or shortages of court personnel and services.

Reliable crime statistics are not maintained by the states of FSM, nor are any data available on what groups are most victimized. Available data suggest that common violations include disturbing the peace, illegal possession of alcohol (e.g., on a Sunday or holiday without a permit), traffic violations, assault and battery, and malicious mischief.

Traditional customs distinguish persons on the basis of status and sex. Because of their traditional status and role, women and children tend to be victimized to a greater degree than men. There are no specific laws against domestic abuse, or governmental or private facilities to support women in abusive situations. Family pressures and a perception that police will not actively investigate abuse have resulted in underreporting of this behavior, which is viewed in both official and popular contexts as a "private" problem. Many islands also continue to observe caste systems, with those of lower caste status being more likely to be subject to assault, battery, and sexual assault.

The role of government and social organizations has not supplanted that of the traditional extended family in protecting and supporting the citizens of FSM. Citizens have preferred to rely on customary and traditional remedies in the resolution of criminal and civil matters. For example, traditional and customary structures provided strong protection for women and children from violence, abuse, and neglect, such activities being deemed offenses against the (extended) family and therefore dealt with by a complex system of familial sanctions. Traditional systems, however, have been challenged by urbanization, monetization, and breakdown of the extended family structure. Cultural resistance to formal litigation and incarceration as methods of maintaining public order have resulted in some individuals acting with impunity, with some cases of serious assault not going to trial. Traditional law provides victims with a strong role in prosecution and sentencing. Traditional social control methods have also been effective in resolving conflicts between families. Traditional methods of dispute resolution follow what has been termed in Western contexts a "restorative" model of justice, with an emphasis on the victim, the community, and the shaming of offenders.

Prison data for 2003–2004 indicate that there were 39 prisoners throughout FSM, which in per capita terms represents 34 prisoners per 1,000 people.

Crime indicators

Indicators	1995	1996	1997
Total	5,445	5,943	6,622
Misdemeanor	2,188	1,299	2,188
Minor traffic	1,725	2,633	1,789
Felony	817	931	1,602
Juvenile	516	546	489
Other	199	534	554

Source: Division of Public Safety, Attorney General's Offices in the respective states

Prison conditions generally meet international standards. Each of the four state jails includes separate cells for female prisoners. However, these are rarely used for their purpose, given the low rate of women detainees, and are regularly used to separate disruptive inmates from the general inmate population. Juvenile crime is rare, and there are no specific juvenile correctional facilities.

Police Profile

Background

Formalized policing throughout FSM began during the period of German colonial rule of the then-Caroline Islands, commencing in 1899. German authorities initially recruited a Malayan force to police the Islands, consisting of approximately 30 personnel. They were largely employed to contain tribal warfare and control the illegal trade in guns and liquor, which had been a feature of the Spanish colonial period. Early policing allowed for the disarmament and the pacification of much of the Carolines, and was carried out as part of a larger German policy to "modernize" the islands.

Malayan police were gradually dismissed, and a process of local recruitment began, although the Germans would occasionally bring Melanesian police to the Carolines to quell uprisings and civil disturbances. German administrators believed that locals would make ideal police, owing to their strong physical build and familiarity with warfare. The recruitment of locals was also a means of indoctrinating them in the language and laws of the colonial regime, so that they could become brokers of government when their service ended. Police strengthened the links between local political system and the German administration by simultaneously serving the interests of chiefs while upholding German law. Former policeman could continue to serve the government as interpreters, Island chiefs, or their assistants. The police force was used by the government as an educational tool in the absence of public schools. Police were recruited from local chiefly families and were sent to Pohnpei, where they received a salary of 16 marks ($4.00) a month in addition to board and lodging. In addition to military drills and rifle practice, police were trained in trades such as bricklaying and carpentry.

Under the Japanese colonial rule (1914), police continued to form the backbone of the colonial administrative apparatus. Police not only enforced government regulations and kept the peace, but they also provided a regular point of contact between remote islands and villages and the colonial administration. Police collected taxes, passed on public information, supervised road building and dock construction, and provided public health education.

The Japanese police structure had three tiers. At the top was the Superintendent. Below the Superintendent were three Police Inspectors and Assistant Inspectors. Below these were the policemen. Each branch of government in the islands used this structure.

While the police formed the lowest rung of the Japanese colonial bureaucracy, it was a prestigious appointment, being one of the highest positions to which an indigenous man could aspire and involving careful selection and vigorous training. The "native constabulary," while inferior in rank to their Japanese supervisors, were outfitted in white uniforms (not unlike their superiors in the colonial administration), were provided with three months' training in the Japanese language and police methods, and were paid a generous income of 25–30 yen (US$12.00–15.00). Recruits were males under the age of 40 who were in good health and had completed at least five years of primary school.

Under Japanese rule, there seems to have been little corruption of police, despite their relative isolation at the fringes of Empire. However, police treatment of locals was often severe and brutal, inspiring much fear and dislike. During World War II, many police were ordered to resign and take up jobs considered more vital to the war effort.

Under the American administration, the local police force remained an avenue to attain prestige. The contemporary Island constabulary was first organized in 1947. Police were drilled and inspected regularly after an initial six-week training period conducted by a non-commissioned military officer. The uniform was khaki shorts and shirts, with bluish helmets. A chevron appeared on the shoulder, and the name of the unit was stenciled on the shirt. Initially, the police were armed with salvaged Japanese weaponry. Initially, police during the U.S. administration occupied a ceremonial position, as crime rates were low during the postwar period. The few problems that did arise were effectively handled by traditional authorities.

Organizational Description and Functions

FSM has national and state-level police and prosecutors, each branch overseen by a national or state Minister of Justice. The national government has a small national police force reporting to the Department of Justice. All four states have a state police agency, which carries out most public order functions and is supervised by a Division/Bureau of

Public Safety, divided into patrol, detective, corrections, traffic, and fire divisions. The structure and organization of these policing agencies are consistent between states. Conflict between national and state police has been known to occur. For example, during 2002 when national police were sent to Chuuk to enforce a search warrant on a public official, Chuuk state police physically interfered with the execution of the warrant.

The President of FSM is the highest law enforcement official in the nation. The Attorney General of FSM is the President's chief law enforcement officer. The Attorney General is nominated by the President and is ratified by Congress. The Attorney General is assisted by seven assistant Attorneys General, two of whom are responsible for civil and criminal litigation. The remaining assistants are responsible for legislation, international treaties, and other documents. The Attorney General also oversees the Department of Security and Investigation (DSI). The DSI is the national police force, responsible for protection of national property, officials, and national law enforcement. The Attorney General also oversees the Division of Marine Surveillance (DMS), which is responsible for patrolling territorial waters. The Chief of State Police is appointed by a state governor but is accountable to the national Attorney General.

Below the Attorney General is the Director of Public Safety, appointed by state Cabinet. Prior to 1991, the national government was responsible for the prosecution of major crimes. An amendment to the Constitution gave jurisdiction to prosecute most crimes to the states. Because of the relative small size of many island communities and the strong communal bonds that exist among island inhabitants, states occasionally request that the Attorney General's office assume a "special" role in investigating and prosecuting what would normally be defined as a state crime.

There are approximately 30 DSI and 35 DMS officers. Kosrea has 35 officers in its Bureau of Public Safety. Yap has approximately 50 officers in its Division of Public Safety. Chuuk has approximately 150 officers in its Division of Public Safety. There are between 100 and 150 officers in Pohnpei's Department of Public Safety.

Training

While no formal qualifications are essential to becoming a police officer in FSM, agencies prefer to recruit high school graduates. Occasionally, officers have university or college qualifications, and a few have received training through the Federal Bureau of Investigation (FBI) Academy in the United States. Prior to 1992, when a cessation of funding from the U.S. Department of Interior led to its closure, the Micronesian Public Safety Academy trained federal and state officers. The DSI and DMS recruit officers from across the islands, while the states employ their own citizens as law enforcement officers. All law enforcement officers at national and state levels are Micronesian, with the exception of a large number of prosecutors.

Women are involved in policing at the state and national levels. Training in the use and maintenance of electronic equipment is provided through seminars sponsored by the U.S. Department of Interior.

Police Use of Firearms

DSI and state officers are provided with sidearms. A small number of shotguns and rifles are also available to police. The DMS has two 100-foot surveillance boats with mounted machine guns.

Each state is also provided vehicles: Kosrea has five vehicles, four used for patrol and one assigned to the Attorney General; Chuuk has 12 patrol vehicles and two surveillance boats, all equipped with radio communication; Yap has four patrol vehicles, each equipped with radio communication. A few states are equipped with traffic radar equipment; however, it is poorly maintained.

Complaints and Discipline

Police may use only "reasonable" force when making an arrest. In order to stop/apprehend a suspect, reasonable suspicion must be established; probable cause is required for arrests. Warrants are required, but are rarely sought because of the possible disruption they may pose to community cooperation and harmony. As such, police mostly dispose of situations informally, with strong cultural and community structures increasing the likelihood of immediate disposition. Similarly, while warrants are required for searches, they are rarely sought. There have been instances in which traditional or political loyalties have resulted in a failure to enforce warrants of search and arrest. Confessions are allowed with adherence to strict procedures, which, among other things, allow the accused a right to counsel when subjected to custodial interrogation.

While the police forces are generally considered to be relatively free of corruption, some levels of police have displayed a lack of professionalism and competency. There have also been occasional reports of physical abuse carried out by police. In terms of managing unlawful police conduct, some police departments have an internal affairs division. Alternately, complaints may be directed to an offending officer's supervisor, the Attorney General. Civil remedies are also available. Complaints against police can be ignored and are seldom dealt with expeditiously. Despite this, there have been instances in which complaints of police mistreatment have resulted in victim compensation and the dismissal of the officers involved. Traditional loyalties have also resulted in a failure to adequately police complaints against relatives of police officers.

The small size of some forces and the lack of a centralized approach to training have made it difficult to establish an *espirit de* corps evident in a disciplined police service. In Chuuck state, there have been reports of police favoritism in the recruitment processes, particularly towards family members. This has led to the police force being oversized and underqualified.

International Cooperation

Irregular air surveillance is provided by Australia and New Zealand in coordination with DMS. The DSI has four radio-equipped vehicles.

Police Education, Research, and Publications

This information is nonexistent and/or unavailable.

JOHN SCOTT

Bibliography

Bureau of Democracy, Human Rights, and Labor. *Micronesia, Federated States of,* Country Reports on Human Rights Practices, US Department of State, www.state.gov/g/drl/rls/hrrpt/2002/18254.htm 2003.
Federated States of Micronesia, The Division of Statistics. www.spc.int/prism/country/fm/stats/Statistics/Social/Crime/Crime.htm, 2004.
Government of the Federated States of Micronesia. *Legal Information System of the Federated States of Micronesia.* www.fsmlaw.org/, 2002.
Hall, D. E. "Federated States of Micronesia." *World Factbook of Criminal Justice Systems.* US Department of Justice, Office of Justice Programs. www.ojp.usdoj.gov/bjs/pub/ascii/wfbcjfsm.txt, 1993.
Hezel, F. X. *Strangers in Their Own Land: A Century of Colonial Rule in the Caroline and Marshall Islands.* Honolulu, University of Hawaii Press, 1995.
Larmour, P., and M. Barcham. *Transparency International Country Study Report: Federated States of Micronesia.* Asia Pacific School of Economics and Government, Australian National University, Canberra, 2004.

MOLDOVA

Background Material

The Republic of Moldova is located in the south-central part of the European continent, bordered on the west by Romania, and on the northeast and south by Ukraine. The total surface is 33,845 sq km.

According to data available in July 2004, there are 4,446,455 inhabitants. The population is composed of the following ethnic groups: Moldovan (64.5%); Ukrainian (13.8%); Russian (13%); Bulgarian (2%); Jewish (1.5%); Gagauz and others (5.2%).

Moldova's major cities are: Chişinău, the capital, with a population exceeding 850,000 inhabitants; Tiraspol, population 184,000; Balţi, population 162,000; and Bender, population 132,000.

The main religion is Eastern Orthodoxy, which is practiced by 98% of the population. Small minorities also adhere to Judaism, the Christian Baptist faith, and others.

Moldavian is the state language. Russian, Ukrainian, Bulgarian, and Gagauz (a Turkish dialect), are all spoken.

The GDP per inhabitant is US$420. Moldova is an agrarian-industrial country. About 50.8% of the country's active population work in agriculture. The main agricultural crops are: cereals, sugar beet, sunflower, tobacco, vine, vegetables, and fruits. Food production represents about 60% of export trade.

Industry is focused mainly on the processing of crops; other industries include: textile, chemistry, wood processing, and car and machinery manufacturing. Heavy industry, whose market is mainly by Russia (cement factories and metallurgy), is focused in Transnistria, and it is dependent on raw materials. The main focus of industry is the processing of food products (especially wine and cigarette production, tobacco, and agricultural products). The country benefits from the limited raw resources of black coal, oil, and metals for the construction industry.

Contextual Features

Moldova's government is a parliamentary Republic.

The nation declared its independence on August 27, 1991. This day was declared National Independence Day. On July 29, the Constitution was adopted. According to the Constitution, the President is the Chief of the State.

The Parliament is the supreme representative body and the only State legislative authority. The right of legislative initiative belongs to the deputies, to the Moldova Republic President (except the initiative of changing the Constitution), and the Government. Accordingly, the Deputies and the President submit law projects and legislative proposals, and the Government presents law projects.

The Magistrates Superior Council, consisting of 11 magistrates with a five-year mandate, ensures the appointments, movements, promotions, and sanctions of the judges. The Council nominates the Ministry of Justice, the Supreme Court Chief Justice, the Appeals Court President, the Economic Court President, and the General Prosecutor. Three of the members are elected, through secret vote, by the United Colleges of Supreme Court; three are elected by Parliament from a group of university professors. The courts operate in districts set up by the Parliament according to the proposal of Magistrates Superior Council.

According to the statistics presented by the police (Ministry of Internal Affairs, www.mai.md), the main crimes that take place in Moldova Republic are larcenies (almost 35% from both private and public properties), followed by robberies, armed robbery, extortions, con jobs, frauds, narcotics crimes, and sexual crimes.

The court rules on all cases regarding civil, administrative, and criminal-judicial relations, as well as other cases for which the law does not mention another judging body. By implementing justice, the courts protect the estate and constitutional order of Moldova.

The local courts handle all those causes regarding crimes mentioned in the special part of the Penal Code, unless they are supposed, according to the law, to be judged by other courts. The military courts judge those cases that involve soldiers, sergeants, or officers of the National Army; members of the Carabineers Troops from the Internal Affairs Ministry, Exceptional Situations Departments, or the Information and Security Service; the members of the Border Police, the State Protection and Guarding Service, or the correction staff; and those who are in the military service.

The appeals courts are concerned with cases regarding crimes against peace and humanity, war crimes, crimes against public order and security, and crimes against public authorities and state security. Also, these courts hear appeals of decisions established at local courts, including military courts. Claimants can also seek recourse against the court's decisions that by law cannot be appealed. Appeals courts also resolve issues related to conflicts over court jurisdiction. In addition, they review cases as required by law.

The Supreme Court tries cases relating to crimes committed by the Moldova Republic President, and also acts as an appeals court regarding decisions made by the appeals court. This court asks the Constitutional Court to determine issues regarding the constitutionality of judges' rulings, including the uniform implementation of the judicial process.

Police Profile

Background

In Moldova, the police are part of the Internal Affairs Ministry. The police are divided into the following structural departments:

- Operative Services Department (includes the Organized Crime, Criminal Police, Transbordering & Informational Crimes, and Special Missions units);
- Public Order Department (includes the Public Order Police General Unit, Court Police Unit, Illegal Migration Office, Minors Placement General Center, and the Traffic Police Unit);
- Penal Surveillance Department;
- State Guard General Department;
- Transport Police Department;
- Technical Forensic Department;
- Information & Operative Statistics Department;
- K-nine Unit;
- "Stephen the Great" Police Academy;
- "Thunder" SWAT Brigade;
- Police Commissariats;
- "Shield" Patrol & Sentinel Division.

Organizational Structure

Moldova's police are divided into State Police and Municipal Police. The State Police operate throughout the country, while the Municipal Police are restricted to their respective administrative units.

Based on the proposal of the Ministry of Internal Affairs (MIA), the government approves the structure and the organization of the State Police, while for the Municipal Police, these decisions are made by the local authorities (the Ministry of Internal Affairs at the request of the District Police Commissioner, the Head of the Internal Affairs Direction, and the Commissioner of Kishinev Municipal Police). The State Police are subordinate to the Ministry of Internal Affairs, while the Municipal Police are subordinate also to the local authorities.

The Ministry's order issued on March 4, 2004 established the following ranks in the Moldova Republic Police: Police General-Colonel, Police General-Lieutenant, Police General-Major, Division General, Police Colonel, Police Lieutenant-Colonel, Police Major, Police Captain, Police Lieutenant-Major, Police Lieutenant, Police Adjunct Plutonier, Police Major Plutonier, Police Plutonier, and Police Major Sergeant.

Citizens over the age of 18 can be members of the police force. When the person enrolls, he/she has to be sworn in. Also, the person will be subjected to various compulsory tests, according to law.

Appointment to certain jobs in different police services, units, or departments can be determined by competition or through contract signing, as established by the Ministry of the Internal Affairs. Employment, transfer, and dismissal from police forces are done according to police law, in accordance with the Labor Code and other applicable laws.

Those who hold a rank in the police force are obliged to complete courses at educational institutions overseen by the Ministry of Internal Affairs.

The activities of the criminal investigation system are important in ensuring the legality and order of law, the respect of civil rights, effective crime fighting, and protection of the State's interests.

The criminal investigation branch of police activity was created in July 2003, and continued the activity of the Preliminary Investigation Service, which was founded in 1963.

Currently, investigation bodies are a police subunit system established according to the Penal Procedure Code, the Government's Decision in regard to the organizational structure, and Internal Affairs Ministry Regulation.

In the Ministry of Internal Affairs, the penal investigation bodies are represented by the Penal Investigation Department, the Penal Investigation Unit of the Fighting Against Organized Crime Direction within the Operative Security Department, the Penal Investigation Unit of the Internal Affairs Direction–Administrative Territorial Unit, Gagauz Yri, the penal Investigation Unit of the Transport Police Direction, the penal investigation unit of the

Police General Commissariat of Kishinev, penal investigation units of the district, regional, municipal commissariats, and the penal investigation bureaus of the transport police commissariats.

The "Thunder" SWAT Brigade was established on December 1, 1991 as a unit within the Ministry of Internal Affairs, located in Kishinev, based on the proposal submitted to the Government by the Ministry of Internal Affairs.

This subdivision is the special intervention unit, consisting of three special interventions and actions branches: a subdivision for counterattacking terrorism and criminal acts, a commanding and technical service subdivision, and a subdivision that directs all subordinating services.

Functions

The Moldova Republic Police is an armed body, part of the Ministry of Internal Affairs, whose role is to protect citizens' life, health, and civil liberties, and to protect society's and the State's interests from criminal attempts and other illegitimate attacks.

The strengths of the Moldova Republic Police are represented by its fight against organized crime, according to the *Fighting Against Organized* Crime General Direction. The priorities of the Direction are focused on the following issues:

- Fighting organized crime and corruption;
- Counterattacking human trafficking;
- Fighting drug use and trafficking;
- Cooperating with civil society and community police.

Based on the way the units are organized, the criminal investigation officers have to actively work with the police forces in order to prevent criminality, in the following ways:

a. By performing qualitative, timely inquiries about the crimes in their area of responsibility; and legally charging all the guilty persons;
b. By adopting adequate measures in order to restore the material damages caused to the owner as result of the crimes;
c. By, during the criminal investigation process, establishing the causes and circumstances of the crimes; and by developing and employing crime-prevention measures.

Training

Police employees are trained in the specialized educational institutions overseen by the Ministry of Internal Affairs, and in civil education institutions with majors corresponding to the services within the Moldova Republic Police. The education, training, and improving of their professional level can be done also, as it is specified in the contract with other states' educational institutions.

"Stephen the Great" Academy is the only higher education institution belonging to the Ministry of Internal Affairs. It ensures the instruction, education, and further training of the specialists from all the subdivisions of the Ministry of Internal Affairs. Also, the Academy provides scientific and methodological support for the Ministry's structures.

The Academy was founded through the Government's Decision no. 276 of August 17, 1990, and also operates based on the Education Law, Police Forces Law, and on the Academy Statute approved through the order of Ministry of Internal Affairs no. 65 on March 29, 1999.

The structure of the Police Academy includes the Law School, which awards graduates a License Degree in Law Sciences; "Dimitrie Cantemir" Police College, whose graduate cadets receive a special Medium Level Degree; and "St. George" Cadets High School, whose graduates receive a high school diploma.

There is also a Scientific Research Center, which provides scientific and methodological support to all Ministry of Internal Affairs (MIA) units; and the Perfecting Staff Center, which trains and instructs specialists from all MIA units on a rotating basis.

Police Use of Firearms

Police employees have the right to possess, to carry permanently, and to use weaponry. The weapon can be used only as an extreme measure by the police employees in the following circumstances:

- In order to protect citizens or for self-protection against attacks that are a real danger for their life or health, and also in order to prevent their capture through usage of the weapon;
- In order to reject a group attack or an armed attack on police forces, on other persons on duty or whose duty is to maintain the public order and to fight crime, as well as to reject attacks of any nature that endanger their life or health;
- To free hostages, even if their life or health is in danger;
- In order to rebuff group attacks or armed attack on important buildings that are guarded, to reject attacks on civilians' living quarters and household quarters, on the public authorities and civil organizations headquarters, on enterprises, institutions, and organiza-

tions, if there is a real danger for the life or health of the persons within, and to reject attacks on military personnel and police forces on duty;
- In order to restrain a person resisting the army, or a person who is surprised while committing a serious crime, or in order to restrain a delinquent who escapes from arrest or an armed person who refuses to obey the legal request of handing over a gun, when it is impossible to break the delinquent's resistance or to restrain the person through other ways and manners.

The weapon can be used without warning in case of surprise attack, or attack by usage of war techniques, of transport means, of flying devices, river ships, in case of hostage releasing, or escaping from arrest with the support of the gun, or by usage of transport means, as well as during the escaping from transport means while driving.

The weapon is not to be used against women, minors, and elderly, or against physically disabled people, except in cases when they have committed an armed attack, or are threatening the life and health of people. In these circumstances, the weapon can only be used by a police officer if these attacks cannot be rejected through other means. In any circumstances in which the gun is used, the police employee has the duty to adopt all the possible measures that will ensure the security of the citizens, and to do everything possible to ensure that the damages caused to their health, honor, dignity, and assets will be as small as possible, and to provide urgent medical assistance to the victims.

Complaints and Discipline

Police officers are held responsible for questionable behavior or illegal actions according to the legislation and the Internal Affairs Body Disciplinary Statute, approved by the Government.

If there is no other way, specified by legislation, to resolve the matter, the citizens' complaints about the police officer's actions that affected the liberties, rights, and legitimate interests of the citizens will be examined and resolved by the manager of the unit where the officer works. If the citizen is not satisfied by the adopted decision, he/she has the right to pursue the resolution of the matter in court.

The police officers preserve discipline by obeying the regulations established through the current laws, and by obeying the Oath, the statutes, regulations, and orders adopted by the Ministry of Internal Affairs.

Discipline in the internal affairs bodies is preserved through:

- The forming and development of high moral and professional qualities, of a hard-working attitude towards the fulfillment of job duties in police officers;
- Maintaining the regulating order;
- Ensuring the strict following of laws, statutes, regulations, instructions, and orders provisions;
- The constraint exercised by bosses towards their subordinates, just application of conviction and constraint measures, and a subtle combination of care and esteem towards subordinates;
- Personal example provided by bosses and superiors.

The following disciplinary sanctions can be applied to the police forces:

- Remark;
- Scorning/warning;
- Severe scorning/warning;
- Reduction in qualification rank;
- Demotion in position;
- Downgrade in special rank by one level;
- Notification of the partial adaptation to the position;
- Dismissal from the internal affairs bodies.

In the education institutions belonging to the Ministry of Internal Affairs, besides the sanctions mentioned above, the following disciplinary actions are applied to the cadets:

- suspension of free time for a period of 30 days;
- nomination in the services earlier – up to five services (with the exception of guarding service);
- expulsion from the institution.

All police officers who study at the "Dimitrie Cantemir" Police College are enrolled in "Stephen the Great" Police Academy. Continued professional training takes place at the Perfection Center within the Police Academy, which has on the curriculum the subject "The Juridical Protection of Human Rights in the Activity of Police Forces." With the support of some NGOs and the UNDP, some courses have been developed by active police officers at the Ministry of Internal Affairs.

The Internal Security unit investigates complaints relating to a breach of human rights. This unit is a subdivision of the main body of the Ministry of Internal Affairs, and it is directly subordinated to the Minister of Internal Affairs. The unit was established in 1997, and its main functions are to prevent, discover, and stop the crimes committed by police officers against the police forces, legislation, work discipline; crimes of failure to protect and ensure citizens' rights and legitimate interests; crimes against the honesty and dignity of police officers and citizens.

Terrorism

The Division of Counterattacking Terrorism and Criminal Acts is part of the "Thunder" SWAT Brigade. This unit is a special intervention unit, and it acts through special methods and procedures throughout all of Moldova.

The main duties of this unit are:

- Fulfilling missions of counterattacking diversion, terrorist, and criminal acts;
- Intervening through specific procedures and methods in severe felonies, as well as in capturing or neutralizing really dangerous offenders;
- Implementing special activities for releasing hostages and kidnapped persons, and arresting organized criminal groups;
- Performing protection services for personnel from the Ministry of Internal Affairs, or for foreign state police chiefs visiting the Moldova Republic;
- Supporting the other Ministry of Internal Affairs units during highly dangerous police activities and searches;
- Participating in eliminating mass riots, violent acts, and disturbance of public order;
- suppressing mass rebellions in withholding and detention facilities that result in victims or hostages taken from the correction staff;
- Rescuing victims of natural catastrophes, calamities, or in case of special events.

No terrorist acts have occurred in Moldova. No terrorist activities have been observed in Moldova.

Police Education, Research, and Publications

A number of valuable materials on police activities have been published and are listed below:

The State and Police, a monograph paper by Law PhD holder, university professor Ion Guceac, professor at the National University of Moldova; paper published at "Cartier" Publisher, Kishinev, 68, Bucharest St.

Starting from the *Police Officer's Behavior Code,* Mr. Guceac makes certain statements regarding the human way of performing as a police officer: that police in the penal justice system have to be representative, caring, and responsible towards society; there should be a better-elaborated law system that will establish the ethical standards for police officers that should be accepted due to their human character; each police officer in the criminal justice system should have prevention and crime control as his/her goal, and his/her behavior should reflect upon the whole judiciary system; police activity should be subject to public examination. The book is published in Romanian.

- *Policeman Guide,* a reader of legislative papers, in two volumes, co-authors: Cebotar Victor Ion, Magistrate, Reader at the Police Force Law Department at "Stephen the Great" Academy; and Plotean Nicolae, PhD Student, Reader at Real Sciences and Informational Technologies Department – "Stephen the Great" Academy. Book published at "Stephen the Great" Academy Publisher & "Elena – V.I." Publisher, located on MD 2028, Kishinev, 3, Academiei St.

The *Guide* is a reader of legislation regarding the police force's activity, and it is written for the commanding troops from MIA and police commissariats, but also for the faculty and cadets of the MIA education institution. It presents international documents in which Moldova Republic is a part, and national documents, all selected according to the main police activity directions. Totally, the guide consists of 107 legislative documents, out of which 16 are international papers. The book is published in Romanian.

- *State Administration Problems*, a textbook in two volumes, co-authors: Law PhD holder, university professor Victor Gutuleac, President of "Stephen the Great" Academy between 1997 and 2001, retired Police Colonel; and Balmus Victor, Law PhD holder, superior scientific researcher in the State and Law Section at the Philosophy, Sociology and Law Institute belonging to Moldova Science Academy.

The book focuses on the management of internal affairs activities—an independent and specific object in state administration. The goal of this work is to provide theoretical arguments and practical recommendations in order to optimize the competence and the structure of the public security bodies. The book is published in Romanian.

- *Interpol: History and Present*, a monograph paper, co-authors: Radomir Garlea, Magistrate, Reader at the Public Law Department; and Alic Clefos, Reader at Police Force Law Department, both at the "Stephen the Great" Academy. Published at the "Stephen the Great" Academy Publisher and "Elena – V. I." Publisher, located on MD 2028, Kishinev, 3, Academiei St.

The books presents a clear image regarding the organizing and operating services and of the main activities of Interpol and the Moldova Republic National Central Interpol Bureau. Book published in Romanian.

- *Terrorism and Counterterrorism*, a monograph paper; co-authors: Oleg Balan, Associate Professor, Law PhD holder, Director at the Public Administration Department within the Public Administration Academy belonging to the Moldova Republic Presidency; and Grigore Besleaga, retired Police Colonel. Published at the "Stephen the Great" Academy Publisher located at 21, Gh. Asachi St., Kishinev, MD 2028.

The book presents from a research point of view all aspects referring to terrorism: the issues of illegal plane hijacking, hostage taking, prevention and stopping of terrorism acts against persons that benefit from international protection. It also mentions the regulations regarding international terrorism in the legislation from the Moldova Republic and Romania. It also treats the structure of the intervention units and procedures that are designed to prevent and fight aggressive national diversion and terrorist types of activities; as well as the training and usage of units in emergency situations and in antiterrorist activities. The book is published in Romanian.

Different NGOs and Moldova "Soros" Foundation, as well as the Ministry of Internal Affairs are making funds available to sponsor research studies in the police field. MIA is editing the *Order & Law Magazine*, which is the only review in the police field with a scientific and law practical approach. The founders of the magazine are MIA and "Stephen the Great" Academy. It was founded on January 30, 2002. The magazine's address is: Moldova Republic, Kishinev, 75, Stefan cel Mare si Sfant Blvd. E-mail: ordine&lege@mail.md. The magazine is published in Romanian.

OLEG BALAN AND THEODORA ENE (TRANSLATOR)

MONACO

Background Material

The Principality of Monaco is a small state with a territory of just 2,900 acres on the Mediterranean coast between France and Italy. Its history goes back to the Middle Ages when François Grimaldi seized the castle by trickery and occupied the rock of Monaco. In 1861, a treaty between France and Monaco reaffirmed the sovereignty of Monaco already recognized on several occasions by the kings of France. In 1911, the first constitution was promulgated, and in 1918 a treaty of protective friendship between France and Monaco was signed. In 1993, Monaco became a member of the United Nations.

Monaco has 32,000 inhabitants, including 6,000 nationals (the non-nationals come mainly from France, Italy, United Kingdom, Switzerland, Belgium, and the United States). Monegasque nationality is recognized under very restrictive conditions. The official language is French, but Italian is also spoken. The Roman Catholic church is the state religion. From an economic and financial point of view, Monaco has become a dynamic place; gross national product (GNP) per capita was US$27,198 in 2002. The economy is based on revenues coming directly from industry, trade, and tourism.

Contextual Features

Monaco is a sovereign state, a hereditary and constitutional monarchy, within the framework of the general principles of international law and particular conventions with France. The Prince represents the Principality in matters of foreign policy. The government is headed by the Minister of State, who directs the executive services, including the police force, and chairs the Government Council. The Minister of State and the Government Counsellors are responsible to the Prince for the administration of the Principality. The legislative power is shared by the Prince, who initiates laws, and the National Council, which is elected by popular vote and decides on the initiatives. The Directorate of Judicial Services, organized in 1918 separately from the administrative authority, has an important role to ensure the proper administration of justice.

Monaco is not a member of the European Union (EU) but is integrated into many European policies. For example, Monaco adopted the Euro currency and is a de-facto part of the EU Schengen territory as regards immigration. It conducts significant diplomatic activity everywhere in the world.

The Constitution affirms that the Monegasques are equal before the law and guarantees the independence of judges. The legal system is founded on the principle of "delegated justice." The judicial power belongs to the Prince, who delegates its full exercise to the courts. The constitution states that individual freedom and safety are guaranteed and that no one can be made prisoner except in the cases envisaged by the law. The criminal laws ensure the respect of the rights of the person and cannot have retroactive effect. The principle of the presumption of innocence is respected. The Monegasque constitution guarantees many political and social rights. Moreover, any legislative or legal text as well as administrative decision infringing on fundamental rights and liberties of the person may be subject of an appeal to the Supreme Court, which may reverse such a decision.

Monaco encounters problems of small and average delinquency (robberies, scooter and vehicle thefts, etc.) often imported from nearby towns. The richness of the principality and its offer of leisure activities (casinos, restaurants, cultural events, and sports) attract large numbers of people, requiring the police force to remain particularly vigilant. Money laundering is also a concern for Monaco, which hosts many banking and financial institutions.

The number of offenses varies between 1,000 and 1,500 per annum, and the crime volume per 100,000 inhabitants between 3,336 and 4,396. The rate of homicides is low (between zero and one murder per year since 1997).

The hierarchy of criminal justice courts is established by the law on the organization of the judiciary of 15 July 1965.

The "*Juge de police*" judges alone and treats the least serious offenses ("*contraventions*" punished by very short imprisonment or by payment of a fine).

The Court of First Instance is a collegial panel of judges that rules in cases of more serious offences (so-called "*délits*") and those committed by minors (less than 18 years old). It also rules over appeals filed against decisions of the "*juge de police*." The examining magistrate ("*Juge d'instruction*"), whose role it is to gather and examine evidence, is attached to this body.

The Court of Appeal ("*Cour d'appel*") rules on appeals against the judgments delivered by the Court of First Instance by virtue of the principle of the double degree of jurisdiction. The Criminal Court ("*Tribunal criminel*") is authorized to rule over the most serious offenses, so-called "*crimes*." The maximum penalty is the life sentence. Composed of professional magistrates and people from civil society, the Criminal Court's decisions cannot be challenged. Nevertheless, its decisions can be contested before the Court of Revision ("*Cour de revision*"), which can review the definitive decision adopted by all the courts under legal aspects but does not constitute a third level of jurisdiction. It also rules on the requests for reopening of proceedings.

The Office of the Public Prosecutor ("*Ministère public*") is in charge of the preservation of law and order, of investigating and of prosecuting offenses, and of ensuring the implementation of laws and decisions of the courts. Placed under the authority of the "Directorate of Judicial Services," it is represented at all the courts. It constitutes the "*Parquet general*," whose head, the General Attorney, is assisted by Deputies.

The Judge of Guardianship ("*Juge des tutelles*") is assigned to rule on family questions and the protection of minors. In penal matters, the judge plays an essential role in the rehabilitation of delinquent minors, according to the special legal system instituted in 1963.

No one may be subject to cruel, inhuman, or degrading treatment, and the death penalty was abolished in 1962. Forms of punishment are fines, confiscation, expulsion from the territory, and imprisonment. The Judge of Penal Implementation ("*Juge d'application des peines*") follows the execution of judgments. Monaco has only one prison with capacity for 100 prisoners, which is used for provisional detention (before judgment), administrative detention (while waiting for a decision of extradition or expulsion), and for imprisonment up to a maximum of six months. Other penalties of imprisonment are carried out in France as soon as the judgment becomes final.

Police Profile

Background

The police force consists of the "Public Security Force" (*Sûreté publique*), the "*Carabiniers*," and the Municipal Police. The "*Sûreté publique*" finds its origin in 1858 with the first appointment of a police chief assigned to ensure safe funds transfers in the framework of emerging tourism, and to control the movements of people in the casino. The modern Monegasque police force dates back to the sovereign ordinance of 1902 when the Prince, Albert I, decided to replace the "Directorate of the police force" by a Directorate of "*Sûreté publique*." The "*Compagnie des carabiniers*" (created in 1817) ensures the safety of the Prince and his family in the palace and, occasionally, outside as a guard of honor. The tasks of the Municipal Police force include, in particular, administrative investigations, general surveillance, respect of the temporary occupation of public space, and monitoring of regulated parking.

Organizational Description

Today the "*Sûreté publique*" is a force of approximately 500 police. It has significant equipment (about 30 motor vehicles, 50 two-wheeled vehicles, and 3 high-speed motorboats). It is organized in five divisions.

The Division of Administrative Police consists of five units. The Administrative Investigations section carries out investigations and collects information regarding industrial legislation or relating to the character of people requesting the creation of commercial companies. It serves administrative decisions to the persons concerned (e.g., measures of removal from Monegasque territory). The Office of the Assistants (social service assistants) ensures the legal protection of adults with limited competence, carries out social investigations on minors implicated in criminal activity or at risk, and processes requests for adoption. The Office of Naturalizations handles requests for Monegasque citizenship. The Office of Residence control examines requests for certificates of residence in Monaco (fiscal mutual assistance with France). Lastly, the Section of the Residents delivers the residence permits.

The Division of Administration and Training consists of the sections for human resources, general affairs, and logistics. The human resources section includes the center of recruitment and training, the personnel office, the office of training courses, the office of studies and planning, as well as the sports hall and shooting range.

The Division of Criminal Investigation searches for and identifies offenders, and gathers evidence to present to the legal authorities. It receives complaints and collects, at the request of the princely Government, economic or social information to support decisions by the political or legal authorities. It consists of five brigades and sections. The Public Highway Brigade ensures contact with the public, including receiving complaints and reports. They also assume part of the evening duty and maintaining police presence in public places. Each of its groups is specialized in a particular field, such as "cybercrime," vehicle theft, and art trafficking. The Research and Intervention Brigade includes the anti-drug group, the anti-gang group that fights the Mafia and organized crime, and the anti-crime group for small and average criminality. The Economic Investigations Brigade targets money laundering. The Files Section complies with requests for verification of identity, for example, on the public highway or for labor purposes. The Criminal Records Section accommodates the services of technical and scientific police as well as the "National Interpol Bureau."

The Division of Urban Police covers safety on public highways. It is the best-equipped division in terms of human resources, with more than half of the staff of the *Sûreté publique*. Due to its direct contact with the public, this staff is under particularly close observation by the hierarchy in regard to compliance with rules of discipline. The Order, Employment and Discipline Office coordinates the activities of the division. The Technical and Operational Command Post serves as an interface between all the divisions of the Monegasque police force. It centralizes radio transmissions and video monitoring systems, thus helping to coordinate interventions on the ground.

The units in uniform supervise public places, and patrols and fixed stations are spread throughout the Principality in order to prevent and to intervene in cases of criminal behavior. They take care of parking and traffic control and react to calls for help by citizens. They are also responsible for tasks such as general preservation of order and the search for school drop-outs. The service includes one night and two day shifts.

The Maritime and Airport Police Division was created in 1960; it has the following responsibilities: preservation of law and order in the port, creation of smooth contacts between the users and the administration, control of the maritime border, rescue and help at sea, civil maritime protection, and control of maritime labor. It is also in charge of general safety at heliports.

The Director of the *Sûreté publique* directs the whole of the police services. He acts under the control of the Adviser for the Interior in charge of police questions, general administration, and religious matters. The Police Chiefs (Division Commissioner, Principal Commissioner, Commissioner) are in charge of the management. The senior police officers (Lieutenant, Captain, Commander) are responsible for the command. The uniformed staff members (Police agent, Brigadier) execute orders.

The great majority of magistrates on duty in Monaco are French under the terms of the 1930 Treaty between France and Monaco. This document also reserves the more important jobs related to public safety, law and order, and foreign relations, to detached executives of the French administration. The other police officers are recruited by competition.

Functions

Police staff have numerous administrative functions. In criminal matters, powers are attributed to them by the code of penal procedure (identity check, right of administrative detention of persons for a limited duration, generally with the agreement of a magistrate). However, the main role of the police lies in the development of preventive strategies that include the permanent and visible presence of police staff in public places, identification of suspicious persons, or supervision of night clubs. It uses the powerful technical device of video monitoring; more than 110 cameras have been permanently installed in such public places as elevators, car parks, stations, and streets.

Training

The Director of *Sûreté publique* is a senior official from the senior management of the French National police force. The Police Chiefs are either deployed from the executive level of the French police force or are Monegasques who have completed the courses of the Higher National School of the Police Chiefs in France and have successfully passed the tests of the training course. The other police officers are recruited by way of a selection exam. Requirements for taking the exam include possession of civic rights, good moral standards, physical capability, minimum/maximum age, minimum level of studies. The exams are both written and oral tests. Priority of employment is reserved for Monegasques, but few nationals join the Sûreté publique (only 5% of police officers have Monegasque nationality; the rest are French). The senior police officers are trained in a French police academy. The uniformed staff is trained within the Monegasque center of recruitment and training.

Police Use of Firearms, and Complaints and Discipline

Police staff have the right to carry weapons, but the goal of the Monegasque police is to act from a preventive point of view in order to preserve the positive public image of the principality. Violence committed by a civil servant constitutes an offense under the penal code. There is no independent organization especially created to control police powers and action (such as Amnesty International). For the Monegasque authorities, this absence of structures is explained by the small size of the country and by the very broad jurisdictional control exercised by the Supreme Court.

International Cooperation

Monaco, although not a member of the European Union and related arrangements such as the Schengen and Europol conventions, represents a de-facto part of the EU-Schengen territory. It carries out the Schengen immigration and visa checks at its external borders and participates in the close police cooperation mechanism established for this purpose by the EU-Schengen member countries.

Monaco is a member of Interpol and collaborates closely with the French police forces (provision of data on offenders, cooperation in the management of tunnels, information exchange, data-processing connections and telephone). Monaco was accepted into the Council of Europe in 2004.

Police Education, Research, and Publications

Monegasque laws are published in the *Monegasque Official Journal* and the French law publication *Editions du Juris-Classeur*. A complete collection of the legal texts is available for consultation and copying at the Bibliothèque Louis-Notarie, Monaco. It is possible to find certain elements on the website of Law Library of Congress. Today, there is no specific publication on Monaco's police force. The only data available are delivered by international organizations such as Interpol. It is also possible to find short descriptions on the internet sites of the Principality of Monaco.

BRUNO DOMINGO

Bibliography

Code pénal et code de procédure pénale monégasques. Paris: Editions du Jurisclasseur.
City of Monaco: www.monaco-mairie.mc/.
François, Norbert. *Introduction au droit monégasque* (Introduction to the Law of Monaco). Baden-Baden: Nomos Verlagsgesellschaft, 1998.
Interpol. *International Statistics Series, Monaco.* (www.interpol.int).
Law Library of Congress: www.loc.gov/law/guide/monaco.html.
Monaco government: www.gouv.mc/ (available in English).
Municipal police: www.monaco-mairie.mc/03_services_communaux/admin/police.php.

MONGOLIA

Background Material

Mongolia is located in northern Asia, between China and Russia. The Mongols under Genghis Khan conquered a sizeable Eurasian empire in the thirteenth century. The empire was divided into several states after Khan's death, although these weakened and broke apart in the fourteenth century. The Mongols came under Chinese rule. With Soviet support, Mongolia won its independence in 1921, and a Communist administration took power in 1924.

During the early 1990s, the ex-Communist Mongolian People's Revolutionary Party (MPRP) gradually yielded its monopoly of power to the Democratic Union Coalition (DUC), which defeated the MPRP in a national election in 1996. Since then, parliamentary elections returned the MPRP overwhelmingly to power in 2000 and produced a coalition government in 2004.

The population of Mongolia is 2,751,314 (2004 est.). The population is composed ethnically of Mongol, mostly Khalkha: (94.9%); Turkic, mostly Kazakh: (5%); other, including Chinese and Russian:

(0.1%) (2000). Religions practiced include Buddhist Lamaist (50%); none (40%); Shamanist and Christian (6%); and Muslim (4%) (2004).

Economic activity traditionally has been based on agriculture and breeding of livestock. The GDP per capita is $1,800 (2003 est.).

Mongolia joined the United Nations in October 1961. Mongolia also belongs to the Economic Council for Asia and the Far East, the Interparliamentary Union, the World Peace Council, the International Labour Organization, the World Federation of Trade Unions, the International Telecommunications Union, the Universal Postal Union, the International Association for Mongol Studies, and the International Red Cross.

Contextual Features

Mongolia has a mixed parliamentary/presidential type of government. The country is divided administratively into 21 provinces and 1 municipality.

The legal system combines aspects of the Soviet, German, and U.S. systems of law.

The chief of state is the President, and the head of government is the Prime Minister. The legislative branch is the unicameral State Great Hural, which has 76 seats. Members are elected by popular vote to serve four-year terms. A Cabinet is appointed by the State Great Hural in consultation with the President.

The Supreme Court serves as an appeals court for people's and provincial courts but rarely overturns the verdicts of the lower courts. Judges are nominated by the General Council of Courts and approved by the President.

The first criminal code was adopted on October 21, 1926. It is made up of 227 articles in 31 chapters. That code was replaced on September 23, 1929, by a new criminal code. The 1929 code remained in effect for five years. It was replaced by the 1934 criminal code, which was adopted in two stages in 1934. The 1934 code was in turn replaced on January 17, 1942, by a code adapted to needs during World War II. The 1942 code remained in effect until January 31, 1961, when a new code was adopted. This code is still in use.

Mongolia's first Constitution, adopted on November 26, 1924, established a national structure based on the Soviet system. The 1924 Constitution was replaced by the 1940 Constitution, closely modeled on the 1936 Soviet Constitution. The 1940 Constitution was replaced by the Constitution adopted on July 6, 1960.

According to the Constitution, the courts must: uphold the Constitution, administer justice according to the law, protect the state, protect state property, and protect citizens' property.

The court system consists of the Supreme Court, *aymag* courts, city courts, and special courts. Except in special cases, all cases are tried by permanent judges in the presence of assessors. The assessors are elected, and they sit on the bench with the judge, hearing evidence, questioning the prosecutor, defendant, and witnesses, and they participate in sentencing.

According to the Constitution, the Supreme Court is the highest judicial body. The Supreme Court oversees the lower courts. It shapes national legal policies.

Mongolia maintains both prison camps and correctional or educational colonies There are detention camps for minor offenders that focus on rehabiliation via labor, which includes tasks such as street cleaning and building repair. Local prisons are availble for brief detentions of intoxicated persons and those awaiting indictment.

Police Profile

Organizational Description

The Ministry of Public Security is the top security and policing body in the government. The central Militia Office is directly under it in the hierarchy, followed by: the police departments, called militia departments; the State Security Administration; the Fire Prevention Administration; the Border and Internal Troops Administration; and the offices handling correctional organizations.

The entire national policing structure is commonly referred to as the militia. The militia is responsible for the registration and supervision of the internal passports that all citizens aged 16 and older are required to carry. A passport is necessary for travel within the country, and persons wishing to travel first have to obtain permission from the militia. After arriving at their destination, they have to register with the militia.

The militia must also carry out criminal investigation duties. Militia units, together with local assemblies, administer compulsory labor sentences of convicted criminals. Militiamen, as well as the executive committees of local governments, have the authority to put intoxicated persons into detention houses for 24 hours or less and to fine them.

Each militia office had a motor vehicle inspection bureau. Each of these bureaus has detectives who focus on investigating vehicular accidents. Militia members direct motor traffic, and they are also stationed along the railroads.

The Ministry of Public Security also oversees the Fire Prevention Administration and the State Security Administration. The Fire Prevention Administration carries out fire-prevention and firefighting duties.

The State Security Administration is a counter-intelligence organization. It focuses on combating espionage and sabotage activities.

The Border and Internal Troops Administration is in charge of 15,000 troops responsible for border patrol, for guard duties, and for immigration control. Border defense troops are equipped with fixed-wing aircraft, helicopters, tanks, motor vehicles and motor-cycles, radio communications equipment, engineering equipment, and automatic weapons.

Various organizations not associated with the government assist the militia. Public police brigades have been organized to help the militia fight crime. Block, district, and parents' committees in schools have also been organized to help fight crime. There are also administrative committees, special police courts, and anticrime commissions in the larger cities and towns.

The Crime Fighting and Crime Prevention Councils are party organizations operating without paid staff. These councils are advisory only; that is, they cannot replace or usurp law enforcement or judicial bodies. They discuss crime problems and how best to combat them.

Bibliography

"Mongolia." *CIA World Fact Book*. www.cia.gov/cia/pub lications/factbook/.

"Mongolia." *Library of Congress Country Studies*. http://lcweb2.loc.gov/frd/cs/.

MONTENEGRO

Background Material

Montenegro currently exists in a loose federation with Serbia. The republics plan to hold a referendum on whether to move to full independence in 2006. The republics operate separate police systems.

Montenegro is situated in the western part of southeast Europe, opening onto the Adriatic Sea with 277 km of shoreline. It covers an area of 13,812 sq km. According to the last census (2001), Montenegro has a population of 648,000, or 47 inhabitants per sq km. The population of Montenegro consists of Montenegrins: 380,484 (61.84%); Serbs: 57,176 (9.29%); Muslims: 89,932 (14.62%); Albanians: 40,880 (6.64%); Yugoslavs: 25,854 (4.20%); Croats: 6,249 (1.02%); Macedonians: 860 (0.14%); Slovenes: 407 (0.07%); and others: 13,425 (2.18%). However, the demographic structure of Montenegro has changed over the past decade due to migrations caused by wars.

The official language in Montenegro is Serbian in its so-called *ijekavski* dialect. Both the Cyrilic and Latin alphabets are used. In municipalities where the majority or a significant portion of the population consists of national minorities and ethnic groups, their respective langages and alphabets are also in official use.

There are two religions in Montenegro: Islam and Christianity, with believers oganized in three religious groups: Orthodox Christian, Roman Catholic, and Islamic. Most citizens are Otrthodox Christians.

The gross national product per capita amounted to US$1400 in 2001. The economy of Montenegro, particularly industry, is currently in its initial stage of development, and it is based on its own raw material resources (production of aluminum, construction materials, black metallurgy). The freedom of economy and enterprise is limited by environmental protection. Cattle breeding is the main branch of agriculture in Montenegro. The geographic location, configuration of the soil, the proximity of the sea on one hand and high mountains, cut by river valleys, on the other, as well as the value of cultural and historic monuments make the territory of Montenegro exceptionally attractive for the development of tourism.

Contextual Features

By order of the Constitution, Montenegro is a parliamentary democracy. The head of state is the President of the Republic, elected for a single five-year term. Legislative power is bestowed on the legislature of Montenegro, consisting of 75 members. The government consists of the Prime Minister and 18 Ministers, and it is responsible to the legislature. The judicial power in criminal, civil, and other cases is exercised by 15 courts of general jurisdiction, located in the larger municipalities. There are two higher-level courts: an Appellate Court and the Supreme Court of Montenegro.

There is also an Administrative Court, as well as a Court of Commerce.

The independent Public Prosecutor performs prosecution duties in the entire territory of the Republic, and prosecutors and senior prosecutors act on his behalf before the respective courts. Both judicial and prosecuting roles are provided for by legislation (*Law on Courts* and *Law on Public Prosecutor*).

Criminal sentences are carried out by prisons and institutions for implementation of criminal sanctions. The Ministry of Justice passes regulations regarding the control and legal functioning of these institutions. The Ministry of Justice determines which institutions are in charge of data and statistics related to crime (e.g., prosecutor and court statistics, police statistics).

Since the end of war in the former Yugoslavia, a slight decline in crime rates has occurred. Nevertheless, there has actually been an increase in certain types of crimes, such as illegal manufacturing and trafficking in drugs, especially among the young.

There were 8,934 criminal offenses in Montenegro in 2002. As compared to the previous year, this was a 5.5% overall increase. This slight increase reflects a 1.1% increase in general crimes and a 20% increase in commercial crime.

Police Profile

Background

Montenegro has made great advances toward modernizing legal and administrative systems. The Montenegrin police force was formed and developed as a mainstay of the autocratic governments that once ruled the Montenegrin state. At the same time, police institutions created in the first half of the nineteenth century had an executive power that reached across the divisions of individual tribes. This undoubtedly contributed to increased awareness of the historical, state, political, and administrative unity of the Montenegrin territory, laying the foundation of the contemporary Montenegrin state.

After World War II, the Montenegrin police were absorbed into the greater Yugoslav federation. Today, the police of Montenegro are organized as the Public Security Service, within the Ministry of the Interior of the Republic of Montenegro. This Ministry also includes: the State Security Service; the Service for Administrative, Technical and Common Tasks; and the Service for Legal and General Tasks.

Demographics

Members of the police are recruited from among Montenegrins, Muslims, Serbs, Albanians, and other ethnic groups living in the territory of Montenegro. Managerial positions in the police are given to members of minority ethnic groups in the communities where their respective ethnic groups are prevalent, including: Croats (0.3%), Albanians (1.5%), Serbs (2.5%), and Moslems (5.63%). The remaining positions are held by Montenegrins.

During previous periods of war and instability, the Montenegrin police mainly performed functions related to defense, requiring an increased number of officers. Following the democratic reforms in Serbia of October 5, 2000, the process of reducing the number of police personnel of Montenegro began; this was also influenced directly by the modernization and professionalization of the police. The ratio of police officers to citizens is 1:115.

Ninety percent of police employees have a secondary education; 4% have college degrees, and 6% have university degrees.

Women compose 2.62% of the entire police force.

The police can employ a person who has had no criminal record and against whom no criminal proceedings have been instituted. A novice police officer must have at least a secondary education, must possess the required mental and physical abilities, and must be younger than 25. Depending on the nature of the tasks, certain work experience or specialized training may be required.

Organizational Description

The Public Security Service in the Ministry consists of the Criminal Police Department (non-uniformed) and the Police Department, which are organized on the local level in centres and departments of security.

The Department of Criminal Police includes the Centre for Forensics, the Centre for Suppressing Drug-Related Crime, the Department for Border and Aliens, and some special units. Departments at the Ministerial level supervise, coordinate, and guide the work of local police forces, which includes supervision (administrative and inspectoral), immediate assistance; and, in complex security situations, managing the actions of police. Within the existing departments (crime investigation and uniformed police), special teams have been formed for combating specific forms of organized crime (e.g., drugs, trafficking in human beings, extortion, kidnapping).

A draft bill on police that is in the process of being passed in the legislature envisions a new organizational structure of the Ministry of the Interior. It proposes the establishment of the General Management of the Police, headed by the General Manager. Within the General Department of the Police, sub-departments for performing specific police tasks are to be established (criminality, road traffic safety, border work). At the local level, police departments are to be organized (as well as police stations, departments of police, and inspectorates) for specific lines of duty.

Functions

Within the bounds of statutory powers and activities of the Ministry of the Interior, legislation establishes the following police tasks: protection of the security of citizens and their constitutional freedoms and rights; protection of property; prevention of perpetration of criminal acts; resolving criminal cases and violations; searching for the perpetrators of criminal offenses and securing their surrender; keeping public order; ensuring the safety of public meetings and other conventions of citizens; security of VIPs and objects; surveillance and control of road traffic safety; surveillance and control of the state border safety; control of aliens; and other activities provided for by statute and related regulations.

The draft bill on police lists the following powers: gathering intelligence; gathering, processing and using personal data; establishing identity and identification of objects; searching persons; temporary confiscation of objects; searching of premises and objects; securing and investigating crime scenes; searching means of transportation, passengers, and luggage; entering apartments and other premises; temporary limitation of movement in limited spaces; counterterrorist check; access to business books and other documentation; giving warnings and issuing orders; summoning; guarding; arresting; use of force; use of other persons' motor vehicles and telecommunications; protection of victims, witnesses, and other persons; and any other powers that may be granted by statute.

Police Use of Firearms

Only when other means are not sufficient, firearms may be used in the following circumstances: to protect the lives of people; to prevent the escape of a person caught in the perpetration of serious criminal offenses, if there is reasonable cause to believe that the person possesses a firearm and that he may use it; to prevent the escape of an arrested person or a person for whose arrest a warrant has been issued; for self-protection from an imminent attack that endangers the officer's life; and to repel an attack upon an object or a person the officer is supposed to secure.

A new feature of this legislation concerns protection of the victim and the witness, and counterterrorist checks. Gathering, processing, and using personal data are powers that are used exclusively with a view to prevent and resolve criminal offenses and violations, and to arrest their perpetrators.

Legislation concerning firearms is very restrictive with respect to granting permits for buying and owning firearms. Firearms can be granted only to a person who actively enjoys hunting as a member of a huntsmen's association or intends to do so. Permission for acquiring hunting rifles or shotguns can be issued for reasons of self-protection to organizations, enterprises, and institutions that have organized security services; and to a person in need of possessing and carrying such weapons for reasons of protecting privately owned property (flocks, herds, crops).

In 2002, there were 58 reports of illegal possession of firearms, and 337 weapons were confiscated for illegal possession. Authorities also confiscated 775 weapons due to use in perpetrating violence or other criminal offenses.

Complaints and Discipline

When exercising police power, a law enforcement officer shall obey the rules of legality, publicity, and cooperation. In 2002, 136 citizen complaints against police officers were lodged. Of all these complaints, 36 were determined to be legitimate.

Starting from the principle of transparency of work, legislation and related regulations are aimed at adjusting the work of the police to European standards, as a public service of citizens.

The practice of immediate or indirect communication with the public and informing the citizens about police work has been stepped up on all levels, and there are opportunities for citizens to address the police in person or in writing in cases where they believe that the conduct and actions of the police endanger their rights and freedoms.

Measures of disciplinary and material liability can be taken against members of the police. Solutions offered in the draft bill on police are essentially different from the existing ones. They parallel European standards, particularly with respect to the code of conduct of law enforcement officers;

and with respect to the limits on police powers, control, transparency, and use of force.

Terrorism

According to the available data, no organized terrorist groups or activities have been detected in the territory of Montenegro. Despite this, a special preventative counterterrorist unit was formed. Its task is to oppose the activities of terrorist organizations, groups, and individual terrorists.

International Cooperation

Cooperation with international organizations (OSCE, Council of Europe) and associations is evident, not only in the preparation of the law on police, but also in the fields of international police cooperation, internal control, and organized crime, to which end a special organizational unit has been formed within the Ministry of the Interior.

Besides cooperation with and active participation in the work of Interpol, the police of Montenegro have developed numerous other forms of international cooperation, especially with the police agencies of neighboring European countries, concerning security issues and human rights protection.

Police Education, Research, and Publications

Police personnel training and education are based on the basic values of democracy, the rule of law, and the protection of human rights. The High School of Internal Affairs is in charge of basic police training; it also organizes professional courses and seminars. Courses are mainly taught by experts from the police of Montenegro; associates from civil and police educational and scholarly institutions from neighboring countries also participate.

Some of the police staff members are educated at university and college-level institutions of the Ministry of the Interior of Serbia.

Together with OSCE, the International Committee of Red Cross, and other international and NGO's, training aims to meet the developmental needs of the Montenegrin police, especially in the domains of human rights and freedoms, public relations, and education of educators.

In the context of reforming the police and police education in Montenegro, the High School of Internal Affairs is expected to undergo a transformation and become a Police Academy that would provide well-planned, deliberate, complete police training at the basic, additional, expert, and specialist levels.

The leading authors in the scholarly work concerning the police are (in the alphabetic order):

Prof. Budimir Babović, Ph.D.;
Čedo Bogićević, Ph.D., Justice of the High Court of Montenegro;
Husnija Redžepagić, Principal of High School of Internal Affairs;
Mićo Orlandić, Assistant Minister for Public Safety of the Republic of Montenegro MI;
Prof. Milo Babović, Ph.D., Law School Podgorica;
Miodrag Vilotijević, Ph.D., Republic of Montenegro Ministry of Interior;
Mladen Milosavljević, Ph.D., Faculty of Crime Studies in Sarajevo;
Stanka Jelić, Head of Security Centre in Bijelo Polje;
Prof. Vladimir Krivokapić, Ph.D., Police Academy Belgrade.

Research and development programs are not very developed in the police of Montenegro. These are done on a voluntary basis by a number of police members, who are granted assistance in publishing their works.

In the sphere of crime suppression and prevention, there have been projects for suppressing possession of and illegal trafficking in drugs on a national level, combating trafficking in persons at the national level, and the project of preventing motor vehicle thefts at the level of the Ministry of the Interior and Customs.

The first issue of a journal for police, *Perjanik*, was published by the High School of Internal Affairs in 2002. Its address is: The Ministry of the Interior of the Republic of Montenegro, the High School of Internal affairs, 81410 Danilovgrad, e-mail: skolamup@cg.yu.

ZORAN KEKOVIC AND HUSNIJA REDEPAGIC

Bibliography

Bogdanović, Branko: *Razvoj policije u knjaževini i kraljevini Crnoj Gori* (*Development of the Police in the Dukedom of Montenegro*) Istorijski zapisi, godina LXXIII, 2000/3-4.

Crna Gora i Crnogorci (Montenegro and Montenegrins)– DOB, Podgorica, 1999.

Pavićević, Branko: *Stvaranje crnogorske države (The Creation of the Montenegrin State)*, Beograd, 1955.

Pismo Petra II Petrovića od 6/18 decembra 1831 Jeremiju Gagiću (The letter of Petar II Petrovic dtd 6/18 December, 1831 to Jeremije Gagic), Arhiv državnog muzeja u Cetinju.

Policijski pravilnik u knjaževini Crnoj Gori (Police Regulation Book in the Dukedom of Montenegro). K.C. Državna tamparija, Cetinje, 1907.

Živković, Dragoje: *Kancelarijsko poslovanje i arhivska služba u Crnoj Gori (Office Work and Archives in Montenegro)*. GCM V, Cetinje, 1972.

MOROCCO

Background Material

Unlike other North African nations, the Kingdom of Morocco has been largely occupied by one group of people for as long as recorded history can recall. The Berbers, or *Imazighen* (men of the land), settled in the area thousands of years ago and at one time controlled all of the land between Morocco and Egypt. Divided into clans and tribes, they have always jealously guarded their independence. It is this fierce independence that has helped preserve one of Africa's most fascinating cultures.

The early Berbers were unmoved by the colonizing Phoenicians, and even the Romans did little to upset the Berber way of life after the destruction of Carthage in 146 BC. All the same, the Romans ushered in a long period of peace during which many cities were founded, and the Berbers of the coastal plains became city dwellers. Christianity arrived in the third century AD, and again the Berbers asserted their traditional dislike of centralized authority by following Donatus (a Christian sect leader who claimed that the Donatists alone constituted the true church).

Islam burst onto the world stage in the seventh century when the Arab armies swept out of Arabia. Quickly conquering Egypt, the Arabs controlled all of North Africa by the start of the eighth century. By the next century, much of North Africa had fragmented, with the move towards a united Morocco steadily growing. A fundamentalist Berber movement emerged from the chaos caused by the Arab invasion, overrunning Morocco and Muslim Andalucia (in Spain). The Almoravids founded Marrakesh as their capital, but they were soon replaced by the Almohads. Under these new rulers, a professional civil service was set up, and the cities of Fès, Marrakesh, Tlemcen, and Rabat reached the peak of their cultural development. But eventually weakened by Christian defeats in Spain, and paying the price for heavily taxing tribes, the Muslim (or Moorish) rule began to wane. In their place came the Merenids, from the Moroccan hinterland, and the area again blossomed—until the fall of Spain to the Christians, in 1492, unleashed a revolt that dissolved the new dynasty within 100 years.

After a number of short-lived dynasties rose and fell, the Alawite family secured a stranglehold in the 1630s that remains firm to this day. Although it was rarely a smooth ride, this pragmatic dynasty managed to keep Morocco independent for more than three centuries. Enter the European traders in the late nineteenth century, and a long era of colonial renovations. Suddenly France, Spain, and Germany were all keen on hijacking the country for its strategic position and rich trade resources. France won out and occupied virtually the entire country by 1912. Spain clung to a small coastal protectorate, and Tangier was declared an international zone.

Relatively speaking, the first French Resident-General, Marshal Lyautey, respected the Arab culture. He generously resisted the urge to destroy the existing Moroccan towns and instead built French *villes nouvelles* (new towns) alongside them. He made Rabat on the Atlantic coast the new capital and developed the port of Casablanca. The sultan remained, but as little more than a figurehead. Lyautey's successors were not so sensitive. Their efforts to speed French settlement prompted the people of the Rif Mountains, led by the Berber scholar Abd el-Krim, to rise up against both colonial forces. It was only through the combined efforts of 25,000 Spanish-French troops that Abd el-Krim was eventually forced to surrender in 1926. By the 1930s, more than 200,000 French had made Morocco home. World War II saw Allied forces use Morocco as a base from which to drive the Germans out of North Africa.

With the war over, Sultan Mohammed V inspired an independence party, which finally secured Moroccan freedom in 1956. Tangier was reclaimed in the process, but Spain refused to hand over the northern towns of Ceuta and Melilla (to this day they remain Spain's last tenuous claim on Africa). Mohammed V promoted himself to king in 1957 and was succeeded four years later by his son, Hassan II. This popular leader cemented his place in Moroccan hearts and minds by staging the Green March into the Western Sahara, an area formerly held by Spain. With a force of 350,000 volunteers, Hassan's followers overcame the indigenous Sahrawis to claim the mineral-rich region as their own. But by the 1960s it had become clear that the 100,000 or so inhabitants of the "territory" wanted independence. Western Sahara's Popular Front for the Liberation of Saguia al-

Hamra and Rio de Oro (Polisario) did not take kindly to the invasion, and embarked on a long and gruesome war of independence against Morocco. In 1991, the United Nations brokered a ceasefire and more recently decided to "remain seized of the matter." In other words, Western Sahara's official status remains in question, thanks to Morocco's continued muscle flexing. While the Moroccan masses applauded the southern invasion, it left nearby Algeria about as happy as the Western Saharans themselves. Morocco's relations with this particular war-torn neighbor have been poor ever since. In July 1999, King Hassan II, who had served as absolute monarch (despite recent, semi-democratic changes to the constitution) for 38 years, was succeeded by his son, Crown Prince Sidi Mohammed. King Mohammed VI has promised to purge corruption from the government, allow more freedom of the press, and institute democratic reform just as soon as he gets a chance. Approximately 13 of his father's co-workers have indeed been discharged, and Mohammed did pardon a couple of journalists imprisoned for questioning the Prime Minister's policies, although seven newspapers were subsequently shut down after they mistook the King's leniency for true editorial autonomy. Much-anticipated democratic reforms are a rocky proposition in this country still stuck in a feudalist rut, but it looks like the young King may well give it his best shot.

In summary, Morocco's long struggle for independence from France ended in 1956. The internationalized city of Tangier was turned over to the new country that same year. Morocco virtually annexed Western Sahara during the late 1970s, but final resolution on the status of the territory remains unresolved. Gradual political reforms in the 1990s resulted in the establishment of a bicameral legislature in 1997. Parliamentary elections were held for the second time in September 2002, and municipal elections were held in September 2003.

The population of Morocco is 32,209,101 (2004 est.). Ninety-nine per cent of the population is Arab-Berber, and 0.2% is Jewish (0.7% is other). Arabic is the official language, although Berber dialects are spoken, and French is often the language of business, government, and diplomacy. Islam is practiced by 98.7% of the population; 1.1% practice Christianity, and 0.2% practice Judaism.

Morocco faces the problems typical of developing countries: restraining government spending, reducing constraints on private activity and foreign trade, and achieving sustainable economic growth. Despite structural adjustment programs supported by the IMF, World Bank, and the Paris Club, the *dirham* is only fully convertible for current account transactions. Reforms of the financial sector are being contemplated. Droughts depressed activity in the key agricultural sector and contributed to a stagnant economy in 2002. Morocco reported a large foreign exchange influx from the sale of a mobile telephone license and partial privatization of the state-owned telecommunications company and the state tobacco company. Favorable rainfall in 2003 led to a growth of 6%. Formidable long-term challenges include: preparing the economy for freer trade with the Europian Union and the United States. Improving education, and attracting foreign investment to boost living standards and job prospects for Morocco's youth.

The GDP per capita is US$4,000 (2003 est.) Primary industries include phosphate rock mining and processing, food processing, leather goods, textiles, construction, and tourism.

Contextual Features

The Kingdom of Morocco, known locally as Al Mamlakah al Maghribiyah, is a constitutional monarchy. The Capital city is Rabat.

The administrative division of the government is divided into 37 provinces and two *wilayas*: Agadir, Al Hoceima, Azilal, Beni Mellal, Ben Slimane, Boulemane, Casablanca, Chaouen, El Jadida, El Kelaa des Sraghna, Er Rachidia, Essaouira, Fes, Figuig, Guelmim, Ifrane, Kenitra, Khemisset, Khenifra, Khouribga, Laayoune, Larache, Marrakech, Meknes, Nador, Ouarzazate, Oujda, Rabat-Sale, Safi, Settat, Sidi Kacem, Tanger, Tan-Tan, Taounate, Taroudannt, Tata, Taza, Tetouan, and Tiznit. Three additional provinces of Ad Dakhla (Oued Eddahab), Boujdour, and Es Smara, as well as parts of Tan-Tan and Laayoune, fall within Moroccan-claimed Western Sahara.

As part of a 1997 decentralization/regionalization law passed by the legislature, 16 new regions (listed below) were created, although full details and scope of the reorganization are limited: Casablanca, Chaouia-Ourdigha, Doukkala-Abda, Fes-Boulmane, Gharb-Chrarda-Beni Hssen, Guelmim-Es Smara, Laayoune-Boujdour-Sakia El Hamra, Marrakech-Tensift-El Haouz, Meknes-Tafilalet, Oriental, Oued Eddahab-Lagouira, Rabat-Sale-Zemmour-Zaer, Souss-Mas-sa-Draa, Tadla-Azilal, Tangier-Tetouan, and Taza-Al Hoceima Taounate.

On March 2, 1956, the Kingdom of Morocco won its independence from France. The National holiday is known as "Throne Day," which commemorates the accession of King Mohamed VI to the throne on July 30, 1999. The Constitution was formed on March 10,

1972, revised on September 4, 1992, and amended (to create a bicameral legislature) in September 1996.

The legal system is based on Islamic law and on the French and Spanish civil law system; judicial review of legislative acts is conducted in the Constitutional Chamber of the Supreme Court. Suffrage is 18 years of age; it is universal as of January 2003.

The principal branches of Morocco's government are: Executive, Legislative, and Judicial. In the Executive branch, there is the Chief of State (King Mohamed VI, since July 30, 1999). The head of the government is the Prime Minister (Driss Jettou, since October 9, 2002). The Cabinet is composed of a Council of Ministers appointed by the monarch. The monarchy is hereditary, and the Prime Minister is appointed by the monarch following legislative elections.

The Legislative branch is a bicameral Parliament, which consists of an upper house or Chamber of Counselors (270 seats; members elected indirectly by local councils, professional organizations, and labour syndicates for nine-year terms; one-third of the members are renewed every three years), and a lower house or Chamber of Representatives (325 seats; 295 by multi-seat constituencies and 30 from national lists of women; members elected by popular vote for five-year terms). Elections for Chambers of Counselors were last held on October 6, 2003, and will next be held in 2006; Chamber of Representatives: last held September 27, 2002, and next to be held in 2007.

The Judicial branch is composed of the Supreme Court, and judges are appointed on the recommendation of the Supreme Council of the Judiciary, presided over by the monarch. Each province is headed by a governor appointed by the King.

Political parties and leaders are as follows: Action Party or PA [Muhammad el-Idrissi]; Alliance of Liberties or ADL [Ali Belhaj]; Annahj Addimocrati or Annahj [Abdellah el-Harif]; Avant Garde Social Democratic Party or PADS [Ahmed Benjelloun]; Citizen Forces or FC [Abderrahman Lahjouji]; Citizen's Initiatives for Development [Mohamed Benhamou]; Constitutional Union or UC [Mohamed Abied (interim)]; Democratic and Independence Party or PDI [Abdelwahed Maach]; Democratic and Social Movement or MDS [Mahmoud Archane]; Democratic Socialist Party or PSD [Aissa Ouardighi]; Democratic Union or UD [Bouazza Ikken]; Environment and Development Party or PED [Ahmed el-Alami]; Front of Democratic Forces or FFD [Thami el-Khyari]; Istiqlal Party (Independence Party) or PI [Abbas el-Fassi]; Justice and Development Party (formerly the Constitutional and Democratic Popular Movement) or PJD [Abdelkrim el-Khatib]; Moroccan Liberal Party or PML [Mohamed Ziane]; National Democratic Party or PND [Abdallah Kadiri]; National Ittihadi Congress Party or CNI [Abdelmajid Bouzoubaa]; National Popular Movement or MNP [Mahjoubi Aherdane]; National Rally of Independents or RNI [Ahmed Osman]; National Union of Popular Forces or UNFP [Abdellah Ibrahim]; Parti Al Ahd or Al Ahd [Najib el-Ouazzani, chairman]; Party of Progress and Socialism or PPS [Ismail Alaoui]; Party of Renewal and Equity or PRE [Chakir Achabar]; Party of the Unified Socialist Left or GSU [Mohamed Ben Said Ait Idder]; Popular Movement or MP [Mohamed Laenser]; Reform and Development Party or PRD [Abderrahmane el-Kouhen]; Social Center Party or PSC [Lahcen Madih]; Socialist Union of Popular Forces or USFP [Mohammed el-Yazghi].

Political pressure groups and leaders: Democratic Confederation of Labor or CDT [Noubir Amaoui]; General Union of Moroccan Workers or UGTM [Abderrazzak Afilal]; Moroccan Employers Association or CGEM [Hassan Chami]; National Labor Union of Morocco or UNMT [Abdelslam Maati]; Union of Moroccan Workers or UMT [Mahjoub Benseddik].

International organization participation: ABEDA, ACCT, AfDB, AFESD, AMF, AMU, EBRD, FAO, G-77, IAEA, IBRD, ICAO, ICC, ICCt (signatory), ICFTU, ICRM, IDA, IDB, IFAD, IFC, IFRCS, IHO, ILO, IMF, IMO, Interpol, IOC, IOM, ISO, ITU, LAS, MONUC, NAM, OAS (observer), OIC, OPCW, OSCE (partner), PCA, UN, UNCTAD, UNESCO, UNHCR, UNIDO, UNITAR, UPU, WCL, WCO, WHO, WIPO, WMO, WToO, WTrO.

Morocco has a moderately high crime rate in urban areas. Criminals have targeted tourists for robberies, assaults, muggings, thefts, purse snatchings, pickpocketing, and scams of all types. Most of the petty crime occurs in the Medina/market areas, transportation centers, parks, and beaches. The U.S. Embassy and Consulate have also received reports of thefts occurring in the vicinity of ATM machines. Other reported crimes include falsifying credit card vouchers and shipping inferior rugs as a substitute for the rugs purchased by the traveler.

The Kingdom of Morocco claims and administers Western Sahara, whose sovereignty remains unresolved. UN-administered cease-fire has remained in effect since September 1991, but attempts to hold a referendum have failed, and parties thus far have rejected all brokered proposals. Polisario, Algeria, and European supporters agreed to the latest U.S.-brokered UN proposals for limited temporary autonomy for four to five years, followed by a referendum on independence, but Morocco's final response is pending. Morocco protests Spain's control over the coastal enclaves of Ceuta, Melilla, and Penon de Velez de la Gomera, the islands of Penon de Alhucemas and Islas Chafarinas, and surrounding waters. Morocco also rejected Spain's unilateral designation of a median line from the Canary Islands in 2002 to set limits to undersea resource exploration and refugee interdiction, but agreed in 2003 to discuss a comprehensive maritime delimitation. Morocco serves as the primary launching area of illegal migration into Spain from North Africa.

According to the DEA, Morocco is an illicit producer of hashish. Trafficking is increasing for both domestic and international drug markets, and shipments of hashish are mostly directed to Western Europe. It is also seen as a transit point for cocaine from South America destined for Western Europe.

Police Profile

Reliable and accurate information on the police force in Morocco is inaccessible.

MICHELLE HARRIGAN

Bibliography

Anderson, B., *Imagined Communities. Reflections on the Spread and Origins of Nationalism* (2nd ed). London: Verso, 1991.

Anderson, M., *Policing the World*. Oxford: OUP, 1989.

Bantekas, I., and S. Nash. *International Criminal Law*, (2nd edition). London: Cavendish publishing, 2003.

Bennett, R., "Government Legitimacy and Policing Styles: The Effect of Corruption on Citizen's Willingness to Report Crimes." Paper given at The University of The West Indies, Kingston & Ocho Rios, Jamaica, 2004.

Bowling, B., and J. Foster, "Policing and the Police" in M. Maguire, R. Morgan and R. Reiner (eds.), *The Oxford Handbook of Criminology* (3rd edition). Oxford: OUP, 2002.

Bowling, B., C. Phillips, A. Campbell, and M. Docking, *Human Rights and Policing*. Geneva: UN Research Institute for Social Development, 2001. www.unrisd.org.

Chan, J., "Changing Police culture." *British Journal of Criminology*, 36: 109–34, 1996.

CIA, *The World Factbook*. www.cia.gov/cia/publications/factbook/geos/html, 2004.

DEA Resources, For Law Enforcement, *Transnational Policing: A practical Approach for the Future*, DEA -02014, webster/dea/pubs/intel/02014/02014.html, (2002).

Findlay, M. *The Globalization of Crime: Understanding Transitional Relationships in Context*. Cambridge: Cambridge University Press, 1999.

Giddens, A. *Runaway World; How Globalization is reshaping our lives*. London: Profile Books ltd., 2002.

Hirst, M. *Jurisdiction and the Ambit of the Criminal Law*. Oxford: Oxford University Press, 2003.

McLaughlin, E and Muncie, J. *The Sage Dictionary of Criminology*. London: Sage, 2001.

Nadelman, E. *Cops across borders: the internationalization of US law enforcement*. University Park, Penn.: Pennsylvania State University Press, 1993.

Newburn, T. and Sparks, R. *Criminal Justice and Political Cultures, National and international dimensions of crime control*. London: Sage, 2004.

OECD-DAC, "Helping Prevent Violent Conflict: Orientations for External Partners." Supplement to the DAC Guidelines on Conflict, Peace and Development Co-operation on the Threshold of the 21st Century, EXECUTIVE SUMMARY. May 2001, Paris: Organization for Economic Co-operation and Development, Development Assistance Committee, 2001.

Sheptycki, J. "The Global Cops Cometh" *British Journal of Sociology*, 49/1:57–74, 1998b.

Sheptycki, J. *Issues in Transnational Policing*. London: Routledge, 2000.

Taylor, I. *Crime in Context*, Cambridge: Blackwell Publishers Ltd., 1999.

UNDCP, *United Nations Convention Against Transnational Organized Crime*, http://untreaty.un.org/Eng lsih/Treaty Event2001, 2000.

World Bank, *Governance: The World Bank's Experience; Development in Practice*. The World Bank, Washington DC., 1994.

MOZAMBIQUE

Background Material

Mozambique was a Portuguese colony for almost five hundred years. It achieved independence in 1975. The new nation's development was hindered by large-scale emigration by whites, economic dependence on South Africa, a severe drought, and a prolonged civil war. The ruling Front for the Liberation of Mozambique party (FRELIMO) abandoned Marxism in 1989, and a new constitution promulgated in 1990 provided for multi-party elections and a free market economy. A UN-negotiated peace agreement between FRELIMO and the rebel Mozambique National Resistance (RENAMO) forces ended the fighting in 1992.

Mozambique is located in southeastern Africa, bordering the Mozambique Channel, between South Africa and Tanzania. It has a total area of

801,590 sq km, and a population of 18,811,731 (2004 est.) Ethnically, the vast majority (99.66% of the population) belongs to one of the following native groups: Makhuwa, Tsonga, Lomwe, Sena, or others. The rest of the population is composed of Europeans, Euro-Africans, and Indians. Half of the population adheres to indigenous beliefs (30% Christian, 20% Muslim).

Portuguese is the official language. It is spoken by 27% of the population as a second language. Makhuwa, Tsonga, Lomwe, Sena, and numerous other indigenous languages are also spoken.

At independence, Mozambique was one of the world's poorest countries. Socialist mismanagement and a brutal civil war from 1977–1992 exacerbated the situation. In 1987, the government embarked on a series of macroeconomic reforms designed to stabilize the economy. These steps, combined with donor assistance and with political stability since the multi-party elections in 1994, have led to dramatic improvements in the country's growth rate. The GDP per capita is $1,200 (2003 est.).

Contextual Features

Mozambique is a republic, organized administratively into 10 provinces. The President is the Chief of State, and the head of the government is the Prime Minister. There is also a Cabinet.

Mozambique has a unicameral Assembly of the Republic, or Assembleia da Republica. It has 250 seats, and members are directly elected by popular vote on a secret ballot to serve five-year terms.

The Supreme Court is the court of final appeal. Some of its judges are appointed by the President, and some are elected by the Assembly. Other courts include an Administrative Court, customs courts, maritime courts, courts martial, and labor courts. Although the Constitution provides for the creation of a separate Constitutional Court, one has never been established; in its absence, the Supreme Court reviews constitutional cases.

Police Profile

During the first decade of independence, the Mozambique security forces, including the police, had virtually unlimited powers of arrest, detention, and torture (usually inflicted against suspected members of RENAMO). The police were poorly trained. They were expected to support FRELIMO unconditionally. In the aftermath of the civil war, violent crime remained a major problem. The police were faced with the challenge of moving from a political role to an anti-crime role, which proved difficult.

By the mid-1980s, some reforms began to appear. By the end of the decade, torture was less frequent, and flogging and the death penalty were abolished.

However, after the UN withdrew after the 1994 election, the crime rate rose significantly. In October 1994, the levels of crime rose alarmingly. In the transition to a market economy, thousands of demobilized soldiers increased the already high numbers of unemployed, and criminals had easy access to weapons. The police did not have the resources to properly address the crime wave. The police have been responsible for injuring and killing people with excessive uses of force.

Demographics

The *Polícia da República de Moçambique* (PRM), or Police of the Republic of Mozambique, has approximately 18,000 members. The paramilitary *Polícia da Intervenção Rápida* (PIR), or Rapid Intervention Police, has several thousand officers, most of whom are former soldiers.

Training

Police officers are generally poorly trained, receiving six months of education at most. Procedures for registering complaints with the police are inadequate. The police are under-resourced in terms of buildings, vehicles, and equipment. They are poorly paid, which may explain why some turn to crime themselves.

International Cooperation

During the peace-keeping operation, the UN decided to seek assistance from the international community for the restructuring and retraining of the police. An agreement was signed in June 1997 for a five-year program in which the Spanish *Guardia Civil* would help to restructure the police. They also agreed to organize a program to train police trainers and to retrain 4,000–5,000 police officers. Spain and the Netherlands have provided a total of US$11 million for the program. Italy has also been involved with the training of the Mozambique police.

Bibliography

"Mozambique." *CIA World Factbook.* www.cia.gov/cia/publications/factbook/.

"Mozambique: Human Rights and the Police." *Amnesty International.* http://web.amnesty.org/library/Index/ENGAFR410011998?open&of=ENG-380.

"Mozambique: Security Information." *Institute for Security Studies.* www.iss.co.za/AF/profiles/Mozambique/SecInfo.html.

MYANMAR

Background Material

Since 1989, the military authorities in Burma have promoted the name Myanmar as a conventional name for their state. However, this decision has not been approved by any sitting legislature in Burma.

Britain controlled Myanmar (Burma) over a period of 62 years, from 1824 to 1886. Burma was administered as a province of India until 1937, when it became a separate, self-governing colony; independence from the Commonwealth was attained in 1948. Despite multi-party legislative elections in 1990 that resulted in the main opposition party, the National League for Democracy (NLD), winning a landslide victory, the ruling *junta* refused to hand over power. NLD leader and Nobel Peace Prize recipient Aung San Suu Kyi, who was under house arrest from 1989 to 1995 and from 2000 to 2002, was imprisoned in May 2003, and she is currently under house arrest. In December 2004, the *junta* announced it was extending her detention for at least an additional year. Her supporters, as well as all those who promote democracy and improved human rights, are routinely harassed or jailed.

Myanmar is located in southeastern Asia, bordering the Andaman Sea and the Bay of Bengal, between Bangladesh and Thailand. It has a total area of 678,500 sq km and a population of 42,720,196 (2004 est.). The population is Burman (68%), Shan (9%), Karen (7%), Rakhine (4%), Chinese (3%), Indian (2%), Mon (2%), and other (5%). The religions practiced are: Buddhist (89%), Christian (4%), Muslim (4%), animist (1%), and other (2%). Burmese is the official language, although numerous minority ethnic groups also speak their own languages.

Myanmar has a GDP per capita of US$1,800 (2003 est.).

The capital of Myanmar is Rangoon.

Contextual Features

The Constitution was promulgated on January 3, 1974. However, it has been suspended since September 18, 1988. A national convention convened in 1993 to draft a new Constitution, but it was dissolved without achieving its goal in 1996. The convention reconvened in 2004, but the democratic opposition is barrred from taking part.

The chief of state is the Chairman of the State Peace and Development Council. The head of government is the Prime Minister. The Cabinet is referred to as the State Peace and Development Council (SPDC). It is essentially a military *junta*. Elections are not held.

A unicameral People's Assembly, or Pyithu Hluttaw, has 485 seats. Members are elected by popular vote to serve four-year terms. An election was last held in 1990; however, the SPDC did not allow the Assembly to convene.

Some vestiges of the British-era legal system are in place, but there is no guarantee of a fair public trial for citizens. The judiciary branch is not independent of the executive branch.

Police Profile

It is difficult to obtain reliable and accurate information regarding police activities in Myanmar. The lack of democratic processes in the nation makes it unlikely that the police force is answerable for its actions against the citizenry. The Myanmar police force maintains an official website at http://www.myanmar.com/Ministry/Moha/MPFmain.htm.

Bibliography

"Burma." *CIA World Fact Book. www.cia.gov/cia/publications/factbook/geos/bm.html.*

Myanmar Police Force (official website of the Myanmar Police Force). www.myanmar.com/Ministry/Moha/MPFmain.htm.

N

NAMIBIA

Background Material

Namibia is located on the west coast of southern Africa and is bordered by South Africa to the south, Botswana to the east, Angola to the north, and Zambia to the extreme northeast. With its surface area of 824,268 sq km, Namibia is the 31st largest country in the world. It has a population of 1.8 million, and a population density of just 1.7 people per sq km, one of the lowest in the world. The country was previously known as South West Africa during the colonial era.

English is the official language, but the country's constitution stipulates the promotion of the more than eleven indigenous languages. People commonly speak two or three languages, and more than 50% of the population speaks Oshiwambo. Due to the colonial history, Afrikaans, the language of the colonizers, is still widely spoken. Namibia has a small number of Khoisan-speaking people, known as the "Bushmen" or San.

Close to 95% of Namibians are believed to be Christians.

Namibia's 1998 per capita income was US$1908, which is a high figure compared to other African countries.

The Namibian economy is based on a free market and private initiatives. The government regards the private sector as the engine of economic growth and has put in place policies and a legislative framework designed to stimulate private-sector production. The economic structure of Namibia is characterized by a dominance of primary industry and is largely influenced by the international economic environment. The economy is also influenced by the South African and international business cycles, due to its dual dependency on imports and exports. It is also susceptible to climatic conditions. Mining is the backbone of the economy, followed by fishing, tourism, and agriculture.

Namibia is a member of the following organizations: the World Trade Organization, the Lome Convention with the European Union, the South African Customs Union, the Southern African Development Community, and the Common Market Area for Eastern and Southern Africa. The country's policies aimed at creating and enabling the investment climate have been formulated and implemented with notable success.

Contextual Features

Upon attaining its independence on 21 March 1990, the Republic of Namibia adopted a Constitution that is the fundamental law of the country. Article 1 of the Constitution characterizes the Republic as a "sovereign, secular, democratic and unitary state founded upon the principles of democracy, the rule of law and justice for all." The constitution also promulgates a multi-party democracy with a series of fundamental rights and freedoms.

In accordance with the doctrine of separation of powers, the government is divided into three branches: Executive, Legislative, and Judiciary. The legislative branch is responsible for making laws, which are implemented by the executive branch and interpreted by the judiciary branch. The executive branch is headed by the President, who is democratically elected by popular majority vote.

The bicameral legislature consists of the National Assembly and National Council, which reviews bills passed in the first chamber. The National Assembly has 72 members elected through the proportional representation electoral systems where contesting parties are allocated seats in accordance to the votes gained in the multiparty election.

The President appoints an additional six members based on their expertise. The National Council is made up of 26 Regional Councilors, two from each geographic region, as nominated by their respective regions. A two-thirds majority is required to enact proposed laws.

The judicial branch of the government consists of the Supreme Court, the High Court, and the Lower Courts, such as the Magistrate Courts and District Labour Courts. All courts are independent and subject only to the Constitution and laws governing the country.

The Supreme Court is headed by a Chief Justice; this court judges and deals with appeals from the High Court and also rules on judicial matters concerning the Constitution. Decisions from the Supreme Court are binding on both the High and Lower courts plus all persons in Namibia.

The High Court consists of a Judge-President and additional judges. It deals with civil disputes and criminal prosecutions, including those cases that involve the interpretation, implementation, and upholding of the Constitution and fundamental guaranteed rights.

The Lower Courts are presided over by a Magistrate, and they deal with smaller cases.

The Namibian legal system is modeled on its Constitution, which is the supreme law. It incorporates Roman Dutch law and statute law as well as customary law. It is required that all laws be consistent with the terms of the Constitution.

The most prevalent serious crimes that are generally committed in Namibia are murder, rape, armed robbery, breaking and entering, commercial crimes, stock theft, and assault. Armed robberies, mainly in urban areas, have increased recently. In response, the Namibian Police have established the Serious Crime Unit to deal specifically with these types of crime. Flying Squads or Quick Response Units have also been set up.

The Namibian Prisons and Correctional Services was established under an Act of Parliament (Act 17 of 1998) and is provided for in Chapter 15 of the Namibian Constitution, Articles 121 to 123. This marked the departure of the colonial prison system, which was purely for incarceration.

The main objective of the Ministry had been the safe custody of people committed to imprisonment by the country's courts of law, and to ensure their rehabilitation and ultimate reintegration in society. With this new focus on rehabilitation, all the prisons' operations were conducted in a humane way in accordance with national and international laws and codes of conduct, which directed that inmates be cared for in a compassionate manner by affording them the opportunity to regain their self-respect as a logical way for their rehabilitation.

The Ministry also played a meaningful role as an instrument of the country's criminal justice system by protecting law-abiding citizens from criminal elements. This task has been accomplished through incarceration of offenders and their rehabilitation for the eventual reintegration into society, while exercising reasonable safe and secure control. For purposes of maintaining law and order, the Ministry worked together with other agencies of the Criminal Justice System and gained support from the community, nongovernmental organizations, and other governmental agencies. Furthermore, the Ministry has been striving to operate in an efficient, effective, and economic manner by emphasizing self-sufficiency in food production and by making contributions to government revenue.

The Division of Inmate Rehabilitation falls under the Office of the Commissioner of Prisons, and it has the function of rehabilitating prisoners in order to enable them to lead law-abiding lives after reintegration into society. The Division is charged with the function of creating and rendering social work services to inmates and further evaluating social work programs.

Juvenile Rehabilitation Centres have been designed for young offenders aged eighteen and under who, by international standards, are not supposed to mix with adult offenders. The Elizabeth Nepemba Juvenile Centre near Rundu is currently under development.

Plans are underway to establish Remand Prisons in the country for the detention of those awaiting trial. The earmarked places include the Windhoek, Oshana, and Kavango regions. Currently, such offenders are usually detained in police cells. The establishment of Remand Prisons is perceived a positive step in improving the existing system, which gives the police responsibilities of arresting and detaining suspects.

As a positive approach to rehabilitation, classification of offenders has been based on lengths of sentences, offenses, character, age, gender, and criminal history. In this arrangement, first offenders are not allowed to mix with hard-core criminals. Such a system has provided a mechanism for controlling overcrowding, and it reduces prisoner idleness by engaging them in productive agricultural and industrial work.

Police Profile

Background

The first formal policing in the country was done by the German *Kaiserliche Schutztruppe* as part of their overall responsibilities. However, on 1 March 1905, the first police force was established in the form of the *Kaiserliche Landespolizei fur Deutsch Sudwestafrika*. During 1907, this force consisted of 400 members, and during the same year it took delivery of its first motor vehicle. However, the horse and camel remained for years the standard means of transport. Camels were mostly used at places like Stampriet, Tsinsabis, and Witdraai. The last camels were withdrawn from service just after World War II.

The period of policing by the *Landespolizei* ceased with the South African invasion during World War I, after which policing again was part of the military. Five regiments of the South African Mounted Rifleman stayed in the country on garrison and policing duties after the withdrawal of the South African Main Force. In the meantime, the recruiting of a military police force commenced in Bloemfontein (South Africa), and during February 1916, the new force took over policing functions with 52 officers and 1,100 other ranks.

Also during 1916, a Training Centre with 16 instructors was established for training of the members, who were mostly young and inexperienced. They were subjected to a five-month intensive training course. The Training Centre also trained police dogs, following the model of the *Landespolizei,* who also used dogs for detection purposes. The military police force was disbanded on December 31, 1919, and the members were absorbed into the South West African Police Force. A detective unit was established in May 1920.

Mounted police patrols in the *Khomas Hochland* normally lasted for three weeks at a time, and some of the camel patrols lasted as long as 65 days. During 1939, the South West African Police Force was disbanded, and policing responsibilities were taken over by the South African Police.

On April 1, 1981, policing functions were transferred from the South African Police to a newly established South West African Police Force. On 21 March 1990, the country became independent; with the birth of the new Namibian nation came the new Namibian Police Force.

Demographics

As of December 31, 2001, the Namibian Police (Nampol) had a manpower strength of 10,981 staff members, including civilian personnel. Of this number, 2,848 are regular police personnel, and 6,955 are members of the Special Field Force.

Organizational Description

The Criminal Investigation Department is primarily responsible for the investigation of a variety of crimes. The division has several specialized units that provide support services to the regular activities of the other operational units within the force.

The Inspector General is the overall commander of the Namibian Police. He is appointed by the President, as stipulated by Article 32(4)(C) of the Constitution.

With regard to commercial crime such as fraud, a Joint Security and Fraud Committee of Financial Institution was established to co-ordinate the quick detection of these cases and to facilitate smooth investigation by the police.

Each specialized unit has a unique crime-prevention strategy, and the commanders are required to report to the management about its implementation on a monthly basis.

The Specialized Crime Investigation Units include:

- Crime Investigation Unit;
- Drug Law Enforcement Unit;
- Motor Vehicle Theft Unit;
- Commercial Crime Investigation Unit;
- Protected Resources Unit;

- Serious Crime Unit;
- Women and Child Protection Unit;
- Scene of Crime Unit;
- Criminal Record Centre/Fingerprint Unit;
- Dog Unit.

There are other divisions of Nampol worth noting. The Special Field Force is responsible for the protection and guarding of borders, and it serves as a support unit in crime prevention. The Special Reserve Field Force primarily focuses on issues relating to public order, strikes, and special operations. It is also involved in general crime prevention. The V.I.P. Division protects all dignitaries throughout the country, as well as government buildings and property.

Functions

Nampol was established by an Act of Parliament (Act 19 of 1990). Nampol's main duties are:

- To prevent crime;
- To investigate any offense or alleged offense; and
- To maintain the internal security of the Republic of Namibia.

Nampol supports the principles and philosophy of the rule of law, and, as such, the Force serves citizens of Namibia and foreign nationals residing within the borders of the Republic. Members of the Force ensure the maintenance of law and order, and they protect human life and public and private property. They are expected to render at all times the necessary quality services as laid down in Chapter II of the *Namibian Police Act,* with due consideration for fundamental rights and freedoms, without compromising the tenets of law and order and the safety and security of law-abiding persons. They must be diligent and honest in their work, sparing no efforts to pursue the truth and ensure that justice is done. To preserve internal security and in maintaining law and order in Namibia, every member of Nampol is charged with the duty to take the necessary steps which, on reasonable grounds, appear to him/her to be correct and necessary for the following:

- Preservation of internal security and peace;
- Prevention of crime;
- Protection of human life;
- Protection of properties from malicious damage;
- Detection and suppression of crime;
- Apprehension and timely booking of offenders;

- Suppression of and peaceful solution for all forms of civil disturbance.

Training

The Israel Patrick Iyambo Police College is the only institution of advanced police training in the country. The objectives of the Police College are to provide basic training to police students, advance training, in-service training, and on-the-job training to members and officers of the Force; and also to render training assistance to other government departments and institutions. It has broadened its scope of training to equip investigators with legal knowledge in order to carry out their respective duties with confidence. It is also vital to note that police officers can also pursue a Police Science Diploma offered by The Polytechnic of Namibia, which is the second-highest tertiary educational institution in Namibia.

Police Public Projects

The Namibian Police Force, via the public relations office within its structure, plays an important role in informing the public of all types of crimes. They do so by liaising with the local media. The Namibian Police has established its own publication, the *Police Journal*, with the purposes of making itself visible and encouraging mutual communication with the public and all other stake holders. The Police Force has created and maintained a harmonious working relationship with the media, taking into consideration the influence the media have on the public.

In carrying out their duty, Nampol members must combine proactive and reactive methods of policing, with an emphasis on the involvement of the community in information gathering. To this end, Community Policing is seen and should be accepted as the guiding philosophy in the fight against crime and in the maintenance of law and order.

The public should be instrumental in getting rid of criminal elements and their activities in all neighborhoods in villages, towns, cities, and anywhere else, by assisting and cooperating with the members of the Force. The Namibian Police Force, as a servant of the Nation accountable to the community it serves, is expected to deliver quality service, to uphold the principles of the rule of law, to demonstrate a national commitment and unwavering patriotism and respect for the supreme law of the Republic of Namibia. Members of Nampol must be guided by the principles of Uniformed

Organizations discipline, norms of human behavior, the Police Act and regulations pertinent to the Act.

Police Use of Firearms

According to law, the use of firearms by members of the Police Force is only justified in the following circumstances:

1. Self-defense, in the case of immediate and lethal attack;
2. Defense of another person under immediate lethal attack;
3. In circumstances according to section 49 of the *Criminal Procedure Act* of 1977 (Act 51 of 1977).

In criminal proceedings, a claim of self-defense will only succeed if:

1. The attack was a positive and unlawful act or interference.
2. The act of "self-defense" was against a threat to life or personal injury.
3. The attack had already commenced or was imminent.
4. The act of self-defense was directed against the attacker, was necessary to avert the attack, and did not use excessive force in reply to the attack.

Before shooting another person in the circumstances as described above, the following steps must be followed chronologically:

1. Establish if it is one of the Schedule One offenses (high treason, sedition, murder, rape, robbery, assault when a dangerous wound is inflicted, breaking or entering any premises).
2. Determine whether there is intent to commit an offense or to escape from lawful arrest for committing a Schedule One offense.
3. The offender must be audibly warned to stop fleeing or resisting the arrest.
4. If the offender is known and could be arrested at a later time, he/she must be allowed to flee.

If there are male bystanders aged between 16 and 60, they must be requested to help with the arrest. If the offender cannot be arrested and all steps above were followed, at least three warning shots should be fired.

As a last resort, the offender may be shot in the leg. If under any circumstances a member fires or orders the firing of a firearm, he/she must immediately report the shooting incident to his/her immediate superior, any senior member at the police station in the area where the incident took place. The officer to whom the incident was reported must immediately arrange to visit the scene and compile a factual report on the shooting incident. Although the law sanctions the use of firearm under certain circumstances, the onus still rests upon the officer to prove beyond reasonable doubts that it was justifiable.

Complaints and Discipline

This unit was established in 1992 with the primary purpose of investigating all types of cases brought against the Namibian Police, including any claims of misconduct by members within the institution. It also has the mandate to enforce discipline within the rank and file of the force, and this is done through the respective supervisors of Divisions and Units. The Division has Units deployed around the country in all 13 police regions, and it has legal officers who serve as advisors on legal matters to the Inspector General. These legal officers also have the responsibilities of checking that civil claims against the police are promptly investigated. Criminal cases against the Namibian Police are investigated in accordance with the provisions of the *Criminal Procedure Act 51* of 1977 as amended, the *Namibian Police Act, Act 19* of 1990 and its subsequent regulations, as well as the legal framework of the Namibian Constitution. The Namibian Police remains committed to upholding the principles of human and fundamental rights. If its members fail to recognize such constitutionally guaranteed rights while executing their duties, the complaint would be investigated impartially and professionally. Once the case is opened against the member, the docket will be forwarded to the Office of the Prosecutor General after the investigation, for a decision about whether to prosecute or not. To date, frequent criminal cases against police-members are assault, pointing of firearm, and attempted murder.

Terrorism

Namibia does not have any terrorist organizations within its borders, but compliance with international organizations is in place to respond to their requests in tracking down terrorist groups that would use Namibia as a hiding place.

International Cooperation

Nampol is a member of various international organizations, such as the United Nations LC.P.O.

(Interpol), counterparts in member countries of the Non-Aligned Movement, the Organization of African Unity currently renamed African Union, the neighboring countries organized in SARPCCO within the SADC framework, and the Joint Permanent Commission on Defence and Security for a Crime-Free Neighbourhood.

Police Education, Research, and Publications

The Research and Development Unit was established to serve as a critical structure to gather and analyze data for strategic policy formulations and implementation. Researchers are appointed to spearhead this component of the Namibian Police to render meaningful and goal-directed research projects as might be deemed necessary. These, as a result, would be used to reform policies, to restore community-Police relations and confidence, to improve resource allocation, to facilitate sector reform and reorganization, and to review sector coordination and networking. The Police Force budgets funds for such research projects, but their implementation can also be co-funded by other donor agencies.

L.N. UUSIKU

NAURU

Background Material

There is little known about Nauru prior to the arrival of British Captain John Fearn, who named it Pleasant Island. In 1888, the name was changed to Nauru. At that time, it was annexed by Germany and became part of the Marshall Islands Protectorate. In 1900, a British company discovered phosphate on the island and negotiated with Germany for mining rights. In November 1914, the Germans surrendered the island to Australian troops, and in 1920 it became a mandated territory and remained in British control until 1921. In 1947, the island was placed under United Nations Trusteeship, and Australia resumed administration on behalf of the three partner governments: Australia, New Zealand, and Great Britain. Nauru became an independent Republic on 31 January 1968, and adopted a modified version of parliamentary democracy. The unicameral parliament consists of 18 members chosen from 14 constituencies. The President, who is Chief of State and Head of Government, is chosen by the Parliament from among its members. In 2001, Nauru accepted A$10 million from the Australian government to accommodate indefinitely the majority of asylum seekers rescued by the Norwegian vessel, the *Tampa*. In December 2001, Nauru agreed to the Australian government's request that it accommodate a further 400 asylum seekers.

Nauru is the smallest republic in the world, with a total area of only 21 sq km. The phosphate supply, the source of Nauru's wealth, is near depletion. Nauru has an unreliable water supply, and the phosphate mining that has dug out the centre of the island has made it prone to erosion. Rehabilitation of the land is an ongoing urgent issue, and with the highest point on the island being only 61 m above sea level, it is also vulnerable to rising sea levels. The OECD has alleged that Nauru is a major money laundering and tax evasion centre. This has resulted in the OECD Financial Task Force charging Nauru in February 2002 with being negligent in its efforts to stamp out money laundering practices.

Nauru, like other small Pacific Island nations, is vulnerable to being used and manipulated by criminals and unscrupulous financiers. The offshore banking industry, which is poorly regulated, is attractive to those wishing to launder money. Nauru's failure to implement effective regulations led to it being blacklisted by several American international banks. Such blacklisting has the potential to cause considerable financial problems for the tiny island nation.

As of July 2001, the population was 12,088. Nauru has a young population, with 40.33% under the age of 15. Fifty-eight percent of the population are Nauruan; 26% Pacific Islanders; 8% Chinese; and 8% European.

Nauruan, which is a hybrid of Polynesian, Melanesian, and Micronesian, is universally spoken. English is used for commercial and government matters and is widely used and understood.

Christianity is the dominant religion, with approximately two thirds Protestant, and one third Roman Catholic.

GDP per capita was estimated at approximately US$5000 in 2000. Phosphate mining and offshore banking are the major economic activities. Unlike other small South Pacific Islands, the tourism market is underdeveloped.

Contextual Features

Nauru has a written Constitution that is the supreme law in Nauru. In addition, laws are passed by the Parliament, and some have been inherited from previous jurisdictions (especially Australia, PNG, and England). The system of law consists of subordinate legislation, common law, and customary law.

There do not appear to be any official statistics that detail the most common crimes in Nauru. However, the Nauru Police Force reports that the most common crimes are theft, unregistered driving of motor vehicles, and alcohol-related assaults. In 2001, Nauru was listed by the Financial Action Task Force on Money Laundering as among the "least cooperative jurisdictions" (http://www1.oecd.org/fatf/fatdocs_en.html).

The High Court of Australia has jurisdiction to hear appeals from the Supreme Court of Nauru in relation to any final first instance judgment. It also hears appeals with leave of the trial judge or the High Court against an interlocutory order or judgment, and can hear an appeal from the Supreme Court exercising jurisdiction in appeals from the District Court.

"Ordinary" appeals may be made to the Australian High Court by those convicted by the Supreme Court on questions of fact, mixed questions of fact and law, or a question only of law.

Appeals can also be made to the High Court of Australia against a sentence, unless it is one that is fixed by law.

The Supreme Court has unlimited original civil jurisdiction. Even though the Courts Act does not specify, it is virtually assumed that it has original criminal jurisdiction. It can hear civil and criminal appeals of final decisions of the District Court, and criminal appeals can be based on questions of fact or of law.

The District Court hears and determines all civil cases involving not more than A$3,000. While the Courts Act does not specify any particular parameters for the criminal jurisdiction of the District Court, the general jurisdiction is sufficiently wide to encompass criminal jurisdictions associated with comparable courts (e.g., the Magistrates' Court) in other jurisdictions.

The Family Court is a separate court, and its proceedings are not open to the public.

No data are available on the corrections system in Nauru. Detention centres have recently been established for asylum seekers from Australian waters.

The death penalty is nominally in force.

Police Profile

Background

Before 1888, chieftains were responsible for social order. When Germany gained control of modern Nauru in 1888, it appointed a series of executive officers who exercised policing authority, among other powers. In 1900, the Police Force consisted of three Nauruans. It grew steadily until 1914, when Australian authorities comprehensively restructured the force. In 1927, Thomas Cude was appointed Director of Police, a position he held for 27 years. The first native Nauruan Director of Police was appointed in 1977.

Demographics

The force consists of 75 persons, including the Director. There are nine female police officers and 66 male officers.

Organizational Description

The Police Department comes under the Ministry for Justice. The Director of Police is the overall head of the Department. The Station Office, Administration, Operation, Crime, Prosecution, and Traffic Branches are under his direct supervision. The Station Officer holds the rank of Superintendent of Police and Officer-in-Charge of the Police Station and Prison Unit. He is also the Officer-in-Charge of the Crime Branch. The Administration and Operation units are under the supervision of a Sub-Inspector; the Prosecution and Traffic Units are under the supervision of a Police Inspector.

The ranks in the Police Force of Nauru are: Director of Police, Superintendent of Police, Assistant Superintendent of Police, Senior Inspector, Sub-Inspector, Senior Sergeant, Sergeant, Senior Constable, and Constable.

The Prosecution unit is separate from the Crime and Traffic units. The supervising Inspector liaises with the Director of Police and the Justice Department, and can recommend whether police or justice department prosecutors are better suited to pursue prosecutions.

Functions

There is only one police agency in Nauru. Its legislated functions are to protect life and property; enforce law and order; provide Aide-de-Camp to the President; administer the prisons; provide a paramilitary force; and provide all guards of honour for ceremonial occasions.(Nauru has no military.)

Training

Police are initially selected on the following criteria:

- University qualification desirable, school leaver's certificate otherwise;
- Medically fit;
- Of sober habits and without criminal convictions;
- Having a command of the English language;
- Aged between 17 and 25;
- Of pleasant temperament;
- Able to carry out orders and work diligently.

Recruits receive six months' training in the basic law of the land (the Constitution of Nauru) and other laws and ordinances. Officers are instructed on the rights of citizens.

While recent training has been neglected, the Director of Police has initiated new training programs covering supervision, communication, law, criminal procedure, and general policing. This is being done with the assistance of the University of the South Pacific.

Promotion is by exam, and the process recognizes outstanding performance and/or long service.

Police Use of Firearms

Police do not use firearms in operational service. Firearm crime is an occasional problem.

Complaints and Discipline

Complaints are dealt with internally. The Director of Police appoints a senior inspector to investigate all allegations. The Director then decides whether to proceed with disciplinary procedures.

No program exists to investigate allegations of human rights abuses. However, the U.S. Department of State finds that Nauru generally has a good human rights record. Amnesty International did not report on Nauru in 2002.

Terrorism

There have been no terrorist incidents in Nauru. The Police, Fire and Rescue Services, Customs and Immigration, and Civil Aviation have participated in joint drills and seminars on terrorism prevention.

International Cooperation

The Police Force is a member of Interpol. It was a founding member of the annual South Pacific Chiefs of Police Conference, and continues to participate in that forum. It is also a member of the South Pacific Security Committee of the South Pacific Forum and the South Pacific Island Criminal Intelligence Network; the Force also regularly cooperates with the Australian Federal Police and the Federal Bureau of Investigation.

The South Pacific Chiefs of Police Conference is designed to foster cooperation, share information that will help to combat crime, and provide formal liaison among police in the South Pacific. In 2003, delegates to the annual conference finalized a four-year strategic plan, which establishes key law enforcement priorities for the region.

Police Education, Research, and Publication

Institutions

Nauru has no police training academy. Training is performed overseas at the University of the South Pacific, http://www.usp.ac.fj/ (Institute of Justice and Applied Legal Studies (IJALS), Laucala Campus, Fiji).

Researchers

Newton, T. (1998). *An introduction to policing in the South Pacific region.* University of the South Pacific School of Law Working Papers.

Leading Journals

Journal of South Pacific Law. http://easol. vanuatu.usp.ac.fj/jspl/current. There is no funding for police research available in Nauru, nor are there any major police publications, nor any police-related websites.

COLLEEN LEWIS

Bibliography

Identifying Non-Cooperative Countries and Territories, FATF (Paris: 2001). www1.oecd.org/fatf/fatdocs_en.htm.

"Nauru." *The World Factbook*. www.cia.gov/cia/publications/ factbook/ geos/ nr.html#Geo.

Ranmuthugala, Douglas (2002). "Security in the South Pacific – the law enforcement dimension." *Platypus*, No 77, December 2002, 10-17.

SBS World Guide, 9th edition, Hardie Grant Books, 2001.

South Pacific Chiefs of Police Conference, AFP. http://www.afp.gov.au/page.asp?ref =/news/events/spcpc.xml.

NEPAL

Background Material

The Kingdom of Nepal is located in southern Asia between India and China, with a total area of 140,800 sq km. The population is 27,070,666 (2004 est.).

Ethnic groups represented include Brahimin, Chetri, Newar, Limbu, Sherpa, Tharu, Magar Tamang, Rai, and others. The religious composition of the population is as follows: Hinduism: 86.2%; Buddhism: 7.8%; Islam: 3.8%; other: 2.2%. Nepali is officially spoken by 90% of the population, although about a dozen other languages and about 30 major dialects are also represented.

Nepal is a poor and underdeveloped country, with nearly half of its population living below the poverty line. Agriculture is the mainstay of the economy; almost 78% of the population depends on agriculture, and it accounts for 41% of the GDP. Textile and carpet production account for about 80% of foreign exchange earnings in recent years. Nepal has considerable possibilities for accelerating economic growth by exploring its potential in hydropower and tourism.

The GDP per capita (purchasing power parity) is $1,400 (2003 est.).

Contextual Features

Nepal is a parliamentary democracy and a constitutional monarchy. The legal system is based on Hindu legal concepts and English common law; Nepal has not accepted compulsory ICJ jurisdiction. The Head of State is the King, and the head of the government is the Prime Minister. The monarch is hereditary. Following a legislative election, the leader of the majority party is usually appointed Prime Minister by the monarch.

The cabinet is made up of members appointed by the monarch on the recommendation of the Prime Minister. The legislative branch is a bicameral parliament consisting of the National Council and the House of Representatives.

The Supreme Court is the judicial branch of the national government.

Sovereignty is vested in the people of the Kingdom of Nepal (Constitution 1990). That being the case, everything that is done in Nepal, in accordance with the Constitution, should be done by and for the people; it is the duty of every person to "uphold the provisions of [the] Constitution."

Subject to the sovereignty of the people, His Majesty the King is "the symbol of Nepalese nationality and the unity of the Nepalese people" (preamble to the 1991 Constitution). The King's Constitutional role is to "preserve and protect [the] Constitution by keeping in view the best interests and welfare of the people of Nepal." In addition, the King is the Supreme Commander of the Royal Nepal Army, and, on the advice of the Council of Ministers, he is responsible for appointing Nepal's ambassadors overseas. The King is obliged by the Constitution to appoint a *Raj Parishad*, or Royal Council, which has the duty of proclaiming succession to the throne, and of creating a regency when necessary. The King is also able to appoint a Standing Committee of the *Raj Parishad* to submit recommendations on matters referred to it by him.

The Prime Minister is appointed by the King to head the government and should be the leader of the party that commands a majority in the House of Representatives. The Council of Ministers has the responsibility of "issuing general directives" and "controlling and regulating the administration" of Nepal. The Council of Ministers is appointed by the Prime Minister to serve under his chairmanship. The members of the Council of Ministers are collectively responsible to the House of Representatives, and individually responsible to the Prime Minister and the House of Representatives for the work of their respective ministries.

State Ministers can be appointed by the King on the recommendation of the Prime Minister, and Assistant Ministers can be appointed to assist any minister in carrying out his responsibilities. The conduct of government business by the Prime Minister, Ministers, State Ministers, and Assistant Ministers must be carried out according to rules approved by the King.

New legislation can be introduced by a member of either the House of Representatives (the lower house of Parliament, consisting of 205 members) or the National Assembly (the upper house of Parliament, which has 60 members) and processed according to the legislative procedure set out in the Constitution. Any Nepali citizen who satisfies the conditions for candidacy may stand as a candidate for election to the House of Representatives. The House of Representatives (Election of Members) Act 1991 was promulgated on March 11, 1991.

Members of the National Assembly are selected as follows: 10 are appointed by the King; 35 are elected by members of the House of Representatives; and 15 are elected by regional Electoral Colleges, as stipulated by The National Assembly (Election) Act 1991, which was promulgated on 6 June 1991.

Each house of Parliament regulates its own procedures, and the House of Representatives may form any number of committees to conduct business. Joint committees of both houses can be formed to regulate joint business. A Parliamentary Secretariat, appointed by the King on the recommendation of the Speaker and the Chairman of the National Assembly, deals with day-to-day business in Parliament.

The Courts in Nepal are responsible for exercising judicial functions. The Supreme Court is the highest court in the land, and only Military Courts are not subject to its jurisdiction. A Chief Justice (appointed by the King on the recommendation of the Constitutional Council) and up to 14 other judges sit in the Supreme Court. The Supreme Court has jurisdiction to hear and determine any suit filed by any citizen of Nepal in relation to Constitutional matters. For enforcing fundamental rights guaranteed by the Constitution, the Court may make any appropriate order. The Supreme Court Act 1991 was promulgated on November 14, 1991.

Appellate Judges and District Judges (who derive their powers from the Constitution and subsidiary legislation) sit in Appellate Courts (currently 18 in number) and District Courts (75) in different districts of Nepal. Provisions relating to the administration of Civil and Criminal Justice (*adalati bandobast*) are contained in Part 2 of the *Muluki Ain* (National Code) 1963, as amended. The Appellate and District Court Judges (Remuneration, etc.) Act 1992 was promulgated on April 20, 1992.

A Judicial Council and a Judicial Service Commission regulate the appointment of judges and the work of Gazette Officers of the Judicial Service. The Judicial Council Act 1991 was promulgated on 11 April 1991, and the Judicial Service Commission Act 1991 was promulgated on November 14, 1991.

The Commission for the Investigation of the Abuse of Authority exists to investigate alleged wrongdoing by any public official. The Abuse of Authority Investigation Commission Act 1991 was promulgated on November 20, 1991.

The Auditor-General is responsible for auditing the accounts of government offices and constitutional bodies.

The Public Service Commission identifies suitable candidates for work in the Civil Service. The Civil Service Act 1993 was promulgated on May 17, 1993.

The Election Constituency Delimitation Commission and the Election Commission, respectively, have responsibility for setting the boundaries of electoral constituencies throughout Nepal and for supervising the conduct of elections within those constituencies. The Election Constituency Delimitation Act 1990 was promulgated on December 9, 1990, and the Election Commission Act 1991 was promulgated on February 11, 1991.

The Attorney General is the chief legal advisor to the Government. He is responsible for determining whether to bring or defend actions where the government is in dispute with another party, and for giving opinions on Constitutional and legal matters.

The Constitutional Council has responsibility for making recommendations in accordance with the Constitution and for appointing officials to Constitutional bodies (except the Attorney General, who is appointed by the King on the recommendation of the Prime Minister).

While the Constitution provides the framework for the government of Nepal on a national level, not all of those responsible for administration have their powers set out in the Constitution. "Extra-Constitutional" national bodies could be categorized as: (i) the Police and Civil Defense authorities; (ii) the Civil Service; (iii) the National Planning Commission; and (iv) other central government agencies.

The prison process begins with the arrest of a suspect. Police are authorized to take him or her into custody for 24 hours without the approval of the court, generally the district court. With the permission of the court, the custody period could extend up to a maximum of 25 days, but the court generally remands custody for 7 to 15 days at a time. During police custody, a suspect is imprisoned in the police station. After completing the investigation, the police submit an investigation report and case file to the District Attorney, who has to decide either to charge or to discharge the suspect.

After the filing of the case and the production of the accused before the court, the statement of the accused is recorded before the judge. The judge has to decide whether to keep the accused in judicial custody until trial, or set him or her free on bail. If the judge rejects bail, then the accused is sent to jail as an under-trial prisoner, forced to prepare his or her defense behind bars. In Nepal, studies show that more than 60% of the jail inmates are under-trial detainees.

The percentage of under-trial prisoners in Nepal is very high compared to other parts of the world, since judges seem to be very conservative in granting bail. The judges, too, have been influenced by social values. In Nepalese society, people are happy once the suspect faces a prison term.

This affects the very basic human and fundamental rights of the accused, because the right to defend his or her case is limited by imprisonment. In many instances, under-trial detainees are eventually found to be innocent. There is no law to compensate for this loss of liberty. The chance for abuse of power is much greater for a case under the Commission of Investigation of Abuse of Authority (CIAA) because it is empowered to exercise both the power of the police and the prosecution. The CIAA starts its investigation by first presuming the accused to be guilty; he or she is then taken into custody, and then the CIAA starts an investigation. It can take people into custody for the maximum period of six months, subject to the approval of the Special Court.

Although Article 14(6) of the Constitution of the Kingdom of Nepal 1990 provides for the production of the arrested person before the judicial authority within 24 hours, the provision is ineffective. Those in custody are often denied the right to consult a lawyer or judicial authority. The District Courts and Special Court do not rush to scrutinize the evidence and related documents while granting remand for detention.

In legal terms, no person is considered guilty unless his or her crime is proved. But there is a belief in Nepalese society that anyone who returns from prison or custody is a criminal. Family members of such detainees have to face discrimination, humiliation, and hatred.

Most of the prisoners are poor and powerless, since they cannot hire a lawyer to challenge the verdict given by the Lower Court. In the course of investigation and delivering the verdict, nobody tries to understand what motive impelled them to the crime. The prisoners' condition clearly shows that the causes were their miserable economic condition, unemployment, and helplessness. In the prison and outside, they have to face similar hardships.

A large number of inmates understand the difference between detainees and convicts, once they are sent to prison. Although the Central Prison is in the heart of the city, over 60% of the prison population is detainees under trial. According to the Central Prison, among 1,538 prisoners in the three units, more than 800 are under-trial detainees.

The situation in other districts and remote areas is worse. In the Central Prison, non-governmental organizations and other bodies visit the premises and listen to the inmates' problems.

The prisons are overcrowded and congested. The rooms are small, since the buildings of most of the jails are a century old. Even the buildings added since the 1950s are congested and small. So, there is little space for recreational activities. A high-level Prison Reform Committee formed by the State Affairs Committee of the House of Representatives recommended improvement in infrastructure. The studies by more than half a dozen committees formed after the restoration of democracy in 1990 presented a similar picture, but no improvements have been implemented.

All committees have made similar recommendations, such as improvement of the room conditions, more space for recreational activities, separate rooms for the patients with deadly diseases, but no government has provided an adequate budget to implement them. Some committees have recommended reforming the penal system to deliver speedy judgment and to create an alternative system for petty crimes.

According to the prison administration in the Central Jail, they are compelled to place all kinds of detainees and prisoners, including those infected with hepatitis B, HIV/AIDS, cholera, and typhoid, in the same units. "There must be separate units for such inmates," says a senior official. The average age of prisoners at the Central Prison is 30, and most of the prisoners are illiterate as well as poor.

Under pressure from human rights organizations, Parliament, and donors, the government is taking steps to improve the physical conditions in many prison units, adding schools and other vocational training components. But the prisoners get few opportunities for rehabilitation. Most of the prisoners released in petty theft cases, girl trafficking, drugs, and other social offenses tend to return to jail. This shows that prisoners do not get the opportunity to reform themselves and that punitive action alone is not enough to deter crime.

The prison system in Nepal began in 1914, when the present Central Jail was established in Kathmandu, under the control of the military general. After the popular movement of 1951, the prison's administration was shifted to the Ministry of Home Affairs. The prison centers are now under the control of District Administrative Offices. They are still regarded as places for inflicting punitive treatment.

Nepal's prison units are governed under the Prison Act and Prison Regulations 1962 AD and 1963 AD. The Act has been amended twice, and the regulations seven times.

With the restoration of democracy, the Prison Section of the Ministry of Home Affairs was upgraded to the status of department, but one cannot see substantial changes in prison management. Instead of creating an efficient system, the department has created more complications and increased bureaucratic layers. According to the present system, the department has no authority over the prison units, whose management comes under the District Administration Office. For the welfare of the prisoners and reform in the units, the department has little to do.

Managed by untrained personnel, the prison units are ill equipped with basic facilities. There are 73 prisons established in 72 districts in the kingdom. The prisoners are placed into four categories. Prisoners are further divided into two groups on the basis of food allowances of category A and category B. Convicted persons and those under trial are distinguished as prisoners and detainees, respectively.

The prisoners and detainees receive similar facilities without distinction. They are provided with clothing two times a year. Daily necessary commodities are supplied based on the category that the prisoners or detainees are placed in. Those placed in category A are entitled to 700 grams of rice and Rs.20 (25 cents) a day. With the Rs.20, a prisoner has to purchase vegetables, cooking oil, salt, milk, and many other daily commodities. With the 700 grams of rice, the prisoner has to support his or her subsistence three times a day. Those falling into the category B obtain 700 grams of rice and Rs. 15 (20 cents). Other facilities like schools and sports exist at the Central Prison, which is known as the equivalent of a five-star hotel among the prisoners.

As the courts are filled with an overload of petitions, it takes a long time to settle pending trials. In many cases, the verdict appears when the person concerned has already spent more time in prison than the sentence. According to a Supreme Court report, more than 65,000 cases are pending in three levels of courts. Even if speedy justice is given, it will take many more years to settle the cases of more than 4,000 under-trial detainees.

According to the Annual Report of the Attorney General 2001/2002, among the 29,445 petitions filed in the court in 2001, only 15,550, or 52.48%, were settled. In the settled case, they are successful to win 8,279, or 53.24% of the cases. In the district courts, where most of the preliminary hearings begin, the success rate is 43.17% or 2,007 cases among the 8,131 petitions. In the appellate court, the success rate is higher in defending the petitions. In total, the success was 43.17%.

Despite the change in the political and other systems, only a few persons care about human rights and human dignity. The old Civil Code Act is still guiding the law in the criminal justice system. There are possibilities of reforming the old Act through the interpretation of the court, but the country is now moving toward acquiring another penal system.

Of the 41 different types of offenses, the highest number of police cases is related to murder. According to the 2001 police report, there were 938 murder cases filed in the courts. The second highest incidence related to 2,169 cases of pubic offense. Some 185 cases related to rape, and 125 cases related to girl trafficking. The police records show that criminal activities continue to increase moderately.

Police Profile

Background

Although no direct provision is made in the Constitution for Police powers and other civil defense matters, the Police Act 1955, the Essential Services Act 1957, the Customs Act 1962, the Anti-State Crimes and Penalties Act 1989, and the Public Security Act 1989, all of which predate the Constitution, have not been repealed and remain in force by virtue of the fact that the Constitution states that, subject to the "inconsistency" proviso, all laws in force at the commencement of the Constitution shall remain in force until repealed or amended.

The Police Act of 1955 stipulates that there shall be one or more than one Police Force for the Kingdom of Nepal. The composition and the number of police employees shall be as specified by His Majesty's Government. His Majesty's Government shall have power to control, guide, and give directives to police, and it shall be the duty of each police to abide by the order and directives of His Majesty's Government. The responsibility of police administration shall lie upon the Chief of Police and the Assistance Chief of Police, as deemed proper by the Government.

Organizational Description

Although the appointment of suitable candidates to the Civil Service, after examination, is governed by the Constitution, the day-to-day workings of the system and the powers of individual officials are not dealt with in the Constitution itself.

Each Ministry, as well as Ministerial policy, is operated by civil servants. The Senior Official in each Ministry is the Secretary. Each Secretary has Joint Secretaries working directly beneath him. Each Ministry has a spokesman and various levels of staff, down to Section Officers. Within most Ministries, there are different Departments with responsibility for a distinct part of Ministerial business. Each Department is headed by a Director General, who has responsibility for the staff below him.

The Government of Nepal has divided the Police of Kingdom of Nepal into two main divisions: the Armed Police Force and the Civil Police Service.

These two discrete police forces have their absolute different mandate and responsibilities as outlined by the law, including specific Acts, regulations, and charters. The newly established Armed Police Force came into existence in 2000, with a very explicit mandate. A seven-year Maoist uprising in the country forced the Nepalese government to form a different well-equipped and well-trained Police Force to combat the insurgents. The Government of Nepal, Ministry of

Home Affair remains in command of and governs the general functions of both Police Forces.

Functions

The Civil Police Act of 1955 and regulations from 1992 define the role of police. The functions of the Armed Police Force are:

- To control armed conflict;
- To control insurgency, rebellion, or a separatist movement;
- To control terrorist activity;
- To resolve any religious and communal riots;
- To render assistance to the relief of natural calamities or epidemics;
- To rescue an abducted person and control heinous and organized crime;
- To control serious crimes;
- To provide border security;
- To provide security for VIPs and vital installations;
- To provide assistance in case of external intervention;
- To perform other duties as prescribed by the Government.

Terrorism

The Terrorism and Disruptive Activities Control and Punishment Ordinance issued by the King has defined terrorism in the context of Nepal. It has described the following acts as terrorism and disruptive activities:

1. Any act or plan of using any kinds of arms, grenades, or explosives, or any other equipment or goods with the objective of affecting or hurting sovereignty or the security and law and order of the Kingdom of Nepal or any part thereof or the property of the Nepalese diplomatic missions abroad thereby causing damage to property at any place or any act causing loss of life or dismemberment or injury or setting fire or hurting physically and mentally or any act of poisoning goods of daily consumption causing loss of life or injury, or any other aforesaid acts thereby causing panic among the people in motion or assembled; acts of intimidation or terrorizing individuals at any place or in any vehicle or abducting them or creating terror among them by threatening to abduct them from vehicles and places or abduction of people traveling on such vehicles as well as activities like taking the life of others, causing physical mutilation,

injury and harm or causing other types of damage by using substances mentioned in the relevant section in that connection or by threatening to use such substances or any other substances other than those mentioned in that section or threatening to use them, or, Acts like the production, distribution, accumulation, peddling, import and export, marketing or possession or installation of any kind of arms and ammunition or bombs or explosive substances or poisonous substances or any assistance in this connection, and; Acts of gathering people or giving training for this purpose; Any other acts aimed at creating and spreading fear and terror in public life; Act such as extortion of cash or kind or looting of property for this purpose, forcibly raising cash or kind or looting property in pursuit of the said purpose. Any attempt or conspiracy to engage in terrorist or disruptive activity, or to encourage or force anyone to take up such activity, gathering more than one individual for such purpose, constituting any group to the same end, or assigning anyone to such activity or participating in such activity with or without pay or engaging in publicity for such activity, causing obstruction to government communications systems, or giving refuge to any individual engaged in terrorist or disruptive activity, or hiding any person doing any of this things.

2. Anyone indulging in crime in Nepal while residing abroad will also be subject to punishment.
3. The government can declare a terrorist-affected area or terrorist individuals.
4. House arrest can be used to prevent any terrorist and disruptive act.
5. Cases will be heard in a court constituted or designed by His Majesty's Government.
6. Arrangements will be made for reasonable expenses for treatment and compensation in case of the maiming or death of security personnel or police assigned to control or investigate terrorist and disruptive activities.
7. Cases instituted under this ordinance will not be subject to any statute of limitations.
8. Individuals arresting or helping in the arrest of any terrorist will be suitably awarded.
9. Despite the State of Emergency, expression of views, running of presses and publications, migration and operation of communications systems can take place as usual without, however, infringing on the Terrorist and Disruptive Crimes Control and Punishment Act and the Constitution of the Kingdom of Nepal.

RANJAN KOIRALA

THE NETHERLANDS

Background Material

The history of the Kingdom of the Netherlands as a unified nation can be traced back to the fifteenth-century Union of Utrecht, in which the seven "free" northern provinces agreed to continue a united struggle in the Eighty Years War against Spain. William of Orange, the founder of the Dutch House of Orange, led the revolt against Spain. In 1648, when the Spanish signed the Treaty of Münster, the sovereignty of the Dutch Republic of the United Provinces was recognized.

The Golden Age (1600–1700) was an important period in Dutch history. The newly formed state experienced a period of unprecedented economic, cultural, and scientific development. This was linked to the United East India Company (VOC), set up on the initiative of statesman Johan van Oldenbarnevelt. The religious freedom established during this period of the Republic continues to attract immigrants fleeing religious persecution.

After a struggle, the Patriots proclaimed the Batavian Republic, which became a unitary state with a modern Constitution. Yet only after the Napoleonic era, the annexation of the Kingdom of Holland to France, and the Belgian independence (1830) did a constitutional reform (1848) force King William II to adopt a liberal stance, and

Thorbecke drafted the new Constitution, which introduced the doctrine of ministerial responsibility for the actions of the monarch (http://www.history-netherlands.nl).

The Netherlands remained neutral for the duration of World War I. During World War II, the Netherlands was occupied by Nazi Germany. Both the Queen and the government Ministers escaped to England. Over 75% of the Jewish population of the country were deported and exterminated. In 1945, the country was liberated by the Allied Forces. During this war, the Japanese occupied the Dutch East Indies, and the local Dutch population were interned by the Japanese in camps, or were deported and forced into slave labor. At the end of World War II, Sukarno's *Partai Nasional Indonesia* (PKI) declared independence from Holland.

"Pillarisation" was the most important feature of Dutch politics in the last century. Different groups (Orthodox Protestants, Catholics, Social Democrats) form "pillars" to ensure political stability (Lijphart, 1968 in Pennings, 1993). Conflicts are settled by consensus. Lijphart characterizes Dutch society and politics as a "pacification democracy" (1968). The "school conflict" (1879–1917) was the start of this segregation of the parties that dominated Dutch politics for decades to come. In 1894, the Social Democratic Labour Party (SDAP) was founded; it was a modern political party destined to be a major force in twentieth-century Dutch politics. After World War II, a part of the political elite tried to eliminate the religiously based social and political divisions in the Netherlands. The attempt to establish a major progressive non-confessional party failed when the country voted overwhelmingly in favor of the old parties in the 1948 general election. "Pillarisation" returned. Until 1958, the Netherlands continued to be ruled by coalitions between Catholic and Socialist parties (*www.history-netherlands.nl*).

A new generation of progressive young people entering politics in the 1960s is one of the reasons why Dutch social legislation is now among the most extensive and generous in the world. The general election of 1967 brought religious-centered parties their first defeat in many years. The era of religious domination came to a halt. Democrats '66 (D '66), a new party advocating a more transparent administrative system and an elected Prime Minister, was one of the victorious parties. As the three religious-centered parties continued to lose votes, they decided to join forces, and in 1980 they formed a new party, the Christian Democratic Alliance (CDA) (*www.history-netherlands.nl*).

In the Wassenaar Agreement, the government and the social partners agreed on pay restraint to strengthen the position of Dutch exports. After seven years, the coalition between the Christian Democrats and the Liberals broke down. The Social Democrats formed a governing coalition with the Christian Democrats.

In 1994, a new coalition was formed between Liberals, Social Democrats, and Democrats. This "purple coalition," as it was known, brought the Christian Democrats to the opposition for the first time in half a century. In 2002, the right-wing populist leader Pim Fortuijn was shot dead, just before new elections were held. This led to political and social turmoil. His party, the *List Pim Fortuijn* (LPF) became one of the three parties that formed a new coalition government. This coalition broke down in the autumn of 2002. In the first half of 2003, a new coalition of Christian Democrats, Liberals, and Democrats was established.

The population of the Netherlands numbers 16 million, of which 10% are non-western minorities (CBS 2002). The capital city, Amsterdam, is home to over 200 different nationalities. The Netherlands is becoming a multicultural society accommodating a host of communities of different ethnic origin. The main groups of immigrants are: Turks (330,709), Surinams (315,777), Moroccans (284,124), and immigrants from the Dutch Antilles and Aruba (124,870). The major religions are Catholic (31%), Protestant (21%), Muslim (4%), Other (3%), and None (41%).

The per capita income amounts to greater than $23,500. Major economic activities contributing to the GDP are: services (45.2%), manufacturing (17.9%), trade (13.1), public sector (11.3%), transport and communication (7.3%), other (5.2 %) (*http://www.cbs.nl*).

Contextual Features

The Netherlands is a constitutional monarchy with a parliamentary system, with Queen Beatrix serving as the official Head of State. The Prime Minister is Head of the Cabinet. After a general election, the Queen and the Prime Minister have a role in forming the government, with the Sovereign (formally) appointing Ministers, and the Cabinet deciding on policy and exercising executive power. There are six tiers of government — the European Union, the national government, the provincial governments, the local or municipal councils, the waterboards, and the sub-local councils, which have certain powers in parts of the major cities in the Netherlands. The National Parliament consists of two chambers. In 1848, at the instigation of lawyer and statesman Thorbecke

NETHERLANDS, THE

(1798–1872), the Lower House obtained its set of rights, which formed the basis of the Dutch constitutional monarchy.

The main political parties represent liberal (VVD), labour (PvdA), green (Groen Links), and confessional (CDA) views.

The Netherlands operates three types of law: (1) Civil law, also known as private law. It sets out the rules governing relationships between people. Examples of civil law are the law of persons, family law, commercial law, rent law, and employment law. (2) Criminal law, which lays down the rules every citizen is required to adhere to. If a person breaks these rules, he is committing a punishable offense (a summary offense or a criminal offense) and, if the public prosecutor so wishes, he will be charged and will have to appear in court. (3) Administrative law describes the rules that prescribe how government agencies are required to make decisions. Examples of government agencies are the local and provincial authorities and central government (*www.rechtspraak.nl*).

Most Common Crimes

In the Netherlands, there are various places where justice is administered, including the cantonal courts, the district courts, the courts of appeal, and the Supreme Court. If one of the parties does not agree with the court's decision, he or she can appeal and request a new decision from a higher court. The cantonal court deals with labor and rent cases and cases for amounts up to 5,000. The district court deals with cases in individual and family law, commercial law, and cases for amounts above 5,000. The court of appeal only deals with appeal cases against verdicts of the court. And, as the occasion arises, the Supreme Court judges whether lower courts have applied the law correctly and have adhered to legal precepts. In the most extreme case, one can turn to the European Court of Justice in Strasbourg (*http://www.ministerievanjustitie.nl*).

The Public Prosecution Service is accountable to two separate authorities. On the one hand, the courts review the conduct of the Public Prosecution Service and the police services. But at the same time, the Minister of Justice has political responsibility for the Department's conduct and performance, and he may be called upon to render account to both Houses of the Dutch Parliament. Policy is therefore always on the agenda in consultations between the Public Prosecution Service and the Minister.

The Minister is concerned with general policy on investigation and prosecution. Only rarely does this entail intervention in individual cases, although instructions may be issued to the Department's officers after consultation with the Board of Procurators General. The Public Prosecution Service's highest authority, the Board of Procurators General, lays down policy on investigation and prosecution. The committee and its staff form the Department's head office.

The organization of the Public Prosecution Service corresponds to the various types of law court in the Netherlands. First, there are sub-district courts, followed by the district courts, the courts of appeal, and finally the Supreme Court (*http://www.openbaarministerie.nl*).

There are 19 law courts in the Netherlands, each covering what is known as a court district.

For young people between 12 and 18 years old who commit a misdemeanour or a crime, there is a special Juvenile Penal Law. Children under 12 years old are not criminally prosecuted. Penalties imposed on those found guilty include: fines, learning penalties, task penalties, or prison sentences. The Ministry of Justice is responsible for the execution of sentences. Where penalties restrict the offender's freedom, the Ministry considers his/her eventual reintegration into society. In so doing, the Ministry wants to prevent detainees from entering or returning to a criminal environment after their penalty (*www.ministerievanjustitie.nl*).

Police Profile

Background

The Netherlands Police is composed of 25 regional forces, and the Dutch National Police Agency (KLPD) consists of five divisions. In all, over 40,000 persons are employed with the police; there are 30,000 executive police officers, and 10,000 administrative officers. They serve a population of 16 million people, which equals one police officer for every 400 citizens. The total of female police officers reached 18.4% in 2001. It is estimated that 5.8% of Dutch Police employees have an immigrant background (Ministry of Justice and Ministry of Interior Affairs and Kingdom Relations 2002: 48-9).

The tasks of the Dutch Police are described in the Police Act 1993, which is the statutory basis for the police organization. Briefly summarized, the Act states that the police must see to a safe and liveable society, and assist those in need. That means that the police must be visibly present in the street; tackle crimes, such as car crime and burglaries; deal with youth and vice issues; and fight violent and serious crime. The basic police work roughly consists of the following tasks: daily

Total Netherlands

Period	1994	1995	1996	1997	1998	1999	2000	2001
Type crime	Absolute figures							
Total-General	1,313,577	1,226,677	1,189,217	1,225,964	1,223,500	1,284,328	1,305,635	1,357,617
Criminal law offences (Wetboek van Strafrecht totaal)	1,206,128	1,126,659	1,076,074	1,104,760	1,102,670	1,152,068	1,173,688	1,219,655
Violence (Geweldsmisdrijven)	67,077	65,284	67,479	74,691	76,666	86,587	90,944	101,143
Theft (Vermogensmisdrijven)	978,299	904,871	834,381	846,445	842,415	872,362	887,829	919,262
Public order (Vernieling en Openbare orde)	155,684	152,793	170,706	180,350	179,100	188,242	189,779	192,921
Other crimes (Overige misdrijven Wetboek v. Strafrecht)	5,068	3,711	3,508	3,274	4,489	4,877	5,136	6,329
Traffic / roads (Wegenverkeerswet) totaal	92,849	89,433	100,819	99,799	105,465	117,087	117,800	120,283
Economic crime-act (Wet op Economische Delicten totaal)	4,389	2,283	1,359	3,187	3,134	3,709	3,528	3,595
'Opium-act' / drugs (Opiumwet totaal)	4,452	4,248	7,331	13,675	7,690	7,613	7,474	10,380
Weapons and ammunition-act (Wet Wapens en Munitie totaal)	3,139	2,147	2,477	3,202	3,372	3,432	2,966	3,508
Other acts (Overige wetten) total	2,620	1,907	1,157	1,341	1,169	419	179	196

police surveillance, giving prevention advice, handling traffic problems, simple crime investigation tasks, rendering assistance, and law enforcement.

Organizational Description and Functions

The 25 Regional Police Forces are responsible for police care in their respective region in the Netherlands. The size of a regional police force differs, depending on population size, crime level, and building density. Each Regional Police Force breaks down into a number of Districts or Divisions, each headed by a District or Division Commander with a small staff. Each District is composed of a number of Basic Units or Bureaus.

Apart from the daily work, the police have a number of specialist tasks. They are either separate tasks or tasks carried out in support of the basic police care. In theory, each Police Force has a number of specialized branches. Basic Units include: Routine Police Surveillance, Investigative Work, Crime Prevention, Traffic Duties, Environmental Monitoring, and Implementation of Special Legislation. Special Divisions include: Criminal Investigation, Technical Branch, Records Service, Criminal Information Service, Juvenile & Vice Unite, Aliens Police, Management Support, and Public Relations (*www.politie.nl/home/engels/default.htm*).

Cooperation between Police Forces is indispensable for an effective and efficient approach to common police issues. Exchanging knowledge and experiences is essential in this respect. Moreover, cooperation reinforces the effectiveness of separate measures and reduces the risk of crime moving to other places. The Netherlands Police Institute supports this cooperation by developing joint new policies and non-operational coordination.

The Netherlands Police Institute is a foundation whose board is composed of the chairmen of the three police boards: (1) the Board of Police Force Administrators, (2) the Board of Chief Public Prosecutors, and (3) the Board of Chief Commissioners.

The National Police Agency is composed of five divisions, which include:

1. Mobility: Traffic Police, Aviation Investigation Unit, and River Police;
2. Royal & Diplomatic Security: Guarding members of the Royal Family and VIPs;
3. NCIS: National Criminal Intelligence Service, collects and processes data relevant to the fight against (organized & international) crime, National Central Bureau for Interpol and Europol, and National Schengen Information System;

4. Logistics: Purchase of clothing, arms, vehicles, and other police equipment;
5. Support: Mounted & Canine Unit, Information & Communication Centre, and Aviation Unit.

(*www.politie.nl/home/engels/default.htm*).

The responsibility for the Police Force and the National Police Agency is structured as follows:

- Maintaining Public Order: the mayor (local level), Queen's Commissioner (monitoring function of public order and the Minister of Interior Affairs and Kingdom relations (national level);
- Investigating Criminal Offenses: Minister of Justice (national), Procurator General (Monitoring function: Investigations), and Public Prosecutor.

From this structure springs a Triangle of Authority at the local level to discuss policing issues and local policy. The components of this triangle are: (1) the Mayor, (2) the Public Prosecutor, and (3) the Chief of the Police Force (Chief Constable). Together, they prioritize police activities; they are responsible for public order, and they are the decision-making body in critical or crisis situations.

The authority to give orders for the carrying out of tasks is vested with the Mayor, for the maintenance of public order and care. The Mayor is accountable to the City Council. If the police are deployed for investigation into a punishable offense, the police follow the instructions of the Public Prosecutor, who is a member of the Public Prosecution Department. The Public Prosecution Department, which falls under the Ministry of Justice, is responsible for maintaining legal order where it concerns violations of the Criminal Code.

The Minister of the Interior and Kingdom Relations is responsible for the central administration of the Police in the Netherlands. One of the Mayors in a region (often the Mayor in the biggest municipality) is the Force Administrator. Together with the Chief Public Prosecutor, he has the ultimate responsibility for administering the Police Force.

Day-to-day management is in the hands of the Regional Chief of Police. The Regional Board makes decisions about the principal lines of policy. The Board consists of all of the Mayors in a region, as well as the Chief Public Prosecutor. Policies are worked out in detail in the so-called tripartite consultations, in which the Force Administrator, the Chief Public Prosecutor, and the Chief of Police in the region in question participate (*www.politie.nl/home/engels/default.htm*).

Training

The Police Education and Knowledge Centre (LSOP) is responsible for general information on the police, national selection and recruitment of future policemen/women, education and training of the police, organization and advice on education, research for police education, and examination of police education. (The LSOP Police Education and Knowledge Centre P.O. Box 834, 7301 BB Apeldoorn. Phone: +31 (0)55-5392000. E-mail: info@lsop.nl).

Its various tasks are carried out in co-operation with the regional police forces, and in these LSOP-institutes:

a. National Selection Centre of the Police (LSCP);
b. National Police Education Centre;
c. The Netherlands Police Academy (NPA);
d. Criminal Investigation School;
e. Police Traffic Institute (PVI);
f. Police Institute for Public Order and Safety (PIOG).

The requirements to be admitted to an educational program, depending on the level of police profession the education aims for, vary between a certificate of vocational/professional or occupational training to a high school diploma, including OAC levels-preparation for university.

There are three types of basic police training in the Netherlands:

Surveillance Officer (six months' training).

Duties: Monitoring and Prevention. Training can be extended through optional modules. Surveillance officers have the authority to investigate offenses.

Police Officer (16 months' training).

On-the-job training is a crucial course component, thus reducing the gap between theory and practice. There are five basic Training Institutions in the Netherlands.

Senior Police Officer (2–4 years).

Designed to equip senior police officers for management positions. There are four types of courses and three study trajectories. A course takes between two and four years, depending on candidates' qualifications and experience. The educational institute for this training is the Netherlands Police Academy.

Only recently has the structure of Dutch police education been drastically modified. Police education is now more compatible with regular higher education in the Netherlands. Police education is based on five job profiles and is structured around the combination of learning and working.

(*http://www.minbzk.nl*).

The ranks from lowest to highest are: Police Trainee, Police Patrol Officer, Constable, Constable First Class, Police Sergeant, Inspector, Chief Inspector, Commissioner, and Chief Commissioner.

Police Public Projects

The Ministry of Justice has formulated four forms of crime prevention:

1. A balanced upbringing;
2. Controlling power of the social environment;
3. Preventing crime situations;
4. Deterrence through criminal law.

(*www.minjust.nl*).

Besides this, the police conduct many different campaigns to inform citizens about such things as how to protect themselves against burglary and theft, and how to keep their neighbourhoods safer.

The Netherlands Police Museum in Apeldoorn contains educational material on the Dutch Police, mainly intended for high school pupils. The lessons include information about such topics as: the daily tasks and challenges of a surveillance officer, police and society, various positions within the police force, and the role of the police in a democracy. In addition, there are various films and guided tours through the museum (*http://home-3.tiscali.nl*). Moreover, in some regions police officers appear in school classes to educate pupils on the police and their responsibilities.

Police Use of Firearms

Police officers in the Netherlands carry firearms routinely. Training is compulsory and should be repeated annually. If training is not sufficient, officers are not allowed to carry their firearm.

The police actual use of firearms 1998–2000 is as follows:

1998: 364 cases;
1999: 485 cases;
2000: 359 cases.
(Naeyé, Timmer, and Beijers, 2001: 9).

Complaints and Discipline

Each regional Police Force follows a structured complaints regulation. The handling of complaints is a process that resembles a customer service and integrity policy, which is professionally structured and implemented (Ministry of Justice and Ministry of Interior affairs and Kingdom Relations 2002: 51). Complaints can be filed at the police station concerned, and be treated on a local level, but may, depending on the severity of the issue, be presented to the Public Prosecutor (*http://home-3. tiscali.nl*).

The Netherlands acknowledges Human Rights as stated in the Council of Europe, Strasbourg, and participates in the "Police and Human Rights—Beyond 2000" Program, following its mission as stated below:

> The underlying goal of the programme "Police & Human Rights 1997–2000" is for all police officers in the member States of the Council of Europe to be able to acquire a sound knowledge of human rights standards which have important implications for policing—in particular those embodied in the European Convention on Human Rights and the European Convention for the Prevention of Torture and Inhuman or Degrading Treatment or Punishment—and to acquire the skills that will enable them to apply these standards to their daily working practice. Aimed at raising awareness, developing training tools and building networks for police and human rights in Europe, the programme brings added energy and a strategic approach to co-operation with and between national police authorities across Europe.

> (*http://www.coe.int*)

In addition, the Netherlands has a National Police and Human Rights Co-ordinator, positioned at the Ministry of Interior Affairs and Kingdom relations, and the country is active in Human Rights training on a national and international level (*http://www.coe.int*).

Terrorism

The Netherlands' Constitution does not include a definition of terrorism, and no official list of terrorist organizations exists. Yet as part of the European Union, The Netherlands acknowledges the Eurolist of terrorist organizations.

The General Intelligence and Security Service (AIVD), a department of the Ministry of Interior Affairs and Kingdom Relations, is in charge of research on terrorism in the Netherlands, stressing a preventive policy (General Intelligence and Security Service 2002: 41). Currently, the AIVD has described a number of extremist groups active in The Netherlands, mainly from Algeria, Egypt, and Turkey:

- *Algerian radical-Islamic groups*: *Groupe Salafiste pour la Prédication et le Combat* (GSPC) and Takfir Wal Hijra (TWH);
- *Egyptian radical-islamitic groups: Al Jamaá al Islamiyya* (AJAI) and the Egyptian Islamic Jihad (EIJ);
- *Turkey:* Kaplan.

International-oriented radical Islamic groups and networks:

- *Al-Qaeda*: terrorist attacks;
- *Network of Mujahedeen, including Groupe Islamique Armé* (GIA) *Algiers* and *Libyan Islamic Fighting Group* (LIFG): radicalising of Moslems to support violent activities;
- *Al Aqsa*: collects money for the radical Islamic Palestinian organisation Hamas;
- *DHKP/C (Revolutionary Peoples Party Front)*: organizes protest actions to show solidarity to fellow victims in Turkey;
- *New People's Army* (NPA): responsible for violent actions in the Philippines;
- *Mujahedin-e Khalq* (MKO): an Iraqi group that launches violent assaults on the Iranian government in order to destabilise the Iranian society.

(Ministry of Interior Affairs and Kingdom Relations 2002:39–47).

International Cooperation

The Netherlands Police Centre for International Police cooperation is in charge of international cooperation.

Acting on requests by foreign governments and international organizations (mostly the OSCE and the UN), the Netherlands yearly sends out a number of police officers to former crisis areas. The aim is to lend assistance to the local police or contribute to the reconstruction of the police force.

In 1999, the EU decided to make a structural contribution to non-military support (CIVPOL) in former crisis areas in the near future. Various responsible Ministries in the Netherlands have together produced a policy note recommending that the Netherlands should supply a maximum of 250 officers for this purpose on a yearly basis. Starting in 2003, the total European capacity will be 5000. The officers will be supplied predominantly by the Ministry of Defence (Royal Marechaussee), which has wide experience in this area. The contribution of the regular police has been fixed at 0.1% of the national capacity.

With the aim of increasing safety for citizens, the Netherlands police have been cooperating with other countries for a long time. This cooperation (bilateral as well as multilateral) can be subdivided into three main categories:

1. Cooperation between fellow member states of the European Union is directed towards increasing safety in these countries, and therefore in the Union as a whole. This form of cooperation fits

in with the member states' objective of creating a European common space of freedom, safety, and justice. Within the European Union, cooperation in the Netherlands-German and Netherlands-Belgian border areas takes up a pre-eminent position. In addition to this, there is structural bilateral police cooperation with Belgium, Germany, and France at the national level. Intensifying contacts with other European Union member states is currently high on the agenda.

2. Cooperation with countries in Central and Eastern Europe is chiefly directed towards supporting accession to the European Union. A focus of attention is the extent to which these countries meet the criteria formulated in the area of Justice and Home Affairs. Central and Eastern Europe has been a priority area for police cooperation for over 10 years. The Netherlands police actively support Estonia, Hungary, Poland, Slovakia, and the Czech Republic by transference of knowledge and exchange of experience. In addition to this, the Netherlands plays a role in developing police institutions in these countries. Besides bilateral cooperation, the Netherlands is also involved in European programs that support the candidate countries in specific fields of interest.

3. Cooperation with other countries often stems from political, operational, and/or professional reasons. In recent years, there has been growing interest in this kind of cooperation. In the past, the Netherlands police have, among other things, trained Indonesian police officers in traffic law enforcement. Other training activities have been organized for the Palestinian and South African police.

To reinforce European cooperation at police-professional level, the European Council of Tampere (1999) decided to institute a Taskforce of European Heads of Police. This Taskforce meets twice a year in the member state holding the EU Presidency. Its aim is to exchange professional information and formulate advice on priorities to be set for operational cooperation within the EU. NCIPC supports the Netherlands' delegation in the Taskforce. The delegation consists of three Chief Commissioners, the Commander of the Royal *Marechaussee* (military police), and the director of NCIPC (*www.ncips.nl*).

Europol is the European law organization, which aims at improving the effectiveness and co-operation of the responsible authorities in the member states in preventing and combating terrorism, unlawful drug trafficking, and other serious forms of international organized crime.

In co-operating with the International Police Organisation, The Netherlands hosts a National Central Bureau of Interpol. This allows the Netherlands Police Force to participate in an international police network of approximately 178 countries worldwide.

Police Education, Research, and Publications

Institutions of Higher Education of the Police

Netherlands Police Academy (NPA)
P.O. Box 1202, 7301 BL Apeldoorn, the Netherlands. Phone: +31 (0)55-5397000. Fax: +31 (0)55-5397100. E-mail: npa@lsop.nl

Centre for Police Sciences (CPW)
Vrije Universiteit Amsterdam, Department of Criminal law and Criminology, Room 5A-42, De Boelelaan 1105, 1081 HV Amsterdam, The Netherlands. Phone: +31 (0)20-444 6231. Fax: +31 (0) 20-444 6230

The Association of European Police Colleges (AEPC) / Secretariat AEPC.
Rijksstraatweg 127, 7231 AD Warnsveld, The Netherlands. Phone: +31 (0)575 580058. Fax: +31 (0)575 580099. E-mail: info@aepc.net

Stichting Politie Vormingscentrum
P.O. Box 110, 8170 AC Vaassen, The Netherlands. Phone +31 (0)578 573 703. Fax: +31 (0)578 571 830. Internet: *www.spvc. nl*, E-mail: info@spvc.nl

Leading Researchers/Authors/Reporters/Columnists

Prof. Dr. F. Bovenkerk; Dr. M. den Boer; Prof. Dr. G.J.N. Bruinsma; Prof. dr. H. van den Bunt; Dr. A. Cachet; Prof. Dr. D.J. Elzinga; Prof. Dr. C.J.C. Fijnaut; Prof. Dr. A.B. Hoogenboom; Prof. Mr. Dr. E.R. Muller; Prof. Dr. J. Naeyé; Prof. Dr. M. Punch; Prof. Dr. U. Rosenthal; Prof. Mr. T.M. Schalken; Prof. Dr. C.D. van der Vijver.

Extent and Sources of Funding for Police Research

Police research is funded by the Ministry of Interior Affairs and Kingdom Relations through a program called "Police and Science/Social Studies," hosted by the LSOP/NPA at the Samuel Esmeijer Institute, P.O. Box 1201, 7301 BL Apeldoorn.

The main outlines of the research are:

1. Exploring relevant social developments and their possible consequences for the police;
2. Investigating current police practices;
3. The development of promising concepts in cooperation with the police.

Yearly research topics, which represent priority areas, should be approached with these outlines in mind. Research areas for 2002 include:

Supervision; Gathering of intelligence; Chain cooperation; Treatment of the public; Management styles.

Police Publications

Het Tijdschrift voor de Politie/Elsevier bedrijfsinformatie, P.O. Box 16500, 2500 BM The Hague, The Netherlands. Phone: +31 (0)20-4415166. Periodical for the Police.

ABP, Algemeen Politieblad/Ministry of Justice and Ministry of Interior Affairs and Kingdom Relations. Schedeldoekshaven 100, P.O. Box 20301, 2500 EH The Hague, The Netherlands. Phone +31 (0)20-3706507.

General Police Journal.SEC/Ministry of Justice. P.O. Box 20301, 2500 EH The Hague, The Netherlands. Phone +31(0)70-3706542. Journal about society and criminology.

1. Tijdschrift voor Criminologie/SISWO, Plantage Muidergracht 4, 1018 TV Amsterdam, The Netherlands. Phone: +31 (0)20-5270600. E-mail: tvc@siswo.uva.nl Journal of Criminology.

Police-Related Websites

The Dutch Police: *www.politie.nl/* (links to 25 regional Police Forces)
Korps Landelijke Politiediensten: *www.klpd.nl*
Ministry of Interior and Kingdom Relations (BZK): *www.minbzk.nl/*
Netherlands Centre for International Police Cooperation: *www.ncips.nl/*
Police Education and Knowledge Centre (LSOP): *www.lsop.nl/*
Politie en Wetenschap: *www.ppenw.nl*

MARTIJN SCHILSTRA

NEW ZEALAND

Background Material

New Zealand was first settled approximately 1,000 years ago by peoples from Eastern Polynesia, now collectively known as Maori. In 1642, the Dutch explorer Abel Tasman briefly sailed along the west coast of New Zealand, and in 1769, Captain James Cook's British scientific expedition aboard the *Endeavour* circumnavigated and charted the country.

After Cook, the British began colonizing New Zealand, and relations between Maori and the settlers (*Pakeha*) became problematic. In 1840, Maori and the Crown signed the Treaty of Waitangi, which ceded sovereignty of New Zealand to Britain in exchange for Maori having protection and guaranteed possession of their lands. War broke out between Maori and the settlers and lasted until 1872.

The discovery of gold in the late nineteenth century and the introduction of wide-scale sheep farming brought prosperity to New Zealand. Dominion

status in the British Empire was given in 1907, and autonomy was granted by Britain in 1931. Independence was not formally proclaimed until 1947.

At the last census (March 2001), the population was 3,737,280; English and Maori were the two official languages, and 61% of New Zealanders identified themselves as Christian. The ethnic make-up of the New Zealand population has become more diverse in recent years. Between 1991 and 2001, those in the resident population identifying themselves as European declined from 83% to 80%, while those identifying as Mäori rose from 13% to 15%. In 2001, the Pacific Peoples ethnic group comprised 6.5% of the population, up from 5% in 1991; the Asian ethnic group comprised 7%, up from 3% in 1991.

New Zealand's primary economic activity still centers on agriculture, exporting wool, meat, and dairy products. Viticulture, fishing, forestry, fashion, tourism, and manufacturing are also economically significant.

Contextual Features

New Zealand's Parliament, located in Wellington, deoveloped from the Westminster system. The Queen of England is the Head of State and is represented by the Governor-General. Parliament has one chamber with 120 Members (MPs) elected for a three-year term by New Zealanders aged 18 years and over.

The 1996 general election was the first held under the mixed member proportional representational system (MMP). Under the MMP, voters have two votes: a party vote and an electorate vote. The party vote elects parties to Parliament; the electorate vote is for a local MP. New Zealand is divided geographically into 61 general electorates and 7 Maori seats. People of Maori descent can choose to be on the Maori or general electoral rolls.

The independence of the judiciary is an important principle of the New Zealand constitution. Parliamentary rules prohibit MPs from criticizing judges, whose role is to apply the law to every case and develop the law by interpreting it wisely. The Governor-General appoints judges from lawyers with at least seven years' experience.

The New Zealand legal system is based on the English system and consists of common law (law built up from decisions made in the United Kingdom and in New Zealand) and Statute law made by Parliament. Civil law covers disputes between individuals, companies, and other parties. The police usually bring criminal prosecutions. Under criminal law, the accused has the right to legal representation and to have the evidence against him or her heard in an open court and tested by cross-examination. The offense must be proved beyond reasonable doubt. If convicted, a person will be sentenced in accordance with the law and may appeal against conviction and sentence.

The Treaty of Waitangi is a constitutional document that establishes and guides relationships between the New Zealand Government and the Maori. It promises to protect a living Maori culture; to enable Maori to continue to live as Maori, while simultaneously conferring on the Crown the right to govern in the interests of all New Zealanders. The Waitangi Tribunal provides a forum for historical and contemporary grievances regarding treaty breaches.

In the District and High Courts, the Judge sits alone or with a jury. A jury is composed of 12 citizens selected at random from the jury roll (based on the electoral roll), and its function is to decide questions of fact. The Judge directs the jury on the law.

The adversarial system is used, with the Judge acting as a neutral referee while each party presents evidence and arguments in support of its case. Rules of evidence determine what can and cannot be presented to the court. The verdict is given after all evidence and arguments have been presented.

Dishonesty offenses (including burglary) made up the bulk of crime (59%) in New Zealand. The total number of offenses reported to Police was 440,129. There were 3,508 recorded sexual offenses and 122 homicides (murder, manslaughter, attempted murder, infanticide, abortion, and aiding a suicide or pact).

The Department for Corrections manages custodial and non-custodial sentences imposed by the courts. It also provides information to the judiciary to inform decision-making, and it provides support services to the New Zealand Parole Board.

The Department operates 17 public prisons, 12 Community Probation Service area offices (with 144 staffed locations nationwide), and eight Psychological Service offices. There are also prison-based units: three drug and alcohol units; two sex offender treatment units; a violence prevention unit; five Maori focus units; and four youth units.

Within the Department, the public prisons service is responsible for the containment of sentenced and remanded inmates, managing the sentences and rehabilitation of each offender. The Probation and Offender Service is responsible for the Community Probation Service (CPS), Psychological Service, and Intervention Services. The CPS manages approximately 38,000 community-based sentences annually, provides information, reports to judges to assist them in sentencing and release decisions, and provides rehabilitative programs.

Police Profile

Background

A paramilitary Armed Constabulary Force was established in New Zealand in 1867. Its members served in the New Zealand Wars as well as keeping civil order. Provincial governments operated civil police forces between 1853 and 1872, initially in cities and later in rural communities. Forces were small, and duties consisted mainly of keeping the peace among drunken sailors and bush settlers.

The New Zealand Constabulary Force was formed in 1877, formalizing the civil police branch (the former Provincial Forces) and the military branch (Field Force) as separate entities in the one organization. The new force was unarmed. Women were admitted to the police in 1941, but it was not until 1973 that they were fully integrated.

A proposed visit to New Zealand of a South African rugby team in 1973, and massive public demonstrations against their actual tour in 1981, led to a need for change in policing tactics, to be able to cope with large, often violent crowds.

In 1992, the Police combined with the Traffic Safety Service, which had previously had primary responsibility for policing the roads.

Public opinion polls in New Zealand always place police close to the top of the list of organizations in which the public has the most faith and trust.

Demographics

As of 30 June 2002, there were 9,054 full-time employees of the New Zealand Police. Of those, 7,037 (78%) were sworn members, and 2,016 (22%) were non-sworn members. In addition, there were 127 recruits.

The majority of sworn staff (86%) is male while the majority (69%) of non-sworn staff is female. Nine percent of sworn staff and 7% of non-sworn staff are Maori; 73% of sworn male staff and 89% of sworn female staff hold the rank of Constable.

Organizational Description

The New Zealand Police Force is divided into 12 geographic districts, each headed by a District Commander responsible to the Commissioner of Police at Police National Headquarters in Wellington. There are two Deputy Commissioners (one is non-sworn), three Assistant Commissioners, and four General Managers, who formulate and monitor planning policy and partnerships, public affairs, cultural affairs, general finance, human resources, and Counter-Terrorism. There are five ranks below the Assistant Commissioner: Superintendent, Inspector, Senior Sergeant, Sergeant, and Constable.

There are three Police branches: General Duties Branch, Criminal Investigation Branch, and Road Policing; these branches are assisted by a number of specialist units, including: Intelligence, Forensic, Armed Offenders (supported by negotiation teams and specially trained police dogs and handlers), Strategic Traffic, Special Tactics, Diplomatic Protection Crash Teams, Maritime, Air Support, and Dog Section.

Functions

The function of the New Zealand Police is articulated in its mission statement: "To serve the community by reducing the incidence and effects of crime, detecting and apprehending offenders, maintaining law and order and enhancing public safety." The Police Oath requires sworn officers to preserve the peace, to prevent offenses against the peace, and to carry out their duties lawfully.

Training

To join the New Zealand Police, applicants must:

- Pass mathematical, literacy, and computer skills tests and undergo a psychological assessment;
- Pass prescribed fitness and medical tests, and maintain fitness with retests every two years of service;
- Have good eyesight (defined as a minimum visual standard of 6/12 unaided in each eye, correctable to 6/6 with contact lenses or eyeglasses);
- Notify the recruitment office of asthma, any significant operations, or knee, neck, back, or joint injuries;
- Notify the recruitment office of any previous criminal or traffic convictions (people convicted of serious crimes – including drink driving – are not eligible to join);
- Hold a current Driver's Licence.

Recruits attend the Royal New Zealand Police College near Wellington for approximately 19 weeks. After graduation, the recruits begin a two-year on-the-job training program as Probationary Constables and enroll in two compulsory university classes. Permanent appointment is conferred at successful completion of the on-the-job competency assessments and academic papers.

Police Public Projects

The police promote police-community involvement through a number of specialist units. A number of liaison units ensure responsiveness to Maori and Pacific peoples. Local Police managers and staff work in partnership with government and non-government organizations to develop public projects aimed at preventing crime and reducing victimization. These include: Matapihi (Maori Wardens), Liquor Ban, and Violence Free Workplaces. The Police Youth Education Service delivers crime prevention programs to schools and school communities. Their programs include: crime reduction and social responsibility, drug abuse resistance education, school road safety education, and violence prevention.

Police Use of Firearms

In general, police officers in New Zealand do not carry firearms in the course of their duties. However, all staff are trained in the use of firearms as well as empty hand tactics, handcuffs, OC (pepper) spray, and Asp baton. The Glock 9-mm pistol and Remington .223 rifle are the standard frontline issue, although alternatives to the rifle are currently being evaluated. Frontline staff are supported by specialist Armed Offenders Squads (trained and equipped to cordon and contain offenders and negotiate) and the Special Tactics Group (trained and equipped to confront the offender).

Sworn members are issued firearms to respond to specific incidents and are the subject of specific orders (Fire Orders). Officers are personally responsible for ensuring that they are fully conversant with relevant law and policy. Police should not use a firearm except:

- To defend themselves or others if they fear death or grievous bodily harm (GBH) and cannot protect themselves or others in a less violent manner;
- To arrest a person if it is believed the person poses a threat of death or GBH, and the arrest cannot be made in a less violent manner;
- To prevent the escape of a person who is believed to pose a threat of death or GBH to any person, and the escape cannot be prevented in a less violent manner;
- The offender should be called upon to surrender unless circumstances make it impracticable or unsafe to do so;
- Regardless of previous actions, there is no legal justification to shoot a person who is no longer a threat to life;
- Warning shots should not be made except in exceptional circumstances. They must be clearly aimed so it is clear that it is a warning shot.

Complaints and Discipline

The Police Complaints Authority (PCA) was established to deal with complaints about misconduct or neglect of duty by police officers and to investigate incidents involving death or serious bodily harm that involve police.

By June 1 of 2000, 2,905 complaints had been received from 11,781 individual complainants: 2,428 were accepted for investigation; 477 were withdrawn, refused, not pursued, or not within the PCA's jurisdiction. Investigation had been completed for 1,213 complaints: of those, 674 (55%) were not sustained; 380 (31%) were resolved; and

159 (13%) were sustained or partly sustained. The use of physical force and attitude/language were the most common complaints.

As of 30 June 2000, 1,965 assaults on police had been reported, 59 involving weapons (19 involving firearms). In 2001, this increased to 1,997, with 66 involving weapons (18 firearms).

Terrorism

As in other jurisdictions, urgency has been given to creating an effective response to counter terrorism. New Zealand is bound by Resolution 1373, passed by the United Nations Security Council. Its primary focus is to prevent financing and support for terrorist organizations. A bill passed in December 2002 made it an offense to fund or recruit terrorists. It allows freezing of terrorist assets and the prosecution of New Zealanders for terrorist acts outside of New Zealand.

New Zealand shares intelligence to detect and prevent terrorist actions. Terrorism is an aggravating factor for sentencing under the Sentencing Act 2002. Police can seek authority to use electronic tracking devices. A 10-year jail sentence or a $500,000 fine applies to offenses relating to possessing, using, or making plastic explosives; and transporting, improperly obtaining, or threatening to use nuclear material.

International Cooperation

The New Zealand Police belong to Interpol. Officers of all ranks are eligible for international exchange.

Police Education, Research, and Publications

The Royal New Zealand Police College is the leading provider of education for police from entry-level to postgraduate training. Courses offered include basic intelligence analysis, supervision, and armed offender training.

Each district has a senior officer representing the college; he or she is responsible for training programs within that district. District training is compulsory for officers and updates them in areas such as law changes, first aid, staff safety, and weapons training.

The rank system relies on qualifications; therefore, officers seeking promotion must study through university and the Police College. The Police force encourages higher education for all employees, providing generous study leave and contributions to fees. Currently, a number of members are enrolled at universities throughout New Zealand and Australia.

Ten One is the major New Zealand Police magazine, published under the Commissioner's authority every two weeks. It incorporates personnel notices, general instructions, policy, news, and editorials.

The aim of the New Zealand Police Association, established in 1936, is to improve working conditions and to promote the general welfare and contentment of members. It is open to all Police employees. The NZ Police Managers Guild was formed in 1955 and aims to represent police managers up to the rank of Deputy Commissioner.

CATHERINE CASEY AND CATHERINE COLLINSON

Bibliography

WWW sites:
The Department of Corrections: www.corrections.govt.nz.
The Department for Courts: www.courts.govt.nz.
The Ministry of Justice: www.justice.govt.nz.
The New Zealand Police Association: www.policeassn.org.nz.
The New Zealand Police: www.police.govt.nz.
Statistics New Zealand: www.statistics.govt.nz.
Books:
Statistics New Zealand (2002). *New Zealand Official Yearbook 2002* (103rd edition). Auckland, NZ: David Bateman.

NICARAGUA

Background Material

Until 1821, Nicaragua was part of the Spanish colony known as the Captaincy General of Guatemala. After independence, Nicaragua entered a phase of modernizing economic activity, accentuating the already severe class polarization and exploitation (Burns, 1991). This phase also saw the beginning of recurring foreign interference. England and the United States quarreled over control of the region; in the mid-1850s, an eccentric American, William Walker, declared himself President. Walker was soon overthrown and executed, but his reign signaled increasing U.S. involvement. By 1912, U.S. Marines occupied the country, and only after the patriot Augusto César Sandino waged a long, frustrating guerrilla war, did U.S. forces withdraw in 1932.

After U.S. withdrawal, the National Guard was turned over to a Nicaraguan, Anastasio Somoza García. Young and fluent in English, he had ingratiated himself with the occupying Americans. Somoza quickly consolidated power. For the next four decades, the Somoza family controlled Nicaragua. Anastasio ruled until his assassination in 1956; his eldest son, Luís Somoza Debayle, ruled until 1967; and Luis's younger brother, Anastasio Somoza Debayle, took control until overthrown in 1979

(Walker, 1991) as the result of a short-lived civil war that brought the Marxist Sandinista guerrillas to power in 1979. Nicaraguan aid to leftist rebels in El Salvador caused the United States to sponsor anti-Sandinista contraguerrillas through much of the 1980s. Free elections in 1990, 1996, and again in 2001 saw the Sandinistas defeated. The country slowly rebuilt during the 1990s, but suffered under Hurricane Mitch in 1998.

Nicaragua has 5,023,818 inhabitants (July 2002 est.), most of whom live in the Pacific basin. The majority (69%) of the population is *mestizo* (mixed Amerindian and white), with the following minorities: white (17%), black (9%), and Amerindian (5%). The official language is Spanish and is often laced with words of Nahuat origin. Miskito, Creole English, and Rama are spoken on the Caribbean coast. Mestizo English is not widely spoken. The religion is predominantly Roman Catholic (85%) with a growing Protestant minority.

Nicaragua is one of the Western hemisphere's poorest countries, with per capita income of $484 in 2001, flagging socio-economic indicators, and huge external debt. Nicaragua suffers from persistent trade and budget deficits and a high debt-service burden, leaving it highly dependent on foreign assistance as much as 25% of the GDP in 2001.

Exports were $640 million in 2001. Although traditional products such as coffee, meat, and sugar continued to lead the list, the fastest growth is in nontraditional exports: *maquila* goods (apparel); gold; seafood; and new agricultural products such as peanuts, sesame, melons, and onions. Nicaragua also depends heavily on remittances from Nicaraguans living abroad. Nicaragua is primarily an agricultural country, but construction, mining, fisheries, and general commerce also have been expanding during the last few years. Foreign private capital infusion topped $300 million in 1999, but due to economic and political turmoil, it fell to less than $100 million in 2001. Rapid expansion of tourism has made it the nation's third-largest source of foreign exchange. Some 60,000 Americans visit Nicaragua yearly–primarily business people, tourists, and relatives.

Contextual Features

The Nicaraguan Constitution was ratified January 1, 1987. It established a democratic system of government with a mixed economy based on a separation of powers. The 1995 constitutional reforms established a more equal distribution of power and authority among the four co-equal branches of government. The President heads the executive branch; he is both Head of State and Head of Government, as well as Supreme Chief of the defense and security forces; he also appoints the Cabinet. The Vice President has no constitutionally mandated duties or powers. Both the President and Vice President are elected to five-year terms by direct popular vote, with the possibility of a runoff election between the top two candidates if one does not obtain at least 35% of the vote on the first ballot. The Constitution does not permit the President to hold consecutive terms.

A single-chamber National Assembly exercises legislative power. In 1996, voters chose 93 members, including 20 deputies from nationwide lists, 70 from lists presented in each of the 15 departments and the two autonomous regions, and three defeated presidential candidates who obtained a minimum percentage of the national vote. The Supreme Court is an independent branch of government; members are selected for six-year terms by the National Assembly from lists submitted by the President, who also selects the head of the Supreme Court. The Constitution also provides that the Supreme Court justices appoint judges to the lower courts. Supreme Court justices can only be removed constitutionally "for reasons determined by law."

After the Sandinista victory in 1979, the FSLN government enacted by decree a Statute on the Rights and Guarantees of Nicaraguans. Among many provisions, the decree banned the death penalty, all forms of torture, and cruel and degrading punishment. The maximum sentence for any crime was set at 30 years. Basic procedures were outlined for arrest and detention, including a defendant's right to legal counsel. Arbitrary violation of an individual's personal integrity, home, or correspondence was prohibited. These principles were gradually eroded by a series of measures. The Law of National Emergency in 1982 legalized prolonged detention of government opponents and imposed constraints on political opposition and labor groups. An expanded State of Emergency, announced in 1985, suspended all civil liberties, including the prohibition against arbitrary imprisonment, the presumption of innocence, the right to a fair and speedy trial, the right to trial, and *habeas corpus* (Rosset, 1986).

The judicial system comprises both civil and military courts. The 16-member Supreme Court is the system's highest court. In addition to administering the judicial system, it also is responsible for nominating all appellate and lower court judges. The Court is divided into specialized chambers on administrative, criminal, constitutional, and civil matters. Under the Law of the Child and Family, which took effect in 1998, the Attorney General's office, rather than the police, investigates crimes committed by and against juveniles. The 1994 military code requires the civilian court system to try members of the military charged with common crimes.

A five-year administration of justice reform program was instituted in 1997. A Judicial Organic Law, which took effect in January 1999, contains a provision establishing minimum professional standards for judicial appointees. The Supreme Court commission supervising the revision of the country's outdated criminal codes and procedures continued its work, in coordination with the National Assembly's judicial commission. Reform of these codes is intended to reduce judicial delays and resulting excessive pretrial detention (see Section 1.d.). By November 2002, the National Assembly finally approved a Criminal Procedures Code.

One problem of the current system is that military courts are responsible for dealing with crimes committed by or against members of the armed forces or police. Proceedings are secret, although information can be released at the discretion of the military. According to the U.S. Department of State's annual human rights reports, convictions by military courts are rare, and when soldiers are convicted, sentences are light or not enforced.

Procedures for the arrest of criminal suspects are set forth in the Police Functions Law. The law requires police to obtain a warrant before detaining a suspect, but the warrant is issued by a police official, rather than a magistrate. The law also permits police to detain suspects for up to nine days. Police are required to inform families when persons are detained but rarely do so, and detainees are not granted access to legal counsel. The Reform Law of Penal Procedures, passed in 1991, provides for a maximum of three days' detention, but police continue to follow the Police Functions Law, which has not been amended. The 1991 reform law also provides for bail; previously, only compelling reasons such as ill health qualified accused criminals to remain at liberty while awaiting trial (Central American Report, 1992).

Defendants have the right to legal counsel at their trials. Although indigents are entitled to *pro bono* counsel, public defenders do not exist. In spite of the constitutional right to a speedy trial, arrested persons often spend months in jail before appearing in court. Under the 1991 law reforming penal procedures, jury trials have been restored. However, the jury system has proven ineffective, partly because prospective jurors seek to evade jury duty, delaying trials. Those convicted have the right of appeal.

In Nicaragua, violent acts are generally placed into two categories: so-called "common crime"; and violence, which originates in unresolved political conflict. In many cases, both types involve the misuse of firearms. Common violent crime has shown strong increases over the last several years, according to police.

The capacity of the Nicaraguan prison system was greatly expanded during the Sandinista period to keep pace with the incarceration of political prisoners. By 1985, the country had nine penitentiaries, holding cells in 48 local police stations, and some 23 DGSE detention centers. By the government's own estimate, there were 5,000 prisoners in

1984, of whom 2,000 were National Guardsmen or others accused of cooperation with the Contras. An independent human rights group in Nicaragua, the Permanent Human Rights Commission, claimed in 1986 that 10,000 were incarcerated, 70% of whom were political dissidents. The International Committee of the Red Cross, which periodically visited prisons, counted more than 1,000 guardsmen and 1,500 others accused of pro-Contra activity in early 1988. An estimated 500 to 600 additional persons were in DGSE facilities. After the release of 39 inmates in February 1990, no further political prisoners were believed to be in Nicaraguan jails.

In late 1990, President Chamorro created a National Penitentiary Commission to oversee and improve the penal system. Conditions in jails and holding cells remained harsh. Police station holding cells were severely overcrowded. Suspects often were left in these cells during their trials, since budgetary shortfalls often restricted the use of fuel for frequent transfers to distant courtrooms. At the Bluefields jail, there were only two showers and four toilets for more than 102 prisoners. At the Corn Island jail, six cells (each holding six detainees) frequently were filled to capacity. The authorities occasionally released detainees when they no longer could feed them.

Only Managua has a separate prison for women; outside Managua, women are housed in separate wings and guarded by female custodians. As of September 2001, females made up 4% of the prison population. The Public Defender's office assigned two full-time employees to work with the women's prison system to help ensure its proper functioning.

Police Profile

Background

The collapse of the Somoza administration in 1979 left Nicaragua without any agency of public order because the National Guard had performed police services. For a brief period, FSLN veterans,

Crimes against persons 1990–1999

Type of Crime	1990	1991	1992	1993	1994	1995	1996	1997	1998	1999
Assassination	202	259	325	331	326	313	296	254	254	180
Homicide	470	473	501	431	399	394	366	425	385	396
Assault	4,568	5,599	6,747	7,274	8,991	10,121	11,617	14,230	15,824	18,604
Sexual assault	344	427	527	712	906	1,037	1,095	1,249	1,249	1,367
Others	1,756	2,634	3,972	4,341	4,878	6,069	6,447	7,666	8,092	9,382

Source: Annual Reports, National Police Force.

Crimes against property 1990–1999

Type of Crime	1990	1991	1992	1993	1994	1995	1996	1997	1998	1999
Violent robbery	966	1,180	1,294	1,580	1,859	2,020	2,400	2,785	3,074	3,513
Robbery using intimidation	1,567	1,879	2,350	3,018	2,954	2,615	2,849	2,761	2,773	3,058
Robbery using force	7,192	6,423	6,754	8,112	8,067	7,775	8,990	10,061	9,805	10,486
Theft	4,570	4,430	5,232	6,526	7,655	7,965	9,300	10,541	11,575	12,187
Swindling	848	1,339	1,755	1,752	1,864	1,931	1,972	2,064	2,184	2,290
Rustling	3,566	3,819	3,367	4,200	4,249	3,395	3,538	3,652	3,405	3,097
Others	1,235	1,311	1,839	2,023	2,537	2,976	3,134	3,879	4,198	4,845

Source: Annual Reports, National Police Force.

working with the Sandinista Defense Committees and other mass organizations, provided rudimentary police functions, but this improvised system failed to quell organized criminal activity, armed robbery, and attacks by youth gangs. Easy availability of weapons also contributed to the breakdown of law enforcement. A professional police force was eventually established with help from the Panamanian National Guard and Cuban government. Panama also donated vehicles and equipment and accepted several hundred Nicaraguans in its police training academy (Uhlig, 1991).

Under the newly established Ministry of Interior, the Sandinista Police (*Policía Sandinista–PS*) resembled a military staff organization, headed by a former FSLN Brigade Commander. Individual operating sections were responsible for traffic, public safety, prisons, communications, surveillance, legal processing, and embassy protection. Women made up a substantial proportion of the force.

Organizational Description

Known as the National Police after 1990, the police force has continued to be controlled by Sandinistas, despite the turnover of power to President Chamorro. The Sandinista Police Commander, René Vivas Lugo, remained its head. Police matters come under the Ministry of Government, which replaced the Ministry of Interior. According to recent statistics, the National Police's total complement is given as 11,000 (Informe Nacional de Policia, 1999) with an officer to resident ratio of 1:1,000. In order to meet the increasingly difficult task of crime control in the 1990s, the National Police contracted voluntary citizens in several precincts, providing them with uniforms, and even guns at the discretion of the police chief. Voluntary police do not receive a salary from the state and do not receive any professional training. Due to sustained criticism of voluntary police for their involvement in human rights violations, in August 2000, the

former Chief of Police, Franco Montealegre, approved a new police statute terminating the employment of all voluntary police in Managua. Government authorities report that as of October 2002, there were still 2,170 voluntary police throughout the country; several were implicated in human rights abuses.

Training

An eight-month training course for police cadets included a heavy dose of military training; during national emergency, the PS was expected to aid in national defense. The police were also called on to combat Somoza's corrupt social legacy by enforcing morality and public welfare laws, later assisted by Revolutionary Vigilance Patrols organized by neighborhood Sandinista Defense Committees.

Complaints and Discipline

According to human rights groups, almost 1,000 persons remained unaccounted for at the close of the Contra war in 1990. Numerous secret gravesites–most ascribed to the Sandinistas but some to the Contras–were discovered. At one site, Correntada Larga on the south Caribbean coast, witnesses reported the torture and killing of 67 peasants by the DGSE during a two-week period in 1981. The end of armed conflict in 1990 brought improvements in human rights; however, sporadic incidents of political killings continue. Rural violence is often associated with disputes in which demobilized Contras and peasants seek to negotiate a share of state-owned cooperatives, clashing with police. The number of violent deaths of former Contras at the hands of the police, the army, or FSLN militants rose in 1993. In some incidents in which civilians were killed, government security forces were provoked by unruly, violent protesters. Nevertheless, even when it seems that the police have used disproportionate force or committed wanton murder, police actions are rarely investigated or punished.

Arbitrary arrest and detention are problems. The Police Functions Law requires police to obtain a warrant prior to detaining a suspect and to notify family members within 24 hours of the detainee's whereabouts. Over the last several years, authorities received fewer reports of arbitrary arrests and illegal detentions, largely due to pressure from internal affairs and support from the Chief of Police. Detainees do not have the right to an attorney until they have been formally charged with a crime. Local human rights groups are critical of the law for providing inadequate judicial oversight of police arrests.

Terrorism

Although there are no confirmed cases of specific terrorist organizations operating out of Nicaragua, reports indicate at least some terrorist activity. In 1993, one of the suspects in the first World Trade Center bombing was caught with five passports from Nicaragua, a nation he had never visited. That same year, an explosion that rocked a Managua auto body shop revealed a cache of arms, passports, and evidence of an international kidnapping ring. The current government supports the international fight against terrorism; however, there is no specific police body in charge. Terrorism is most typically used as a political issue; FSLN connections with terrorism, for example, have been used to derail comeback hopes of the Sandinistas. In the electoral campaign of 2001, newspaper ads showed Ortega with photographs of Castro, Gadhafi, and Saddam Hussein.

International Cooperation

At the beginning of 2000, when the U.S. policy of limiting support to Nicaragua was revised, a police assistance project was inaugurated to develop the investigative capabilities of the Criminal Investigations Department (DIC) and improve the training capacity of the police.

The focal point of U.S. security assistance to the hemisphere in the late 1980s and early 1990s, Central America has since been eclipsed by the Andean ridge drug source countries. A wide variety of U.S. military operations continue in the isthmus, however, and Washington continues to offer a great deal of aid to the region's police forces and militaries.

Many of these activities have a counter-drug mission; the White House Office of National Drug Control Policy estimated, for instance, that 59% of South American cocaine en route to the United States passed through the "Mexico-Central America corridor" (Report no. NSAID-00-09, Washington, DC: Dec.1999). This mission predominates especially in Nicaragua, Guatemala, Panama, and Costa Rica, which are receiving significant amounts of counter-narcotics police and military aid, and in El Salvador, which is hosting a staging area for aerial U.S. counter-narcotics operations. The U.S. Southern Command also continues to offer non-drug-related aid, largely training and engagement activities, regular exercises, and humanitarian assistance.

Police Education, Research, and Publications

The history of the Nicaraguan Police from the country's beginnings until the first years of the Sandinista era is traced in *Armed Forces of Latin America* by Adrian J. English. *Revolution and Foreign Policy in Nicaragua* by Mary B. Vanderlaan reviews the Sandinista military buildup and defense policy during the Sandinistas' first six years. Supplementary information on the Sandinista People's Army can be found in an article by Stephen M. Gorman and Thomas W. Walker in *Nicaragua: The First Five Years*. The brief article, "Nicaragua in Crisis," by Julio Montes in *Jane's Intelligence Review* summarizes the effects of the tremendous cutback in the armed forces since 1990.

Much of the data on the Nicaraguan weapons inventory can be found in *The Military Balance, 1993-94* from the International Institute for Strategic Studies, and in *Jane's Fighting Ships, 1993-94*.

The Nicaraguan internal security situation, law enforcement, and conditions in the court and prison systems have been surveyed in various reports of Americas Watch and in the U.S. Department of State's annual *Country Reports on Human Rights Practices*. (For further information and complete citations, see the Bibliography.)

Leading inside sources are Vision Policial and Boletin Policial. Relevant sources for police research on the Nicaraguan police include:

- United States, Department of State, Background Notes: Nicaragua, (Washington: Department of State: March 1998) *www.state. gov/www/background-notes/nicaragua-0398-bg n.html*
- United States, Central Intelligence Agency, *The World Fact Book* 1999, (Washington: Central Intelligence Agency: 1999) *www.odci. gov/cia/publications/factbook/nu.html*
- United States, Arms Control and Disarmament Agency, World Military Expenditures

and Arms Transfers 1996, (Washington: ACDA: 1996) *www.acda.gov/wmeat96/wmeat96.htm*

- United States General Accounting Office, "Drug Control: Assets DOD Contributes to Reducing the Illegal Drug Supply Have Declined," Report no. NSAID-00-09 (Washington, DC: December 1999) *http://frwebgate.access.gpo.gov*
- United States, Department of Defense, Defense Security Cooperation Agency, Humanitarian and Civic Assistance Program of the Department of Defense, Fiscal Year 1999, (Washington: Department of Defense, March 1, 2000)
- United States, Department of State, "Report to Congress," Washington, DC, July 27, 2000 *www.ciponline.org/colombia/aid/080102.htm*

Leading publications containing police reports include:

- The World Bank. *World Development Report, 1999.* New York: Oxford University Press, 1999.
- Inter-American Development Bank. *Economic and Social Progress in Latin America: Annual Report.* Washington: 1991.
- *Statistical Yearbook for Latin America and the Caribbean, 1999.* Santiago, Chile: 1989.
- United States. Agency for International Development. *Country Development Strategy, Nicaragua, 1991–1996.* Washington: 1990.
- Central Intelligence Agency. *The World Fact book, 1999.* Washington: GPO, 1999.
- United States. Agency for International Development. *Latin America and the Caribbean: Selected Economic Data.* Washington: 1999.
- Embassy in Managua. *2000 Foreign Economic Trends.* Washington: GPO, 2000.
- United States. Arms Control and Disarmament Agency. *World Military Expenditures and Arms Transfers, 1990.* Washington: GPO, 1991.
- United States. Congress. 102nd, 2d Session. Senate. Committee on Foreign Relations. *Nicaragua Today: A Republican Staff Report to the Committee on Foreign Relations, United States Senate.* Washington: GPO, 1992.
- Department of State. *Country Reports on Human Rights Practices for 1990.* (Report submitted to United States Congress, 102d, 1st Session, Senate, Committee on Foreign Relations and the House of Representatives, Committee on Foreign Affairs.) Washington: GPO, 1991.
- Department of State. *Country Reports on Human Rights Practices for 1991.* (Report submitted to United States Congress, 102d, 2d Session, Senate, Committee on Foreign Relations and the House of Representatives, Committee on Foreign Affairs.) Washington: GPO, 2001.
- Department of State. *Country Reports on Human Rights Practices for 1992* (Report submitted to United States Congress, 103rd, 1st Session, Senate, Committee on Foreign Relations and the House of Representatives, Committee on Foreign Affairs.) Washington: GPO, 2000.
- Department of State. *Background Notes: Nicaragua.* Washington: GPO, 1999.
- *Human Rights in Nicaragua under the Sandinistas: From Revolution to Repression.* Washington: GPO, 1986.

MARIA PIA SCARFO

Bibliography

Burns, E. Bradford. *Patriarch and Folk: The Emergence of Nicaragua, 1798-1858.* Cambridge: Harvard University Press, 1991.

Carr, Albert H.Z. *The World and William Walker.* Westport, Connecticut: Greenwood Press, 1975.

Castro, Vanessa, and Gary Prevost (eds.). *The 1990 Elections in Nicaragua and Their Aftermath.* Lanham, Maryland: Rowman and Littlefield, 1992.

Child, Jack. *The Central American Peace Process, 1983-1991: Sheathing Swords, Building Confidence.* Boulder, Colorado: Lynne Rienner, 1992.

Rosset, Peter, and John Vandermeer (eds.). *Nicaragua: Unfinished Revolution. The New Nicaragua Reader.* New York: Grove Press, 1986.

Skidmore, Thomas E., and Peter H. Smith. *Modern Latin America.* (3d ed.) New York: Oxford University Press, 1992.

Spalding, Rose J. (ed.). *The Political Economy of Revolutionary Nicaragua.* Boston: Allen and Unwin, 1987.

Stimson, Henry Lewis. *American Policy in Nicaragua: The Lasting Legacy.* New York: Markus Wiener, 1991.

Stone, Doris Z. "Synthesis of Lower Central American Ethnohistory." Robert Wauchope (ed.), *Handbook of Middle American Indians,* 4. Austin: University of Texas Press, 1966. 209-233.

Uhlig, Mark A. "Nicaragua's Permanent Crisis: Ruling from Above and Below," *Survival,* 33, September/October 1991, 401-23.

United Nations. Economic Commission for Latin America and the Caribbean. *Damage Caused by Hurricane Joan in Nicaragua: Its Effect on Economic Development and Living Conditions, and Requirements for Rehabilitation and Reconstruction.* New York: December 2, 1988.

Walker, Thomas W. (ed.). *Nicaragua: The First Five Years.* New York: Praeger, 1985.

———. *Revolution and Counterrevolution in Nicaragua.* Boulder, Colorado: Westview Press, 1991.

Williams, Mary Wilhelmine. *Anglo-American Isthmian Diplomacy 1815-1915*. (American Historical Association series.) Gloucester, Massachusetts: P. Smith, 1965.

Woodward, Ralph Lee, Jr. *Central America: A Nation Divided.* (2nd ed.) New York: Oxford University Press, 1985.

Wyden, Peter. *Bay of Pigs: The Untold Story*. New York: Simon and Schuster, 1979.

NIGER

Background Material

The Republic of Niger is a landlocked country located in West Africa. It lies southeast of Algeria; south of Libya; west of Chad; north of Nigeria, Benin, and Burkino Faso; and east of Mali. The country covers an area of 1.267 million sq km, which makes it almost twice the size of the state of Texas. It has one of the hottest climates in the world. The northern four fifths of the country form part of the Sahel and the Sahara Desert; however, in the south and in the Niger River Valley, the country is tropical and fertile. The capital of Niger is Niamey, which is located in the southwest of the country on the Niger River.

There is evidence that there was a human presence in the area that is now Niger 600,000 years ago. In more recent times, the nomadic Tuareg and Hausa peoples dominated the area. In the nineteenth century, European exploration led to the incorporation of Niger into French West Africa in 1896, but indigenous resistance ensured that the country did not become a French colony until 1922. It became an autonomous republic in the French Community in 1959 and gained full independence in 1960.

During the 1970s uranium production ensured a flourishing economy, but a fall in demand and prices in the 1980s brought the short-lived prosperity to an end. In addition, Niger underwent a number of violent regime changes, most recently in 1996 and 1999. A new Constitution was approved in 1999, and free elections were held in 2000 and again in 2004. The country has thus attained some degree of stability and democracy.

The multi-ethnic population of Niger is 11.36 million. The largest group is the Hausa, which constitutes 56% of the population. The Djerma represent 22%; the Fula 8.5%; the Tuareg 8%; the Kanouri 4.3%; and the Arab, Toubou, and Gour-

mantche together comprise 1.2%. There are also about 1,200 French expatriates in the country. Eighty percent of the population is Muslim, and the rest are Christian or hold indigenous beliefs. The official language is French, but Hausa and Djerma are also spoken.

Niger is one of the poorest countries in the world. There is little infrastructure or services, and the government relies on foreign aid to pay for operating expenses and public investment. About 63% of the population lives on less than $1 a day, and per capita income is less than $200 a year. Only 70,000 of the total population receive regular wages or salaries. Life expectancy at birth is 42.18 years. The literacy rate is about 18%. Both life expectancy and the literacy rate are lower for women.

Agricultural products include cotton, cowpeas, peanuts, and other crops as well as livestock. Industrial activity includes uranium mining, cement, brick, textiles, food processing, chemicals, and slaughterhouses. Exports go mainly to France, Nigeria, Japan, and Spain. In 2004 and 2005, drought and locust invasions led to food shortages; hunger affected 3 million people in 3,000 villages, and many children suffered from malnutrition.

Niger is a member of the Economic Community of West African States (ECOWAS), Interpol, and the United Nations.

Contextual Features

Under the 1999 Constitution, a President is elected by direct universal suffrage for a term of five years, which can be renewed once. The President is Head of State; he is also head of the administration and of the armed forces. The legislative authority is the unicameral National Assembly. It is composed of 113 seats, elected every five years. The Prime Minister is chosen by the President, and while he is the titular head of the government, he shares that responsibility with the President. The government is responsible to the National Assembly.

There is a Constitutional Court of seven members, which has jurisdiction over constitutional and electoral matters, and rules on the constitutionality of laws and ordinances, as well as compliance with international treaties and agreements. A High Court of Justice is responsible for trying crimes or misdemeanours committed by public officials. Its members are chosen from the National Assembly. An independent National Communications Institution is responsible for ensuring the freedom and independence of electronic and print media, while the independent National Committee for Human Rights and Basic Liberties promotes human rights and verifies and reports on human rights violations.

The legal system of Niger is based on the French civil law and on customary law. The Appeals Court hears questions of fact and law, and the Supreme Court reviews only the application of the law. According to the Constitution, the judiciary is independent but does not always act independently for reasons associated with family and business ties. Legal thinking, practices, and the criminal laws show a marked resemblance to those that prevailed in France during the colonial period.

The customary law is used in family matters, such a divorce and inheritance. Traditional chiefs are responsible for the customary law, although they are permitted only to mediate and not to arbitrate. They are paid a stipend and also collect local taxes. There are customary courts located in large towns, headed by a practitioner with basic legal training who is advised by someone with knowledge of social traditions.

While there are constitutional safeguards for human rights, they appear at times to be observed more in the breach than the application. There are large backlogs in the judicial system, and suspects may languish in pretrial detention for months or years without being charged. Freedom of speech and the press have been limited on occasions. Despite slavery having been declared illegal, there are also the remnants of a caste system in some ethnic groups that virtually enslaves men and women to others of a higher caste. Women, children, ethnic minorities, and the disabled live under a number of disadvantages. Widows and divorced women cannot be considered heads of households, and, among the Hausa, their mobility is restricted. In rural areas, they do most of the subsistence farming, water and wood gathering, and child rearing. Few have the opportunity for education. In urban areas, there are few women in professional or government employment, and few women have served in the Cabinet.

Despite unrest and harsh conditions, crime in Niger is low compared with developed countries. Analysis of 1996 Interpol data for Niger showed that the total rate for the offenses of murder, rape, robbery, aggravated assault, burglary, larceny, and motor vehicle theft was 59.07 per 100,000 compared to 1,280.58 per 100,000 for Japan, and 5,078.93 per 100,000 for the United States. Domestic violence is common but not often prosecuted, and female genital mutilation is also practiced by several ethnic groups. There is also some prostitution near mining and military camps. Niger is a transit and destination point for human trafficking for labor and sexual purposes; and there is some drug, oil, and arms trafficking across the borders with neighboring countries.

While prisoners are separated by gender and age, conditions in the 35 prisons in Niger are said to be poor and life threatening. The prisons are underfunded, understaffed, and overcrowded. In 2003, there were 550 prisoners in the civil prison in Niamey, which was built for 350. Of the number incarcerated, 400 were in detention awaiting trial, since pretrial and convicted prisoners are not separated. Nutrition and health conditions are poor, and there have been deaths from AIDS, tuberculosis, and malaria. Corruption among prison staff is reported to be rampant, probably because salaries of criminal justice workers are often not paid for months.

Police Profile

Organizational Description and Functions

The policing system in Niger is modeled on that of France. There are two police organizations in the country: the National Gendarmerie and the National Police. The Gendarmerie is part of the Armed Forces and comes under the Ministry of National Defense. The National Police is a civilian police organization, which comes under the authority of the Ministry of the Interior and Decentralization. The Gendarmerie operates mainly in rural areas, and it also acts as the military police. The National Police operates in the cities. The role of both organizations is administrative and preventive; that is to say, they maintain public order, safety, well-being, and peace.

Given that the Gendarmerie is dispersed throughout the country, it has the greatest responsibility for quelling unrest, particularly in the north, where the Tuareg have resisted the central government. It can be deployed where needed and operates from detachments located throughout the country. As a military force, it is also better equipped than the National Police, although the poverty of the country means that being better equipped is only relative.

When members of either of the two police organizations engage in investigation of criminal offenses, they are said to be acting in a repressive, as opposed to a preventive role. In the repressive role, they acquire the status of judicial police and come under the authority of the courts. In this role, their responsibilities are to investigate and identify offenses and suspects, collect evidence, and, when proceedings have begun, to act as delegates of the Public Prosecutor and the examining Magistrates. Under the Penal Code, it is the court officials who have charge of an investigation, and they can take it over at any time.

There are two levels within each police organization: higher-ranking officers and lower-ranking agents (gendarmes and sub-officers). Officers receive more initial training and enter at a higher level in the organization than agents, gendarmes, and sub-officers. When they become judicial police, the lower ranks act as assistants in the investigative process in collecting information for the officers, although they are also under the authority of the Public Prosecutor.

In its role as judicial police, the Gendarmerie has jurisdiction outside population areas and in those urban areas where there are no national police. The judicial police in the Gendarmerie also investigate forestry, customs, economic, fiscal, fishing, hunting, and military offenses. The separate responsibilities of the two organizations are generally complementary, but on occasion they are not clear cut. For example, if a member of the military commits an offense in the jurisdiction of the National Police, it is the National Police who do the investigation.

Complaints and Discipline

The weakness of the system of judicial police is the dual accountability to the courts and to the two police organizations. While the courts have authority over the investigative activities of the judicial police, they have no influence over their performance or discipline because they report hierarchically to their respective police services, and it is in those organizations that rewards such as promotion reside. Moreover, because the courts are understaffed and underfunded, the Public Prosecutor or the examining Magistrates are frequently not able to assert practical authority over the police. For this reason, the police can extend pretrial detention without the required authority of the public prosecutor and act without the authority of warrants.

The question of human rights violations by the police is being addressed with training, aided by the international community. The Danish Institute for Human Rights has done a study on the perception of human rights by the police in Niger, and developed a training manual on human rights for the police, which has been incorporated into the curriculum at the National Police Training Academy. The United States has also contributed to training in such matters as the control of human trafficking, and France also provides advanced training.

International Cooperation

The police engage in cooperative relations with the police of neighboring countries to combat human trafficking, drug trafficking, and arms smuggling, and they take part in joint operations. Niger is also participating in the organization of Police Chiefs of the Economic Community of West African States (ECOWAS) to encourage intelligence sharing and joint efforts against crime. Niger has also supplied police for United Nations peacekeeping operations in Africa.

TONITA MURRAY

Bibliography

Juriscope (1999). *La direction de la police judiciare et son contrôle par les autorités judiciare de Sénégal.* www.juriscope.org/publications/etudes/pdf-polive/OK.NIGER.pdf. February 28, 2005.

Niger, Embassy of. *Organization of the Government of Niger.* www.nigerembassyusa.org/govt.html. February 28, 2005.

Schwab, Peter. *Africa: A Continent Self-Destructs.* New York: Palgrave Macmillan, 2002.

United States, Central Intelligence Agency (2005). "Niger." *The World Factbook.* www.cia.gov/cia/publications/factbook/geos/ng.html. February 28, 2005.

United States, Department of State (2004). "Niger." *Country Reports on Human Rights Practices 2003.* www.state.gov/g/drl/rls/hrrpt/200, February 28, 2005.

Winslow, Robert (n.d.). "Niger." *Crime and Society: A Comparative Criminology Tour of the World.* www.rohan.sdsu.edu/faulty/rwinslow/Africa/Niger.html. February 26, 2005.

NIGERIA

Background Material

Nigeria is situated on the west coast of Africa and is regarded by many as the pillar of Africa because of its natural resources, high population density, and presence on the world political and economic stage. This reputation is being challenged, however, by credible and consistent reports of corruption, fraud, oil theft, and drug trafficking. The country's land size is 923,768 sq km, with the southern boundary set by the Gulf of Guinea and Bights of Benin. The population is 137,253,133 (2004 est.). The country shares its borders in the east with the Nation of Cameroon, Chad Republic in the northeast, Niger Republic in the North, and the Republic of Benin in the west.

The close proximity to these neighboring countries and the fact that there has not been a formal agreement regarding lines of demarcation between them have created land disputes, especially with Cameroon in the east, where the discovery of oil deposits has further exacerbated the dispute. Nigeria is not different from most of contemporary African countries in that the country was transformed geographically into its present demographic status by western scramblers. The country's name is derived from its predominant physical feature, the Niger River, and it was suggested by a British journalist, Flora Shaw, in the 1890s. Nigeria is a bundle of ethnic groups with varying traditions and dialects.

Though the country may be seen as being composed of similar cultural values, Nigeria can be divided into five cultural zones: north, south, east, west, and midwest. The north is associated with the Hausa-speaking groups, who inhabit a majority of the region. The Kanuri and the nomadic Fulani also occupy the region. The western region is inhabited by the Yoruba-speaking people, and the east is occupied by Igbo-speaking people. The south is occupied by a blend of what can be regarded as the melting pot of Nigeria: the Edos, Ijaws, Esan, Eksako, Urhobo, and Bendel Ibos; a minority of Yoruba speaking groups; and a mix of other cultural groups. The midwest is the economic base from which the other regions of the country draw economic energy, since the national economy is mostly dependent on the natural oil in the midwest and south regions.

Nigeria's official language is English, which is used in the operations of government, in classroom instruction, and in the popular news media. There is a variety of the English language referred to as "broken" English or pidgin English by Nigerians. Today, this dialect is regarded by many Nigerians educated in the United States as the African slang version of the English language. This version of English helps facilitate communication, especially in the streets and traditional marketplaces. It also helps communication among the different tribal groups. It is estimated that the country is composed of at least 250 ethnic groups that share between 350 and 400 varying dialects.

The relationship between the tribal entities has been a dominant issue in the Nigerian political, social, and economic debate. Though ethnic relations in Nigeria's culturally diverse society are sometimes politically volatile and even violent, reliance on ecological, social, and economic resources has encouraged peaceful interactions among ethnic groups. The strife of civil war in the 1960s taught the country a valuable lesson. Nigerians now know that ethnic conflicts are a destructive force in nation building and can lead to war. However, ethnic stereotyping still remains a major national issue in this country of diverse traditions. Ethnic friction is visible in the manner that the national resources are shared among the regions of the country and in the hiring practices of the different federal, state, and local government agencies.

The nation has an oil-rich economy with a purchasing power of $114.8 billion dollars (2004 est.) and a 7.1% real growth rate (2003 est.). Petroleum is a crucial aspect of the national economy. In fact, petroleum products account for two thirds of the energy consumed. The country also boasts substantial resources in the form of hydroelectricity, timber, coal, charcoal, and lignite. Yet close to half (45%) of the nation's population live below the poverty line and use wood as a source of energy. The agricultural economy comes from exports of cash crops, including cocoa, palm oil, rubber, cotton, peanuts, and other domestic products.

Nigerian religions are as follows: Muslim: 50%; Christian: 40%; indigenous beliefs: 10%. Northern Nigeria is populated by a majority of Islamic worshippers. Islam was introduced to the Hausa states or northern Nigeria in the fifteenth century and began to dominate the country after the *jihad* of 1804, which extended Islamic influence to most parts of the north and portions of other parts of the country. A good number of the Yoruba tribe in the west are also faithfully Islamic.

Nigeria gained independence from British imperial rule on October 1, 1960. The government of Nigeria has been dominated by military rule for most of its years of independence. Abuja became the national capital in 1991, when it was officially transferred from Lagos. Since then, most of the federal agencies have transferred their headquarters to the new capital.

Contextual Features

Nigeria is a federation of 36 states and the Federal Territory of Abuja. The executive branch of government is headed by the Chief of State, who is also the President of the country. He is elected by popular vote to a four-year term, and can serve no more than two terms. The 1999 Constitution provided for a bicameral National Assembly. There are 109 seats in the Senate, three allocated to each of the 36 states and one from the Federal Territory. Members of the Senate are elected by popular vote to serve four-year terms. The House of Representatives is made up of 360 seats, and members are also elected by popular vote to serve four-year terms. The Constitution also provided for a Senate and a House of Representatives in each state.

Each state in the Republic is zoned into counties that are referred to as local government areas, administered by a Chairman and a Council of at least 20 Council Members. Within this system of government, the traditional chiefs and village heads are also in positions of authority, based on family title inheritance. A good working alliance between the traditional leaders and the officially elected County Chairman and Council is necessary.

The Nigeria legal system is based on English common law, Islamic *shariah* law (mainly in some parts of the north), and traditional law. Nigeria is composed of separate federal and state courts, and a Supreme Court. The nation's judicial system is tripartite, and the English-style judicial system applies only to the common law courts.

The Islamic and customary law courts are not under the jurisdiction of the common law courts. Like the United States, the Nigerian criminal legal procedure is based on an adversarial system. Whereas the Islamic and customary courts use the French style of an inquisitorial system, the adversarial approach of the state and federal courts places the burden of proof on the accused.

The history of Nigeria's criminal justice cannot be understood without revisiting the country's problems as a British colony. The fundamental tenet of the Nigerian criminal justice system was derived from English law. When Lagos was annexed in 1849 by the British Empire, the other regions of the country were declared protectorates, and the Royal Niger Company became manager of the country's affairs. The Royal Niger Company was chartered by the British Empire to rule Nigeria until 1900. It was not until 1899 that the British Government revoked the charter granted to the Royal Niger Company Limited and took over direct administration of Nigeria in 1900 (Ebbe, 1999; Niven, 1957; Burns, 1929).

The Nigerian Protectorates in 1861 were assigned a Legislative Council by the British Consuls and the Royal Niger Company Limited. The Legislative Council was set up to make laws capable of controlling the citizens of these Protectorates, and to control and regulate economic activities.

The Royal Niger Company did establish courts of justice and also created an armed constabulary to enforce laws and regulations, as expected of colonialists and imperialists. The British government established 10 different courts with four devoted to criminal procedures. The four courts included the Supreme Court/Police Magistrate Court, the Court of Civil and Criminal Justice, the West African Court of Appeal, and the Privy Council (Elias, 1963). These courts implemented policies and legislation that were of no consequence to the cultural values of the people of Nigeria.

In 1904, Lord Luger, the Governor of the northern protectorate, introduced the Criminal Code, which was modeled after the code introduced by Britain to Queensland, Australia in 1899. According to Oloyede (1972), the Queensland Criminal Code was based on a criminal code drafted by a Briton, Sir James Fritzstephen, who was then living in Jamaica. However, the Criminal Code of 1904 was not enforced or applicable to all Nigerians, even after the addition of the southern and northern protectorates in 1914 (Elias, 1954; Adewoye, 1977). The Criminal Code was not applicable to northern Nigeria, partly because of illiteracy and the difficulty of negotiating with the Emirs, who were the traditional leaders of Moslem groups in the north. Because northern Nigeria, even in 1959, lacked professional personnel trained in criminal law (Ebbe, 1998), British representatives decided to create a panel of jurists who were charged with the introduction of a penal code that will be compatible with Islamic doctrines, values, and customs.

This panel of jurists modeled the Penal Code for northern Nigeria after the Sudanese Penal Code (Nwabueze, 1963). Northern Nigeria Administration, however, was at this time patterned after the Emirate rule. As a result, any one who prosecuted under the Penal Code had to answer to a Moslem judge in the Alkali court according to Muslim laws. It was no secret that a majority of people who settled in northern states were Moslems. This became the guiding principle of the Penal Code—that it was applicable to all in the northern region.

In 1916, while the Nigerian Criminal Code was applicable to all, Moslem criminal cases were still governed by "native law and custom." This created not only competition but also friction between the two systems of justice. This friction was especially troublesome in the northern states, where the Moslem laws were particularly incompatible with the English law. Okonkwo and Naish (1964) argued that "the northern laws were not acceptable under the English law ... the offense of homicide, punishable by death, includes any assault ending in death, regardless of intent ... in effect, the crime of manslaughter under the country's criminal code is prosecuted under the *maliki* law as murder." To remedy this confusing administration of a dual system of justice, an attempt was made to abolish the customary courts in 1933. The British administrators abandoned this idea, however, and instead introduced what was known as Section 10 of the Native Courts Ordinances, which allowed the Native Courts to administer customary law, provided that the punishment did not include mutilation or torture and was "not repugnant to natural justice, equity, and good conscience."

Nigeria uses a tripartite system of criminal law and justice: the Criminal Code (based on English common law and legal practice); the Penal Code (based on Maliki law and the Muslim system of law and justice); and customary law (based on the customs and traditions of the people). In southern Nigeria, the native laws are informal, unwritten agreements, and the northern region has codified Muslim laws.

Since independence, Ebbe and Elias report, "both the Nigeria criminal code and the Northern Nigeria Penal Code have added many amendments to reflect the norms, values, and standards of the Nigerian people ... one result of having the Nigerian criminal code based on the English common

law tradition was the criminalization of some of the Nigerian customs ... for example, section 370 of the Nigerian criminal code prescribes a seven year prison sentence for any person who marries another while his/her marriage partner is still living ... according to this section, Bigamy is the contracting of a second marriage during the lifetime of one's first wife/husband ... section 35 of the marriage act declares such a second marriage as void, and sections 47 and 48 prescribe penalty for such violation." Ebbe states that such normative standards in Nigeria that were criminalized by the Colonial Administration have since been revoked; for example, the bigamy law in the Nigerian Criminal Code was declared null and void in 1970. The revocation was not surprising, especially since Nigeria is a country that condones polygamy and polyandry due to existing traditions and cultural values of its different ethnic groups.

Crimes are classified in Nigeria according to the severity of the criminal action. The Nigerian legal system classifies crimes as felonies and misdemeanors. Felonies are serious crimes such as murder, armed robbery, carjacking, and drug offenses; and misdemeanors are less serious offenses such as verbal insults, and trespassing.

The law enforcement community, because of their responsibility to protect and serve and because they must interact with a blend of tradition and culture, classify crimes into offenses against persons and properties; victimless crimes; and crimes against customary laws or local ordinances.

The Nigerian Criminal Code considers any person who has reached 17 years of age and above as an adult, making this the true age of criminal responsibility. Adolescents between 12 and 16 are treated as juvenile offenders. Those between the ages of 7 to 11 are usually considered children, but they can be classified as juveniles if they violate customary law. The country is a transit point for heroin and cocaine intended for Europe, East Asia, and North America. It is also a safe haven for Nigerian narcotics traffickers operating worldwide and a major money-laundering center. Massive corruption and criminal activity, along with unwillingness of the government to address the deficiencies in its anti-money-laundering regime, make money laundering a major problem.

Recently, the Nigerian government has embarked on strict enforcement of drug-related violations. The sale or possession of controlled substances such as heroin, powder cocaine, marijuana, and crack cocaine are now serious felonies. Drug trafficking of marijuana was first observed in the 1960s, during the turbulent Biafra war (a tribal war between the Ibos and the Hausa, who were supported by the rest of the country). Between 1979 and 1988, some 14,883 Nigerian traffickers were arrested worldwide (Obot, 1992). In the late 1990s, the U.S. State Department determined that Nigerian gangs controlled 80% of heroin imports to the east coast of the United States. The government responded by first passing legislation that led to the formation of the National Drug Law Enforcement Agency (NDLEA) in 1989; its sole responsibility was the eradication of controlled substances. The number of drug violation arrests increased from 456 in 1993 to 2,814 in 1998.

Corruption and bribery are also significant crimes in Nigeria. A Corrupt Practices and Other Related Offences Act was enacted in the year 2000. This Act established for the first time a statutory body charged with fighting corruption in the country. The body was referred to as the Independent Corrupt Practices Commission (ICPC), and the Act granted the Commission considerable power to investigate, arrest, and prosecute. The Act gave the Commission the power to deal with presumption of corrupt enrichment, prohibition of gifts to public officers, duty to report bribery transactions, applicability to the private sector, protection of informers, the power to independently investigate the President and other high political office holders, and power over cross-border offenses. The Commission's dependence on the ability of the Nigerian police to enforce the law may impede the implementation of the policy. Some observers have argued that unless the police force is reformed and resources provided to the Commission, the implementation may be derailed.

The most widely noted, discussed, and publicized crime in Nigeria is what is now popularly known as "419" fraud. It involves requests for up-front money to secure victims' involvement in a financial transaction, and the process is usually marked urgent or confidential. The U. S. Secret Service refers to "419" fraud as "Nigerian advance fee fraud." The goal of the perpetrators is to delude the target into thinking that he/she is being drawn into a very lucrative, albeit questionable, arrangement. The "419" fraud has further damaged the integrity of the country. The 2001 Corruption Perception Index survey (CPI) ranked Nigeria as the second most corrupt country in the world. This type of categorization can affect foreign confidence in investing resources for business ventures in the country.

The following is a discussion of available data of crime statistics in Nigeria, which must also be considered unreliable and incomplete. Criminal statistics in Nigeria are compiled by the Nigerian Police and are based on numbers of crimes reported by citizens and those observed by police. Though robbery is a very common crime in Nigeria, the police recorded only 30%, and indicate that lack of reporting and inadequate record keeping may skew the data. Sam Olukoya, in "Crime war rages in Nigeria" (2003), states that the battle between police and armed robbers for control of Nigerian streets is proving a costly one for both sides. According to the writer, police statistics show that between August of 2002 and May of 2003, armed robbers killed 273 civilians and 84 policemen, and injured 133 others. The writer reported that criminals have been operating with impunity, snatching cars on highways, raiding banks, and breaking into homes.

The 1991 Library of Congress data indicate that serious crime grew to nearly epidemic proportions, especially in the country's big cities such as Lagos and Benin City. This situation is blamed on stark economic inequality and deprivation, social disorganization, lack of social services, and distrust of law enforcement. This source argued that "Published crime statistics were probably grossly understated, because most of the country was virtually unpoliced." The law enforcement resources were concentrated in the urban areas and neglected the other parts of the country. There is widespread underreporting of crime in the country. Furthermore, it is estimated that at least 60% of the crimes are disposed of informally in customary courts.

The annual Report of the Nigerian Police Force presents the data for some crimes, including murder. In 1989, there were 928 cases of murder reported to police, at a rate of 1.07 per 100,000 population. *Travel Phobia* (2000) ranks Nigeria among the world's most dangerous countries, with an average of four murders daily in the nation's most populated city of Lagos. Amnesty International recorded over 100 executions of violent criminals in 1994 alone. The nation's crime rate was 300 per 100,000 in the 1970s, and it has steadily increased. The 1989 Nigeria Police Annual Report indicated that there were 69,454 cases of theft, at a rate of 81.2 per 100,000; 1,032 cases of rape were reported to the police, at a rate of 1.20 per 100,000. Date rape or rape of wife by husband is not prosecuted as a crime. However, because of the inadequate record keeping and the fact that the country lacks a centralized database for compiling criminal incidents, these figures must be considered unreliable.

Statistical data for criminal events are not yet provided by the only officially known source of information of criminal victimizations. To date, the Nigerian police have no technologically organized way of data collection. As a result, there are no reliable victimization data in terms of geographic distribution. It can be argued, however, that property crimes would be more prevalent in the southern states than the northern states, not only because there are more business activities in this region, but also because the northern states are governed by the *Sharia* laws that usually recommend mutilation of body parts for thieves. Furthermore, there are no deliberately specified records of victimization or incident-based reporting in terms of ethnicity, gender, age, social economic status, and other demographic characteristics. Many correctional reports indicate generally that a majority of crimes occur intra-ethnically, and that males are more likely to be perpetrators and victims. Ebbe in 1985 reported that a survey of inmates of maximum and minimum security prisons showed that 68% of the subjects were 30 years old or younger at time of the offense, and 62% of them victimized older persons.

The nation's criminal procedures provide for witnesses of crimes to be regarded as crown witnesses during the trial. Unfortunately, the country lacks the victim assistance programs seen in the United States, and victims are not given the opportunity of obtaining compensation. The self-defense statute does prescribe that a victim may take extraordinary action against any perpetrator who seriously threatens life or property. Recently in Nigeria, vigilantism has increased, especially because of lack of law enforcement protection. The private security business has grown tremendously for those who can buy the services. Others resort to vigilantism and instant justice.

Police Profile

Background

If there is any society where the law enforcement agency is designed to control the masses for the main purpose of drowning any voice for change, it is Nigeria. Marxist theory is prevalent in Nigeria even today. Furthermore, there is no known agency that collects data for research on police activities including crime rates, trends, and victimization. The Nigeria Annual Abstract of Statistics collects information on police and prison industry performance rather than criminal statistics. This inadequacy in data collection makes it virtually impossible to conduct reliable research studies. For example, in early 2004, the International Centre for Prison Studies provided information related to prisons in Nigeria. The prison population in September 2003 was estimated by the Ministry of Internal Affairs at 40,447 (official

capacity listed as 42,681 in the year 2000). Based on the estimated national population in 2003, the prison population per 100,000 is 33. In 2002, 63% of the prisoners were pretrial detainees, and 1.9% were female prisoners. There are reports of an increasing prison population.

The Nigerian Police structure is provided for in Section 214(2) (9) and Section 215(2) of the Constitution of 1999. The Police Force is specified by Section 194 of the 1979 Constitution as the National Police with exclusive jurisdiction throughout the country. The Nigerian Constitution further provides for the establishment of separate branches of the National Police Force. Specifically, this branch "forms part of the armed forces of the federation or for the protection of the harbors, waterways, railroads and airfields." An example of such wing of the NPF is the Port Authority Security Police, reported to have manpower strength of 1,500 and 12,000 personnel.

The Nigerian Police started with a 30-man consular guard formed in Lagos in 1861. The armed Paramilitary Hausa Constabulary was formed in 1879, and the official Police Force was first established in Lagos in 1896, in Calabar in 1894 under the Niger Coast Protectorate, and in Lokoja in 1888. The contemporary Nigerian Police was born when the country's northern and southern regions were added in 1914; and the Police Forces of the two regions merged in 1930, forming what is regarded today as the Nigerian Police Force. Though headquartered in Lagos, the Colonial Police Force was under the local authorities. It was in the 1960s that the first Republic reorganized and nationalized the NPF.

The NPF structural pattern was designed to meet the constitutional expectations of the police in order to be able to perform the duties of law enforcement. Section 215(2) states that "The Nigeria police force shall be under the command of the inspector-general of police and any contingents of the NPF stationed in a state shall; subject to the authority of the inspector-general of police, be under the command of the commissioner of police of that state." Based on the above Constitutional provision, three different structures in the NPF emerged. The first was the command structure, sometimes referred to as the authority structure. This structure is grounded on the regimental nature of the NPF and conducted according to badges of ranks.

Organizational Description and Functions

The NPF is divided into six administrative departments, each charged with specific management duties. The main responsibility of the Administration Division is to lead in the direction, supervision, and coordination of the various departments within the Directorate of the NPF. This Division also manages the policies, procedures, and administration of NPF budget, review of regulations, discipline, conferences, monitoring finances, research and publication of the annual police report, computer, and liaison between the different divisions of the NPF.

Directives, instructions, and authority flow from the Inspector-General of the NPF through the chain of command to the officer in the street. The Deputy Inspector-General is second in command, as provided by Section 7(1) of the Police Act, established not by the Constitution but by the National Assembly. Section 5 of the Police Act provides for several Deputy Inspector-General positions. The Nigeria Police Council is responsible for appropriating those positions as requested by the Inspector-General. Section 215 (2) of the Constitution establishes the position and office of the Commissioners, and Section 5 of the Police Act provides for every other rank in the NPF.

The NPF plans and organizes internal security measures, and oversees the monitoring and execution of these policies. The Operations Office directs and coordinates policies on crime prevention, implementation of K-9 unit and other force animals' care, traffic control policies, communication networks, joint operations, tactical planning and operation regarding crime prevention and control, inspections of the various operational units, antiterrorism, disasters, suppression of conflicts, and preparation of annual budgets.

The Logistics and Supplies Department is responsible for procurement of all technical and other equipments crucial to the operation of law enforcement. This Department provides the NPF with aircraft, communications, armaments, transportation, and stationery. They are also responsible for the allocation and distribution of procured equipment and constructions, maintenance of police buildings, and provision of arms and ammunitions.

The Investigation and Intelligence Division is very specialized. This branch of the NPF consists of both the criminal investigation and intelligence units, the Interpol liaison unit, narcotics, and forensics, and it also handles the criminal prevention policies and crime records, and assists in prosecution of offenders. The most important unit of this department is the CID, or Central Intelligence Division, which is responsible for crime detection and prevention. NPF also has a paramilitary unit, known as the Mobile Police, who are responsible for prevention and control of violent and chronic offenders, especially highway robbers and international smugglers. The Special Constabulary and the Traffic Warden Service are responsible for maintaining order and traffic control.

The Training and Command Department of the NPF is responsible for the formulation and implementation of supervision of police training policies. This branch of the NPF supervises and coordinates the activities of the force and the police staff training colleges. There is also a Research and Planning Unit and an Office of the Force Secretary. The Nigerian Police Force is organized into seven operational units: the force headquarters, 10 zonal headquarters, 36 State Commands Headquarters, Divisional Police Headquarters, Police Stations, Police Posts, and Village Police Posts. The Nigerian Police Force is a national and unified force controlled by the federal government. Each state is assigned a squadron of the NPF. The Inspector-General has command over all of the police squadrons in Nigeria.

Training

Nigeria has been managed for years by different careless military dictators who answer to no one. As a result, no one has been bold enough to challenge the authorities about the lack of data collection regarding any public or private agencies. In such a dictatorship, the military is often consumed with protecting their power instead of assisting public agencies or dealing with citizens' needs. Furthermore, between 2002 and 2003, oil workers were engaged in a long strike, and public spending in Nigeria exceeded its revenues, leading to the suspension of foreign debt payments. The Nigerian Police were therefore ignored, until the recent civilian regime, which must now embark on developing the NPF and providing them with necessary resources, including expenditures, technology, investigative tools, forensics, and other law enforcement needs.

However, police recruits in Nigeria pass through a rigorous boot camp-like training at the four major police colleges. Usually, the minimum requirement to be admitted to the Police College is a high school diploma, but corruption has contributed and set a stage for eighth graders to be admitted without challenge. Police training in Nigeria is controlled from the headquarters by a Deputy Inspector General, designated as Commander. Recruits are trained at the Oji River, Maidugiri, Kaduna, and Ikeja police colleges. NPF also has specialized in-service training schools and facilities in Guzuo for mobile forces, the detective college in Enugu, the dogs service training center, and the mounted training center. The

Nigerian Police Academy in Kano offers a five-year academic and professional degree program for new cadets and an 18-month intensive course program for college graduates interested in the NPF.

Technical assistance is obtained mainly from the U. S. and Britain. For example, in 2003, the United States Department of Justice announced its operational plans to provide 5.8 million dollars to train members of the NPF for more effective crime prevention and control, and to bring the force to adequate standards of operation worldwide.

This assistance helped develop contemporary curricula for the police training institutions, training for trainers, establishment of database systems, criminal records database to improve report tracking and statistical analysis, election security, civil disorder management, field training, community policing, and provision of qualified police activities managers. In November 2003, the U.S. government also gave an additional 1.1 million dollars to the Nigerian government to assist in modernizing and upgrading the NDLEA training facility in Jos.

Complaints and Discipline

The skepticism and distrust of the Nigerian Police are based on past corruption, which is common at all levels of government in Nigeria. This corruption facilitates narcotics trafficking and money laundering, and it hinders counter-narcotics efforts. There are credible reports of violent crimes, bribery, and corruption in the Nigerian Police Force. A number of domestic human rights groups report deaths of suspects in custody and the practice of legitimized robbery in the form of forced contributions at too many police posts and checkpoints. Victor Dike (2003) classified corruption in Nigeria into political, bureaucratic, electoral, embezzlement, and bribery. According to Dike, becoming corrupt in Nigeria is almost unavoidable, because morality is relaxed in the society, and many people struggle for survival without assistance from the State.

Police corruption is not new; neither is it unknown to government authorities. There are several reports of elements within the Nigerian Police involved in kidnappings, murders, gang-like executions, highway robberies, home invasions, and bribery.

Decisions to arrest are based on probable cause that a crime has been committed. However, because of the state of corruption and the lack of accountability on the part of the NPF, many arrests are made without any legal grounds. As a result, a lot of cases brought to the office of the Director of Public Prosecution are settled outside the legal system through bribery, corruption, or plea bargains. In some instances, the police actually prosecute cases themselves, and the Prosecutor's Office handles the more serious offenders. Serious criminal cases are sometimes dismissed by the Police and the Director of Public Prosecutions on order or request from politicians, wealthy citizens, and other government officials. As a result of the corruption and inconsistencies, the data on the proportion of cases going to trial are not reliable.

Offenders in Nigeria can be held for trial for long periods, especially if they do not have the resources to post bail, do not have an attorney, or they lack adequate resources for bribery.

Terrorism

Nigeria has remained steadfast and determined to repress and quell terrorism in the country. Nigeria is committed to the global war on terrorism, and the country has continued diplomatic efforts in both global and regional theaters concerning counterterrorism issues. The President of Nigeria, Olusegun Obasanjo, and other African Heads of State founded the new Partnership for African Development to sustain development in Africa and to provide resources to African countries to combat terrorism. Nigeria has been helping the United Nations to monitor terrorism on the west African coast. Nigeria has also been able to monitor and thwart several threats to the U. S. interests and citizens, and the country is cooperating with U.S. authorities in tracking and freezing terrorists' assets. There is, however, the threat of the spread of radical Islamism, especially in northern Nigeria. Recently, the Yobe state uprising, led by a group calling itself Taliban, headed by Mullah Umar, to demand an Islamic state, was cut down by the Nigerian military. Credible reports of foreign groups' aid to domestic extremist Islamic groups who want the institutionalization of Islamic law are suspected to be from foreign Islamic radicals. There are credible reports of extremist Islamic foreign group involvement in the 2001 *bauchi* state violence, which led to the arrests of six Pakistanis and the arrest of an Iranian diplomat found taking pictures of sensitive sites in January of 2004 in the new Nigerian capital, Abuja. The following counties are suspected of sponsoring radical Islamic activities in Nigeria: Saudi Arabia, Syria, Iran, Libya, Chad Republic, and Pakistan.

Police Education, Research, and Publications

The NPF has four police colleges and an academy, all but one of which are located in northern or near northern Nigeria. The Nigerian firefighters also train in Maryland, in the United States. Members of the Economic Community of West African States (ECOWAS) usually will exchange prisoners on the cooperative bases between the countries. The information regarding police activities is truly scanty. It is, however, possible to find relevant materials from the NPF website. To conduct a reliable and valid study of this country, one has to have access to the necessary favorable network of agency officials and be physically present in the country.

There are several individuals and sources that can be regarded as reliable to study Nigerian law enforcement affairs. However, based on available information, the following list is tentative at best: Declan Onwudiwe, Emmanuel Oyenyinli, and Jonathan Odo (University of Maryland, Easternshore); Obi Ebbe (University of Tennessee, Chattanooga), Evaristus Obinyan (Fort Valley State University, Fort Valley, Georgia); Usiwoma Enuku (University of Benin, Benincity, Nigeria.); Tori Olori (Inter Press Service News Agency); Paul Marshall (*National Review Online*); Jean-Luc de Vere (*Jihad Watch*); Emmanuel Obe (*Nigeria Punch*), Kayode Oluyemi (*Journal of Police Chief*), A. K. Greene (University of Oxford); Oyeleye Oyediran (University of Lagos), Hoover Institution Journal of Democracy; Bureau of Public Enterprises, International Centre for Prison Studies, Drug Enforcement Administration, Law Enforcement Executive Forum, *The International Journal of African Studies*, Library of Congress Country Studies, *www.nigerdeltacongress. com*, *www.fas.org*, *www.webstar.co.uk*, *www.pbs.org*, ALLREFER.COM, *www.workmll.com*, NIGERIA NEXUS, *www.internews.org*, *www.freemaninstitute. com*, *www.ecoi.net*, *www.motherlandnigeria.com*, *www.nigeriapolice.org/press.html*, *WorldAtlas. com; The World Fact-Book*; United States Department of State, Central Intelligence Agency, *www. state.gov/g/drl*, *www.carnelian-international.com*, *www.gamji.com/NEWS*.

EVARISTUS OBINYAN

Bibliography

Achebe, Chinua. *The Trouble with Nigeria*. Enugu: FIRST Dimension, 1983.

Adewoye, Omoniyi. *The Judicial System in Southern Nigeria 1854–1954: Law and Justice in a Dependency*. New Jersey: Atlantic Highlands, Humanities Press, 1977.

Aguda, Akinda T. *The Law of Evidence in Nigeria*. London: Sweet & Maxwell, 1974.

Alemika, Etannibi, E.O. "The Smoke Screen: Rhetoric and Reality of Penal Incarceration in Nigeria." *International Journal of Comparative and Applied Criminal Justice*. vol. 1(1983): 137–149.

Allott, A.N. Th*e Future of Law in Nigeria*. London: Sweet and Maxwell, 1963.

Ames, Walker L. *Police and Community in Japan*. Berkeley: University of California Press, 1976.

Arikpo, Okoi. Th*e Development of Modern Nigeria*. Baltimore: Penguin Books, Inc, 1967.

Bayley, David H. *Patterns of Policing: A Comparative International Analysis*. New Jersey: Rutgers University Press, 1985.

Brett, Lionel, Sir, and Ian McLean. *The Criminal Law and Procedure of Lagos, Eastern Nigeria and Western Nigeria*. London: Sweet and Maxwell, 1963.

Burns, Alan Sir. *History of Nigeria*. London: George Allen & Unwin Limited, 1929.

Constitution of the Federal Republic of Nigeria, 1963, Sec. 111(2) and Sec. 1(1). *Criminal Procedures Ordinance (Nigeria) 1960. Customary Courts Edict (No. 2)*, 1966.

Das, Dilip K. *Policing in Six Countries Around the World: Organizational Perspectives*. Chicago: University of Chicago Press, 1993.

Diamond, Larry. "The Social Foundation of Democracy: The Case of Nigeria." Unpublished PH.D. Thesis, Stanford University, 1980.

Dike, Kenneth O. *Trade and Politics in the Niger Delta, 1830–1891*. Oxford: Oxford University Press, 1959.

Director of Prisons. "The Correction of Imprisoned Offenders in Nigeria." Paper presented at the International Conference on Crime and Crime Control in Developing Countries. Ibadan, Nigeria: University Conference Center, 1980.

Ebbe, Obi N.I. *Crime in Nigeria: An Analysis of Characteristics of Offenders Incarcerated in Nigerian Prisons*. Ann Arbor, Michigan: University Microfilms International, 1982.

Ebbe, Obi N.I. "Power and Criminal Law: Criminalization of Conduct Norms in a Colonial Regime." *International Journal of Comparative and Applied Criminal Justice,* vol. 9, no. 2, 1985a. 113–122.

Ebbe, Obi N.I. "Juvenile Justice System in Southern Nigeria." *International Journal of Comparative and Applied Criminal Justice*, 12, no. 2 (1988): 191–204. www.ojp.usdoj.gov/bjs/pub/ascii/wfbcjnig.txt.

Elias, Oluwale Taslim. *The Groundwork of Nigerian Law*. London: Routeledge & Kegan Parel, Ltd, 1954.

Elias, Oluwale Taslim. *The Nigerian Legal System*. London: Routeledge & Kegan Paul, Ltd, 1963.

Elias, Oluwale Taslim. *The British Commonwealth: The Development of Its Law and Constitution-Nigeria*, vol. 4. London: Steven & Sons, Limited, 1967.

Elias, Oluwale Taslim. *The Prison System in Nigeria*. Lagos: University of Lagos Press, 1964.

Elias, Oluwale Taslim. *The Nigerian Magistrate and the Offender*. Benin City: Ethiope Publishing Company, 1972a.

Elias, Oluwale Taslim. ed. *Law and Social Change in Nigeria*. Lagos: Evans Brothers Ltd, 1972b.

Ibginovia, Patrick E. "The Chimera of Incarceration: Penal Institutionalization and Its Alternatives in a Progressive Nigeria." *International Journal of Offender Therapy and Comparative Criminology*. 28, no. 1 (1984): 22–36.

Igbinovia, Patrick E. "Nigeria." *World Encyclopedia of Police Forces and Penal Systems*. ed. George Thomas Kurian. New York: Facts on File, 1988.

Iwarimie—Jaja, Darlington. "Corrections in Nigeria: A System in Need of Reform." *Criminal Justice International*, 5, no. 5 (1989): 13–19.

Karibi-Whyte, A.G. "Some Recent Amendments to the Criminal Code (Nigeria)." *Nigerian Law Journal*. 10 (1964): 156–164.

Kasumu, A.B. *The Supreme Court of Nigeria.* London: Heinemann, 1978.

Kayode, Oluyemi, and Etannibi O. Alemika. "An Examination of Some Socio—Economic Characteristics of Inmates of a Nigerian Prison." *International Journal of Comparative and Applied Criminal Justice*, 8, no. 1 (1984): 85–91.

Keay, E.A., and S.S. Richardson. *The Nature of Customary Courts in Nigeria.* London: Sweet & Maxwell, 1966.

Law of Northern Nigeria. Lagos: Government Printing Press, 1963.

Law of Northern Nigeria, 1963. Revision Section 3(1), Court of Resolution Law, Cap. 28.

Lugard, Frederick Sir. *Sir Frederick Lugard: Political Memorandum.* Ibadan: National Archives Library, University of Ibadan, 1913.

News Agency of Nigeria: *Nigeria News Update,* December 8, 1992 and 1993.

Nigerian Police Force Annual Reports 1986–1989.

Niven, C.R. *A Short History of Nigeria.* London: Longmans, Green & Co., Ltd 1957.

Northern Region Law Report, 94 of 1960.

Nwabueze, Boniface B., *The Machinery of Justice in Nigeria.* London: Butterworths, 1963. www.ojp.usdoj.gov/bj s/pub/ascii/wfbcj nig.txt.

Obilade, A.O., "Reform of Customary Law Court Systems in Nigeria Under the Military Government." *Nigerian Law Journal,* vol. 3, 1969.

Obilade, A.O. *The Nigerian Legal System.* London: Sweet and Maxwell, 1979.

Okediji, Francis, and Oladejo, Okediji. "Nigerian Prison Inmates," in Taslim O. Elias (ed.). *The Prison System in Nigeria.* National Conference on the Prison System. University of Lagos, July 1–5.

Okonkwo, Cyprain O. *The Police and the Public in Nigeria.* Lagos: African University Press, 1966.

Okonkwo, Cyprain O., and Michael Naish. *Criminal Law in Nigeria (Excluding the North).* London: Sweet and Maxwell, 1964.

Rotimi, Adewale R. "Prison Administration in Modern Nigeria." *International Journal of Comparative and Applied Criminal Justice* 9, no.1 (1982): 73–83.

NORTHERN IRELAND

See **United Kingdom**

NORWAY

Background Material

Norway extends further north than any other European country. It covers 386,958 sq km, and with only 14 inhabitants per sq km is one of the most sparsely populated countries in Europe. Lying on the westward rim of the Scandinavian peninsula, its width ranges from 6 km to 430 km. The distance from the northernmost to the southernmost points is 1,752 km; the coastline is 2,650 km long. Norway, with its 19 counties, and 454 municipalities, shares borders with Russia (196 km), Finland (725 km), and Sweden (1.619 km). To the west lies the North Sea.

The Nordics did not play a prominent part in European history until the Viking Age (800–1030 CE) when Swedes, Danes, and Norwegians set sail for far-off destinations. The Vikings were expert shipbuilders, able seamen, skilled warriors, tradesmen, and explorers. They founded cities and built new empires. They looted and plundered wherever they set foot in Europe, and brought Christianity back with them to the North. Norway was united in 1030. During the Late Medieval Period (1319–1537), Norway and Sweden were united for a brief spell (1319–1355). The plague broke out in 1349, and it was brought to Norway on a ship from England. Spreading swiftly, it decimated the population. The Kalmar Union united Norway, Sweden, and Denmark from 1397 to 1523, but after Sweden's secession and a period of civil unrest, Norway was tied to Denmark until 1814, a period popularly known as the Four Hundred Year Night.

Norway's modern Constitution, based largely on French and American prototypes, dates from 17 May 1814. It enshrined the sovereignty of the people and the separation of powers between the legislative, executive, and judicial functions: parliament (*Storting*), monarch, and courts. The Constitution provided for Norwegians to elect a monarch of their own choosing. Parliament was divided into two chambers. In late July 1814, King Karl Johan of Sweden led a military assault on Norway; in November of that year, Norway, as a constitutional monarchy and retaining much of its independence, entered into a union with Sweden.

The nineteenth century witnessed a sharp rise in Norway's population: towns multiplied in number and size. The Industrial Revolution picked up speed, promoting trade with the outside world. Although there had been sporadic emigration in the first half of the 1800s, the 1860s mark the beginning of mass emigration. Between then and 1930, 800,000 Norwegians left the country for the U.S. Emigration declined steadily until the 1960s. Today, there are as many Americans of Norwegian descent in the US as there are Norwegians in Norway.

Norway's union with Sweden came to an end in 1905. A new king—a Danish prince—was elected by popular vote, and Norway could finally celebrate independence. After World War II (1940–1945), Norway prospered in virtually every area. The first two decades were politically stable, as the government set about rebuilding the country through central economic planning. Several large state-owned factories were founded, a range of social reforms introduced, and health and education expanded. Offshore oil production commenced in the 1970s, and this had a great effect on Norway's economic progress. The number of women in the workforce grew; equality has remained an important consideration since

the 1970s. Student numbers rose dramatically in the late 1980s. State-sponsored welfare continued to expand.

Norway is a relatively stable country with only 22 governments between 1945 and 2001. Norway is also the home of the annual Nobel Peace Prize.

The population of Norway is 4.6 million (2004 est.); the population grows at a rate of around 0.5%, with immigration accounting for as much as the domestic birth rate. Predictions suggest that Norway will eclipse five million by 2020, an increase fueled mostly by immigration.

The immigrant population (defined as persons whose parents are both immigrants, and children born in Norway to non-Norwegian parents) makes up 6.9% of Norway's population or 349,000 individuals (2004). They have come to Norway as refugees, labor immigrants, or family relatives from more than 200 different countries, with Pakistan, Sweden, Denmark, Vietnam, and Yugoslavia in the lead. Every municipality in Norway has some immigrants, though most live in Oslo (114,000 or 22%).

Norway has two official written languages: *Bokmål* (Dano-Norwegian) and *Nynorsk* (New Norwegian). They have equal status, and are used by government, schools, churches, radio, television, and the print media. The differences are not great. Nynorsk is based on local dialects.

Norway has an established church—the Protestant Lutheran Church of Norway—of which about 86% of the population are members. Another 8% are members of other non-state-funded confessional communities. About six percent do not belong to any of the confessions supported financially by the state.

Norway is economically prosperous. The Gross National Product (GNP) in 2003 was NOK$1,564 billion, or NOK$260,000 per capita ($41,000/32,500). Only Luxembourg tops Norway in Europe, adjusted for differences in country price levels. Norway's 2003 trade surplus was NOK$213 billion, about 14% of the GNP. Norway is the world's third biggest oil producer, after Saudi-Arabia and Russia. Oil exports account for 44% of Norway's foreign trade. Gas is produced in significant amounts, too. Fish exports are considerable.

Norway has a Sami population as well. The Sami are an indigenous people who live mostly in the north of the country. They have their own language, a long history, and a distinct culture. The Sami are partially self-governing with their own 39-member Sami Parliament (*Samitinget*). The first Sami elections to the newly founded Parliament were held in 1989.

Contextual Features

Norway's system of government is a parliamentary democracy, based on the rule of law. Authority rests with the people to delegate their freely elected representatives to Parliament. The two chambers of the Norwegian Parliament (*Storting*) are the *Lagting* and the *Odelsting*. Parliamentary elections are held every four years. After the 2005 election, the *Storting* will have 169 members of Parliament (MPs); 47 percent of MPs are women.

The Cabinet has 18 members or ministers, including the Prime Minister. At the regional level, county authorities headed by a County Governor carry out government business in each of the 19 counties, while civic authorities at the municipal level attend to local government through the popularly elected local councils. The political head of the civic corporation and its legal representative is the Mayor. Local councils are elected every four years. The crucial issue is that municipalities are run by the local populace. Taxation and central government grants fund local government spending.

Nine political parties are represented in Parliament, the largest of which are the Labour Party (*Arbeiderpartiet*) and the Conservative Party (*Høyre*), with nearly 50% of MPs between them. Local and general elections are held every other year.

The Norwegian Constitution of 1814 is considered *lex superior*. The principle of *lex superior* underpins the Norwegian judicial system: it means that certain laws stand above others. The structure of laws can be compared to a pyramid, and in the event of conflict between laws, lower-order laws must give way to higher-order laws. Bills are proposed by the various ministries and passed into law by the *Storting*. In addition to legislation enacted by the *Storting*, many rules, regulations, and guidelines are put in place by the Government, ministries, directorates, and local councils.

In Norway interpretation of the law is based on sources of law: the Constitution, legal texts, legal practice, precedent, and custom. The primary consideration is the wording of the law itself; then authorities consider the law's preparatory works (*travaux préparatoires*), meaning the business of the *Storting* leading up to the adoption of the law in its present form. Adjudication procedures regularly refer to these sources. The weight lent to the preparatory works demonstrates the strength of the bond of allegiance between legislator and interpreter.

In the interpretation of statutes and when issues not previously regulated by law require a solution, it is customary to explore legal practice in the area, where it exists. Decisions of the Supreme Court are considered preeminent. That verdicts can influence later considerations means that the courts both influence and refine the law of the land.

The courts are not the only authorities empowered to take decisions on legal questions. In criminal cases, for instance, the police and public prosecutors may decide whether an action represents a violation of the law and whether proceedings should be initiated. Other public authorities are also empowered to make decisions in certain areas of the law. Jurisprudence also affects legal practice.

Norway's legal system is divided into two main domains: public and private law. Public law deals with rules and regulations relating to the state and its legal relations with the citizens. It also regulates relations between public authorities and the practice of authority. Private law regulates legal relations between citizens. Far from being entirely separate, the two domains interact in many areas.

Public law is characterized by its wider scope and greater stringency. It is divided into constitutional law, administrative law, criminal law, and procedural law. Private law covers law of persons, family law, law of inheritance, and law of obligations and property.

There are three ordinary instances in civil cases: the district or city court, the court of appeal, and the Supreme Court. In certain cases, an agency of mediation, the conciliation board, may also deliver judgment. A special committee under the Supreme Court—the Interlocutory Appeals Committee (Høyesteretts kjæremålsutvalg)—acts as a court on occasion and is authorized to make a number of decisions.

Legal procedure in criminal cases takes the form of adversarial proceedings. On side, there is the public Prosecuting Authority, and on the other the person charged and his defense, if any. The Prosecuting Authority, headed by the Director General of Public Prosecutions (*Riksadvokaten*), answers directly to the King (i.e., the Government) and is independent of the Ministry of Justice. Norway has ten Chief Public Prosecutors, each of whom heads one of the Public Prosecutor Offices. The Director General of Public Prosecutions, the Chief Public Prosecutors, and the Public Prosecutors are qualified lawyers and appointed by the King.

Norway has a special system whereby senior police officials—generally chiefs of police (*politimestrene*), the highest-ranking officers in the police force in each district, are part of the Prosecuting Authority. Chiefs of police and virtually all of the aforementioned officials are qualified lawyers.

The prosecution of senior officials for criminal acts committed by them in their official capacity is a matter to be decided by the King, who must also make decisions regarding prosecution in certain other cases, as specified by statute. Serious offenses are punishable by imprisonment of up to 21 years, the maximum penalty under the Penal Code. If the offense was directed against public authorities, or is of particular public interest, decisions concerning prosecution must be made by the Director General of Public Prosecution. He must also decide whether to prosecute serious offenses. In the vast majority of minor offenses, the decision to prosecute is generally made by the Public Prosecutor in that district. There are many instances of what one might call everyday crime, and in these cases the district Chief of Police, or his deputy, may initiate proceedings.

These officials also decide whether to institute a prosecution in cases of minor offenses. They also have other powers conferred on the Prosecuting Authority by statute, such as the right to carry out an investigation, to apply to the courts for a person charged to be remanded in custody, or for a search warrant. As a rule, an appeal may be lodged by the authority who has instituted a prosecution.

Besides imprisonment, the most common penalties are detention, community service, and fines. Verdicts in criminal cases may also include seizure of money or belongings. This is not considered a penalty. A demand for confiscation may also be put forward without demanding a penalty.

When a person is found guilty, the court may decide to postpone sentence, in which cases, probation of two to five years (the latter in special circumstances) will be ordered. If the convicted person violates the terms of his probation, and prosecution is instituted or an application made to have the case adjudicated by the court of examination and summary jurisdiction within six months after the probation period expires, a combined immediate sentence may be imposed for the second offense.

Police statistics show a steep rise in most types of crime over the past 25 years. Some of the increase has to do with changing behavioral patterns, but the public are also more likely to report incidents, and judicial practices have changed as well. Other statistics paint a less dramatic picture. For instance, it appears that the rate of violent crime fell in recent years, and the public are apparently less apprehensive about falling victim to crime.

Every year, about 450,000 crimes are reported to the police, of which over 320,000 are felonies (crimes warranting a prison sentence of more than three months) and over 120,000 are offenses (traffic violations, for instance). This adds up to 1,200 reported crimes every day. The actual ex-

tent of crime is unknown, but is assumed to be very high indeed.

Investigated crime has increased eightfold since 1960. Taking into account the growth in population of about a million, this would adjust it to a sixfold rise. Investigated crime affects today about 70 people per 1,000. Part of the rise has to do with higher reporting rates among the public (theft, for instance) and the streamlining of police statistics and reporting systems.

Between 180,000 and 190,000 incidents of theft are reported annually. Together with other forms of economic crime, theft accounts for two thirds of all crime. The steep rise in the theft statistics largely explains the rise in crime since the middle of the last century. Thefts from and of motor vehicles number 50,000–60,000 annually, along with about 60,000 traffic offenses involving motor vehicles directly or indirectly, account for 25% of total crime.

Fifteen percent of all reported crime is drug related. Since the late 1960s, the figure has grown from 200 to 48,000 incidents annually in 2001. This rise needs to be considered in relation to legislative changes and intensified police investigations. More than 90% of reported drug-related charges are brought by the police, and a significant share of the rise in charges can be attributed to increased police commitment in this area. The highest increase is in petty crime (possession and use of drugs). Serious drug-related crime accounts for only 2% of all crime. While sentencing severity for drug-related crime rose steadily over many years, it has leveled off recently.

Violent crime has risen sharply and accounts today for almost 6% of all reported crime. Here too, minor offenses such as threats and assault dominate.

Most violent crime is reported by the young, especially young men. Between 1995 and 1998, statistics show that members of ethnic minorities are the most frequent victims of violence.

In 2002, there were 53 murders and 71 attempted murders, an increase over the average for 1991–2001. Murder rates vary from year to year, however, and it is impossible to say whether the increase is symptomatic of a wider trend.

In the mid-1980s, almost half of those charged with an offense were juveniles (under 21). The number of juveniles charged remained relatively unchanged between the late 1980s and mid-1990s. The under-21s accounted for less than a third of all persons charged in 1997. Since then, statistics turned upwards again, and in 2001 more than 6% of the juvenile population aged 18–20 was charged for some offense or other.

In past years, most juveniles arrested by the police were suspected of theft. The same applies today, though police statistics do not suggest that the young steal more than they did before. About half are charged with drug-related offenses. From 1998–2001, the number of juveniles apprehended for drug-relate offenses rose by 72%, and today, half of all juveniles apprehended by the police are charged with using drugs.

Statistics for the past 10–20 years show that drug use, and the problems associated with it, are growing in Norway, especially among the younger generation.

In 1960, four out of 10 crimes were solved. From then until the late 1980s, the figure fell 50%. It has risen since then again. In 2001, 33% of all crimes were solved. Eight out of ten summary offenses are solved. But the proportion of solved cases varies widely across the different categories of crime. Virtually all unlawful deaths are solved, as are drug-related offenses. But only about a tenth of all thefts are solved.

Norway's many preventive options range from a residence restriction order (*forvisning*) or ban on alcohol, to confinement in an institution for preventive supervision, imprisonment, and, for the mentally ill, confinement at a psychiatric hospital. The court decides the scope of the preventive measures.

Prisons in Norway are financed and run by the State. Lengthy prison sentences are served in five central institutions. There is one prison for women only. In addition to these institutions, there are 38 regional prisons, auxiliary prisons, and work camps.

Norwegian prisons can house a total of 2,959 inmates; 2,033 in closed facilities, and 926 in open facilities. Prison staff put in the equivalent of 2,519 person-years.

The average number of prisoners in 2001 was 2,800, the highest ever. This had little effect on the prison queue, however, as the number of unconditional prison sentences rose at the same time.

Prison statistics showed a significant rise in imprisonments in 2000–2001. About 12,000 were recorded in 2001, 8% more than the previous year.

Little separates the statistics for 2001 from the year before, in terms of imprisonments to custody or persons in custody at any particular time. This means that the rise in the prisoner population over that period must have been caused by an increase in the number of persons admitted to serve a sentence. On an average day, 612 persons will be detained in Norwegian prisons.

In 2003, more sanctions were meted out in Norway than ever before; the 2003 figure was also 25% higher than the previous year. The jump is largely due to increased vigilance on the part of the traffic police and a 30% rise in on-the-spot fines to traffic offenders.

Fines (those decided by court verdict, and ticket fines, the two types of fines in Norway) accounted for 92% of all sanctions in 2003. The most common sanction was on-the-spot fines for minor traffic and customs offenses. Ticket fines accounted for 71% of all sanctions.

Of the 211,000 persons punished in 2003 with reliable identity information, 105,000 (49%) had been punished in one or more of the preceding five years; 56,000 (27%) had been punished in one of those years, while less than 1% had been punished each of the preceding five years. The likelihood of incurring additional sanctions was highest among those punished for drug-related crime in 2003. Three out of four persons punished for drug-related offenses had also been punished during the previous five years. Regarding the large group of persons punished for crimes of gain and traffic misdemeanors, the percentages of previous offenders were 66 and 47, respectively. Ten percent of the sanctions were handed down to non-Norwegian nationals.

Police Profile

Background

Between the late seventeenth and mid-eighteenth centuries, small police forces, emulating French or Prussian models, were established in the four main cities (Trondheim, Bergen, Christiania (now Oslo), and Christiansand) to augment but not replace the old watch.

The last half of the nineteenth century marked the beginning of a cautious modernization of the Norwegian Police, following the English pattern. Towns and cities got their own Police Chief. There were about 50 district Police Chiefs across the country, including urban areas. A few years later, constabulary forces of the English type were on duty in the major cities, replacing the former town watchmen.

With an increasing urban population, these constabulary forces also grew and became more specialized.

Trade unions were founded towards the end of the nineteenth century, though for a number of reasons the policemen's unions remained relatively powerless. Police officers came mainly from the upper working and lower middle classes, in particular owner-farmers. As former non-commissioned officers, which most of them were, their civilian education was also good, compared with that of the general public.

In 1934, the Parliament decided that the State should take over the administration of the police.

Demographics

About 12,000 people work in the Police Force in some capacity or other (2004); 8,000 are police officers. Almost 450 are trained lawyers. About 2,700 are civilian employees. About 35% of police employees are female.

Organizational Description

The Norwegian Police are well educated and trained. The service is also well equipped.

Norway has one police service, structured on the principle of coherence, meaning that all functions are collected in the one organization. There are 27 local police districts, each under command of a Chief of Police. The Chiefs of Police head all kinds of policing in their district. Each police district has its own headquarters and several police stations. The districts are divided into rural police districts, under the command of a Police Chief Superintendent (formerly *lensmann*). All police officers are trained as generalists, able to fulfill every aspect of ordinary police work, including criminal investigations, maintaining public order, and community policing.

The Norwegian Police and Prosecuting Authority follows a parallel-track system, where responsibility for combating crime is shared between the Ministry of Justice and the Director General of Public Prosecutions.

The Director General of Public Prosecutions is in charge of criminal prosecutions. All other responsibilities come officially under the Ministry of Justice, mainly in its incarnation as the National Police Directorate.

The principle is that the Prosecuting Authority shall operate independently of politics and the rest of the civil service. No other professional authority, not even the Minister of Justice, may instruct the Prosecuting Authority.

Command structure

Norsk politi	Norwegian Police Service
Politidistrict	Police District
Særorgan	Service
Driftsenhet	Unit
Avdeling	Department
Seksjon	Section
Avsnitt	Subsection
Gruppe	Group
Kontor	Office

The National Police Directorate is organized under the Norwegian Ministry of Justice and acts under the Minister's constitutional responsibility. The National Police Directorate provides professional leadership, management, and development of the Norwegian Police Service. The Directorate is responsible for overseeing and managing the police districts and the special agencies. It plays a key role in combating international and organized crime. The National Police Directorate has a staff of about 120. The ongoing Police Reform is changing the police more than any other measure in the past 100 years. In 2002, the number of police districts was reduced from 54 to 27, a step deemed necessary to channel more resources to operative police duties and fewer to management.

Functions

The impact and growth of organized crime and the mobility and internationalization of criminal networks are matters of considerable concern, which require a concerted effort domestically and internationally. The National Police Directorate is in charge of organized crime, which includes working with other national police forces and managing Norwegian liaison officers abroad. The Directorate conducts what is known as "intelligence-led policing." It analyzes and assesses threat, and passes information on to the operative police force. Such analyses and assessments represent a crucial element of the strategies put in place to fight organized crime. The Task Force on Organized Crime (*Rådet for samordnet bekjempelse av organisert kriminalitet – ROK*) represents another important element of the fight against organized crime, especially when several Police Districts are involved.

Training

The National Police Academy, in Oslo, is the only police training body in Norway. It was established as an institution of higher education in 1992. In 2004, the basic training was recognized as a bachelor degree and gives 180 credits.

The first police school dates back to 1919. Training lasted three months, increasing to 4.5 months in 1925. By 1952, it took two years to qualify as a policeman, three years since 1992.

This three-year basic training equips future policemen with the general knowledge required by the police service. In-service training and further studies offer all groups within the police service an opportunity to update, develop, and widen their competence in various fields and areas of police work.

The basic education offers a combination of theory and practice. The first year is spent on studies at the National Police Academy. Then there is a year of practice at one of the 27 police districts. The third and last year involves more studies at the Police Academy.

In the first year, the students are taught elementary policing, law, and sociology, which aim at giving the students the knowledge they need to carry out their year of practice in an efficient and proper manner. In the second year, the students work under the guidance of seasoned police officers. In the third year, the students have the opportunity to reflect on the knowledge and skills picked up during the practice year, and to study some subjects in depth.

Further training is grouped into three areas: policing, detection, and management.

The Research Department designs and conducts studies of relevance to the police, publishes findings, and maintains a high academic standard. Studies feed into basic police training and the judiciary as a whole. The department has a permanent staff of four.

The Police Directorate heads the National Police Academy; it appoints members to the Board of the Academy, the majority of whom are not connected to the police, but represent the interests of society at large. Other members represent the students, teaching and other staff, and the school management. The Board deals with strategic plans, the budget, guidelines, and training.

The Academy is headed by a Director and a Deputy Director. It has five departments: a basic training department; a department at Bodø in the north of the country; a department of further education, and one each of research and administration. There is a staff of about 150, and about 1,100–1,200 students altogether. Yearly about 2,000 law enforcement personnel follow programs in basic or higher training.

Police Use of Firearms

Norwegian police officers are not routinely armed, though they may bear weapons in critical situations. The Norwegian Police Force is therefore one of the very few non-armed police forces in the world.

The 1989 regulations on the use of weaponry by the police issued by the Ministry of Justice, under powers set out in the 1936 Police Act, specify training, arming procedures, and use of weapons. They also specify how reports on situations requiring armed police are to be filed.

Between 1990 and 1991, 307 such incidents were reported to the Ministry and filed in the Ministry archives (Strype and Knutsson, 2002). Of these, 16 (5.2%) involved the firing of shots at targets. In 249 incidents, the police gave warning that they were prepared to open fire, but without that coming to pass.

The Oslo Police District differs from other Police Districts in terms of the incidence of use of weapons and reports filed at the Ministry of Justice, which have increased in recent years. The basic rule is that Norwegian police officers seldom fire. No more shots were fired in the period under study, though there appears to have been a rise in the number of situations where the police have warned that weapons could be used. Situations requiring the arming of the police tend to involve violence or threats of violence, robbery, and sightings of armed persons.

Complaints and Discipline

Human rights is an integrated element of police training, and is covered by several courses, such as law, community awareness, policing, and ethics. Courses on ethics and human rights are also separate programs. It is difficult to state the number of hours or the extent of training in human rights.

Norway has been criticized by Amnesty International on one occasion, and that concerned the use of isolation in custody, whereby a person in custody is denied newspapers, may not write or receive letters, or receive visitors.

The Special Investigation Branch (*De særskilte etterforskningsorganene* – SEFO) heads investigations of suspected offenses committed by police officials and police officers in the course of duty. SEFO heads investigations in cases in which the Prosecuting Authority has reason to suspect members of the police or Prosecution Authority of breaking the law in the course of duty.

There are currently twelve Special Investigation Branch units, one under each of the nine District Public Prosecutors, and three under the Oslo Public Prosecutor. Each unit has three members; they are headed by a Justice of the Supreme Court, or a person with equivalent qualifications. The other two members are a lawyer with experience from criminal cases, and an experienced police detective. Each SEFO unit has a deputy unit, also with three members. Members are appointed for a four-year term, and can be re-appointed for one more term.

In 2005, SEFO was phased out and replaced by a special investigation unit that looks into irregularities and brings charges where necessary against members of the police and Prosecuting Authorities. It is known as the Police Crime Unit (*Spesialenheten for politisaker*). It has fewer branches throughout the country, and it operates more independently from the police.

Terrorism

International terrorism continues to affect Norway's security policy as it does other nations'. The threat of international terrorism varies over time, but can change quickly. As of early 2004, the general terrorist threat to Norwegian interests was considered to be low. For certain foreign interests, the threat is considered to be slightly higher. Terrorist acts in 2003 showed that international Islamic extremists are intent on and have the capacity to conduct acts of terrorism against western and other targets. Certain core western targets remain particularly at risk from extremist Islamic groups.

European countries will continue to attract international Islamic extremists, both as a haven for various affiliated groups, and as a target for new attacks. Security services of several countries have frustrated planned terrorist actions, but the threat stemming from al-Qaeda in May 2003 showed that al-Qaeda also considers Norway a legitimate and profitable target.

Al-Qaeda, or groups inspired by al-Qaeda, were behind a range of terrorist actions in recent years, all of which feature the following:

- They used basic, conventional means, such as motor vehicles, bombs, small firearms, and hand grenades.
- They were largely executed by suicide terrorists, either alone or with others, or in combination with armed personnel, to ensure a successful outcome.
- They are characterized by high precision, careful planning, and coordination.

Norway's prominent international profile comes with a higher risk of terrorism and sabotage, espionage, and other criminal activities. Likely targets are diplomatic representations, economic interests, and Norwegian nationals abroad.

Rising international threat levels might also mean higher risks for Norwegian interests abroad. The level of threat will vary, and it is difficult to accurately predict or assess on a short-term basis.

The Police Security Service (PST) is a special branch of the police. PST answers directly to the Ministry of Justice, although in certain matters it answers to the Director General of Public Prosecutions and Offices of the District Public Prosecutor.

PST prevents and investigates crime related to terrorism; espionage; dissemination of weapons of mass destruction and equipment, material, and technology for their manufacture and use; and violent extremism. The service advises Norwegian authorities on matters concerning the security and sovereignty of the Norwegian State, and conducts assessments of threat. Such assessments are classified under Norwegian law, and are only communicated to the Ministry of Justice and other relevant authorities to apprise them of the current situation and as an element in decision making.

In addition to the Police Security Service, there is a special police unit of personnel trained and equipped to deal with and thwart terrorist attacks on Norwegian soil. It is known as the Counter Terrorism Force (*Beredskapstroppen*), and is part of Oslo Police District. It can be deployed to other Police Districts and Svalbard.

Every Police District employs specially trained officers for special duties. There are 800 such officers. The Police can also call on police reservists when required.

International Cooperation

International police cooperation is essential to effective combating of crime. In addition to membership in international organizations and collaboration between operatives, importance is attached to ensuring that Norwegian officers gain experience of foreign services, outreach activities, and networking.

Norway joined Interpol in 1931. Norway also takes part in meetings and on working parties in connection with Interpol. Norway currently chairs Interpol's European group and Interpol's Working Party against Traffic in Women.

Europol is the European Union's mainstay in the fight against organized crime. Norway entered into a cooperative agreement with Europol in 2001 and has two liaison officers stationed at The Hague. Europol works to improve the effectiveness of the fight against serious international crime and to enhance cooperation among responsible authorities. The gathering and exchange of intelligence information is a key element of Europol's work, which also offers comprehensive crime analyses and can assist member states' investigations of international crime with expertise and technical support.

The Schengen Agreement removed checkpoints at common points between State Parties to the Agreement, replacing them with external border checks. Compensatory measures aim to simplify cooperation between the police and judiciary within member states. Norway has participated since 2001. The Schengen Information System (SIS) has yielded good results for the Norwegian Police.

The five Nordic countries (Denmark, Finland, Iceland, Sweden, and Norway) have a tradition of close cooperation, which has resulted, among other things, in a Nordic agreement on police cooperation. The police of the Nordic Countries participate in a number of different Nordic forums. On the initiative of, among others, the National Police Commissioners in the Nordic countries, a special Nordic Working Group for Witness Protection was set up to draw up guidelines and manage collaboration in cases concerning the protection of witnesses.

Norwegian police officers have been taking part in international peacekeeping operations such as CIVPOL (Civilian Police), the UN-administered international police force deployed in peacekeeping and humanitarian operations, since 1989. Most operations have been UN-led and bilateral. About 800 Norwegian police officers have served in various areas of conflict in all.

The Nordic countries collaborate with the Baltic States. Together with Sweden, Finland, and Russia, Norway is a member of the Barents Region, in addition to various expert committees organized under the auspices of the Baltic Sea Task force.

Norway is currently involved in a joint project in Serbia, and has worked with a number of former eastern bloc countries, in particular the Czech Republic, Slovakia, Bulgaria, and Romania, to advance the Norwegian Government's Plan of Action for Applicants for Membership of the European Union.

Police Education, Research, and Publications

Major Norwegian Studies include:

PHS Forskning 1995:2 *Politiet i parken*
Johannes Knutsson.
PHS Forskning 1995:3 *Beruselse,*
utelivsdeltakelse og utsatthet for vold
Leif Petter Olaussen.
PHS Forskning 1997:1 *Karakteristika ved*
ungdomskriminalitet og unge lovovertredere
Hilde Pape.
PHS Forskning 1997:2 *Kriminalitetsforebygging*
i et situasjonelt perspektiv Johannes
Knutsson.

PHS Forskning 1997:3 *Det kriminalitetsforebyg-*
gende siktemål
Ola Erstad.
PHS Forskning. 1998:1*Kriminalitetsforebygging.*
Justisdepartementet forskningskonferanse 1997.
PHS Forskning 1998:2 *Hvorfor går ungdom inn i*
rasistiske grupper – og hvordan kommer de seg
ut igjen?
Tore Bjørgo.
PHS Rapport 1998 *Norges Kriminalstatistikk*
1789 – 1799
Ferdinand L. Næshagen.
PHS Forskning 1999:1 *Ungdom og Kriminalitet.*
Justisdepartementets forskningskonferanse
1998.
PHS-Forskning 1999:2 *SEFO - Det særskilte*
etterforskningsrgan
Gunnar Thomassen En empirisk belysning.
PHS-Forskning 1999:3 *Kvaliteten på politiets*
etterforskning
Ragnar Hatlem.
PHS-Forskning 1999:4 *Ride to live- live to ride*
Kåre Rørhus. En oversikt over sentral
forskning om outlawbikerkulturen.
PHS-Forskning 1999:5 *Fra selvtekt til*
demokratisk politi
Ferdinand L. Næshagen.
PHS Forskning 2000:1 *Politi og publikum.*
Justisdepartementets forskningskonferanse
1999.
PHS-Forskning 2000:2 *Ranere*
Kåre Rørhus.
En studie av raneres tenkemåte og mentalitet.
PHS-Forskning 2000:3 *Voldsalarm*
Katja H-W Skjølberg
En programevaluering av et forebyggende
tiltak mot gjentatt kvinnemishandling.
PHS-Forskning 2000:4 *Det vanskelige*
*politiarbeidet.*Justisdepartementets
forskningskonferanse 2000.
PHS-Forskning 2000:5 *Innbrudd, tyvegods og*
marked
Gunnar Thomassen. En eksplorativ undersøkelse.
PHS Forskning 2001:1 *Politiets*
fjernsynsovervåking ved Oslo Sentralstasjon
Stig Winge—en evaluering av kameraenes
effekt på kriminalitet og ordensproblemer.
PHS-Forskning 2001:2 *Politiarbeid på godt og vondt.*
Forskningskonferansen 2001.
PHS-Forskning 2002:1 *Politiets bruk av*
skytevåpen Jon Strype og Johannes Knutsson.

PHS-Forskning 2002:2 *Polititjenestemann og akademiker?*
Forskningskonferansen 2002 Arne Skodvin (red.).

PHS-Forskning 2003:1 *Åsta-ulykken*
Elin Karlsen Mestring og psykisk helse hos personell i politiet etter kritiske hendelser.

PHS-Forskning 2003:2 *Korrupsjon i politiet*
Former årsaker og mottiltak Gunnar Thomassen.

PHS-Forskning 2003:3 *Det utfordrende politiarbeidet*
Trond Myklebust og Forskningskonferansen 2003 Gunnar Thomassen (red.).

PHS-Forskning 2004:1 *Forsøk med Ungdomskontrakter*—en alternativ reaksjonsform rettet mot unge lovbrytere Marit Egge.

PHS Rapport 1995:1 *Om drapsutviklingens flertydighet*
Leif Petter Olaussen.

PHS Rapport 1995:2 *Mer synlig politi?*
Johannes Knutsson.

PHS Rapport 1996:1 *Kriminalstatistikk og virkelighet*
Leif Petter Olaussen.

PHS Rapport 1997:1 *Voldens rolle i filmfortellingen.*
Delrapport 1—Volden for øyet— Unge, vold , medier og oppvekst Arnt Maasø.

PHS Rapport 2001 *Antisosial atferd og risikofaktorer i familien til to grupper unge.*
Delrapport 3—Volden for øyet—Unge, vold, medier og oppvekst Klara Øverland.

PHS Rapport 2002 *Politihundens rettslige beskyttelse*
Tor Erik Heggøy.

RUNE GLOMSETH

Bibliography

Administration of Justice in Norway, a brief presentation, published by the Royal Norwegian Ministry of Justice and the Police in collaboration with the Royal Norwegian Ministry of Foreign Affairs, Oslo, 1998.

Aftenposten: Hvem, hva, hvor, aktuelt leksikon, 2004.10.24 Stortinget i navn og tall, 2001–2005, Universitetsforlaget, Oslo, 2002.

Christensen, Tom og Egeberg, Morten: Forvaltningskunnskap, forvaltningen i samfunnet, Tano forlag, Oslo, 1992.

Christensen, Tom, Egeberg, Morten, Larsen, Helge O., Lægreid, Per og Roness, Paul G: Forvaltning og politikk, Universitetsforlaget, Oslo, 2002.

Eide, Per: *Lost in Norway*, Dinamo forlag, Oslo, 2003.

Hagen, Terje P. Og Sørensen, Rune J.: Kommunal organisering, effektivitet, styring og demokrati, Tano Aschehoug, Oslo, 1997.

Hellevik, Ottar: Nordmenn og det gode liv, norsk monitor 1985 – 1995, Universitetsforlaget, Oslo, 1996.

Klausen, Arne Martin (red.): Den norske væremåten, Cappelen forlag, Oslo, 1984.

Knophs oversikt over Norges Rett, Universitetsforlaget, Oslo, 1975.

Libæk, Ivar og Stenersen, Øivind. Norges historie, fra istid til oljealder, Grøndahl, Oslo, 1991.

Næshage, Ferdinand: *Norway's Democratic and Conservative Tradition in Policing*, paper in Scandinavien Journal of History 25.

Norwegian Statistics, 2004 (www.ssb.no).

Østerud, Øyvind: Statsvitenskap, innføring i politisk analyse, Universitetsforlaget, Oslo, 1999.

Politiet: The Police in Norway, National Police Directorate, Oslo, 2004.

Politiet: Årsrapport 2003, *National Police Directorate*, Oslo, 2004.

Samfunnsboka, Statens informasjonstjeneste, Universitetsforlaget, Oslo, 1994.

Strype, Jon og Knutsson, Johannes: Politiets bruk av skytevåpen, PHS, 2002:1.

O

OMAN

Background Material

The conventional long form of the country's name is Sultanate of Oman and the local long form is Sultanate Oman. The country is regarded as one of the oldest and more traditional in the Arab world. Until recently, the Sultanate of Oman was the most isolated country in the gulf region. The Sultanate of Oman is in the southwestern part of Asia, and the country sits on the southeast corner of the Arabian Peninsula. Oman shares borders with Saudi Arabia and the United Arab Emirates in the west, the Republic of Yemen in the south, and the Strait of Hormuz in the North Arabian Sea in the east. The coast is 1,700 km long from the Strait of Hormuz in the north to the borders of the Republic of Yemen in the south, and overlooks three seas including the Arabian Gulf, Gulf of Oman, and the Arabian Sea. Oman is very accessible via the sea and the gulf. The Sultanate of Oman is very protective of territorial integrity, and access to the country is deliberately controlled with a net migration rate of 0.29 migrants per 1,000 population.

With 309,500 km of total land area, Oman is the third largest country on the Arabian Peninsula. The country is regarded as dry desert with hot and humid temperatures along the coast, hot and dry in the interior, and strong southwest summer monsoon in the far southern periphery. At one point, the country had its own empire extending down the east African coast and contended with Portugal and Great Britain for supreme influence in the Gulf and Indian Ocean.

The country has a population of 2.81 million people (estimates derived from Central Intelligence Agency, 2003) and a population growth rate of 3.38%. Oman's strategic location on the Musandam Peninsula and adjacent to the Strait of Hormuz, a vital transit point for global crude oil, makes it a commercial oil business point. The people of Oman are collectively referred to as "Omanis," and the individual citizen as "Omani."

The Sultanate of Oman's official language is Arabic with English, Baluchi, Urdu, and Indian dialects spoken by a very small minority. The country has four major ethnic groups, including Arabs, Baluchi, South Asians (Indian, Pakistani, Sri Lankan, Bangladeshi), and Africans.

The capital of the country is Muscat with a population of 797,000 people in the metropolitan area and 53,800 in the city. The country's monetary unit is the Omani ryal.

Three-fourths of the Omani Arabs in Oman belong to the Ibadaya Muslim sect that follows

Abd Allah Ibn Ibad. Ibadism is a moderate sub-sect of the Kharijite movement, which seceded from the principal Muslim body after the death of Prophet Muhammad in 632 CE because they opposed emerging patterns of early caliphal succession in the seventh century. There are also Sunni and Shi'a Muslims, with the latter being the largest minority (25% of the population). The Ibadis live primarily in the mountainous regions of Oman. The Sunnis live in the coastal villages, and the Shiites are located in the cities. The Shi'a minority includes the Khojas, Baharina of Iraq or Iranian descent, and the Ajam, whose origin is traced to Iran.

The Ibadi leadership is vested in an Imam who is regarded as the sole legitimate leader and combines religious and political authority. The Imam is elected by a council of Shaykhs. The practice of and adherence to Ibadism may be responsible for the country's historical isolation. Oman is the only country in the Islamic world with a majority Ibad hi population known for its moderate conservatism. The most distinguishing feature of the Ibadi practice is the choice of rulers by communal consensus and consent. Ibadi is considered a heretical form of Islam by the Sunni Muslims (those who established caliphal succession in Islam). Historical accounts suggest that Oman adopted Islam in the seventh century CE when the Prophet Muhammad explored the area and that Ibadism became the dominant religious sect in Oman by the eighth century CE.

Oman's economy has grown tremendously, and the growth is attributable to the upturn in oil prices. The government moved toward privatization of utilities and development of a body of commercial law to facilitate foreign investment. The continuous liberalization of Oman's markets and acceptance into the World Trade Organization have contributed significantly to economic growth. In 2000, Oman's purchasing power reached $19.6 billion with a real growth rate of 4.6%. The country's main industries are in the area of crude oil production and refining, natural gas production, construction, cement, and mining of copper and other minerals. The people of Oman enjoy a decent standard of living. The economy is based on free market policies established by Sultan Quaboos. Oman mostly imports food, especially because agriculture accounts for less than 1% of exports. Oil production is owned by the Omani government (60%), Royal Dutch Shell (34%), and a few other oil companies (6%). Oman has embarked on economic diversification by encouraging investments in mineral resources such as copper, asbestos, coal, and marble. Another area of economic growth is tourism. Oman is becoming an increasingly open country. New hotel construction by multinational corporations such as Hilton and Radisson and youth hostels invite tourists to visit and better understand the culture. In 1997, Oman set up an international commerce center, the Omani Center for Investment Promotion and Export Development (OCIPED), to place the country as one of the key global centers for trade and industry as part of the economic diversification efforts. The country gives fair incentives to businesses for investing, including diverse tax exemptions, and waivers on foreign exchange controls.

In the ninth century BCE, there was great migration of Arabs to the capital of the geographical entity known as Oman. The conversion to Islam occurred in the seventh century CE. The country was occupied by the Portuguese from 1508 to 1648. The Ottomans overwhelmed the Portuguese in 1659, but were defeated and forced out in 1741 by Ahmad ibn Said of Yemen, who founded the present royal line. The major international issue for Oman was a dispute with the United Arab Emirates over its northern tip. The Musandam Peninsula forms the country's northern tip, which is separated from the rest of the country by the United Arab Emirates' (UAE) eastern coast and includes the only coast Oman has on the Persian Gulf. The Omani enclave of Madha is entirely surrounded by the UAE and lies halfway between the Musandam Peninsula and the rest of Oman. The boundary agreement was signed and ratified with the UAE in 2003 for the entire border area, including Oman's Musandam Peninsula and the Al Madhah enclaves.

In the eighteenth century, Oman became the object of Franco-British rivalry. However, in the nineteenth century Omani leaders managed to sign several treaties of friendship and commerce. For example, in 1908 the British entered into an agreement of friendship and the traditional association was completed in 1951 through a new treaty of friendship, commerce, and navigation. This treaty led to the recognition of the Sultanate of Oman as a fully independent state. In 1718 CE, the Imam, Sultan bin Saif II, died, and civil war broke out over the election of his successor. This war lasted for eighteen years and two factions emerged: one supporting the leadership of Saif bin Sultan, who was, at the time, a young boy; and the other supporting Muhanna bin Sultan, who held the necessary qualities to be an Imam. In the mid-1700s, the first ruler of the present dynasty (Al-Busaid) gained power, and in 1786 the capital was moved to Muscat. At the same time, the Al-Busaid adopted the title of Sultan, which continues to this day. The

Omani Empire prospered in the mid-nineteenth century under Sultan Said bin Sultan (ruled from 1804–1856). When Sultan Said bin Sultan died, the empire split in two due to rivalry over the succession: one son became the Sultan of Zanzibar and the other the Sultan of Muscat and Oman. The prosperity of Oman collapsed due to this split, and Britain took control of the island in 1890. In 1932, Sultan Said bin Taimur came to power at the age of twenty-two on his father's abdication, and ruled until 1970. On July 23, Sultan Qaboos bin said ascended the throne after his father abdicated and went to live in England. Sultan Qaboos had not only the vital responsibility to bring peace and stability to the nation, but also the responsibility of dealing with the growing problems of underdevelopment, including disease, illiteracy, and poverty. The new sultan initiated new policies. He abolished his father's harsh restrictions, which had led to thousands of Omanis leaving the country. He offered amnesty to opponents of his father's regime. He further established a modern government structure. For the first time in the history of the sultanate, he launched a major developmental program that upgraded education, health facilities, and developed the country's natural resources with modern infrastructure. The 1974 insurgency, a separatist revolt that began in the Dhofar province, was aided by communist and leftist governments, notably the People's Democratic Republic of Yemen, who encouraged the rebels to form the Dhofar Liberation Front. To quell the insurgency, Sultan Quaboos expanded and modernized and re-equipped the armed forces and granted amnesty to all surrendering rebels, while also dealing with the war in Dhofar. Sultan Quaboos requested and received military assistance and direct support from the United Kingdom and Islamic states, including Iran and Jordan. The guerrillas responsible for the insurgency were defeated in 1975. Sultan Quaboos has embarked on balancing tribal, regional, and ethnic interests in erecting a national government. Since 1975, Oman has devoted its attention to progress and modernization.

Contextual Features

The Sultanate of Oman is an Arab, Islamic, and fully independent state with Muscat as its capital. According to the 2003 census, Oman is divided into three *muhafazat* (singular: *muhafazh*; governorate) and five *minṭaqat* (singular: *minṭaqah*; regions). The three *muhafazat* are Muscat, Dhofar, and Musandam. The five regions include Al Batinah, Adh Dha-hirah, Ad Dakhiyah, Ash Sharqiyah, and Al Wusta. These regions are divided into fifty-nine administrative districts called *wilayat* (districts), and each *wilaya* is governed by a *wali* and a local council who reports to the Ministry of the Interior.

The sultan is the chief of state and head of the cabinet. In 1981, he established a Consultative Assembly, whose members he selected, to advise him. In 1991, Qaboos replaced the assembly with a Consultative Council, a body intended to give broader participation to Omani citizens. In 1994, membership in the Consultative Council was expanded from fifty-nine to eighty (with the larger districts represented by two members) and women candidates were permitted. In November 1996, thé Basic Law, in effect a constitution, was promulgated to regulate several important areas of governance. The law called for the creation a bicameral system of an upper chamber, the Council of State (Majlis al-Dawala), which together with the Consultative Council (Majlis al-Shura) form the Council of Oman. The Majlis al-Dawla is appointed by the sultan and has advisory power, while the Majlis al-Shura is elected via limited suffrage with the exception of the president, who is appointed by royal decree. The last elections were held in 2003. The Basic Law also outlines a process for choosing a successor to Quaboos, who has no heir; forbids government ministers from holding positions in private companies, in an attempt to separate political and economic power; and affirms the rule of law and the independence of the judiciary. Oman has no political parties.

Oman has no developed judicial branch. Islamic Sharia, combined with tribal laws, English common law, and a nascent civil court system, is administered by the *wali* (governor) or *qadi* (judge) in each region/district. Alongside the Basic Law, the sultan mandated the establishment of the Supreme Court and other courts to interpret the law. He maintained power over the judiciary and judicial decisions. Appeals are made to the Sharia Chief Court in Muscat, and subsequent appeals are made directly to the sultan, who determines matters brought before him in accordance with his own notions of justice.

The public prosecutor's office, established in 1999, was headed by the Royal Oman Police (ROP) inspector general. The new decree placed the entire court system under control of the Ministry of Justice, and it separated the prosecutor's office from the ROP. The decree of 1996 formally established the judiciary as an independent, hierarchical check and balance system composed of a supreme court, an appeals court, primary court or regional courts, and divisional courts that encompass courts that deal with commercial, civil, penal, labor, taxation, general, and personal (Sharia) cases. The Sharia court hears cases according to Ibadi doctrine. The new bills and legislation also enacted policies that are relevant to the welfare of children. For example, the criminal procedure law of 2000 states that persons under eighteen must be assisted by a guardian, and a controlled substances law stipulates that sometimes the death penalty may be applied to minors for trafficking in illegal drugs.

Crime in Oman is low. Traffic laws are strictly enforced, and this has led to a dramatic reduction in vehicle accidents in the Sultanate. Oman has intensified a campaign to reduce white-collar crime, and instituted anti-money-laundering legislation, which is mostly related to proceeds from illegal drugs. Although the country is not a producer of narcotics nor known for trafficking, drug-related offenses increased in 2002. The most significant offenses are in the areas of embezzlement, counterfeiting, and smuggling of gold and diamonds. From January 2002 to December 2002, for example, there were eight suspects arrested for robbery, six arrested for using forged credit cards, and five jailed for violating residency laws. In 2003, there were sixty-four road accidents killing three, and in the first five months of 2004, eleven had been killed in road accidents. The country expanded the scope of the death penalty to include drug-related crimes. The Sultanate's criminal procedures provide for fair trials, but within the framework of Sharia law. Although presumed innocent, the offender cannot be detained for longer than twenty-four hours without judicial review of violations by a magistrate. The defendant can be represented by a public defender. There are no jury trials or rights to public trial and (according to Islamic Sharia's dictate of Qadi justice), only the judge examines witnesses at trials, and only sentences of more than US$1,000 can be appealed. The legal profession is regulated, and citizens may study at the College of Sharia and jurisprudence located in Muscat to specialize in Sharia jurisprudence.

Correctional institutions, according to U.S. State Department reports, are harsh. Prisoners complain of physical abuse and torture, extreme temperatures, and other minor complaints. The death penalty is reviewed by the grand mufti of the Sultanate, who can declare a religious death sentence before it is issued and approved by the courts. Death sentences are carried out in private. The U.S. Department of State reports indicate that torture and cruel and unusual punishment are not institutionalized, and the traditional punishment authorized by Sharia laws such as amputation of limbs and stoning are not imposed.

Police Profile

Background

There is evidence of police presence in the country dating back to the seventh century CE. In fact, the Sultanate of Oman at one time had no internal security. During this period, security was the responsibility of the local *walis* and Askers (Police Force). The social organization of security in the past was simple: the Askers were responsible for simple policing work such as guarding the markets and enforcing the law. Every *wilaya* in the country had its own group of government-appointed Askers. The Askers were not regularly trained; they had no uniforms but carried rifles and ammunition. The highest-ranked Asker was the *aged* or colonel. Policing was limited to the big cities, especially to Muscat and Muttrah. The present ruler, Sultan Quaboos, is credited with the establishment of a modern, competent, skilled, and technologically advanced force, which is regarded as one of the best in the Arab League countries.

The Royal Oman Police became known as such in 1974. The ROP are subject to and controlled by police laws issued in a royal decree in 1990 prescribing responsibilities and accountabilities of police personnel. The decree defined the position of the inspector general of police and customs and the role and responsibilities of the ROP.

Demographics

Women are becoming a permanent feature of the Oman police relative to other police forces in the Arab League countries. In 1974, the first group of female officers was trained and commissioned. ROP officers numbered nearly 7,000 in 1992, but have since increased to about 8,000.

Organizational Description

Although the ROP is under the command of the Sultan, it is administratively under the auspices of the Ministry of the Interior, which has overall responsibility for public safety, security, law, and order. ROP organization begins with Sultan Quaboos Bin Said, supreme commander. The Inspector General of Police and Customs is next in the hierarchy, and serves as the day-to-day commander of the ROP appointed by the Sultan. This is a ministerial position, and is supported by Directorate General of Development, Legal Affairs, Police and Customs, and a Special Branch. The assistant inspector general of police and customs handles operational schedules, and an assistant inspector handles general office duties. The ROP is headquartered in Qurum. There are also governorate or regional headquarters as well as special task force headquarters in Muscat, Dhofar, Musandam, Al Wusta, Al Sharqiyah, Al Batinah, Al Dihirah, and Al Dakliyah. The directorate general is comprised of the directorate general of financial affairs, human resources, maintenance and projects, logistics and supplies, information and technology, Sultan Quaboos Academy for Political Sciences, transportation, customs, civil defense, airport security, prisons, and inquiries and criminal investigation. There are also specialized directorates, including the director of police officers' club, social welfare, music band, public relations, and aviation. The ROP has three specialized police divisions, including the special security police, mounted police, and police coast guard.

Oman police also includes eight other directorate generals. The Directorate General of Operations is responsible for securing special events in the Sultanate, public and vulnerable buildings, and order. The Criminal Investigation Directorate General is responsible primarily for detecting criminal transactions, and investigates crimes with the use of specialized units such as crime control, narcotics, forensics, criminal evidence, quality control, information and crime analysis, license section, and an international and Arab police liaison directorate that cooperates with Interpol. The Immigration Directorate General deals with visitors to the country and immigration laws. The Customs Directorate General enforces customs laws, especially those related to smuggling. The Civil Directorate General focuses on public awareness regarding hazards and dangers that citizens might be exposed to, and operates fire and rescue emergency facilities. The Traffic Directorate General is responsible for, among other duties, enforcing traffic laws very stringently. The Civil Status Directorate General is responsible for birth and marriage registration, residency permits, and other interior matters. The Legal Directorate General drafts laws and regulations and formulates administrative decisions, and is responsible for developing the framework and studies used in policing. ROP also boasts of two specialized directorates: Directorate of Police Aviation, and Directorate of Public Relations (music, medical services, social welfare, and officers, club).

Functions

One of the functions of the Sultan in Article 42 of the 1996 royal decree is "taking prompt measures to counter any threat to the safety of the citizens, territorial integrity and interests of the people." Furthermore, the Sultan shall assure internal and external security, maintaining rights and freedoms of citizens and the rule of law, and guiding the general policy of the state. Based on the principles of the state, the Sultan is the supreme commander of the ROP. The present emphasis is on community policing and development of a well-trained force to protect the society from those who violate the laws. The development of adequate trained personnel is important, especially because the ROP use the latest technology in carrying out their duties. Over the years, the ROP have set up several police stations and posts, and strive to provide vital services to the communities. The ROP's departmental goals include administrative efficiency, crime prevention, and rescue operations on land and sea. The ROP work closely with the business community, government agencies, and with the public at large to achieve such goals.

Training

The main training institute located in the Al-Wataya area of Muscat was established in 2000, and is one of the main training institutes for the ROP.

Terrorism

Oman has been subject to terrorist attacks in the past. The ROP cooperate with the international community for the elimination of terrorists everywhere, and have taken steps to ratify and implement relevant U.N. policies, and to criminalize financing of terrorism, terrorist organizations, and terrorist acts.

Police Education, Research, and Publications

The following are police-related websites:

www.rop.gov.om/
www.law.emory.edu
www.lexicorient.com/e.o
www.omanet.com
www.nationmaster.com
www.gulf-news.com
www.omanobserver.com
www1.oecd.org/fatf/ctry

EVARISTUS OBINYAN

Bibliography

Al, Maamiry, and Ahmad Hamoud. *Oman and Ibadhism.* New Delhi, 1989.

OMAN

Ballantyne. *Commercial Law in the Middle East: The Gulf States*. 1986.

Carter, John. *Tribes in Oman*. London, 1982.

Central Intelligence Agency. *The World Factbook*. 2003.

El, Amin. *Middle East Legal System*. Glasgow, 1985.

Kechichian, J. A. *Oman and the World: The Emergence of an Independent Foreign Policy*. 1995.

Mahmood. *Statutes of Personal Law in Islamic Countries*. 1995.

Maurizi, Vincenzo. *History of Sayd Said, Sultan of Muscat*. Cambridge, 1984.

Morris, Jan. *Sultan in Oman*. 2004.

Riphenburg, Redden. *Modern Legal Systems Cyclopedia*. Vol. 5, 1990.

Tore, Kjeilen. *Oman Political Situation: Encyclopedia of the Orient*. 2004.

Wilkan, Unni. *Behind the Veil in Arabia: Women in Oman*. London, 1982.

P

PAKISTAN

Background Material

The Islamic Republic of Pakistan gained independence on August 14, 1947. The capital is Islamabad. The nation has a total area of 888,102 sq km. As of 2004, the population was approximately 150 million. Pakistan is bounded by, going clockwise from the west, Iran, Afghanistan, China, and India. Ethnicities include Punjabi, Sindhi, Pashtun (Pathan), and Baloch. The religious composition of the population is 97% Muslim (Sunni 77%, Shia 20%), with the remaining 3% comprised of Christians (mostly Catholics), Hindus, Zoroastrians, and others. The official languages are Urdu and English.

Contextual Features

Pakistan's government is parliamentary with a strong executive branch and a federal republic. The executive branch is composed of the prime minister and the cabinet. The legislative branch is a bicameral parliament consisting of an upper house (Senate) and a lower house (National Assembly). A parliamentary constitution was promulgated on April 10, 1973. The country is administratively divided into four provinces, including Punjab, Sindh, North-West Frontier Province, and Balochistan. Federal territories comprise Islamabad Capital Territory, Federally Administered Tribal Areas (FATA), Azad Jammu and Kashmir, and the Northern Area.

The following are the laws regulating the criminal justice system in Pakistan: Pakistan Penal Code, 1860; Criminal Procedure Code, 1898; Qanun-e-Shahadat, 1984; Islamic Hudood Laws, which include Offence of Zina (Enforcement of Hudood Ordinance), 1979; Offences Against Property (Enforcement of Hudood Ordinance), 1979; Prohibition (Enforcement of Hudood Order), 1979; and Qisas and Diat Ordinance.

The Pakistan Penal Code was framed by the Indian Law Commission, transplanting Anglo-Saxon law concepts into a Pakistani sociocultural milieu. By this code, the colonial masters curbed the crime. It has been kept up-to-date with many subsequent amendments. The Pakistan Law Commission, Islamic Ideology Council of Pakistan, and the Federal Shariat Court also review it.

The prevalent Islamic Hudood Laws of Pakistan prescribe the following punishments for offenders. Hudood are punishment for major crimes as prescribed by the Holy Quran and practiced by the

Holy Prophet (Peace Be Upon Him). These are stoning to death, chopping of hand from wrist, chopping of one hand and opposite foot, whipping, death, and life imprisonment. The standard of proof required in these cases is, however, so high that offenders are rarely subjected to these extreme punishments.

Tazeer are flexible punishments in the form of fines, whipping, death sentence, or imprisonment, as may be prescribed by Islamic state in the light of analogies of the Jurists of Islam.

Criminal offences in Pakistan are of two kinds: cognizable and non-cognizable. In cognizable offences, the accused may be arrested by the police without a warrant. In non-cognizable offences, the police are not empowered to arrest without a warrant from a competent court.

There are 511 sections in the Pakistan Penal Code (PPC); of these about 210 sections are cognizable, but the number and types of offences most frequently reported to the police do not surpass 20.

Prisoner categories follow:

- Convicted criminal prisoners: A person found guilty of a crime after adjudication of his offence in a criminal prosecution in a court, and sentenced to undergo imprisonment as punishment proportionate to his guilt, as adjudged by the court.
- Juvenile prisoners: Any prisoner who has not attained the age of eighteen years (Section 27 of PPC).
- Habitual prisoners: Any person convicted of an offence whose previous conviction taken in consideration with the present conviction shows that he habitually commits offences, punishable by law, or he/she is proved by habit to be a member of gang of *dacoits* or thieves, or is a bad character. The punishment of such habitual offenders could also be enhanced (U/S 75 PPC).

The crime codes in Pakistan classify some felonies as noncognizable for police action, and many others as noncompoundable for police arrest. Some offences are also bailable before arrest. Accused persons also have a remedy for bail before arrest from courts.

Crime statistics are collected by police departments at the level of the police station. The record is tabulated for each district, each province, and for the country as a whole. Crime data are published in tabular, graphic, regional, demographic, periodic, descriptive, and many other types of presentations. Comparative crime figures for 2001, 2002, and 2003 appear in the following table.

In the Police Order of 2002, the investigation branch has been separated from the operational

Offence	2003	2002	2001
Crimes against persons	65,971	62,586	63,281
Murder	9,346	9,462	9,593
Attempted murder	11,562	10,920	11,594
Hurt	28,703	27,874	27,281
Rioting	2,673	2,636	3,315
Assaults on public servants	2,900	2,605	2,668
Zina	2,415	2,148	2,176
Kidnapping/abduction	8,197	6,753	6,487
Kidnapping for ransom	175	189	167
Crimes against property	65,484	58,991	58,342
Highway dacoity	80	75	65
Bank dacoity	41	25	8
Petrol pump dacoity	6	9	14
Other dacoity	1,939	1,520	1,295
Highway robbery	179	189	184
Bank robbery	319	228	24
Petrol pump robbery	31	46	77
Other robbery	10,042	7,738	7,429
Burglary	13,049	13,306	13,146
Cattle theft	6,742	5,402	5,569
Other theft	20,189	17,151	18,641
Traffic accidents	11,606	10,886	11,232
Fatal accidents	4,619	4,640	4,651
Nonfatal accidents	6,987	6,246	6,581
Miscellaneous	79,787	74,037	83,315
Total PPC crime	222,848	206,500	216,170
Arms Act	72,696	92,407	68,661
Prohibition Order	71,592	72,835	68,736
Local and special laws	33,544	27,267	27,092
Total recorded crimes	400,680	399,006	380,659

or prevention branch. The head of the investigation branch at the provincial level is an officer of the rank of Additional Inspector General of Police. A complete hierarchy of investigation branch down to police station level has been organized. The head of the investigation branch of subdivisional level, who is a gazetted officer of the rank of ASP/DSP, entrusts the investigation of criminal cases to police officers not below the rank of ASI. These investigating officers are legally bound to finalize the investigation of the cases within seventeen days after the arrest of the accused.

When an investigation is completed after arrest or nonarrest of the accused, the full facts of the case are submitted to the prosecutors (legal branch or district attorney) of pertinent criminal courts of the jurisdiction according to Challan number under 173 CrPC for adjudication.

The 2002 Police Order envisages establishment of a separate independent prosecution agency for each police organization in the country. However, a marked improvement over the colonial legacy had been made a decade ago when the prosecution of heinous cases was taken from the Police Department and transferred to the Law Department.

Criminal courts in Pakistan consist of judges of different classes; first-class magistrates/judicial magistrates having original jurisdiction to try all types of police-registered penal and nonpenal (traffic) offences. The additional sessions judges and the sessions judges in each district play the crucial role of trying serious crimes and offences under Islamic law. Sessions judges are also the first appellate courts for punishments awarded by junior judges up to three years with fixed fine.

First-class magistrates/judicial magistrates are law graduates appointed by provincial governments, after undergoing competitive examinations conducted by provincial public service commissions.

The introduction of criminal justice reforms has brought fundamental positive change, including abolishment of the most conspicuous pillar of the British colonial masters, that is, executive magistracy. Although separation of the judiciary from executive in 1996 was also a gigantic step forward, this step by the present government has put an end to lingering controversy, and executive magistrates no longer exist.

In Pakistan, there are eighty-eight prisons of various types. At present, more than 80,000 people are confined in these jails, including convicted prisoners, defendants in trial, foreigners, women, and juveniles. Most of the jails are overcrowded and lack good facilities.

Pakistan has the following legislation for operation of probation and parole, as well as regulation of noninstitutional treatment of young offenders:

• Reformatory Schools Act, 1897
• Punjab Borstal Act, 1926
• Good Conduct Prisoners' Probational Release Act, 1926
• Probation of Offenders' Ordinance 1960
• Sindh Children Act, 1995
• Punjab Youthful Offenders' Ordinance, 1983

Reclamation and probation directorates operate in all provinces under the Probation of Offenders' Ordinance, 1960, and Good Conduct Prisoners' Probational Release Act, 1926, respectively.

Drug Abuse and Trafficking

Pakistan has been a producer of opium for domestic consumption for several centuries. In 1979, the government responded to the problem of increased illicit opium production and trade by passage and enforcement of the Hadd Ordinance. This ordinance brought existing law in line with Islamic

injunctions, and prohibits trafficking, financing, or possession of more than ten grams of heroin or one kilogram of opium. In 1979, all poppy cultivation (licit and illicit) was banned, and all government-controlled processing plants and detail outlets for licit opium were closed. As a result of the Hadd Ordinance and partly because of massive stockpiling of opium following the bumper harvest in 1979, opium cultivation and production sharply declined in the 1980s.

The government's commitment to make Pakistan drug-free increased efforts in law enforcement, the impact of alternative development assistance from the international community, and a drop in retail prices of opium gum due to the massive increase in production in Afghanistan, are major factors that contributed to a further decline in opium cultivation since the mid-1990s. The analysis of poppy harvesting trends reveals a decline in the amount harvested from 9,441 hectares in 1992 to less than 284 hectares in 1999. Of the three main poppy-growing areas, Dir district (where the United Nations Office on Drugs and Crime [UNODC] has been active since 1985) accounted for approximately 60% of the opium harvested in the country. Over this period, UNODC spent US$34 million on alternative development projects in this district. Alternative development interventions coupled with demonstrated government commitment led to a decrease in opium poppy cultivation in Dir District from over 3,500 hectares in 1992 to near zero in 2000, making the Dir project one of UNODC's most successful alternative development projects.

Pakistan continues to be one of the major conduits for heroin/morphine base/opium and hashish originating from Afghanistan, the world's largest opium producer. Iran and the adjoining Central Asian states are also used for trafficking purposes.

Pakistan's Anti-Narcotics Force and other agencies with a drug control mandate such as Customs, Police, Frontier Corps, Rangers, and Coast Guard seizures from 1997 to 2000 are summarized in the following table.

Pakistan has a significant drug abuse problem. Trends in drug use patterns indicate a marked increase in heroin consumption that emerged in

Year	Opium	Heroin	Hashish
1997	8,502 kg	5,076 kg	108,500 kg
1998	5,021 kg	3,363 kg	65,909 kg
1999	15,469 kg	4,672 kg	80,505 kg
2000	8,780 kg	9,400 kg	129,913 kg

Source: Anti-Narcotics Force, Pakistan.

the 1980s. The 1993 National Survey on Drug Abuse (albeit results have been disputed) estimated the number of drug users at 3 million, of which approximately 50% were addicted to heroin. According to provisional results of the 2000 National Assessment Study on Drug Abuse, the number of hardcore heroin addicts had swelled to 500,000.

Police Profile

Background

The Police Department was established in the Indian subcontinent under the 1861 Police Act. In accordance with this act, the comprehensive Police Rules were framed in 1934, under which the police force remained functional. In response to persistent public demand, the present regime promulgated the Police Order in 2002 by repealing the 1861 Police Act. In the new order, an elaborate mechanism was provided to ensure the neutrality of police and its functional autonomy, in addition to its democratic control.

Demographics

The strength of the police force in the provinces is determined by respective provinces according to their needs. A reasonable ratio is maintained between the force and the area of its responsibility (see next table) except for the Islamabad Capital Police, where a large force is deployed for protection duties of diplomats and the diplomatic enclave and other important government functionaries and buildings.

Organizational Description

The Islamic Republic of Pakistan is a federal republic. Constitutionally, policing is a provincial/regional function. Accordingly, police forces have been organized on provincial and administrative unit (territorial) bases, namely:

- Punjab Police
- Sindh Police
- NWFP Police
- Balochistan Police
- Islamabad Capital Territorial Police
- Azad Jammu and Kashmir Police
- Northern Areas Police

Other police organisations are organized on a functional basis for specific specialized jobs such as the following:

- Pakistan Railway Police: Prevention and investigation of offences committed on railway tracks and trains.
- National Highways and Motorways Police: Prevention of offences and regulation of traffic on motorways and national highways.
- Federal Investigation Agency: Investigation of white-collar and organized crime and performing immigration responsibilities at entry and exit points. Interpol also functions under this agency.
- Intelligence Bureau: Collection and collation of intelligence and analysis.
- Anti-Narcotics Force: Prevention and investigation of offences related to drug production and trafficking and liaison with other government agencies.

In accordance with the 2002 Police Order, all police establishments are being organized in the following branches and divisions:

- Watch and Ward
- Intelligence
- Investigation
- Criminal Identification
- Reserve Police
- Personnel Management
- Education and Training
- Finance and Internal Audit
- Traffic Planning and Management
- Information Technology
- Transport
- Research and Development
- Legal Affairs
- Welfare

Functions

According to Article 4 of the 2002 Police Order, following are the duties of every police officer:

- Protect life, property, and liberty of citizens.

Police to area ratio, 2003

Area	Sanctioned Police Strength	Area (sq km)	Police Officers per 10 sq km
Punjab	110,149	205,344	5.4
Sindh	89,151	140,914	6.3
North-West Frontier Province	33,322	74,521	4.5
Balochistan	18,862	347,190	0.5
Islamabad	7,244	906	80.0
Northern Areas	3,037	72,496	0.4
Azad Jammu and Kashmir	6,401	13,297	4.8
Total	268,166	854,668	3.1

- Ensure that the rights and privileges, under the law, of a person taken in custody, are protected.
- Prevent the commission of offences and public nuisances.
- Collect and communicate intelligence affecting public peace and crime in general.
- Regulate and control traffic on public roads and streets.
- Detect and bring offenders to justice.
- Apprehend all persons legally authorized to apprehend and for whose apprehension sufficient grounds exist.
- Perform other duties and exercise powers as are conferred by this order, the code, or any law for the time being in force.
- Aid and cooperate with other agencies for the prevention of damage to public property by violence, fire, or natural calamities.
- Prevent harassment of women and children in public places.

Police officers shall make every effort to:

- Afford relief to people in distress situations, particularly women and children.
- Provide assistance to victims of road accidents.

Training

Training enhances skills and knowledge, and brings positive changes in the attitudes of trainees. Since policing is a very challenging profession, the necessity of providing the best training to police officers, particularly new entrants, cannot be over-emphasized.

The government and policymakers are increasingly recognizing the importance of police training in the country. Since the 1990s, successive governments have made very serious efforts to provide better training facilities to the Police Department.

After a quarter century of neglect, establishment of the National Police Academy, Central Planning and Training Unit (CPTU), and the National Police Training Management Board are real milestones in the right direction. Creation of CPTU has helped in the analysis of training needs for police and designing curriculum at police training institutions under the supervision of National Police Training Management Board, which is composed of all heads of police organizations in the country.

The National Police Academy is now considered a premier police training institution according to international standards. Besides catering to the training needs of young recruits and in-service courses for senior police officers, it has also started providing training opportunities to police officers of friendly countries.

Complaints and Discipline

The role of the police in a democratic society is pivotal, if the rule of law is to remain meaningful and human rights are to be protected and enjoyed by everyone. It is not contradictory to say that the police are essentially protectors of human rights in a democratic society, but the nature of their work can also make police officials responsible for human rights abuses through excessive use of force or through discriminatory practices.

Police in Pakistan are increasingly incorporating human rights training in its curriculum and syllabi. The National Police Academy has made human rights training an important component of its activities. Special emphasis on the subject is given during the nine-month training period required for assistant superintendents of police at the Academy.

Senior police officers, judges, lawyers, and members of civil society are invited to deliver lectures on various aspects of human rights, with the help of international agencies like the International Committee of Red Cross (ICRC), Norwegian Aid Agency (NORD), Save the Children Fund, and others. The police in Pakistan are also trying to enhance awareness among officers of human rights through a series of training programmes, seminars, and workshops.

Seminars and courses are now being organised regularly to raise human rights awareness among the general public and among professional groups who are likely to be confronted with situations involving human rights violations in day-to-day police activities. These seminars and courses aim at illustrating the importance of human rights awareness for police in order fully to ensure respect for human rights in a democratic society.

Terrorism

Terrorism exists in different forms such as ethnic, sectarian, political, and internationally sponsored terrorism. Pakistan has been a target of terrorism fundamentally from outside the country for over twenty years. Starting from Afghanistan in 1980s during the occupation of that country by the Soviet army, cross-border terrorism has continued unabated with outside support.

The September 11, 2001, terrorist attacks against the United States have radically and permanently changed the balance of power politics in the whole world, particularly in south and west Asia. Fundamental changes have taken place in Pakistan's foreign policy by reversing its previous position as far as its relations with Afghanistan are concerned. It has thrown its lot with the U.S.-led international antiterrorist coalition. Pakistan condemned the attacks and pledged "unstinted cooperation."

War on terrorism has had a profound impact on Pakistan's domestic and international policies. Occupation of Afghanistan by the U.S.-led coalition, in which Pakistan was its main ally and provided all logistic support, ended Taliban rule. As a result, hundreds of Taliban and al-Qaeda fighters fled Afghanistan to seek refuge in the tribal belt adjoining Pakistan. The country's law enforcement agencies with the help of information provided by U.S. intelligence are combing the border areas adjoining Afghanistan to capture these elements.

In the wake of its status as a front-line state against terrorism, Pakistan is being targeted by various terrorist groups, primarily religious extremists. Pakistan has been victimized by international as well as domestic terrorist groups. The foreign agencies have infiltrated religious and ethnic organizations, and are exploiting extremist elements on religious and linguistic bases, respectively. Their destructive activities have resulted in heavy losses of life and property, and are shaking the foundations of civil society.

Presently, much emphasis is being given by the government of Pakistan at both operational and training levels to fight terrorism. In this regard, relevant laws have also been made very stringent.

A new antiterrorism wing has been created in the Federal Investigation Agency (FIA). At the provincial level, the Criminal Investigation Department (CID) has been tasked to carry out antiterrorism measures.

Police Education, Research, and Publications

Established in 1977 in the Ministry of Interior, the Bureau of Police Research and Development (BPRD) was tasked to conduct research on different aspects of crime, policing, and police reforms in Pakistan. Similarly, issues like training, coordination, and modernisation of the police were also dealt with by BPRD.

In November 2001, it was decided to give the Bureau several functions, and change its name to the National Police Bureau (NPB). According to Police Order 2002, NPB is a statutory body, which is to act as the Secretariat for National Public Safety Commission as well as National Police Management Board. The principal task of the NPB is to assist the Ministry of Interior to make evidence-based policy decisions on all police-related matters.

The NPB is tasked to oversee the implementation of police reforms. It acts as a national focal point for coordination with provincial governments on police matters. It is at present working to standardise police training, telecommunication, computerisation, and forensic science facilities in Pakistan. It is also working to establish the Automated Fingerprinting Identification System (AFIS) and National Criminal Justice Database.

The National Police Bureau (NPB) is part of the federal Ministry of Interior, and is headed by an officer of the rank of inspector general of police, who is designated the NPB director general. He is assisted by a director, several deputy directors, and other support staff.

A. QADIR HAYE

PALAU

Background Material

The Republic of Palau (known as Balau to inhabitants) encompasses a cluster of some 300 islands in the southwestern corner of the Mariana Archipelago in the northern Pacific Ocean about 500 miles north of New Guinea, southeast of the Philippines, and southwest of Guam. It also lies 500 miles north of the Equator. Palau territory occupies 458 sq mil, which makes it two and a half times the size of Washington, DC. It had an estimated population of 20,006 in July 2004. Eighty percent of the people are native Palauans, and the remainder are Asians, primarily Filipinos. About half the population is Roman Catholic. The climate is tropical, hot, and humid.

The main Palau island is Babelthuap. The capital is Koror (sometimes identified as Oreor), but a new capital site is being constructed about twenty miles to the northeast of the current location. English is the primary language, and U.S. dollars are the islands' currency.

Contextual Features

Until it gained independence in 1988—the last of the post-World War II trust territories to do so—Palau was under foreign control from the late 1880s onward. It came under Spanish domination in 1886, and three years later was sold to Germany. In 1914, as a reward for its participation on the Allied side during World War I, Japan was given control of most of the Mariana Islands, including Palau. The invasion of the Japanese-defended outer island of Peleliu in the Palau Archipelago by the U.S. Marines and Army in September 1944 is regarded by some military historians as the bloodiest encounter for American forces throughout World War II. After the war, the United States was granted trusteeship control over Palau under the auspices of the United Nations, an arrangement the United States insisted upon in order to protect itself from possible enemy incursions, most notably from the Soviet Union.

Bitter controversy prevailed before Palau was able to secure independence, with fiery disputes focusing primarily on a provision in the Palau Constitution found nowhere else in the world. Article XIII, Section 5, specified: "Harmful substances such as nuclear, chemical, gas or biological weapons intended for use in warfare, unclean power plants, and waste materials therefrom, shall not be used, tested, stored, or disposed of within the territorial jurisdiction of Palau without the express approval of three-fourths of the votes cast in a referendum submitted on the specific question." A succession of referenda came close but never reached the 75% approval level.

The country's first elected president, Haruo Remeliik, was assassinated in 1985 by gunmen hired by a political opponent during the conflict over ratification of the Compact of Free Association with the United States. The instigator of the killing was caught, given a life sentence, and died in prison in 2003. Two years after the Remeliik murder, the father of an outspoken Compact opponent was shot in his house after the assassins failed to kill his son. Then the second elected president, Lazarus Solii, committed suicide in 1988, for reasons never altogether clear, although there is strong suspicion that he was plagued by a guilty conscience over questionable political machinations. President Tommy E. Remengesa, Jr., was elected to his second four-year term in November 2004.

The pact with the United States, signed in 1993, provided Palau with a subsidy of $700 million to be paid over fifteen years. In return, the United States is accorded specified military facilities for fifty years, and the right to expel any unwelcome foreign forces from Palau. Palau itself does not have an army; its defense lies in U.S. hands.

The two notorious assassinations of political figures gained the territory an undeserved reputation as a particularly violent society. Neither killing was solved until the United States insisted during the Guam Accord negotiations in 1989 on the appointment in Palau of a special prosecutor and a public auditor, both of whom would be paid with U.S. funds. They are named by the Palau president and must be confirmed by the country's Congress. The Compact also provided funds for drug education and prison rehabilitation programs.

The first special prosecutor was dismissed when it was learned that he had been suspended from the practice of law in Florida after a disciplinary action. Jerry Massie, his successor, brought about the conviction of a former vice president of Palau and his wife for the murder of President Remeliik. The killers had forewarned the police that they intended to shut off power to the city so as to enable them to carry out the assassination, but the officers had not taken them seriously.

There is considerable involvement of Palau as a way station for counterfeit American money printed in the Philippines. Studies also indicate that 95% of crime in Palau now is either drug or alcohol related, a figure reflected in statistics showing that more than three-quarters of admissions to hospital emergency facilities have to do with conditions related to alcohol. The records for 1999, the latest available, show the following breakdown of crimes known to the police: grand larceny, 298 cases; assault and battery, 255 cases; burglary, 173 cases; and drunk and disorderly conduct, 164 cases.

The considerable presence of illegal drugs on Palau islands was indicated by a 2004 police raid on the outlying islands of Peleleu and Amguar where the police destroyed more than 4,000 marijuana plants found on thirty-eight plantations. At a meeting of Micronesia police leaders in late 2004, the head of the Bureau of Public Safety in Palau identified alcohol-related vehicle accidents and drugs as the islands' most pressing enforcement problems. Some help with these and other crime issues has been offered by the recent installation of a database system by an outside consultant who spent seventeen months on Palau designing the hardware. Among other things, the system allows computerized tracking of all criminal citations issued by the police, and permits the trial court to have access to the prior records, if any, of those who appear before it.

The legal system is largely derived from existing U.S. law, and the country's judiciary has a reputation for integrity and fairness. The court system features the Supreme Court, National Court, and Court of Common Pleas. Common Pleas handles small claims, traffic violations, and other minor incidents. Proceedings in Common Pleas normally are carried out in the Palauan language, and the higher courts are particularly attentive to concerns of customary village traditions when they adjudicate civil and criminal matters. Palauans are said to be quite litigious, and keep their courts busy.

A murder during the 2003 Christmas season shocked politicians and the public, killings being unprecedented in recent times. The case highlighted the reliance on outside specialists to help deal with serious offenses, since the autopsy was done by an imported doctor and Federal Bureau of Investigation agents were brought in from Guam to work on the case. A forty-two-year-old Seventh-Day Adventist pastor who had come to Palau the year before from Brazil as well as his wife and teenage son were bludgeoned to death by an intruder who had sought to steal their television and VCR. His eleven-year-old daughter was taken by car from the murder scene, sexually assaulted and strangled, and thrown onto the roadside from the murderer's car. The offender claimed that he had been high on methamphetamine. The strongest penalty he would face was life imprisonment; Palau does not have a death penalty.

The U.S. Department of State in its outline of conditions in Palau notes that the crime rate is "moderate," but calls attention to the PROTECT statute (an acronym for Prosecutorial Remedies and Other Tools to End the Exploitation of Children Today) enacted by the U.S. Congress in 2003, which allows the prosecution in the United States of commercial sexual acts committed by American citizens or permanent residents on foreign soil with a person under the age of eighteen.

Police Profile

Background

The island had its first jail constructed during the German interregnum. The Germans also estab-

lished a school for policemen in 1902, with instruction in the German language as well as in reading, writing, and arithmetic. With the exception of several mission facilities, this was the first vocational school open to local people. By August 2004, nearly 40,000 commercial-grade coconut trees had been planted in Palau under German authority, and police officers were required to check the groves at least once a month. Fines were levied against people when trees in their care had yellowed leaves. In the criminal realm, the Germans carried out the execution of a man who had killed two Chinese workers, a move that is said to have intimated the native population.

Under the Japanese, the police were the only part of the government that employed a significant number of Palauans. These were typically men of high clan status. The village police were charged with reporting the outbreak of epidemics and other unusual events in their assigned territory and with submitting a semiannual report on local conditions. Crime was uncommon during the Japanese period. The most common offenses were tied to alcohol, fights, stealing, and breaking into the homes of the Japanese. A majority of these incidents were handled informally by the police rather than being submitted to the courts, especially since arrested persons frequently were tortured by the Japanese. Sentences of those who confessed or were convicted generally involved several months spent building roads or other forms of hard labor such as work in the phosphate mines.

Organizational Description

Palau today is divided into sixteen states, each with its own police unit. Title 34 of the National Code provides for "a uniformed and trained group of persons in sufficient numbers and ranks to efficiently maintain law and order within the Republic." The police are located in the Bureau of Public Safety; the Bureau director is equivalent to a chief of police. Subordinate ranks are designated as captains, sergeants, and patrolmen. The director of the Bureau is appointed by the president of the Republic and is responsible to the president. The term in office is three years, but the incumbent may be reappointed for further service. The director is specifically exempt from liability for damages resulting from enforcement of the law while carrying out his assigned duties, although the Code provides that "he shall act upon his own private accountability for all excesses of his official powers and for any departure from the lawful provisions of any process in his hands."

Police captains are also presidential appointments. They are selected from a roster of nominees put together by the director of public safety. Their term of office is two years, "unless sooner removed for cause or by reason of a reduction in force." They may be reappointed. Special police captains can be appointed by the director in emergencies, and they serve until released by the director.

Functions

Police captains on outer islands "shall act in all respects as though they were the director and shall be liable for his acts or failure to act in the same extent as the director would in like circumstances."

The police are responsible for the supervision of the prisons and jails, and for "the receipt and proper treatment, housing, feeding and clothing of all prisoners." They also serve as fire marshals and court bailiffs.

There are five specific agencies under the supervision of the Bureau of Public Safety. Duties of the Patrol Division are specified in Executive Order No. 203 as follows:

(a) Provides necessary patrol services to the states, controls traffic, provides protection at public functions, and enforces all laws and performs other duties that may be assigned.
(b) Provides manpower necessary to fight fires, operates ambulance services, and responds to emergencies.
(c) Conducts investigations and prepares reports regarding traffic and misdemeanor offenses.
(d) Provides security as required at the Republic of Palau airports. (Inadequate airport security is regarded as one of the major current deficiencies in Palau's law enforcement efforts today).
(e) Maintains maritime navigational aids.

Provision also is made for a Division of Criminal Investigation and Drug Enforcement which has the responsibility for enforcing laws pertaining to the cultivation, distribution, transport, and sale or use of illicit drugs, as well as control over the sale and use of tobacco and alcoholic beverages. The Division of Fire and Rescue and the Division of Corrections have duties congruent with their titles. The latter, more specifically, is required to provide a workforce for public and government projects. There is a specific stress on rehabilitative programs in prisons, with designation of the need for training in gardening, fishing, woodcarving, and handi-

crafts. The Division of Marine Enforcement is charged with surveillance over what the guidelines regard as the 200-mile Exclusive Economic Zone of Palau, a claim disputed by other countries, which say that Palau's control can legally extend only the usual twelve-mile distance from its shores recognized in international law. The Australian government provides assistance to this unit. Finally, the duty of the Division of Fish and Wildlife Protection is to see that animals and plants designated as endangered species are adequately protected.

Training

Police training is the responsibility of administrators of the Trust Territory of the Pacific agency and the Palau government. Basic training is provided on the Palau Community College campus, while specialized courses are offered to Palau police off-island.

Complaints and Discipline

In 1999, the state department report on human rights in Palau noted that there were "creditable complaints" that the police pursued and prosecuted crimes that had been committed against Palau nationals more vigorously than those against the foreign residents who constitute 30% of the population and 46% of the country's workforce.

Corruption is far from rampant in Palau, but law enforcement has to deal with complaints of nepotism, cronyism, and favoritism, all exacerbated by the relatively inbred characteristics of so small a country. Matters of corruption are handled by the special prosecutor (SP), who acts as an ombudsman for citizen complaints, although the ethos in Palau, which favors indirectness in human relations, often serves to inhibit formal protest against wrongdoing.

The special prosecutor's office seems understaffed with only the prosecutor, two investigators, and two secretaries. The present SP mentioned that he had been the object of harassment, his dog had been poisoned, his car tires had been slashed, and obscene words had been painted on his car. The prosecutor's efforts currently are aided by an especially effective watchdog radio personality who tends to focus on corruption. Over the years, three of the announcer's cars have been firebombed; in each instance, a different wealthy citizen replaced the vehicle, indicating the tension between forces that try to thwart what are regarded by some as legitimate, time-sanctioned practices, and seen by others as unacceptable corruption.

When the SP filed charges in 2002 and 2003 against virtually all members of the National Congress for falsifying travel reimbursement requests, the Congress attempted to declaw the office by legislative mandate, but ultimately failed, and ended up paying fines that came to a total of a quarter of a million dollars to settle the allegations of impropriety.

In the five years before 2005, a Transparency International report indicates that at least fifteen police officers have been terminated, thirty to forty suspended; and two are now in jail for law infractions. Complaints against law enforcement personnel are handled by the Police Practices Committee, which is made up of three persons from the police force, the attorney general, and three civilians. Serious cases of police misconduct also may be brought directly to the attorney general or the special prosecutor.

GILBERT GEIS AND BRYAN VILA

Bibliography

Leibowitz, Arnold H. *Embattled Island: Palau's Struggle for Independence.* Westport, CT: Praeger, 1996.

Rechelei, Elizabeth Diaz, and McPhetres, Samuel. *History of Palau: Heritage of an Emerging Nation.* Koror: Ministry of Education, 1997.

Shuster, Donald R. *National Integrity Systems. Transparency International Country Study Report: Republic of Palau 2004.* Canberra, Australia: Transparency International Australia and Asia Pacific School of Economics, Australian National University, 2004.

PANAMA

Background Material

The Republic of Panama is located in Central America, bordering both the Caribbean Sea and the North Pacific Ocean, between Colombia and Costa Rica. It has a strategic location on the eastern end of an isthmus forming a land bridge connecting North and South America. Panama controls the Panama Canal, which links the North Atlantic Ocean via the Caribbean Sea with the North Pacific Ocean.

The population of Panama is 3,000,463 (July 2004 estimate). The following ethnic groups are represented in the population: mestizo (mixed Amerindian and white) 70%, Amerindian and mixed (West Indian) 14%, white 10%, and Amerindian 6%. The population is Roman Catholic (85%) and Protestant (15%). Spanish is the official language, although 14% of the population speaks English.

Panama's economy is based primarily on a well-developed services sector that accounts for three-fourths of GDP. Services include the Panama Canal, banking, the Colon Free Zone, insurance, container ports, flagship registry, and tourism. A slump in Colon Free Zone and agricultural exports, the global slowdown, and the withdrawal of U.S. military forces held back economic growth in 2000–2001. The government plans public works programs, tax reforms, and new regional trade agreements to stimulate growth. GDP per capita purchasing power parity is US$6,300 (2003 estimate).

Contextual Features

Panama is a constitutional republic. The nation achieved independence from Spain on 28 November 1821, and from Colombia on 3 November. The constitution was promulgated on 11 October 1972, and major reforms were adopted in April 1983.

The president is both the chief of state and head of government. Members of the Cabinet are appointed by the president. The legislative branch of government is a unicameral Legislative Assembly or Asamblea Legislativa (seventy-one seats; members are elected by popular vote to serve five-year terms). Legislators from outlying rural districts are chosen on a plurality basis, while districts located in more populous towns and cities elect multiple legislators by means of a proportion-based formula. The judicial branch is the Supreme Court of Justice (Corte Suprema de Justicia), composed of nine judges appointed for ten-year terms. There are also five superior courts and three courts of appeal.

The legal system is based on the civil law system, with judicial review of legislative acts in the Supreme Court of Justice. It accepts compulsory International Court of Justice jurisdiction, with reservations.

The Criminal Code and the Administrative Code define crimes against public order, public security, public trust, decency, the person, and property, as felonies (*delitos*) or misdemeanors (*faltas*), depending on the seriousness of the crime.

Capital and corporal punishment are prohibited. The most severe penalty permitted for a single offense is twenty-year imprisonment, and prison sentences are differentiated as to place of confinement. All prisoners can be required to perform prison labor whether or not it was included in a sentence.

A conditional penalty (*condena condicional*) is a suspended sentence used at the discretion of a court in the sentencing of a first offender, except on a major felony charge. The sentence requires residing at a fixed address and reporting any change, frequent visits to the court, and checks by the police on the offender's conduct.

Provisions for appeal exist in the system, and many categories of cases required automatic review in a higher court. Time limits are set on the preparation of appeals, and court action on them as well as on the time taken for automatic review. Few cases can be appealed to the Supreme Court; an appeal usually requires that an error be shown in handling by a lower court. Prosecutors also have the right of appeal.

The cases of minors are handled in a special system designed to combat juvenile delinquency and to keep young offenders from contact with lifelong criminals. The Guardianship Court for Minors (Tribunal Tutelar de Menores), established in 1951, works closely with various social agencies to handle the cases of young offenders and to provide them with guidance and assistance if possible. Cases involving persons under age eighteen are not made public.

Article 27 of the Constitution declares that the prison system is based on the principles of security, rehabilitation, and the protection of society. Provisions have been made to establish training programs designed to teach skills and trades that will afford prisoners the opportunity of reentering society as useful citizens after they complete their sentence. The same article also prohibits physical, mental, and moral abuse of prisoners. Juvenile offenders who were sentenced by a court were cared for in a special system that provided protection and education and attempted to rehabilitate minors before they came of age. Women are also segregated in the penal system.

The Department of Corrections was established in 1940 to administer the country's penal system for the Ministry of Government and Justice. Operation of the prisons had previously been a direct function of the National Police. The intention of the government officials who established the Department of Corrections was to end inherent abuses in the system, but the new department was never properly staffed, and police had to be used as jailers.

In comparison to the conditions under which male prisoners served sentences and awaited trial, women receive much better care. The Women's Rehabilitation Center (Centro Feminino de Rehabilitación) in Panama City appears to be an ideal prison. The center is under the supervision of the Department of Corrections, as are all prisons in Panama, but it is operated by nuns who have established a reputation for discipline tempered by humaneness and decency.

Police Profile

Background

The rivalry between civilian elites and the Panamanian military, a recurring theme in Panamanian political life since the 1950s, developed into a grave crisis in the 1980s. Prompted by government restrictions on media and civil liberties, in summer 1987 more than 100 business, civic, and religious groups formed a loose coalition that organized widespread antigovernment demonstrations.

Panama's developing domestic crisis was paralleled by rising tensions between the Panamanian government and the United States. When national elections were held in May 1989, Panamanians voted for the anti-Noriega candidates by a margin of over three to one. Although the size of the opposition victory and the presence of international observers thwarted regime efforts to control the outcome of the vote, the Noriega regime promptly annulled the election and embarked on a new round of repression.

By fall 1989, the regime was barely clinging to power. An unsuccessful Panamanian Defense Forces (PDF) coup attempt in October produced bloody reprisals. Deserted by all but a small number of cronies, and distrustful of a shaken and demoralized PDF, Noriega began increasingly to rely on irregular paramilitary units called Dignity Battalions. In December 1989, the regime's paranoia made daily existence unsafe for U.S. forces and other U.S. citizens.

On December 20, President Bush ordered the U.S. military into Panama to assist the Panamanian people in restoring democracy, and to bring Noriega to justice. The U.S. troops involved in Operation Just Cause achieved their primary objectives quickly, and troop withdrawal began on December

27. Noriega eventually surrendered to U.S. authorities voluntarily. He is now serving a forty-year sentence in Florida for drug trafficking.

Panamanians moved quickly to rebuild their civilian constitutional government. On December 27, 1989, Panama's Electoral Tribunal invalidated the Noriega regime's annulment of the May 1989 election and confirmed the victory of opposition candidates under the leadership of President Guillermo Endara, and Vice Presidents Guillermo Ford and Ricardo Arias Calderon.

On 10 February 1990, the government of then-President Endara abolished Panama's military and reformed the security apparatus by creating the Panamanian Public Forces; in October 1994, Panama's Legislative Assembly approved a constitutional amendment prohibiting the creation of a standing military force, but allowing the temporary establishment of special police units to counter acts of "external aggression."

Organizational Description

The Republic of Panama is divided in nine provinces and several Indian reservations called *comarcas*. Each province is a police zone, except for Panama Province, which is divided into seven police zones, and Veraguas Province, which is divided into two zones. Each police zone is divided in small "police areas." Altogether Panama has seventeen police zones.

Special support units of the Panamanian National Police include:

- Prison security service
- Riot police unit
- Support to the regular service unit
- Special force unit
- Childhood and adolescence police
- Information and investigation police
- Traffic police
- Tourism police

The Panamanian National Police have the following ranks and hierarchies:

Board of Directors: General director (a civilian appointed by the president), deputy director (a police officer in the rank of commissioner)
Senior officer: Commissioner and deputy commissioner
Junior officer: Major, captain, lieutenant, and sublieutenant
Patrolmen: 1st sergeant, 2nd sergeant, 1st corporal, 2nd corporal, and agent (beginner patrolman).

Promotion to the next rank is granted by the president, prior recommendation from the National Police general director and the Ministry of Government and Justice (Ministry of the Interior), and after passing an examination.

Functions

The Panamanian National Police works within the legal framework of the constitution and the law. The main mission of the National Police is to protect life, dignity, possessions, and others rights and liberties; uphold internal public order, and keep the peace and security of all the inhabitants, as well as guarantee the observance of the constitution and the law.

Training

The mission of the Panamanian Police Academy (PPA) is to provide timely, contemporary law enforcement training, education, and development from basic to advanced levels. Today, the law enforcement professional is challenged to acquire a wide variety of skills necessary in a fast-changing society. The PPA provides the means to obtain the necessary skills.

Offering both full-time and in-service training programs, the Institute trains dedicated people who want to enter the field of law enforcement, and offers advanced training to those already experienced in law enforcement. The Police Academy trains students for a career in police. The police science program combines contemporary knowledge, state-of-the-art technology, and field learning.

In addition to its full-time programs, the Institute offers courses in specialized areas for law enforcement professionals working in the field. These courses are delivered at advanced levels both at the PPA and in the field for any agency involved with professional enforcement.

Complaints and Discipline

The protection of human rights is of critical importance for the police service and reinforces values already at its core.

The government generally respects the human rights of citizens; however, there continue to be serious problems in several areas. Police and prison guards on occasion use excessive force against detainees and prisoners, and on occasion police use force against protesters. Credible reports of human rights violations have contributed to some police dismissals.

The Panamanian National Police, in cooperation with the Inter-American Institute for Human Rights, UNESCO, and Danish International Development Agency, has developed a comprehensive national plan of action for human rights education in police academies, which includes a survey on the state of human rights education in schools, a revision of textbooks, training of teachers, workshops, establishment both of a network of human rights trainers, and of a National Commission to Promote Human Rights Education and Learning.

Terrorism

Panama has not suffered terrorist incidents linked to extremist Islamic groups or any other organizations. However, the National Police has special units that are able to face such incidents, including the special bombing unit, the anti-kidnapping unit, and the special force unit (SWAT).

The National Security Council, the Information and Investigation Police (Panamanian National Police), and the Judicial Technical Police are charged with preventing and investigating terrorism activities. They also make suggestions to the executive branch related to terrorism policy.

VICTOR MANUEL GARCIA

Websites

Interior Ministry (Spanish): *www.gobiernoyjusticia.gob.pa*
National Police official website (Spanish): *www.policia.gob.pa*
Panamanian government official website: *www.pa*

Bibliography

Police law (Spanish): Ley #18, 3 June 1997.

PAPUA NEW GUINEA

Background Material

Papua New Guinea (PNG) was settled approximately 30,000 years ago. The first official sighting by Europeans was by the Portuguese in 1512. It was named New Guinea by the Dutch.

In an attempt to protect their East Indies empire, the Dutch in 1929 formalised their claim to sovereignty over the western part of the Island (Irian Jaya). In 1884, Germany took possession of the northern part (New Guinea). The British exercised a protectorate over the southern section (Papua) and annexed it in 1888.

British New Guinea became the territory of Papua in 1906, and was transferred to Australia. In World War I, Australia took control of German New Guinea, and in 1920 it became a League of Nations mandated trust under the trusteeship of Australia. In 1942, Japan occupied part of New Guinea, but by 1944, American and Australian forces had defeated the Japanese.

In 1951, the first Legislative Council embracing the combined territories was formed. Indonesia took control of Dutch New Guinea in 1963, and it was incorporated into the Indonesian state as the province of Irian Jaya.

In 1964, a House of Assembly consisting of sixty-four members came into being. In 1968, the House was enlarged to ninety-four, and was further enlarged to 100 in 1972. Self-governance was declared in 1973, and in 1975 Papua New Guinea (PNG) became independent and adopted a parliamentary system of government.

Since then, PNG has been ruled by a series of unstable coalitions that have been formed by patronage rather than political ideology. Governments have been constantly threatened and brought down by motions of no confidence. PNG has also struggled with problems of law and order and ethnic tension, most notably the long conflict over the island of Bougainville. It has also experienced declining economic prosperity.

The head of state is the British Queen, who is represented by the governor-general. The prime minister is the head of government. There is a unicameral parliament of 109 members, who are elected for (up to) a five-year term. There are nineteen provinces in PNG, and each has its own provincial government.

Law and order is a major challenge for PNG, particularly in urban areas. In an effort to deal with the problem, the death penalty was introduced in 1999 for major crimes, including murder and rape.

Environmental problems, including tsunamis and floods, cause many deaths and have a severe effect on the economy.

In 2004, the population was 5,420,280. Thirty-nine percent were under fifteen, and 58% were aged between fifteen and sixty-four. Four percent of the population was over sixty-five. The life expectancy for male and females is fifty-eight.

There are over 800 indigenous languages spoken with English, Pidgin, and Motu being the three official languages, and English being used as the official language in schools, government, and business.

Sixty-four percent of the population are Protestants (Lutheran, Presbyterian, Methodist, London Missionary Society, Anglican, Evangelical Alliance, Seventh-Day Adventist) and 33% are Roman Catholics. Indigenous beliefs are also widespread, with traditional rituals being an integral part of Papua New Guinea's culture.

Annual GDP per capita is US$2,500. PNG has a wide range of natural resources, including forestry and mineral products, but development of the economy has been hampered by remoteness and the country's rugged terrain. PNG is a resource-rich nation, and mineral deposits including oil, copper, and gold account for 72% of export earnings. Contrary to most developing South Pacific countries, economic activity in PNG has been characterised by boom years followed by equally disastrous years.

Contextual Features

The PNG Constitution is the supreme law, and the Parliament has enacted a considerable body of law. Common law, as developed by the PNG courts, also has effect.

The legal system, which in large part reflects that of Australia, is based on the English system. However, customary law based on traditional village law is applied in certain areas.

There are several levels of courts. Most minor civil, criminal, and customary legal matters are dealt with by local and village courts. Magistrates preside over District Courts and have jurisdiction over less serious criminal cases that involve relatively short prison sentences.

The National Court is the court of first instance for all criminal and civil cases that are beyond the jurisdiction of the lower courts. It also acts as a court of appeal in relation to decisions of the lower courts.

The Supreme Court is the highest court in the land and is the final court of appeal. It can review all decisions of the National Court and also has original jurisdiction with respect to constitutional matters. Papua New Guinea does not have a jury system.

Approximately half of the serious and petty crimes that are reported in PNG are committed in the capital, Port Moresby. Police arrest statistics show that about 90% of offenders come from squatter areas on the outskirts of the capital. In 2000, there were 13,292 recorded crimes. The most common were robberies (3,394) and burglaries (2,618), with the total recorded major assaults numbering 1,351. Total recorded rapes were 1,295. Violence against women, including domestic violence and rape, is a serious problem.

Findings from the UN Interregional Crime and Justice Research Institute survey confirmed that cities in Papua New Guinea stand out among other developing world countries for their high levels of violence (assaults/threats).

There are nineteen prisons in PNG, but only seventeen are operational. They house some 3,300 prisoners, of which 90% are males. Male and female prisoners are housed separately, but there are no separate facilities for juvenile offenders. Some prisons provide separate sleeping quarters for juveniles.

Police Profile

Background

Papua New Guinea has a national police force, the Royal Papua New Guinea Constabulary, which is headed by a commissioner of police. Functions of the Department of Police include assisting in the development of police policy and its implementation (including the use of force), providing investigatory, research, executive, administrative, and financial management and providing services to other organisations as they relate to police functions.

In 2002, a new commissioner was appointed. In an effort to address entrenched corruption and inefficiency problems, he replaced many of the senior levels of the force. However, corruption remains a problem. Effectiveness is also impeded by a lack of resources and clan rivalries. Clan loyalty is also a problem, as police are reluctant to undertake disciplinary action against members of their own clan.

Australia has assisted the Royal Papua New Guinea Constabulary since PNG gained independence in 1975. This has been done through consultancies, training courses, attachments, and the Australian Aid Project. The Project has focused on institutional strengthening, specialist advisory assistance, and funding. To assist with the organised crime threat, the Australian Federal Police stationed two officers in Port Moresby. This followed an agreement between Australia and PNG in 2001. In December

2003, the two countries agreed on a new Enhanced Cooperation Program which, among other things, includes sending up to 230 Australian police personnel to PNG.

Demographics
In 2000, the Police Department consisted of 5,462 members (5,175 men and 287 women).

Organisational Description
The establishing legislation provides for the following ranks and establishment strength, for a total force size of 5,864:

Commissioner, 1
Deputy commissioner, 1
Assistant commissioner, 4
Senior superintendent, 10
Superintendent, 20
Inspector (first class), 30
Chaplain, 3
Inspector (second class), 82
Inspector (third class), 69
Subinspector, 115
Cadet officer, 175
Sergeant (first class), 39
Sergeant (second class), 83
Sergeant (third class), 202
Senior constable, 575
Constable (first class), 3,956
Constable, 499
Probationary constable, 500

According to the Act, the force is to consist of a Regular Constabulary Branch, a Field Constabulary Branch, and a Reserve Constabulary Branch. The commissioner is appointed by the head of state.

Training
After a state of emergency was declared in the National Capital District in 1985, the Australian government pledged more assistance. A study was commissioned to assess the developmental needs of the Constabulary (Miller Report). Phase one of that report began in 1989, and phase two in 1993. An objective of the phase one report was to improve the quality and effectiveness of police training.

Police Public Projects
In an effort to enhance cooperation between the police and the community, since 1998 the Peace Foundation Melanesia has provided training programs and supported community-based projects.

Police Use of Firearms
The Royal Papua New Guinea Constabulary is an armed police force.

Complaints and Discipline
The commissioner or a commissioned officer deals with minor breaches of discipline. Minor breaches incur a caution, reprimand, small fine (two kina), or two weeks' confinement to barracks. The more serious penalties listed need to be confirmed by the commissioner.

The commissioner, after providing a written summary of the accusation, may decide on penalties for more serious offences. The penalties include a fine of forty kina, pay cuts, demotion, transfer, and dismissal. Appeals in relation to the commissioner's penalty are to the Police Appeals Tribunal, which consists of a judge or magistrate. The Tribunal effectively acts as a court and has power to administer oaths, call witnesses and subpoena documents.

Terrorism and International Cooperation
In 1970, the South Pacific Chiefs of Police Conference was founded. The forum facilitates cooperation and information sharing to help prevent crime. It also facilitates formal liaison among police in the South Pacific. In 2003, the conference theme was "Terrorism—the Wider Law Enforcement Context." At the conference, a four-year strategic plan was finalised that will assist in establishing key law enforcement priorities for the region.

Police Education, Research, and Publications
Institutions

Bomana Police Academy, Papua New Guinea
University of Papua New Guinea (*www.upng.ac.pg*)

Researchers and Publications

Abru, Elly. "Policing the Wild West." *New South Wales Police News* 82, no. 4 (April 2002): 34–36. Abstract: Papua New Guinea's undermanned and underfunded constabulary is struggling to hold back a tide of lawlessness. Travel and communications are difficult; violent crime and drug abuse are spreading; and tribal fights are conducted with sophisticated weaponry.

Banks, Cyndi. "'We Have to Prove We Are Not Just Women': Policewomen in Papua New

Guinea." *International Journal of Comparative Criminology* 1, no. 1 (2001): 40–76.

Dangoume, Joan. "Royal Papua New Guinea Constabulary Women Police, 1977–96." *International Journal of Police Science & Management* 1, no. 3 (1998): 308–312.

Dinnen, Sinclair. "Community Policing in Papua New Guinea." *Criminology Australia* 4, no. 3 (January/February 1993): 2–5.

Dinnen, Sinclair. *Criminal Justice Reform in Papua New Guinea*. Canberra: Australian National University, National Centre for Development Studies, 1998.

Dinnen, Sinclair. "Breaking the Cycle of Violence: Crime and State in Papua New Guinea." In *Developing Cultural Criminology: Theory and Practice in Papua New Guinea*, edited by Cyndi Banks, 51–78. Sydney: Sydney Institute of Criminology, 2000.

Dinnen, Sinclair. *Law and Order in a Weak State: Crime and Politics in Papua New Guinea*. Adelaide: Crawford House Publishing, 2001.

Gammage, Bill. "Police and Power in the Pre-War Papua New Guinea Highlands." *Journal of Pacific History* 31 (1996): 162–177.

Ibrum K. Kituai, August. *My Gun, My Brother: The World of the Papua New Guinea Colonial Police, 1920–1960*. Pacific Islands Monograph Series, No. 15. Honolulu: Center for Pacific Islands Studies, University of Hawaii, May 1998.

Newton, T. *An Introduction to Policing in the South Pacific Region*. Suva, Fiji: University of the South Pacific School of Law, 1998.

Richardson, B.L., Wuillemin D.B., and Moore, D.W. "Ranking of Crime Seriousness by the People, the Law, and the Police in Papua New Guinea." *Melanesian Law Journal* 15 (1987): 49–65.

Leading Journal

Journal of South Pacific Law (*http://easol. vanuatu.usp.ac.fj/jspl/current*)

Police-Related Website

PNG Police: *www.police.gov.pg/index.htm*

COLLEEN LEWIS

Bibliography

O'Collins, Maev. *Law and Order in Papua New Guinea: Perceptions and Management Strategies, State, Society and Governance in Melanesia Project*. 2000. Working Paper 00/1. Australian National University. Available at: http://rspas.anu.edu/au/melanesia/naev2.htm.

Sikani, Richard. "The Criminal Threat in Papua New Guinea." In *Australia and Papua New Guinea: Crime and the Bilateral Relationship*, edited by Dino Docha and John McFarlane, 35–56. Canberra: Australian Defence Studies Centre, June 2000.

United Nations Office on Drugs and Crime. *The Seventh United Nations Survey on Crime Trends and the Operations of Criminal Justice Systems (1998–2000)*. Available at: www.unodc.org/unodc/crime_cicp_survey_seventh. html.

Wan, Jan. "Overview of AusAID Assistance to the Royal Papua New Guinea Constabulary, 1988–1998." *Australia/Papua New Guinea: Crime and the Bilateral Relationship*, 2000.

Zvekic, U., and A. Alvazzi del Fratem. *Criminal Victimisation in the Developing World*. United Nations Interregional Crime and Justice Research Institute publication No. 55, 1995. Available at: www.unicri.it/icvs/publications/index_pub.htm.

PARAGUAY

Background Material

Paraguay, located in central South America, is divided into the eastern region composed of hills and fertile valleys (Amambay, Mbaracayú, and Caaguazú mountain range), and the western region (Chaco Boreal Plain), bordered in the south by the Pilcomayo River surrounded by sandy hills of no more than 100 meters in altitude. To the north, the country shares borders with Bolivia and Brazil, to the east with Brazil and Argentina, to the south with Argentina, and to the west with Argentina and Bolivia. Administratively, the country is divided into seventeen departments. It has a surface area of 406,752 sq km, and a population of 6,191,368 (July 2004 estimate). Most of the population is located in the eastern region.

There are two official languages: Spanish and Guaraní. Paraguay's main economic activities are agriculture, livestock raising, and hydroelectric power generation.

Contextual Features

Paraguay is a unitary republic with a democratic representative government. The government is composed of the executive, legislative, and judicial branches. The executive branch consists of the president, who is selected via popular ballot for a five-year term. He is in charge of enforcing the laws of the country.

The legislative branch is composed of the bicameral National Congress: the Senate, with forty-five regular members and thirty replacements, and the House of Representatives, with eighty regular members and the same number of replacements. The judicial branch is composed of the Supreme Court of Justice, the Counsel of the Magistracy, the Public Ministry, and the High Court for Electoral Justice. The Supreme Court of Justice is composed of nine members and is organized in chambers: constitutional, civil, and penal. Its members are named as ministers and they can handle any cases while working in their posts.

Police Profile

Background

On September 20, 1840, the dictator José Gaspar Rodrigues de Francia died, marking the beginning of a new era in the country. Soon afterward the second consulate was formed by Carlos Antonio López and Mariano Roque Alonzo, both assigned as consuls. This second consulate on March 8, 1841, created the police.

The new national constitution that was elaborated by the same National Constituent Assembly was in force since June 20, 1992. New bodies were created and among them, the National Police Article 172, clearly cites that the public forces are composed mainly and exclusively by the military and police forces. Article 175 establishes that the National Police is a professional institution organized as a permanent body dependent on the executive power, and responsible for the internal security of the nation. Within the context of the constitution and the law, the police have the following missions: maintaining public order and the rights and security of people and entities and their personal properties; preventing crimes/infringement of laws; executing the mandate of the competent authority and under the judicial leadership in investigating offenses. Finally, it is established that the law will rule its organization and attributes.

The cited constitutional article states that the National Police will be headed by a senior police office, and that the police will not participate as an affiliate in a political party or movement or carry out any political activity.

In virtue of the 1992 Constitution, Decree 15/108, General Commissioner Germán Gabriel Franco Bargas was appointed as chief of the police of the capital. The National Police force was implemented during the Juan Carlos Wasmosy administration; Mario Agustin Sapriza Nunes was appointed general commissioner via Decree 1734 on December 29, 1993.

Organizational Description

The National Police are organized under law 222/93, Article 149 into Commando, General Office, and Offices units. The Commando unit is responsible for direction, planning, and coordination through the commandant and the subcommandant. The National Police commandant is appointed by the executive office, and is known as the general commissioner commandant.

The General Office for Order and Security is responsible for enforcement, composed of six police zone offices and technical support. Each zone consists of several police offices at the department (province) level. They are in charge of planning, organizing, and executing police activities for maintaining public order, the preservation of security of the people and their goods, and the prevention and investigation of offenses.

The Office for Technical Support is in charge of planning, organizing, and executing technical and scientific support in the following offices: Investigation of Offenses, Interpol, Judicial, Communications, Migrations, Narcotics, and Family Affairs.

The Tactical Support Office is in charge of supporting police operations for the various police branch offices. They are composed of the following groups: Specialized, Security, Motorized, Firefighters, Riders, Environmental and Rural Protections, Waterways, and Air.

Functions

The functions of the National Police are as follows:

- Protect the life, integrity, safety, and freedom of persons and properties.
- Anticipate the combat of crimes by means of the technical organization, information, and alertness.

- Investigate, under judicial direction, crimes committed anywhere in the national territory, whether on land, sea, or air.
- Collect, distribute, and archive evidence of crimes.
- Request of judges the corresponding authorization to level domiciles in cases of crime, inquiries, or suspect detention. This authorization will not be necessary to enter to establishments open to the public in circumstances foreseen under the law.
- Request presentation of police accreditation as necessary.
- Arrest and detain persons in conformity with the law (regarding time period and form).
- Detain persons caught during the commission of crimes in the form and in the time established by law; suspects must be informed of the reason for their arrest and their rights, putting them at the disposal of competent Judge.
- Support and organize throughout the country the service of personal identification, files and records of precedents, and of the domicile of persons.
- Distribute bonds of identity, passports, certificate of precedents, of life, of domicile, of residence, and other documents as necessary.
- Exercise alertness and control of persons in border areas.
- Organize foreigners' records and to control their entry and exit of these in conformity with the law.
- Pursue the search for missing persons, as well as of property lost or stolen, and to return the latter to legitimate owners.
- Guard over good customs and public morality, and suppress illegal games and activities prohibited in agreements under the law.
- Regulate weapons possession by civilians, and organize respective records in conformity with the law.
- Guarantee order during meetings in public places and protecting the rights of third parties.
- Communicate to judicial authorities the deaths of individuals without known relatives, and adoption of first measures to protect such persons' goods.
- Cooperate and coordinate with the responsible organism in the control and prevention of the production, marketing, sale, consumption, use, and possession of drugs and narcotics under international agreements and domestic law.
- Fight fires and other disasters that endanger the life, safety, and property of persons.
- Prevent and deter activities related to trafficking of persons, especially in women and children, under existing law.
- Control activities of private detectives, vigilante and security companies, and related activities.
- Control, under judicial order, individuals' records in hotels, accommodations, and related establishments.
- Cooperate with responsible parties in the control of minors' assistance for rooms of games of random and public spectacles for major.
- Control in conformity with the law the expenditure and the consumption of alcoholic drinks.
- Regulate the use of uniform, arms, equipment, and materials of the institution.
- Form reserves for the national defense.
- Exchange information at national and international levels and to cooperate with similar institutions in crime prevention and investigation. Assist persons and institutions that legally need it. Cooperate in meeting requests by the courts or other national organisms regarding facts related to crimes.
- Fulfill laws, bylaws, and other dispositions related to functions assigned to the police by law.
- Coordinate with municipalities and other institutions traffic control on public roadways.
- Fulfillment of judicial mandates.

Training

The General Department of Police Teaching Institutes oversees planning, organizing, coordinating activities, and refinement in the technical and scientific fields as well as cultural aspects of police personnel. This department controls various police teaching institutes, including the country's largest, the Police Officers Training College. Several other institutes provide professional, development, and promotional courses.

For noncommissioned officers, there is also a Training School where candidates study for one year. There are also other institutes where the officers can study to improve their professional knowledge, and of course these courses are also geared toward promotion. Included here are the School of Command and Police Advice, School of Physical Education, School of Officials' Application, School of Training for Officials, Course of Officials of Reservation, School of Sub-Officials' Application, and School of Sub-Official Sgto. Ayte. Jose M. Sarabi.

For promotion or career development, police officers can also access specialization courses, such as courses in instruction, investigation, special police operations, mounted police, police intelligence, drugs and narcotics, and antiterrorism.

Human Rights

The National Police have taken part in diverse training sessions to ensure that the police display respect for human rights. The positive results of these efforts are already apparent. From 1997, the Police Officers College included human rights in the curriculum. "Human rights of the minor" is studied in the first, second, and third years of cadet training.

Terrorism

Police work with the Counterterrorism Department, which is charged with investigating and anticipating terrorism. According to sources and information available at the time of writing, Paraguay has not experienced any international terrorism.

JUAN CARLOS VALENZUELA SANCHEZ

Bibliography

Police Magazine, Policia Nacional del Paraguay, Asunción, Paraguay.
Policía Nacional Law Number 222, Police College "Gral. Jose E. Diaz", Luque, Paraguay, 1998.
The Book about Nacional Police History. Police College "Gral. Jose E. Diaz," Luque, Paraguay, 1992.

PERU

Background Material

The Republic of Peru is located in the central and western part of South America, and has a total land area of 1,285,216 sq km. In the sixteenth century, the conquest of Peru began with the arrival of the Spaniards. In 1821, after a series of armed conflicts between Spaniards and Peruvians (the latter had the support of external forces), the independence of Peru was proclaimed and the Peruvian state was born, with its capital established in Lima. In 1879, after having been defeated in the Pacific War, Peru was bankrupt. After many military governments, Peruvian democracy has been slowly developing in recent decades.

In 2004, the Republic of Peru had a population of 27,546,574 people, composed of 72.3% urban inhabitants and 27.7% rural inhabitants; the population was made up of 50.3% men and 49.7% women.

A multitude of native languages coexist in Peru. Although Spanish is the language of common use, Quechua is an important inheritance of the Incan past, and in many regions of the country it is still used, with slight regional variants. The language breakdown follows: Spanish, 80.3%; Quechua, 16.2%; other native languages, 3.0%; and foreign languages, 0.2%.

Peru has a great diversity of beliefs, and freedom of religion is manifested in a variety of festivities and rituals that have been influenced by Catholicism, which is part of the Spanish heritage. Statistically, the distribution of religious affiliation follows: Catholic, 89%; Evangelical, 7%; other, 6%.

The average annual per capita income is US$3,600. The main economic activities in Peru are agriculture, mining, fishing, construction, and trade. The majority of exports are raw materials or primary products (69.5%), followed by manufactures (29.6%), and services (0.9%). In 2004, total exports were expected to surpass US$11.5 billion.

Contextual Features

The Republic of Peru has a presidential, unitary, and decentralized government system. The most recent political constitution was promulgated on October 31, 1993.

The government of the state is divided into three branches: the executive has its head in the president of the Republic, who is elected to a five-year term, and has the power to appoint ministers; the legislature is comprised of the unicameral Congress, made of 120 members elected to serve five-year terms; the judiciary is made up of the Supreme Court, headquartered in Lima, Superior Courts whose jurisdiction is at the district level, and the Courts of the First Instance, which sit in provincial capitals.

The judiciary is in charge of administering justice according to the law, and has autonomy in its functional exercise of political, administrative, economic, and disciplinary issues, and is independent in its jurisdictional constraints under the constitution.

Within the Peruvian legal system, the duty executed by the Public Ministry is also of great importance. The Public Ministry represents and defends society by investigating crime, emitting opinions, and taking part in civil and family processes; and in actions for the prevention of crime and in legal medicine issues, it offers scientific information for the fiscal process.

The Public Ministry carries out the following main duties through the public prosecutors:

- To promote by act of authority or upon request, action for the rule of law
- To supervise the autonomy of jurisdictional organs and strict administration of justice
- To represent society in judicial processes
- To conduct crime investigation from the beginning
- To exercise penal actions by act of authority or upon request

The most common crimes follow:

- Against property 42.6%
- Against public administration 12.4%
- Against life, body, and health 11.3%
- Against collective safety 10.9%
- Against public faith 9.0%
- Against freedom 6.6%
- Other crimes 7.1%

In Peru, the generic crimes with highest incidence are crimes against property, in which swindles, theft, illicit appropriation, and robbery are the most common. In second place are crimes against public administration, particularly embezzlement and abuse of authority. In third place are crimes against life, body, and health, being the most common injuries, and homicides. In fourth place are crimes against collective security like crimes of public danger and against public health. Finally, the last group is crimes against freedom, including violation of sexual freedom, violation of individual freedom (kidnapping), and forced entry.

For 2003, the Crimes Commission found significant variations in other types of crimes, such as crimes against economic order and public tranquility, which increased 77.9% and 57.9%, respectively. Crimes against property increased 6.2%, and crimes against public security increased 22.2%, whereas crimes against the public faith decreased 5.5%.

The acts and responsibilities of individuals are governed by laws whose observance must be enforced by the judicial branch. Justice must serve the nation, and this statement is the reason for a judicial system to exist as an organization that allows citizens to have access to justice at different levels and instances depending on the gravity of the violation or crime.

The judicial instances are distributed as follows:

- Minor Courts ruled by non-lawyers: Investigation and sentencing in cases of minor infringements, according to a court's competence
- Minor Courts ruled by lawyers: Resolve appeals submitted against the sentences pronounced by Minor Courts ruled by non-lawyers, and investigate and sentence in cases of infringement, according to its competence
- Specialized or Mixed Courts: Investigate or proceed in submitted cases (ordinary processes), investigate and sentence in summary and special processes, resolve appeals submitted against sentences pronounced by Minor Courts
- Superior Courts: Conduct judgments or oral judgments within ordinary processes and resolve the appeals submitted against sentences pronounced by Specialized or Mixed Courts
- Supreme Court: The last instance to which every judicial process submitted by any Superior Court of Justice can be appealed

The National Institute of Prisons (INPE) is a decentralized public organization of the justice sector, which is head of the National Penitentiary System. INPE's mission is to manage and control technically and administratively the National Penitentiary System, assuring an accurate penitentiary policy directed to the reeducation, rehabilitation, and reintegration of the prisoner back into society; and the establishment and maintenance of the penitentiary infrastructure, as well as of the security framework needed for the processes and programs that it implements. For the accomplishment of these functions, INPE runs eighty-six penal establishments with support by the Peruvian National Police. Peru's prison population is estimated at 32,572.

Penitentiary rehabilitation is focused basically on the following subjects:

- Education and work
- Health
- Social assistance
- Legal assistance
- Psychological assistance
- Free environment and limited punishment

The general functions of the National Institute of Prisons are stated in the Code of Penal Execution and its Regulation:

- To propose and grant penitentiary benefits specified in Article 42 of the Code of Penal Execution
- To carry out the actions related to penitentiary treatment
- To develop the proceedings for postpenitentiary assistance in coordination with regional and municipal governments
- To keep records of the background of the accused, and of limits on freedom and rights penalties of the sentenced.

Police Profile

Background

During the 1825–1839 period, the first police forces were created in the form of night watchmen and other watchmen under control of the Armed Forces. In 1872, Manuel Pardo y Lavalle reorganized the police forces by subdividing them into three main fields: Neighborhood Organization, Special Police Services, and Regular Police Force, which was divided into the Civil Guard and Gendarmerie (on horseback with rural policing duties).

From then on, Peruvians witnessed the establishment of three police forces with specific missions and functions: the Civil Guard, Investigative Police, and Republican Guard. An important change took place in 1985 when the government began reorganizing the police forces based on Law 371, the same law that established a unique commando unit and a single training center for the instruction of police officers and a training school for guards.

The new political constitution of Peru was promulgated in 1988. This constitution recognized for the first time in the history of Peru, the purpose of the Peruvian police, which was clearly specified to be the maintenance of internal order. After strengthening the police integration policy, a constitutional amendment based on Law 24949 resulted in the creation of the National Police of Peru (PNP). This new police unit assumed the organization and functions of the former institutions (Civil Guard, Republican Guard, and Investigative Police), with all their rights and obligations. Thus began a new era in the history of the Peruvian police.

The 1980s and 1990s were difficult for the police, who faced serious problems of drug trafficking, terrorism, and delinquency. The contributions of the police toward defeating the terrorist organizations Tupac Amaru Revolutionary Movement (MRTA) and Sendero Luminoso (Shining Path), and of international organizations of drug traffickers, are historical achievements that deserved the recognition of the national and international community.

Demographics

Peruvian police personnel total 92,433, distributed in eleven police regions. Of the total, 91,116 are uniformed, and 1,267 are civil personnel, meaning that they have not received a military education. Of the uniformed personnel, 86.7% are men and 13.3% are women. There is one police officer for every 298 inhabitants.

Organizational Description

The general direction of the police (PNP) is under the control of the Interior Ministry and its organization as follows:

Managing Directorate
General Directorate of the PNP (DIRGEN)
Control Directorate
Inspector General (IG)
Consultancy Directorate
Staff Chief (EMG)
Support Directorates
Managing Executive Directorate (DIREJADMI)
Logistics Division (DIRLOG)
Economic and Finance Division (DIRECFIN)
Telematic Division (DIRTEL)
Human Development Directorate (DIREJDESHUM)
Human Resources Division (DIRREHUM)
Training Division (DIREDU)
Welfare Division (DIRBIE)
General Secretariat (S. GRAL.)
Intelligence Division (DIRINT)
Police Air Force Division (DIRAVPOL)
Information Division (DIRINFO)
Criminology Division (DIRCRI)
Family and Community Participation Division (DIRFAPACI)
National Central Interpol Division (Interpol)
Health Division (DIRSAL)
Executive Directorates
Special Operations Directorate (DIREJOPE)
Specialized Divisions (DD.EE)
Counter-Terrorism Division (DIRCOTE)
Counter-Corruption Division (DIRCOCORR)
Criminal Investigation and Support to Justice Division (DIRINCRI)
Police Prosecutors Division (DIRPOFIS)
Tourism and Environmental Police Division (DIRPOLTURE)
Public Security Division (DIRSEPUB)
State Security Division (DIRSEST)
Prisons Security Division (DIRSEPEN)
Regional Divisions (DIRTEPOL) (DD.TT)
Regional Division Piura
Regional Division Chiclayo

Regional Division Trujillo
Regional Division Moyobamba
Regional Division Iquitos
Regional Division Pucallpa
Regional Division Lima
Regional Division Huancayo
Regional Division Ayacucho
Regional Division Cuzco
Regional Division Arequipa

The principal divisions of the PNP follow:

DIRANDRO, Anti-Drugs Division: In charge of the fight against illegal drug trafficking.

DIRCRI, Criminology Division: Chief department of the PNP's Scientific System, whose mission is to provide technical scientific support to the command and competent authorities through experts and police identification reports that may allow them to fight against crime and impede impunity when trying to clarify the truth about crimes committed and determine the presumed author's identity.

DIRAVPOL, Police Air Force Division: Responsible for controlling all aeronautic equipment of the PNP.

DIRCOCOR, Counter-Corruption Division: In charge of investigating and denouncing corruption crimes.

DIRINCRI, Criminal Investigation and Support to Justice Division: Responsible for investigating, identifying, capturing, and denouncing people involved in crimes committed against life, body, and health.

DIRCOTE, Counter-Terrorism Division: Best indicator of the optimal job that the PNP has executed against terrorism.

DIRPOFIS, Police Prosecutors Division: Responsible for preventing, investigating, denouncing, and fighting within national jurisdiction, the crimes committed against customs, intellectual rights, cultural patrimony, finance and monetary order, public administration, and economic order.

Functions

The following are functions of the PNP:

- To maintain public security and harmony in order to allow free exercise of individual fundamental rights decreed in the Peruvian Constitution
- To prevent, fight, investigate, and denounce crimes established in the Penal Code and in special regulations persecuted by authority act
- To guarantee public security
- To investigate the disappearance of naturalized citizens
- To guarantee and control free vehicular and pedestrian circulation on public roads and highways
- To participate in the security of penitentiary establishments, as well as in the transportation of prisoners, according to law
- To participate in the fulfillment of regulations referring to protection and conservation of natural resources and the environment, and the security of the archeological and cultural national patrimony
- To participate in national defense, civil defense, and economic and social development of the country
- To execute people's identification for police purposes

Training

The PNP has the following training facilities:

School for Officers of the National Police of Peru, where a five-year curriculum is required for obtaining the rank of second lieutenant

School for Sub-Officers of the National Police of Peru, where a three-year curriculum is required for obtaining the rank of third major sergeant of the PNP

The requirements for entering into PNP training schools follow:

- Peruvian citizenship
- Eighteen to twenty-five years old
- Minimal height: men 1.65 meters, women 1.60 meters
- Appropriate weight for height (according to table)
- Marital status: single without children
- Completion of five years of middle education
- Complied with pertinent military service and electoral law
- Faultless behavior and morality, no criminal record
- Absence of subjection to judicial processes in common or military law, and sentence of freedom limitation
- Absence of expulsion or suspension from school of middle or advanced education, or suspension due to disciplinary measures or psycho-physical deficiencies at any of the armed forces and police schools

- Physical and mental health compatible with police activities

The enrollment of people who already have a previous technical or advanced professional education is also possible. In this case, the students would enter one level above the minimum, according to the study level that they would have finished or are going to finish.

Complaints and Discipline

Respect for human rights is a guiding principle in PNP activities, in accordance with the Peruvian Constitution and the Universal Declaration of Human Rights (United Nations).

In this area, the police count on the Human Rights Directorate as regulator, with jurisdiction at the national level through the Human Rights Offices. The Human Rights Directorate is responsible for guiding and informing PNP's personnel, so as to prevent, as much as possible, complaints and objections related to the violation of human rights.

The regulations and proceedings dictated by the Directorate try to make Peruvian police officers conscious of the obligation of acting in every moment with deep respect toward the human person, guaranteeing life and physical integrity, and without discriminating based on race/ethnicity, gender, religion, point of view, language, or age.

The Record of Human Rights approved by the Institutional Command is a guide and instrument of great value for PNP personnel, who have a permanent commitment to protecting human rights. Nevertheless, in the event of violation by a police employee against the fundamental rights of a person or in the case of corruption acts, complaints and evidence can be turned over to the PNP investigation center. Communication with the PNP can be made by phone, e-mail, or written statement.

Terrorism

Peru has domestic terrorist organizations: Sendero Luminoso and the Tupac Amaru Revolutionary Movement, whose principal leaders have been in prison for more than ten years.

Sendero Luminoso was the result of a long dogmatic, sectarian, and violent purge that had its roots in communism. Sendero Luminoso tried to take control of the country through the use of arms, bringing the violence that started in rural areas to the city, with the purpose of placing its leader Abimael Guzman Reynoso in power. The national leadership of this movement seduced thousands of young people who tried to change the unjust reality in which they lived, thereby justifying a campaign of terror. It is said that this organization was absolutely vertical and instilled hate for life, punished minor discrepancies against dogma, and demanded complete submission. After the capture of Guzman and a significant number of the movement's leaders in the early 1990s, the influence and power of Sendero Luminoso has slowly disintegrated; today it exists primarily as small bands in rural areas.

The Tupac Amaru Revolutionary Movement, a subversive organization, was created as a result of groups of Marxist and nationalist inspiration, and it used arms to cause chaos and terror. This organization used to finance its terrorist activities with the kidnapping and extortion of wealthy well-known people in Peruvian society, and maintained links with drug trafficking organizations in the Peruvian central forest. The MRTA was founded in 1982, but most of its activities took place between 1985 and 1995. During this period, the MRTA was responsible for a total of 1,852 terrorist incidents, including sabotage, assassination, and military operations. Additionally, the organization caused 2,232 nonviolent acts of proselytism. As of 1996, more than 1,300 members were captured. In December of that year, the dramatic capture of the Japanese ambassador's residence took place, which ended after 126 days with the deaths of a hostage, two commandos, and fourteen MRTA members.

Both terrorist organizations had connections with the main drug trafficking organizations of the sierra and Peruvian rain forest, providing the drug traffickers with security and receiving financing from the traffickers. In addition, both Sendero Luminoso and MRTA had connections with the Revolutionary Armed Forces of Colombia (FARC), with the MRTA having a closer relationship.

International Cooperation

The PNP receives technical support from the international community, allowing its police personnel training in foreign countries, as well as training in Peru by foreign instructors. This training is focused in fields such as antinarcotics, antiterrorism, criminology, and investigation. The field most favored by this international support is the one dedicated to the fight against drugs, which in addition to technical training, has also received logistic support such as airplanes, technical equipment, vehicles, telecommunications, and trained dogs, among other things. The countries that have offered this support have been fundamentally the United States, United Kingdom, and Germany. An exchange of police personnel also exists with the border countries, basically in the antinarcotics field.

Police Education, Research, and Publications

The School of Police Training and Specialization (ECAEPOL) is in charge of the training and specialization of PNP's civil and police personnel.

The PNP has also a training center known as Superior School of the PNP (ESUPOL), which provides one-year curricula to superior officers such as:

CUSCAP: Superior Course for Command and Police Advising, directed at officers with ranks of commandant and major

CACOP: Training Course for Police Officers, directed at officers with rank of captain

Finally, the PNP has the National Institute of Advanced Police Studies (INAEP), which provides training for officers with the rank of colonel.

Within the Peruvian communication media, the most distinguished journalists are the following:

Angel Páez, Edmundo Cruz, and Ernesto Guerrero, newspaper *La República*

Cecilia Valenzuela, *Agenciaperú.com*

Carlos Orbegoso, Maribel Toledo-Ocampo, and Heidi Grossmann, TV program "Cuarto Poder"

Cesar Hildebrant and Elizabeth Rubianes, TV program "La Boca del Lobo"

The change in the course of Peruvian history was determined in several cases by the achievements of the Peruvian National Police, especially in the fight against subversion. Especially important in the suppression of the two terrorist organizations was the capture of their principal leaders, including Victor Polay Campos on 9 June 1992, and Abimael Guzman Reynoso on 12 September of the same year. These captures constitute a fundamental contribution in attaining the strategic defeat of subversion and terrorism.

With respect to the fight against narcotics, the PNP has disarmed important organizations of drug traffickers that were related to the cartels of Colombia and Mexico, by capturing hundreds of involved people and confiscating property, vehicles, and tons of drugs.

Finally, with respect to social security, the PNP has also disarmed known criminal organizations that have been responsible for kidnapping and extortion, through the capture of its prin-cipal leaders.

Notable books include:

La Crisis de los Rehenes en el Perú—Base Tokio. Publisher of newspaper *Comercio.*

Jiménez, Benedicto. *Inicio, Desarrollo y Ocaso del Terrorismo en el Perú.*

Jiménez, Benedicto. *Manual de Inteligencia Operativa Policial.*

National Police is the name of the police newspaper, which is published on a regular basis by the General Directorate of the National Police of Peru, through its Public Relations Division.

Notable websites include:

Educared Perú: *www.educared.edu.pe/ estudiantes/geografia/tema3_2_1.asp*

General Directorate of Security Services Control: *www.mininter.gob.pe/article/ articleview/905*

Interior Ministry: *www.miniter.gob.pe*

Judiciary Branch of Peruvian Government: *www.pj.gob.pe/AVANCE% 20INFORMATIVO.htm*

National Institute of Statistics and Informatics (INEI):*www.inei.gob.pe/perucifrasHTM/banner/ documentos/Proyecciones/Cuadro026.xls*

National Penitentiary Institute (INPE): *www. inpe.gob.pe/proyectoestadistica/RESUMEN/ Cabecera.asp*

National Police of Peru (PNP): *www.pnp.gob.pe/ conociendo/historia.asp*

Peruvian government website: *www.peru.gob.pe/ frame.asp?dsc_url_web = http%3a//www.peru. org.pe/historia.asp*

Peru Virtual.net: *www.peruvirtual.net/moeue/ texto-aboutperu.htm*

Public Ministry, National Attorney General's Office: *www.mpfn.gob.pe/info_general.php*

DANIEL LINARES RUESTRA

Bibliography

Cueto, Manuel. Lawyer. "Generalidades del Ministerio Público" (General Facts of the Public Ministry). Interview by author, November 10, 2004.

Del Busto, Javier. Colonel of the PNP. "Generalidades de la Policía Nacional" (General Facts of the National Police). Interview by author, November 14, 2004.

Linares, Antonio. Colonel of the PNP. "Las Direcciones Especializadas de la PNP" (The Specialized Divisions of the PNP). Interview by author on October 15, 2004.

Zamora, Enrique. Lawyer. "El Sistema de Justicia Peruano" (The Justice System of Peru). Interview by author, October 10, 2004.

PHILIPPINES

Background Material

Little is known about early human settlement on the islands of the Philippines; however, scientific evidence has suggested that the first human settlement on the island began shortly after the last ice age, the Pleistocene Epoch. When sea levels were low at this time, land bridges connected the South Asian mainland to some of the present islands of the Malay Archipelago, south of the Philippine Islands. The primary hunter and food gatherers to arrive in the Philippine Islands were ancestors of the present-day people of the Aeta and Agta tribes, who were thought to have crossed the land bridges following herds of wild animals.

The people of Malay descent, who now make up the majority of the population, are thought to have settled in the Philippines in several waves of migration in the third century BCE. The Philippines have a long history of colonial influence, primarily from Spain and the United States. Original Spanish explorers, led by Miguel Lopez de Legazpi settled in Cebu City, which became the capital of the new Spanish colony after defeat of the Muslim ruler Rajah Soliman, who had controlled an area that the Spanish explorers sought to establish as their port to the east. Spain had a threefold objective in colonising the Philippines: first, to secure a share in the lucrative Filipino spice trade; second, to provide a base from which they could convert Asians to Christianity; and third, to convert the people of the Philippine Islands. However, limited success was obtained in all three areas, as the Muslims of southern Mindanao and the Sulu Archipelago were never baptized, and resisted Spanish rule throughout its 300 years of rule.

The nineteenth century saw the arrival of the Industrial Revolution, which transformed the means in which industries operated throughout the world. Modern techniques in production and transportation left the Philippines in a unique position for economic development. Demand for agricultural crops such as sugar, tobacco, and abaca led to increased economic activity and interest by Britain, France, Holland, and North America in the Philippines.

A clear distinction between the natives and the Spanish settlers began to emerge in the mid- to late nineteenth century, when higher education was only afforded to the "Ilustrados," that is, the Spanish settlers. After the Spanish revolution of 1868, the Ilustrados sought to establish the same democratic construction of equality of civil and political rights that had been brought about in Spain for the Filipinos. However, the Catholic Church resisted such changes, as they would lead to the end of the Church's control of indigenous diocesan priests in places successfully converted to Christianity. In these areas, which were Catholic strongholds, the Church functioned as a form of local government, controlling local services and education, as well as the largest landowner. Following a number of campaigns for social and political reforms that led to waves of civil unrest, the Spanish colonial power managed to retain its power in the Philippines. However, after a bitter war fought between Spain and the United States over their competing imperialist interests, negotiations led to an agreement that left the United States with colonial power over the Philippines. U.S. influence over the region left an indelible mark on the justice system, legal code, civil service, and police force. On attaining power, the United States established a political administration with the goal of preparing the Philippines for eventual independence. The way in which the land was purchased from the Catholic Church and then sold to the wealthy Ilustrados ruling class, resulted in alienating a large portion of Filipinos for several generations, as this move prevented them from achieving economic stability and the wherewithal to ensure a subsistence standard of living. U.S.-unrestricted free trade with the Philippines had a decisive influence on the Filipino economy. Crops of sugar, abaca, copra, and tobacco had the effect of making the ruling landowner class rich. Additionally, the United States also established a military base at Subic Bay near Manila as a strategic stronghold for U.S. forces based in the Pacific.

After a number of U.S. presidents pursued different policies regarding how and when the Philippines should be made a republic, on July 4, 1946, the Philippines finally declared itself a republic with Manuel Roxas as its first president. In the aftermath of World War II, the Philippines faced staggering problems, as Japanese and American fighting had produced severe structural damage in the Philippines. The United States granted large war damage and rehabilitation aid to the Philippines in return for generous use of Philippines natural resources. While the Philippines had achieved independence, it became heavily dependent on U.S. aid, which meant that the United States retained strong influence in the country. After several presidents in the Philippines followed various objectives in attempts to stabilize the country and return economic well-being, high debt, political corruption, and colonial influences made this an impossible task. Despite limited constitutional reforms in 1988 and limited changes to the land tenure system, problems still are rampant with dissatisfaction among the poorer classes. Parallel to these problems, Muslims in the southern parts of the Philippines were demanding independence and the establishment of an Islamic state. Political corruption, highly concentrated land ownership, Muslim separatists, and poor infrastructure underscore the fundamental problems that face the Philippines today.

The Philippines is a diverse country of culture and traditions, which has been impacted largely by its colonial history. The Malayan peoples had early contact with traders who had Chinese and Indian influences. Islamic traditions were first introduced to the Malays of the southern Philippine Islands in the fourteenth century. The Spanish imposed a foreign culture and tradition steeped in Catholicism. The architectural impact from the Catholic Church was intense, with most emphasising religious iconography. While some of the local people converted to Catholicism, many in the upland tribes maintained cultural independence. During the first half of the twentieth century, U.S. influence made the Philippines one of the most Westernized countries in Southeast Asia. In the aftermath of the Philippines attaining independence, Filipino artists while drawing on Western forms, still depicted distinctly Philippine themes. Therefore, many traditions of the Malay have survived despite centuries of foreign rule. Muslims and upland tribal groups maintain distinct traditions in music, dance, and sculpture. In addition, many Filipino artists incorporated indigenous folk motifs into modern forms.

Filipinos are primarily descendants of the Malayan peoples who migrated to the islands thousands of years ago. The Philippines had a population of almost 65 million in 1990, with an average growth of 2% per year, with a population of almost 87 million in 2004. As the Philippines has a high population growth rate, this has contributed toward a young population, with 38% below fifteen years of age. The projected population for 2010 is 93.9 million, and in 2025, 113.5 million. The current infant mortality rate is 34 per 1,000 births. Life expectancy for men is sixty-five years of age, and for women, sixty-eight. The male adult literacy rate currently stands at 95%, and female literacy, 94%. A total of 47% of the population lives in cities, with 45% of the labour force engaged in agricultural activities.

The Philippines is located in Southeast Asia, 15 degrees north, 121 degrees east, with an area of 298,160 sq km; Manila is the capital city.

The principal economic activity in the Philippines is agriculture, with the main crops being rice, coconut, corn, sugar cane, bananas, pineapples, mangoes, pork, eggs, beef, and fish. Major industries are electronics assembly, textiles, pharmaceuticals, chemicals, wood products, food processing, petroleum refining, and fishing.

The Philippines was severely affected by the Asian financial crisis of 1998, with a GDP growth rate that year of 0.6%, increasing to 2.4% in 1999, and 4.4% in 2000. However, it slowed again to 3.2% in 2001. GDP growth in 2002, 2003, and 2004 was 4.4%, 4.2%, and 4.5%, respectively.

However, due to high population growth and unequal distribution of income, it will take higher sustained economic progress to achieve poverty alleviation. The national debt in 2004 ran at 77% of GDP. The current administration of Macapagal-Arroyo has promised to continue economic reforms, particularly improving infrastructure, strengthening tax collection, further deregulation and privatization of government assets, enhancing the viability of the economy, and strengthening trade with major trading partners. Prospects for coming years depend on two things: the economic performance of the United States and Japan, and increased confidence among investors.

Filipinos are divided generally along linguistics, geography, and religious lines. Different linguistic groups developed as a result of original settlement patterns. As the Malayan peoples spread throughout the archipelago, they dispersed into separate groups, each developing a distinct vernacular or regional language. The primary religious groups are Christians and Muslims; due to Spanish colonialism, the Philippines is one of the few places in Southeast Asia that is predominately Christian. About 94% are Christian, 5% are Muslims; and the remainder are Buddhists, animists, or nonbelievers. Approximately 84% of all Filipinos are Roman Catholic; another 10% belong to other Christian denominations, most notably the Igelsia Filipina Independiente (Philippine Independent Church). Smaller groups of Christians also exist, including Protestants and revivalist groups. The Muslim population of the Philippines lives mostly on the southern islands of Mindanao and Sulu Archipelago. Islam predated Christianity in the region, spreading to the Sulu Archipelago in the fourteenth century and Mindanao in the fifteenth century.

Nearly eighty indigenous languages and dialects are spoken in the Philippines. These languages belong to the Malayo-Polynesian group of the Austronesian language family. The most widely spoken languages are Tagalog, Cebuano, Ilocano, Hiligaynon, Bicol, Waray-Waray, Pampangan, Pangasinan, and Maranao. English and Filipino (formerly spelled "Pilipino") are the official languages. While Filipino is widely used in schools, English is more commonly used in higher education.

Contextual Features

The Philippines has been a democratic republic since 1946, and is currently governed by the 1987 constitution, which is modeled on the commonwealth constitution of 1935 that established a system of government similar to that of the United States. The head of state and chief executive of the Philippines is the president, elected by popular vote to a nonrenewable term of six years. All Philippine citizens over eighteen years of age are eligible to vote. The president and vice-president are directly elected by separate ballot and may belong to two separate parties. The president nominates appointments for heads of government departments or ministers to form the government. The Commission on Appointments, composed of twenty-four members of Congress, reviews and votes on the nominations. The approved cabinet oversees the day-to-day functions of government, with the president having limited emergency powers; martial law cannot be claimed for more than sixty days. The Philippines has a bicameral legislature called the Congress of the Philippines. The upper house or Senate has twenty-four members who are directly elected to serve six-year terms. Senators are limited to two consecutive terms. The lower House of Representatives has a maximum of 260 members who serve three-year terms; 208 are directly elected and 52 are indirectly elected from party list nominees of indigenous minority groups. House members are limited to three consecutive terms. A two-thirds majority vote of Congress is required to overrule a presidential veto of proposed legislation.

For administrative purposes, the Philippines is divided into sixteen regions and seventy-nine provinces. Each province is headed by a governor who is directly elected to a three-year term. Additionally, there is an Autonomous Region of Muslim Mindanao (ARRM), encompassing four provinces in Mindanao. The ARRM is a quasi-self-governing region that was formed in 1989, result of an agreement between Muslim separatists and the Philippines government. It has an elected legislative assembly that is headed by a governor with limited executive powers.

The highest tribunal in the Philippines is the Supreme Court, consisting of a chief justice and fourteen associate justices, all appointed to four-year terms by the country's president. Other judicial bodies include a court of appeals, court of first instance, and municipal courts.

The Philippine legal system is hybrid in nature, which is a reflection of the country's colonial history. It has combined elements of Roman civil law from Spain and Anglo-American common law introduced by the United States. The influence of Spain is clearly evidenced in private law, including family relations, property matters, and contracts. The areas of law most influenced by the United States are constitutional law, taxation, and banking and corporate law. Islamic law is applied in the Muslim area of the south of the country.

The Philippines has had a history of chronic crime linked to a variety of social and cultural factors, in addition to the widespread poverty and high population growth. With high population rates, a shortage of jobs in rural areas causes large migrations to the cities. The police have pointed to the rapid growth of slums and squatter areas and high rates of firearms ownership as a direct consequence of high crimes rates. Drug trafficking has grown since the 1980s, particularly in marijuana. Cultivation was widespread with large parts of the mountainous regions of Luzon and the central Visayas being the major growing centres. The Philippines remains a centre of drug trafficking and transshipment. Cannabis growers export their product to Hong Kong, Japan, Australia, and the United States, and Filipino waters have routinely been used by other smugglers as a transshipment point for Southeast Asian marijuana bound for North America. Additionally, corruption remains a serious problem for the Philippines. Despite consistent anticorruption efforts, petty graft is commonplace, and high-level corruption scandals periodically rock the government. As part of continuing efforts by the government to root out official malfeasance, the Sandiganbayan, a special anticorruption court, was established.

Police Profile

Background

Prior to the 1970s, the Philippine Constabulary alone was responsible for law enforcement on a national level. However, after a major restructuring of the nation's police system was embarked upon, independent city and municipal police forces took charge of maintaining peace and order at the local level, calling on the Constabulary for aid when the need arose. In 1966, the National Police Commission was established to improve professionalism and training of local police, and was given loose supervisory authority over the police. However, some fundamental defects began to emerge in this system of policing, including jurisdictional limitations; lack of uniformity and coordination; and disputes between police forces and partisan political involvement in police employment, appointments, assignments, and promotions. Local political bosses routinely used police forces as private armies, protecting their interests and intimidating political opponents.

To correct these fundamental defects in the system, the 1973 Constitution sought to provide for the integration of the police, fire, and jail services in the nation's more than 1,500 cities and municipalities. On 8 August 1975, Presidential Decree 765 officially established the joint nationwide command and staff structure. The chief of the Philippine Constabulary serves jointly as the director general of the Integrated National Police. As Constabulary commander, he reported through the military chain of command, and as head of the Integrated National Police, he reported directly to the minister of national defence (which was later changed to secretary of national defence). The National Police Commission was transferred to the Ministry (later Department) of National Defence, retaining its oversight responsibilities, but turning over authority for training and other matters to the Philippine Constabulary and Integrated National Police.

The Integrated National Police was assigned responsibility for public safety, protection of lives and property, enforcement of laws, and maintenance of peace and order throughout the nation. To carry out these responsibilities, it was given powers "to prevent crimes, effect the arrest of criminal offenders and provide for their detention and rehabilitation, prevent and control fires, investigate the commission of all crimes and offences, bring the offenders to justice, and take all necessary steps to ensure public safety." In practice, the Philippine Constabulary retained responsibility for dealing with serious crimes or cases involving distant jurisdictions, and the Integrated National Police took charge of less serious crimes and local traffic, crime prevention, and public safety.

The Integrated National Police's organization paralleled that of the Constabulary. The thirteen Philippine Constabulary regional command headquarters were the nuclei for the Integrated National Police's regional commands. Likewise, the constab-

ulary's seventy-three provincial commanders, in their capacity as provincial police superintendents, had operational control of Integrated National Police forces in their respective provinces. Provinces were further subdivided into 147 police districts, stations, and substations. The Constabulary was responsible for patrolling remote rural areas. In Metro Manila's four cities and thirteen municipalities, the Integrated National Police's Metropolitan Police Force shared the headquarters of the constabulary's Capital Command. The commanding general of the Capital Command was also the director of the Integrated National Police's Metropolitan Police Force, and directed the operations of the capital's four police and fire districts.

As of 1985, the Integrated National Police numbered some 60,000 people, a marked increase over the 1980 figure of 51,000. Approximately 10% of these staff were fire and prison officials, and the remainder were police. The Philippine National Police Academy provided training for Integrated National Police officer cadets. Established under the Integrated National Police's Training Command in 1978, the academy offered a bachelor of science degree in public safety following a two-year course of study. Admission to the school was highly competitive.

The Integrated National Police was the subject of some criticism, and the repeated object of reform. Police were accused of involvement in illegal activities, violent acts, and abuse. Charges of corruption were frequent. To correct the Integrated National Police's image problem, the government sponsored programs to identify and punish police offenders, and training designed to raise their standard of appearance, conduct, and performance.

Dramatic changes were planned for the police in 1991. The newly formed Philippine National Police (PNP) was to be a strictly civilian organization, removed from the armed forces and placed under a new civilian department known as the Department of the Interior and Local Government.

Local police forces were supported at the national level by the National Bureau of Investigation. As an agency of the Department of Justice, the National Bureau of Investigation was authorized to "investigate, on its own initiative and in the public interest, crimes and other offences against the laws of the Philippines; to help whenever officially requested, investigate or detect crimes or other offences; (and) to act as a national clearing house of criminal records and other information." In addition, the bureau maintained a scientific crime laboratory and provided technical assistance on request to the police and constabulary.

Local officials also played a role in law enforcement. By presidential decree, the justice system in the *barangays* empowered village leaders to handle petty and less serious crimes. The intent of the program was to reinforce the authority of local officials, and to reduce the workload on already overtaxed Philippine law enforcement agencies.

The Philippine National Police (PNP) is the central organising unit that takes care of its own police recruitment, located at its headquarters in Manila. There are several different obstacles for potential recruits to pass before entry into the force will be offered. Recruitment management is performed under the Civil Service Commission, each department and agency evolves its own screening process, which include tests and fitness standards in accordance with general guidelines. The general requirements for admission to the Philippine National Police force follow:

Philippines citizenship.

Good moral conduct.

Pass psychiatric/psychological, drug, and physical tests to be admitted by the PNP or by any National Police Commission (NAPOLCOM)-accredited government hospital for the purpose of determining physical and mental health.

Formal baccalaureate degree from a recognized institution of learning (A baccalaureate degree is an examination taken at the conclusion of a student's secondary school studies, to enable entry into university.)

Eligible in accordance with the standards set by NAPOLCOM.

Absence of dishonorable discharge from military, or dismissal for cause from any civilian position in the government.

Absence of conviction by final judgment of an offence or crime involving moral turpitude.

Height of at least 1.62 meters for men, and 1.57 meters for women.

Weight of no more or less than five kilograms from the standard weight corresponding to his or her height, age, and gender.

For new applicants, between twenty-one and thirty years of age.

Except for the last qualification, the above-mentioned qualifications shall be continuing in character, and an absence of any one of them at any given time shall be grounds for separation or retirement from the service, provided that PNP members who are already in the service upon the effectivity of RA 8551 shall be given at least two years to obtain the minimum education qualification and one year to satisfy the weight requirement.

Screening Committees are established by the chief of police to be responsible for the determination of fitness for applicants. Provincial, regional, and national Screening Committees ensure the eligibility of candidates. The screening process usually begins with an interview, test of physical fitness, and medical/psychological fitness and character background investigation, with one final interview.

Police Public Projects

One innovative approach in fighting crime that the police adopted in 2002 was the introduction of reporting crime via text messaging, which enable citizens to report wrongdoing by police officers and to report general crime. Unfortunately, no cost data are available on the text messaging system, but some performance indicators are known. In its first six months of operation in 2003, the text 2920 system received just over 29,000 messages. Of these, 33% were requests for assistance; 25% were reports of illegal drug use or gambling; and 13%—more than twenty messages per day—were reports on wrongdoings by police officers.

Terrorism

Threats of terrorism remain at a high risk factor for the Philippine Islands. Director General Edgardo Aglipay, PNP chief, has admitted to the ABS CBN News Group that the country is still vulnerable to terrorist attacks, especially from extremists from Thailand, Indonesia, and Malaysia. Intelligence-gathering operations have intensified, but the nonexistence of antiterrorism laws makes it difficult for authorities, leaving them with the option of only filing charges of illegal possession of firearms and possession of explosives and violation of immigration laws against possible suspects.

Police Education, Research, and Publications

Current research on police development and training is performed by the National Police Commission, which has the stated goal of evolving "highly professional, competent, disciplined and creditable Philippines National Police Force." Additionally, the Commission is there to supervise the Philippines National Police Force toward its continual professionalisation and to foster citizen participation in crime prevention, thereby ensuring the attainment of peace, order, and development.

NOEL McGUIRK

Websites

www.pnp.gov.ph/
www.napolcom.gov.ph/
www.unescap.org/stat/meet/iags/iags_status_w&m.pdf
www.egov4dev.org/text2920.htm
www.vic-info.org/RegionsTop.nsf/0/
　23737e3e1ad607ae0a256d6f00078fe9?OpenDocument
www.alsagerschool.co.uk/subjects/sub_content/geography/
　Gpop/HTMLENH/country/ph.htm
www.gov.ph
www.doj.gov.ph/
www.philippinebusiness.com.ph/surveys_forecasts/
　survey_of_forecasts.htm
www.classbrain.com/art_cr/publish/philippines_economy.
　shtml
www.makati.gov.ph/contents/geninfo/economics.php

www.cia.gov/cia/publications/factbook/geos/rp.html#Econ
www.abakada.com.ph/phil_link.htm#goverment
www.philippineembassy-usa.org/other/links.htm
www.abs-cbnnews.com/FlashNewsStory.aspx?FlashOID
　= 24186

Bibliography

Colbert, Evelyn. *United States and the Philippine Bases.*
　Lanham, MD: Rowman & Littlefield Publishers, 1988.
Thompson, Winfred. *Introduction of American Law in the
　Philippines and Puerto Rico, 1898–1905.* Fayetteville:
　Arkansas: University of Arkansas Press, 1990.
Walton, Clifford Stevens. *Civil Law in Spain and Spanish
　America: Including Cuba, Puerto Rico, and Philippine
　Islands.* Union, NJ: Lawbook Exchange, 2003.

POLAND

Background Material

The Republic of Poland is located in Central Eastern Europe. Its neighbors are Russia (Kaliningrad District), Lithuania, Byelorussia, Ukraine, Slovakia, the Czech Republic, and Germany. Poland has an area of 312, 685 sq km. and a population of 38,626,349 (July 2004 estimate).

The capital of Poland is Warsaw, and the official language is Polish. The nation is administratively structured into sixteen large provinces (*voivodeships*), 373 counties (*powiats*), and 2,489 municipalities (*gminas*). The gross domestic product per capita in 2002 was 5,177 euros.

Contextual Features

From 1989 to 2003, the number of all crimes increased from almost 550,000 to more than 1,466,000, or from 1,400 to 3,800 crimes per 100,000 inhabitants. The substantial increase in crime since 2000 is the result of changes in traffic regulations, according to which driving a vehicle with a blood alcohol level of more than 0.05% since 2001 is treated as a crime (earlier it was a misdemeanor).

Juveniles commit from 63,000 (2002) to 83,000 (1995) punishable acts per year. After 1989, the number of such felonies grew uninterruptedly up to 1995. Since then a downward tendency remains discernible.

Organized crime remains a dynamic phenomenon. During the first half of 2003, the Central Investigation Office registered 459 criminal groups (including 367 Polish groups) active in Poland. The principal dangers posed by organized crime affect businesses and the government treasury.

Police Profile

Demographics

In 2003, police personnel included a total of 99,919 police officers and 19,487 civilian employees. Poland has on average one police officer per 380 inhabitants. The percentage of commissioned officers is 17.4%; ensigns, 27.7%; noncommissioned officers, 34.1%; and constables, 20.8%. The majority of Polish police officers are under the age of forty (73% of total staff). Seventy-four percent of Polish police officers have secondary education, with 24% having college education, and 2% with vocational education.

A total of 57% of police officers are employed in the prevention service, 32% in the criminal service, and 11% in the support service. Women make up over 10% of police officers, and they hold managerial positions at all organizational levels of the police.

The police in Poland consist of the following branches: criminal, preventive, and support services, which provide administrative, logistics, and technical support. A separate service, established by the chief commander of police upon the approval of the government minister in charge of internal affairs, as provided by the law, is the investigative force. The structures of the police also include the Court Police, Police Academy, training centers, and police schools, separate prevention squads, and antiterrorist squads, as well as research and development units.

A separate service working against organized crime is the Central Investigation Bureau, or the investigative service, which operates in the General Police Headquarters.

The organizational structure of the police is as follows:

- General Police Headquarters
- 16 Voivodeship police headquarters, plus the metropolitan police headquarters
- 270 County police headquarters
- 65 municipal police headquarters
- 618 police stations
- 15 Specialized police stations

Organizational units of the police also include the Police Academy, four police schools, twenty-one prevention squads, ten antiterrorism squads, and fourteen training centers.

The fundamental duties of the Police include:

- Protection of people's life and health, and their material possessions against unlawful attempts in breach of these values
- Protection of law and order, including maintenance of order in public places and on public transport, as well as on public roads and waters
- Initiating and organizing activities aimed to prevent crime and misdemeanors as well as any situations or behavior that lead to crime, and to cooperate in this respect with government authorities, local self-government bodies, and community organizations
- Detection of crime and offences and prosecution of the perpetrators

Training

Police officer training is modular and alternating at all training levels. Theoretical training is alternated with periods of acquiring specific police skills through performing practical tasks in the field.

The first fifteen-week phase of basic training applies to officers in all police services. Upon completion of this phase, police officers in support services may be appointed to a specific job position within the service.

Police officers in prevention and criminal services must go through the second phase of basic training, called the profiled training, which takes about four months depending on the training profile. The curriculum for this training phase matches the specialization assigned to each specific group of trainee officers, that is, prevention, road traffic, investigative operations, forensic techniques, and operational techniques.

The next phase is specialized training carried out in Police Schools. Police officers in the prevention service are trained in the Police Schools in Slupsk and Katowice, within the following specializations: district constable, duty officer, head of patrolling and intervention unit, and platoon commander of a prevention squad.

Police officers in the criminal service are trained in the Police School in Pila, within the following specializations: intelligence and operational investigation and inquiry, and economic crime.

The Police Training Center in Legionowo provides training to police officers in the services that provide the Police with administrative, logistics, and technical support, within one comprehensive specialization. The Training Center also provides courses for the officers in the prevention service within the scope of road safety and juvenile delinquency, as well as training for police dog guides and training for criminal service officers with regard to forensic techniques and operational techniques.

Police Use of Firearms

In Poland, conditions and type of firearms use by the police are regulated by order of the Council of Ministers dated May 21, 1996. Before using firearms, police are obliged to adhere to precisely defined procedures, such as calling on a suspect to immediately comply with the law, to provide a warning of intent to use firearms, and to shoot warning shots.

Situations where police officers are allowed to use firearms are strictly defined in Article 17 of the Police Act of April 6, 1990, published in the *Journal of Law of the Republic of Poland*. They may use firearms only if other means are ineffective. When deciding about the use of firearms, police officers are obliged to act with great deliberation, treating firearms as a special and ultimate method of direct constraint.

Police Education, Research, and Publications

College-level professional education takes place in the Police Academy in Szczytno. During the three-year course of study, the curriculum offers subjects in criminal and prevention service, law and social studies, and management studies.

Training provided in the Police Academy is profiled, which takes into account the statutory division in different services (criminal and prevention service). The Police Academy also runs a training and professional development program for police officers employed in managerial positions and so-called "independent positions," such as management courses for police managerial staff. Within the Academy, the Centre for Management Studies prepares commissioned police officers for taking up the job duties of managerial positions.

Bibliography

General Police Headquarters. *Police in Poland*. 2002.

Holyst, B. *Kryminologia* (Criminology). 8th ed. Warsaw, 2004.

Holyst, B. *Crime in Poland in 1989–2002, Forecast up to 2008*. Warsaw, 2004.

Holyst, B. *Kryminalistyka* (Criminalistics). 10th ed. Warsaw, 2004.

The author wishes to express sincere appreciation to inspector Piotr Calinski for his help in information acquisition.

PORTUGAL

Background Material

Portugal lies in the southwest of Europe, occupying approximately one-sixth of the Iberian Peninsula. Its total area is 92,446 sq km. Besides its continental area, Portugal includes two archipelagos in the Atlantic Ocean: Azores and Madeira.

A nation since 1143, Portugal was a leading world power in the fifteenth and sixteenth centuries. Much of its wealth and status were lost with the destruction of Lisbon in the 1755 earthquake, occupation during the Napoleonic Wars, and the independence in 1822 of Brazil as a colony. After the 1910 revolution and abolition of the monarchy, repressive governments ran the country during the next six decades. The republican period is characterized by three different phases: unstable democracy (before 1926), dictatorship (1926 until April 25, 1974), and representative democracy (since 1974). In 1975, Portugal granted independence to all of its African colonies. Portugal became a member of the European Union in 1986.

The last census indicated a population of 10.318 million inhabitants. There are about 190,000 foreigners living in Portugal (2000). Much crime is attributed to second-generation immigrants from former Portuguese colonies in Africa that arrived after the independence of their countries (approximately 90,000); the same applies to illegal immigrants from recently independent states in Eastern Europe (especially Moldavia and Ukraine) and Romania.

Roman Catholicism is practiced by 94% of the population, with the rest of the population divided between Protestantism and others that are generally related to specific ethnic/religious groups. Portuguese is the official and, practically, only used language.

Portugal has a thriving market-oriented economy with a per capita GDP of US$19,400 in 2002. The country is a member of the European Monetary Union (EMU), launching the euro on 1 January 1999. The government is working to reform the tax system, and to increase the country's competitiveness in the increasingly integrated world markets. Improvement of the education sector is a critical factor in terms of the long-run catch-up process.

Contextual Features

Portugal is a unitary state without any elements of state or federal pluralism. Administratively, it is divided into eighteen districts and two autonomous regions (the aforementioned archipelagos), which are subdivided into municipalities.

Portugal is a parliamentary democracy with a legal system based on a civil law system. Executive power is exercised by the president of the Republic (elected by popular vote for a five-year term) with the Council of State as a consultative body, and by the government, which through the Council of Ministers approves its decisions. Legislative power lies in principle with the unicameral Assembly of the Republic. The president has the prerogative to veto legislation adopted by the Assembly and send it to Constitutional Court for a review of its constitutionality.

Besides the Constitutional Court, the following categories of courts exist: Supreme Court of Justice and judicial tribunals of first and of second instance; Supreme Administrative Court and other administrative and fiscal tribunals; Court of Accountancy, and optionally, Marine courts, courts by arbitration, and judges of the peace.

The judicial courts are generally competent in civil matters, but they do not exercise jurisdiction in areas attributed to other judicial branches. Portuguese territory is divided, for the purpose of the administration of justice, in judicial districts and subdistricts.

The Supreme Court of Justice is the superior organ in the hierarchy of judicial courts. Located in Lisbon, it consists of sections in civil, penal, and social matters. It operates, under the direction of a president, in the plenary, in addition to specialized sections and sections. The civil sections are competent for cases that not attributed to other sections; the criminal sections judge cases of the same nature; the social sections judge cases falling under the competence of the Labor Courts. The Supreme Court of Justice, except for other legally consecrated, only analyzes matters of law.

Crime rates are increasing, mainly due to thefts, in particular vehicle theft and inside-vehicle theft, and to simple physical offences. Property offenses seem to be mainly focused on cellular phones (and the establishments that market them). Most of this crime is related to drug trafficking/consumption, which presents, in the largest districts, a growth tendency.

A growing use of firearms by criminals, namely in robberies, assaults on banks and commercial establishments, and in encounters with police, illustrates increasing violence in urban society in recent years. Nevertheless, crimes such as murder still have a low rate (58 in 2001 and 69 in 2002).

Gang crime focuses on robberies and thefts at fuel stations, computer stores, and large shopping facilities, showing a growing specialization and mobility (juvenile delinquency records a decrease in the number of cases reported, partly due to the growing group element).

Imprisonment and fines are the most widely applied penalties (the maximum penalty that can be applied to anyone in Portugal is twenty-five years in prison). Once a sentence has become final, without any further appeal possible, the execution falls under the responsibility of the Ministry of Justice; during the proceedings, some restrictive measures may also be taken by the court, such as home detention and preventive detention. This ends the role of the court, which is, in accordance with the institutional powers, strictly confined to the dispensation of justice.

The Ministry of Justice supervises the correctional system through Prison Services, including the penitentiary facilities (for imprisonment sentences) and sentences management (the system in Portugal is outward directed, which means that day releases and parole may be granted) are considered.

Police Profile

Background

The word "police" originally meant the global activity of a state whose aim was to secure its legislative, executive, and judicial powers. In Portugal, the first document referring to the administration of justice dates from the fifteenth century (Alphosine Ordinations, 1447), although the "quadrilheiros" (recruited by force among the strongest men by the Town Councils since 1383) are considered the first approach to a police corps. In the last quarter of the eighteenth century, the Lisbon earthquake led to the creation of a genuine police force, the Royal Police Guard. During the turmoil of 1800s, many police forces were created, extinguished, or merged; however, 1867 is accepted as the date for the creation of the Public Security Police (PSP), as it marks the birth of the Civilian Police Corps. The National Republican Guard (GNR), in accordance with its denomination, was created directly after the arrival of the Republic in 1910, although both its origins and those of the PSP have a common root. The first decades of the fragile republic emphasized the military character of the GNR, which it had always maintained in both operational (it even had artillery until 1926) and doctrinal aspects, whereas the PSP covered the remaining aspects of internal security.

Organizational Description

The internal security of the Portuguese state is incumbent upon a group of forces and services at national level, dependent in its majority on the Ministry of the Interior (MAI). They are generally acting in uniform and follow a clear hierarchical structure. The concept of "public security" is based on two police forces: the PSP and the GNR.

Other services, with civil structures, also represent important elements in the internal security system, and include the following:

- Service of Foreigners and Borders (SEF), with police competencies and as a main mission to control the entry and stay of foreigners in national territory

- Security Information Service (SIS), without police competencies and responsible for collecting and processing intelligence destined to guarantee internal security and to prevent sabotage, terrorism, espionage, and other acts directed against the rule of law
- Judiciary Police (PJ) under the Ministry of Justice, a mainly investigative police force in charge of the most complex and most severely penalized crimes and endowed with the necessary operational competencies to fight it

Functions

The NRG is a special body of troops with administrative and criminal police competence similar to that of other European (France, Italy, and so on) "gendarmerie"-type forces.

It has jurisdiction over the entire national territory, with special importance in rural areas. Besides four brigades with territorial competence, there are two special brigades (traffic and fiscal) as well as two reserve units and a Practical School. The whole organization is coordinated by a general command with headquarters in Lisbon.

GNR personnel number approximately 23,000, divided into the following ranks: general senior officers (superior management); colonel, lieutenant colonel, and major (complex units commanders); captain, lieutenant, second lieutenant (smaller units commanders); sergeant (supervising); and soldier (operational execution).

The GNR mission consists of the following:

Maintain and reestablish citizens' safety and of the public, private, and joint property, and preventing illicit acts against them
Collaborate with judiciary authorities
General execution of laws and regulations, namely, those connected with traffic
Combat fiscal infringements
Assist in control of entry and exit of foreigners in the national territory
Help and protect citizens and to defend and preserve property in situations of danger, resulting from human or natural causes
Assist in implementation of national defense policies

The PSP is defined as an armed and uniformed force, with a civilian status. It is competent in the entire national territory, but executes its mission mainly in the most important and populated urban areas of the country.

There are eighteen police commands, which are located in district capitals on the continental territory, and two regional commands, in the Azores and Madeira. Besides the territorial units, there are three special units: the Anti-Riot Corps used in special circumstances to ensure the maintenance of public order (such as during football matches or demonstrations); the Special Operations Group for counterterrorism and high-violence special missions; and the Close Protection Corps, in charge of guaranteeing the security of special entities. The latter force has two training establishments, the Police Sciences Superior Institute and Police Practical School. The coordination body for the entire organization is the National PSP Directorate, located in Lisbon.

The PSP staff comprises approximately 21,500 officers in the following ranks: senior management—11 chief superintendents; complex units commanders—36 superintendents; 32 intendants and 83 subintendants; small unit commanders— 204 commissioners and 408 subcomissioners; supervising ranks—1,977 chiefs and 509 subchiefs; and operational execution—17,920 officers.

The mission of PSP is somewhat similar to that of the GNR, but with two functions attributed exclusively to this force: (1) control of the manufacture, possession, trade, use, and transportation of all firearms and explosives (military excluded); and (2) close protection of special entities. There is also a special mission regarding the security and safety of civil airports.

Police forces when carrying out their missions have to have to bear in mind the triple perspective of repressive, preventive/proactive, and administrative action. To that end, the penal procedure attributes several powers to police, which have to be seen in light of the support role granted to police, in relation to judicial authorities, and in the application of criminal justice. In this sense, the police take initiative to gather evidence of crime, investigate authorship, and ensure that all acts to preserve evidence are undertaken. Portuguese law accepts a wide definition of means of proof, stating that all legally relevant facts for the existence, or not, of a crime, should be so considered, unless they are obtained through torture or in any way that can be morally or physically offensive, excluding the exceptions that concede police forces their ultimate power and very special status within society. These allow police forces to arrest, detain, question a person; to conduct home searches, to listen to private communications; and to seize objects. All of these powers are subject to very strict limits (limited period of validity, requirement of a court mandate, and so on). The administrative action takes place in accordance with the regulations applicable to the specific sector of activity (for example, selling of arms, control of hunting). In case of infringement, less severe penalties apply (generally fines); however, disrespect of such regulations may lead to a special form of criminal behavior, and therefore penal rules became applicable in the fullest sense.

Training

Training for security forces is a strategic necessity, as this represents a decisive factor in promoting motivation and modernization. Significant human and financial resources as well as material invested have allowed to meet the demanding challenges of contemporary society. The modernization of training establishments and consolidation of educational projects, practice orientation, qualification of trainers, and a new training dynamic are characteristic for this important investment. This effort has resulted in a better service rendered to citizens.

The central mechanisms for the coordination of training are the Advisory Council for the Training of Security Forces and Services (CCFFSS), Training Section of the GNR, and Training Department of the PSP. In the National Directorate of PSP, the latter consists of two divisions: Training, Improvement, and Specialization (planning and coordination of all training); and Methods of Recruitment and Selection (study, planning, and implementation of selecting methods for PSP candidates). Basic training in the various security forces is quite similar; for officers in the PSP and soldiers in the GNR it is almost identical.

Recruitment into the PSP takes place for two different careers. For the officer career, it occurs at the lowest position in the hierarchy, and for the senior officer career, also at the first position of this career, that is, the subcommissioner.

The training of PSP senior officers is carried out at the Superior Institute of Police Sciences and Internal Security (ISCPSI). The creation of this school in 1979 was motivated by gradually substituting the army officers that rendered service in the PSP. In 1993, the Superior School of Police obtained the right to grant a degree in police sciences to the graduates of the Training Course of Police Senior Officers (CFOP).

The CFOP lasts five years, with the first four marked by a strong theoretical component. The fifth year, labeled as apprenticeship, is destined to provide students with closer contact to the functions that they will carry out during their career. At the end of the apprenticeship, the students present a thesis on a police-related subject.

The general areas of the CFOP curriculum are legal sciences (e.g., constitutional law); languages (Portuguese language and literature, French, English); social and political sciences (human rights, political science, political philosophy); exact sciences (mathematics); administration and management (administration and accounting); and police sciences and technology (communication techniques, computer science, armament).

Nonpolice trainers or teachers are experienced university scholars; ISCPSI has developed close cooperation with a number of institutions through the promotion of lectures, seminars, and partnerships.

Following similar recruitment requirements, the GNR senior officers' training takes place, at the Military Academy (alongside army senior officers), and is directed in a much more military style, even if the course is specially designed for GNR needs and is internal-security oriented. It grants a degree in military sciences and also lasts for five years.

The mission of training PSP officers is conferred to the Police Practical School (EPP), and GNR soldiers to the Guard Practical School (EPG). The main difference regarding requirement relates to the school level (eleventh grade). Selection practices also require candidates to take knowledge tests, medical examinations, psychological exams, and physical tests. The main subject areas are legal training, general training, police techniques, physical activities, and psycho-social training.

As of this writing, progression training is currently under reevaluation. It is intended to limit promotion courses to the passage from one group of ranks to the following one (officers, subchiefs, senior officers in PSP and soldiers, sergeants, and senior officers in GNR). This accompanies another change that will make promotions depend on training, service evaluation, professional curricula, and functions performed instead of the seniority system that would promote people just by achieving a certain number of years in a certain rank.

Specialization training is required for certain functions that demand specific skills or specialization. The relevant courses are held in the special units of the security forces, or staff members are deployed to attend such courses in similar forces or external entities. Course examples follow:

- Personal safety (9 weeks).
- Public order (7 weeks). This course can be combined with another related to dog training.
- Special operations. Staff training for the "antiterrorist and combat of high violence unit" (6 months).
- Specialist in deactivating explosives (6 months).
- Traffic control and regularization (12 weeks).

- Criminal investigation. As a consequence of the new attributes in the framework of criminal investigation given to PSP and GNR, 6-week courses are held in both practical schools, for all staff that carry out functions in this area (around 7% of all police staff). In addition, some very specific courses are given by the PJ.

Refresher courses are carried out through implementation of a program of training of improvement embracing all staff and encompassing essentially technical subjects. This program follows general orientations of National Directorates, and is the responsibility of each of police command.

There is also a "distance-learning" program, coordinated by the CCFFSS. This program consists of distributing videotapes to each police unit/department, whereby senior officers with previous specific technical and pedagogical training take over the presentation. With the aid of support texts, staff members carry out self-study of the subjects; weeks later, another session takes place and the subject is widely analyzed. The subjects concern mainly psycho-social and behavioral areas, and aim for a better understanding and approach of the citizen.

There is also a computer training program set up by the Ministry of the Interior, which aims to equip every staff member to operate with a personal computer.

In the field of training, the Annual Shooting Plan should be mentioned, which is scrupulously fulfilled. In order to overcome difficulties with shooting ranges that belong mainly to the Army, mobile shooting ranges were acquired. This equipment complements existing fixed ranges.

Police Public Projects

Concern for individual rights is expressed by the community policing approach developed by the Ministry of the Interior in conformity with a general police trend towards social intervention. Police forces are also involved in a series of social programs and partnerships that cover special risk groups and activities, such as the Secure School, Elders in Security, Domestic Violence, Support to Victims of Crime, and Secure Trade.

Police Use of Firearms

The use of firearms is the most common cause to criticize police action, and legislation is not entirely unambiguous about the situations in which it should or can be used. A police officer may use a firearm in nine stated, but widely drafted circumstances (to repel aggression, make an arrest or prevent escape of someone suspected to have committed a crime punishable by more than three years imprisonment, to free hostages, as an alarm device when no other method can be used, and so on). But use is justified only when, cumulatively, in any of the previously mentioned circumstances, one of the following three conditions is observed: to repel an actual and illegal aggression aimed at the agent or another person, with imminent danger of death or serious threat to physical integrity; to prevent a very serious crime that endangers human lives; and to arrest or avoid escape of someone who represents a threat and resists police. Practice has shown tremendous difficulties of judgment for the officer who faces such a situation and tries to frame it under these parameters. This provision essentially reveals the difficulties experienced by police officers through the dilemma of having the power to use firearms against persons, but at the same time being obliged to ultimately respect human life.

Complaints and Discipline

Portugal offers little concern to organizations that deal with this subject. Amnesty International is among the most active, although in recent years complaints were confined to three cases of people killed in dubious circumstances after police pursuit, and poor conditions in prisons, whereby the latter is a political rather than a police issue. Also, the adoption of measures against racism was recognized, even if their implementation was not yet considered totally effective. One of the major Portuguese institutions is Fórum Justiça e Liberdades (Forum Justice and Liberties), which undertakes to denounce judicial/police malfunctions or disrespect for equal access to justice and weaknesses of law that do not grant sufficient rights to people. Police forces do not have any special link to any of these organizations.

In cases of alleged police violation of human rights, investigation is conducted (besides the one that is ordered by the competent court) by the IGAI, an autonomous inspection service of the Ministry of the Interior composed, for this purpose, of lawyers.

The very low rate of human rights violations mirrors a society that generally sees police action in this area very positively. This excludes certain groups with more frequent encounters with police due to their proximity to the world of crime. These groups, often supported by the media, try to represent themselves as the victims of police.

Due to new methods of recruitment, a considerably lower average age of police officers, and a thorough training in human rights and citizenship, complaints about police staff have dropped drastically in recent years. Quality training in this field is achieved by calling on police trainers who have completed specialization courses in foreign police institutions or highly regarded university institutions.

All police forces, regardless of their institutional status, are now subject to similar disciplinary regulations. This is the case after the military rules formerly applicable to GNR members were adapted to the more civilian approach of discipline, penalties, and rewards valid for the other security forces and services. These regulations state a wide range of duties (for example, loyalty, proficiency, zeal, secrecy, obedience, assiduity, punctuality) that have to be strictly followed in both private and professional life. Reprimand, fines (in PSP), suspension, aggravated suspension, early retirement, and removal from office are the penalties that can be applied in accordance to the seriousness of the infringement or crime committed, and after the respective disciplinary or criminal process is complete. A Deontological Chart for the Police Service recently approved by the government sets out a number of principles valid for duty-related contacts with persons and respect of fundamental rights. Since the Chart is part of the disciplinary codes, any infringement of it is to be punished according to the same rules as general disciplinary offenses. Where the disciplinary fault also represents a crime, generally the disciplinary action does not proceed until the judicial decision has been taken.

Terrorism

Terrorism is nonexistent in Portugal. The last counterterrorist police action dates from the mid-1980s, concerning an intervention against an Armenian commando at the Turkish embassy in Lisbon. Activity regarding this issue generally occurs through the occasional arrest of members of Europe-based terrorist organizations that come to Portugal for other purposes than terrorist action, and that operate mainly in Spain (Basque country) and France (Corsica). Internal forms of terrorism ceased in the early 1980s after the dismantlement of the 25th of April Brigades, a leftist extremist group, which after the 1974 revolution threatened the country with assassinations, bank hold-ups, and bomb attacks to sabotage the process of democratization. Although PSP, GNR, PJ, and SIS cooperate closely in this area, SIS is the organization mainly responsible for gathering, analyzing, and coordinating terrorism-related data.

International Cooperation

Portugal is one of the fifteen members of the European Union Schengen Agreement, and thus is included in its intelligence system. The latter is controlled, at the national level, by the national SIRENE cabinet, which divided data management between the various security forces and services: SEF with responsibility for filing nonadmissible foreigners and blank documents, GNR with missing persons, PSP with firearms and stolen vehicles, and PJ with bank notes, surveillance, and detention for extradition requests. Besides this, in a more operational perspective, the national SIRENE is also responsible for controlling mutual assistance requests for prevention and investigation of criminal actions, strengthening police cooperation in border areas, cross-border pursuit, and provision of intelligence to other European police services that can be useful in crime prevention. The exchange of liaison officers is also managed under the Schengen Agreement, which falls under the responsibility of SEF. Schengen also covers cross-border surveillance, which is conducted operationally in a particular way, due to their specific competences, by PJ and the Customs Directorate General.

Further cooperation concerns Europol and Interpol, with national cabinets as contact points under the responsibility of PJ; this cooperation mainly relates to intelligence on wanted criminals and terrorism.

A senior officer nomination for the UN mission in Bosnia-Herzegovina in March 1992, at the beginning of the Balkan conflict, marked the beginning of Portugal's very successful involvement in international police assignments. The missions carried out by the police forces have been particularly rewarding as they included restructuring and training of local police, technical assistance to international organizations and local institutions, protection of the safety of persons and goods, participation in humanitarian actions, and election preparation.

The missions involved the following destinations: Bosnia, Albania, Croatia, Guatemala, Kosovo, Macedonia, Mozambique, Central-African Republic, Democratic Republic of Congo, and Western Sahara. Posts held by Portuguese police representatives included the first two commissioners of police in the UN missions to East Timor, chief of logistics of the Bosnia mission, and, in a behind-the-scenes capacity, deputy director of the police division of peacekeeping operations of the United Nations in New York. The PSP also took part in the first European Union Police Mission (EUPM) to Bosnia from January 2003.

A final aspect of international cooperation is the one maintained with the former colonies. PSP has long experience in this respect being responsible for the training of senior officers from Angola, Cape Verde, Mozambique, and São Tomé, and now East Timor, since 1995, through the CFOP. Some specialization and progression courses also included police staff from these countries in the same period. Another item in this cooperation is the supply of police material, namely, to Angola (publications), Cape Verde (publications, public order equipment, vehicles), and São Tomé (vehicles). Institutional support has also been granted to some of these countries, with the permanent presence of a senior officer in Mozambique and São Tomé, as technical assessor, producing legislation and establishing easier channels of communication.

Police Education, Research, and Publications

Despite remarkable activities developed in the areas of operations and training, the police are not very productive in terms of specific research. Certain senior officer courses or training establishments have thus far allowed the publication of studies on an individual basis, away from any definitive structured and institutional project. Nevertheless, the theses required for the completion of training courses are beginning to build up a reliable scientific basis in doctrine and science regarding police interaction with social and criminal sciences, strategy, management, law, and other disciplines. Apart from this, scientific police-related articles with innovative subjects are frequently published in the police reviews of the two forces (*Pela Lei e pela Grei* of the GNR and *Polícia Portuguesa* of the PSP).

Protocols with universities were signed in recent years, providing a basis for developing specific studies in social (psychology, sociology, criminology) and legal areas. The publications obtained are mainly used in training centers or to develop studies in central departments. There is also an exchange of expertise insofar as some graduate courses on police matters are established by universities; senior police officers are in turn requested as lecturers.

Publications follow the same path, as their periodicity and quality are beginning to show up in a more consistent way, whether they are published by the police forces for themselves, or for the general public. Recognizing the importance of this information source in police matters, as focused on policing techniques, law and order, social intervention, the Ministry of the Interior undertakes to coordinate the publication of all books presented by the police forces.

With more or less regular updates, various internet sites also provide valuable information on security forces and services (partially in English). The most important follow:

Ministry of the Interior: *www.mai.gov.pt*
Public Security Police: *www.psp.pt*
Superior Institute of Police Sciences and
    Internal Security: *www.esp.pt*
National Republican Guard: *www.gnr.pt*
Service of Foreigners and Borders: *www.sef.pt*
Security Information Service: *www.sis.pt*
Judiciary Police: *www.policiajudiciaria.pt*

JOÃO JOSÉ RAMALHETE MARQUES PIRES

Bibliography

Amnesty International. *Amnesty International Annual Report 2002*. New York: Amnesty International, 2003.
Barreto, Mascarenhas. *História da Polícia em Portugal* (History of Portuguese Police). Lisbon: Braga Editora, 1979.
Dias, Jorge Figueiredo. *Comentário Coimbricense ao Código Penal* (Coimbra Commentary on Penal Code). Coimbra: Coimbra Editora, 2001.
Escola Superior de Polícia. *Polícia Portuguesa* (Portuguese Police). Lisbon: Escola Superior de Polícia, 1998.
Gonçalves, Manuel Lopes Maia. *Código de Processo Penal* (Penal Procedure Code). Lisbon: Editora Almedina, 1999.
Ministério da Administração Interna. *Relatório Anual de Criminalidade* (Annual Crime Report). Lisbon: Ministério da Administração Interna, 2003.
Neves, Pedro Mendes. *Leis das Polícias e Forças de Segurança* (Laws on Police and Security Forces). Lisbon: Legis Editora, 2001.
Reis, António. *Portugal Contemporâneo* (Contemporary Portugal). Lisbon: Alfa, 1992.
Sampayo e Mello, António. *A Guarda Nacional Republicana* (The National Republican Guard). Lisbon: Comando Geral da GNR, 2001.
Serrão, Joaquim Veríssimo. *História de Portugal* (History of Portugal). Lisbon: Verbo Editora, 1995.
Serras, Júlio. *Leis dos Profissionais do Foro e dos Tribunais* (Laws of Legal Practitioners). Lisbon: Júlio Serras Edições, 2001.
Trindade, Diamantino Sanches, and Jesus, Manuel dos Reis. *Subsídios para a História da Polícia em Portugal* (Short History of Police in Portugal).

Q

QATAR

Background Material

Qatar is a small country in the Middle East, bordered by Saudi Arabia and the Persian Gulf. Humans inhabited Qatar as far back as 50,000 years ago. Qatar, once a British Protectorate, is now an independent state (gained independence in 1971). The form of government in Qatar is a traditional monarchy ruled by an emir. Besides leading the country, the emir also heads the Ministry of Defense and is commander-in-chief of the armed forces. The Al Thani family has ruled Qatar since the mid-1800s.

Qatar has a total area of 11,437 sq km (all land), and a population of 840,290 (as of July 2004). The capital is Doha. Ethnic composition follows: Arab 40%; Pakistani 18%; Indian 18%; Iranian 10%; and other 14%. Arabic is the official language, and English is common as a second language. A vast majority (95%) of the population practices Islam.

Per capita income is US$21,500. Major economic activities include crude oil production, fertilizers, petrochemicals, and cement.

Contextual Features

Qatar's government is a traditional monarchy, ruled by an emir. In 1972, a provisional constitution was enacted, and in 1999 the drafting of a permanent constitution began. The new constitution was scheduled to go into effect in summer 2005. Currently, the emir has discretion over the law of the country. Civil codes are being introduced and Islamic law rules all family matters.

The emir and chief-of-state of Qatar is Emir Hamad bin Khalifa Al Thani. Under the supervision of the emir, the prime minister runs Qatar's government. The prime minister is assisted by the first deputy prime minister and the second deputy prime minister. The emir has a cabinet (Council of Ministers) of at least twelve members, all of whom he appoints. Since the monarchy is hereditary, there are no elections.

An Advisory Council was created in 1972 to debate matters referred to it by the Council of Ministers. There are thirty-five elected members on the council. The emir regularly seeks advice from the Advisory Council before rendering his final decision.

Islamic tradition is the basis of Qatar's customs and laws. Violation of Qatari law may result in arrest, imprisonment, or expulsion for the country. Illegal drug charges may result in long prison sentences and/or heavy fines. Driving while under the influence of alcohol is a serious offense, and may result in expulsion from Qatar or a long term of imprisonment. Homosexuality is a criminal offense in Qatar, and any individual convicted of homosexual behavior may receive a lashing as well as a custodial sentence.

Photographing government buildings/institutions is prohibited by law. The use of obscene gestures and/or language often results in arrest and fines, even if the incident is between private parties. Since the law is based on Islamic traditions, all individuals in Qatar (including visitors) are expected to dress in a modest fashion. Sleeveless shirts, halter tops, shorts, and other forms of revealing dress are not tolerated.

Although occurrences are rare, Qatar's laws allow leniency for a male who commits a "crime of honor." This may include a violent assault on a woman perceived to be defiant or immodest. Trafficking and prostitution are illegal in Qatar. Trafficking of children for the purpose of camel race jockeying was a growing problem in Qatar. Although the practice of using children as jockeys is not illegal, issues arose about the age and welfare of some of the jockeys. Consequently, laws were implemented in 2001 that require camel jockeys to wear helmets and safety belts. The government also opened a school for the children who participate in camel jockeying. In 2002, the Camel Racing Association implemented a mandatory minimum weight for the children who jockey the camels.

Before 2004, there were two court systems in Qatar—the Adlea Court and the Shari'a Court. The Adlea Court had jurisdiction in commercial, security, trafficking, and criminal matters. The Shari'a court's jurisdiction encompasses family, deportation, wrongful injury, and most civil matters. Most principles tried in the Shari'a Court fell under principles found in the Family Status Law. Juvenile matters also fell under the Shari'a Court.

In 2004, the Adlea and the Shari'a Courts united to form a Supreme Judiciary Council, responsible for trying all civil and criminal matters, including violations of Islamic law. All defendants have the right to appeal their case. The Court of Appeals is the highest court in Qatar.

All judges are appointed by the emir for a three-year term. Qatar citizenship is not required to be a judge. Many of Qatar's judges are foreign nationals who possess residency permits. Approximately 50% of Qatar's judges are actually citizens of Qatar.

Criminal cases are normally tried within two or three months. Individuals may be released on bail, except in the case of violent offenders. Foreigners released on bail are prohibited from exiting the country until their case is tried.

Punishment for a convicted offender is harsh in Qatar. Prison and jail sentences are often very long.

There is no system of parole in Qatar. Many criminal penalties follow Islamic law. Most forms of corporal punishment are allowed by the government. Lashings and floggings are common forms of punishment. Neither amputation nor physical mutilation is allowed. Punishments are not viewed by the public. The death penalty is allowed under Qatar's law and the last execution took place in 2000. In 2000, three individuals were executed. Before this, the last execution was in 1990.

Prisons in Qatar meet international standards. The government of Qatar allows human right groups to monitor their prisons. The prison system is divided so that women are separate from men, juveniles are separated from adults, and individuals awaiting trial are separated from convicted offenders.

Police Profile

Demographics

Men have historically dominated the Police Force in Qatar. Before 2003, there were only thirty female officers on the Force. Qatar, determined to be the first country in the Middle East to support women's rights, is working to change its policies. In 2003, 107 women graduated from Qatar's police academy. This event marked the first time in history that an entire female squadron participated in the graduation ceremony. Women receive the same pay as men, although their benefits differ slightly. At times, women receive less compensation for transportation and housing.

The entire Police Force is composed of 2,500 individuals. This includes all ranks and officers. The Police Force is highly visible throughout the country, and the police patrol the entire nation of Qatar.

Organizational Description

At the top of the Police Force is the emir, who oversees all actions of the force and approves all laws that are enforced. The Ministry of Interior (in the emir's cabinet) has complete control over the force. The Civilian Security Force is composed of the police and the General Administration of Public Security. The General Administration of Public Security (formerly known as the Criminal Investigation Department) is solely responsible for investigations of criminal activities.

Qatari State Security (QSS) was formed when the Mubahathat (Secret Police Office) combined with the Mubahith (Investigation and State Security Service). Qatari State Security, now a branch of the Ministry of Interior, handles all matters concerning sedition and espionage. The intelligence sector of the QSS is responsible for the interception and arrest of terrorists as well as keeping watch over political disputes.

Functions

Qatar's local police force is responsible for enforcing the laws of Qatar and arresting law violators. The police also monitor communications between suspicious individuals, especially when there could be security risks. Warrants are required for the police to conduct a search in all cases except those involving national security. At times, severe force may be used when investigating political or national security cases. Suspects can be detained without being charged, although this rarely occurs.

Training

Education in Qatar is free from primary school through the university level. Literacy (those age fifteen and older who can read and write), which was a major problem in the early 1900s, is at a high of 82.5% throughout the entire country. The majority of Qatari police officers are well educated.

Aside from public education, Qatari police officers are required to attend the Police Academy in Doha. During their training at the Academy, women undergo the same rigorous training as men. Cadets are trained in areas concentrating on police work and the skills needed to become a professional police officer.

Complaints and Discipline

There are no reported complaints against the Qatari Police Force. Due to the fact that the Qatari government imposes some restrictions on the right of free speech (concerning individuals speaking out against the government), the public may not openly voice complaints about the police.

The prisons in Qatar meet international standards and no reports of prisoner mistreatment by security personnel have been reported. Qatar is open to investigations by human rights groups. Overall, Qatar's human rights violations are minimal as the country continues to make significant progress in the area of human rights.

Amnesty International, an organization opposed to the death penalty, voiced concern when Qatar began using the death penalty again in 2000. This group feels that the death penalty is a violation of human rights.

Terrorism

It has been alleged that in the past, Qatar was a supporter of the Palestine Liberation Organization (PLO), both politically and economically. If this was true, Qatar has now cut all ties with this organization, and condemns the PLO. No proof has been offered that supports the idea that there are terrorist cells operating in Qatar. However, Qatar's location in the Middle East makes the country a viable hideout for terrorist groups.

On February 13, 2004, the former Chechen president, Zelimkhan Yandarbiyev, was assassinated when an explosion in Doha was aimed at his car. His son was also wounded in the attack. This is the first reported terrorist attack in Qatar, and the group responsible is presently unknown.

Qatar's television network, Al-Jazeera Satellite Channel, is privately owned and claims to be free of government influence. The government has paid some of the costs for running Al-Jazeera. Although the terrorist group al-Qaeda is known to use Al-Jazeera to broadcast information, no connection between al-Qaeda and Qatar has been discovered.

The police have jurisdiction when dealing with the possibility of terrorism. Police have full discretion when monitoring prisoners believed to pose a threat to national security. It is not uncommon for the police to monitor communications and/or phone lines of individuals believed to pose a threat to Qatar.

International Cooperation

After Qatar declared independence in 1971, the United Kingdom, most Arab states, and the United States were among the first countries to recognize Qatar. Qatar also gained admittance to the United Nations and the Arab League in 1971. In 1988, Qatar settled disputes and established diplomatic relations with the Soviet Union and China. Although Qatar and Saudi Arabia have been known to engage in minor disputes, relations between the two countries are improving.

Qatar's relationship with the United States remains strong. The two countries are working together to increase security in the Gulf. Qatar willingly allowed U.S. forces to use their land and military bases during the U.S.-led Operation Enduring Freedom.

Qatar is a member of many international organizations, including (but not limited to) Interpol, World Health Organization, International Labor Organization, International Civil Aviation Organization, and the United Nations.

681

Police Education, Research, and Publications

Higher education is Qatar is mainly obtained at the University of Qatar, in Doha. There is no specific degree for police education, but all members of the police force are educated at the police training academy in areas dealing with police work. Carnegie Mellon University in Qatar also offers degrees in business and computer science.

Publications in Qatar were monitored by the Ministry of Information and Culture until 1998. In 1998, this ministry was dismantled and duties were taken over by other ministries. Publishing works containing criticism of the ruling family and government is prohibited. There are four private newspapers in Qatar. Three are printed in Arabic: *Ar Rayah* (The Banner), *El Watan*, and *Ash Sharq* (The East). One newspaper, *Gulf Times*, is printed in English. The acting editor-in-chief of *Gulf Times* is Paul Cowan (P.O. Box 2888 Doha, Qatar; edit@gulf-times.com).

Information about Qatar, including information about the police system, is available at www.qatar-info.com. Statistical information about Qatar is available at www.cia.gov/cia/publications/factbook/geos/qa.html.

AMANDA MARIE SHARP

Bibliography

Aman News Center. "More Women Join Qatar Police Force." 2005. Available at: www.amanjordan.org/english/daily_news/wmview.php?ArtID=1667. Accessed January 17, 2005.

Central Intelligence Agency. *CIA World Factbook. Qatar.* Available at: www.cia.gov/cia/publications/factbook/geos/qa.html. Accessed January 3, 2005.

Freedom House. *Freedom in the World 1998–1999. Qatar.* Available at: http://freedomhouse.org/survey99/country/qatar.html. Accessed January 22, 2005.

Qatar Information. "Political System." Available at: www.qatar-info.com/general/politica.htm. Accessed January 22, 2005.

Terrorism Knowledge Base. *Qatar.* Available at: www.tkb.org/Incident.jsp?incID=18069. Accessed January 26, 2005.

U.S. Department of State. *Country Report on Human Rights Practices: Qatar.* 2004. Available at: www.state.gov/g/drl/rls/hrrpt/2003/27936.htm. Accessed January 3, 2005.

U.S. Department of State. "Consular Information Sheet: Qatar." 2005. Available at: http://travel.state.gov/travel/cia_pa_tw/cis/cis_1003.html. Accessed January 20, 2005.

R

ROMANIA

Background Material

Romania is located in southeastern Europe and covers an area of 238,391 sq km, distributed almost symmetrically on both sides of the Carpathian Mountains. Romania's population currently totals 22,355,551 inhabitants (2004 estimate), 89.4% of which are Romanians. The majority of Romanians are Christian, specifically Eastern Orthodox (88%), although Roman Catholicism (6%), Protestantism (5%), and other religions (1%) are represented.

While the official state language is Romanian, other national minorities' languages are also used in day-to-day life in specific areas, such as Hungarian, German, Turkish, Russian, and other languages. The Romanian economy, with a full-fledged privatization process underway, is based on industry, agriculture, construction, and services. The per capita annual GDP is 6,000 euros.

Contextual Features

Since 1991, when the entire nation voted in favor of the adoption of a new constitution, Romania has been a parliamentary democracy. The head of state is president of the Republic, and is elected by direct vote for a four-year term and for a maximum of two mandates.

The legislative authority is the Parliament, composed of the Deputies Chamber and the Senate, the two chambers having equal powers. The 345 deputies and 140 senators are elected for a four-year mandate on the basis of a system providing for national representation.

The executive branch of the government consists of the prime minister and other ministers. The prime minister, appointed by the president, appoints the other ministers and the government is subject to validation by the Parliament.

Between 1990 and 2002, the fundamental goal of the Ministry of Interior was to reform, reconstruct, modernize, and optimize its structures, as well as to achieve interoperability with similar structures of the European Union states.

The reform process is ongoing. The need to reevaluate the role and the place of the Romanian Police, and of the other structures of the Ministry of Interior in the context of the radical changes sustained as of December 1989, remains urgent.

Police Profile

Background

One cannot fully grasp the significance of the reform of the Romanian Police without some background information on what this institution represented at the beginning of the 1990s. In this respect, after a half-century under the totalitarian regime established after World War II, the Romanian Police system was under the political control of the Communist Party. Politics played a key role in the functioning of the police and mostly at the executive level, since in each police unit there was a political structure. Although frequently the obligations and directives assigned for the police by the Communist Party coincided with actions stipulated by laws, in many cases those exceeded the legal limits because Party policies had to be observed and implemented, irrespective of the methods and means required to implement them. Party membership was a sine qua non condition to enter the system, and hierarchical promotion to executive positions was closely related to an individual's and record with the Party.

Another essential characteristic of the early 1990s police system was its organization and functioning on a military model. Almost all personnel were military, and military discipline and regulations represented not only the premise for a clockwork precise operation, but also the constraining instruments guaranteeing its functioning in the exclusive interest of the ruling Party. The need to hold military status resulted in a significant reduction of the number of women in the police force, and those accepted were confined to administrative functions. Obviously, the psychological impact of a military organization over civil society was fully exploited by Party structures.

At the same time, the police system was based on excessive centralization, intended to ensure a single command for all component structures, and also to ensure the instruments for implementing Party policies down to the lowest levels.

The total isolation behind the Iron Curtain, and the lack of transparency at the level of the nation was also manifest at the level of the police system. While some achievements in preventing and countering crime were made public exclusively for propagandistic exploitation, the dynamics of crime represented one of the most important secrets of the Romanian government, on the basis of the doctrine that there are no crimes in socialism.

Implicitly, the total lack of transparency led to the absence of communication with civil society. In fact, the way the system had been established obstructed communication, with the place and the role of the police force strictly enforced and the Party's dispositions excluded from public debate.

The closure and the rigidity of the police system resulted also in the weak cooperation with the judiciary. In this respect, even if the law stipulated the functional subordination of police structures to the Public Ministry, often this was not the case in practice.

The adoption of Law 40/1990 on the organization and operation of the Ministry of Interior was a first step toward reform. The Ministry of Interior became the central body of the executive power that exercises, according to the law, attributes regarding public order; defends fundamental rights and liberties, public and private property; and prevents and reveals crimes. In this way, the Ministry contributes to the establishment of a democratic society in Romania and preserves its independence, national suzerainty, and territorial integrity.

The year after the adoption of the law on the organization and operation of the Ministry of Interior in 1990, mostly based on the need for change imposed by necessities of the moment, the reform process stalled, and only in 1994 was a new law on the organization and operation of the Romanian Police adopted, Law 26/1994, which aligned the attributes of the police to the provisions of the 1991 Constitution.

The new law represented the first substantial steps towards reform, succeeding, even though sometimes only partially, in resolving some essential problems. First, normality status was regained regarding the role of this institution within the rule of law, providing the fact that the Romanian Police as the specialized state institution that exercises within national territory attributes regarding the protection of the person's fundamental rights and liberties and of public and private wealth, prevention and detection of crime, and maintaining the public order. This rearrangement of the priorities regarding the values that the Romanian police system aims to defend and protect, as well as stipulating the fact that the activity of the Romanian Police is exclusively conducted on the basis of and with a view to enforcing the law, represented the starting point of the real reform process.

Another important step was the inclusion of a constitutional provision regarding the depoliticization of the police system, within the abovementioned normative act, by forbidding its personnel membership in political parties and bodies, while the right to vote remains as guaranteed by the constitution.

After the adoption of this law, the strategy on the Romanian Police reform became more consistent, and actions have been taken according to the following strategic directions:

- Preparing the conditions necessary for transforming the Romanian Police
  into an institution with civilian statutes
  and underlining its role as public service

- Increasing response capability to meet the requirements of the operational situation dynamics by increasing the flexibility of the organic structures, eliminating intermediary links, and decentralization of decision making at the functional-operative level, simultaneous to centralization of strategic decision making at the strategic level
- Changing of organizational culture, renewing and professionalization of personnel based on unitary and coherent programs
- Focusing international relations activity on the accomplishment of this institution's task within the preparations for Romania's accession to the European Union and Euro-Atlantic structures

The above strategic activities were organized and conducted to achieve the following goals:

- Creating the legal framework required for exercising specific missions in optimal conditions
- Institutional reconstruction, decentralization of decision making, responsibilities, and allocation of the resources, up to the level where maximum efficiency and operational response capability can be reached (concentrated at territorial level)
- Modernization of working methods and adjustment to the democratic society's requirements
- Assessment and ensuring of efficient logistic support performance
- Management of human resources and protection of personnel (salaries, life and health insurance, bonuses, holiday houses, leisure activities, and so on)
- Cooperation with public authorities from the defense sector, national security, public order, and justice
- New efficient instruments for planning, organizing, and controlling, adequate to the dynamics of the overall operative situation, in order to ensure an improved management of activities, even under austerity conditions
- Increasing the interoperability level within similar bodies of the European Union in order to maintain the regional stability

The first steps in legislation toward achieving these objectives were taken with the abrogation of all administrative regulations that harmed fundamental human rights and liberties, at the same time as adhering to relevant international legal instruments, such as the European Conventions against torture and for protection of fundamental human rights and liberties, and so on, which were signed and ratified.

The legislative process was conceived and accomplished in two major directions: ensuring a modern legal framework, elastic and perfectly adjusted to the present exercise of the rule of law authority, as well as the harmonization of the internal legislation according to the specific documents initiated by the European Union, especially those of the European Councils of Amsterdam and Helsinki, that aim at alignment to European Union standards. Therefore, a series of high-level normative acts were elaborated and adopted (laws, government decisions, government ordinances) aiming at organization and operation of the Romanian Police and its major component subsystems, the firearms and ammunition regime, countering the illicit traffic and abuse of drugs, precursors' regime, corruption, organized crime, money laundering, trafficking in human beings, and so on. There was also elaborated, on a hierarchical level, a series of internal normative acts, on the basis of the law, which are to allow improved enforcement of high-level legal acts and Romanian Police tasks.

Activities developed to promote and observe human rights and humanitarian international law materialized in improved collaboration with the Romanian Institute for Human Rights and the Romanian Association of Humanitarian Law and with other nongovernmental organizations, organizing intercounty courses, elaborating 120 specific materials for the Ministry of Interior structures, concluding protocols with organizations and institutions, and solving notifications received from natural persons or nongovernmental organizations on violations or alleged violations of human rights.

Without doubt, legislative reforms and enactments reached their highest point in 2002 with the new law on the organization and functioning of the Romanian Police (Law 218/2002), as well as with the Law of the Statute of the Police Officer (Law 360/2002).

Demographics

Presently, the Romanian police system consists of a civilian force—the Romanian Police having 52,000 personnel; a military force—the Romanian Gendarmerie, having around 18,000 personnel; and the community police—Public Guards with 20,000 personnel, subordinated to city halls, conducting activities related to the public order.

Organizational Description and Functions

The new law on the organization and functioning of the Romanian Police stipulates a series of principles and provisions derived from the European Code of Police Ethics. For instance, with regard to police objectives, besides its traditional tasks, new tasks such as preventing and countering terrorism, illegal migration, illegal traffic with radioactive materials, and aspects on providing assistance and service functions to the public were taken into account, by stipulating that Romanian Police activity is a public service, and is carried out in the person's and community's interest, as well as for supporting public institutions, exclusively on the basis of law and through the enforcement of laws. This provision modified the police role, transforming it into a mechanism of community service, ceasing to be exclusively an instrument of coercion.

The law on the police officer statute is the first legal provision regulating the police profession and its position in relation with other professional communities.

Fundamental changes within the structure and tasks of the Romanian Police were conceived as a gradual process, which has to develop from inside, coherently and organized, with clearly defined stages and objectives, based on logical criteria, and in a permanent adjustment to the dynamic of the social reality.

In this respect, the legislative rebuilding actions aimed to:

- Continue the reorganization and restructuring process, seeking to eliminate the parallelisms and the intermediary links, to reduce overdimensioned bodies, to accomplish the concordance between the units tasks and the organizational structure, to increase their interoperability level with the European Union states similar structures
- Correlate new organizational charts with similar structures of the states with advanced democracies, according to the European bodies' recommendations, assumed by the Romanian government, regarding the institutional reform, acknowledged as one of the conditions for accession to the European Union
- Make operative structures more efficient by a rational redistribution of the personnel, in order to increase the efficiency in accomplishing their tasks

The Romanian Police were reorganized into three basic components: Judiciary Police, Public Order Police, and Administrative Police.

The main organization changes consisted of establishing the following structures: Institute for Crime Research and Prevention, Compartments for Human Rights, Brigade for Countering Organized Crime, specialized antidrugs, countering cyber criminality, trafficking in human beings, money laundering, corruption, traffic with radioactive materials, cross-border crime compartments, and Rapid Response Unit in Bucharest and within thirteen county police inspectorates. The Road Police Brigade was reorganized and is now responsible for registration, issuing permits, and drivers' records. The national Europol structure was established within the General Inspectorate of the Police, in order for the Romanian Police to participate in European Community activities for countering organized crime.

The law on the organisation and functioning of the Romanian Police stipulates the establishment of a new structure: the Territorial Authority for Public Order, specially conceived in order to ensure the involvement of civil society in the achievement of its own security environment by contributing to the elaboration of the activity plan and to the settlement of objectives and minimal performance indicators, aiming to protect the community's interests, and to ensure the public safety climate; by notifying and proposing measures for eliminating police activity deficiencies, by organizing consulting meetings with the members of the local community and with nongovernmental organizations regarding individuals' safety and public order priorities by an annual elaborated report on the efficiency of police unit activity, which is to be made public, and so on.

Training

Reconstruction of the Ministry of Interior educational system was completed by transforming the School for Active Officers into an educational institution at the university level, accredited by the Ministry of Education and Research. Within the Police Academy A. I. Cuza, there are four-year courses for training police officers, gendarmes, and firefighters. Upon completion of their studies, individuals graduate with licenses in law, business, or engineering. The Police Academy also offers two-year postgraduate courses or six-year doctoral courses in police specializations.

On the basis on the new law on the organization and functioning of the Romanian police, special attention was directed toward police personnel training by focusing on crime prevention, countering organized crime, humanitarian law and human rights, use of force, intelligence, investigation and undercover activity, and protection of victims, especially women and minors. Actions have also been taken to redistribute the police force in territories according to specific problems and needs, to decrease the average age of the personnel, to increase the force's quality and its compatibility with the specific tasks and missions, to hire minority nationals, and to increase the proportion of women in the police forces.

Police Public Projects

Romania has embraced a new conception of the police that has developed in Europe in recent years: community police. The entire community, in cooperation with the police, plays a role in preventing and combating crime.

One of the basic goals of the Romanian Police is to transform itself into a public service, and to be recognized as such by society in general.

In order to align itself with international standards of community policing, the Territorial Authority for Public Order and the Consultative Council were established. Members of these bodies include police and other representatives of public institutions, as well as civilian representatives, all focused on improving police services by adapting activities to the community's requests and needs. Concurrently, relations between the police and the local public administrative authorities were re-established on a new basis by decentralizing the police.

Police Use of Firearms

Initiatives have been adopted to demilitarize the police. The police officer is defined as an armed civil servant.

The demilitarization of the Romanian police, a unique initiative in southeastern Europe, is a sine qua non condition for transforming the role that the police will play in Romanian society. In their new role, the focus of the police is on public service, without neglecting the judicial function of the police.

Complaints and Discipline

The Ministry of the Interior and the Romanian Police entered into a short-term partnership program with the Ombudsman and domestic nongovernmental organizations (Organization for Human Rights Defense, Association for Human Rights Defense—Helsinki Committee) in order to ensure the protection of human rights. Pursuing the goal of transforming the Romanian Police into a public service, the necessary means for ensuring democratic control of its activity were created. Aware of the need to create mutual confidence between the police and the com-

munity, it is recognized that maintaining the integrity of police personnel integrity is a priority. Therefore, integrity tests are being developed and implemented.

The need for some external control of the police has been recognized as necessary to guarantee a real and objective control of police activities, and to ensure a degree of professionalism and respect for the public. This control is exercised both by the civil authorities—Parliament, Public Ministry, judicial courts—and also by the citizenry through mass media and nongovernmental organizations.

External control is exercised by the legislative branch of the government by its ability to approve budgets, the activities of the Commissions for Defense, Public Order and National Security, and the establishment of special investigative commissions. The administrative branch of the government exercises control through the activities of the Prime Minister's Control Body. The judiciary branch supervises the activities of the Public.

The Court of Counts exercises permanent control over how the Ministry of Interior, including the police, uses the public funds allocated to it. External control of the police is exercised by the citizenry through the constitutional rights afforded to all citizens to register complaints regarding the police.

International Cooperation

Aware that an authentic democracy cannot be achieved outside a greater democratic region, special attention was given to the development of international cooperation and relationships. Particular attention has been paid to establishing and developing such relationships in connection with police structures. The main goals have been cooperation with neighboring countries, and relationships with member states of the European Union, Europol, Cepol, Eurojust, and other states. In order to achieve these goals of cooperation, two positions have been established: that of the liaison officer and that of the internal affairs attaché.

PAVEL ABRAHAM

Bibliography

Abraham, Pavel. *Comunitatea, poliţia şi tranziţia.* Bucharest: Editura Naţional, 1996.

Abraham, Pavel. *Valori democratice şi respectarea drepturilor omului în activitatea de poliţie.* Bucharest: Editura Naţional, 1995.

Abraham, Pavel, Craciun Adriana, and Lucica Rizon. *Legislatie in asistenta sociala.* Vols. 1–2. Bucharest: Editura Naţional, 2003.

Abraham, Pavel, and Ioan Hurdubaie. *Conventii europene in materie penala.* Bucharest: Editura Naţional, 2001.

Abraham, Pavel, Nicolăescu Victor, and Iaşnic Bogdan. *Politia comunitara*. Bucharest: Editura Expert, 2002.

Abraham, Pavel, Nicolăescu Victor, and Iaşnic Bogdan. *Introducere in probatiune*. Bucharest: Editura Naţional, 2001.

Bădescu, Ilie, ed. *Geopolitica integrarii europene*. Bucharest: Editura Universităţii din Bucureşti, 2002.

Carjan, Lazar, ed. *Istoria Politiei Romane de la origini si pana in 1949*. Bucharest: Ed. Vestala, 2000.

Cartea Albă a Ministerului de Interne, 1990–2000, Editura Ministerului de Interne, 2001.

Convenţia pentru Apărarea Drepturilor Omului şi a Libertăţilor Fundamentale, amendată prin Protocoalele nr. 3,5 şi 8 şi completată prin Protocolul nr. 2.

Constituţia României—modificată, MO nr. 767/2003.

Hotărârea Camerei Deputaţilor nr. 8/1994 privind adoptarea Regulamentului Camerei Deputaţilor a României, MO nr. 50/1994.

Hotărârea Guvernului nr. 137/1991 privind organizarea şi funcţionarea Academiei de Poliţie Alexandru Iona Cuza.

Hotărârea Guvernului nr. 314/2001 privind înfiinţarea, organizarea şi funcţionarea comisiilor de dialog social în cadrul unor ministere şi prefecturi.

Hotărârea Guvernului nr. 438/2004 privind adoptarea Codului deontologic al poliţistului.

Hotărârea Senatului nr. 16/1993 privind apdoptarea Regulamentului Senatului României, MO nr. 58/2001.

Legea pentru organizarea serviciului administraţiunii centrale, 19 aprilie 1892.

Legea Ministerelor din 1929, MO nr. 168/08/02/1929.

Legea nr. 40/1990 privind organizarea şi funcţionarea Ministerului de Interne, MO nr. 146/12/18/1990.

Legea nr. 92/1992 pentru organizare judecătorească, MO nr. 197/08/12/1992.

Legea nr. 80/1995 privind statutul cadrelor militare, MO nr. 155/07/20/1995.

Legea nr. 26/1996 privind organizarea şi funcţionarea Poliţiei Române.

Legea nr. 35/1997privind organizarea şi funcţionarea instituţiei Avocatului Poporului, MO 048/03/20/1997.

Legea nr. 195/2000 privind constituirea şi organizarea clerului military, MO nr. 561/11/13/2002.

Legea nr. 90/2001 privind organizarea si funţionarea Guvernului României şi a Ministerelor, MO nr. 116/2001.

Legea nr. 195/2001 privind voluntariatul, cu modificările ulterioare.

Legea nr. 128/2002 privind organizarea şi funcţionarea Poliţiei Române.

Legea nr. 360/2002 privind Statutul Poliţistului, MO nr. 440/06/24/2002.

Legea nr. 656/2002 privind organizarea asistenţei şi protecţiei martorilor.

Legea nr. 39/2003 privind prevenirea şi combaterea crimei organizate, MO 050/01/29/2003.

Ordonanţa Guvernului nr. 26/2000 cu privire la asociaţii şi fundaţii.

Ovidius Paun, ed. *Politia Romana—1990–1996*. Bucharest: Tipografia Inspectoratului General al Politiei Bucuresti, 1997.

RUSSIA

Background Material

Since becoming an independent state in 1991, Russia has undergone far-reaching changes to its political, economic, and legal systems. While reforms have created opportunities, they have also led to a high degree of uncertainty and insecurity in previously taken-for-granted areas, such as employment, education, and health. And whereas society may as a whole enjoy greater civil liberties, some groups continue to face repression from the country's law enforcement agencies. Greater freedom has also generated growth in nationalist and separatist movements, the most serious being the prolonged and bloody conflict in the Chechen Republic (Chechnya). Rising crime levels throughout the 1990s also generated much concern among the public and politicians alike, fueling demands for police reform, which is now on the government agenda.

Russia is the world's largest country, extending from Saint Petersburg on the Baltic Sea to the Pacific Ocean port of Vladivostok across eleven time zones.

The population of Russia is 143,782,338 (July 2004 estimate). Of all the former Soviet states, the Russian Federation is the most ethnically diverse and includes (figures for 2000) Russians (81.5%), Tatars (3.8%), Ukrainian (3%), Chuvash (1.2%), Bashkir (0.9%), Belarussian (0.8%), Moldavian (0.7%), and other groups (8.1%). The official language is Russian, although around 100 other languages are spoken by the country's numerous ethnic groups.

Per capita annual income is US$1,660 (2000 estimate); and purchasing power parity, US$8,900 (Central Intelligence Agency 2002 estimate). Major economic activities include mining and extraction (coal, oil, gas, chemicals, metals); machine building;

shipbuilding; road and rail transport equipment; communications equipment; agricultural machinery; and construction equipment.

Contextual Features

The Russian Federation is the largest of the fifteen successor states that emerged from the dissolution of the Soviet Union in 1991, following several years of attempts to reform the communist system that had existed since 1917.

The federation comprises 89 federal jurisdictions (*subzhekty*), including 49 *oblasts* (provinces), 21 autonomous republics, 10 autonomous *okrugs* (districts), 6 *krais* (territories), 2 federal cities (Moscow and Saint Petersburg), and 1 autonomous *oblast*. In 2001, an additional layer of administration was added with the creation of seven federal regions.

Reform was initiated in the mid-1980s by Mikhail Gorbachev, then General Secretary of the Communist Party of the Soviet Union, whose name became synonymous with his polices of "glasnost" (openness) and "perestroika" (restructuring or reform). The process of reform continued under Boris Yeltsin, Russia's first president, who oversaw the privatisation of state enterprises and the development of market relations, which had far-reaching economic and social consequences for Russia's people. For a minority, the liberalisation of the economy created vast wealth, while for many it led to growing impoverishment. The financial crisis of August 1998 aggravated the situation further. Although the economic situation appears to have stabilised, Russia still faces significant problems and challenges, primarily linked to the lack of legal order.

Although many legal reforms have been introduced, critics argue that commitment to the rule of law in Russia is half-hearted and that the judicial and legal systems are obstacles to the fight against crime and corruption, problems that undermine the economy and society as a whole, as well as obstructing the protection of human and civil rights.

Official crime rates more than doubled between 1988 and 2001. Economic and social instability has been blamed for this increase, but other factors are relevant, including weaker police and gun control, and escalating levels of drug-related crime, including trafficking, which is one of the country's biggest international problems. Among Russia's other crime problems, organised crime figures prominently. Russia also boasts some of the highest murder rates in the world, earning it a reputation as a violent country.

Less serious crimes have also increased, especially property-related offences, which are the most commonly recorded crimes.

Corruption was endemic during the Soviet era and continues to permeate Russian society. According to Transparency International's annual corruption index, Russia ranks among the world's most corrupt countries. Within Russia, the militia (police) are considered the most corrupt agency by the public, making them appear part of the crime problem rather than the solution.

The Constitution of the Russian Federation was adopted on 12 December 1993, establishing Russia as a federal presidential republic with a bicameral legislature. Since then, many legal reforms have been introduced, including the adoption of new Criminal (1997) and Civil Codes (1995). In spite of such progress, critics argue that reforms have not gone far enough to resolve the problems facing the criminal justice system.

The government consists of three branches: the executive, legislative, and judicial branches. The executive branch is headed by the chief of state—the President—who is elected by popular ballot for a four-year term. The government comprises the premier (prime minister), four deputy premiers, ministers, and other agency heads, all of whom are appointed by the president.

The legislative branch is the bicameral Federal Assembly (Federalnoye sobraniye), composed of the Federation Council (Sovet federatsii) upper house and the State Duma (Gosydarstvennaya duma) lower house. Members of the Federation Council are appointed for four years by the chief executives and legislative officials in each of the eighty-nine federal jurisdictions. Members of the State Duma are elected by direct popular vote for four years.

The judicial branch comprises the Constitutional Court, Supreme Court, and Superior Court of Arbitration (Commercial Court).

The court system in Russia is governed by the Justice Ministry, which has territorial branches throughout the Federation. The country's highest judicial body is the Supreme Court of the Russian Federation, which has the right of legislative initiative. The next level of the judiciary encompasses the supreme courts of the federal jurisdictions. Most cases (98% to 99%) are judged by general courts at the lowest level—the people's courts located throughout the country—which are also responsible for judging administrative offences, complaints about unlawful behaviour and arrest, and implementing court decisions.

Most cases are heard by judges, who must act independently, basing their decisions on the rule of law (Law "On the status of judges," 1992). However, their independence is often questioned, as Russian judges may find it difficult to act independently of political structures, upon whom they are dependent not only for their jobs, but in many cases for their homes, cars, medical coverage, and so on.

The legal system has long been criticised for providing wide powers to prosecutors and few rights to defendants, but this may change as, following a pilot project, jury trials were scheduled to be phased in across much of the federation during 2003/2004.

The Russian legal system is a civil law system and based on judicial review of legislative acts. Sources of law include the Russian Constitution, federal constitutional law, federal laws, and the laws of the federal jurisdictions. Since the adoption of the Russian Constitution, many new laws and amendments have been introduced, suggesting that the rule of law is being established in Russia. However, the criminal justice system is far from the independent and law-based structure necessary for the rule of law to prevail. For example, although many new laws have been introduced, they are not necessarily adhered to, and even where court rulings are made they may not be applied. As a result, in areas such as business, people may bypass the court system in favour of informal mechanisms to resolve disputes and seek redress. Such mechanisms include private arbitration and enforcement through the use of the militia, private security guards, or criminal groups.

All crimes are indicated in the Russian Criminal Code (1997), which is the sole source of criminal legislation. The Code classifies crime into various categories that determine how offenders are sentenced and the type of correctional institution to which they may be sent:

- Serious offences (*tyazhki* or *osobo tyazhki*) include rape, kidnapping, treason, espionage, crimes against the justice system, serious violent crimes, and murder.
- Minor offences (*nebol'shoi* or *srednei tyazhesti*) include property offences, hooliganism, and offences against public order.

Official statistics from the Ministry of Internal Affairs (MVD: Ministerstvo Vnutrennykh Del) put the total number of crimes recorded in 2001 at 2,968,255 (MVD 2002). This represented an increase of 0.5% over the previous year, but some types of offences had increased to a greater extent than others, including certain serious crimes such as murder (up 5.5%) and grievous bodily harm (up 12%). The most commonly recorded crime was theft of property, which accounted for 43% of all recorded offences, while economic crime (fraud, extortion, etc.) represented 13%. The number of crimes recorded in connection with the illegal trade in drugs increased by 45%, accounting for 11% of crime. In addition to criminal offences, the Russian police annually process 75 million administrative offences. Official statistics, however, only tell part of the Russian crime story, mainly as a result of the way in which militia performance has traditionally been measured, using clear-up rate targets, which makes many officers reluctant to record incidents that they have little chance of clearing. The MVD estimates that less than one-quarter of all crimes committed are officially recorded by the militia, but victim surveys suggest that actual crime rates are much higher (Zvekic 1998; Beck and Robertson 2002).

The role of the penal system is largely to punish offenders, sometimes through hard labour. Although the law does provide for rehabilitation services upon completion of sentences, insufficient funding means that those released from prison are largely left to fend for themselves.

The prison system is governed by the Main Directorate of Administering Punishment (GUIN: Glavnoe upravlenie ispolneniya nakazaniya), which was transferred from the MVD to the Ministry of Justice in 2000. The prison system encompasses various types of correctional establishment (IU: Ispravitel'no-trudovoe ucherezhdeniye) for sentenced and remand prisoners. Conditions and restrictions depend upon the level of security of any given IU, to which prisoners are sentenced by court order.

As of January 1, 2002, 976,000 inmates were being held in Russia's penal institutions, 23% of whom were on remand. With 638 inmates per 100,000, Russia occupies third place on London's Home Office World Prison Population List after the United States and the Cayman Islands.

Police Profile

Background

The police as a key state institution first appeared in Russia during the early nineteenth century, prior to which police functions were carried out alongside other judicial and administrative functions by various state bodies. During their long history, police bodies have undergone many changes, but their central function of maintaining public order and fighting crime has ensured continuity in their development.

The history of the police system in Russia can be divided into four main stages of development:

Stage 1 covers the ninth to the beginning of the eighteenth century, during which time groups existed that carried out police, as well as other functions. The first investigative groups appeared during the fifteenth century, when special local crime-fighting offices were created along with a central investigative unit, the Razbojniye prikaz.

Stage 2 lasted from the early eighteenth century to the 1917 Great October Revolution. During this period, a regular police force was developed as a specialised body released from other duties except for those directly required for the establishment of the organisation. In 1802, the Ministry of Internal Affairs was created as the central body in command of the police. Between 1860 and 1880, city and district police groups were merged, conditions of service were changed, and the functions of the police were narrowed.

Stage 3 covers the establishment and development of the Soviet militia (1917–1991). The Soviet authorities perceived the chief function of the militia not to protect public order and fight crime, but to operate as their agents and suppress opposition, be it political, ideological, or economic. The militia initially existed as informal units of workers, including Red Guards, voluntary people's brigades, special guard units, and public order units. These units were consolidated by a decree from the People's Commissariat of Internal Affairs (the NKVD) in October 1917. One year later the NKVD and the People's Commissariat of Justice (NKYu) ratified the "Instructions for the Organization of a Soviet Workers' and Peasants' Militia," thus establishing an official state body for the maintenance of public order. The militia was characterised by a centralized management apparatus, which excluded any control on the part of the public, a high level of militarization, and an extensive range of powers regulated not by laws, but by directives. This paved the way for widespread abuse and made the militia strictly dependent upon the ruling elite. Between the 1930s and 1950s, the rigid centralization of militia control was consolidated, and a strict policy of political repression largely determined its functions and activities. The sociopolitical "thaw" under Khrushchev (late 1950s/early 1960s) marked a special period in the history of the Soviet militia, resulting in some positive shifts, but limited and inconsistent structural change or efforts to fight illegal behaviour within its ranks. The 1970s and 1980s witnessed an improvement in the status of the militia and the beginning of a process of specialisation. During the late 1980s, efforts were made to improve police training and discipline, and to devolve control of the police throughout the Soviet Union, with the aim of responding better to local needs and dealing more effectively with serious problems such as drug trafficking and organised crime. Although

some progress was made, the militia remained authoritarian and further reforms were hampered by the redirection of MVD resources to groups such as the OMON (Otryad militsii osobogo naznacheniya), the Special Designation Police Detachments (see below).

With the collapse of the Soviet Union in 1991, Stage 4 in the development of the militia began with the formation of a sovereign Russia and the declared intention to create a legal state. This has proved far from easy. During the early 1990s, President Yeltsin expanded police powers, but with little effect, and crime continued to increase. Although some of the security agencies, such as the KGB (Komitet gosudarstvennoi bezopasnosti: the State Security Committee), were reorganised, law enforcement agencies have remained largely unchanged, perhaps because they are not equipped to deal with the changes to policing required (Shelly 1999). They remain in need of radical reform.

Demographics

The secretive nature of the MVD makes it difficult to obtain precise information on personnel levels, but using the data available and a process of extrapolation, it is estimated that around 1.1 million people are employed in the MVD system, including its teaching establishments. Women represent around 12% of all staff in the MVD system, including 20% of teaching and research staff at MVD establishments. High turnover is reported to be a serious problem, caused by poor pay and conditions and low morale. Officers leave the militia to work in related spheres such as the private security industry, where pay and conditions are considerably better. However, many of those who remain in the militia also engage in other activities, both legal (such as providing security services, and retail trade or taxi services) and illegal (taking bribes, registering stolen cars, dealing in drugs and arms, selling fake passports) to supplement their wages (Kosals 2003).

Organizational Description

The militia form part of the MVD, which is responsible for regular police functions such as maintaining public order, investigating and preventing crime, and traffic control, but also for vehicle registration, transportation security, and issuing visas and passports. The MVD operates at both central and local levels: The central apparatus is administered from Moscow, but MVD organisations exist throughout the Federation.

Command Structure

- MVD Ministerstvo vnutrennykh del (Ministry of Internal Affairs)
- GUVD (Glavnoe upravlenie vnutrennykh del) Main Internal Affairs Directorate (a major city police command)
- UVD (Upravlenniya vnutrennykh del) Directorate of Internal Affairs
- (Police HQ in each of the administrative Divisions of the Federation) OVD (Otdel vnytrennykh del)
- Internal Affairs Department (generally a subcommand of an UVD) GOVD (Gorodskoi otdel vnutrennykh del) and ROVD (Raionnyi otdel vnutrennykh del) City and District Internal Affairs Departments (Local police command: generally subordinated to an UVD or GUVD)
- OM (Otdel militsii) Police Department (police station/precinct)

The Ministry of Internal Affairs is in charge of all militia officers. The militias of the administrative divisions of the Russian Federation are controlled by the ministers of internal affairs of the republics (heads of GUVDs, UVDs), who are appointed and removed from office by the Minister of Internal Affairs in agreement with the chief executives of the federal jurisdictions. In the districts, cities, and territories, the militias are headed by the chiefs of internal affairs departments (OVDs). As part of the trend toward decentralisation, some cities such as Moscow have formed their own militias, which are locally financed and work together with their MVD counterparts. A law has been drafted on the creation of municipal forces throughout the country to work alongside a federal police force, federal investigations service, and national guard.

Functions

The Russian militia is a public agency, part of the executive branch of government. Its overall functions are to protect the life, health, rights, and freedoms of the public; and to protect property and the interests of the state and society from criminal and other unlawful infringements. The militia's main tasks are contained in the 1991 Law on the Militia and include ensuring individual safety; preventing crimes and administrative offences; detecting and clearing crimes; maintaining public order and safety; protecting personal, state, municipal and other forms of property; and rendering assistance to individuals and groups to protect their rights and legal interests. They are expected to defend the rights and freedoms of everyone, irrespective of gender, race, nationality, mother tongue, place of birth or residence, property or position, religious beliefs, membership of public organisations, or other circumstances.

The militia are subdivided into the Public Security Militia (Militsiya obshestvennoi bezopasnosti) and the Criminal Militia (Kriminal'naya militsiya), both of which are subordinated to the Federal MVD and the MVDs of the federal jurisdictions. The Public Security Militia is also subordinate to local authorities.

The public security or local militia run police stations, temporary detention centres, and the State Road Safety Inspectorate. They deal with crimes outside the jurisdiction of the criminal militia (including those not requiring a preliminary investigation) and are responsible for maintaining law and order. Their main functions are to prevent crime; react to offences and detain suspects; guard property; assist the criminal militia and other police services to detect crimes and apprehend offenders; and to maintain order and security during public meetings, demonstrations, and other events. The PSM are also responsible for issuing administrative penalties.

The number of militia officers required in any area is established on the basis of norms; for example, in cities and towns the norm is one officer per 1,000 to 1,500 inhabitants, while in rural areas the norm is one officer per 120 to 150 households.

The largest service within the PSM is the Patrol Service (Patryl'no-postovaya sluzhba), which is the "beat" element of the Russian militia and subdivided into post and patrol units:

- A post is a unit comprising one or several police offices responsible for maintaining public order in a specific location (beat).
- A patrol is a mobile unit comprising one or several officers who carry out duties assigned to them on a specific patrol route (by bicycle, boat, car, helicopter, motorbike, or on horseback).

The PSM encompasses other services, including:

- The State Road Safety Inspectorate (GIBDD: Gosygarstvennaya inspektsiya bezopasnosti dorozhnogo dvizhenyia), which is responsible for road and vehicle safety.
- The Extra-Departmental Guard Service (UVO: Upravleniye vnevedomstvennoi okhrany), which receives no funding from the MVD, but provides security guard services to companies and individuals purely on a commercial basis. As such, it is generally much better equipped and pays higher wages than the regular militia.
- Passport and visa services.
- Secret and classified objects militia (guards).
- Transport and special transportation militia (guards).

- Department of Work with Juvenile Delinquents (Otdel po pabote s nesovershennoletnimi pravonarushitelyami).

In towns and cities where the population exceeds 200,000 or the crime situation is perceived to be serious, Special Designation Militia Detachments (OMON) also exist. These units were first created in 1987 to deal with terrorist incidents and serious criminal activities, and to maintain order during mass public unrest. OMON units are regarded as having the best and most up-to-date weapons and equipment available.

The Criminal Militia (CM) are responsible for preventing, disclosing, and detecting criminal offences. They also search for missing persons, escaped prisoners, and others seeking to avoid questioning, trial or punishment. The CM includes detectives, scientific and technical support, and other departments required to fulfil its duties.

The CM include the Criminal Investigations Department (OUR: Otdel ugolovnogo rozyska), which is subdivided in accordance with the needs of each regional or district police department along the following lines of activity:

- Property crimes—fraud, arson and intentional property damage, robbery and burglary, car theft, illegal sale of firearms, and explosives.
- Crimes against people's health and life—murder, intentional cause of serious injuries, rape.

The CM also includes units responsible for fighting particular types of crime, such as:

- Directorate for Combating Economic Crime (UBEP: Upravleniye po bor'be s ekonomicheskimi prestupleniyami)
- Directorate for Combating the Illegal Trade in Drugs (UNON: Upravleniye po bor'be s nezakonnym oborotom narkotikov)
- Directorate for Combating Organised Crime (UBOP: Upravleniye po bor'be s organizovannoi prestupnost'yu)

In addition to the PSM and CM, other MVD units include:

- Transport Militia, responsible for policing the country's rail, water, and air transport systems.
- Internal Troops of the Ministry of Internal Affairs (VV: Vnutrennie voiska), which are part of the armed forces, but subordinated to the MVD. Their job is to defend the interests of individuals, society, and the state, as well as the constitutional rights and freedoms of members of the public from criminal and other unlawful infringements. They also participate in counterterrorist activities.
- The Spetsnaz (Voiska spetsial'nogo naznacheniya), which are the Internal Troops' special forces. These came under the control of the MVD in 1992 and are primarily deployed in trouble spots to deal with local conflicts. Spetsnaz units have gained notoriety for activities during "counterterrorist" campaigns in the Chechen Republic.

Training

To join the Russian militia requires a period of professional training in specialised MVD training or educational establishments. Candidates must be between eighteen and thirty-five, have completed secondary (high) school, and have no prior convictions. Recruits serve a probation period of between three months and one year, depending on their level of education and the post to which they are appointed.

MVD educational establishments include:

- The MVD Academy of Management in Moscow, which provides senior-level training, lasting for three years. Cadets are usually selected from among serving officers with a law degree and work experience in the militia, but exceptional graduates of MVD higher educational establishments may also be accepted.
- Higher MVD Educational Establishments provide a 4.5-year course on law-enforcement activity, which largely follows the typical five-year law degree programme provided by civilian institutions, but with special training in the use of firearms, and intensive physical and self-defence training. Militia personnel with no legal training or education may also study by distance learning: courses last for five years and are conducted in study schools ("sessions"). Militia personnel with a high school law education (two years) may study by distance learning for three years to gain a law degree.

Militia high schools provide legal education at the secondary level. Training is provided on campus only for two years. Entrance requirements for high schools are the same as for entrance to the militia's higher educational establishments.

Militia training centres provide six-month basic training for new militia employees with no legal education. Students study such subjects as basic law, criminal law, the legal process and forensics, use of weapons, police behaviour in extreme situations, self-defence, and physical education.

Police Public Projects

Public opinion polls repeatedly show that the public is dissatisfied with the militia, do not trust them, think they are corrupt, and doubt their abilities to prevent and solve crimes, which adversely affects relations between them. Surveys also show, however, that the public are prepared to work with the militia, provided that the right conditions exist for such cooperation (Beck and Robertson 2002). In 2002, a Centre for Social Partnership between Law Enforcement Agencies and the Public was set up at the Smolensk branch of the Moscow MVD University to study the theory and practice of police/public cooperation.

Police Use of Firearms

Militia officers are routinely armed and entitled to use firearms to defend themselves and members of the public, gain the release of hostages, detain suspects, and prevent escapes. The use of firearms and other special means are not permitted against pregnant women, the disabled, and juveniles unless they are in a group, armed, or presenting a clear danger to others. Militia officers must undergo special training and also regular checks on their capacity to act in situations where they may be required to use firearms. Any officer who discharges a firearm must inform their chief within twenty-four hours of the incident. A total of 759 cases of deaths and injuries sustained by police use of firearms were recorded in 2001. During 2002 more than 350 regular militia officers were killed while on duty.

Complaints and Discipline

Members of the public who consider that militia activity or lack thereof has infringed on their rights, freedoms, or legal interests may complain to the Internal Security Service (Sluzhba sobstvennoi bezopastnosti), which polices the militia, or the prosecutor's office, which works closely with the militia on a daily basis. The militia are responsible for any illegal activity or for failing to act when called upon to do so, and may be held liable for any losses consequently suffered by individuals or organisations. Compensation may be payable in accordance with civil law. In 2002, 61,000 claims were made against the militia, around half of which were upheld.

Corruption is by far the greatest problem within the militia, and for many taking bribes is considered normal practice. Many factors play a role in militia corruption, including low wages, poor legal consciousness, and lack of respect for the law (Shelley 1999). More than 21,000 police officers were censured for criminal and other offences in 2002, 17,000 of whom were sacked.

The militia have come under much criticism for human rights violations, particularly from Amnesty International (2002), which claims that torture and ill treatment are routine in Russian police stations. They partly blame inadequate training, poor pay and conditions, and pressure to clear crimes quickly (by getting confessions, for example), but argue that such practices continue because the perpetrators are never brought to justice. Human Rights Watch has lodged complaints against the militia for their treatment of ethnic minorities, who tend to be stereotyped as "terrorists" and "drug dealers." Although Russia is a signatory to international human rights conventions, well-documented incidents of abuse suggest that very little is done to ensure respect for human rights either inside or outside the militia. Programmes have been developed and implemented to raise awareness of, and respect for, human rights among the militia, and courses exist for cadets and officers, but usually as special noncompulsory rather than core courses.

Terrorism

The Federal Security Service (FSB: Federal'naya sluzhba bezopasnosti) is the main organisation charged with fighting terrorism, although it relies on the assistance of many other organisations, including the regular militia, Internal Troops, and Spetsnaz units. In March 2003 a presidential reshuffle strengthened the role of the FSB with a view to increasing efficiency between government agencies in fighting terrorism. Recent terrorist acts include the hostage taking by Chechen rebels at the Moscow theatre in October 2002, which resulted in 120 deaths, including all the hostage takers. In July 2003, female suicide bombers struck Moscow, killing 13 and injuring many more. Prior to this, more than 300 people lost their lives in a series of apartment bomb blasts in Moscow, Buinaksk, and Volgodonsk in 1999. The Russian government blamed Chechen terrorists and used the blasts to justify its second military campaign in the breakaway republic.

International Cooperation

Russia has borders with many different countries, including Azerbaijan, Belarus, China, Estonia, Finland, Georgia, Kazakhstan, Latvia, Mongolia, Norway, and Ukraine. The Russian enclave of Kaliningrad, which is cut off from the rest of Russia, borders Poland and Lithuania. With so many borders, cooperation with neighbouring countries is vital. Bilateral agreements and pacts between law enforcement agencies exist to tackle various issues, particularly those of an international nature, including organised crime, money laundering, drugs and human trafficking. For example, the United States and Russia cooperate on drugs, with attachés from the Federal Bureau of Investigation, Drug Enforcement Agency, Customs, and Secret Service posted permanently in Russia. There are also more than thirty branches of Interpol in Russia.

International cooperation exists in many fields, including training and education, research, and practice. Links have been developed between training academies in Russia and colleagues in Europe (France, Finland, Germany, United Kingdom), the Far East (China, Japan, Vietnam), and North America (United States). Cooperation takes the form of joint research projects, conferences, symposiums, seminars, training, and personnel exchanges. Topics covered include human rights issues, organised crime, counterfeiting, economic crime, computer crime, international banking, working with the public, and public safety. Organisations involved include the International Human Rights Federation, the Federal Bureau of Investigations, Central Intelligence Agency, Red Cross, the U.S. State Department, United Nations, and the Council of Europe.

Many overseas government agencies, educational establishments, and other organisations have provided training assistance to Russian law enforcement agencies. The scope of such assistance is wide, and has included counternarcotics assistance from the United States, focusing on improving law enforcement capacities and developing judicial reforms as well as reducing drug demand; courses and study tours at the International Law Enforcement Academy in Budapest; training the trainer courses facilitated by the European Union's Tempus Tacis programme and training links between the United Kingdom's Peel Centre at Hendon and the Saint Petersburg MVD University.

Exchanges have included delegations of Russian and American police cadets and trainers under the auspices of Project Harmony. Research or study tours are more common and law enforcement officers, cadets, and the trainers have visited countries such as Austria, Belgium, China, France, Hungary, United Kingdom, and the United States to improve their qualifications and exchange professional experience. In March 2002, at the initiative of the MVD, the Volgograd MVD Law Academy established the Centre for the Adaptation and Introduction of Foreign Law Enforcement Experience with the aim of improving both the training and activity of law enforcement staff by using the latest Russian and overseas experience and methods.

Police Education, Research, and Publications

The MVD Academy of Management in Moscow is the country's top militia educational establishment. The Ministry also has four MVD Academies (Moscow, Nizhny Novgorod, Omsk, and Volgograd); two MVD Universities (Moscow and Saint Petersburg); and more than twenty MVD institutes, fifteen colleges/higher schools, and 136 training centres throughout the country. The MVD has its own research institute, the MVD National Scientific Research Institute, which is based in Moscow.

Leading authors include:

V. Chernikov, Head of MVD Directorate

Y. Gilinskiy, Professor of Law, Saint Petersburg Law Institute of the General Prosecutor's Office

A. Ivashchenko, Professor of Criminology and Crime Prevention, Faculty Chief, Omsk Law Academy

I. Kilyaskhanov, Faculty Chief, Moscow MVD University

V. Kvashis, MVD National Scientific Research Institute, Moscow

P. Ponomarev, MVD National Scientific Research Institute, Moscow

V. Revin, MVD Academy of Management, Moscow

V. Seliverstov, Deputy Presidential Ombudsman for Human Rights

Y. Solovei, Rector, Omsk Juridical Institute

A. Zubkov, MVD Academy of Management, Moscow

Apart from Gilinskiy, very few Russian academics publish outside Russia or in English, making access to texts difficult.

Specific information on Russian sources of funding is not available, but overseas organisations that have funded research on policing in Russia include the U.S. Agency for International Development, the United Kingdom's Department for International Development (DfID), the Open Society Justice Initiative, and the European Union. Areas of recent research include police corruption, human rights training, and burglary prevention.

Relevant journals and magazines include:

Rossiskaya yustitsiya (Russian Justice). V.N. Rudnev (Ed.), 38/40 Zemlyanoi val, Moscow, 103064, Russia

Zhurnal Rossiiskogo prava (Journal of Russian Law). V.N. Ryabinin (Ed.), 34 B. Cheremushkinskaya Street, Moscow, Russia

Pravovedeniye (Law). I.Yu. Kozlikhin (Ed.), 26 23rd Liniya Street, Saint Petersburg, 199026, Russia

Zakonnost' (Rule of Law). I.P. Zaikin (Ed.), 6/9 B. Dmitrovka Street, Moscow, 101999, Russia

Gosudarstvo i pravo (State and Law). B.N. Topornin (Chair of Editorial Commission), 10 Znamenka Street, Moscow, 119992, Russia

Militsiya (The Police). A.V. Azarov (Ed.), 24 Ivanovskaya Street, Moscow, 127434, Russia

Shchit i mech (The Shield and the Sword). V. Kulik (Ed.), 24 Ivanovskaya Street, Moscow, 127434, Russia

Police-related websites

MVD: *www.mvdinform.ru*
Federal Traffic Police: *www.gai.ru/*
Extra-Departmental Guards: *www.uvo.ru/*
Moscow Police Trade Union:
   www.prof-police.ru/
Ministry of Justice: *www.scli.ru/_mjrf.asp*

ADRIAN BECK AND ANNETTE ROBERTSON

Bibliography

Amnesty International. Amnesty International Report on Russia. 2002. Available at: www.amnesty.org/russia/briefing.html. Accessed March 21, 2003.

Beck, A., and Robertson, A. *Public Attitudes to Crime and Policing in Three Russian Cities: Burglary, Victimisation and the Police Response*. Research Report for the Department of International Development. Leicester: Scarman Centre, 2002.

Beck, A., and Robertson, A. "Crime in Russia: Exploring the Link Between Victimisation and Concern About Crime." *International Journal of Crime Prevention and Community Safety* 27–46 (2003).

Central Intelligence Agency. The World Factbook. "Russia." 2002. Available at: www.cia/gov/cia/publications/factbook/print.rs.html. Accessed January 7, 2003.

Federation of American Scientists. *World Factbook of Criminal Justice Systems*. 1995. Available at: www.fas.org/irp/world/russia/docs/wfbcjrus.htm. Accessed August 19, 2002.

Gilinsky, Y. *Crime and Deviance: Stare from Russia*. St. Petersburg: St. Petersburg Branch of Institute of Sociology of the Russian Academy of Sciences, Baltic University of Ecology, Politics and Law, 2000.

Gustafson, T. *Capitalism Russian-Style*. Cambridge: Cambridge Univeristy Press, 1999.

Human Rights Watch. *Briefing Paper on the Situation of Ethnic Chechens in Moscow*. 2003. Available at: www.hrw.org/backgrounder/eca/russia032003.htm. Accessed April 4, 2003.

Kosals, L. "Informal Economic Activities of the Police in Russia: Sociological Analysis." Moscow: Institute of Population Studies, 2003.

Lotspeich, R. "Crime in the Transition Countries." *Europe-Asia Studies* 47, no. 4 (1995): 555–589.

Moscow Centre for Prison Reform. Available at: www.prison.org/english. Accessed May 23, 2002.

Shelley, L. *Policing Soviet Society: The Evolution of State Control*. London: Routledge, 1996.

Shelley, L. "Post-Socialist Policing: Limitations on Institutional Change." In *Policing Across the World: Issues for the Twenty-first Century*, edited by R. I. Mawby, London: UCL Press, 1999.

Timoshenko, S. "Moscow (Russia)." In *Understanding Crime: Experiences of Crime and Crime Control*, edited by Alvazzi del Frate, A., Zvekic, U., and van Dijk, J., 605–614. Publication No. 49. Rome: United Nations Interregional Crime and Justice Research Institute, 1993.

Timoshenko, S. "The International Crime Victim Survey in Moscow (Russia) 1996." *The International Crime Victim Survey in Countries in Transition: National Reports*, edited by Hatalak, N., Alvazzi del Frate, A., and Zvekic, U., 459–476. Publication No. 62. Rome: United Nations Interregional Crime and Justice Research Institute.

Walmsley, R. *World Prison Population List*. London: Home Office, 2003.

Zakon, RSFSR. "O militsii" (Law on the militia). 1991. Available at: http://zakon.kuban.ru/sayt/milo1.shtml. Accessed March 7, 2003.

Zvekic, U. *Criminal Victimisation in Countries in Transition*. Rome: United Nations Interregional Crime and Justice Research Institute, 1998.

RWANDA

Background Material

Rwanda, or the Rwandese Republic, is situated in the Central African Great Rift Valley, about two degrees south of the Equator. Because of its elevation, the climate is relatively temperate. Rwanda is surrounded on the east and west by Tanzania and Zaire, respectively, and is bordered on the north by Uganda. The Akanyaru River to the south and the Kagera River Valley to the east splits Rwanda from neighboring Burundi. Rwanda has a total area of 26,338 sq km.

The population of Rwanda is 7,954,013 (July 2004 estimate). The capital is Kigali. Languages spoken include Kinyarwanda (official), French (official), English (official), and Swahili. A majority (56.5%) of the nation is Roman Catholic, followed by Protestant (26%), Adventist (11.1%), Muslim (4.6%), and an adherence to indigenous beliefs (0.1%).

According to published accounts and legends, beginning in the fifteenth century, Tutsi herdsmen began relocating to Rwanda from the Horn of Africa, and slowly subjugated the Hutu populations. The Hutus were the original inhabitants of the land. They established a dynastic rule that was headed by a *mwami* (king) and a feudal hierarchy of Tutsi aristocrats and gentry. According to the folklore, early contact between the Hutus and the Tutsis was peaceful. However, through an agreement known as *ubuhake*, the Hutu farmers promised their loyalties and offerings to a Tutsi lord in return for the loan of cattle and use of pastures, as well as arable agricultural fields. Allegedly, this contract resulted in the Tutsi capacity to reduce the Hutu to virtual serfdom. As history has demonstrated, this comparative advantage of the Tutsis did not last forever. This is, primarily, because along with the demise of the Tutsi hegemony, the boundaries of race and class became less important in the region.

Relative to other African societies, the colonial period for Rwanda was short-lived. It included the reigns of three African rulers, including Yuhi Musinga (1896–1931), Mutara Rudahigwa (1931–1959), and Kigeri Ndahindurwa (1959–1962). The colonial period also encompassed two European powers—Germany (1898–1916) and Belgium (1916–1962). The first European who was reported to have immigrated to Rwanda was German Count Von Goertzen in 1894. Others who visited the country included missionaries, generally regarded as "white farmers." In 1899, the *mwami* rulers surrendered to German governance without a struggle. In 1915, Belgian armies from Zaire forced German soldiers out of Rwanda and instituted Belgian control in the country.

While the area is endowed with fertile and abundant land for herding and agriculture, Rwanda remains one of the poorest countries in Africa, with a per capita annual income of US$270. Important sources of economic stagnation lie in the perpetual pressures of exploding population in the region, the scourge of war and genocide that has disturbed progress in the country, and a command economy where the government owns and controls the land. With a population of about 8 million people, Rwanda is purported to have the highest population density in Africa—248 people per square mile. The Rwandan economy is concentrated largely in agricultural production. The nation possesses few natural resources and has minimal industry. The major food crops are beans, peas, sorghum, cassava, maize, and bananas for the fermenting of beer. Indeed, agribusiness accounts for 50% of Rwanda's GDP and 70% of its exports. Tea accounts for 60% of foreign exchange, followed by coffee and pyrethrum. Additionally, if they can be developed as a tourist attraction, mountain gorillas can generate revenue for the country. However, the 1994 genocide continues to have a negative impact on the Rwandan economy. This tragedy devastated Rwanda's weak economic base, severely impoverished the population, particularly women, and eroded the country's capacity to attract internal and external investments.

The international community has not ignored Rwanda since the war and genocide of 1994. Rwanda is an active member of the African Union (AU) and the United Nations. About a dozen countries participated in the UN Chapter Six peacekeeping operation under the umbrella of the UN assistance mission in Rwanda (UNAMIR). Most of the UN development and humanitarian agencies have also operated in Rwanda. Many African countries maintain diplomatic relations with Rwanda. Some West European nations, Canada, China, Russia, the Vatican, and the European Union also maintain diplomatic missions in Kigali.

Most importantly, since 1995, the United States has not only contributed humanitarian aid, but also focused its attention on avoiding neighboring conflict, renewed economic growth, and the endorsement of domestic stability. It also maintains a cultural center in Kigali. Furthermore, the United States has contributed about $11 million to the removal of landmines in Rwanda. Through the auspices of the U.S. Agency for International Development (USAID), the United States plans to accomplish three strategic objectives in Rwanda:

- Increased rule of law and transparency in governance
- Increased use of health and social services and changed behavior related to sexually transmitted infections and human immunodeficiency virus, and maternal and child health by building service capacity in target regions
- Increased ability of rural families in targeted communities to improve household food security

Contextual Features

According to published reports, in 1959, prior to gaining political independence from Belgium on July 1, 1962 (primarily due to Hutu political agitation), the majority Hutu ethnic group overthrew the Tutsi ruling king. Subsequently, thousands of Tutsis were murdered, forcing about 150,000 Tutsis to flee into neighboring countries. The children of these exiles later formed a rebel group, the Rwandan Patriotic Front (RPF), which started a civil war in 1990. The war exacerbated ethnic tensions and culminated in the 1994 genocide. The genocide claimed the lives of about 800,000 Tutsis and moderate Hutus. Suffice it to say that the Tutsi rebels defeated the Hutu regime and ended the massacre in July 1994.

The problems that Rwanda faces could cause endemic problems for the formation of any stable government. After its victory in July 1994, the RPF formed a Broad Based Government of National Unity. The law governing the creation of this coalition government was based on a combination of the June 1991 Constitution, the Arusha Accords, and the political declarations of various political parties. Some political parties were also outlawed. Amnesty International reported the alleged disappearances of some political figures who belonged to certain defunct political parties and some parliamentarians of the National Assembly.

Rwanda is a republic, characterized by an executive presidential branch and a multiparty legislative system. There is a president, who is the chief of state, and a prime minister, who performs the role of head of government. In the United States, these functions are performed by the president alone. Rwanda's legislative branch of government consists of an eighty-seat chamber of deputies and a twenty-six-member senate. Together, these legislative bodies and the president were elected in the 2003 elections. In May 2003, Rwanda approved a new constitution, which guaranteed the rejection of references to ethnicity and paved the way for elections. On August 25, 2003, Paul Kigame was elected to a seven-year presidential term. Today, many problems confront the government of Rwanda. The challenges include strategies to encourage more democratization in the country, judicial reform, prosecution of participants in the 1994 genocide, controlling insurgency, and economic development.

Provisions of the 1978 Constitution dictate that the judicial system be reorganized to include a Supreme Court, Constitutional Court, Council of State with administrative jurisdiction, Supreme Court of Appeals, Court of Accounts responsible for examining all public accounts, and courts of appeal, courts of first instance, and provincial courts. It must be emphasized that the country's legal system was rooted in a Belgian jurisprudence of procedures and precedents. Custom-

ary law is observed in some administrative jurisdictions. The judicial system is hierarchical, with the Supreme Court at the apex. The judiciary is statutorily independent, but the executive president has the authority to name and discharge judges. Rwanda has three detached court systems for criminal and tort litigations, military matters, and state security concerns, such as treason. Based on its jurisprudence, all citizens have fundamental constitutional rights to legal representation. In Rwanda, due to the dearth of lawyers, family and other types of nonlawyers are permitted in court for legal representation.

Preceding the genocide of 1994, the capacity of Rwandese prisons was 18,000. The construction of new prisons and remodeling of old accommodations for inmates has not kept pace with the intake and arrests of genocidal defendants. According to published reports, between mid-1994 and mid-1996, the prison population in Rwanda increased to more than 90,000. It rose again to about 124,000 between 1997 and 1998. Approximately 70% of the inmates are held in Rwanda's nineteen prisons, and the remaining 30% are held in *cachots* (detention centers). Although the government has slowed the pace of incarcerating genocide perpetrators, the prison population remains high. Currently, Rwandan prisons have a total population of about 80,000 convicts. In 2003, the government decided to close down four of its prisons because of environmental hazards that they pose to prisoners and the general population. This policy is timely since the government intends to accelerate the release of thousands of detainees and the construction of modern prisons.

While few criminal statistics are collected and recorded in the country, reports indicate that domestic violence is a perennial problem in Rwanda. It is a crime that demands police attention in order to protect victims of domestic violence. According to published accounts, domestic violence has existed in Rwanda for a long time, but police interventions are hampered because of deep-rooted cultural aspects that prevent women from reporting such abuses. Domestic violence has always been regarded as a family affair, and the Rwandan police are committed to curbing the traditional focus on "silence" between the people and their police. Allegedly, domestic violence in Rwanda consists of emotional and psychological abuse, physical abuse such as beatings and knife attacks, sexual abuse including rape, and denial of access to needed resources for survival. A police training school has been established in the northern part of the country to help officers to become more effective in controlling these types of offenses.

Police Profile

Background

In 1960, when Rwanda was seeking its political independence, Colonel Guillaume Logiest established an emergency police and national security patrol known as the Garde Territoriale. This police organ of an initial 650-man security force came from the ranks of the country's ethnic groups. Since the Hutus represented the majority, it was primarily a Hutu police force. The new police recruits, who came from all parts of the country, were required to have at least a primary education. Also, in 1960 officers' training was conducted under the leadership of Colonel Logiest. Although there is a dearth of information on the history and formation of the Rwandan police, the National Police (Police Nationale) replaced the Belgian Force Publique on July 1, 1962.

Under the auspices of the minister of police and the National Guard, the National Police was administered by a director general. The majority of the 1,500-strong force was consigned to the ten prefecture divisions. Primarily, they were accountable to the police command center in issues of discipline, promotion, instruction, and wide-ranging policies.

Allegedly, communication and equipment facilities are not up to date. Weapons resemble the police arsenal of the Belgian regime.

Organizational Description

The prefect and his assistants provide operational guidelines to the various prefecture detachments. Each police unit (commune) has a separate police force, which is supervised by a brigadier, who is responsible to the mayor. The mayor has the duty of requesting police assistance from the commune in times of unrest and during any form of disorder.

Indeed, the government of Rwanda inherited many dilemmas because of the aftermath of the war and the 1994 genocide, which in turn demands the presence of a strong national police. The new government endeavors to re-invigorate a new police force that can maintain peace and tranquility in the country.

As a result, in June 2000, the government abandoned the old police structure that included the National Gendarmerie and the communal police. In their place, the Rwandan National Police was established to combine the duties of the various police organs. The National Police falls within the auspices of the Ministry of Internal Affairs under the leadership of a commissioner general.

The commissioner general has two appointed deputies charged with administrative and operational responsibilities. It is the responsibility of the commissioner general to plan, organize, lead, coordinate, and control all the functions of the National Police. The commissioner general determines the deployment of the officers of the police force, promotes the general welfare of the police departments, ensures that the police work according to the laws of the land, and develops and implements police force policies.

The new National Police consist of three main units, including a territorial unit, located in Kigali, Gitarama, Butare, and other areas; a support unit consisting of medical services, canine brigade, police band, and police air wing; and a specialized unit of traffic police, guard and protection, airport security, fire brigade, air and border police, and the navy police.

Functions

The National Police are charged with ensuring that individual rights are observed and protected under the mandates of the constitution. In addition to serving as agents of law who have the authority to safeguard the right to life and property of all individuals, the police are also charged with performing other duties that include the enforcement of the law, crime prevention, order maintenance, road and airport security, providing firefighting services to the community and the nation, and combating terrorism.

Training

The National Police training school is located in Ruhengeri, a northern province of the country, and in the vicinity of the provincial hospital. The academy is in the location of a former Belgian medical training center. It is situated about ninety-four kilometers from Kigali and twenty kilometers from the Virunga National Park. Established in 2001, the National Police Academy assumes the principal role of giving instructional seminars on professional policing. It also provides instructions to police cadres on different areas of law enforcement, such as officer cadet courses, higher training courses in many disciplines, supervisory seminars, and senior command lectures. The academy encourages educational trainings that recognize the community as a support system in the fight against crime. The stated vision of the academy is designed to proceed with the advancement of police knowledge in order to enable the Rwandan people and visitors to achieve a sense of a modicum of security in the nation.

The government of Rwanda supports efforts geared toward the training of an efficient professional police.

Complaints and Discipline

According to public accounts, between 1994 and 2001, about 11,000 prisoners and detainees allegedly died in prison facilities because of problems of overcrowding, disease, and malnutrition. It has also been reported that detainees have died in custody because of physical abuse by custodial officials. In 1999, Amnesty International reported that seventeen prison directors were fired because of allegations of corruption and physical abuse of prisoners. Fifteen of the directors received jail sentences. The government of Rwanda is steadfast in its efforts to ameliorate the poor conditions of the country's prison system.

Terrorism

Rwanda, like most other African nations, has condemned international terrorism. However, it faces domestic pressures at home in the form of internal insurgencies. On April 6, 1994, it was reported that the airplane transporting President Habyarimana and the president of Burundi was bombed by insurgents at the Kigali airport as it was preparing to land. Both presidents died. Their assassinations sparked violence by military and militia groups that resulted in the killing rampage against Tutsis and political moderates without regard for their ethnic affiliations. The prime minister and her ten security guards were among the initial victims. The killings also engulfed all parts of the Rwandan Republic. Some terrorism experts argue that this form of unprecedented genocide, which claimed the lives of as many as 1 million Rwandees, constitutes terrorist acts of violence. Amnesty International aptly described the 1994 genocide and the torture of innocent and unarmed civilians by a government as a catastrophe of orchestrated mass slaughter, representing one of the nastiest humanitarian horrors in recent memory.

International Cooperation

The government has formed partnerships with several countries, including Sweden, the United Kingdom, Canada, and Kenya, to help train its police force. Additionally, the Rwanda National Police belongs to the Eastern Africa Police Chiefs Committee (EAPCCO). The EAPCCO has provided assistance in the training of the police, information dissemination, and general strategies of crime prevention.

IHEKWOABA D. ONWUDIWE AND
KENETHIA L. MCINTOSH

Bibliography

Banks, S. Arthur, and Muller, Thomas C. *Political Handbook of the World: Governments and Intergovernmental Organizations*. New York: CSA Publications, 1998.

Central Intelligence Agency. *The World Fact Book*, "Rwanda: Country Facts Sheet." 2004. Available at: www.cia.gov/cia/publications/factbook/geos/rw.html. Accessed 12 June 2004.

Dorsey, Learthen. *Historical Dictionary of Rwanda*. Metuchen, NJ, and London: Scarecrow Press, 1994.

The Europa World Year Book. London: Europa Publications Limited, 1999.

Ingleton, D. Roy. *Police of the World*. New York: Charles Scribner's Sons, 1979.

Kiernan, Ben. "The Rwanda Genocide." In *Century of Genocide: Critical Essays and Eyewitness Accounts*, edited by S. Totten, W.S. Parsons, I.W. Charny, 395–414. New York: Routledge, 2004.

Kurian, George Thomas. *World Encyclopedia of Police Forces and Penal Systems*. New York: Facts on File, 1989.

Legun, Colin. *Africa: Contemporary Record*. New York and London: African Publishing Company, 1992–1994.

Mars-Proietti, Laura. *Nations of the World: A Political, Economic and Business Handbook*. Millerton, NY: Grey House Publishing, 2004.

Onwudiwe, Ihekwoaba D. *The Globalization of Terrorism*. Aldershot: Ashgate Publishers, 2001.

Ramsay, Jeffress. *Global Studies: Africa*. Guilford, CT: Dushkin Publishing Group, 1993.

Internet Resources

Amnesty International. 2004. "Rwanda: Further Information on Fear for Safety/Possible Disappearances." Available at: *http://web.amnesty.org/libraryprint/ENGAFR 470032004*. Accessed September 13, 2004.

National Police, Rwanda. "Rwanda, National Police Challenges." 2004. Available at: *www.police.gov.rw/challe. htm*. Accessed February 18, 2005.

U.S. Department of State. "Background Note: Rwanda." 2004. Available at: *www.state.gov/r/pa/ei/bgn/2861.htm*. Accessed June 12, 2004.

S

ST. KITTS AND NEVIS

Background Material

St. Kitts and Nevis are two islands located in the northern part of the Leeward Islands in the Eastern Caribbean.

St. Kitts is 23 miles long and 5 miles across at its widest point, encompassing an area of 68 sq mi. The island's highest elevation is Mt. Liamuiga at 3,792 feet. Nevis, the smaller island, lies to the south and is approximately 7 miles in diameter, covering a total of 36 sq mi.

Christopher Columbus first sighted St. Kitts on his second voyage in 1493 and named it "St. Christopher" after his patron saint of travelers. Over the years, the island has become known as "St. Kitts," a shortened version of this name. It is said that when Columbus first sighted Nevis, with its central mountain covered in white mist, he named it "*Nuestro Senora del las Nieves,*" which means "Our Lady of the Snows" because it reminded him of a snow-capped peak. As with St. Kitts, this name became shortened.

St. Kitts was the first island in the West Indies to be colonized by the English in 1623. Both islands have experienced a tumultuous past because of intermittent warfare between the British and French throughout the seventeenth century. Both islands reverted to Britain by the Treaty of Versailles in 1783. After a long period of British Colonial rule, St. Kitts and Nevis attained full political independence and became a two-island Federation on September 19, 1983, adopting the parliamentary form of democratic government. To a large extent, the educational, legal, judicial, and political institutions have been inherently British by tradition. St. Kitts and Nevis is a member of the regional Organization of Eastern Caribbean States (OECS) and Caribbean Common Market (CARICOM).

St. Kitts and Nevis, like most of its Caribbean counterparts, faces increasing levels of crime, particularly among its youth. Additionally, the Federation's ability to shape the course of the twenty-first century will depend largely on poverty reduction and the productivity of the workforce. Democratic trends characterized by declining birth-rates, technological changes, the threat of HIV/AIDS, and international competition are already creating a shortage of skilled workers. While part of the difficulty is attributable to a low employment rate, it is also the result of a "skills gap," an inadequate supply of workers with the skills required by employers. A major challenge to the Federal Government is to find the mechanisms to adjust to the new realities. There is no option but to continue to upgrade the economic and social infrastructure—

including human resources—which, along with the natural resources of sun, sea, and sand, are the basis for international competition in this small open economy.

The population is 46,111 (St. Kitts: 34,930; Nevis: 11,181, 2004 est.). The ethnic composition is 95 percent black; 2.6% mixed; 1.4% white; 0.7% East Indian. The official language is English. Thirty-three percent of the population adheres to Anglicanism; the remainder are Roman Catholic, Methodist, Baptist, Adventist, Moravian, and Jehovah's Witnesses.

The per capita income is EC$20,114 (market prices). The official currency is the Eastern Caribbean dollar, which is tied to the U.S. dollar at approximately $2.70 EC per US$1.00. Major economic activities include tourism, construction, light manufacturing, sugar production (rum products), and financial services.

Contextual Features

The legal system is based on English common and civil law. The judicial system in St. Kitts and Nevis consists of a hierarchy of Courts. The Magistrate Court is a court of Summary Jurisdiction that derives its authority purely from statute. The Eastern Caribbean Supreme Court (High Court) exercises jurisdiction over felonious offenses and civil offenses that are beyond the jurisdiction of the Magistrate Court; unlike the lower court (Magistrate), it is a court of pleadings. The Eastern Caribbean Court of Appeal handles matters of appeal from the High and/or the Magistrate Courts; and, finally, the Judicial Committee of the Privy Council in the United Kingdom is the Final Court of Appeal (*CDB News*, 2003).

By 2004, the Caribbean Court of Justice (CCJ) is to be established in the region. In addition to its role as a court of original jurisdiction, the CCJ will replace the Privy Council as the final court of appeal in both civil and criminal matters from common law courts (Caribbean Community Secretariat). The CCJ is to be a hybrid institution, that is, a municipal court of last resort and an international court with compulsory and exclusive jurisdiction with respect to the interpretation and application of the treaty under which CARICOM functions.

The correctional system consists of Her Majesty's Prisons, which are under the jurisdiction of the Ministry of National Security and operate under the Prison Ordinance, Chapter 205 (July 1956) of the Revised Laws of St. Christopher and Nevis and Anguilla. There are no established reform institutions at this time.

The most common crimes in St. Kitts and Nevis are house and building break-in, larceny, wounding, possession of controlled drugs, malicious damage, and burglary. Since the 1990s, there has been a significant increase in drug-related crimes and other crimes involving firearms, car breakings, and crimes involving violence and anti-social behavior, particularly among young offenders.

The following percentage increases and decreases were observed over a five-year period 1999 – 2003:

In 2000, the number of serious crimes committed increased by 4.9% in comparison with 1999.

In 2001, the number of serious crimes committed decreased by 21.1% in comparison with 2000.

In 2002, the number of serious crimes committed increased by 18.7% in comparison with 2001.

In 2003, the number of serious crimes committed decreased by 15.3% in comparison with 2002.

Police Profile

Background

The Royal St. Christopher and Nevis Police Force was established on January 1, 1960. Prior to that, St. Kitts and Nevis, along with Anguilla, as part of the British West Indies colonies, constituted Division B of the Leeward Islands Police Force with headquarters in Antigua. The island of Dominica was a member of the Leeward Island Police Force for the purpose of administration. The Royal St. Christopher and Nevis Police Force is a typical medium-size Caribbean law enforcement organization with responsibility for law enforcement and security. In the Federation of St. Kitts and Nevis, the Police Force comes under the Ministry of National Security and is commanded by a Commissioner of Police, who reports to the Minister of National Security through the Permanent Secretary in that Ministry.

The Commissioner of Police has the administrative and operational responsibility of managing the Police Force. He is assisted by a Police High Command, which consists of a Deputy Commissioner and an Assistant Commissioner, and also works in consultation with the Senior Gazetted Officers (Inspectors and above) and middle managers, known as the Policy Advisory Group or (PAG). The Police Force has a complement of 400 uniformed personnel and 22 civilian personnel. In St. Kitts and Nevis, immigration/emigration comes under the responsibility of the Commissioner of Police, and therefore police officers perform duties as immigration officers at the various points of entry into the Federation.

The powers and duties of the police are authorized under the Police Ordinance, Chapter 181, Sections 22 & 23 of 1962. In May 2003, a new Police Act, No. 6 of 2003 was passed into law to amend and consolidate the Police Act, No. 181.

For the purpose of administration and operational control, the Federation is divided into three sectors called Police Divisions (A, B, and C). Divisions A and B are on the island of St. Kitts; the island of Nevis is Division C. Each Division is headed by a Divisional Commander, who is responsible to the High Command for the general administration and operational management of his respective area of operations. The purpose of the Royal St. Christopher and Nevis Police Force is to uphold the law fairly and without fear or favor, to prevent crimes, and to pursue and bring to justice those who break the law. Additionally, it is to keep the peace; to protect, help, and reassure residents and visitors; and to do all this with integrity and impartiality.

Demographics

There are 282 male officers and 118 female officers (a force of 400) who make up the Royal St. Christopher and Nevis Police Force. The Force is predominantly Afro-Caribbean and is a National Law Enforcement Agency with 22 Civilian Personnel. The educational attainment in the Force ranges from secondary school graduation to university level, with some specialized training obtained overseas at police academies and similar institutions.

Organizational Description

The Commissioner of Police has operational command of the Police Force and is directly responsible to the Permanent Secretary in the Ministry of National Security. The Commissioner has a Deputy Commissioner, an Assistant Commissioner, and the Force Personnel Officer to form the Police High Command. The hierarchy of the Police Force is made up of: the Commissioner of Police, Deputy Commissioner of Police, Assistant Commissioner of Police, Superintendents, Inspectors, Sergeants, Corporals, and Constables.

The Government has embarked on a policy to introduce more civilians into the Force. This decision has had a significant impact from a human resource perspective. Previously, police officers of various ranks, in whom considerable training had been invested, were deployed in various clerical, accounting, and middle management positions. The release of these officers from non-police operational roles resulted in an increase of officers available for actual police functions (*Police Force Manpower Plan,* 2001–2003).

There is an Interview Board that considers qualifications for promotion. To be upgraded from Constable to Sergeant, the officer must pass Intermediate Level Exams; promotion of Sergeants to Inspectors requires Advance Promotion Exams. Promotion from the rank of Inspector to Superintendent is considered when the applicant attains additional qualifications of higher learning (that is, an Associate Degree, diploma in Police Management, or higher). In addition, each rank is required to engage in a promotion process that includes application, Interview Board, Personal Performance Appraisal Reports, and level of experience.

The Criminal Investigation Unit is responsible for the investigation and detection of all serious crimes in the Federation. It is a non-uniformed unit with members of wide experience and backgrounds in extensive investigation and related skills. The Special Services Unit (SSU) is a special tactical unit with military and other specialized training to respond to terrorism, internal security situations, riots, and related public emergencies.

The Anti-Narcotics Unit is in the forefront of the anti-drug campaign and is the primary investigative arm for drug interdiction and other contraband items/products. Like the members of the SSU, personnel in this unit receive special military and drug investigative training and are part of the special response unit for special tactical emergency situations.

The St. Kitts and Nevis Defence Force supports the police on a regular basis for routine operations and also in national emergencies.

Functions

The Royal St. Christopher and Nevis Police Force provides service and protection by prevention and detection of crime, controlling traffic, immigration, internal security operations, and keeping public order. The police handle criminal law in respect to the investigation of offenses and bringing perpetrators to court. The police have powers of arrest and investigation, and they can detain for questioning.

Training

The minimum entrance requirement for the Police Force is the Secondary School Certificate (CXE, GCE qualifications/O Level passes or equivalent) together with any other academic and/or specialized training as obtained by the applicant upon enlistment. The police recruit then spends 26 weeks of initial training at the Police Academy before graduation and posting to operational units for supervised on-the-job training for a probationary period of three years.

Police Public Projects

The police are engaged in a number of public projects, such as Youth Education and Awareness (DARE) and daily radio public service announcements on traffic and crime prevention information. A school liaison officer program is in effect in which a police officer is assigned to a school and files situation reports on a monthly basis. In addition, there are traffic wardens and a Community Policing Program.

Police Use of Firearms

The police are regulated by the Force Standing Orders (FSO) and Regulations, Standing Order. No. 90 *Use of Force Policy,* which provides procedures and guidelines for the use of deadly force (firearms): "... to be used in the most exceptional circumstances, when no other means remain open to him/her to effect his/her lawful object." Additionally, there is a Force Policy governing firearm use and the use of deadly force. The police have statutory authority under the Police Ordinance, CAP 181, Sections 22 & 23, which outlines their powers and duties. Other circumstances in which use of firearms is justified include: when force is employed for the defense of the Federation against external aggression, CAP 181, Section 4, CAP 181, Section 23(i).

Complaints and Discipline

Complaints against a police officer are handled in accordance with Force Standing Order (FSO) No. 63 and guided by the 1996 Force policy relating to reports or complaints made by a member of the public against a member of the Police Force. The policy clearly outlines the procedures to be followed and defines the responsibilities of officers executing the process. An officer shall be appointed and is required to maintain a register of complaints received, including details of results of subsequent investigation and or disposal.

Discipline and control over Gazetted police officers is provided under the provision of Section 55 (1). The manner and procedure to be followed in the exercise of the power of disciplinary control shall be prescribed by regulation by the Governor-General, acting in accordance with the recommendation of the Police Service Commission. The power of dis-

ciplinary control for non-Gazetted ranks (below Inspectors) is exercised by the Commissioner of Police, in accordance with the recommendation of the Police Service Commission.

The Police Force has no formal or regular training in place regarding human rights. Some elements of human rights training are covered in other programs, such as the Regional Security System (RSS), and in courses that police officers are required to attend from time to time. There have been no formal reports, allegations, or violations of human rights to date.

Terrorism

There are no known terrorist organizations or cells operating in St. Kitts and Nevis. The Special Services Unit (SSU) is a special tactical unit within the Police Force with specialized training to respond to any terrorist or related threats. It is the primary response unit for terrorist acts and other internal security emergencies in St. Kitts and Nevis. In addition, there is also a Task Force of Police and Military Units for national incidents.

International Cooperation

St. Kitts and Nevis is a member of the Barbados-based Regional Security System (RSS), established by treaty in 1982. Member states are Antigua & Barbuda, Barbados, Dominica, Grenada, St. Lucia, and St. Vincent and the Grenadines. The purpose of the RSS is to promote cooperation among the member states in the prevention and interdiction of traffic in illegal drugs, national emergencies, search and rescue, immigration control, fisheries protection, customs and excise control, maritime policing duties, natural and other disasters, pollution control, combating threats to national security, the prevention of smuggling, and the protection of off-shore installations and exclusive economic zones.

A treaty with the U.S. government called the Shiprider Program and Enforcement Agreement, also known as the Shiprider Agreement, concerning maritime counter-drug operations, came into force in April 1995. This agreement between the governments of St. Kitts and Nevis and the United States was an effort to promote greater cooperation between the two countries in combating illicit maritime drug traffic. In addition, assistance in training is received mainly from the United States, United Kingdom, and Canada in such areas as maritime issues, special police training in fingerprinting, K9 handlers, officer development courses, police management, and other related subjects.

Police Education, Research, and Publications

In addition to training received locally at the Police Training Academy, officers attend study programs at Bramshill in the United Kingdom, the Federal Bureau of Investigation (FBI) National Academy in the United States, the Jamaica Police College in Jamaica, Canadian Police College, and the University of the West Indies.

Leading Police Journals/Magazines/Newsletters

- *Royal St. Christopher Nevis Police Annual Report;*
- *Police Force Manpower Plan.*

IVOR W. BLAKE

Bibliography

Caribbean Community Secretariat, carisec2@caricom.org.

Caribbean Development Bank, *CDB News, Vol. 21,* (April–June 2003).

Force Personnel Department, *Manpower Plan 2001–2003* (December 2000).

Kairi Consultants Ltd July 2001, *Poverty Assessment Report – St. Kitts and Nevis.*

Royal St Christopher-Nevis Police, *Comparative of Crime Statistics, 2003.*

Statistical Division Planning Unit, *Preliminary Estimates,* St. Kitts, 2001.

United States/St Kitts & Nevis, *Shiprider Program and Enforcement Agreement,* April 1995.

SAINT LUCIA

Background Material

St. Lucia has an area of 238 sq mi. It is located between the islands of Martinique and St. Vincent. St. Lucia became an independent nation on February 22, 1979. The capital city is Castries. St. Lucia has two towns and six villages. It has a unique history influenced by both British and French rule. St. Lucia has a bicameral system of government, with an Upper and Lower House of Parliament and Senate. The country operates under the Westminster-style parliamentary democracy, with three main branches: executive, legislative, and judicial. General elections are constitutionally due every five years. There is a Governor General, who is the Head of State, and a Prime Minister, who is the Head of the Government.

St. Lucia, like other Caribbean countries, faces economic challenges. The demand for employment is highest on the list. This is as a result of the very young population of St. Lucia. Efforts are being made to have the farmers diversify in their agricultural produce.

St. Lucia has a population of 160,260 (78,629 males and 81,991 females). Statistics show that out of this population, 126,723 (78.9%) are below the age of 45.

The ethnic composition is: Black: 82.4%; East Indian: 2.5%; Mixed: 12.0%; and other: 3.1%.

The main language spoken in St. Lucia is English, with Creole as a second language. However, French and Spanish are taught in the schools.

St. Lucia is predominantly (67.5%) a Roman Catholic country. Other religions are:

The per capita income is $6,969.00; Eastern Caribbean Currency (E.C.).

St. Lucia's economy is based on tourism and agriculture, with some input from small-scale manufacturing. Tourism accounts for 13% of the GDP; agriculture, 7.9%; industry (manufacturing), 5.5%.

Contextual Features

The legal system is based mainly on English Common Law. Civil law is based on both English and French law, whereas criminal law is predominantly English.

The types of crime in St. Lucia are placed into six categories, namely: crime against lawful authority; crime against public morality; crime against the

Religion	%	Religion	%
Seventh Day Adventist	8.4	Bahai	0.1
Pentecostal	5.6	Muslim	0.2
Evangelical	2.0	Brethren	0.1
Rastafarian	2.1	Salvation Army	0.1
Anglican	2.0	Hindu	0.2
Baptist	1.9	Methodist	0.5
Jehovah	1.1	No Religion	4.5
Church of God	1.4	Not stated	1.5
		Other	0.8

person; crime against property; firearm offenses, and drug offenses. However, the most common crimes are crimes against property (19,568 reports in a three-year period), and crimes against person (14,890 reports over the similar period).

In each category, the most common offenses were assault and threats (against the person), stealing (general), and house-breaking (against property).

An analysis of criminal activity over the period 2001–2003 showed that the year 2001 had the highest activity. There was a decline in 2003 in all areas except firearm offenses. In 2003, there was a decline in reports in some areas, but the categories of crime against lawful authority, crime against person, and firearm offenses showed increases.

The judicial system of St. Lucia consists of the Magistrate's Court, the High/Supreme Court, the Court of Appeal, and the Privy Council, soon to be replaced by the Caribbean Court of Justice, which will be the final Appellate Court.

These institutions are located within the Ministry of Home Affairs and Internal Security. The average population of the adult prison is 431, broken down into 422 males and 8 females. The average intake is 10 persons per week, and the age ranges between 16–36 years.

Police Profile

Background

In the police system of St. Lucia, law enforcement was carried out by expatriates during the colonial period. From 1967, locals were groomed to take over. The core of the force consisted mainly of Barbadians. At Independence, the first local Commissioner was appointed in the person of Mr. E. Lawrence. The system is patterned after the British Metropolitan Police system. The Royal St. Lucia Police Force is under the Ministry of Home Affairs and Internal Security. The Force is presently undergoing reform.

Demographics

The total number of persons employed in the police system in St. Lucia is 727; 643 males, and 84 females. The ethnic representation is mainly persons of African descent (95%). There are 36 civilians performing administrative functions.

Organizational Description

The ratio of police to citizens averages 1:220. The Ministry of Home Affairs and Internal Security has jurisdiction over The Royal St. Lucia Police Force. The methods utilized for the selection/promotion for each rank are examination, interview, and appraisal. The Criminal Investigation Unit carries out investigative work only. The Special Response Units respond to emergencies and civil disorder; the Immigration Department, Traffic Department, and Community Relations Department provide support services.

Functions

The functions of the Police consist of the protection of life and property, investigations, and preservation of peace. Police powers include arrest with warrants, as stipulated under section 62 b–64 of the Criminal Code.

Training

Entry into the Royal St. Lucia Police Force requires 5 CXC General Proficiency level passes at Grades 1, 2, or 3, or Basic at Grade 1. English language is compulsory. Applicants must be in the age range of 18–35 years old.

During the 32-week training period, recruits receive instruction in physical training, police duties, computer application, swimming and life-saving, drill, and firearm training. Special instructions are received in handling domestic abuse cases, as well as dealing with mentally challenged persons.

Police Public Projects

The Royal St. Lucia Police Force has embarked on a number of projects with the aim of improving their relationship with the public.

The Community Relations Branch is engaged in school liaison exercises. Officers visit schools in their districts and lecture the students in all aspects of being law-abiding citizens. Special emphasis is placed on the Anti-Drug Programme.

The introduction of the Community Policing Programme is being vigorously pursued with town hall meetings in all the districts. The public response is very encouraging.

Police Use of Firearms

The use of firearms by the police is outlined in the Police Standing Orders of 1990. Section 45 details the principles governing the use of firearms as follows:

(i) Firearms are to be used only where there is reason to suppose that a Police Officer may have to face a person who is armed or otherwise so dangerous that he could not safely be retained without the use of firearms, for protection purposes or for the destruction of dangerous animals.

(ii) Firearms are to be used by authorized and trained Police Officers only as a last resort where conventional methods have been tried and failed or must from the nature of the circumstances obtaining be likely to succeed if tried. They must be used for example when it is apparent that a Police Officer cannot achieve the lawful purpose of preventing loss of life by other means.

Permission to use a firearm must be obtained from an Officer not below the rank of Assistant Superintendent, except when circumstances render it impractical.

Complaints and Discipline

In order to enhance the relationship between the police and the public, no efforts are spared to ensure that officers receive specialized training, especially in relation to human rights violations. In this regard, a Police Complaint Unit has been established within the force, allowing the public an avenue to make their complaints against the police. Legislation has also been passed establishing the Police Complaints Act No. 6 of 2003.

Terrorism

There are no known terrorist organizations in St. Lucia.

International Cooperation

The areas of international cooperation and the countries involved are Interpol, Association of Caribbean Commissioners of Police (ACCP), United Kingdom, and the United States of America. The Federal Bureau of Investigations (FBI) has assisted in the training of police in St. Lucia. There is no exchange of officers among countries at this time.

Police Education, Research, and Publications

Institutions for Higher Education for Police

The Jamaica Staff College, the Sir Arthur Lewis Community College and R.S.S Training, Bramshill, FBI National Academy, and UWI School of Continuing Studies are the institutions available for the education of the police in St. Lucia.

Police-Related Websites

www.rslpf.com.

LINWALL JAMES

Bibliography

Annual Reports. Government Statistical Department.
Government of Saint Lucia–Standing Orders 1990, Castries, Ministry of Home Affairs and Internal Security.
Institutional Appraisal and Strategic Review of the Royal St. Lucia Police Force.
Police Complaints Act No-6 of 2003.
Police Standing Order–1990.

ST. VINCENT AND THE GRENADINES

Background Material

St. Vincent and the Grenadines is a multi-island country in the Caribbean, with the Atlantic Ocean on the Eastern Coastline and the Caribbean Sea on the western side. The mainland is approximately 133 sq mi, with the Grenadines accounting for another 17 sq mi. The Grenadines consists of 34 islands and cays. The main islands in the Grenadines chain are Bequia, Mustique, Canouan, Mayreau, Union Island, Palm Island, and Petit St. Vincent. The island is mountainous, with a backbone of mountains running through the island and nearer the western side, making the western side of the island more rugged. The highest peak is the LaSoufriere, towering to over 4,048 feet, with the LaSoufriere volcano clutched in its bosom. The volcano is presently dormant; it last erupted in 1979. The country has a rich cultural history, which dates back to the early seventeenth century.

The first natives were the Caribs, who in their struggle for independence, endured the wrath of the early French and British colonial settlers.

The island attained political independence from Britain on October 27, 1979, and has a Westminster Parliamentary Democracy system of government. This democratic system of government allows for general elections to be held every five years. The economy of the State is dependent mainly on agriculture and tourism. Financial services and information technology have also been targeted as possible growth areas. Conscious of the vulnerability of the country to external shocks and natural disasters, the government of St. Vincent and the Grenadines is pursuing a strategy of economic diversification. This is intended to lessen the dependence on agriculture, which has traditionally been the mainstay of the economy. The contribution of tourism to the GDP in 2000 was 2.35%, represented by contributions from the hotels and restaurants in the National Accounts.

The major challenges facing St. Vincent and the Grenadines are the economic downturn in agricultural and tourism earnings, the impact on the offshore financial sector by the OECD, and the trafficking of illegal drugs.

The total estimated population for St. Vincent and the Grenadines is 112,000, with ethnic composition of 90% Negroes (African descendants), and the remaining 10% a mix of East Indians, Europeans, and Indigenous peoples (Caribs).

The language spoken is English. Major religions are Anglican, Methodist, Roman Catholic, Evangelical, Pentecostal, Spiritual Baptist, and Seventh-Day Adventist.

The per capita income is $2,900.00 (2002 est.). Major economic activities include agriculture, tourism, offshore financial services, and information services.

Contextual Features

The legal system is based on English common law and is adversarial in nature.

The most common crimes are theft, burglary, robbery, wounding, and possession of dangerous drugs.

The judicial system of St. Vincent and the Grenadines consists of a hierarchy of courts: the Magistrate's Court, Supreme Court, Court of Appeal, and the Judicial Committee of the Privy Council (both civil and criminal).

The correctional system consists of Her Majesty's Prison Service, established under the Prison Act, CAP 281 of the Revised Edition of the Laws of St. Vincent and the Grenadines, 1990. The Prison Service is under the jurisdiction of the Ministry of National Security.

Police Profile

Background

The Royal St. Vincent and the Grenadines Police Service grew out of the colonial era of policing handed down from Britain. The present structure and legal framework under which it operates have not changed much, even after 24 years of political independence. The Service is at present undergoing restructuring, including a revision of the Legislature. The management of the Service has responsibility for the Fire Brigade, Coast Guard, Immigration, and Transport (licensing), in conjunction with its normal policing duties of crime and security. The island has no defense force, so the Police also have responsibility for matters that require a military and paramilitary response.

Demographics

The Royal St. Vincent and the Grenadines Police Service is made up of 854 officers. The Service is predominantly Negro, with 837 uniformed officers and 17 civilians. Educational attainment ranges from secondary school graduation to university level, with some specialized training obtained abroad at police academies and similar institutions.

Organizational Description

The Commissioner of Police controls the Police Service. Selection and promotion are based on the recruits having at least five "GCE or CXC" passes, with Promotion Examinations held up to the rank of Inspector, approval by the Police Service Commission up to the rank of Deputy Commissioner of Police, and based on training and recommendation.

The criminal investigation unit is a detective branch that investigates all crimes. The Special Response Unit is a uniformed section that responds to serious crimes, especially those involving the use of firearms and other weapons.

Functions

The Royal St. Vincent and the Grenadines Police Service ensures the preservation of public peace, and the protection and detection of crimes and offenses. The officers arrest offenders who have committed or who are suspected of committing a crime. They regulate traffic, processions, and assemblies in public places. The Service preserves order in public places, excises quarantines, enforces emigration and immigration laws, and preserves order at the ports in the state. Police officers execute summons, warrants, subpoenas, commitment, or other quasi-criminal processes issued by the Court. They conduct prosecutions, and they protect life and property. They are also responsible for keeping order at the Courts and escorting prisoners to and from prison. Every member of the Police Service has authority, privilege, protection, and advantage under the Common Law of England or any law that is in force in St. Vincent and the Grenadines. The Police handle Criminal Law, and they investigate, arrest, and prosecute offenders.

Training

The entrance requirements for the Police Service include being a national of St. Vincent and the Grenadines, between the ages of 19 and 30 years (male or female), the ability to pass a qualifying test or having obtained at least five passes in "GCE or CXC" O'levels; and applicants must be physically fit.

Police Public Projects

The Royal St. Vincent and the Grenadines Police Service conducts a weekly radio program *On the Beat,* which covers all aspects of public concern (traffic, crime prevention, fire). A Drug Awareness Reduction Education (DARE) program in primary schools is also a major part of the Police Service's public outreach/education program.

Police Use of Firearms

The Royal St. Vincent and the Grenadines Police Service is guided by the Firearms Act, No. 12 of the Laws of St. Vincent and the Grenadines, 1995. The use/discharge of firearms is guided by Force policies.

Complaints and Discipline

Reports are made to the Police/Ministry and allegations investigated. Findings of a criminal nature are dealt with by the Court, through the Director of Public Prosecutions.

Police officers receive basic training in internationally recognized Human Rights. Training includes lectures, seminars, and workshops conducted by the Human Rights Association (visiting Lecturer).

The police have come under criticism for human rights violations. The programs that exist in this country to control and investigate human rights violations are the Police Public Relations and Complaints Department, Courts, and Police Oversight Committee. To ensure a climate of respect for human rights inside its organizations, any alleged improper conduct is investigated; anyone found guilty is disciplined. To ensure a climate of respect for human rights outside its organizations (in regard to the public), allegations are investigated; and offenders, if guilty, are dealt with under the law.

Terrorism

There are no known terrorist organizations in St. Vincent and the Grenadines. The police agencies charged with responding to terrorism are the Special Services Unit, the Rapid Response Unit, and the Special Branch.

International Cooperation

The Royal St. Vincent and the Grenadines Police Service participates in the exchange of information and cooperation, particularly in the area of drug trafficking and money laundering, with the United States of America, Britain, and Canada. International assistance is also received for training in Drug Interdiction and Financial Investigation. There is no exchange of officers among countries.

Police Education, Research, and Publications

Institutions for Higher Education for Police

Police pursue higher education at the Jamaica Police Staff College, the Regional Police Training School in Barbados, the Royal Canadian Mounted Police (RCMP) College in Ottawa, and the Federal Bureau of Investigations (FBI) National Academy in the United States of America.

Leading Researchers/Authors/Reporters/Columnists with Affiliations

None available.

Extent Sources of Funding for Police Research

None available.

Leading Police Journals/Magazines/Newsletters

None available.

Major Police Publications

None available.

Police-Related Websites
Under construction.

WILLIAM HARRY

Bibliography

Crime Statistics – Royal St. Vincent and the Grenadine Police Service (unpublished).

Laws of St. Vincent and the Grenadines, Revised Edition, 1990, Cap. 280.
St. Vincent and the Grenadines' Statistical Digest, 2001.

SAMOA

Background Material

Samoa was invaded by Fiji in the early part of the thirteenth century, but no detailed records were kept until the arrival of John Williams from the London Missionary Society in 1830. In 1900, the islands were divided. Under the Tripartite Treaty of 1899, Germany took over Western Samoa, and the United States acquired American (Eastern Samoa). Britain renounced all previous claims, and in 1914 New Zealand annexed Western Samoa. It administered it on behalf of the League of Nations and United Nations until 1962.

Moves towards self-government and independence commenced in 1947, and in 1962 Western Samoa gained independence. It joined the United Nations in 1976 and gained universal suffrage in 1991.

In January 2000, Samoa and the unincorporated territory of American Samoa signed a memorandum of understanding in relation to matters of health, trade, law enforcement, education, and agriculture.

Samoa is vulnerable to natural disasters. It has active volcanoes, and because of its geographic position it is subject to significant tropical storms.

The OECD named Samoa as a harmful tax haven in June 2001.

As of July 2001, the population was 179,058. The two official languages are Samoan (a Polynesian dialect) and English. Virtually the whole population (99.97%) are Christians, with half being affiliated to the London Missionary Society. Other Christian religions are Roman Catholic, Methodist, Mormon, Seventh Day Adventist, Protestant, Anglican, Jehovah's Witnesses, Baha's, Peace Chapel, Assembly of God, and Baptist.

The GDP per capita is US$3,200. Coconut products are a major component of Samoan agriculture. It employs two thirds of the population and provides 90% of its export earnings. Tourism is a growing industry.

Contextual Features

Samoa has a unicameral system of government. The *O le Ao O le Malo*, the Head of State, acts as a constitutional monarch and appoints the Prime Minister (the Head of Government) on the recommendation of the 49-member Parliament (the *Fono*). The Head of State (with the exception of the present incumbent His Highness Malietoa Tanumafkil II, who has tenure for life) will be selected by the Parliament for a five-year term of office.

On independence, Samoa inherited a body of English and New Zealand Acts and regulations, which remain in force except where they are inconsistent with the Samoan Constitution. The Samoan Parliament has also added to, and in some cases repealed, this body of law. Common law also exists where consistent with the Samoan Constitution. There is scope for recognizing customary law, but generally the courts have declined to do so, except for some property and title issues.

The death penalty is nominally in force.

News reports from the *Samoa Observer* (27 October 2002) indicate that possession of marijuana was the most common offense dealt with by Samoan courts.

Appeals go from the Supreme Court to the Court of Appeal.

If the court has given leave, it will consider "further" criminal appeals from the Magistrates' Courts.

The Supreme Court has unlimited original civil and criminal jurisdiction and jurisdiction to hear civil appeals from a Magistrate's Court. It can hear criminal appeals brought except for the payment of costs.

The Magistrate's Court has jurisdiction to hear and determine minor civil matters regarding tort or contract.

The Magistrate's Court also has jurisdiction over offenses punishable by a fine, a penalty, forfeiture, or a period of imprisonment, except for those offenses that are punishable by a term of imprisonment exceeding five years. Customary land is excluded from Magistrate's Courts jurisdiction.

The Village *Fono* has the power to deal with village affairs in accordance with village custom. This jurisdiction applies only to persons who ordinarily reside in the village. Appeals from Village *Fono* regarding land are heard by the Land and Titles Court.

This court has a separate jurisdiction in all matters relating to Samoan chiefly titles and in all claims and disputes relating to customary land. It hears appeals from the Village *Fono*. Appeals from the Land and Titles Court are presided over by a court composed of the President and two Samoan judges appointed by the President. There is no right of appeal in relation to such judgments.

In mid-1998, the Samoan prison system housed 173 prisoners.

Police Profile

Background and Demographics

The Police Service of Samoa was established in 1962. In 2000, it had 330 police personnel with six police outposts. Units within the Police Service include a Special Branch and a Police Band.

Organizational Description

The *Police Service Act 1977* (Western Samoa) lists the following ranks:

- Commissioner;
- Deputy Commissioner;
- Superintendents;
- Chief Inspectors;
- Inspectors;
- Senior Sergeants;
- Sergeants;
- Corporals;
- Senior Constables;
- Constables;
- Cadets.

Section 5 of the *Police Service Act* states that the Commissioner of Police must have served in the force for 10 years, and have been a commissioned officer,

before he or she can be appointed Commissioner. The position is for three years and is a renewable term.

Promotions are recommended by an internal Appointment and Promotion Board made up of a Superintendent, a Chief Inspector or Inspector, and a subordinate officer. All are appointed by the Commissioner of Police (Section 12).

Functions

Although the legislation does not specifically state the functions of the Samoan Police Service, they include the preservation of order and peace throughout Samoa and the prevention of offenses.

Training

New Zealand provides training for the Samoan Police. This has included training the Samoan civilian police for deployments to the United Nations in East Timor.

In February 2004, the Australian government announced a major Australian policing initiative to support the Samoa Police Service. AusAID will contribute $9 million to help strengthen the operational, administrative, and investigative capacity of the Samoa Police Service. This will include a new combined Police Headquarters and Central Police Station, together with a community education campaign designed to enhance police-community relations. The project will complement the recently established Australian–led Pacific Regional Policing Initiative (PRPI), announced by the Prime Ministers of Australia, New Zealand, and Fiji at the Pacific Islands Forum in August 2003.

Police Use of Firearms

The Samoan Police are usually unarmed.

Complaints and Discipline

The Commissioner may refer complaints against officers to a tribunal. For subordinate officers, the tribunal consists of a superior officer; for inspectors, the tribunal is made up of a peer within the police service and two external members. The tribunal can recommend sanctions ranging from dismissal to exoneration.

The Commissioner and Superintendents can be dismissed for disciplinary breaches by Samoa's Head of State.

All tribunal findings can be appealed. However, it appears that the Commissioner and Superintendents are not able to appeal their dismissal. However, they can be restored to their position by the Head of State if necessary (Sections 23–29).

Terrorism

In 1970, the South Pacific Chiefs of Police Conference was founded. The forum facilitates cooperation and information sharing to help prevent crime. It also facilitates formal liaison among police in the South Pacific. In 2003, the conference theme was "Terrorism—the Wider Law Enforcement Context." A four-year strategic plan was finalized to assist in establishing key law enforcement priorities for the region.

International Cooperation

The Honiara Declaration is the basis for law enforcement cooperation in the Pacific region.

Samoa is a member of Interpol, the Pacific Islands Forum's Regional Law Enforcement Capacity Development and Cooperation Program, the South Pacific Islands Central Intelligence Network, and the South Pacific Chiefs of Police.

Samoan Police are involved in international peacekeeping work serving as part of the UN force in East Timor.

Other examples of international cooperation include a Police contingent of 40 deployed to the Solomon Islands in 2003. After a request from the United Nations in October 2003, Samoa sent 15 police personnel to the mission to help rebuild Liberia's police force.

Police Education, Research, and Publications

Institutions

University of the South Pacific, www.usp.ac.fj/ (Institute of Justice and Applied Legal Studies [IJALS], Laucala Campus, Fiji).

Researchers

Bevan, Colin Russell, *Report on probation and parole in Western Samoa*, Canberra: Australian Institute of Criminology, 1977.

Findlay, Mark, 'Decolonising restoration and justice: restoration in transitional cultures' *Howard Journal*, 39(4) Nov 2000; 398-411.

Newton, T. (1998). *An introduction to policing in the South Pacific region*. University of the South Pacific School of Law Working Papers.

Leading Journals

Journal of South Pacific Law, http://easol.vanuatu.usp.ac.fj/jspl/current

Police-Related Websites

Samoa Police Project, AusAid www.ausaid.gov.au/media/release.cfm?BC=Media&Id=2925_2989_8265_171_3189

COLLEEN LEWIS

Bibliography

AusAID media release, www.ausaid.gov.au/media/release.cfm?BC=Media&Id=2925_2989_8265_171_3189.

Ingram Seal, Leigh. 'Samoa' November 23, 2003. www.orbat.com/site/orbats/data/samoa/samoa.pdf.

SBS World Guide, 9th edition, Hardie Grant Books, 2001.

SAN MARINO

Background Material

A small state (61 sq km) located in central Italy, San Marino claims to be the world's oldest Republic. According to tradition, San Marino was founded by Marino, a Dalmatian stonemason who took cover on Mount Titano, part of the Appennine range, and established a Christian community in September 301 AD. It is certain that the area had been inhabited since prehistoric times, even though the first official documents date back only to the early medieval period. In memory of its founder, the land was called "Land of San Marino" first, then "Community of San Marino," and finally "San Marino Republic."

By the middle of the fifteenth century, San Marino became a Republic ruled by a Grand Council composed of 60 members taken from a self-governed assembly known as the *Arengo,* or assembly of families. In the same century, the Republic entered into a period of political alliance, which contributed to the territorial expansion and the strengthening of the frontiers. Since then, the size of the country has remained the same.

The autonomy of San Marino has been threatened on various occasions, particularly by Cesare Borgia in the sixteenth century, but the Republic tenaciously and wisely defended its freedom and independence, building a reputation for being a land of freedom and political asylum. Among the most famous refugees was the Italian national hero Giuseppe Garibaldi in 1849. In 1862, a friendship treaty with Italy reinforced San Marino's independence. After World War I, a Fascist Party seized power and started a transformation of the state, using Italy as model. During World War II, the Republic maintained a neutral position and became a refugee state for 100,000 people. In 1992, San Marino joined the United Nations.

Today, San Marino is a wealthy country that benefits from its close relationship with its only neighbor, Italy. With a population of about 26,000 inhabitants, the growth rate of the population is 1.38% per year; the median age is 39.6 years (male, 39.2; female, 40); and the life expectancy is 78 years for men and 85 years for women. The ethnic groups are Sammarinesi (great majority) and Italians. The religion is Roman Catholic, and the language is Italian. Literacy is high (96%).

Tourism contributes considerably to the GDP (more than 3 million people visited San Marino in 1998). The major economic activities are banking (the country attracts a large inflow of cash from Italy and other countries), ceramics, furniture, and craft goods. The main agricultural products are wine and cheese. San Marino has no mineral resources, and most of its territory is cultivated or covered by woods. The country has a long tradition for stamps, postal stationery, and coins; the first official Postal Service in the world was created in San Marino in 1607. The standards of living are comparable to those of the most prosperous regions of Italy. In 2001, per capita income was about $34,000. The monetary unit is the Euro.

Contextual Features

According to the *Declaration of the Rights of the Citizens and of the Fundamental Principles of San Marino Regulations* (Law decreed on 8 July 1972), sovereignty is in the people. The Republic is headed by two Heads of State, called Captains-Regent, who are elected by Parliament every six months. At the end of their mandate, they are subject to the "Regent's Union" (*Sindacato della Reggenza*), which can open a trial in the case of citizen allegations. San Marino's Parliament, called the Great and General Council (*Consiglio Grande e Generale*), is composed of 60 members and is elected every five years by direct, popular vote (all adults, including residents abroad can take part). Parliament is unicameral; it exercises legislative power, ratifies treaties with other states, grants pardons, and adopts the budget.

The Congress of State (*Consiglio di Stato*) is the government of the Republic and asserts executive power. Composed of 10 members, it is elected by the Great and General Council. Judicial power is exercised by the Council of Twelve (*Consiglio dei XII*), which is headed by the two Captains-Regent. Members of the Council of Twelve are also chosen and elected by the Great and General Council. This body exercises civil, criminal, and administrative functions; and, as regards civil matters, it plays the role of a judicial body by hearing appeals from the Judge of Appeal.

The legal system is based on a *sui generis* common law system in which customary law norms are mixed with a civil law system based on statutes and prescribed text.

With the exception of the Justice of Peace Judge (*Giudice Conciliatore*), judges must not be San Marino citizens and are nominated by the Great and General Council. The aim of this provision is to ensure impartiality. Judges hold the office for three years, but they can be re-nominated.

Court proceedings for criminal cases start with the Investigator of the Law (*Commissario della Legge*), who handles less serious criminal cases (those in which the sentence does not exceed three years of imprisonment). The next level is the Criminal Judge of First Instance, who hears and determines all other types of criminal cases. Then there is the Judge of Appeal, who hears and determines appeals from decisions of the Judge of First Instance. Civil matters are handled by the Justice of Peace Judge, when the amount in dispute is not more than 1 million Italian lire (about 500 Euro), and by the Investigator of the Law in all the other cases. The Judge of Appeal of criminal cases hears the appeal and, in some cases, the Council of Twelve may function as final appeal.

The law prohibits arbitrary arrests and detention. Consequently, a suspect can be arrested only if there is a probable cause. The defendant is guaranteed an impartial and speedy jury and, after trial, has the right to appeal. The main principle of the criminal procedure is that there can be neither crime nor punishment without a law first.

San Marino has a very a low rate of criminality, although there were some signs of increase in the early 1990s. Property crimes are the most common: there were 50 cases in 2002 and 15 cases between January and October 2002 (statistics provided by the Gendarmerie of San Marino). No bank robbery occurred in the period between 1988 and 2002. The second most common crime is drug trafficking and consumption. Violent crimes are extremely low (one murder in 2002). Frequently, those who break the San Marino law try to cross the border and enter into Italy, where it is more difficult to conduct investigations.

The prison system policies are quite liberal. Capital punishment and life sentences were abolished since they were considered to be inconsistent with the purpose of punishment, namely, the rehabilitation of prisoners. According to the Criminal Code, prisoners can serve from three months to 35 years. According to a 2002 report of the *Bureau of Democracy, Human Rights, and Labor* of the U.S. Department of State, the conditions of the San Marino prison meet international standards (male prisoners are held separately from female prisoners, and juveniles from adults). Quite often, convicted persons do not serve the full sentence but are granted conditional early release. For petty crimes, law breakers can receive a period of probation instead of prison time.

Police Profile

Background

San Marino has three police forces: two military police forces (the Gendarmerie and the Fortress Guard) and the Civil Police. The oldest corps is the Fortress Guard (*Guardia di Rocca*), which was established in 1754. At that time, the Fortress Guard was a military unit with the specific purpose of defending the First Fortress of San Marino, which functioned as a prison. Later, the Fortress Guard nearly disappeared, only performing ceremonial duties with their red trousers and green jacket parade uniforms. However, in 1956 the government assigned it the task of protecting the frontiers of the state.

The Gendarmerie was created in 1842. Its own statute established that its task was the maintenance of public order, the enforcement of the law, and the investigation of all crimes that occurred in the country. The fulfilment of the mission sometimes proved to be difficult, and the Gendarmerie was aided by a group of Italian military policemen from the *Carabinieri* Army, particularly in the periods between 1921 and 1936 and 1962 and 1984. Today, the Gendarmerie performs its functions autonomously, but its commander is still a Colonel of Italian *Carabinieri*. The Civil Police is the newest force. Created in 1945 from a split with the Gendarmerie, the Civil Police initially worked as traffic police and then started performing some public order functions in 1982.

With the exception of the Commander of the Gendarmerie, all policemen are citizens of San Marino. It is worth noting that San Marino citizenship can be obtained only after 30 years of residence. The ratio of officers to citizens is 1:250. Besides these forces, there are two Voluntary Military Forces (the Guard of Honour and the *Compagnia Uniformata delle Milizie*), which basically perform ceremonial duties and limited policing.

Organizational Description and Functions

The Gendarmerie is the biggest force in size. Composed of nine Brigades (one per each municipality or *castello*), it has about 100 members, six of whom are women. There are two officials, the Commander and the Vice-Commander. The Commander is responsible for all activities and is accountable to the Ministry of Foreign Affairs. The duties of the Gendarmerie are the protection of lives and property, the maintenance of order, crime prevention, investigation, and other law enforcement services. Altogether, it has quite a large range of activities: standard police work and crime detection, anti-drug and narcotics investigations, prison guarding, and monitoring of websites promoting illicit activities within San Marino. Moreover, the Gendarmerie performs administrative tasks, such as the issue of gun licences and residence permits.

The main department units are Emergency, Crime Prevention, Anti-Drugs, Narcotics, and Administration. The Emergency unit operates 24 hours a day and responds to emergency calls through two phone lines (112 and 113). All alarm systems of banks and main shops are linked to the Headquarters, where there is also an electronic data collection system. In addition, the Emergency unit is responsible for routine proactive patrol of the towns. The Crime Prevention unit is responsible for investigations into crimes, ranging from burglary to homicide. Following magistrates' instructions, the unit analyzes crime scenes and collects evidence. The Anti-Drugs and Narcotics units are responsible for the investigation of narcotics violations and the enforcement of the laws pertaining to dangerous drugs. Periodically, their officers give lectures in schools to inform students about drug-related risks.

Members of the Gendarmerie must be citizens of San Marino and have attended at least eight years of middle school and another five years of high school in order to become an official. After selection, there is a six-month training course in a police school, taught by policemen and magistrates. After the course, there is a one-year apprenticeship before becoming an officer. For officials, the training is different, as they have to attend a school for officials. Periodically, there are training courses and workshops.

Officers of the Gendarmerie are equipped with a Beretta gun and a M12 rifle. In addition, the patrols are equipped with shotguns with both lead and rubber ammunition. However, the Gendarmerie promotes prudent use of firearms in order to protect the lives of civilians, and officers rarely resort to weapons to perform their duties.

As a military force, the Gendarmerie organization takes care of its men during their years of active service, developing a sense of institutional self-identification and discipline. The Gendarmerie tends to see itself as a national institution that belongs to the tradition of San Marino life.

Possible violations of civil rights are controlled not only by officials, but also by a delegation of the Council of Europe from Strasbourg that periodically visits the Gendarmerie Headquarters, the Fortress Guard station, the Civil Police Headquarters, and the prison.

The Gendarmerie keeps close contacts with the Italian police and cooperates with other police according to international agreements. It is a member of the International Police Association (IPA), an independent body composed of members of other countries' police forces. The IPA is committed to the principles set out in the *Universal Declaration of Human Rights* adopted by the United Nations in 1948.

The Civil Police is the second biggest police force of San Marino. It has 78 members, ten of whom are women. There are two officials who are equivalent to Chief Superintendent. One of them is the Commander of the Civil Police, who is accountable to the Ministry of Interior.

Its tasks involve the control of traffic and tourism, inspection of industrial establishments for workers' safety, and investigation into food and drink adulteration. It also performs fire brigade duties, interventions in cases of natural disasters, and a limited amount of public order functions.

The main units are the Division Commander, Traffic, Fire Brigade, and Emergency. The Traffic unit has a responsibility to help keep traffic moving safely, ensure safety of pedestrians, and document traffic collisions. Its officers visit schools to educate students about road safety. The Emergency unit patrols the territory and intervenes during incidents ranging from car crashes to natural disasters.

Members of the Civil Police must be citizens of San Marino and have attended at least eight years of middle school and another five years of high school to become officials. Cadet officers follow a six-month training course in a police school first, and then a one-year apprenticeship before becoming officers. Periodically, there are training courses.

Members of the Civil Police were unarmed until 1997. Nowadays, they are equipped with a Beretta Stoch gun. Like the Gendarmerie, possible violations of civil rights are controlled not only by internal officials, but also by a delegation of the Council of Europe from Strasbourg that periodically visits the Civil Police Headquarters.

The Civil Police force is a member of the International Police Association (IPA).

The Fortress Guard has 30 members, none of whom are women. The Commander is the only officer and is ranked Captain. He is accountable to the Foreign Ministry. In addition, there are a number of volunteers who join the force during parades (the main parade takes place on 3 September, Republic Day). Besides ceremonial duties, the Fortress Guard is responsible for the external defense of the state and occasionally assists the Gendarmerie in criminal investigations. Moreover, in recent years the force began to help the judiciary in investigating tax crimes.

All members of the Fortress Guard are citizens of San Marino and should pass a physical and psychological exam and attend a training course (between six months and one year) before becoming officers. They are equipped with a Beretta gun and a M12 rifle. They have also Enfield English muzzle-loader 1860 rifles for the parades.

The Fortress Guard is also a member of the International Police Association (IPA).

Police Education, Research, and Publications

The three police forces of San Marino do not invest particular funds for police research. They do not have any journal, magazine, or newsletter to publish police articles. A website on the San Marino police is under construction.

FRANCESCO MARELLI

Bibliography

BBC, *Country Profile: San Marino*, 2003, http://news.bbc.co.uk/2/hi/europe/country_profiles/2669927.stm.

Captains-Regent San Marino, *Regolamento del Corpo dei Gendarmi*, San Marino, 1880.

Central Intelligence Agency, "San Marino." *The World Factbook 2003*, www.cia.gov/cia/publications/fact book/geos/sm.html.

Edwards Adrian, and Chris Michaelides. *San Marino*, World Bibliographical Series, No. 188. Oxford: Clio, 1996.

Martini Luca. *La Repubblica di San Marino: brevi cenni sulle peculiarità istituzionali e sul particolare regime societario e tributario*, www.filodiritto.com/diritto/pubblico/internazionale/nomrativasanmarino.htm.

Omnyway, Il portale della repubblica di San Marino, www.omniway.sm.

US Department, Bureau of Democracy, Human Right, and Labor, *2002 Report*, www.state.gov/g/drl/rls/irf/2002/13959.htm (Accessed December 1, 2003).

SÃO TOMÉ AND PRÍNCIPE

Background Material

This small island country is situated off the coast of Guinea in the Horn of Western Africa. The Portuguese claimed the discovery of São Tomé and Príncipe in the fifteenth century. São Tomé and Príncipe were separate islands colonized by Portuguese imperialists, whose intention was to use the islands as a slave trade route.

As the scramble for land and natural resources in Africa became a deliberate effort by European nations, several slave countries and colonialists occupied São Tomé and Príncipe until the two islands were united in 1753 as a Portuguese crown colony.

The location of the country was particularly attractive to visitors who were interested in the sugar economy. The two islands are situated on land in the Gulf of Guinea, straddling the equator to the west of Gabon. The country is more than five times the size of Washington, DC, with an estimated population of 181,565 in 2004. The nation also includes the islets of Cabras, Gago, Coutinho, Pedras Tinhosas, and Rolas. They all lie approximately 1,001 km off the coast of Gabon. The two islands and the several islets sit on inactive volcanoes, making the country vulnerable to tsunamis.

The country consists of rugged and undulating landscapes peaking at 6,639 feet with dense tropical vegetation and forests with virgin, palm-fringed beaches. So this is a rare land of unspoiled beauty, isolated from the pollution of Western civilization. But economic hardship unfortunately puts the country in a position that makes it impossible to remain totally untouched by the vices of being Western civilization.

The history of this tiny nation is dominated by the scramble for African land and exploitation for slave trade and slave-managed sugar, coffee, and cocoa plantations. The purported discovery of the islands by Portuguese navigators in 1469 and 1472 conflicts with historical information dating the first true settlements of São Tomé and Príncipe in 1493 and 1500, respectively.

Alvaro Caminha received the land as a grant from the Portuguese crown, and, with the aid of his co-settlers and the sweat and blood of slave labor, he turned the islands into a dominant exporter of sugar. As expected of the colonialists, the islands were formally seized and ruled by the Portuguese crown in 1522 and 1573, respectively. In the middle of the 1600s, the country was relegated to a ship port after the decline of sugar cultivation in the previous years. Since then, the country has continued to struggle economically and politically. Like neighboring Nigeria, São Tomeé and Príncipe is politically unstable because of the unpredictability of the government and history of political coups. However, local administration of the country was established by 1951; it became autonomous in 1974, and gained independence in 1975.

Several hundred Black African workers were slaughtered during labor protests/riots by Portuguese land owners in an event called the "Batepa Massacre" in the early 1950s. The success of independence movements in other African countries motivated native São Tomé and Príncipe and other freedom-loving citizens to establish in 1960 the Nationalist Liberation Organization, which demanded an end to Portuguese rule. This organization was reorganized in 1972 to reflect the consensus and cooperation of the African natives of the two islands. The birth of MLSTP facilitated the process of independence. The country gained independence on July 12, 1975, with Dr. Manuel Pinto da Costa as the country's first President. In 1978, there was a coup organized by mercenaries from neighboring Gabon.

The total population is 181,565 (2004 est.) The principal ethnic majority are Black Africans. The State Department identified six popular groups in this island nation. The *Mestico* are descendants of African slaves who arrived in the country during the early years of slave trade from the African nations of Benin, Gabon, and the Congo. This group is referred to as *Filhos da terra* or "sons of the land." The *Mestico,* or mixed blood, claim ancestral and spiritual guardianship of São Tomé and Príncipe. The *Angolares* are the descendants of Angolan slaves, known for surviving a shipwreck in 1540 and who now make their living in the fishing industry.

The *Forros* are descendants of freed slaves after slavery was abolished. The *Servicais* are contract laborers from African nations such as Angola, Mozambique, and Cape Verde. The *Servicais* are temporary immigrants. The *Tongas* are the children of *Servicais* who are born on the islands. Finally, there are Europeans, mostly remnants of Portuguese imperialists. The return of many Sao Tomean refugees from Angola in the 1970s and the exodus of the Portuguese led to a Luso-African culture.

Forros is a national language or "language of freedmen" that is becoming extinct. However, Portuguese, São Tomense, and Principense are the official languages of the country. São Tomense is spoken on São Tomé Island. This language is classified as Portuguese-based Creole and spoken in a heavy Creole dialet. Most people on the island speak Portuguese, the language of social identity in most São Tomé social networks. The *Angolares* speak São Tomense also. Angolar is spoken on the southern tip of São Tomé Island. Graham (1999) contends that there are few Principenses on Príncipe Island who speak Príncipense.

São Tomé and Príncipe is a Christian nation. Most of the citizens are Roman Catholic. Evangelical Protestants and Seventh-Day Adventist churches have been a growing phenomenon in the country. This religious phenomenon is a reflection of the colonial power supervision by Portugal. Christians make up 84% of the population; all others practice some form of local native tribal beliefs, sometimes referred to as traditional African religion.

The local currency is the Dobras. The economy of the country cannot be understood without knowledge of plantation agriculture, in which acres of land are propagated for a specific cash crop. São Tomé's economy has been based on plantation agriculture since the 1800s. The colonialist Portuguese controlled at least 90% of the plantations. Cocoa is the dominant export cash crop, representing 95% of exports. The government is small and accounts for 11% of São Tomé's employment.

Fishing is the main economic activity other than agriculture, and a small industrial sector processes local agricultural products. São Tomé and Príncipe had a centrally directed economy, especially following the country's independence, when the means of production was owned and controlled by the federal government. Prior to independence, the Constitution guaranteed "Mixed Economy." Like a number of African nations, São Tomé's economy failed to progress, and it became stagnant in the 1980s and 1990s, when the redistribution of land led to decreased cocoa production, and international cocoa prices decreased.

In order to reform the economy, the nation implemented an international monetary fund structural adjustment program. The government embarked on privatization for state-run agricultural and industrial sectors. The government invited and encouraged greater participation in management of the *parastatals* and in the agricultural, commercial, banking, and tourism sectors.

Since independence in 1975, the country has been relegated to a welfare state. The government has traditionally depended on foreign assistance from various donors, including the United Nations Development program, World Bank, European Union, Portugal, Taiwan, and African Development Bank. The International Monetary Fund, for example, approved funds for poverty reduction for the country in the year 2000. In the same year, São Tomé qualified for significant dept reduction under the IMF World Bank's heavily indepted poor countries (HIPC) initiatives.

Political instability has left the reform efforts stagnated. Sixty-nine percent of the country's government expenditures for 1997, for example, were financed by external assistance. The nation's economy increasingly is dependent on the production and exportation of cocoa. The strengthening cocoa prices have helped tremendously to boost export earnings in the past two years. The newly found oil production may actually change the course of the São Tomé and Príncipe economic future.

Contextual Features

São Tomé began to embark on constitutional changes in 1987. These changes included universal adult suffrage. But in 1988, a faction of the exiled São Tomé National Resistance Front led by Alfonso Santos attempted to overthrow the government. The disgruntled elements were arrested and imprisoned.

Since independence and the subsequent decolonization, the country has experienced a period of two main fundamental changes to its political and economic system. São Tomé had previously embraced Soviet-style socialism and a centralized economy upon independence. However, in 1990 the country introduced liberal democracy and a free market economy from an authoritarian socialist one-party state. In the same year, a new Constitution was introduced that provided for the formation of opposition parties and multi-party elections. The country is proud to announce the comfortable victory of an independent candidate, Fradique de Menezes, in the most recent Presidential election in 2001. A democratically rooted political atmosphere has prospered in the country since the last election. There have been some sporadic coup attempts, most recently in 2003. The July, 2003 military coup led by Major Fernando Pereira took over power. The coup was in part a response to the administration's private dealings with various oil corporations. After elaborate negotiations, Pereira's *Junta* signed an agreement with the former leaders and stepped down. Menezes and das Neves resumed power.

The Constitution of 1990 vested legislative power in the National Assembly, elected by popular vote for a period of four years. The President governs with the assistance of the Council of Ministers. Unlike the U.S. system of government, the President's tenure is limited to two successive five-year terms. The National Assembly granted political and administrative autonomy to Principe. However, the island's seven-member Regional Assembly and five-member Regional Government remain accountable to the government of São Tomé.

The Democratic Republic of São Tomé and Príncipe is a multi-party democracy. The government is composed of an executive branch and a unicameral legislature, known as the General Assembly. The President appoints the Prime Minister and delegates authority to the Prime Minister to appoint Ministers of Government. The President is the Chief of State and is elected by popular vote for a five-year term. The 1990 Constitution officially ended one-party rule. Transition to democracy was a peaceful one. Since this constitutional change, there have been seven elections, with the National Assembly divided among the country's several political parties. There are organizations such as associations of small-scale land holders or fishermen. These organizations are an increasingly visible part of the new political atmosphere, and voter participation has also increased. The country is made up of six districts that are composed of district councils, and the Island of Príncipe, which now an autonomous region.

The country is a member of the United Nations, ACP group, African development bank, non-aligned group of nations (G-77), International Bank of Reconstruction and Development, International Monetary Fund, INTERPOL, and OAU.

The legal system of the São Tomé and Príncipe is based on the Portuguese legal system and customary law. Like many countries, São Tomé and Príncipe has not accepted compulsory ICJ Jurisdiction. The judicial system is regarded as inefficient, especially because of its inability to prevent and control violence and because of discrimination and crimes against women, child labor, and harsh labor practices. The Constitution provides for an independent judiciary, but it is subject to political influence and manipulation, as it is in many third world countries.

The highest level of justice administration is the Supreme Court. But the National Assembly is the supreme body of the state and the highest legislative body. The Supreme Court was in the past responsible to the National Assembly until the new Constitution provided that the judiciary be independent. The São Tomé Courts system has two basic levels: Circuit Courts and the Supreme Court. The Supreme Court is the appellate court of last resort. The country's court system is divided into seven municipal districts, with six in São Tomé and one in Príncipe. In each of these districts are governing councils that maintain a limited number of autonomous decision-making powers, and they too are elected every five years.

The Constitution provides for an independent judiciary, but the government has important powers relating to the judiciary, including powers to decide on salaries of judges.

The São Tomé and Príncipe Constitution is very clear on the provision for the right to fair trial, appeal, and legal representation. On paper, this is a fair representation of democratic principles; however, the political influence on the judiciary makes it less than fair. The judicial infrastructure suffers from painful budgetary constraints, inappropriate and inadequate facilities, and shortage of trained judges and lawyers.

The budgetary situation of the judiciary causes a backlog of cases and results in the unfortunate three- to nine-month procedural delay for court cases, impeding adequate investigations of cases. The Constitution provides for freedom of speech and press, peaceful assembly and association, freedom of religion and movement, political rights, and human rights. It also provides for the equality of all citizens, regardless of race, sex, origin, political affiliation, creed, or ideology.

Men and women have equal political, economic, and social rights; and access to government, education, and business opportunity. There are laws prohibiting trafficking in persons. The Constitution also provides for a law that prohibits forced labor or bonded labor by children or any citizen. There are several kinds of criminal activities on the island. Most common among them are burglary, pickpocketing, and armed robbery.

Penalties for possession, use, or trafficking of illegal drugs are very strict, and convicted offender can be expelled; long jail sentences and heavy fines are sometimes imposed.

Police Profile

Organizational Description

São Tomé and Príncipe has a national police system. The Police are organized in eight districts. The Agua Grande district includes the country's capital. Other districts include Mezochi, Lemba, Lobata, Cantagalo, Caue, and the Island of Príncipe (administratively known as Pague).

The minister of National Defense, Security and Internal Order is responsible for Military services, Immigration, and the Police. The Police force is grossly underfunded.

Training

The National Police force has a cooperative training program with the Angolan National Police. This program has been helpful in elevating the competence of the São Tomé and Príncipe National Police.

Complaints and Discipline

The government proclaims the protection of human rights. Yet, there are instances of gross violation of this rule. Security forces on several occasions violate citizens by beating and abusing detainees and disperse peaceful protests with violence. Prison conditions are harsh. Fernandes Pires Correia encouraged special training for riot and traffic police.

EVARISTUS OBINYAN

Bibliography

São Tomé and Príncipe. International Buisness Publication, USA, 2004.
São Tomé and Príncipe Business Law Handbook. IBP, USA, 1999.
U.S Department of State. Bureau of Public Affairs. Office of Public Communication 1997, 2003, 2004.
Warne, Sophie. Gabon, São Tomé and Príncipe: Travel Guide. Bradt Travel Guide 2003.
www.greekorthodoxchurch.org.
www.worldbank.org.
www.usemb.se/human/human1998/saotomep.html.
www.un.org/webcast/ga58.
www.countrywatch.com.
www.phrasebase.com.
www.saotome.com.
www.cia.gov.

SAUDI ARABIA

Background Material

The Kingdom of Saudi Arabia, with a land mass of 1,960,582 sq km, is the largest among nine other countries (Yemen, Oman, Bahrain, United Arab Emirate, Kuwait, Iraq, Jordan, Syria, and Lebanon) that comprise the Arabian Peninsula, a vast stretch of land in the Middle East region that separates the African continent from Asia. Saudi Arabia shares borders with Yemen on the south; Oman, Bahrain and Kuwait on the east; Iraq on the northeast; and Jordan on the north.

Topographically, although the Arabian Peninsula is located between the Red Sea to the west, Indian Ocean to the south, and the Persian Gulf to the east, Saudi Arabia has coastal lines with the Red Sea and the Persian Gulf, but not with the Indian Ocean. Although surrounded by large bodies of water and in close proximity to the Indian Ocean, Saudi Arabia is an arid land, especially in its interior, which is known as the *Rub' al-Khali* (the Empty Quarter).

However, the country is endowed with huge oil and natural gas reservoirs, making the Kingdom a very important country in the Middle East region.

The 2004 population of Saudi Arabia was estimated at 25,795,038, with an annual growth rate of 2.44%, giving the country one of the fastest population growth rates in the world. Arabic is the major language of the country. The Kingdom's ethnic makeup is 90% Arabs with another 10% of Afro-Asian extraction. According to official statistics, 92% adhere to the Sunni branch of Islam, and 8% to Shii.

Saudi Arabia is a monarchy founded by a warrior-tribal chief, Abdul Aziz bin Abdul Rahman al Saud in 1932 (thus the designation of Saudi); it has been ruled ever since by Ibn Saud's male lineage. The document known as the "Basic Law," composed of 83 Articles, defines (I) General Principles (articles 1–4), (II) System of Government (articles 5–8), (III) Constituents of Saudi Society (articles 9–13), (IV) Economic Principles (articles 14–22), (V) Rights and Duties (articles 23–43), (VI) Powers of the State (articles 44–71), (VII) Financial Affairs (articles 72–78), (VIII) Institutions of Audit (articles 79–80), and (IX) General Provisions (articles 81–83). A synopsis of the eight parameters of the Basic Law is provided below as a prelude to exploring Saudi Arabia's police system and philosophy.

The General Principle articles depict the Kingdom as an Islamic state founded on Islam's Sacred Law, and the Traditions of the Prophet Muhammad, proclaiming Islam as the official religion of the country, Arabic as its language, and Riyadh as its capital city. In addition, the shape, color, and the motto of the Saudi Arabian flag is designated.

The System of Government articles depict the structure and the sources of authority, power, and legitimacy of the State, as well as the manner in which citizens' acquiescence and loyalty to the monarchy is procured through the Islamic institution of voluntary pledge of allegiance (*biya*) to the kings of the House of Ibn Saud. These articles declare that the Saudi form of governance is a truly Islamic one modeled on the advice of the Koran and the Traditions of the Prophet Muhammad. In addition, the laws that are passed by the Saudi State are portrayed as verbatim Koranic laws. The right to rule as a monarch belongs to the sons of the founder of the Saudi State, provided that the ruler is the most upright among his brethren. The Kings have to rule with justice and in accordance with the guiding principles of the Koran and the Traditions of the Prophet.

The Constituents of the Saudi Society articles give to the family a central role in the raising of the generations of the Saudi citizens obedient to God, and to the teachings of the Prophet Muhammad and those in the position of authority. The State is deemed responsible for disseminating the true Islamic and Arab values in strengthening the family and its bonds to society. The Saudi citizens are duty-bound to work hard to foster a set of values that would foster unity, benevolence, and mutual assistance, engendering national unity and a sense of brotherly love and compassion towards one another.

The Economic Principles articles proclaim that the country's resources as well as revenues accrued through the utilization of such resources belong to the State as specified by law. Recognizing private property, capital, and labor as the fundamentals of the Saudi free-market economy, private rights have to be in harmony with the criteria specified by Islam's Sacred Law, the *Sharia*. In addition, confiscation of public or private property is forbidden, unless allowed by law and if fairly compensated. Any taxation and/or imposition of fees is subjected to the principle of fairness and shall apply if such needs were to arise.

The Rights and Duties articles give primacy to the State's responsibilities in protecting Islamic Creed, safeguarding the application of the principles of the *Sharia*, perpetrating the Islamic principle of good deeds and avoidance of evil as expressed in the Koran. The State is also obligated in the propagation of Islam and of its Call (*Da'wa*), accordingly. Of special significance is Article 26, which stipulates that the State shall protect human rights in accordance with the *Sharia*. The article does not specify how the Islamic *Sharia* articulates human rights as we understand this concept as a modern one that emerged in the aftermath of the French Revolution in 1789. However, other articles specify that the State is responsible for the provision of proper care to Saudi citizens during illness, old age, or public emergencies.

The Powers of the State articles define the powers of the judiciary, the executive, and the organizational branches of the government. Although these powers are bestowed on these branches to perform their duties, it is the King who is legally the ultimate source of all State authorities according to Article 44. The King is assisted by a tribunal of religious experts who have reached expertise in Islamic law and thus are authorized to issue sound religious opinions in resolving public issues and concerns that are brought to the attention of the King for final resolution. The judiciary is declared as autonomous bowing to no one other than the principles of the *Sharia* (Article 46). Everyone is entitled to equal right to litigation, be it a Saudi citizen or a foreigner (47). The main responsibility of the courts is the proper application of the *Sharia* and the Traditions of the Prophet Muhammad (Article 48). There is a Supreme Judicial Council empowered to propose to the King (based upon law) who shall be appointed to, or dismissed from office (Articles 51 and 52). There is a Board of Investigation and Public Prosecution that carries out the prosecutorial functions in relation to both investigation and prosecution of crime in fourteen provinces of the Saudi Arabia (54).

The Saudi King is more than a symbolic figure; he has full executive powers. He also assumes the responsibilities of the office of the Prime Minister assisted by the Council of Ministers. The Council includes, among other members, those officials who assume ministerial posts (a total of 23) in the Kingdom. These are the Ministries of Agriculture, Civil Service, Commerce and Industry, Communication and Information Technology, Culture and Information, Defense and Aviation, Economic Planning, Education, Finance, Foreign Affairs, Haj, Health, Higher Education, Interior, Islamic Affairs, Endowment, Dawa and Guidance, Justice, Labor, Municipal and Rural Affairs, Petroleum and Mineral Resources, Social Affairs, Transport, Water and Electricity, and General Presidency of Youth Welfare. The Law of the Council of Ministers specifies various aspects, functions, powers, and jurisdiction of this body, including the duties of the Ministers (57). All government officials, from the Deputy Prime Minister to Cabinet Ministers and their deputies, including officials designated as "excellent grade," are appointed to, or dismissed from, office by the King's royal decree. All are accountable to the Prime Minister, who is the King himself. The King is also the Supreme Commander of the Saudi Arabian armed forces; he appoints military officers to, or dismisses them from, their posts. The King is also authorized to declare war or a state of emergency, as well as general mobilization (Articles 57 and 60). When traveling abroad, or in times of ill health, the King is authorized to delegate parts of his authority to the Crown Prince through a royal decree (65 and 66).

Financial Affairs articles of the Basic Law regulate the manner in which state revenues are procured and deposited with the General Treasure of the State, and how they are budgeted for public expenditures. These articles also regulate various fiscal and monetary policies of the state.

Institutions of Audit articles specify the manner in which state audit shall apply, the results reported to the Prime Minister, and charges of mismanagement of public funds investigated. Finally, the General Provisions articles ensure that the application of various articles of the Basic Law shall not be in contravention of the treaties or agreements that the Saudi government has signed or reached with other States.

The Kingdom is divided into 13 provinces, each under a Provincial Governor who carries the rank of a Minister under the Ministry of Interior and headquartered in the respective Provincial Capitals. The 13 Saudi Provinces (known as Regions) are Riyadh, Makkah, Madinah, Qasim, Eastern, Asir, Tabouk, Hail, Northern Border, Jizan, Al-Barah, and Al-Jouf. The Provinvial Capitals carry the name of the Regions, except for Qasim, Asir, Eastern, Northern, and Al-Jouf. Each Governor is responsible for matters related to policing and security concerns of the region under his jurisdictional authority.

Contextual Features

The Kingdom is an Islamic state. Reading the country's Basic Law articles, one gets the distinct impression that Islam is an intrinsic part of the Saudi society, government, and polity structure, playing a central role in fostering an Islamic base for the operational dynamics of the Saudi social and legal affairs, including its policing and security concerns. In fact, the Saudi monarchy, in its official declarations, portrays itself as the "Protector of the Faith of Islam and of the Two Holy Cities of Mecca and Medina." This designation is due to the fact that Islam originated in Arabia (in the cities of Mecca and Median) in the early decades of the seventh century AD. In addition, this designation is important for a better appraisal of the Saudi political establishment's view of the role and function of the police and policing philosophy, from the time of its modern foundation in 1932 to present. The Saudi police's primary function is to serve and protect Islam and its values according to its official mandate stipulated by the Ministry of Interior.

In addition to being the birth place of Islam, a feature which gives to the Kingdom its privileged position in the eyes of the larger world of Islam, the Kingdom is the largest producer of crude oil among the OPEC (Oil Producing and Exporting Countries). Oil was discovered in 1930 in Saudi Arabia, enabling the Kingdom to gradually change its status from a ramshackle patch of Arab tribal societies that King Ibn Saud brought together in the early decades of the twentieth century, into the status of a prosperous stable nation. The Kingdom has played an important role in the Middle East region due to its strategic location and its abilities to forge a close alliance with American oil and natural gas industries from the time of Ibn Saud to present. The ARAMCO (Arab-American Oil) is the principal oil venture in the Kingdom that is involved in the exploration, refinement, and export of Saudi Arabian crude, which is one of the finest in the world. The venture has been beneficial for both parties according to official declarations giving to the Kingdom a very important place and role in OPEC. In addition, because the Kingdom's main source of revenue is petrodollars, it has played an important role in the world's financial markets. Following the advice of the International Monetary Fund (IMF) in 1958, the Kingdom has implemented five developmental plans during a 25-year period commencing in 1970, and ending in 1995. The budgeted expenditure of the First Developmental Plan (1970–1975), budgeted at a modest US$9.2 billion, rose to 21 billion due to an unprecedented rise in the price of the crude oil in 1973. During the Second Plan (1975–1980), it rose to the staggering amount of US$142 billion. Absorbing this huge amount of revenue and putting it in different factors of the Saudi economy created a number of bottlenecks for the Saudi economy, upsetting the pre-oil traditional Saudi economic structure and social relationships. One such problem was inflation; another was the inability of the Saudi customs, warehousing, and transportation systems to handle the amount of imported goods that included perishable food and other consumable items. To remedy some of these economic bottlenecks, the Third and Fourth Developmental Plans (1980–1990) reconsidered the overall budgeted expenditures. Another blow to the ambitious Saudi development plan came in 1986, when a sudden crash occurred in crude oil prices, forcing the Kingdom to take some corrective measures in its planned expenditures.

Despite the positive results of the five-year development in improving the Kingdom's agriculture, education, health and human service, tourism, water, electricity, and road and transportation networks, the Saudi society and state remain deeply religious entities. The vast majority of the population adheres to a strict branch of Sunni Islam, the Wahhabi, which from its foundation in the eighteenth century has been proposing a return to Islam's basic values by emulating the Prophet Muhammad's model of governance in the City of Meddinah (R. 622–632). To do so, the founder of the Wahhabi sect, Abdul Wahhab, proposed that an Islamic government is duty-bound to base its social, political, economic, and legal affairs on Islam's Sacred Law, the *Sharia* as it was practiced under Muhammad. Following this view, the offi-

cial rhetoric of the Saudi Kingdom is that the monarchs of the House of Ibn Saud have tried to shape the country as a true Islamic society at the same time that they have tried to adapt the country to the realities of the modern world—factors such as urbanization and industrialization—as well as changes that have taken place in the Middle East region due to globalization.

Criminal Justice System

The Kingdom's criminal justice system is based on the Islamic *Sharia,* whose mandate is to disseminate justice by applying the principles of the *Sharia* in matters related to law and justice. One principle maintains that those who violate the country's laws and regulations as specified in the Kingdom's Basic Law articles must be apprehended and brought before a court of law for prosecution. If found guilty of capital crimes, the culprit must be punished accordingly. The Ministry of Interior is responsible for crime investigation, apprehension of the suspects, and law enforcement activities. The *Sharia* courts hear cases as presented to them by the Ministry's prosecutors. The punishment regime is quite stern, applying various retributive and/or corporal punishments for crimes based on a strict application of the *Sharia*-based crime and punishment categories. Examples include amputation of finger for theft, public lashing for signs of public intoxication, and public beheading for adultery or premeditated murder. Amnesty International has characterized these as cruel and unusual punishments that are against human dignity. The Saudi Justice system has rejected this criticism, arguing that it adheres to the Koran's principles of just punishment. Defending the system, Saudi dignitaries maintain that the Kingdom controls crime through both formal and informal means.

The formal means are harsh because those who commit crime are beyond help insofar as the efficacy of the informal system is concerned, and thus they must be punished to the fullest extent as allowed by law to jolt them out of criminality. Those criminologists who have studied the Saudi society have recorded a relatively low rate of crime commission in the past. However, the Saudi society is changing, and so is the rate of crime.

The biggest challenge facing the Kingdom is whether the present system of justice, based on a strict reading of the *Sharia*, is amenable to reform. Is it possible for the Kingdom to gradually replace this complex system of justice, especially its harsh punishment regime, without compromising the Kingdom's much-cherished Islamic tradition? Ironically, when we refer to Traditions of the Prophet Muhammad as narrated by authentic Islamic sources, as for instance, Imam Bukhari, we find stories that give us a rather different picture as to the adaptability of the *Sharia*. One story is about the Prophet's judgment on the question of the propriety of the punishment for adultery. Accordingly, a group of Jewish residents of Madinah appealed to the Prophet to adjudicate an adultery case between a Jewish man and a Jewish woman. The Prophet inquired about the customary manner in which adultery was punished among the Jews. They replied that it was customary to blacken the face of the accused with coal and subject him/her to a beating. Hearing this, the Prophet inquired about the punishment of stoning adulterers that Torah had advised. The answer was that such punishment did not exist in the Torah. Hearing this, one of the learned Muslims in the session asked the plaintiff to bring the text of the Torah to the session to show that such punishment had indeed been advised by the Scripture. Although the gist of the story is that the Prophet ordered the punishment of stoning be carried out against the defendant, it was due to the principle of adherence to the law of the Scripture that prevailed among Jewish residents of Madinah then. This adherence does not mean that this Torah-based punishment for adultery has a base in the Koran, too. The Koranic punishment for adultery is flogging of both the male and female involved in adultery that has been eye-witnessed by four reputable witnesses who under oath and the penalty of perjury testify to the act in a court of law. Nowhere in the Koran is there any allusion to stoning those found guilty of adultery, let alone beheading them by sword. The point is that the Saudi justice system is open to much reform without a tangible loss of its Islamic nature.

Police Profile

The Saudi Arabian police system falls under the jurisdiction of the Ministry of Interior. Public information on the Saudi police is extremely rare, and even the most basic information is extremely difficult to access. It seems that there is a national police under the authority of the Ministry of Interior with regional headquarters in the Kingdom's thirteen regions. Besides traditional policing, the Saudi police force seems to be an integral part of the Saudi defense forces, with a wide range of arrest and interrogation authority at its disposal. Anecdotes relating the maltreatment of suspects in police custody abound on the Internet, although generally the veracity of this information cannot be guaranteed.

SCOTLAND

See **United Kingdom.**

SENEGAL

Background Material

The Republic of Senegal is the westernmost country on the African continent. It is situated on the Atlantic Ocean, north of Guinea and Guinea Bissau, west of Mali, and south of Mauritania. It almost completely encapsulates The Gambia, a country which stretches from the Atlantic east into Senegal in a long narrow strip around the Gambia River. The capital city of Senegal is

Dakar, which is situated on the Atlantic coast. From the ninth to the fourteenth centuries, the Tukulor people held sway in the Senegal River Valley. They were converted to Islam in the eleventh century. The Mali Empire expanded westward in the fourteenth century and conquered the Tukulor. This incursion was followed by that of the Jolof Empire, composed of the Wolof and other groups. In the fifteenth century, the Portuguese established trading posts along the coast and developed routes inland. The Portuguese in turn were displaced by the Dutch and, in the seventeenth century, the French. During the Seven Years War (1756–1763), and again in the Napoleonic Wars, the British captured the French posts in Senegal, but they were returned under treaty arrangements. Senegal became a French colony in 1895 and, in 1960, joined with the former French Sudan to form the independent Mali Federation. Shortly after, Senegal withdrew from the Federation and became an independent state within the French Community. Initially, there was considerable unrest, but the country gradually evolved to a multi-party democratic state, which is reasonably stable, except for a chronic secessionist movement in the Casamance Region to the south.

The population of Senegal is 10.8 million, two million of whom live in the capital city of Dakar. It is a multi-ethnic society comprising Wolof (43.3%); Pular (23.8%); Serer (14.7%); and Jola, Mandika, Soninke, and others. The official language is French, but various indigenous languages are also spoken. Ninety-four percent of the population is Muslim, 5% Christian, and the remaining practice indigenous religions.

Life expectancy is 56.5 years, and the literacy rate is slightly more than 40%. The GDP per head is US$1,600. Seventy percent of the population lives in rural areas, and agricultural production and fish processing are the mainstays of the economy. There is also some phosphate and iron ore mining and fertilizer production. The urban areas suffer chronic unemployment, particularly among youth. Nevertheless, the average annual economic growth rate is 5%; over 80% of the economy is privatized; inflation is flat; and full Internet connectivity, achieved in 1996, has created a number of technology-based services.

Contextual Features

The revised Senegalese Constitution of 2001 assures a secular, democratic state, founded on popular sovereignty, where all citizens are equal without distinction of origin, race, sex, or religion. Constitutional rights include the right to life, liberty, security, property, and bodily integrity. A long list of freedoms, including expression, opinion, association, movement, religion, education, health, work, and protest, are also constitutionally guaranteed. Further constitutional provisions include women's rights to inherit and manage their own property, equal treatment in work, pay and taxation, and not to be subject to forced marriage. Children are also protected against exploitation and neglect. In general, Senegal adheres to the human rights principles embedded in its Constitution, and civil society is reasonably well-developed.

The Executive branch consists of a President, who is elected for a term of five years, and his Council of Ministers. The National Assembly is the legislative body. It is elected directly by universal suffrage for a term of five years. The Prime Minister and Ministers named by the President form the government, which conducts and coordinates the national policies set by the President. They are accountable both to the President and to the National Assembly. The judiciary is independent of both the executive and the legislative branches of government.

There are a number of female members of the National Assembly. In 2004, six of 33 ministers were women. A woman has also held the office of Prime Minister. Fourteen percent of lawyers are women. Despite constitutional guarantees, however, women suffer some disadvantages in Senegalese society, particularly in rural areas, where traditional practices are still common. Women have a lower literacy rate than men, and only 20% are in paid employment. They pay higher income taxes than men because they are not considered heads of households. Half of all women are in polygamous marriages.

The system of law is founded upon the French civil law, although there is some use of customary law in family matters. The courts system consists of a Constitutional Council, a Council of State, a Final Court of Appeal, an Accounts Court, and local courts and tribunals.

The Constitutional Court is responsible for ensuring the constitutionality of laws and international agreements, and for ruling on jurisdictional conflicts between the executive and legislative branches of government, or between the Council of State and the Appeals Court.

The Council of State is judge of first and final resort on use of excessive authority by the executive. It is also responsible for decisions on electoral lists and the election of local councils, and hears administrative appeals from lower courts and tribunals. The Court of Cassation, or Court of Final

Appeals, hears appeals from the judgments of the lower courts, while the Accounts Court is responsible for the oversight and audit of public accounts. The lower courts and tribunals are seriously understaffed, thus delaying the processing of cases. The usual time for a case to proceed from charge to trial averages two years, and the interval may be served in detention, since bail is rare. In 1998, the government undertook a special initiative to alleviate the situation by recruiting and training 48 law school graduates for employment as magistrates.

The crime rate in Senegal is low compared with western countries. Crime reports based on Interpol data for the year 2000 put total index offenses at 64.29 per 100,000 compared to 4,123.97 per 100,000 for the USA. The Senegalese rate per 100,000 for murder was 0.33, sex offenses 1.71, robbery 2.07, aggravated assault 6.62, burglary 2.47, larceny 46.98, and motor vehicle theft 4.11. In 2001, Interpol reported that 13,234 cases were known to the police. The Gendarmerie reported in 2004 that during the year it had arrested 7,355 offenders, 690 for drug offenses; resolved 84 crimes out of 95; recorded 5,160 minor crimes; and collected 800 million francs in fines and forfeitures. According to the International Centre for the Prevention of Crime, 76 percent of offenders are between the ages of 20 and 44, although this age group forms only 27 percent of the Senegalese population. Nine out of 10 offenders are men; however, in the 15–19 age group, girls are more likely to offend than boys.

Senegal is a transit point for heroin from Southwest and Southeast Asia, and cocaine from South America destined for Europe and North America. Cannabis is also cultivated for export and local use, and there is some small arms trafficking. Senegal is also a source and transit country for trafficking of women and girls to Europe and the Middle East for labor and sexual exploitation. Sex tourism is also described as an acute problem in some large Senegalese cities, and children are also sometimes held in involuntary servitude by religious institutions to earn their living expenses and those of their teachers. Although female genital mutilation is illegal and the government has public education programs to discourage its use, it is still practiced regularly in some rural areas of the country. Domestic violence, usually wife beating, is common. In 1996, a Canadian study done in Dakar found 87% of 515 women interviewed had suffered from some form of domestic violence.

In 2001, it was reported at a United Nations workshop that the prison population rate in Senegal had been empirically assessed at 53 per 100,000 population, or 5,300 prisoners, but the rate is reported to be climbing steadily. Recidivism rates are also reported to be as high as 90%. Prisons tend to be underfunded and overcrowded, and food and health care poor. While the lengths of pre-trial detention periods are prescribed by law, detainees can be held for months and even years without trial, mainly because of lack of court personnel to process cases. Pre-trial detainees are also sometimes held with convicted prisoners because of lack of space. The 2001 UN report put the rate of pre-trial prisoners at 32.6% of the total prison population.

Women and children are held separately from male prisoners in Senegalese prisons, and international human rights groups are allowed to visit institutions to check on conditions.

The Senegalese prison population suffering from HIV/AIDS is reported to be 2.7%, which is among the lowest in Sub-Saharan Africa. The government has introduced AIDS awareness programs. In the past, it has also experimented with a program of transcendental meditation for both prisoners and staff to reduce violence and recidivism. Extravagant claims for its success were made by western supporters of transcendental meditation, but the results appear to have been inconclusive at best.

Police Profile

Demographics

A particular challenge for the police is shortage of personnel. During 1994 and 2004, little more than 100 recruits a year were admitted. This appears to have been due to budget pressures, but it is also claimed that the extensive involvement of Senegalese police in United Nations peace-keeping operations also contributed significantly to the personnel shortage. There has been considerable outcry because there were only four commissioners of police in Dakar for a population of two million. In 2004, there was some amelioration of the situation, with an intake of over 600 recruits for the police and penitentiaries, and the promise of more in the future.

Organizational Description and Functions

In 1990, Senegal spent 4.5% of the national budget on police and security, compared with 11 percent on education and 6.1% on defense. The policing system is modeled on the French system and is centrally controlled. There are two main police bodies: the National Gendarmerie and the National Police. The Gendarmerie comes under the Gendarmerie High Command and Military Justice Directorate of the Ministry of the Armed Forces, while the National Police comes under the jurisdiction of the Minister of the Interior. The Gendarmerie is a paramilitary organization that operates in rural areas and at borders, while the civilian National Police operates mainly in cities.

In addition to the rural-urban and paramilitary-civilian divisions between the two agencies, there is a functional division within each of the two police forces between the administrative and judicial or investigative police. The administrative police are characterized as essentially preventive, responsible for the protection of persons and property, and the maintenance of order. The judicial police are responsible for the detection of crime, its investigation, and the arrest of suspects. Members of either the Gendarmerie or the National Police can act in both capacities, but when they are acting as judicial police, they come under the authority of the courts, in particular the examining magistrate (*juge d'instruction*) and the prosecutor.

There are two levels of judicial police: higher ranking officers of the Gendarmerie, and commissioners and officers of the National Police are the officers of the judicial police; while lower ranking personnel are agents of the judicial police. Under the delegation of the examining magistrate, officers of the judicial police have the power to detain suspects for questioning for 48 hours (or up to 96 hours if approved by a public prosecutor), to inquire into an offense, to prepare the proceedings of the inquiry, and to receive complaints, charges and declarations of those with an interest in the case. Agents of the judicial police gather information and intelligence as required, and report it to their superior officers.

Training

Higher ranking peace officers or commissioners receive two years of training at the National Police School; and inspectors, police officers, and sub-peace officers receive one year of training. Training starts with technical and legal courses and then proceeds to professional courses. The Senegalese police also receive specialist training from French, American, and some German police training units. The National Police Training School also trains guards for the penitentiary system. Women are accepted into the National Police as well as the penitentiary system.

Police Public Projects

The National Police recognize that fewer than 30% of cases under investigation are ever solved and that only 50% of all offenses are ever reported. The Police force has therefore introduced some innovations in recent years to prevent rising delinquency. These have included some decentralization of policing; partnerships with municipalities and local communities to provide neighborhood policing; and working with women, youth, and the poor to reduce poverty and prevent crime.

Complaints and Discipline

There is some reported concern that police and gendarmes are not particularly effective, that they sometimes act without the necessary authority of warrants and resort to violence to control situations. There is little or no official retribution when police violate human rights.

International Cooperation

Senegal is participating with other West African countries in creating cooperative mechanisms for countering international crime such as smuggling, illegal aliens, financial crimes, child and women trafficking, terrorism, and drug trafficking. Senegal is also a member of Interpol.

TONITA MURRAY

Bibliography

Amnesty International. "Senegal." *Amnesty International Report 2002*, 2002.

France, Ministère des affaires étrangères. *Composition du gouvernement de la République du Sénégal*, Gouvernement du 22 avril 2004. www.diplomatie.gouv.fr/actu/article.asp?ART=29409. October 3, 2004.

Hills, Alice. *Policing Africa: Internal Security and Limits of Liberalisation*. Boulder, CO: Lynne Rienner Publishers, 2000.

International Centre for the Prevention of Crime. "Safety for All ...Equally!" *International Observer*, edition 26, March 2004. www.crime-prevention-intl.org. September 25, 2004.

International Centre for the Prevention of Crime. «La sécurité pour tous ...également», Seminaire sous-régional sur la sécurité des milieux de vie and la prévention de la délinquance, Dakar, 20-13 janvier, 2004. Montreal: International Centre for the Prevention of Crime.

Interpol. *African Member Countries*. www.interpol.int/public/Region/Africa/Members.asp, 2004. October 3, 2004.

Juriscope. *La direction de la police judiciare et son contrôle par les autorités judiciare de Sénégal*, 1999, www.juriscope.org/publications/etudes/pdf-polive/OK.SENEG.pdf. February 28, 2005.

M'Boge, Fatoumatta, and Doe Sam Gbaydee. *African Commitment to Civil Society Engagement: A review of eight NEPAD countries*. Paper no. 6, African Human Security Initiative, August 2004. www.africareview.org. February 25, 2005.

Senegal-online. *Économie nationale*. www.senegal-online.com/francais. October 10, 2004.

United Nations Programme Network Institutes, Technical Assistance Workshop, Vienna, Austria, May 10, 2001. *World Prison Population: Facts, Trends and Solutions*, "Prisons in Africa". www.unicri.it/pdf/un_workshop/kibuka.pdf, February 28, 2005.

United States, CIA. "Senegal." *The World Factbook*. www.cia.gov/cia/publications/factbook/geos/sg.html. September 19, 2004.

United States, Department of State. "Senegal." *Country Reports on Human Rights Practices–2003*. http://us.politinfo.com.

United States, Department of State. *International Narcotics and Law Enforcement: FY 2004 Budget Justification*. www.state.gov/g/inl/rls/rpt/cbj/fy200. October 3, 2004.

Winslow, Robert (n.d.). "Senegal." *Crime and Society: A Comparative Criminology Tour of the World*. www.rohan.sdsu.edu/faulty/rwinslow/Africa/Senegal.html.

SERBIA

Background Material

The State Union of Serbia and Montenegro is the successor of the Federal Republic of Yugoslavia, established by Constitutional Agreement in February 2003. Serbia currently exists in a loose federation with Montenegro. The republics plan to hold a referendum on whether to move to full independence in 2006. The republics operate separate police systems.

Serbia is located in the central part of the Balkans, occupying 88,361 sq km. It contains two autonomous provinces: Vojvodina and Kosovo, and Metohija.

The ethnic population is highly varied as a result of turbulent history. The 1991 census puts the population of Serbia at 9,779,000. Serbs make up 66%, Albanians 17%, and Hungarians 3.5%, followed by Romanians, Romanies, Slovaks, Croats, Bulgarians, Turks, and others. The Constitution guarantees rights for minorities in accordance with the highest international standards. The official language is Serbian, and the alphabet is Cyrillic, as well as Latin. In the areas inhabited by national minorities, the languages and alphabets of the minorities are in official use, as provided by the law.

The main religion is Christian Orthodox, the faith of the Serbs. Other religious communities are Islamic, Roman Catholic, Protestant, Jewish, and others.

The GDP per capita (purchasing power parity) is $3,400 (2001 est.) The main foreign trading partners are Bosnia and Herzegovina, Italy, FYR Macedonia, Germany, Bulgaria, and Russian Federation.

Besides a devastated economy, now in transition towards a market economy, the main challenges facing Serbia are ethnic tensions in Kosovo and Metohija, and south Serbia; and organized crime.

At the beginning of the twentieth century, Serbia formed a kingdom with Croatia and Slovenia that existed until World War II. In the period between 1945 and 1990, Serbia was part of the Socialist Federative Republic of Yugoslavia. This country was enveloped in civil war, and Serbia with Montenegro formed the Federative Republic of Yugoslavia. In 1990, Serbia formally became a pluralistic society and democracy, introducing democratic institutions in the new Constitution. In reality, it was an authoritarian regime headed by Slobodan Milosevic, who was in power until "the democratic revolution" in October 2000. In the province of Kosovo and Metohija, inhabited mostly by Albanians, ethnic tensions between them and Serbs and other nationalities were present for several decades. Albanians, guided by the project of forming "Greater Albania," exerted pressure on other nationalities to move out of the province. In 1990, Serbia suspended autonomy of the province; the resistance of ethnical Albanians grew, so in 1998 they formed the Kosovo Liberation Army (KLA). Clashes between the KLA and Serbian military and police forces expanded. Serbia was under international pressure for excessive use of force. After the breakdown of negotiations, NATO forces intervened in March 1999, and eventually the UN took over the responsibilities for maintaining civil law and order, including establishing local police forces and deploying international police personnel to serve in Kosovo.

Since October 2000, Serbia has been in a process of reforming all the institutions, including the police, with a general aim to become a democratic society, based on the rule of law and other democratic values.

Contextual Features

Constitutionally, the Republic of Serbia is a democratic state for all citizens who live in its territory, founded on the freedoms and rights of man and citizen, rule of law, and social justice. Serbia's constitutional order is parliamentary democracy. Activities on making a new Constitution are underway in Serbia, since the existing one is inherited from the period of Milosevic's rule, and it is in many aspects outdated or incompatible with the intentions of Serbia to become a EU member. Constituent and legislative power is vested in the National Assembly with 250 deputies. Executive power is vested in the Government, which consists of the Prime Minister, Deputy Prime Ministers, and other Ministers. The Government and the Ministers are independent within the framework of their jurisdiction, and are responsible to the National Assembly.

Serbia has a civil law system; its criminal law system could be called mixed or quasi-adversarial. The criminal justice system consists of the courts, the State Prosecutor, the prisons and correctional institutions, and the Police.

The protection of constitutionality, as well as the protection of legality, in accordance with the Constitution, is vested in the Constitutional Court, which is also a protector of the constitutional order of Serbia.

Judicial power is vested in the courts of law with general responsibilities (138 municipal and 30 district), commercial courts (district and Supreme), Court of Appeal, Administrative Court, and the Supreme Court of the Republic, the highest court in Serbia.

The State Prosecutor is an independent state authority responsible for prosecuting cases brought against those suspected of committing criminal offences. There are 109 municipal public prosecution offices, 30 district public prosecution offices, and the Supreme State Prosecutor's Office and Special Prosecutor responsible for organized crime.

The Prison Administration, working within the jurisdiction of the Ministry of Justice, performs administrative and professional tasks related to implementation of penal sanctions; organization and management of prisons and correctional institutions; provision of financial, material, human, technical and other resources for the functioning of prisons and corrective institutions; and the training of personnel to meet the requirements of the implementation of penal sanctions and the exercise of prisoners' rights and discharge of their duties. There are district and regional prisons. According to the level of security measures and treatment of prisoners, prisons are opened, semi-opened, closed, and strictly closed.

The growing trend of criminality dropped by 21.7% in 2002. Property offenses are on the decline, as well as most serious criminal offenses, while the detection of economic crime increased. Main problems include the rise of organized crime (drug trafficking, trafficking in human beings, kidnappings, and political assassinations), violence, and drug abuse among the young.

Police Profile

Background

Frequent breaks in historical continuity have been reflected in police organization. The postwar period saw an ideologically motivated police force with a low level of respect for human rights. After the introduction of a multi-party system, the Ministry of Interior (MUP) became one of the main pillars of the autocratic system of government that blocked transition towards democracy. The police were separated from the people and misused for political aims, principally to protect the regime rather than enforce the law. They were ineffective in fighting crime and operated outside any form of effective democratic control.

After democratic changes, it became apparent that a complete revision of the security concept was a high priority, and that immediate and substantive change in all the organizational and functional sections of the MUP must correct the serious inherited shortcomings (links between some police officials and organized crime, corruption, politicization, militarization, centralization, lack of control and respect for human rights, code of conduct, capable managers, personnel, and equipment).

As a part of the overall social reform, the reform of the MUP was launched immediately, aiming to create a police that will be more democratically oriented and aware of respecting human rights in its actions against crime and the protection of citizens and their property, as well as organized in line with the highest standards, norms, and rules of the EU countries. The reform process has been greatly helped by the international community, primarily the OSCE, Council of Europe, Danish Institute for Human Rights (DIHR), and the national experts of the MUP Advisory Body as the manager of the reform project.

The reform of the MUP has been implemented in three main areas:

- the reform of practice (increasing the efficiency of work);
- legislative reform (drafting of laws and regulations); and
- long-term strategy for the development of law enforcement agencies.

The years 2001 and 2002 witnessed a radical break with the negative legacy of the past. A new organizational structure of the Ministry has been set up, whereby the Republic Security Service has been separated from MUP, and the new Security-Information Agency (BIA) responsible for protection of the national security was placed under the civil control of the Government and Parliament. The guidelines for further reform of the police, including the reform of the relevant legislature, police education, and the plan for the equipment and modernization of MUP, have been clearly defined and validated by the Government. Personnel changes down to the lower managerial levels have been made. The police are more representative of the population. The institute of the beat officer started operating; prevention programs have been launched; and new technologies have been implemented in some fields of police work.

The process of drafting new legislation related to internal affairs started, as a legal basis for a quality and comprehensive police reform. Strategic laws on BIA and on Power of State Bodies in Suppressing Organised Crime have being adopted, and three laws of particularly reformist nature (Law on Police, Law on Police Education and Law on Records of the Security Service) are to be submitted to the Assembly. Pending the passage of the new Law on Police and other police laws and by-laws, only the most necessary organizational changes have been carried out as the initial phase of further and more thorough restructuring of MUP.

Demographics

In Serbia, there are 2.5 policemen per 1,000 inhabitants (with full executive power and authority and Uniformed Police), which is insufficient, considering the complexity of security issues. A particular problem is the lack of highly qualified and specialist staff. According to the Job Classification, the MUP has 51,218 positions, out of which 35,528, or 69.37%, are filled. Out of the total number of employees, there are 3,999 with full executive power and authority (OSL) with ranks similar to military ones; 20,870 uniformed police officers (P); 2,480 officers executing specific duties; 3,045 fire fighters; and 5,009 others. In the Hedaquarters of the Ministry, there are 4,170 employees; and in the field organizational units of the Ministry, there are 31,358 employees. There are 3,540 employees with university degrees, 4,015 with college degrees, 27,066 with secondary, and 1,309 with elementary education. There is a positive trend of increased employment of women (currently 6,777 employed, or 19.1% of the overall number of employees, 251 as senior staff). In context of reforming the police in almost all multinational communities, a multi-ethnic police has been formed.

Organizational Description

The only police organization in Serbia is the MUP. The work and managing of the Ministry are organized horizontally, vertically, and territorially, through the Public Security Sector and 33 territorial organizational units: Secretariats of Internal Affairs, (SUP) comprising 126 Departments of Internal affairs and 31 Police Stations. The units outside the Sectors are the Cabinet of the Minister with three bureaus (for media relations, for international cooperation, and for complaints and suggestions), Directorate for Combating Organized Crime, Inspector General of the Public Security Sector, Directorate for Protection of VIP and Government Premises, Legal and General Affairs Department, Police Academy, Police College, and Police High School.

The Public Security Sector is comprised of 10 departments (Criminal Investigation Department, Police Department, Traffic Police Department, Border Police Department for Foreigners including 37 border police stations, Fire Protection Department, Analytical Department, IT Department, General Affairs Department, Communication Department, and Catering and Accommodation Department) and the Operational Centre, the Helicopter Unit, Special Counter-terrorist Unit, and the Gendarmerie.

The SUP has its own internal division of labor, organizational units for main fields of police work. Organization of the SUP Belgrade (capital and largest city) is the most complex one. The SUP responsible for the territory of Kosovo and Metohija is practically out of function, as this region is under UN administration.

Functions

The MUP carries out administrative affairs, defined in the Law on Ministries, related to: the security of the Republic and detection and prevention of activities directed at subversion or destruction of the constitutional order; the protection of lives and property of persons; the prevention and detection of criminal offences and apprehension of perpetrators and bringing them to competent authorities; the maintenance of public peace and order; securing of assemblies and other gatherings of citizens; securing of certain persons and buildings; traffic safety; border crossings and movements in the Green Line; movement and stay of foreigners; acquisition, possession and carrying of weapons and ammunition; production and circulation of explosive substances, flammable liquids and gases; fire-protection; citizenship; personal identification number; identity cards; travel documents; permanent and temporary residence of citizens; staff training; and other tasks in accordance with law.

Police powers, defined in the Police Act, are to: issue warnings and orders, establish identity and perform identification procedures, examine persons for security reasons, invite, perform security control, prohibit movement, search premises, inspect devices and areas, arrest and detain persons, order stricter police control, confiscate objects, enter premises, use transport and communication means, use secret police measures, coercive means, and use other authorities defined by law. There are no differences in police powers between policemen regarding their functions.

Training

In order to become a police officer, one has to possess appropriate mental and physical abilities, and must be a citizen of Serbia with a permanent address in Serbia, not older than 30 years, free of criminal charges or convictions. One can join the police after finishing one of the police schools, or after completing at least secondary school and completing a police course (basic, for border police, gendarmerie, firemen). To enter a higher rank, a university degree is required.

There is no clearly defined system of career building, monitoring, development, and planning. The only thing that is certain is that working position and rank depend on formal level of education and years of service. A policeman with a secondary school diploma cannot climb up to a medium or high position in the police hierarchy, whatever his performance record. There are no clear relations between in-service training and performance on one hand and promotion on other.

Police Public Projects

There are several police public projects in place. The Project School Policeman program has been introduced in 246 primary and secondary schools, the objective of which is enhancing overall safety in these institutions. A community policing project, based on the experience of EU countries, has been formed and adopted, aiming to establish efficient partnerships between police and citizens in local communities. Several projects of improving traffic safety have been implemented. These include Road Worthy Vehicle, a program that promotes safe driving by offering free technical inspections of car road-worthiness; and Play for Life—No to Alcohol, which is aimed at raising awareness of drunk driving.

Police Use of Firearms

The police are authorized to use firearms only if they cannot otherwise protect lives, prevent flight of a suspect who was caught in the act of serious crime (attack on the constitutional order; undermining of military and defense capability; violence towards highest state officials; armed rebellion; terrorism; diversion; undermining of territorial sovereignty; endangering the safety of flight of aircrafts; murder; armed robbery; robbery; hard cases of theft and robbery); prevent flight of a person who committed other crimes punishable by law if there is a reasonable doubt that he/she has firearms and is going to use them; prevent flight of an arrested person or a person for whom there is an issued arrest warrant for committing serious or other crimes; prevent an attack on persons or property under police protection; or prevent an unlawful attack on police officers that endangers their lives.

Police officers used force in 939 cases (physical force—584, baton—65, firearms—41, and other means of coercion—249) in 2002. As a result of use of coercive measures, five persons sustained serious injuries, and 41 light bodily injury. Only in 12 cases was the use of force unjustified. The main reasons for usage of firearms were preventing assault and preventing a person from fleeing.

Complaints and Discipline

Complaints against the police are handled only by the police, with no participation of the representatives of the public. There is no external control body, and activities of parliamentary bodies are insufficient. In 2002, 2,192 complaints were filed against the work and conduct of police officers, of which 201, or 9.1 percent, had reasonable grounds. Disciplinary proceedings were instituted against 44 officers for serious violation of duty. Each complaint (whether written or verbal, signed or anonymous) was examined and processed.

MUP devotes special attention to lawful use of power and authority, and to proper and professional relations with citizens. Strict measures were taken against all police officers who violated the law and Rules of Service or acted contrary to the professional code of ethics. For 944 serious and 606 minor violations of duty, 1,550 disciplinary proceedings were instituted. Criminal charges were filed against 259 police officers for 523 criminal offenses; 46 officers were arrested, and 214 were suspended on various grounds. For 74 officers, employment was terminated by mutual agreement. In disciplinary proceedings at Ministry level, 43 ended in termination of employment, and 691 ended in other disciplinary measures and sanctions. One of the priority tasks is establishing a General Inspectorate service and instituting reform of the disciplinary system.

Police officers receive training in human rights protection in all forms of police education, and in basic and advanced police training. Length and content of training (performed by teachers of police schools and experienced police officers, and international experts and organizations) are adjusted to work profiles.

Terrorism

The main terrorist organizations are KLA and other paramilitary organizations of ethnic Albanians in the region (e.g., Albanian National Army-ANA). The Ministry is monitoring the security situation in Kosovo, which is still difficult, as a consequence of Albanian terrorist attacks, in order to prevent spreading of terrorist actions into the ground safety zone (GSZ) and other territories of Serbia. The engagement of the multi-ethnic police has prevented tensions and serious conflicts between the members of different nations, as well as possible destabilization of this region.

International Cooperation

The MUP and the State of Serbia have joined the international actions against all forms of terrorism. After the terrorist attacks in the USA, on Bali, and in the Russian Federation, the readiness of all services was raised to the highest level, and precautionary measures against all forms of international terrorism were stepped up to prevent any attempt of organizing and using terrorist organizations and groups in the territory of the Republic; and to protect all important facilities for the Republic (the embassies, diplomatic, consular and other foreign missions) from possible terrorist attacks. Specially trained police units are engaged in fighting terrorism include Special Counter-terrorist Unit for the prevention of hijacking, as the toughest MUP unit for fighting the most serious forms of terrorism; and the Gendarmerie, whose duties include prevention and suppression of internal and international terrorism.

In order to achieve reform objectives, the MUP established intensive cooperation with the police services of foreign countries and international organizations centered on involving the police of Serbia in international police developments. Also important are the exchange of information and experiences, and the coordination of activity, primarily in combating organized crime and international terrorism. These efforts also focus on standardizing border systems in line with EU countries; suppression of human trafficking, smuggling of weapons and narcotics; and the exchange of experience in application of modern information technology and telecommunication systems. A considerable part of these activities are being realized through Interpol, and also through bilateral cooperation.

With the aim of exchange of experience and coordinated activity in combating organized crime in the region and internationally, cooperation has been established with police forces of Great Britain, Germany, Holland, Italy, Croatia, USA (DEA) and with OSCE, Council of Europe, FBI Academy in Budapest, Interpol, Stability Pact for South-East Europe, SECI centre, IACP, UNDCP, IPTF, and UNMIK. Cooperation with the Hungarian, Swiss, Italian, Bulgarian, and Austrian police includes exchange of operational information, as certain organized groups are active in a number of countries.

Officers of the CID of this Ministry took part in numerous seminars, courses, and other forms of advanced and professional training (suppression of cyber crime, suppression of corruption, money laundering, counterfeiting money and forging documents, suppression of smuggling of vehicles, drugs and weapons, courses for divers-demolitionists, unexploded ordnance, and defusing of cluster bombs) both at home and abroad.

Police Education, Research, and Publications

The system of education and training of staff in the MUP is implemented through the Police High School, Police College, and the Police Academy. Candidates for this institution have to satisfy certain psychophysical criteria. After working for the police for four years, the graduate are released from military obligation.

The secondary school education, the duration of which is four years, is gained in the Police High School in Sremska Kamenica. The school enrolls 14-year-old boys. The cadets attend the classes at this boarding school, and they spend their time entirely in school premises.. The school diploma is externally valid. The cadets graduating from this school get employed in entry-level police jobs (police constable and patrol work) but are obliged to pass a state exam after a six-month period of on-the-job training.

Police High School also runs a basic police course, which lasts six months for males and four months for female participants. Teaching is conducted pursuant to the new curriculum for professional training of students enrolling in police schools: a police officer course, with foreign language study and a new course covering UN resolutions and the conventions related to freedoms, rights and duties of man and citizen, as well as the provisions of war and humanitarian law and the Police Code of Conduct.

Police education on the higher level is achieved at the Police College. This education lasts for five semesters. There are two possible regimens of studying: full-time students (who are financed from the budget) and part-time students (who provide the financing themselves). A number of students from Montenegro also attend the College. The College diploma is externally valid. Besides preparing students for the most complicated and complex security jobs for the managing positions of a middle level in the MUP, this diploma provides other work positions in other institutions (the judiciary, penal institutions.) and in security systems for companies. The graduates are not obliged to work in the MUP, unless they had been granted the scholarships.

The other activity of the Police College relates to expert qualifications and improvement for different specialists within the police force. The types of training last from one day up to one week (seminars), and from one week up to six months (courses). The teachers and the associates from the College itself and more than 400 renowned experts on practical work from the Ministry of the Interior and out of its system conduct the training. So far, the College has conducted 30 different courses and seminars for an expert qualification and improvement of the police staff. The most significant courses and the seminars organized by the College are: criminal investigation; commercial crime suppression; forensics; territorial fire-brigade

stations; border police; traffic police; police dogs handling; IT; diving; and martial arts. "Modern policing" (modern policing techniques, work in local community) and "Multiethnic policing" (in context of confidence building measures, democratic policing and human rights in pluralistic environment) have been launched in partnership with OSCE. The Advanced Police Training Centre of OSCE has been established in the Police College.

A four-year university education of police officers is offered by the Police Academy in Belgrade, the highest scientific and educational police institution. Its main activities are providing the basic studies (a university degree), specialized studies, MA and doctoral studies, which are of great significance for the police activities and the security itself.

The studies last for four years, they are free of charge, and all the students receive scholarships similar to the income of a trainee police officer. There are only full-time students, accommodated in the boarding houses, who spend most of their time at the Academy, dressed in uniforms, respecting a strictly defined regimen of life and work, similar to the military. Until the school year 2001/2002, the Academy did not enroll female students. Graduates of this institution are qualified for managing the uniformed police. After graduation, the student gets a title of a graduated police officer and is obliged to spend twice the time of his schooling within the police force. From the formal point of view, this diploma has its external validity, but due to the specific features of such education, in reality the graduates have very few possibilities to be employed in institutions apart from the police. The diploma automatically provides a middle (a commander of the police station of the first category) or even high and the highest positions in the police hierarchy.

The Police Academy provides specialized, MA, and doctoral studies. Experiences with these types of scientific work, at the moment, are comparatively modest.

Besides the above mentioned, every year Department of Police designs an annual training plan. This training is held during the whole school year in the police units. Topics include: security and the specific performance of security jobs and tasks, new regulations adopted by the police, and the application of police authority.

Police education can be estimated as theoretical and inadequate, given the concrete needs of daily police work. The teaching methods are outdated; little attention has been given to education and training based on practice and experience; and there has been a complete lack or insufficient presence of certain topics (human rights, police ethics, police management, domestic violence, inter-ethnical relations, police-media relations, peaceful solution of the conflicts, organized crime, commercial terrorism, communication with the public, first aid). Some of these problems have been addressed. After the passage of the Law on Police Education, reform of police training should continue.

The leading researchers and authors in the area of police and policing in Serbia are (in alphabetical order):

Bogoljub Milosavljevic, Ph.D., Official Gazete;
Budimir Babovic, Ph.D., President of Advisory Body;
Momcilo Talijan, Ph.D., Police College;
Mico Boskovic, Ph.D., Police Academy;
Milenko Milosevic, Ph.D., Police College;
Vladimir Krivokapic, Ph.D., Police Academy;
Zelimir Kesetovic, Ph.D., Police College.

Reporters, who most frequently write on police and policing in Serbia, are (in alphabetical order):

Dragana Arsic, Serbian Radio Television;
Aleksandar Roknic, newspaper Danas;
Milan Galovic, newspaper Politika;

The most reputable columnists who write on issues of the police in Serbia are:

Milos Vasic, magazine Vreme;
Slobodan Ikonic, magazine NIN;

The majority of police research is funded by the MUP. Some funding is available within the Ministry of Science Technology and Development's programs, while another source of funding are donations from NGO. Examples of recent research on police and policing are the following:

Comparative Models of Police Organization by Bogoljub Milosavljevic;
Police Public Relations by Zelimir Kesetovic;
Control as a part of Police Management Process by Momcilo Talijan;
Comparative Survey of Information-security systems by Andreja Savic, Milan Delic and Mladen Bajagic

There are three specialized police journals published in Serbia:

Nauka, bezbednost, policija [Science, Security, Police], published by Police Academy; Editor:

Radojko Milovanovic, Ph.D.; address: Police Academy, Humska 22, 11000 Beograd, e-mail: mica.mdg@Eunet.yu
Bezbednost [Security], published by MUP; Editor: Momcilo Talijan, Ph.D.; address: Police College, Cara Dusana 196, 11080, Zemun-Beograd, e-mail: momcilot@vsup.edu.yu
Nauka-Tehnika-Bezbednost [Science, Tehnic, Security], published by Institute of Security; Editor: Slobodan Jovicic PhD.; address: Kraljice Ane bb, 11000 Beograd, e-mail: stjovicic@yahoo.com

An important source for police scholars and practitioners is *Proceedings of teachers works* published by Police College.

Police newspapers that deal with everyday police activities are:

Policajac [Policeman], published by MUP,
Mladi policajac [Young Policeman], published by Police High School,
Policijski glasnik [Police Herald], published by SUP Valjevo.

The following are police-related websites in Serbia:

www.mup.sr.gov.yu—a website of the MUP;
www.vsup.edu.yu—a website of the Police College;
www.bia.sr.gov.yu—a web site of the BIA;
www.ib.yu—a web site of the Institute for Security.

ŽELIMIR KEŠETOVIĆ, ZORAN KEKOVIĆ, HUSNIJA REDŽEPAGIĆ

Bibliography

General Information. www.mfa.gov.yu/.
Milosavljevic, Bogoljub: *Uvod u policijske nauke* [Introduction to Police Science]. Belgrade: Police Academy, 1994.
Milosavljevic, Bogoljub: *Nauka o policiji* [Police Science]. Belgrade: Police Academy, 1997.
Monk, Richard. *A Report on the Police Work in the Federal Republic of Yugoslavia*, Belgrade. OSCE, 2001.
Police Reform in Serbia, Belgrade. OSCE, 2002.
Slayter, John. A Report on the Evaluation of Human Rights, Ethics and Standards of Police *Functioning in the Federal Republic of Yugoslavia, Serbia and Montenegro*, Belgrade. The European Council, 2001.
Vision Document on the Reform of the Ministry of the Interior of the Republic of Serbia, Belgrade. Ministry of the Interior, 2003.

SEYCHELLES

Background Material

One of the smallest nations of the world, the Republic of Seychelles is an equatorial archipelago consisting of 116 islands comprising about 455 sq km. The nation has but roughly 2.5 times the land mass of Washington, D.C., dispersed over approximately one million sq km in the western portion of the Indian Ocean, north of the island of Madagascar off the east coast of the African continent. Discovered by Portuguese traders in the early sixteenth century, the islands of Seychelles would remain uninhabited until French settlement began with the intention of developing the spice and slave trades in the mid-eighteenth century on what is today the island of St. Anne. The late eighteenth and early nineteenth centuries were witness to a protracted struggle between the French and British governments for control of the islands, with the latter emerging victorious in 1811 by virtue of the superiority of their naval forces, and control was ceded to the British Empire by the Treaty of Paris in 1814. Seychelles would remain under the authority of the British government until 1976, at which time independence was gained from the mother country.

The city of Victoria on the principal island of Mahe is the capital. Seychelles has a population of 82,000 (2004 est.). African, Indian, French, Chinese, and Arabic ethnic groups speak either Creole, English, or French as their official languages. Its citizens enjoy freedom of religious expression, with all major religions finding adherents. Christianity is the dominant religion; about 90% are Catholic, and slightly less than 10% practice Protestant denominations. Seychelles boasts a literacy rate in excess of 90%, and all children have the opportunity to complete the first 10 grades of schooling free of charge. Additional, but non-compulsory, schooling is possible, including vocational schooling. There are no institutions of higher education; those desiring to pursue university courses must do so in foreign nations, typically Britain, America, or France. Gross National Product on a per capita basis is estimated at US$7,800. The tourism and fishing industries predominate, with a small manufacturing sector contributing to the economy.

Contextual Features

With the advent of the Third Republic in 1993, Seychelles made the successful transition from a repressive one-party socialist state to a multi-party republic. Under the new Constitution, the citizens of Seychelles are provided a panoply of rights. Among them are the right to life (the death penalty is proscribed), freedom of expression and association, equal protection under the laws, the right to a fair and public trial, and the right to obtain an education.

The government of Seychelles is tripartite in nature. The Executive branch is headed by the President, who has under his authority the Departments of Defense, Police, Finance, and Internal and Legal Affairs. Under the Seychelles Constitution, the President is a "strong" leader. Head of State and Government, Commander-in-Chief of the Defense Forces, the President is elected by popular vote and may serve up to three five-year terms. Under the umbrella of the Executive branch are the offices of the Vice-President and various ministries typically associated with developed nations, including Foreign Affairs, Health, Environment, Education, and Transport.

The Legislative branch consists of a unicameral National Assembly comprised of 25 members directly elected by means of universal adult (17 years of age) suffrage, with up to 10 additional members elected based on proportional results of national elections held at least once every five years. Bills passed by the National Assembly are forwarded to the President, who by affirmative assent may cause a bill to become law.

The third branch, the Judiciary, is independent under the Constitution. As might be expected given the nation's historical influences, the legal system in Seychelles is based on customary and English common law, although provision for jury trials is made only in cases involving murder or treason. French civil law serves as a basis for tort and other civil litigation. Seychelles courts have been historically staffed by foreign jurists acting on a contract basis, typically from neighboring countries in Africa and Asia, as well as India. Mr. Bernardin Renaud became the first native Seychellois justice with his appointment in January 2004.

The Judiciary consists of four levels, or tiers. The first level of tribunals is the Magistrate Courts. Analogous to small claims courts, these courts consist of three members: one Senior Magistrate and two Magistrates. The Magistrate Courts are themselves subordinate to second-tier courts of original jurisdiction, called Supreme Courts, which, dependent on the nature of the matter to be adjudicated, divide the criminal docket with the Magistrate Courts, and act as an appeals court. Staffed by four justices, including a Chief Justice, Supreme Courts are responsible for the administration of the lower courts.

The third tier is the Constitutional Court. Convening weekly, or as necessity may dictate, this court considers only constitutional issues from the lower courts.

The highest court in the Republic is the Court of Appeal, which is comprised of five justices, the President being among their number. The Court of Appeal has the authority to pass upon any judgment, decision, or order of a lower court, whether civil or criminal in nature. The Court of Appeal convenes three times yearly for a term of two weeks during the months of April, August, and October. The Court hears only cases referred from the Supreme Courts and Constitutional Court. All jurists in all courts are appointed by the President and serve a seven-year term. Judges may be re-appointed for another term by the President, with the concurrence of the Constitutional Appointment Committee.

Under the Constitution, criminal defendants are afforded legal protections considered typical by western standards. Among protections extended to a defendant are: the presumption of innocence, freedom from arbitrary search and seizure, the right to a public trial, the right to counsel even if indigent, the right to confront and cross-examine witnesses, and the right to appeal if convicted. Provision is typically made for bail, and those detained must be brought before judicial authority for charging purposes within 48 hours of detention, with additional time allowance made if transport before the charging authority must be made by boat from an outer island.

The penal system in Seychelles is, like the legal system, based on English common law and French codes; however, information on prisons and corrections is limited. Courts may sentence those convicted of crimes to the Grand Police Camp on Mahé Island, or to the prison on Long Island, where conditions are said to be austere. Although the prison population must of necessity fluctuate, about 150 persons are currently imprisoned by the government. Prisoners are allowed reading material, medical treatment, and monthly family visits. No women or juveniles are currently incarcerated. Probation services are used in place of incarceration in many cases. The Probation Services Section of the Social Affairs Division is charged with providing services typically associated with probationary programs. Among these tasks are: background reports on both adult and juvenile offenders, supervision of persons placed on probation, providing social services to those who are incarcerated, coordination of the Youth Residential Treatment Center, and after-care upon release from incarceration as directed.

Crime in Seychelles presents a mixed picture. The total rate for index offenses is trending downward, with recent (2001) rates showing a decrease over the preceding five-year period from 1459.56 to 1346.98 per 100,000 persons. Rates for both robbery and burglary have dropped significantly, from 61.33 to 17.32 and 916 to 58.15 per 100,000, respectively, while motor vehicle theft has decreased from 40.9 to 1.24. However, the rates for murder and rape have increased from 1.33 to 3.71 and 17.33 to 78.79 per 100,000, respectively, with rates for aggravated assault and larceny increasing from 142.67 to 180.65, and 280 to 1,007 per 100,000. While the some of the rates above may appear striking at first glance, it must remain in the reader's mind that as a small nation having a population of less than 100,000 persons, any increase or decrease will appear magnified, with other admittedly dated statistics from 1990 indicating that only about 34 percent of all reported crime was non-traffic in nature.

Police Profile

Background

The police force in Seychelles is national in character, and is organized along British lines, reminiscent of the colonial background of the country. The department is headed by a Commissioner, appointed by the President with the assent of the National Assembly, and it has a strength of about 500 members assigned to general duty, with an additional 60 assigned to a paramilitary unit.

Organizational Description, Functions, and Complaints and Discipline

The Police Force in Seychelles underwent a major reorganization in 2004, dividing the department into five divisions, each under a single director: Administrative/Personnel and Finance, Special

Branch, Special Support Unit, Operation Command, Seychelles Police Academy.

Seychelles maintains a total of 17 police stations throughout the country, and members of the department share the mission statement, "To uphold the law and provide protection to each and everyone without fear, favour, affection or ill-will." In addition to the mission statement, the Police Force has undertaken to strive for nine listed objectives:

Preservation of the peace;
Prevention and detection of crime;
Apprehension of offenders;
Protection of life and property;
Fire fighting and prevention;
Participation in the national defense;
Enforcement of all laws, acts, regulations, and orders.

With the reorganization of the Police Force, fewer senior officers now oversee the Department from a central command, since the former regional system has been discarded. Along with most western nations, the emphasis of the Police Force is now based on a "community policing" model, with "discipline officers" appointed to address issues of professionalism and standards of performance within the Department. Several civil suits have been filed against the Police, typically on grounds related to unlawful (warrant-less) search and seizure, although legal satisfaction has been largely problematic.

Promotion in the Police Force is from officer to the following ranks, in ascending order: Lance Corporal, Corporal, Sergeant, Sergeant Major, Sub-inspector, Inspector.

Training

Training of the police is initially accomplished at the academy on Praslin Island. The basic training for police recruits consists of a 15-week course, after which time the recruit undergoes a field training regimen. Refresher training is also provided on an as-needed basis, together with supervisory and promotion courses lasting two weeks, with additional in-service courses of four weeks' duration.

Police Use of Firearms

The "regular" Police have, both traditionally and under normal circumstances, gone unarmed. However, the members of the elite unit are equipped with modern weapons, including rifles of 7.62 millimeter caliber.

International Cooperation

The Republic and its Police Force are members of, or parties to, a variety of international institutions and agreements. Seychelles is a member of the Eastern Africa Police Chiefs Cooperation Organization (EAPCCO), formed in 2000 in association with police administrators in Burundi, Djibouti, Ethiopia, Eritrea, Kenya, Rwanda, Sudan, Tanzania, and Uganda; this organization operates under the auspices of the International Criminal Police Organization (Interpol), and it works toward the suppression of cross-border crime. In addition, Seychelles is also a member of the sub-regional bureau for eastern Africa, also administered by Interpol, charged with cooperation in guarding against what its members consider the most pressing crimes in their region: illegal firearms, narcotics, motor vehicle theft, economic crime and corruption, terrorism, environmental crime, and cattle stealing. Seychelles is also a state's party to the International Criminal Court (ICC).

Although terrorist groups are not active in Seychelles, the government has engaged in consultation and training relative to the subject, hosting in 2004 in conjunction with the United States Army a course concerning legal aspects by which terror might be suppressed. Immigration, and document and passport control are seen as key elements by which the county may avert being used as a transit point for international terrorists, crucial in light of Seychelles' air links to middle-eastern nations.

The Seychelles Police Force may be accessed at www.virtualseychelles.sc.

G. Q. BILLINGS

Bibliography

"East Africa, Horn unite to fight organised crime." *Afrol News* www.afrol.com/articles/13953. November 16, 2004. "Police react to youth aspirations."

"Large batch of police officers promoted." *Seychelles Nation Online.* www.nation.sc/index1024.php?art=944.

"Ministries and Departments, Department of Police." www.virtualseychelles.sc/pages/vs_ie.htm. November 11, 2004.

"Ministries and Departments, Ministry of Social Affairs and Employment." www.virtualseychelles.sc/pages/vs._ie.htm. October 28, 2004.

"Security personnel study legal aspects of combating terrorism." www.virtualseychelles.sc/news/news_details.asp?id=451. November 29, 2004.

"Seychelles." *The World Fact Book.* www.cia.gov/cia/publications/factbook. October 16, 2004.

"Seychelles, Legal System and Civil Rights." www.lcweb2.loc.gov/cgi-bin/query/r?frd/cstdy:@field(DOCID+sc0042). December 1, 2004.

Seychelles Nation Online. www.seychelles-online.com.sc/ index800.php?art=1304. November 16, 2004.

"Seychelles, Penal System." www.lcweb2.loc.gov/cgi-bin/ query/r?frd/cstdy:@field(DOCID+sc0067). November 12, 2004.

"Seychelles, State Security Services." www.lcweb2.loc.gov/cgi-bin/query/r?frd/cstdy:@field(DOCID)+sc0064). November 12, 2004.

"U.S. finds Seychelles a worthy partner in war on terror." www.virtualseychelles.sc/news_details.asp?id=421. December 4, 2004.

Winslow, Dr. Robert, and Melissa Francescut. "Crime and Society: A comparative criminology tour of the world." San Diego State University. www-rohan.sdsu.edu/faculty/ rwinslow/africa/seychelles.html. December 2, 2004.

SIERRA LEONE

Background Material

Sierra Leone is a small West African State that shares inland borders with Guinea, Liberia, and with the Atlantic Ocean on the west. It is a tropical climate, with two seasons–dry and rainy. It is divided into western, northern, southern, and eastern Regions. The British initially annexed it as a home for freed slaves, and later declared it a crown colony in 1808. The Queen ruled until independence.

The opposition All People's Congress (A.P.C.) won the 1967 elections, but the Sierra Leone Army intervened. A series of coups followed until 1968, when Siaka Stevens of the APC became the Prime Minister, and subsequently the Republican President on April 19, 1971. His rule was characterized by coups that led to military alienation and reliance on the Sierra Leone Police (SLP). In November, 1985, he handed over rule to Major General Joseph Saidu Momoh.

Civil war broke out in March, 1991, led by Corporal Foday Sankoh of the Revolutionary United Front (RUF). As Major-General Momoh could not contain the war, young Lieutenants led by Captain (Rtd) Valentine Strasser ousted him on April 29, 1992. The international community pressured the soldiers to hand over the country to civilians.

Elections were conducted in February 1996, and Dr. Alhaji Ahmad Tejan Kabbah won. His rule was short-lived. On May 25, 1997, Major (Rtd) Johnny Paul Koroma ousted him.

His reign was not recognized. West African troops removed him and re-instated President Ahmad Tejan Kabbah. His first move was to disband the army and build the SLP. By July 1998, the Commonwealth Police Development Task Force (CPDTF) and the United Nations Civilian Police (UNCIVPOL) had started the process of building the Police Force.

Disgruntled soldiers formed the "West Side Boys." With the RUF, they attacked Freetown on January 6, 1999. West African forces, assisted by locals, repelled the invaders. When peace returned by 1999, UNCIVPOL and the CPDTF, renamed Commonwealth Community Safety and Security Project (CCSSP), became more involved with the SLP. The CCSSP Leader, Mr. Keith Biddle, (British) was appointed Inspector General (IGP) of the SLP in November 1999; he retired in 2003 and was replaced by a Sierra Leonean, Mr. Brima Acha Kamara. Mr. Keith Biddle, through strategic leadership, made significant changes in the SLP. For the first time, there were a Government Policing Charter, a Police Mission statement, and a Strategic Development Plan. Community participation and involvement in policing through Local Needs Policing (LNP) was introduced. Local Partnership Boards were formed, and Police Units were restructured, from Divisions headed by Chief Police Officers (CPO), to Local Command Units (L.C.U.) headed by Local Unit Commanders (L.U.C.).

New Departments like Equal Opportunities; Media; Community Relations; Complaints, Discipline and Internal Investigations Department (CDIID); Corporate Services; and Family Support Unit were created. These Departments changed the SLP from reactive to proactive.

Under the present IGP, the Change Management Process is ongoing, with the assistance of a CCSSP consultant, Dr. Robin Campbell. The Government Policing Charter, the Police Mission Statement, and the SLP Strategic Development Plan

Most common crimes reported, and trends predicted, 2003

S/No.	Offenses	January–June	July–December	Trend
1.	Assault	9,915	8,841	Decrease
2.	Larceny	4,195	4,960	Increase
3.	Fraudulent conversion	2,628	2,658	Increase
4.	House breaking and larceny	822	751	Decrease
5.	Sexual offenses	333	430	Increase
6.	Bburglary & larceny	273	313	Increase
7.	Domestic violence	100	212	Increase
8.	Robbery	172	158	Decrease
9.	Murder	72	69	Decrease

2002 have undertaken twelve programs and some 60 projects over a number of years. Through Project Initiation Documents (PIDS) and Business Case, and through various action plans, the Executive Management and Change Board (EMCB) has been able to monitor and assess the progress of all these projects. To manage the complexity of such a large and diverse portfolio of projects, Top Ease software was introduced by the CCSSP Consultant, Raymond Flanagan.

As the United Nations Adjustment, Drawdown and Withdrawal (ADW) program is in progress, the SLP is expected to consolidate the peace process in a country still confronted with high illiteracy; high unemployment, especially among the youths; poverty, hunger, and disease, including the threats posed by malaria and HIV/AIDS. All of these contribute to a high mortality rate.

The population of Sierra Leone is 5,267,748 (2003 est.). The nation's land mass is 71,700 sq km. The official language is English, although Krio is commonly spoken. The major ethnic groups are the Mende, Temne, Limba, and Krio. Seventy-five percent of the population identifies as Muslim, while 24% are Christian, and 1% practice other religions. The GDP (in millions of *leones*, the national currency) is 2,050,994.25 (2004 est.).

Contextual Features

Sierra Leone is governed by the Constitution of Sierra Leone, 1991 (Act No.6 of 1991), based on the Parliamentary and Presidential systems. A uni-cameral Parliament is in Freetown, with separation of powers among the executive, the legislature, and the judiciary branches. Local government, which had not been in existence for close to 30 years, has been re-introduced. The criminal justice system links the Police, the Judiciary, and the Prisons Department. The Police force prevents, detects, and investigates crimes, and apprehends and prosecutes criminals. The Judiciary dispenses justice through trials, enquiries, and inquests; Prisons Services oversees probationary, custodial, remedial, and corrective programs. The Criminal Justice system is strictly formalized though the Safety, Security and Access to Justice (SSAJ) project funded by DFID, which is also exploring means of ensuring informal mechanisms.

Sierra Leone is a secular state with no religious influence on the law. According to Section 170 (1) of the 1991 Constitution, the laws are based on:

(a) the 1991 Constitution;
(b) laws made by or under the authority of Parliament;
(c) any orders, rules, regulations, and other statutory instruments made by any person or authority pursuant to a power conferred in that behalf by the 1991 Constitution or any other law;
(d) the existing law; and
(e) the common law.

Section 120 (1) (4) of the 1991 Constitution states that the Judiciary shall consist of the Supreme Court, and other inferior and traditional Courts as Parliament may by law establish.

The Supreme Court shall be the final Court of Appeal in and for Sierra Leone and shall have original, supervisory, appellate, and interpretative jurisdiction in all criminal, civil, and constitutional matters. The Court of Appeal has appellate jurisdiction in all Criminal and Civil matters. The High Court has original, appellate, and supervisory jurisdiction in all civil and criminal matters.

According to Section 8 of the Courts Act 1965, the Magistrate Court has original, inquisitorial, and review jurisdiction in all civil and criminal matters arising within the district, area, or place in and for which it is established or transferred to it by the Supreme Courts.

The Courts Act 1963 sets up the Customary Courts. They have very limited jurisdiction in civil and criminal cases, with their main focus being to try cases for which fines are very minimal, cases which do not require imprisonment, or matters that are purely customary and which the Superior Courts of Judicature determines to be under the jurisdiction of the Customary Courts.

The National Prisons has a Director and a Deputy, with Assistant Directors of the four regions. The Prisons department is responsible for incarcerating male and female criminals on whom custodial sentence has been passed.

Remand Homes and Approved Schools were established by Cap 44 of the Laws of Sierra Leone 1960, but the two in Freetown are poorly managed; the SSAJ Project is expected to address the situation.

Police Profile

Background

The SLP was set up in 1808, when Freetown became a Crown Colony, to protect the borders and British colonial interests. Between 1863 and 1906, the West African Frontier Force maintained public order. On October 27, 1894, Captain V.F. Laphan from the British Army was head, and in 1906 British citizen Mr. George Brook became the first Commissioner. In 1948, the present Police Training School (P.T.S.) at Hastings was established to train Sierra Leoneans. The first Sierra Leonean Commissioner of Police was Mr. L.W. Leigh (1963–1969). During his reign, a Police Act was passed by Parliament in 1964, establishing the SLP.

Demographics

The SLP, in response to the UN A.D.W., is to reach the pre-war strength of 9,500 personnel by 2005. The present strength (June 2004) is 7,903; that is, 6,858 males and 1,045 females. The SLP is a national institution with no ethnic discrimination and deliberately no ethnic distribution statistics. Out of the 7,903 SLP personnel, approximately 15 percent are non-uniformed personnel; no civilian component exists, though a civilianization strategy is before the EMCB. The IGP is the strategic focus commanding from the center and assisted by the EMCB. The western region has 4,789 personnel, including 652 females; there are 819 personnel in the south, including 137 females; the northern region has 1,287 personnel, including 183 females; and the east has 1,008, including 73 females. All personnel are expected to read and write English, and are trained as operational officers with the O.S.D., with further training in light weapons.

The SLP strength of 7,903 to a population of 5,267,748 means one officer to every 667 citizens.

Organizational Description

Section 3 of the Police Act 1964 (Act No.7 of 1964) and Sections 155 and 156 of the 1991 Constitution (Act No.6 of 1991) established the SLP and the Police Council, respectively. The SLP is headed by the IGP. The Police Council, chaired by the Vice President, is composed of: the Minister of Internal Affairs (responsible for Police); the IGP Deputy Inspector General (DIGP); the Chairman of the Public Service Commission; a member of the Sierra Leone Bar Association; and two other members appointed by the President, subject to the approval of Parliament.

The Police Council, according to section 158 of the 1991 Constitution, shall advise the President on all major matters of policy relating to internal security, including the role of the Police, Police budgeting and finance, and administration.

The EMCB is the highest policy body in the SLP and is chaired by the IGP, with membership comprising the DIGP and all Assistant Inspector Generals (AIGs) sharing national or regional assignments, with the Heads of UNCIVPOL and CCSSP as observers. The EMCB provides strategic leadership and management of the organization.

The rank structure is stated below:

Junior Ranks
Recruit;
Constable;
Sergeant.
Inspecting Rank
Inspector.
Senior Ranks
Assistant Superintendent;
Superintendent;
Chief Superintendent;
Assistant Inspector-General;
Deputy Inspector-General;
Inspector-General.

From recruit to IGP, several benchmarks have to be fulfilled before promotion. On completion of three months' training, a recruit is elevated to the rank of a Constable. From Constable to Superintendent, personnel to be promoted must have completed at least three years on their present rank with unblemished record and sit for a written examination followed by interview. Successful candidates with sound appraisal by their immediate supervisors are prioritized, based on existing vacancies and funding. If approved by Police Council, personnel will be promoted accordingly. Promotion from Superintendent to Chief Superintendent follows a similar procedure, except that essays on areas of Police interest are submitted instead of a written examination. Promotions from Chief Superintendent to AIG shall be the prerogative of the Police Council as advised by the IGP. The DIGP and IGP are appointed by the President.

Functions

Criminal investigations are the prerogative of the Criminal Investigations Department (CID), with a Director of Crime Services accountable to an AIG for Crime Services. At the National Headquarters, the Director has small specialized units to support the decentralized Criminal Investigation Units countrywide. Summary and misdemeanor offenses are investigated by uninformed personnel.

The pre-war SLP made no distinction between support and operational services. It was during the tenure of Mr. Keith Biddle that an attempt was made to distinguish between support and operational services. For the first time, an AIG Support was appointed to deal with Transport, Communications, Estate, Hospital, Engineering, and Finances.

The SLP is the constitutional body responsible to protect life and property; prevent and detect crime; secure and sustain safety and security; ensure a peaceful society; and reduce conflict, as well as ensure primacy in the rule of law. These are statutory functions for which Police primacy is always expected. The bulk of SLP personnel are trained to handle criminal law, with a small percentage concerned with assisting the strategic tier (IGP and top team) in administration.

Training

All SLP are trained at the Police Training School Hastings. The criteria for recruitment are:

- Citizen of Sierra Leone;
- Aged 18 to 30 years;
- Having completed at least Form 5 or Senior Secondary School II (SSS II);
- Obtain a pass grade in the SLP Recruitment Examination;
- Satisfy character checks;
- Declared fit for Police duties by the Force Medical Officer.

Police Public Projects

Through the Local Needs Policing Strategy, a series of public projects have been undertaken by the SLP through the community Relations Department; they are aimed at sensitizing the citizenry to existing in a relatively safe and secure environment.

Some of these projects are:

- Operation Classroom, aimed at sensitizing school children on road safety;
- Operation Clean City, daytime foot/mobile patrols to protect life/property and ensure safety and security;
- Operation Phoenix, nighttime foot/mobile patrols to protect life/property and ensure safety and security;
- Operation Free flow, unhindered flow of pedestrian and vehicular traffic;
- Operation Zero Tolerance, aimed at no compromise in dealing with anti-social vices like drugs;
- National Union of Sierra Leone Students and Police Partnership Initiative (NAPPI), aimed at bringing the Police and students closer and bridging the misunderstanding gap often leading to violence and breakdown of law and order.

Police Use of Firearms

The SLP is essentially an unarmed police service. Considering that at times, a Police Officer can only maintain his or her constitutional duty of protecting life and property and maintenance of law and order through the use of firearms, a section of about 35 percent of the SLP (known as the Operations Support Division, or OSD) have been trained in the use of firearms and permanently armed. The laws and regulations governing the issue, ownership, and use of arms, ammunition, and explosives are found in the Arms and Ammunition Act and the Explosives Act, both of 1955 as amended. Considering the obsolete nature of these two Acts, a bill to be known as the Arms, Ammunitions, and Explosives Act 2004 is now receiving the attention of the Cabinet. As the bill is yet to become law, much cannot be said about it contents. The principles governing the storage, issue, and use of Police firearms are contained in guidelines approved by the EMCB. Firearms are to be fired by authorized and trained Police Officers, only as a last resort where conventional methods have been tried and failed or must from the nature of the circumstances be unlikely to succeed if tried. The IGP is the authority to permit Police Officers to carry weapons; he may delegate this function to his deputy or the AIG operations. There are published guidelines for the discharge of firearms by Police. Firearms ownership laws are found in the old Act as well as the new Arms, Ammunitions, and Explosive bill.

Complaints and Discipline

The Complaints, Discipline, and Internal Investigations Department (CDIID), headed by a National Director, handles complaints and discipline. The AIG for professional standards at strategic level oversees the Department.

The Police (discipline) Regulations 2001 governs complaints and discipline of police officers. The IGP is disciplined by the President. The Department is expected to maintain professional standards and ethical growth of the organization. Reports are handled as either criminal, disciplinary, or organizational and are impartially investigated. Criminal cases are forwarded to the Director of Public Prosecutions (DPP) for legal advice pending criminal charge or dismissal of the case. For disciplinary matters, if a case is established on the balance of probability against an ASP or above, the file is forwarded to the DPP to draft charges; and for officers below, charges are drafted by the CDIID before presentation to a Disciplinary Tribunal, with the alleged at liberty to solicit a defense counsel from among members of the SLP. There is provision for appeal. The Chairman, at the conclusion of any tribunal, recommends either disposal or punishments ranging from caution to dismissal. Recommendations for officers below the rank of A.S.P. are forwarded to the IGP, and for A.S.P. and above to the Police Council, which shall impose any punishment recommended or as modified as it thinks fit. For organizational investigations, recommendations will be discussed by the EMCB, and the AIG Professional Standards will take action as required.

Post-conflict Sierra Leone saw the intervention of the Commonwealth, United Nations, and other international Non Governmental Organizations (NGOs) collaborating with the SLP. Human Rights Sensitizations were conducted by UNAMSIL. The impact of these sensitizations led to the inclusion of Human Rights training in the police curriculum. Since 1998, all recruits are lectured by trained SLP personnel on Human Rights. With international assistance, two pamphlets, *Human and People's Rights* and *Child Rights and Child Abuse,* are being used as training manuals at the PTS The high influence of the international community in post-war Sierra Leone has created public awareness, especially on human rights issues. Nationwide criticism of human rights violations, though some are incorrect, are levied periodically against the Police. Organizations championing human rights include: the Coalition for Justice and Accountability, the Lawyers Centre for Legal Assistance (LAWCLA), and the independent radio stations.

Government entities dealing with human rights are the Ombudsman, and the National Commission for Democracy and Human Rights (NCDHR). As human rights concerns are taking center stage, the Sierra Leone government (SLG) is in the process of piloting a bill establishing the Human Rights Commission of Sierra Leone, expected to be the statutory body to champion human rights issues.

To ensure a climate of respect for human rights, the CDIID is to investigate human rights abuses reported against Police; L.U.C.s are encouraged to appoint custody officers, who are to monitor detention, detention of minors, refusal to grant bail, or abuse of human rights of persons in custody or under investigations. A lay visitor plan is in progress, whereby influential or concerned members of the community may visit Police detention facilities on short notice and make public their observations. This approach is employed by some international NGOs, like the RED CROSS. The AIG Professional Standards, which also represents the SLP on the SSAJ, having realized the importance of human rights, has appointed a Human Rights Officer.

Outside the organization, the SLP has ensured a lot of sensitization through the Community Relations Department using theatre performances and the Media both print and electronic as well as the partnership boards to sensitize the citizenry.

In short, the human rights abuse reduction strategy in the SLP has really taken a national dimension.

Terrorism

Presently, the SLP is not aware of any domestic terrorist group within the country nor any group that has international connections with terrorist groups in or out the country.

This does not mean that the SLP is not prepared to face internal acts of terrorism. The police agencies charged with responding to terrorism are the:

- Special Branch
- Crime Intelligence Agency
- Criminal Investigations Department
- Operations Support Division.

International Cooperation

Pre-war Sierra Leone benefited immensely from technical co-operation with Egypt in terms of training and still ongoing. Nigeria, England, Canada, America, South Africa, Bostwana, and Ghana have also helped in training SLP personnel. International co-operation with the Commonwealth of Nations led by England and through DFID has resulted to international training and provision of necessities including transport, communications, IT facilities and uniforms.

Through the CCSSP, over 40 senior officers have attended the International Commanders Programme (ICP) and 3 the International Strategic Leadership programme (ISLP) at CENTREX, England between 2001 and 2003. This year (2004) at least 12 senior officers are expected to benefit from CENTREX training.

The SLP is a member of the West African Criminal and Intelligence Bureau; the West African Chiefs of Police Committee and INTERPOL. The SLP and the Guinean Police signed a communiqué on joint security strategy on June 27, 2003. The same is expected with the Liberian Police after the April 8, 2004 visit by the SLP to Liberia. A strong co-operation is being built with the Botswana Police following the visit of the Botswana Police Chief between June 7 and 10, 2004.

At the moment, the SLP is not engaged in any exchange of officers.

Police Education, Research and Publications

At local level, the SLP has established partnership with the Institute of Public Administration (IPAM), University of Sierra Leone to train Police officers in management. Internationally, the Police Academy in Cairo, Egypt and the Centre for Excellence (CENTREX), England are the most frequently used.

Presently, the SLP cannot boast of researchers, authors, reporters, or columnists who have done work relating to the SLP and no budget allocation at the moment for Police research.

The only publication by the SLP at the moment is the SIERRA LEONE POLICE NEWS, a monthly newspaper published by the SLP Media and Public Relations Unit. The Editor is Inspector Khruschev Kargbo with editorial office as Head of Police Media and Public Relations Unit, Sierra Leone Police Headquarters, George Street, Freetown, Sierra Leone, West Africa – Tel: No.00-232-22-221031.

No major publication has been released by the SLP in the last two years.

The SLP website is *www.slpol.org*.

MUSA BOCKARIE LAPPIA

Bibliography

Alie, Joe A.D. *A New History Of Sierra Leone*. London: Macmillan Publishers, 1990.

Butler, A.J.P. *Police Management*. Hants: Gower Publishing, 1984.

Crawshaw, Ralph and Leif Holmstrom, eds. *Essential Texts On Human Rights For The Police: A Compilation Of International Instruments*. The Hague: Kluwer Law International, 2001.

Deveneaux, Gustav H.K. *Power Politics In Sierra Leone*. Ibadan: Pilgrim Books Limited, 1982.

Gwynne – Jones, D.R.G.; P.K. Mitchell; M.E Harvey and K. Swindell. *A New Geography Of Sierra Leone*. Essex: Longman, 1987.

Lappia, Musa B. "National Stability In Sierra Leone, 1961 – 1985". B.A. dissertation, Fourah Bay College, University of Sierra Leone, 1988.

Lengor, Morie. "Crime and Society—The Western Area Of Sierra Leone as a Case Study." LLB dissertation, Fourah Bay College, University of Sierra Leone, 2001.

Lucan, Talabi A.C. *A Visual History Of West African*. London: Evans Brothers, 1988.

Stevens, Siaka. *What Life Has Taught Me*. Bucks: Kensal Press, 1984.

SINGAPORE

Background Material

Singapore's history has long been rich with romance, as well as spice trading, piracy, and colonialism. According to Malay legend, a Sumatran prince encountered a lion on Temasek. He considered it a good omen and founded Singapura, meaning "Lion City." A century later, the island was abandoned after a fierce struggle between Java, Siam, and China, its buildings being reclaimed by the jungle until 1811, when Malays, led by their chief, the Temmenggong settled there. Singapore might have remained a quiet backwater if not for Sir Stamford Raffles' intervention in 1819. As a result of his intervention, Singapore became a British trading base and tariff-free port. Migrants poured in, and Singapore continued to grow into the twenty-first century. One of the greatest losses for the British during World War II was the defeat of Singapore by Japan.

Singapore was under British rule after WW II as part of Malaya, then Malaysia. In 1965, Singapore broke off from Malaysia to become a republic.

The population of Singapore is estimated to be 4,353,893 (2004). The Chinese make up 76.8% of the population; Malays, 13.9%; and Indians, 7.9%. Other ethnic groups account for the remaining 1.4%.

The official languages are Malay, Chinese (Mandarin), Tamil, and English. Malay remains the language of administration. Mandarin is increasing used among the Chinese, replacing the dialects of Fujian, Teochew, Cantonese, Hakka, Hainanese, and Foochow. Besides Tamil, other languages spoken by Indians include Telegu, Malayalam, Punjabi, Hindi, and Bengali (Sing*apore Facts and Pictures* 2000).

The Constitution allows every person the right to profess, practice, and propagate his/her religion. The main religions are: Buddhism, Taoism, Islam, Christianity, Sikhism, Confucianism, and Hinduism.

Singapore's per capita income advanced from S$1,618 in 1965 to S$36,906 in 2002, at current market prices. The contributions of various economic activities are agriculture, negligible; industry, 28%; and services, 72%. The challenge is how to excel in the face of globalization, trading blocs, and protectionism. Singapore has long abandoned labor-intensive industries in favor of high technology industries as well as niche production. More and more, the country is more reliant on the service sector.

Singapore is blessed with a highly developed and successful free-market economy, a remarkably open and corruption-free business environment, stable prices, and the fifth-highest per capita GDP in the world. Exports, particularly in electronics and chemicals and services, are the main drivers of the economy. The main industrial concerns are: petroleum refining, electronics, chemicals and chemical products, machinery and equipment, oil-drilling equipment, rubber processing and rubber products, processed food and beverages, ship repair, financial services, and biotechnology.

Contextual Features

The President is elected by popular vote for a six-year term. Following legislature elections, the leader of the majority party or leader of majority coalition is usually appointed Prime Minister by the President, with the Deputy Prime Minister(s) appointed by the Prime Minister. The Cabinet is appointed by the President and is responsible to the Parliament.

There is a unicameral Parliament with 83 seats. Members are elected by popular vote to serve five-year terms.

The Chief Justice of the Supreme Court is appointed by the President, with advice of the Prime Minister. Other judges are appointed by the President, with advice of the Chief Justice and Court of Appeal.

The legal system in Singapore is adversarial in nature. English common law was superimposed on the existing customary law and Muslim Law. Consequently, the legal system in Singapore can be characterized as pluralistic; while the dominant common law which shaped the Singapore legal system applies to all segments of the population, Muslim law governs the Muslim community in religious and matrimonial matters. Muslim law is administered in accordance with the Administration of Muslim Law Act, Cap.42. (Woon, 1989). The death penalty is still in force. Drug trafficking is a capital offense.

The crime rates are low in Singapore, compared to most countries, and the categories of major crimes are: Immigration Act offenses, motor vehicle thefts, and cheating.

The Judicial power is vested in the Supreme Court and in the subordinate courts. The Supreme Court of Judicature Act established the Supreme Court of Singapore, which consists of the High Court, The Court of Appeals, and the Court of Criminal Appeal. The High Court has unlimited original jurisdiction in criminal and civil matters (*The Europa World Year Book*, 1993).

The Subordinate Court Act incorporated the Subordinate Courts, comprising the District Claims Courts, Magistrate Courts, Juvenile Courts, Coroner Courts, and Small Claims Courts. There are 30 District and Magistrate Court, one Juvenile Court, and one Coroner's Court. District and Magistrate Courts have original criminal and civil jurisdiction. While the District Courts try cases with a maximum 10 years penalty, the maximum term does not exceed three years. Further, the Administration Muslim Law Act established the *Shariah* Court (*The Europa World Year Book*, 1993).

The Juvenile Court was created by The Children and Young Persons Act of 1949. That Act prescribes the method for processing juvenile delinquents between 14 and 16 years old. Proceedings of this court are not open to the public.

The Coroner's Court is appointed by the President on the recommendations of the Chief Justice. The Coroner may issue a warrant for person suspected of causing death.

In 1992, there were 11 judges, including the Chief Justices, and 10 Judicial Commissioners in the Supreme Court (*The Europa World Year Book*, 1993). Subordinate Judges are generally members of the Singapore Legal Service. They do not enjoy the security of tenure. There are 12 district courts and 14 magistrate courts.

The accused is presumed innocent until proven guilty. Under the Singapore Constitution, the accused person must be notified of the grounds for arrest. Every accused person has a guaranteed right to consult and be defended by a legal practitioner of his or her choice. The accused has a right to remain silent in the course of a police investigation (Constitution, Article 9[3].) The Legal Aid Bureau of the government provides legal aid for civil cases. A lawyer of the defense is assigned by the Registrar of the Supreme Court on the Government's behalf. In minor cases, an officer will go to the scene of a crime to investigate the offense and to arrest any alleged offenders. Officers are also authorized to have special powers to initiate investigations of serious offenses. When a police investigation discloses an offense, the Attorney General's Chambers (AG) has the discretion to initiate a criminal prosecution (Mahesh Nalla, *World Factbook of Criminal Justice Systems, http://www.ojp.usdoj. gov/bjs/pub/ascn/wfbcjsm.txt*). Upon completion of the investigation, the prosecutor will initiate the criminal prosecution, and the case will be prepared for trial.

After a review of the case, the Magistrate issues a summons or a warrant of arrest to the accused. An examining Magistrate then conducts an investigation to determine if the case against the accused justifies proceedings in the High Court.

As a general rule, all criminal cases are tried by a single judge, with the exception of capital offense trials, which are conducted by a court consisting of two High Court judges (*World Factbook of Criminal Justice Systems*).

Information on the number and type of prisons is largely derived from the 1970s. The dated material states that Singapore prisons held a daily average of approximately 3,000 prisoners. Prison programs focused on rehabilitation and individualized treatment, and the prisoners were segregated by sex and age (Vreeland et al. 1977).

During the same period, there were four prisons for adult males, one female minimum security prison, and a training school for juvenile offenders between 16 and 21 years old. Juveniles below 16 were sent by the courts to approved homes for girls and boys.

The Queeenstown Remand Prison I, a minimum security prison, serves the purpose of receiving and classifying new convicts and those awaiting trial. The Changi Prison is a maximum security prison for those with a prison sentence exceeding three years. In addition, Moon Crescent at Changi and the Khasa Centres serve as a medium security prison and a detention home for those awaiting trial, respectively. The prison system also includes pre-release centers to assist long-term prisoners with their re-entry into society (Vreeland et al. 1977).

In 1988, the incarceration rate was 183.3 per 100,000 population. Those committed to Drug Rehabilitation Centres were included in this figure (Chieng 1990). The Director of Prisons administers the Prisons Department, which is housed in the Ministry of Home Affairs (Vreeland et al. 1977).

Police Profile

Demographics

The Singapore Police Force has an operationally ready strength of 36,142 officers, consisting of 8,950 regular officers, 854 civilian officers, 3,288 National Service Full-time (NSF) personnel, 21,786 operationally-ready national servicemen (NSmen), and 1,264 Volunteer Special Constabulary Officers (as of 31 March 1999) (*www.spinet. gov.sg/news/spfar/annual9899/p.14.html*).

Organizational Description

The Singapore Police Force is divided into Senior and Junior Officers. Senior Officers occupy the ranks of Commissioner of Police, Senior Assistant Commissioner, Assistant Commissioner, Deputy Assistant Commissioner, Superintendent, Deputy Superintendent, Assistant Superintendent, and Inspector. Junior Officers occupy ranks of Station Inspector, Senior Staff Sergeant, Staff Sergeant, Corporal, and Constable (Harman, 1991).

The organization of the Singapore Police force is as follows:

Airport Police, Commercial Affairs Department, Criminal Investigation Department (CID), Divisional Headquarters (Precinct), Gurkha Contingent, Manpower Department, National Police Cadet Corp, Planning and Organisation Department, Police Coast Guards, Police National Service Department, Public Affairs Department, Service Department and Inspectorate Department, Special Operations Command, Special Projects, Traffic Police, Training Command, and Volunteer Special Constabulary (www.spinet.gov.sg/aboutus/index.html).

There are special units, including the Police Task Force, Special Tactics and Rescue Unit, and the recently established Police Troops to combat illegal immigrants and to tackle regional instability in South East Asia.

Advancement and promotion in the Singapore Force depend very much on the officer's performance and potential.

Functions

The Mission of the Singapore Police Force is to uphold the law, maintain order, and keep the peace in the Republic of Singapore. That is done in partnership with the community to protect life and property, prevent crime and disorder, detect and apprehend offenders, and preserve a sense of security and safety.

Training

Basic training is made up of academic and field work. This includes physical training, weapon training, criminal law, unarmed combat, and basics of investigation.

Junior Officers begin with six months of training at the Police Academy. For Senior Officers, the period of training is nine monthsTraining is under the Training Command (TRACOM). Besides basic training, there is the Continuing Education Centre, providing opportunities for academic awards from advanced programs to university postgraduate degrees. Singapore Police officers are also sent to various institutions around the world for training, including the FBI School.

Trainers not only teach law subjects, they also inculcate value training, instill self-discipline, and prepare the trainees for more challenging and professional roles when they graduate from the Training Command.

Police Use of Firearms

Possession of firearms in Singapore is illegal. Firearms control is very strict. Only police and military personnel are allowed to carry firearms. Normally, Police Officers relinquish firearms when they are off duty.

Complaints and Discipline

The Corruption Prevention Investigations Bureau is charged with investigating complaints about Police. Police Officers are disciplined severely if found guilty of committing crimes. As Law Enforcement Officers, they are expected to uphold the law.

Singapore Police Officers adhere closely to the Sets of Standards Operating Procedures (SOP) and Police General Order (PGO) in the execution of duties. The SOP and PGO are in line with the Constitution and the Criminal Procedure Code in ensuring that the basic dignity of all persons is respected, in a manner that does not compromise crime-fighting efforts.

There are no human rights initiatives or projects. Police Officers are not trained in Human Rights. The Singapore Police Force believes that their standards of training are very high. The Police have not been criticized for human rights violations for a long time. There is no program to control and investigate human rights violations.

Terrorism

The Internal Security Department (Ministry of Home Affairs) is responsible for investigating and preventing terrorism. Terrorist activities in Singapore are rare. Early in the twenty-first century, terrorism arrived in Singapore. The Police and Internal Security prevented disaster by arresting terrorist suspects before targets were hit. The identified terrorist organizations are: Jemiah Islamiayah (JI), with connection to al-Qaeda, and the Communist Party of Malaya.

International Cooperation

The Singapore Police Force is part of the worldwide law enforcement community. It cooperates well internationally with most major international police organizations, including INTERPOL and the United Nations. Regionally, the Singapore Police is part of the ASEANPOL, the Police of the Association of South East Asian Nations.

Police Education, Research, and Publications

The Singapore Police Academy is the basic institution for police education. Besides first level training for entry police officers, there are other advanced courses for serving police officers. The Temasek Polytechnic offers part and full time courses in Police Studies, Security Management, and Law. They are at the Certificate, Diploma, and Advanced Diploma levels. Upgrading to a Bachelor's Degree can be accomplished in Brisbane, Australia at the Queensland University of Technology.

Staff departments in the Singapore Police force possess research capabilities to a certain extent. Departments such as the Criminal Investigation Department have research and planning divisions, albeit still at a nascent stage for the Singapore Police Force. There are few academic researchers at the National University of Singapore and Institute of South East Asian Studies in the area of Law and Justice Studies.

The Police Public Affairs Department (PADF) of the Singapore Police Force handles all police publications. The major publications are: 1. *Police Life* magazine, a monthly journal with scholarly content, 2. *Police Life Annual,* and 3. *Annual Report.* Additionally, in conjunction with The National Crime Prevention Council the "Mr. Policeman" Series was published. This series includes:

"Dear Mr. Police-man," written by Chuah Ai Mee (1986 and 1992); and
"Mr. Policeman is My Friend," written by Chua Hui Ling (1994).

MARKE LEONG

Bibliography

Chieng, LK. "Use of Non-Custodial Sanctions in the Treatment of Law Breakers in Singapore." *Resource Material#38 U.N. Asia and Far East Institute.* Tokyo: UNAFEI, 1990.

CIA. "Singapore." *The World Fact Book 2000.* (www.odci-gov/cia/publications/factbook/geos/sn.html.

Harman, A. "Singapore–From Humble Beginnings, Epitome of Modern Policing." *Law and Order.* April:16–22, 1991.

Nalla, M. "Singapore." *World Fact Book of Criminal Justice Systems.* Singapore. (www/djp.usdoj.gov/djs/pub/asen/wfbcjsm.txt).

Vreeland, N. et al. *Area Handbook for Singapore.* Washington DC: US Printing Office, 1977.

Woon, W. *The Singapore Legal System.* Singapore: Longman, 1989.

———Woon, W. *SBS World Guide 6th Edition.* South Yarra: Ausinfo, HGP, 1989.

———Woon, W. *Singapore Facts and figures 2000.* Singapore: Ministry of Information and The Arts, 2000.

———Woon, W. *Singapore Police Force Annual Report– 1989–99.*

———Woon, W. Singapore Police force Internet. www.spinet.gov.sg/about us/index.html.

———Woon, W. *The Europa World Year Book, Singapore.* London: Europa Publications, 1993.

SLOVAKIA

Background Material

Currently an independent state in Eastern Europe, the Slovak Republic (*Slovenska republika*) existed historically as part of the Great Moravian and Holy Roman Empires, the Austro-Hungarian Empire and, more recently, the Republic of Czechoslovakia. After World War II, Slovakia (*Slovensko*) became part of the Czechoslovak Socialist Republic, within the sphere of the Soviet Union's influence. Following the 1989 overthrow of communism (the "Velvet Revolution"), the nation was reborn as the Czechoslovak Republic, and on January 1, 1993 the Slovak Republic came into existence (sometimes referred to as the "Velvet Divorce"). In 2002, the nation was invited to join NATO as one of seven former Soviet countries, and it was slated for membership in the European Union (EU) in May 2004.

The capital is Bratislava. Slovakia has an area of 49,036 sq km and a population of 5.4 million (July 2003 estimate). The ethnic composition of the nation breaks down as follows: Slovak 4,614,854 (85.8%), Czech 44,620 (0.8%), Hungarian 520,528 (9.7%), Romany 89,920 (1.7%, although some estimates are 4% to 7%); also Ruthenian (0.3%), Ukrainian (0.2%), and German (0.1%). Religions include Roman Catholicism (60.3%), Protestantism (8.4%), and Orthodox Christianity (4.1%). There is also a Jewish population of about 3,000 (mainly in Bratislava and Košice).

Major Industries include mining, metal and metal products, chemicals and manmade fibers, machinery, paper and printing, earthenware and ceramics, transport vehicles, textiles, electrical and optical apparatus, and rubber products.

Contextual Features

The Slovak Republic is a parliamentary democracy with a unicameral parliament, the 150-member *Narodna rada Slovenskej republiky* (National Council of the Slovak Republic). Following elections in

September 2002, a coalition government was formed, composed of four center-right parties.

The legal system in Slovakia is new and is still evolving. It is a civil law system belonging to the family of continental legal systems (built on written law rather than on judicial precedent) and based on Austro-Hungarian codes. It has been modified to comply with the requirements of the Organization on Security and Cooperation in Europe (OSCE) and to expunge Marxist-Leninist legal theory.

In 2002, there were 107,373 incidences of crime in the Slovak Republic, a sharp increase over the previous six-year period of decline. Crime is lower than in most western European countries. Recent figures for the United Kingdom, for example, show just over six million crimes reported, most of them theft, one crime for every 10 residents. In Slovakia, there is one reported crime for every 50 persons. It should be noted that these figures only show reported crime, and in a country where there is a high distrust of the police, it is difficult to estimate the number of crimes that remain unreported.

The most common crimes are theft and burglary, but, following a trend observed in other Eastern European countries after the fall of communism in the late 1980s, drug offenses and related crimes have escalated. While the Slovak Republic has been primarily a transit country for illicit drugs, it is more and more becoming a consumer country as well. There is a disproportionate and growing amount of violence, with about 15,000 gun-related crimes annually; this is comparably high for a country of this size. It is widely believed that many of these and other violent crimes are related to organized criminal activities. Organized crime has become a most serious problem, and while Slovakian gangs are still the most prevalent, Russian, Albanian, and Italian groups are emerging as well. These groups concentrate primarily on economic crime, money laundering, drug trafficking, and illegal migration. Until 1998, the law-enforcement agencies were usually unsuccessful in exposing these illegal activities.

The Slovakian court system is comprised of several layers of state courts: 43 district courts, four regional courts, and a supreme court, all under the jurisdiction of the Ministry of Justice. There are also military courts that deal specifically with military crimes. Most criminal cases and minor civil cases are handled by district courts, while regional courts hear appeals and major criminal and civil cases. The Supreme Court in Bratislava is the court of final review, except for constitutional cases, which are under the exclusive jurisdiction of the Constitutional Court. The function of the Slovak Constitutional Court is similar to that of the U.S. Supreme Court, except the President appoints judges to the Constitutional Court for a single term of seven years.

Judges in state courts are appointed initially for a term of four years and subsequently either reappointed for life or removed from office. State courts have either one judge or a bench/senate composed of five professional judges, and do not have the jury system per se but instead have lay judges, who sit on the bench in courts of the first instance. Judges are independent, and the court hearings are public. Any person charged with a criminal offense is presumed innocent until proven guilty, and an accused person has the right to counsel and may request free legal assistance if needed. The Constitutional Court of the Slovak Republic is an independent judicial body that interprets and safeguards the constitutionality of laws, government decrees, and other legal rules. The Constitutional Court has 20 judges who serve seven-year terms and are appointed by the President and nominated by the Parliament. The Court has jurisdiction over administrative disputes dealing with decisions of central and local governments, and the court is the final arbiter in interpreting the Constitution and constitutional laws.

A new Criminal Code has been adopted, and the new philosophy of penalties will include habitual offender provisions ("three times and that's it"), and provisions for life sentences without parole, for example. The scope of criminal penalties will also be narrowed, because possibilities for non-uniform and often subjective court decisions regarding criminal penalties have often occurred. Mediation and probation opportunities will be introduced into criminal proceedings, and negotiations between the prosecutor and the accused will hopefully reduce the burden on the courts.

The correctional system in the Slovak Republic is administered within the Ministry of Justice under the General Directorate of the Corps of Prison and Court Guard. In 1992, there were 6,311 prisoners (119 per 100,000), increasing to 7,412 in 1995; there were 7,409 in 1998, dropping in 2001 to 6,941 (129 per 100,000). There were 8,829 prisoners (164 per 100,000) housed in 18 institutions in the Slovak Republic in September, 2003. Pre-trial detainees or remand prisoners comprised 33.1% of the prison population; female inmates made up 2.5% of the prison population, and 0.7% were under the age of 18. The official capacity of the prison system is 9,435, and occupancy levels remain between 80–85%.

SLOVAKIA

Police Profile

Background

The Police in the Slovak Republic grew out of the Czechoslovakian National Security Corps, the majority (80% in 1986) of whom came from worker or farm families. The Corps was comprised of both Public Security (SNB), which performed routine police functions at all levels from federal to local, and State Security (the former secret police).

The SNB was an armed force, organized and trained as such, but equipped to perform police rather than military functions. Although precise numbers are not verifiable, in the late 1980s it was reported to be a relatively small force that was augmented by volunteer auxiliary units. Articles in the Slovak press at this time referred to 27,000 auxiliary guards in 3,372 units assisting Public Security in Slovak areas alone. The People's Militia, formed after World War II, was given responsibility for the defense of the socialist society, and militia personnel had powers of arrest equal to those of the regular Police. With the emergence of an independent Slovak Republic in 1993, a national Police Force was formed, which has evolved into the Slovak Police Corps of today.

Organizational Description and Functions

The national Police Corps has sole responsibility for internal and border security. With the exception of the Slovak Information Service (SIS), which reports directly to the Prime Minister, all security forces are under the Ministry of the Interior; Municipal Police report to their individual city councils. Municipal Police wear dark blue or black uniforms, while National Police wear olive green uniforms. Although an accurate number of current Police Corps personnel is unavailable, there were 20,208 in 2000, representing one officer for every 374 citizens; 10% of the officers at that time were women, but that number is increasing. Police officers on average earn Sk 19,375 (US$475) per month (2002 figures); this is higher than the average national salary of Sk 13,000 (US$317).

The Police Corps consists of seven departments or services and is led by the Police Corps President. Departments are as follows: (1) service of the criminal police, (2) service of the financial police, (3) service of the public order police, (4) service of the traffic police (5) service for the protection of premises, (6) service of the border police, and (7) special police services. The Ministry of Interior establishes and abolishes these departments, and it defines their specific roles and duties under the Constitution and constitutional law.

Financial police deal with money laundering and other white-collar crimes. Police officials have said that there was an increase in the incidence of economic and financial crime since the "velvet divorce," in part as a result of a growing awareness and expertise among businessmen in how to commit these crimes. Officers in the special police services are used in terrorist, hijacking, or kidnapping situations, as well as natural disasters and rescue operations. In January, 2004, two special units of the Slovak Police were designated and an office established, specifically for combating organized crime

In 1991, the Slovakian Parliament passed the Municipal Police Act, which began decentralizing many policing activities within the country. While this idea has gained some acceptance by the public and the police themselves, there is still some opposition to this concept. Municipal Police have responsibilities similar to public order police but are relegated to individual towns and cities, issuing parking fines and citations for minor traffic offenses. The Slovakian Municipal Police Chiefs Association (SANMOP) was formed as a professional service provider for Slovakian Municipal Police Departments, who pay special attention to community policing principles. SANMOP is responsible for day-to-day operations of servicing its member departments through the operations of the Slovakian Municipal Police Information Technology Network System (SPINS M).

Volunteer peace officers have also been authorized to assist the border and traffic police services, by supervising the security and efficient operation of automobile traffic on the roads and by patrolling the state borders. The peace officer should be 21 years of age and "enjoy the confidence and respect among citizens."

There are also Police units within the military and, in addition to their military policing responsibilities, they can also be used for civilian law enforcement in times of necessity. Article 70 of the National Council of the Slovak Republic Act No.171 (1993) states that the government can subordinate members of the military on active duty, to the command of the Police Corps if necessary, to safeguard protection of the state border, guarded premises, or public peace. They retain their military uniform with the addition of a police badge or patch.

Training

To be a member of the Police Corps, one must be a citizen at least 18 years of age and must have passed the exit examination at a secondary school or graduate from a Technical College or University. To be appointed as an Investigator, a Police Officer must be 24 years of age, have a law degree or a degree in security services (master's level), must have completed a period of probation of one year, and successfully pass the final investigator's exam. The Minister of the Interior can also appoint a Police Officer as an Investigator who has a degree other than law or security services but who meets all the other requirements. Police training is provided at four Police Colleges in Pezinok, Košice, Bratislava, and Zilina, and the Police Academy, all under the Ministry of Interior.

The Police Colleges in Pezinok and Košice provide one year of elementary police education specializing in security service for entry-level officers (first rank/warrant officers). The institution in Bratislava is for those with elementary police education and at least one year of experience who plan careers in the public order, transport, criminal, or border (alien) police. Successful students graduate in 9-10 months after final examinations in specialized subjects and will qualify for second rank (officer). The Police College in Zilina provides elementary and specialized education in fire protection.

There are numerous opportunities available for those who want careers in policing. One of the more successful programs is the Green Cross Junior Police Venturers, a program that offers Slovakian youth interested in law enforcement careers a chance to become acquainted with the system. This exposure to the judicial and law enforcement systems increases the chances that interested youths are better able to function as future citizens and prospective members of the police force.

Police Use of Firearms

Slovakian Police are armed and authorized to use deadly force. There are strict guidelines for the use of a weapon (specified in Article 61 of Act No. 171, 1993), but a great deal of discretion is left to the individual officer. Incidences of excessive use of force by the Police are rare, with the exception of certain ethnic minorities, especially the Roma.

Complaints and Discipline

The Roma are often the targets, along with other minority groups, of racially motivated violence by citizens as well as authorities. The rate of crime among this group is much higher than among the general population, due primarily to their unfavorable economic situation and levels of high unemployment. Amnesty International and similar groups have also reported numerous instances of forced sterilization of Romani women, physical and verbal abuse by police, racial disparities in quality of health care, and other examples of overt discrimination. There were other reports of violent police raids on entire Romani communities, ostensibly in order to arrest criminal suspects.

In February 2002, the Minister of the Interior, Ivan Šimko, in an attempt to curb corruption, formulated the Code of Ethics of the Police Force Members to guide officers, both practically and philosophically, in the performance of the duties. A 2002 survey published by the Slovak Statistics Office showed that three out of four Slovaks have little or no confidence in the Police, and public support was at one of the lowest levels in the country's short history. This resulted in a high degree of non-reporting of crimes or accidents and of citizens refusing to come forward when they witness crimes. Increasing levels of violence by skinheads and other racist groups led the United Nation Committee on the elimination of Racial Discrimination to recommend that Slovakia strengthen procedures for timely and thorough investigations and effective prosecutions against these organizations.

Slovakian newspapers frequently carry stories of crimes committed by the Police themselves, particularly with regard to drunk driving and collusion with organized crime. Given the levels of improper behavior within Police ranks, there may well be many other crimes committed within the force that go unreported or simply not prosecuted. In 2002, there were 189 offenses committed by officers, 22 involving automobile accidents; about half of these involved drunken Police, including high-ranking officers.

In May 2001, the United Nations Committee Against Torture considered Slovakia's initial report concerning the implementation of the provisions of the *Convention against Torture and Other Cruel, Inhuman or Degrading Treatment or Punishment*. The Committee recommended that the Slovak authorities adopt measures to initiate an effective, reliable, and independent complaints system to undertake prompt, impartial, and effective investigations into allegations of maltreatment or torture by Police and other public officials, and where the findings are warranted, to prosecute and punish alleged perpetrators. It further suggested that the Ministry of Interior continue to provide human rights training for law enforcement and military personnel.

International Cooperation

The Slovak Republic has been quite active in anti-terrorist efforts. The country is party to 11 of the 12 global international conventions signed to combat international terrorism. In 2000, a decision was made to lend support for the European Union's rapid response forces; in addition to military police, artillery units and mine-clearing units were committed as well.

Organized crime, especially by gangs from Ukraine, increased markedly during the 1990s, and Slovakian Police have begun new cooperative efforts with police forces in other countries to combat it. The country has also joined OCTOPUS, a joint European Commission and Council of Europe project to combat organized crime and corruption.

In 1994, several months after the split of Czechoslovakia, the defense ministers of both countries signed an agreement on mutual collaboration in areas such as defense planning, exchange of information on flights of military aircraft, and on the use of military training facilities. In the following year, the two countries signed several documents, including an agreement on cooperation between Czech and Slovak Police, and on cooperation in legislative and legal affairs. By 2000, the countries had signed 15 treaty documents, the most Slovakia has signed with any one country.

The Slovakian Municipal Police Chiefs Association (SANMOP), in addition to its activities discussed above, coordinates international police training and international police officer exchange programs; it also exchanges Police intelligence on wanted and missing persons, maintains international contact with legal Police experts on issues relating to the development of the democratic policing system in the country, and provides other support services.

In collaboration with the Police Academy of the Slovak Republic and the Institute for Continuing Education for Police in Canada, a program in human rights training was established for Slovakian Police. Budgeted at CA$204,090, the objective of this two-year phase 2 Royal Canadian Mounted Police CMP is to contribute to improving management and training of the Slovak Police and to increase their ability to effectively deal with criminal activity. The project assists them in their reform efforts and focuses specifically on developing a strategic plan, professional standards (code of ethics), training systems, and specialized police operations (such as witness protection).

Police Education, Research, and Publications

The Police Academy is a university providing specialization in security service and non-governmental security service for officers at both the Baccalaureate and Master's levels. Entrance examinations consist of knowledge, language, and psychological tests, as well as tests for physical suitability. Those accepted must have graduated from one of the Police Colleges and have a minimum of two years' experience in the field.

Some Slovakian universities offer advanced degrees that are available for Police officers and administrators desiring further education, and Police experience is a prerequisite for these Master's and Doctoral-level programs of study. Programs for Master's degrees take between two and four years, while the Doctoral degree takes between three and five years after obtaining the Master's degree. These are available to both male and female candidates. The Master's and Doctoral degrees do not guarantee a certain rank in the Police hierarchy after completion.

Kriminalistický a expertízny ústav Policajného zboru (abbreviated KEU PZ or Institute) is a part of the Police Investigation and Criminalistic Expertises of the Ministry of Interior. While not actively involved in Police education, the Institute provides expertise in several aspects of forensic science for the Police Corps and other law enforcement institutions.

The major academic journal devoted to policing and police research in the Slovak Republic is *Police Theory and Practise*, a journal published (since 1992) four times per year by the Police Academy. The Editorial Board consists of 12 members from the Police Academy in Bratislava, and includes academics from Austria, Czech Republic, and Germany, as well as several Slovakians. Authors of the articles are primarily teachers, lecturers, and scientists, belonging to the pedagogical and scientific staff of the Police Academy, as well as contributors from other universities in Slovakia, mainly from the Faculty of Law and Pedagogy. Contributions by foreign authors from the Czech Police Academy and other Czech universities are regularly published.

There are a number of academics who write about various aspects of policing in the Slovak Republic. For example, Karol Murdza, a Sociologist at the Police Academy, has published works about Police education, and the relations between citizens and the Police. Matδ© Korba, a Czech academic in Prague, studies the reform of the security forces in the Czech and Slovak Republics. One of the more prolific researchers is Peter Bilsk, also of the Police Academy, who has published extensively in several areas of policing and police education.

CHUCK FIELDS

Bibliography

Baláz, Pavol. *Polícia Slovenskej republiky v transformacnom procese spolocnosti*. Bratislava: Akadâemia Policajnâehozboru SR, 1995.

Crampton, R. J. *Eastern Europe in the Twentieth Century — And After*. London: Routledge, 1997.

Goldman, Milton, F. *Slovakia Since Independence:A Struggle for Democracy*. Praeger Publishers, 1999.

Henderson, Karen. *Slovakia: The Escape From Reality*. London: Routledge, 2002.

Kollár, Miroslav, Grigorij Mesenikov, and Tom Nicholson (eds.) *Slovakia 2002—A Global Report on the State of Society*. Bratislava: Institute for Public Affairs. (Published annually).

Leff, Carol Skalnik. *The Czech and Slovak Republics: Nation versus State*. Boulder, CO: Westview Press, 1997.

Mesenikov, Grigorij, et al. *Slovakia 2001: A Global Report on the State of Society*. Bratislava: Institute For Public Affairs, 2002.

Williams, Kieran & Dennis Deletant. *Security Intelligence Services in New Democracies: The Czech Republic, Slovakia and Romania*. London: Palgrave, 2001.

http://bratislava.usembassy.gov/cis/cisen022.html (Country Reports on Human Rights Practices).

www.minv.sk/en/ (Ministry of Interior, Slovak Republic).

www.minv.sk/en/_private/171.htm (Act No. 171/1993, July 1993 regarding the Police Force).

SLOVENIA

Background Material

Slovenia is a small Central European country, which used to be a part of the former Socialist Federal Republic of Yugoslavia. Slovenia declared its independence on June 25, 1991. The next day, the newly formed state was attacked by the Yugoslav Army. A truce was called after a 10-day war. The European Union recognized Slovenia in the middle of January 1992, and the UN accepted it as a member in May 1992. In February 1999, an association agreement with the EU came into effect, and Slovenia also applied for full membership.

The country is situated on 20,273 sq km between the Alps, the Adriatic Sea, and the Pannonian Plains. It has a population of 1,965,986, of which 87.9 percent are Slovenes. The official language is Slovene. The majority of Slovenes are Roman Catholics, although there are some small communities of other Protestant Christians, as well as Muslims and Jews. The capital city is Ljubljana.

In 1999, the GDP per capita was $10,078, while the standardized rate of unemployment was 7.5. The relatively small Slovenian market directed the orientation of the economy towards export. Main foreign trading partners are Germany, Italy, Croatia, France, and Austria.

Contextual Features

Slovenia's constitutional order is parliamentary democracy. The Head of State is the President of the Republic, popularly elected every five years, for a maximum two five-year terms. The legislative authority is the National Assembly with 90 deputies. The Government consists of the Prime Minister and other Ministers. The Government and the Ministers are independent within the framework of their jurisdiction, and they are responsible to the National Assembly.

Slovenia has a civil law system, while its criminal law system could be called mixed or quasi-adversarial. The criminal justice system comprises the courts, the State Prosecutor, the prisons and correctional institutions, and the Police.

Judicial power in Slovenia is implemented by courts with general responsibilities and by specialized courts. Forty-four District Courts, 11 Regional Courts, four Higher Courts, and the Supreme Court of the Republic of Slovenia are the courts with general jurisdiction. The Supreme Court is the highest court in the state. In addition to courts with general jurisdiction, there are four Labor Courts and the Social Court.

The State Prosecutor is an independent state authority responsible for prosecuting cases brought against those suspected of committing criminal offenses. There are 11 regional public prosecution offices, four higher public prosecution offices, and the Supreme State Prosecutor's Office of the Republic of Slovenia.

The Prison Administration, working within the jurisdiction of the Ministry of Justice, performs administrative and professional tasks related to the following: implementation of penal sanctions; organization and management of prisons and correctional institutions; provision of financial, material, human, technical and other resources for the functioning of prisons and corrective institutions; training of personnel to meet the requirements of the implementation of penal sanctions; and the exercise of prisoners' rights. The Prison Administration encompasses several prisons and one correctional institution.

In 2001, the extent of crime handled by the police increased, which is the result of more consistent filing of complaints for minor crimes, and a larger number of crimes committed by drug addicts. Statistical data indicate that residents of Slovenia are still relatively safe from crime, although the predictions of experts concerning the strengthening of organized and transnational crime, an increase in crime with elements of psychological and physical violence, and the exploitation of new crimes, especially communication technologies and devices for the commission of criminal offenses, have come true. A rise of abuse of illicit drugs and the so-called secondary crime, related to drugs, has continued. What is particularly concerning is a rise of violence and drug abuse among the young (Svetek 2002).

In 2001, the police recorded 74,795 criminal offenses, for which there was a reasonable suspicion that they had been committed in the past year or in previous years, which is 10.6% more than a year before. Among these offenses, the largest rise was in minor property offenses, offenses of illicit drug manufacturing and traffic, simple assault, threat to safety, and maltreatment and sexual assault on a minor under 15 years of age.

Police Profile

Background

After gaining independence from the former Yugoslavia, the new Slovenian state reorganized its political and economical system and started to reorganize its public services, including the Police Force. The Slovenian Police Force is now an independent part of the Ministry of the Interior of the Republic of Slovenia. The Police perform their tasks at three levels: the state, the regional, and the local levels. Organizationally, it is composed of the General Police Directorate, regional Police Directorates, and police stations. The police headquarters are in Ljubljana.

Within the General Police Directorate, there are: the Uniformed Police Directorate (with its sectors taking care of public order, traffic, state borders and foreigners, and the organization and development of uniformed police; it also includes the flight police unit, the center for foreigners and the police orchestra); the Criminal Investigation Police Directorate (with sectors for general, white collar and organized crimes, special tasks, computer crime and criminal analysis, and the Forensic and Research Center); the Operation and Communications Center; the Security and Protection Bureau; the Special Unit; the Common Services; the Informatics and Telecommunications Service; the Personnel Department; and the Police Academy.

On the regional level, there are 11 Police Directorates, located in major cities across Slovenia. Regional Police Directorates supervise the work of police stations on the local level. There are 98 police stations in Slovenia.

Demographics

All together, there were 6,882 police officers and 716 detectives employed by the Slovenian Police in 2001, which gave the ratio of 274 police officers and 36 detectives per 100,000 inhabitants. Their average age was 31 years; the average length of service was 13.5 years. The vast majority (70%) had a high-school-level education, while some 20 percent had education above the high school level (associate, bachelor's, master's, or doctoral degrees). Eighty percent were males.

Functions

Police powers are defined in Article 33 of the Police Act: "In performing their tasks, police officers can issue warnings and orders, establish identity and perform identification procedures, examine persons for security reasons, invite, perform security controls, prohibit movement, perform anti-terrorist inspection of premises, devices and areas, arrest and detain persons, order stricter police control, confiscate objects, enter premises, use transport and communication means, use secret police measures, coercive means and use other authorities defined by law."

The Police Act also specifies the conditions under which the police are authorized to use firearms. They can only use firearms if they cannot otherwise protect lives, prevent from fleeing a suspect who was caught in the act of crime punishable by law by at least eight years of imprisonment, prevent an attack on persons or property under police protection, or prevent an unlawful attack on police officers that endangers their lives.

Training

In order to become a police officer, a successful candidate has to have a high school degree and must possess appropriate mental and physical abilities. He or she has to be a citizen of Slovenia with a permanent address in Slovenia, not older than 30 years, and must be free of criminal charges or convictions. After being employed, each police officer has to complete a year-and-a-half basic training program at the Police Academy.

Pursuant to the law, the police service performs the following tasks:

- protecting life, personal safety and property of people;
- preventing, discovering, and inspecting penal acts and minor offenses; discovering and arresting those committing penal acts and minor offenses, other wanted persons, and their extradition to the authorized bodies;
- maintaining public order;
- control and regulation of traffic on public roads and non-categorized roads used for public traffic;
- protecting the state border and performing border control;
- performing tasks defined in the regulations about foreigners;
- protecting certain persons, bodies, buildings, and districts;
- protecting certain working places and the secrecy of information of state bodies, if not otherwise defined by law; and
- performing tasks defined in the Law on Police and other laws and secondary legislation documents.

Police Use of Firearms

In 2000, the police in Slovenia used firearms on nine occasions, while the average number of cases for previous eight years was 9.4. In the large majority of cases, only warning shots were fired. Only one person lost his life as a consequence of police confrontation in 2000. One of the reasons for these relatively low numbers is that the perpetrators typically do not possess or use firearms. Firearms ownership laws in Slovenia are quite restrictive. As an illustration, firearms were used as a weapon in only 65 out of 474 robbery cases in 2000.

Complaints and Discipline

In 2000, there were 1,552 complaints against the police. Of those, 1,496 were processed by the police, and 201 (13.4 % of the processed complaints) were sustained. A similar trend could be observed during several previous years, as well. A novelty in Slovenia, introduced by the Police Act of 1998, is a participation of the public's representative in handling complaints against the police.

As a part of their basic police training, police officers receive training in human rights protection. There are, however, occasional instances of police violations of human rights. The European Commission, in its Report on Slovenia's progression as a candidate country, accused the Slovenian Police of being brutal and violent in some cases, based largely on the judgments made by some other governmental and non-governmental organizations. The police responded by denying allegations and providing statistics that showed just a slight increase in the number of cases where the police actually used force (1–27 % over the last four years). At the same time, several measures were implemented, including an increased level of control of the use of force, more precise analyses of recorded cases, programs for increasing the level of human rights awareness, and more training in the area of human rights.

Terrorism

While the police have increased their anti-terrorist measures and have been striving to heighten the terrorism awareness after the September 11, 2001 terrorist attacks in the United States, there are neither known terrorist organizations nor any activities of the international terrorist organizations discovered in Slovenia.

International Cooperation

The Slovenian Police have been very active in the area of international cooperation. In addition to bilateral operational cooperation with police forces of the neighboring countries, a close cooperation in the area of training has been developed with the Surrey Police (the United Kingdom) and with the Federal Bureau of Investigation (the United States of America). Slovenia is also a member of the MEPA (Middle European Police Academy) and regularly participates in its training programs. Lately, there has been an increased participation in programs organized by the AEPC (Association of European Police Colleges) and the CEPOL (European Police College).

Police Education, Research, and Publications

The only institution for higher education of the police in Slovenia is the College of Police and Security Studies, which is both a part of the

Ministry of the Interior and an affiliated member of the University of Ljubljana. Currently, the college is offering a three-year program in police and security studies. In 2003, the college will be transformed into the Faculty of Criminal Justice within the University of Maribor and—a year later—will start to offer a four-year program in criminal justice, in addition to the existing three-year program.

The following are the leading researchers and authors in the area of police and policing in Slovenia (in alphabetical order):

- Andrej Anzic, Ph.D., General Police Directorate;
- Anton Dvorsek, Ph.D., College of Police and Security Studies;
- Branko Lobnikar, M.Sc., College of Police and Security Studies;
- Darko Maver, Ph.D., College of Police and Security Studies;
- Gorazd Mesko, Ph.D., College of Police and Security Studies;
- Milan Pagon, Sc.D., Ph.D., College of Police and Security Studies;
- Janez Pecar, Ph.D., College of Police and Security Studies;
- Peter Umek, Ph.D., College of Police and Security Studies.

Reporters, who most frequently write on police and policing in Slovenia, are (in alphabetical order):

- Zarko Hojnik, newspaper Delo;
- Mica Vipotnik, newpaper Dnevnik;
- Damijana Zist, newspaper Vecer.

The most reputable columnists who write on issues of the police in Slovenia are Jakob DEMSAR and Drago KOS, both former high-ranking police officials.

The majority of police research is funded by the research organizations themselves. Some funding is available within the Ministry of Education, Science and Sport's programs, while another source is funding from the city government in larger Slovenian cities. Examples of recent research on police and policing are the following projects:

- *Structural analysis of attitudes and personality characteristics of Slovene police officers, by Gorazd Mesko;*
- *Determinants of police deviance in Slovenia, by Milan Pagon and Branko Lobnikar;*
- *Organizational and interpersonal sources of stress in Slovenian police force, by Milan*

Pagon, Daniel C. Ganster, and Michelle Duffy;
- *Police integrity, code of silence and police corruption: international comparison of different police organization,s by Milan Pagon, Sanja Kutnjak Ivkovich, Carl B. Klockars, Maria R. Haberfeld, and Branko Lobnikar;*
- *Attitudes of Slovene police officers towards foreigners by Peter Umek and Gorazd Mesko;*
- *Sociolinguistic factors in police dealings with German foreigners, by Bojana Virjent;*
- *Moral values of students, police and prison officers in Slovenia and Michigan, by Gorazd Mesko, Joanne Ziembo-Vogl, James Houston, and Peter Umek;*
- *Psychological factors in criminal investigation, by Peter Umek and Igor Areh;*
- *Protection of judges and courts in Slovenia, by Ivan Bele, Gorazd Mesko, Bojan Dobovsek, Sonja Kotnik, Anton Dvorsek, and Andrej Kmecl.*

There are two journals published in Slovenia that regularly contain police articles.

The first one is *Varstvoslovje: Journal of Security Theory and Praxeology,* published by the College of Police and Security Studies; Editor: Anton Dvorsek, Ph.D.; address: College of Police and Security Studies, Kotnikova 8, 1000 Ljubljana, e-mail: revijaVS@vpvs.uni-lj.si.

The second one is *Revija za kriminalistiko in kriminologijo* [Journal of Criminalistics and Criminology], published by the Ministry of the Interior; Editor: Darko Maver, Ph.D.; address: College of Police and Security Studies, Kotnikova 8, 1000 Ljubljana, e-mail: darko.maver@vpvs.uni-lj.si.

Two important sources for police scholars and practitioners regarding policing in Slovenia are the proceedings of two conferences, organized by the College of Police and Security Studies. The first conference is domestic and annual, while the other one is international and biennial. Examples of the latest editions are:

- Pagon, Milan, ed. *Dnevi varstvoslovja: zbornik prispevkov* [Days of Criminal Justice: The Proceedings]. Ljubljana: College of Police and Security Studies, 2002.
- Pagon, Milan, ed. *Policing in Central and Eastern Europe: Deviance, Violence, and Victimization.* Ljubljana: College of Police and Security Studies, 2002.

Another important source regarding the statistical data on police and policing in Slovenia is an annual statistical almanac of the Ministry of the Interior (MoI) and the Police. An example of the latest publication is:

Batis, R., ed. *Statisticni letopis MNZ in Policije* [Statistical Almanac of the MoI and the Police]. Ljubljana: Ministry of the Interior, 2001.

The following are police-related websites in Slovenia:

- *www.policija.si/en*—a website of the Slovenian Police;
- *www.mnz.si*—a website of the Ministry of the Interior;
- *www.vpvs.uni-lj.si*—a website of the College of Police and Security Studies.

MILAN PAGON

Bibliography

General Information. Government Public Relations and Media Office. www.uvi.si/eng/slovenia/facts/general (February 2003).

Kolenc, Tadeja. *Slovenska policija* [The Slovenian Police]. Ljubljana: Ministry of the Interior, General Police Directorate, 2002.

Mesko, Gorazd, ed. *Research at the College of Police and Security Studies*. Ljubljana: College of Police and Security Studies, 2002.

Ministry of Justice. www.gov.si/vrs/ang/government/ministry-of-justice.html (February 2003).

Pagon, Milan, ed. *Policing in Central and Eastern Europe: Comparing Firsthand Knowledge with Experience from the West*. Ljubljana: College of Police and Security Studies, 1996.

——Pagon, Milan, ed. *Policing in Central and Eastern Europe: Organizational, Managerial, and Human Resource Aspects*. Ljubljana: College of Police and Security Studies, 1998.

——Pagon, Milan, ed. *Policing in Central and Eastern Europe: Ethics, Integrity, and Human Rights*. Ljubljana: College of Police and Security Studies, 2000.

——Pagon, Milan, ed. *Policing in Central and Eastern Europe: Deviance, Violence, and Victimization*. Ljubljana: College of Police and Security Studies, 2002.

Pagon, Milan, and Branko Lobnikar. "Police Integrity in Slovenia." *The Contours of Police Integrity*, edited by Carl B. Klockars, Sanja Kutnjak Ivkovich, and Maria Haberfeld. Sage Publications, in press.

Police. www.policija.si/en (February 2003).

State and Political System. Government Public Relations and Media Office. www.uvi.si/eng/slovenia/facts/political-system (February 2003).

Svetek, Stas. *Kriminaliteta in kriminalistično delo v letu 2001* [Crime and crime investigation activity in 2001]. Revijaza kriminalistiko in kriminologijo, 53(2), 99–108, 2002.

SOLOMON ISLANDS

Background Material

Archaelogical research indicates that the Solomon Islands have been inhabited for at least 3,000 years. The Solomon Islands' first contact with Europeans was as early as 1568, when a Spanish explorer visited, but ongoing relations emerged only in the 1860s, when the Solomons' population was targeted by "blackbirders," who forcibly supplied indentured laborers for the plantations of Queensland and Fiji. In 1893, Britain seized control of the eastern islands and made them a protectorate; Germany controlled the west, but ceded control of most of their territory to Britain in 1899. After being the theatre for major battles in World War II, Solomon Islands independence was granted on July 7, 1978. However, ethnic tension caused instability, culminating in a *coup d'état* in June

2000. The Solomon Islands is one of four Melanesian independent states of the Pacific.

Ethnic tensions have been an ongoing challenge on the island of Guadalcanal between the local population and immigrants from the neighboring island of Malaita.

The economy is currently in rapid decline (14% and 25% GDP growth in 2000 and 2001, respectively). The government has suffered ongoing deficits and is essentially bankrupt.

Ethnic violence, government malfeasance, and endemic crime have undermined stability. A government besieged by militias, a state of lawlessness, unpunished murders, and a climate of criminal violence are the primary concerns in this pluralistic society of diverse cultures.

High-powered weapons have enabled renegade members of the Police Force to threaten law and order. The 2003 Australian-led military and policing contingent has disarmed several strategic groups in the Solomons.

Malaria control is a significant health concern.

As there is a lack of will and resources to control the activities of the logging companies, deforestation has emerged as a pressing problem. Other environmental problems include soil erosion and dying coral reefs.

The population is 494,786 (July 2002 estimate). Ethnic groups represented include the Melanesian (93% of the population), Polynesian (4%), Micronesian (1.5%), European 0.8%, Chin 0.3%, other 0.4%. English is the official language, but it is spoken by only one to two percent of the population. Solomon Tok Pisal and 120 indigenous languages are more commonly spoken. Religions practiced include Anglicanism (34% of the population), Roman Catholicism (19%), Baptist (17%), Seventh-Day Adventist (10%), other Protestant denominations (5%), and indigenous beliefs (4%).

The GDP per capita US$2000 (approximately half what it was in 1978, when the islands gained independence). The bulk of the population depends on agriculture, fishing, and forestry for at least part of their livelihood. Seventy-five percent of the labor force is classified as agricultural workers. There are large undeveloped mineral resources (lead, zinc, nickel, gold), but the lack of social stability has stymied development. Severe economic violence, the closure of business enterprises, and a government on the verge of bankruptcy have created serious economic problems, to the point of virtual economic collapse. Teachers and nurses regularly go without pay, and the electricity is often shut down. The country's external debt was estimated as US$137 in 2001.

The Solomon Islands economic situation has deteriorated considerably since the ethnic conflict on the island of Guadalcanal: the economy contracted by an estimated 25% in 2001, and export revenues have fallen by 60% since 1997. Three of the main export operations—the SIPL oil palm plantation, the Gold Ridge gold mine, and the Solomon Taiyo tuna cannery—have closed down because of the law and order situation. Due to social instability, international assistance to the Solomon Islands dropped 70 percent between 1998 and 2001 (*www.abc.net.au/ra/ pacific/places/ country/solomon_islands*).

Contextual Features

The Solomon Islands Constitution is the supreme law of the land, but a considerable body of law was inherited from England on independence. Additionally, legislation, regulations, and common law exist. Customary law is also recognized, and it takes precedence over common law and inherited British and subsidiary legislation.

Like other South Pacific countries' crime statistics, those of the Solomon Islands are limited and flawed. In the first half of 1998, a total of 1,583 criminal offenses were reported; 47.4% of these were property offenses, and 28.9% were offenses against the person. This constituted a 24% decrease on the corresponding period in the previous year (Newton 2000). Drug addiction among young people is increasing at an alarming rate.

The court structure of the Solomons is based on the standard model of inferior courts, superior courts, and appeal courts. Separate courts have been established to deal with customary land and minor local disputes.

The Court of Appeal has jurisdiction to hear civil appeals from any decision of the sitting High Court, including decisions of judges sitting in chambers. The High Court has unlimited original civil and criminal jurisdiction. Appeals can be made to the High Court from all civil judgments, orders, and decisions of any Magistrates' Court, except in certain circumstances. The decision of the High Court is final. The Magistrates' Courts have civil jurisdiction in claims relating to contracts or tort. The criminal jurisdiction of the Magistrates' Courts varies according to the class of magistrate. All classes of magistrates have jurisdiction to try criminal matters summarily (Care et al. 1999).

As a prerequisite to the exercise of Local Court jurisdiction, the court must be satisfied that the dispute has first been referred to the chiefs and that all traditional means of resolving the dispute have been exhausted. Local Courts may pass sentences ordering imprisonment for a term not exceeding six months or may impose a fine not exceeding $200. These village courts are empowered to "administer the law and custom of Islanders prevailing in the local area, as well as to administer punishment according to custom provided it is compatible with natural justice and humanity" (Findlay 1996). The Customary Land Appeal Court is a separate appeal court that has been established to deal with customary land appeals. A party cannot have a matter heard in this court unless the traditional chiefs have certified that the dispute is unsuitable for settlement or that attempts to settle it have failed (Lal et al. 2000).

Police Profile

Background

There are no regular military forces in the Solomon Islands, only the Solomon Islands National Reconnaissance and Surveillance Force. The multi-functional Royal Solomon Islands Police (RSIP) constitutes the national law enforcers. As a result of the coup in 2000, the Solomon Island Police underwent comprehensive restructuring. The notorious Police Field Force that was involved in the 2000 coup was reintegrated into the ordinary police. This paramilitary arm of the RSIP is being replaced with a Special Task and Rescue division. This unit will have high fitness, discipline, and skills, and it will include an elite unit modelled on the Special Operations Group of the Victoria Police (Australia) (*Australian*, October 10, 2002). Assistant Commissioner of Police, Joe Baetolinga, states that the new division will not be a paramilitary organization but a police tactical response unit (ABC Radio, Australia, October 10, 2002).

Ongoing disputes within the Solomon Islands Police Force have made data collection difficult. Police Commissioner Morton Sireheti resigned from the force in a dispute with the government in November 2002. Bill Morrell, a former Deputy Chief Constable from Manchester, became the new Police Commissioner in late January 2003 and immediately pledged to prioritize stability, defense of human rights, and professional policing. Morell acknowledges that the RSIP is beset by tribal rivalries, lack of funds, and involvement in crime.

Some rural and remote communities tend to rely solely on customary law. For example, the bush Kiowo of the Solomons refused to have their territory policed by anyone other than themselves (Newton 1998).

Demographics

In 1998, a research questionnaire distributed to chief officers of police indicated 897 members, resulting in a police to population ratio of approximately 1:390. The same survey revealed a male-dominated force: 96% were male (Newton, 2000).

Organizational Description

The ranks of the Solomon Islands Police Force are:

- Commissioner;
- Deputy Commissioner;
- Assistant Commissioner;
- Senior Superintendent;
- Superintendent;
- Assistant Superintendent;
- Inspector;
- Station Sergeant;
- Sergeant;
- Constable.

The Commissioner is responsible for the day-to-day administration of the Force, including the appointment of the lower-ranking officers. Senior officers are appointed by the separate Police and Prisons Service Commission.

Functions

The functions of the RSIP are to maintain and enforce law and order, preserve the peace, protect life and property, prevent and detect crime, apprehend offenders, and to control traffic. In July 1998, the Police Commissioner identified manpower, transport, and equipment deficiencies caused by financial restraints as the reason for low crime detection rates (Newton 2000). Additionally, the Police Force can be called upon to act in a military capacity, if the security of the Solomon Islands is under threat.

Failure to adequately perform its functions constitutes a major political, economic, and law and order problem in the Solomon Islands. For instance, police in the Western Province in early 2003 were demoralized and inoperative, as they operated without resources, and the judicial system is seriously compromised by a lack of magistrates. Vigilantes and mercenaries have been operating in some communities.

A two-year brutal civil war erupted in the late 1990s and caused some 20,000 Malaitans to flee from Guadalcanal; this conflict resulted in approximately 200 deaths; it brought all economic activity on the island to a standstill and paralyzed the regular police. A rebel coup of June, 2000, backed by the predominantly Malaitan RSIP Force, seized police armories and forced the government's resignation. Law and order collapsed, and foreign investors and expatriates fled the country (*Age* 31, March 2001:24). The government allowed an estimated 2000 militants to keep their high-powered guns, escape justice, and enlist as Special Constables (SCs). SCs cooperated with police in trying to restore law and order, but the SCs were notorious for extortion and brutality to Guadalcanal Liberation Front supporters. The former Police Commissioner said in August 2002, that the government was "scared" of the police, many of whom, he said, were running illegal businesses and had refused to hand in weapons they had stolen from police armories. The RSIP is partly corrupted from within by its role in the ethnic conflict. The SCs were demobilized in 2003.

Police Use of Firearms

RSIP are only permitted to use firearms with the Commissioner's authority, which may only be granted in accordance with the Prime Minister's instructions.

Complaints and Discipline

Offenses relating to mutiny, desertion, obstructing a senior officer, and failing to suppress riot are regarded as the most serious offenses of a police officer; more general disciplinary breaches include disrespect, drunkenness, sleeping on duty, insubordination, cowardice, and misconduct. Inquiries into disciplinary issues are conducted along judicial lines, with rules regarding evidence, due process, and cross-examination. Penalties for disciplinary breaches may include reprimand, a fine of up to 10 days' pay, confinement to quarters, demotion, or dismissal. Police officers penalized by demotion or dismissal may appeal to the Police and Prisons Commission; or for more minor penalties imposed by middle-ranking officers appeal to the Commissioner is possible.

Terrorism

The Solomon Islands has expressed its opposition to all forms of terrorism. The United States listed the Solomon Islands as supporting the "coalition of the willing" in the 2003 Iraqi war, but its Prime Minister denied any such support without UN authorization.

The thirtieth South Pacific Chiefs of Police Conference (SPCPC) in October, 2001 stressed the need to combat terrorism and to prevent its initiation in the South Pacific. The SPCPC resolved to urge Commissioners to seek legislative changes to ban proscribed terrorist groups, to freeze and seek the early forfeiture of assets of proscribed terrorists and their associates, and to facilitate the extradition of known terrorists and their associates. The Nasinoi Declaration of 2002 recommitted Pacific nations to fight terrorism, money-laundering, drug trafficking, people smuggling, and people trafficking.

There were reports of arms movements between Bougainville and the Solomon Islands Western Province. The advent of "failed states" has aroused regional fears of easy facilitation of terrorist transit bases and finances, weapon smuggling, drug dealing, money laundering, and people smuggling. The 2003 Australian-led military and policing force to the Solomons also comprises personnel from New Zealand, Fiji, Papua New Guinea, and Tonga. The operation is directed to rid the Solomons of their gang warfare, disarm the militias, and restore the infrastructure of law and order. One priority is to rebuild the reputation, capacity, and effectiveness of the RSIP. AFP counter-terrorist expert, Assistant Commissioner Ben McDevitt, was deputized as the Deputy Commissioner of the RSIP in late July 2003. During 2003, rival militia leaders, Keke and Rasta, surrendered to the police. About 3,700 weapons have been forfeited. Resistance from warring militia has been minimal. Police posts have been established across the country, and many refugees have been able to return to their homes.

International Cooperation

The Solomon Islands Police Force belongs to two central cooperative policing organizations:

- South Pacific Chiefs of Police Conference; and
- South Pacific Islands Criminal Intelligence Network (SPICIN).

The Solomon Islands Police Force was one of seven founding members when the South Pacific Chiefs of Police Conference began in 1970 in Fiji and determined the need for regional cooperation in law enforcement as a priority for its future endeavors. The annual conference was held in the Solomon Islands in 1972 and 1995. SPCPC is a leading law enforcement organization in the Pacific region, especially with increased international travel, technological advances, the spread of transnational crime, and terrorist threats. Murder, serious assaults, drugs, money laundering, fraud, pedophilia, electronic crimes, people smuggling, weapons control, and official corruption are central concerns for Pacific police leaders. In October 1987, SPICIN was created by the 17 executives of SPCPC at the sixteenth annual conference. SPICIN coordinates and disseminates the exchange of criminal information to combat narcotics trafficking, white collar crime, organized crime, mobile criminals, money laundering, terrorism, and other international crime. The Solomon Islands participate in the annual Pacific Islands Forum. Its Honiara Declaration is the basis for law enforcement cooperation and further liaison in the Pacific (*www.forumsec.org.fj/docs/dolec.htm*).

The Australian Federal Police has maintained liaison officers in Honiara, the capital of the Solomon Islands. The AFP regards the domestic situation in Melanesia as being of importance to Australian police because the poorly developed civil infrastructure of the region makes it prone to exploitation by organized crime (Australian Federal Police, *Annual Report 2001-2002*). Recent programs include the development of an improved training program for South Pacific police forces. Australia assists the RSIP through a Law and Justice Sector Program aimed at strengthening the police, prison, and legal services (ABC Radio Australia, 10 October 2002). In April, 2003, the Solomon Islands Police Minister requested additional assistance for the country's Police Re-strengthening Program. Three bilateral donors (Taiwan, Japan, New Zealand) responded positively by supplementing the existing $190,000 US program.

DAVID BAKER

Bibliography

Australian Federal Police, *Annual Reports 2001-2003.*
"Guns and Money." Liz Jackson reporting, *Four Corners,* ABC television, May 20, 2002.

Care, J., T. Newton, and Paterson, D. *Introduction to South Pacific Law*, Cavendish Publishing, London, 1999.
Findlay, M. *Criminal Laws of the South Pacific*, University of the South Pacific, Suva, 1996.
Lal, B., and K. Fortune, (eds). (2000) *The Pacific Islands: an Encyclopedia*, University of Hawai'I Press, Honolulu.
Newton, T. "Policing in the South Pacific Region." Occasional Paper No.1, School of Law, University of the South Pacific, Suva, 2000.
Newton, T. "Policing in the South Pacific Islands." *Police Journal*, vol.LXX1/4:349-352, 2000.

Websites:

http://pidp.ewc.hawaii.edu/pireport (Pacific Islands Report with archives from 1997-2002)
www.abc.net.au/ra/pacific/places/country/solomon_islands
www.odci.gov/cia/publications/factbook/geos/tn.html
http://abc.net.au/asiapacific/news/GoAsiaPacificBNP_697550. htm

SOMALIA

A government is being established in Somalia, and the country is still experiencing conflict. Fighting between rival warlords and an inability to deal with famine and disease has led to the death of up to one million people. However, in 2004, after protracted talks in Kenya, the main warlords and political leaders signed a deal to establish a new Parliament. The task currently facing the government is formidable: the construction of the necessary departments for the functioning of a democratic state. Fundamentalists still have to accept the peace accord and the new ultimate success or failure of the new framework will hinge on the ability of President Abdullahi Yusuf Ahmed's administration's abilities at securing reconciliation between the factions. While Abdullahi has named his Cabinet, which includes many leading warlords, they remain in exile in Kenya, awaiting security guarantees before returning.

Somalia is located in Eastern Africa and is bordered by Ethiopia, Kenya, and the Indian Ocean. The capital city is Mogadishu; Somalia has a population of seven million and occupies 637,657 sq km of land mass. Major languages include Somali, Arabic, Italian, and English; Islam is the prominent religion. Life expectancy is 45 for men and 48 for women.

Somalia has a long history; scientific evidence suggests that it has been inhabited since 100 AD. The country's name is derived from "Samaal," the ancestral name. By the eighth century, Somalis had developed pastoral nomadism and were followers of Islam. Their first contact with Islam is believed to have occurred when a group of persecuted Muslims from Arabia sought refuge in the region at the time of the Prophet Muhammad in the eighth century. Historically, the area was home to two peoples: (1) pastoral and agro-pastoral groups living in the interior, with informal and varied political structures; and (2) trading communities on the coast, such as Seylac and Berbera in the north, and Merca and Mogadishu in the south, who developed administrative and legal systems based on the Muslim *sharia*.

The Somalis or Samaal consist of six major clan-families. Four of the families are predominantly pastoral—the Dir, Daarood, Isaaq, and Hawiye, representing about 70 percent of Somalia's population; and two of the families are agricultural – the Digil and Rahanwayn, constituting about 20 percent of the population. The remainder of the population consists of urban dwellers and marginal non-Samaal groups, most of whom engage in trade or crafts and who historically have lacked political participation. The Digil and the Rahanwayn are located mainly in the south in the area between the Jubba and Shabeelle rivers, the best agricultural area. The rest of the country consists primarily of arid plateaus and plains, with some rugged mountains in the north near the Gulf of Aden coast. Because of sparse rainfall, nomadic pastoralism has been the principal occupation of clan-families in much of the country.

Historically, Somalis have shown a fierce independence, an unwillingness to submit to authority, a strong clan consciousness, and conflict among clans and subclans, despite their sharing a common language, religion, and pastoral customs. Clans are integral to Somali life. Clan consciousness has been described as centering around the struggle for recognition in all its forms–social, political, economic, and cultural rights and status. Despite this clan consciousness, the Somali community has historically preserved its basic unity because of the relative homogeneity of the society. Over the centuries, the Somali Peninsula and the East African coast were subject to various rulers, including the Omanis, the Zanzibaris, the sharifs of Mukha in present-day Yemen, and the Ottoman Turks. By 1885, there were five mini-Somalilands: the north central part, controlled by the British; the east and southeast, controlled by the French; the south, controlled by the Italians; the Ogaden in the west, controlled by Ethiopia; and the southwestern part that became a part of Kenya. This colonial control continued in various forms until Somalia gained its independence in 1960. The British and Italians followed different courses in their colonial administration. The British regarded northern Somalia mainly as a source of livestock for Aden, the principal supply post en route to India through the Suez Canal; whereas the Italians developed plantation agriculture based bananas, citrus fruits, and sugarcane in southern Somalia. Between 1900 and 1920, while Italy and Britain were consolidating their colonial rule, a Muslim resistance movement arose under Mahammad Abdille Hasan, whom the British called the Mad Mullah. Until he died in 1920, Abdille Hasan, a member of the Salihiyah brotherhood, and his followers constituted a dervish group that waged war originally against Ethiopia, and later against the British, seeking to regain the Ogaden for Somalis.

Early in World War II, Italy invaded British Somaliland and ejected the British. British forces retook the colony in 1941 and conquered Italian Somaliland and the Ogaden as well, placing all three areas under British military administration. The Potsdam Conference in 1945 decided not to return Italian Somaliland to Italy; ultimately, the matter was referred to the United Nations General Assembly, which decided in 1949 to make the southern area an Italian trust territory. Meanwhile, under pressure from its World War II allies, Britain returned the Ogaden to Ethiopia in 1948, to the dismay of Somalis because the majority of the inhabitants were Somalis. Nationalism had been growing in Somalia, largely as a result of the efforts of salaried Somali colonial officials who constituted an urban petty bourgeoisie. In 1943, the first Somali political party, the Somali Youth Club, was created. In 1947, the group changed its name to the Somali Youth League (SYL) and adopted the goals of unifying all Somali territories and opposing clannishness. Partly in response to nationalist pressures, both the Italians and the British took steps to improve education and health facilities, spur economic development, and give Somalis some experience in the political process. Somalia's independence in 1960 faced several obstacles. Economically, the country was obliged to rely on Italian and British subsidies; it also had to obtain other foreign loans to build an infrastructure and to create model farms and livestock improvement programs, all designed to increase exports. Other major obstacles included clan-family and sub-clan rivalries, pressures to incorporate Somalis living in the various mini-Somalilands, and differences between residents of British and Italian Somaliland. These differences were of two main kinds: economic (pastoral nomadism with its tending of flocks as opposed to plantation agriculture) and political (northern Somalis were less experienced in administration and political participation than their counterparts in the south). Furthermore, the new Somali Constitution did not include strategies designed to move citizens away from clan loyalties and toward national objectives. For example, the Iise clan of the Dir clan-family had devised a system by which the smallest clan was given a special role, that of providing the overall clan leader and also of being responsible for settling disputes. Such an approach could have served as a model for the Western framers of the Somali Constitution.

As a result of clan-family dissensions, one of the major objectives of the Somali government after independence became that of national integration. This objective was accompanied by the efforts of the first president, Abdirashiid Ali Shermaarke, to promote a Greater Somalia. In seeking to distance itself from its colonial past, the new government cultivated relations with the Soviet Union and Eastern Europe. Soviet influence prevailed, particularly in the armed forces, and later the German Democratic Republic (East Germany) established the National Security Service (NSS). The Police Force, however, was trained primarily by the Federal Republic of Germany (West Germany) and the United States. The 1969 elections for the National Assembly demonstrated the Somali characteristic of independence: 64 political parties participated, some of them as small as one man. The SYL, however, dominated the field. The elections revealed that various groups, especially the military, had become increasingly critical of government corruption and nepotism. The October,1969 killing of President Shermaarke by one of his bodyguards led the army, which had previously avoided political participation, to take over under army commander Major General Mahammad Siad Barré. The new governing body, the Supreme Revolutionary Council (SRC), named Siad Barré President. Retroactively, to facilitate continued Soviet aid, the SRC indicated it was pursuing scientific socialism, although Somalia lacked the infrastructure appropriate to Marxist socialism. Among the new government's objectives were breaking up the old regions (administrative units) into smaller entities and resettling many of the nomads in farming and fishing cooperatives. The government also sought to promote nationalist and socialist goals by appointing "peacekeepers" to replace the traditional elders and by creating various committees in place of traditional clan groups. With reference to the legal system, Siad Barré eliminated codes that gave clans land, water, and grazing rights. He also abolished the Islamic payment of blood money (*diya*) for injuries. Presumably, all these steps were designed to break down the traditional clan structure and strengthen the personal control of Siad Barré, as well as to weaken the role of religious leaders.

Although Siad Barré proclaimed scientific socialism compatible with Islam, his regime attempted to reduce the influence, particularly in politics, of Muslim leaders. Historically, clans had relied on itinerant religious teachers and on religiously devout males, known as *wadaddo*, who generally were the only literate individuals and who often occupied judicial roles. These religious functions were supplemented by Sufi religious orders or brotherhoods, whose leaders were more learned than the *wadaddo*. The best known of the latter was Mahammad Abdille Hasan, the early twentieth-century leader of the revolt against the British. In the first half of the twentieth century, religious teachers provided most of Somali education through Quranic schools that gave minimal literacy instruction. A major difficulty was the absence of an agreed-upon spelling system for the Somali language until the government decreed one in 1973. The government undertook a huge literacy campaign thereafter and established numerous primary schools, some secondary schools, and a university. As of 1990, Somalia had 4,600 university students. Whereas in its early years the SRC devoted considerable attention to such fields as education and economics, later a major part of its activity related to the political sphere. Despite the SRC's denunciation of clannishness, the clans connected with Siad Barré and his family became sufficiently prominent to be dubbed the MOD (Mareehaan-Ogaden-Dulbahante–the name of Siad Barré's clan, his mother's clan, and his son-in-law's clan, respectively). Initially, the SRC outlawed political parties, but in 1976 Siad Barré dissolved the SRC (it was later revived) and created one national party, the Somali Revolutionary Socialist Party (SRSP). The party in practice occupied a largely ceremonial position; actual power remained with Siad Barré.

To entrench his personal rule and in an attempt to regain the Ogaden, Siad Barré launched the Ogaden War against Ethiopia in 1977. The war officially ended in 1978, but low-level conflict continued with border raids and skirmishes for years afterward. Somalia experienced defeat and the death of 8,000 men, the influx of about 650,000 ethnic Somali and Ethiopian Oromo refugees, and a severe drain on its economy. The economic drain was caused by the purchase of military materials to replace equipment lost in the war—three quarters of Somalia's armored units and one-half of its air force. Having lost its alliance with the Soviet Union, which shifted its support to Ethiopia during the war, Somalia sought military aid from the United States. The latter, following the fall of the Shah of Iran in 1979, was eager to bolster defenses in the Persian Gulf-Indian Ocean area. As a result, in return for the United States provision of arms and military training in 1980, the United States and Somalia concluded a military access agreement by which the United States could use Somali ports and airfields in the event of a crisis. The expansion of its armed forces, which grew from 5,000 troops at independence to 65,000 in 1990, also sapped Somalia's economy. For example, 30% of the national budget went to the military in the mid-1980s. To develop the economy, in the early years of his regime Siad Barré launched several development plans, created agricultural and fishing cooperatives, and began establishing food processing plants. Somalia's foreign debt, however, increased at a tremendous rate as a result of the 1977–1978 Ogaden War. Unable to call on the Soviet Union for aid, the Siad Barré regime turned for economic aid to the West, to oil-producing Arab states such as Kuwait, Qatar, Saudi Arabia, and the United Arab Emirates, and to the *World Bank*. The economic crisis forced Somalia to devalue its currency and to encourage privatization. Economic output from agriculture and manufacturing, however, showed little progress and in some cases declined, partly as a result of intermittent droughts. The country lacked any energy sources, apart from wood and charcoal, despite surveys that indicated the likelihood of oil offshore in the Gulf of Aden. Moreover, its transportation and communications networks were minimal. In addition to livestock and agricultural products, which have constituted the bulk of Somalia's exports, the country did have a number of undeveloped sectors, however. Among the chief of these were forestry (myrrh and frankincense were among Somalia's exports), fishing, and mineral deposits, including uranium.

Following the Ogaden War, Siad Barré recognized that to gain Western support he needed to create a political system that would appear to restore many civil rights that had been eliminated by the military regime. Accordingly, the Constitution of 1979 provided for freedom of speech, religion, publication, and assembly, but these rights were subject to major qualifications. The Constitution made the President Head of State and head of government, with broad powers to conduct foreign affairs, serve as Commander in Chief of the armed forces, appoint various ministers and leading officials, and dissolve the legislature. Members of a single-chamber legislature, the People's Assembly, served a five-year term, with the government drawing up official lists of candidates and the assembly occupying a largely symbolic position. On the local government level, Siad Barré had dissolved all elected bodies following the military coup and required that all candidates for

election be approved by the central government. The Constitution confirmed the National Security Courts introduced by Siad Barré; these courts had jurisdiction over numerous cases and supplemented the regular courts. Siad Barré appointed only military officers to the High Court, thus bringing the judiciary under the executive. Another result of the Ogaden War was the rise of several organized internal opposition movements. To counter them, Siad Barré undertook increasingly repressive measures, including measures that involved numerous human rights violations. After judging a number of Majeerteen members of the military guilty of a coup attempt in 1978, Siad Barré initiated a campaign against the clan-family, using the Red Berets, an elite unit that served as his bodyguard. Several Majeerteen colonels escaped and fled abroad, where in 1978 they formed the Somali Salvation Front, renamed in 1979 the Somali Salvation Democratic Front (SSDF). This was the first opposition movement dedicated to overthrowing the regime by force. Siad Barré then turned on the Isaaq in the north, who were discontented because they felt inadequately represented in his government. Isaaq dissidents in London had formed the Somali National Movement (SNM) in 1981 to topple Siad Barré's regime. In 1982, they transferred their headquarters to Dire Dawa, Ethiopia, from where they conducted guerrilla raids against Somali government-held territory. Siad Barré's campaign against the Isaaq was particularly bloody; it included the 1988 destruction by bombing of Hargeysa, Somalia's major northern city, causing the flight to neighboring countries of tens of thousands of refugees. Next, Siad Barré attacked the Hawiye in the central area around Mogadishu. The Hawiye had meanwhile formed their own opposition movement, the United Somali Congress (USC), which received support from the SNM.

Siad Barré thus progressively alienated an increasing number of clans, including some, such as the Ogaden, that originally had given him strong support. The Ogaden blamed him for Somalia's defeat in the Ogaden War and opposed his 1988 peace treaty and the resumption of diplomatic relations with Ethiopia. As a result of Siad Barré's actions, many Ogaden officers deserted from the army and joined the Somali Patriotic Movement (SPM), an opposition group that had been formed in 1985 and that also received SNM support. The various opposition groups waged relatively intense warfare against the national army during Siad Barré's final three years in office and gained control of extensive government areas: the SNM in the northwest, the USC in the center, and the SPM in the south. Africa Watch reported that 50,000 unarmed civilians were killed in the course of Siad Barré's various reprisals against the Majeerteen, Isaaq, and Hawiye. Thousands more died of starvation resulting from the poisoning of water wells and the slaughtering of cattle. In addition, hundreds of thousands sought refuge outside the country. Following a July 1989 demonstration in Mogadishu in which about 450 persons were killed by government forces, leaders from various sectors of society, representing all clan-families, formed the Council for National Reconstruction and Salvation to press for political change. In May, 1990, they published a manifesto calling for Siad Barré's resignation, the establishment of an interim government representing opposition movements, and a timetable for multi-party elections. Siad Barré ordered the arrest of the 114 signatories, but the security forces could only locate 45 persons. Foreign protests over their detention forced their release. Meanwhile, the opposition groups recognized the need to hold talks among themselves to coordinate strategy; time, however, did not allow mutual trust to develop.

Opposition forces defeated Siad Barré's regime on January 27, 1991. Long before the government collapsed, however, the armed forces, the Police Force, the People's Militia, government ministries, and institutions such as the People's Assembly, schools, and health facilities, for all practical purposes, had ceased to operate. Siad Barré fled Mogadishu, and, after a stay in Kenya, ultimately sought refuge in Nigeria. The USC announced the formation of a provisional government in February 1991, with Ali Mahdi Mahammad of the Hawiye clan-family as President and Umar Arteh Ghalib, of the Isaaq clan-family, as Prime Minister. However, former army commander General Mahammad Faarah Aidid opposed Mahammad's presidency and eventually split off to form his own USC faction. The provisional USC government created a Ministry of Constitutional Affairs charged with planning a constitutional convention and revising the constitution. Meanwhile, provisions of the Constitution of 1979, which had not been specifically voided by the provisional government, remained in force. The provisional government also announced its intention of restoring judicial independence. The USC's establishment of a provisional government angered other opposition groups, who felt they had not been consulted. In the subsequent clashes, the SSDF and the SPM aligned themselves against the USC. In the course of the fight-

ing, control of various towns such as Chisimayu and Baidoa changed hands several times. A number of cease-fires were announced between early April, 1991 and the latter part of 1992, but none remained in effect long.

Meanwhile, in the north the SNM refused to participate in the unity talks proposed by the USC. In May 1991, the SNM proclaimed the Republic of Somaliland as an interim government, pending 1993 elections, and decreedthe *sharia* as its legal base. As of early 1993, the Republic of Somaliland had not been recognized by any foreign government. Moreover, the government has proved ineffective in establishing its authority throughout the region of former British Somaliland that it claims to control. In the Mogadishu area, each of the opposition groups drew support from a particular clan, and each resorted to arms to further its claims. The result was disintegration of government, civil society, and essential services by September 1991, if not earlier. Serious fighting in Mogadishu began in September 1991, intensified in November, and by the end of March 1992 was estimated by Africa Watch to have caused 14,000 deaths and to have wounded 27,000. Mahammad, a member of the Abgaal clan of the Hawiye clan-family and leader of one USC faction that had a force of about 5,000 fighters, gained control of northern Mogadishu. He was challenged primarily by Faarah Aidid, of the Habar Gidir clan of the Hawiye, who led a USC faction of about 10,000 guerrillas that advocated cooperation with the SNM. During 1991 and 1992, outside parties, such as Djibouti, the League of Arab States, the Organisation of African Unity, the Islamic Conference, and the United Nations, made numerous unsuccessful attempts to end the fighting in Mogadishu. The situation in the country as a whole deteriorated rapidly, as a result not only of the civil war but also of the drought in central and southern Somalia that left hundreds of thousands starving. By August 1992, Somali refugees were reliably estimated at 500,000 in Ethiopia, 300,000 in Kenya, 65,000 in Yemen, 15,000 in Djibouti, and about 100,000 in Europe. The civil war destroyed Somalia's infrastructure and brought all economic activities, apart from minimal subsistence agriculture, herding, and internal trade, to a virtual halt. Following an official visit to Somalia in early August 1992 by Muhammad Sahnoun, the UN Special Representative, and Bernard Kouchner, the French Minister of Health and Humanitarian Affairs, an estimate was released that approximately one fourth of the population, about 1.5 million people, was in danger of death by starvation; other estimates ran as high as one third of the population. A United States Centers for Disease Control study further showed that in the city of Baidoa at least 40% of the population had died between August 9 and November 14; relief organizations estimated that as of September, 25% of all Somali children under five years of age had died. The problem of food distribution to the starving was aggravated by armed bandits, frequently under the influence of *qat*, a mild stimulant known to increase aggressiveness, grown in several areas of East Africa. These bandits, who recognized no authority except occasionally that of local warlords, looted warehouses in Mogadishu and other major centers, as well as shipments of food to the interior. The rise of local warlords, who controlled the cities, including harbors and airports, as opposed to traditional clan leaders, clan councils, and clan-recruited militias in the hinterland, was a relatively new phenomenon in Somali society. Their rise has been attributed to the breakdown of central government authority and the lack of strong, well-organized opposition parties. The rise of the warlords was further facilitated by: the availability of vast quantities of arms in the country from earlier Soviet and United States arming of Somalia (between the early 1980s and mid-1990, the United States provided Somalia with US$403 million in military aid), from the large caches of arms gained in gray and black markets, and from the cross-border trade, particularly in ammunition, as well as the military training that the Siad Barré regime required all school and college graduates and civil servants to undergo.

In response to this critical situation, UN secretary general Boutros-Ghali announced in early August that he would send UN soldiers to Somalia to protect food supplies. In mid-August, United States president George Bush ordered a food air lift to Somalia. In implementation of his earlier pledge to protect food aid convoys, on August 28 Boutros-Ghali authorized sending 3,500 personnel in addition to a 500-man Pakistani force already authorized for Somalia. After a number of delays resulting from the opposition of local warlords, on November 10, Pakistani units were allowed to take control of Mogadishu airport. Meanwhile, on November 21, the United States National Security Council decided to intervene in Somalia. It did so because of the scale of human disaster and the realization that the United States was the only nation perceived by Somalis and by the regional states as being in a position to maintain neutrality and with the ability to launch such a large-scale aid operation. The first United States military

units in Operation Restore Hope arrived in Mogadishu on December 9. They were joined by elements of the French Foreign Legion from Djibouti, with others from Belgium, Canada, Egypt, Italy, Saudi Arabia, and Turkey expected. To avoid contact with the foreign forces, Somali armed groups and their "technicals" (vehicles on which an automatic weapon had been mounted) began leaving Mogadishu, thus exacerbating security problems in the hinterland.

United States forces and those of their allies gradually branched out from the airport and harbor of Mogadishu to the surrounding area. In succession, they secured the Soviet-built airport at Baledogle (halfway to Baidoa), Baidoa, and then Chisimayu, Baardheere, Oddur, Beledweyne, and Jalalaqsi. The plan entailed setting up food distribution centers in each of the major areas affected by the famine and bringing in large quantities of food so as to eliminate looting and hoarding. By doing so, the operation would ensure that food was no longer a "power chip," thereby eliminating the role of the warlords. As the provision of food to southern Somalia reached massive proportions, however, it became clear that as a result of the August rains and resultant domestic crop production, it would be necessary to sell some of the donated grain in local markets at a suitable price in order to safeguard the livelihood of local farmers in the hinterland. The question of the security of food shipments proved a difficult one with respect to disarming the population. The commander in chief of the United States Central Command, Marine General Joseph P. Hoar, announced on December 14 that the United States would not disarm Somalis because the carrying of arms was a political issue to be settled by Somalis. However, by January 7, 1993, after completing the first stage of Operation Restore Hope, United States forces began to pursue "technicals" and raid arms depots in order to safeguard the operation and protect United States and allied personnel and Somali civilians.

In the second stage of the operation, United States political officers also began coordinating town meetings in Mogadishu, Baidoa, Baardheere, and Chisimayu, encouraging Somalis to set up their own municipal institutions. Furthermore, United States military personnel cleared streets and restored municipal water systems. Observers noted that Somali women, who displayed a gift for reconciliation, were playing key roles in operating many of the food distribution centers established by nongovernmental organizations. Meanwhile, on the political level, in an effort to further reconciliation, Aidid and Mahammad met several times, as arranged by former United States ambassador to Somalia Robert B. Oakley, who served as special presidential envoy. On December 28, the two Somalis led a peace march along the Green Line separating the two areas of Mogadishu controlled by their forces. Other factors complicating a political settlement were the control of Baardheere by Mahammad Siad Hersi Morgan, the son-in-law of Siad Barré and leader of the Somali National Front, a Mareehaan organization; and the control of Chisimayu by Colonel Ahmad Omar Jess, a leader allied with the SDM and the Southern Somali National Movement (SSNM). Jess was reliably reported to have killed between 100 and 200 individuals whom he regarded as potential enemies before United States forces reached Chisimayu. As a symbol of support for United States forces and their efforts in Somalia, President Bush arrived on New Year's Eve for a one-day visit and received a warm welcome from Somalis. In contrast, the UN Secretary General faced an angry reception from Somali crowds on January 3. The Somalis remembered Boutros-Ghali's former cordial relationship with Siad Barré when Boutros-Ghali served as Egyptian minister of foreign affairs. They also faulted the UN for its long inaction in relieving the starvation in Somalia; volunteer organizations, particularly the International Committee of the Red Cross, had proved more effective than the UN in sending food to Somalia and in setting up kitchens to feed hundreds of thousands daily. Despite this negative reception, on January 4 the leaders of 14 Somali factions attended meetings in Addis Ababa chaired by the UN secretary general at which the United States was represented. After considerable discussion, on January 15 the faction leaders signed a cease-fire agreement and a disarmament pact and called for a national reconciliation conference to be held in Addis Ababa on March 15. Despite the cease-fire, fighting and instability in Somalia continued in late January. Because of the number of foreign forces that had joined Operation Restore Hope—as of January 9 these numbered about 10,000—the first contingent of United States military personnel began to leave Somalia on January 19. Overall, United States forces were scheduled to remain at 25,000 in the immediate future. The long-term goal was to turn over the operation as rapidly as possible to a UN force; it was said that perhaps as many as 5,000 United States logistical, transportation, and engineering personnel might be assigned to the UN force.

With regard to Somalia's future, the role of Islamism, sometimes referred to as fundamentalism, concerned the United States and some of its allies. In the north, Islamic militants, who were well trained and armed and supplied with funds primarily by wealthy Saudis, had at one time controlled the town of Bender Cassim in the northeast but had been driven out by the SSDF. From Bender Cassim, the Islamists spread westward into such SNM areas as Hargeysa. Although Islamic militants, known as the Somali Islamic Union or popularly as Ittihad (Union), had relatively few supporters in Somalia, their numbers appeared to be increasing somewhat. In the latter months of 1992, they became active in Merca, the seaport south of Mogadishu, where they had sought an alliance with clan leaders in the SSNM, which was aligned with that section of the USC led by Faarah Aidid. Time would indicate whether the Islamists could prove effective in providing services that the government was not providing in such fields as education and health. If so, the likelihood of their gaining followers would increase greatly. Other steps toward the creation of what President Bush termed a "secure environment" included a discussion held in mid-January between Aidid and Mahammad on re-establishing a Police Force. The Police Force had traditionally commanded respect in Somalia, and if such a Force could be reconstituted initially in a number of regions but ultimately nationally, it would help diminish the power of the warlords and restore internal order. It was also likely to strengthen the position of traditional clan elders. Such steps would be consistent with the apparent goal of the UN Security Council to create a national government in Somalia with sufficient authority to maintain security but one that allowed considerable autonomy to the various regions. The situation with regard to the relationship of the self-proclaimed Republic of Somaliland in the north and the rest of Somalia in the south remained unclear. Most knowledgeable observers noted that as yet there was no effective government in the northern region that could negotiate with the remainder of Somalia. Therefore, in the near future the establishment of either a federation with Somalia or a unitary state combining the two as in the past was unlikely.

NOEL MC GUIRK

Bibliography

Ahmed, Jimale Ali. *The Invention of Somalia*. New Jersey: Red Sea Press, 1995.

Ali, Taisier M. and Ronald Matthews. *Civil Wars in Africa: Roots and Resolution*. Montreal: McGill-Queens University Press, 1999.

Schmidl, Erwin A. *Peace Operations Between War and Peace*. New York: Frank Cass Publishers, 2000.

Walter, Barbara F. and Jack Snyder. *Civil War, Insecurity and Intervention*. New York: Columbia University Press, 1999.

Woodward, Peter. *The Horn of Africa: Politics and International Relations*. London: I.B. Tauris, 2002.

http://allafrica.com/somalia/.

www-sul.stanford.edu/depts/ssrg/africa/somalia.html.

www.unsomalia.net/.

www.usaid.gov/locations/sub-saharan_africa/countries/somalia/.

SOUTH AFRICA

Background Material

South Africa is a diverse nation, with over 40 million people, and a wide variety of cultures, languages, and religious beliefs.

The nation has nine provinces. Its largest provincial population is in KwaZulu-Natal, with almost 8.5 million counted in the 1996 census, but the most densely populated province is Gauteng, with some 7.35 million people occupying just 1.4% of the country's land area.

The population as a whole is young. Of the total population, about 18% are between 20 and 29 years old.

South Africa is a multilingual country. Besides the 11 officially recognized languages, many others are spoken. South Africa's Constitution recognizes and guarantees equal status to the 11 official languages of the country's diverse peoples and their cultures. The 11 languages are: Sesotho sa Leboa, Sesotho, Setswana, SiSwati, Tshivenda, Xitsonga, Afrikaans, English, isiNdebele, isiXhosa, and isiZulu. English is generally understood across the country, and it is usually used in official and commercial public life. However, it ranks fifth out of the 11 as a spoken language.

According to the 1996 census, iZulu is the mother tongue of 22.9% of South Africa's roughly 40 million people, followed by isiXhosa (17.9%), Afrikaans (14.4%), Sesotho sa Leboa (9.2%), and English (8.6%). Setswana is the mother tongue of 8.2% of South Africans, followed by Sesotho at 7.7%. The remaining four official languages are spoken at home by less than five percent of the population.

In terms of religious affiliation, about two thirds of South Africans are Christian, mainly Protestant. They belong to a variety of churches, including many that combine Christian and traditional African beliefs. Many non-Christians espouse these traditional beliefs. Other significant religions are Islam, Hinduism, and Judaism.

South Africa is one of the most sophisticated and promising emerging markets in the world, with a unique combination of highly developed first-world economic infrastructure and a vibrant emergent market economy. It is also one of the most advanced and productive economies in Africa. It has identified agro-processing, automotive, banking and finance, chemicals, fishing, food and beverages, IT and electronics, mining and minerals, property, tourism, telecommunication, and textiles, among others, as ripe for investment.

South Africa is the world's biggest producer of gold and platinum, and one of the leading producers of base metals and coal; mineral commodities are exported to 80 countries.

Contextual Features

The South African government is constituted at the national, provincial, and local spheres, which are distinctive, interdependent, and interrelated. The powers of the law makers (legislative authorities), governments (executive authorities), and courts (judicial authorities) are separate from one another.

Parliament is the legislative authority of South Africa, and it has the power to make laws for the country in accordance with the Constitution. It consists of the National Assembly and the National Council of Provinces (NCOP). Parliamentary proceedings are open to the public.

The National Assembly consists of no fewer than 350 and no more than 400 members elected through a system of proportional representation.

The National Assembly, which is elected for a term of five years, is presided over by a Speaker, assisted by a Deputy Speaker.

The National Assembly is elected to represent the people and to ensure democratic governance as required by the Constitution. It does this by electing the President, by providing a national forum for public consideration of issues, by passing legislation, and by scrutinizing and overseeing executive action.

The NCOP consists of 54 permanent members and 36 special delegates, and aims to represent provincial interests in the national sphere of government. Delegations from each province consist of 10 representatives.

The NCOP obtains a mandate from the provinces before it can make certain decisions. It cannot, however, initiate a Bill concerning money, which is the prerogative of the Minister of Finance.

Any Bill may be introduced in the National Assembly. A Bill passed by the National Assembly must be referred to the NCOP for consideration. A Bill affecting the provinces may be introduced in the NCOP. After the Council passes it, it must be referred to the Assembly.

A Bill concerning money must be introduced in the Assembly and must be referred to the Council for consideration and approval after being passed. If the Council rejects a Bill or passes it subject to amendments, the Assembly must reconsider the Bill and pass it again with or without amendments. There are special conditions for the approval of laws dealing with provinces.

The President is the Head of State and leads the Cabinet. He or she is elected by the National Assembly from among its members, and leads the country in the interest of national unity, in accordance with the Constitution and the law.

The Constitution of the Republic of South Africa, 1996 (Act 108 of 1996), is the supreme law of the country and binds all legislative, executive, and judicial bodies of the State at all levels of government.

In terms of Section 165 of the Constitution, the judicial authority of South Africa is vested in the courts, which are independent and subject only to the Constitution and the law.

No person or entity of state may interfere with the functioning of the courts, and an order or decision of a court binds all State institutions and persons to whom it applies.

The Department of Justice and Constitutional Development is responsible for the administration of the courts and constitutional development.

It performs these functions in conjunction with the judges, magistrates, National Director of Pub-lic Prosecutions (NDPP), and Directors of Prosecution (DPP), who are independent.

The Department's responsibilities include the provision of adequate resources for the proper and efficient functioning of the criminal and civil justice systems. It provides legislation and gives administrative support for the establishment of institutions required by the Constitution.

The Constitutional Court (CC) is the highest court in the interpretation, protection, and enforcement of the Constitution. It deals exclusively with constitutional matters.

The Supreme Court of Appeal, situated in Bloemfontein, is the highest court in respect to all other matters. It is composed of the Chief Justice, a Deputy Chief Justice, and a number of judges of appeal determined by an Act of Parliament. The Supreme Court of Appeal has jurisdiction to hear and determine an appeal against any decision of a High Court.

Decisions of the Supreme Court of Appeal are binding on all courts of a lower order, and the decisions of the High Courts are binding on Magistrate's Courts within the respective areas of jurisdiction of the divisions.

In terms of Item 16 (6)(a) of Schedule Six to the Constitution, "all courts, their structure, composition, functioning, and jurisdiction, and all relevant legislation, must be rationalized with a view to establishing a judicial system suited to the requirements of the Constitution." The Minister for Justice and Constitutional Development must, after consultation with the JSC, manage this process.

The primary function of the Department of Correctional Services is to keep those detained in prison in safe custody until they are legally released. It is also concerned with the rehabilitation of offenders.

Prisoners are classified into minimum, medium, or maximum custodial categories. Variables taken into account include the type of crime, the length of the sentence, and previous convictions.

Police Profile

Background

At the end of the nineteenth century, there were many independent urban and rural police agencies in South Africa. These included various colonial police forces, such as the Cape Mounted Riflemen, Cape Mounted Police, the Transvaal Police, the Natal Police, the Orange River Colony Police; and several urban police forces, which continued to exist independently even after the establishment of the Union on May 31, 1910.

Towards the end of 1911, it was resolved to organize the Police Force of the Union more or less along the lines of the system used in the Cape Colony. At that time, the Cape Mounted Riflemen patrolled the densely populated "Non-White districts," while the Regular Police Force performed duties in other areas. Initially, it was decided to establish two forces: The South African Police and the Mounted Rifleman (SAMR).

Proclamation 18 of 1913 stipulated that April 1 was the date of establishment of the South African Police (SAP). On April 1, 1920, the Mounted Riflemen were disbanded. Altogether, 1,022 men were incorporated into the Police Force.

World War II saw the SAP actively participating in the battles against Germany. The force became politicized; some members wanted to fight, others did not. Police volunteers travelled to North Africa in 1940.

The Reserve Police Force came into being in 1961, but only started functioning in 1963.

Milestones in the 1970s included the employment of women for the first time, on January 1, 1972.

South Africa became an internationally accepted democracy in 1994, when Nelson Mandela was elected as the new dispensation's first President. This new democratic order, which brought about many changes in the country, also had a substantial impact on policing. Prior to 1995, South Africa was divided into the 10 so-called TBVC states, self-governing territories, and development regions. The TBVC states and self-governing territories were also referred to as homelands.

Each homeland had its own policing agency, bringing the total number of policing agencies in the country to 11 (10 in the homelands *plus* the old SAP). With the adoption of the interim Constitution in 1994, the homelands and old development regions were abolished and integrated into a united South Africa with nine provinces.

Owing to the existence of these 11 different Police agencies and in response to the constitutional obligations placed on him, the Minister for Safety and Security appointed a change management team shortly after the democratic elections of 1994. The new Constitution prescribed a single national police service for South Africa under the executive command and control of a National Commissioner appointed by the President of South Africa (George Fivaz was appointed as the first National Commissioner of the SAPS). The team was to facilitate the rationalization and unification of all the agencies into one service.

The South African Police subsequently changed to South African Police Service (SAPS). Prior to that, it was commonly known as the police "force," indicating that law and order would be maintained by the use of force. Since 1994, the emphasis has been on delivering a safety and security service to all the people of South Africa. To facilitate this fundamental transformation from a rules-bound police force to a results-driven police service, with the emphasis on service delivery, the South African government introduced new laws, regulations, and policies.

The transformation objectives included: (i) restructuring and rationalization; (ii) institution building and management; (iii) inclusiveness and affirmative action; (iv) transforming service delivery; (v) human resource development and training; (vi) promotion of a professional service ethos; and (vii) democratizing the workplace.

A new vision, mission, and value system were developed to render the quality service demanded by the community and members, and to create a safe and secure environment.

Following the appointment of SAPS National Commissioner Jackie Selebi in January 2000 (the second police commissioner in the new service), the SAPS went through an extensive process of strategic planning, during which priorities were reviewed. It developed a strategic plan that focused on the crimes that have the most negative impact on society and government. In addition, it focused strongly on the areas where such crimes were the most prevalent. The priorities defined were to combat crime, including organized crime, and serious and violent crimes, and crime against women and children; and to improve service delivery. Various successes were achieved following the implementation of the SAPS crime-combating strategy. Various initiatives in this regard were implemented, and police members were trained nationwide in the effective use of the Computerized Crime Analysis System. The implementation of these steps led to significantly higher degrees of reliability. By September 2001, an analysis of reported crime trends clearly indicated that within 18 months (April 1, 2000 to September 30, 2001), at least 17 of the 20 prioritized crime trends had been stabilized.

In November 2001, the SAPS announced a plan to institute sector policing in 145 focal points. These focal points were divided into several smaller areas. One of the aims of sector policing is to improve response time when crimes are in progress. This new approach to crime prevention is already reaping benefits, which will increase as the training of newly enlisted members is completed.

Demographics

As of 2003, the SAPS had 129,722 staff members. Of these, 27,327 are civilian members, 43 temporary members, and three contract workers.

The staff component of the SAPS (January, 2003) is as follows: 95,993 males and 33,729 females. The ethnic representation is as follows: 3,529 Indian males and 1,312 Indian females; 8,878 coloured males and 3,738 coloured females; 20,776 white males and 12,798 white females; and 62,810 black males and 15,881 black females.

Organizational Description

In accordance with the South African Constitution, the Minister for Safety and Security is responsible for policing in general and is required to account to Cabinet and Parliament on all matters relating to policing. Important features of the Minister's responsibility include the determining of national policing policy, and the provision of civilian oversight. Minister for Safety and Security Charles Nqakula was appointed in 2002.

A National Commissioner heads the SAPS. National Commissioner Jackie Selebi was appointed in 2000. The National Commissioner appoints Deputy National Commissioners to his office to look after various portfolios, for example human resource management. He also appoints Provincial Commissioners for each province of South Africa and divisional commissioners to oversee the SAPS divisions.

The rank below Provincial/Divisional Commissioner is that of Assistant Commissioner, followed by Director, Senior Superintendent, Superintendent, and Captain. These are all officer ranks in the SAPS. Inspectors, Sergeants, and Constables (which are ranks below Captain) are non-commissioned officers.

Functions

The South African Police Service is part of the service industry in the country. Its main functions are to prevent, combat, and investigate crime; to maintain public order; to protect and secure the inhabitants of the country and their property; and to uphold and enforce the law. To carry out its functions, a medium-term plan has been devised. The main objective of the plan is to focus the role of the police, to ensure efficient utilization of resources, and to establish partnerships with various role-players in government and in communities.

Four key strategic priorities have been established. The first priority is to combat organized crime, focusing on crimes relating to drugs, trafficking in firearms, vehicle theft and hijacking, corrupt public officials, and organized commercial crime.

The second priority concerns the country's levels of serious and violent crime. Strategies have been developed to counter the proliferation of firearms, which fuels levels of violent crime; to improve safety and security in high-crime areas; to combat specific crimes such as gang violence, and faction fighting; and to maintain security at major public events.

The third priority focuses on developing strategies to reduce the incidence of crimes against women and children, while also improving the investigation and prosecution of these crimes.

The fourth priority is to improve service delivery at police stations.

The SAPS divisions are the following: Crime Intelligence, Crime Prevention, Detective Service, Operational Response Services, Security and Protection Services, Personnel Services, Career Management, Training, Legal Services, Management Services, Logistics, National Evaluation Services, and Financial and Administrative Services.

Crime Intelligence is specifically responsible for maintaining an effective, information-gathering, centralized, and integrated information analysis and management function; and a technical intelligence support service, on both tactical and strategic levels.

Crime Prevention is regarded as a line function division of the SAPS specifically responsible for the prevention of crime. Social Crime Prevention is responsible for addressing the root causes of crime, for example, socio-economic factors, and the uplifting of the community through rural development and urban renewal projects. Visible Policing is responsible for combating crime through crime operations, the rendering of a quick response service to crimes in progress, for example, police emergency services, and furthermore through the high visibility and availability of police officials at the grassroots level.

Detective Service is responsible for maintaining an effective crime investigation service. The division's main functions incorporate investigations regarding serious and violent crime, commercial crime, and organized crime.

Operational Response Services is responsible for maintaining public order, conducting high-risk operations, combating rural and urban terror, executing search and rescue flights, stabilizing volatile situations, and preventing cross-border crimes.

Training

The SAPS Training Division presents functional and support training. Functional training consists of basic training (entry level training), and protection services, dog school, public order, border, functional skills, special task force, human rights, and community policing training. At present, recruits undergo a 12-week basic training course, followed by a four-week tactical firearms training course, and then a three-week field training mentorship course.

Support training consists of financial, logistics, career, management, adult basic education, and basic diversity training.

The South African Police Service consists largely of three groups of personnel: functional personnel, Public Service Act personnel (elementary occupations, clerks, etc.), and professionals and managers.

Applicants for appointment as functional police members must meet certain criteria, such as Grade 12 (senior certificate); possession of a valid driver's license; and meeting the post profile of an entry level constable that includes psychometric, physical, and medical tests.

For appointment in any other post in the South African Police Service, the candidate must meet the stipulated requirements as contained in vacancies that are advertized prior to filling.

All promotions in the South African Police Service are post-bound and subject to the availability of funds. Vacant posts are advertized within the department and externally. Personnel whomeet the requirements of the relevant promotion policy are invited to apply for advertized posts.

Police Public Projects

The SAPS has developed a strong focus on partnership policing. The SAPS is mobilizing the community to become involved in various projects to counteract crime. Community policing forums are playing a major role in safeguarding the country. The year 2002 was proclaimed the Year of the Volunteer, and the SAPS was gladdened by the response of the public. Some 70,000 members of the community volunteered their services at police stations across the country.

The SAPS has committed itself to ensuring the safety and security of all communities in the country. It is furthermore dedicated to the betterment of previously disadvantaged communities. The building of community safety centers has consequently been introduced. The focus of the program is on the delivery of basic and easily accessible services (a one-stop service) to communities, especially in far-off rural areas and informal settlement areas.

Other campaigns launched include the Stolen Goods campaign in April 2001. The campaign aims at educating communities about the suffering caused to others when people buy stolen goods. Cross-border operations carried out in conjunction with neighboring countries have been fruitful. Operation Rachel, which the SAPS launched with the help of Mozambique, dealt a severe blow to the illegal firearms trade. The joint operation between the SAPS and the Royal Swazi Police resulted in the massive destruction of cannabis fields in Swaziland.

The police in Mpumalanga (one of the country's nine provinces) have achieved a new milestone: An evaluation of crime in the province indicated that social fabric crimes were mostly committed in rural areas. In searching for ways to address this serious matter, the Mpumalanga police came to the conclusion that traditional leaders could play a major role in combating these crimes. They successfully joined hands with the *Amakhosi*, the traditional leaders, who agreed to help curb crime by encouraging the communities to report any incidents or suspected incidents of this nature to the police; by assisting the police in giving information on the whereabouts of criminals; and by initiating programs to make the community, especially parents, aware of negative trends and to encourage them to take precautionary measures.

The concern over the incidence of attacks on farms has led to the establishment of a Rural Safety Committee. Further, the banking sector has supported the SAPS in curbing bank robberies and cash-in-transit heists. The SAPS reached an agreement with the banking sector to develop a formal mechanism for combating banking-related crimes and cash-in-transit robberies.

Operation Octopus was launched early in 2002 in conjunction with the Airport Company of South Africa to make airports safer for all travelers.

The SAPS established the National Bureau For Missing Persons in October 1994. The main purpose of the bureau is to render a support service to the SAPS official investigating the case, and not to take the investigation into its own hands.

The SAPS also targets the youth. To acquaint children with the police service, it launched, among others, a "Captain Crime Stop" project. The friendly Captain Crime Stop pays regular visits to schools across the country. The aim is to educate children about crimes and to provide them with hints for personal safety, while showing them that the SAPS is an organization that serves and protects the community.

A National Crime Stop number is available to report information on criminals and their activities, as is a national emergency number.

The South African government has recognized the importance of addressing the needs of victims of crime and violence in South Africa. To address these needs, a national victim empowerment program (VEP) was launched. This program aims to make the county's criminal justice system (CJS) more understandable and accessible to victims. It further aims to address the negative aspects of crime and violence through the provision of counseling and other support services. The police force, as the first and often the only criminal justice agency to come into contact with victims, has a vital role to play in the empowerment of victims.

The SAPS is also an important partner in the project that will allow a full-scale interpreting service to be established in the country. South Africa is a multilingual country, in which 11 languages have been accorded official status. The Telephone Interpreting Service for South Africa, also known as TISSA, is a government-approved project aimed at facilitating the linguistic human rights stipulated in the country's Constitution. TISSA makes it possible for all South Africans to have immediate access to information and government services in a language of choice. TISSA has been implemented at many police stations around the country. By making use of this interpreting service, information-gathering in the SAPS will becoming increasingly accurate, and collaboration between the SAPS and community in fighting crime will be enhanced.

Police Use of Firearms

In 1997, the Department for Safety and Security embarked upon putting in place legislation that would address the proliferation of firearms in South Africa. Motivating considerations included creating safer cities, creating job opportunities and prosperity, and creating safer environments for people living in, or visiting anywhere in South Africa.

On the one hand, the government was faced with controlling legally owned firearms, and on the other, dealing with illegal firearms brought across the borders into South Africa. Although operations, such as Operation Rachel, effectively dealt with the latter concern, by, *inter alia*, destroying arms caches, the theft of legally owned firearms remained a concern.

Such concerns led to the formal introduction of the Firearms Control Act (Act 60 of 2000). The issue of accountable and responsible firearm control and ownership, whether privately, in dealerships, or government departments, forms the essence of the Act. The Act now provides for stronger police search and seizure, as well as investigative powers, which in turn strengthen the prosecution processes. Stricter penalties are now in place to deal with the illegal dealing in firearms.

Police members may use firearms in self-defense and in the defense of other persons.

Complaints and Discipline

The South African Constitution has created independent national institutions, subject only to the Constitution and the law, to transform society and to deliver the fundamental rights guaranteed in the Constitution to all in South Africa.

The South African Human Rights Commission (SAHRC) is one such national institution. The SAHRC works with government, civil society, and individuals, both nationally and abroad, and it serves as both a watchdog and a visible means through which people can access their rights.

While the handling and management of complaints concerning human rights violations lies at the heart of the SAHRC's work, it also aims to create a national culture of human rights through its advocacy, research, and legal functions. Furthermore, it implements, monitors, and develops standards of human rights law. Taking up the challenge to be regarded as a model institution on human rights promotion and protection, the SAHRC also works closely with human rights commissions throughout Africa and the world.

The SAPS has a training program on human rights and policing that is aimed at all members of the service. It aims at training all members on how to police in accordance with International Human Rights principles and the Bill of Rights in the South African Constitution.

The Reconstruction and Development Programme (RDP) of the South African government sponsored the training program. International donors and other government organizations, such as the UN High Commission for Human Rights, the European Union, and the Swedish government, sponsored some of the training aids.

The National Secretariat and the Independent Complaints Directorate (ICD) are the civilian oversight bodies that monitor the work of the police.

Terrorism

South Africa has capabilities to deal with terrorism. Counter-terrorism issues are dealt with in the domain of the Division Crime Intelligence of the South African Police Service. Areas of investigation include local fundamentalist, narrow racist, and international terrorist groupings.

International Cooperation

The SAPS has cooperation agreements with France, Argentina, Chile, Brazil, the Russian Federation, Hungary, and the People's Republic of China. Negotiations are ongoing to include more countries on its list of international partners against organized crime.

The SAPS has also signed a multilateral police cooperation agreement involving 12 Southern African countries, which is an important instrument in the fight against organized crime. The agreement culminated in the birth of the Southern African Regional Police Chiefs Cooperation Organisation (SARPCCO). Some successful operations have been accomplished in the past on the basis of regional cooperation.

South Africa is among 179 countries whose police structures are affiliated with Interpol. It has 12 liaison officers based at South African missions abroad to interact on a continuing basis with its counterparts in the detection and prosecution of international crime.

The SAPS International Liaison division serves as a 24-hour clearing house for issues related to: crimes committed against and by the diplomatic corps, requests for protection duties throughout the country, visits by foreign delegates to the SAPS, and general inquiries regarding foreign missions and diplomatic-accredited international organizations.

Police Education, Research, and Publications

The SAPS has the following training colleges: The Pretoria Training College (basic training), the Paarl College for Advanced Training, and the Hammanskraal College (detective training).

Courses in police training are offered at various tertiary institutions, such as the University of Pretoria, Port Elizabeth University, the University of the North, Venda University, the University of South Africa, the SA, and the Pretoria, Vaal Triangle, and Wits technicons, as well as Technikon SA.

Researchers in the SAPS are Dr. C de Kock, Head, Crime Information Analysis Centre; Senior Superintendent J. Schnetler, Head, Research and Development; and Senior Superintendent Nelly Sonderling, Subsection Head, Strategic Communication Research.

Areas of research include evaluation of services rendered to the community by the police, measuring of organizational performance, development of performance indicators for the strategic plan and the budgetary plan, and service delivery in high crime areas. Ongoing research is also undertaken into organized crime, serious and violent crimes, crimes against women and children, and vigilantism.

Countries such as Britain, France, America, and Sweden make donations each year, some of which are allocated to police research. Non-government organizations also make donations for training and research.

Universities and technikons have scholarships available for students studying in the field of policing.

The major SAPS publications are the *SAPS Annual Report*, *SAPS Journal*, and *SAPS Bulletin* (a monthly newsletter for staff).

Other law enforcement-related publications in South Africa include *Servamus*, *Crime and Conflict*, *SA Crime Quarterly*, *SA Rights and Conflict Monitor*, *Acta Criminologica*, and the *ISS Monograph Series*.

NELLY SONDERLING

Bibliography

Burger, Delien, ed. *South Africa Yearbook 2001/2002*. Pretoria: Government Communication and Information System, 2002.

South African Police Service. *Annual Report of the National Commissioner of the South African Police Service – summary 2001/2002*. Pretoria: SAPS, 2002.

South African Police Service. *Focus on safety and security – for a better life for all*. Pretoria: SAPS, s.a.

South African Police Service Website. [available online: www.saps.org.za.].

SPAIN

Background Material

The Kingdom of Spain is one of Europe's largest countries, occupying the majority of the Iberian Peninsula. Celtics arrived to it in the ninth century BC. Then, the peninsula was dominated by the Romans from the second century BC until the Visigoth invasion at the beginning of the fifthcentury AD. In the early eighth century, Muslims from North Africa took control of most of the peninsula. During the following centuries, a slow reconquest took place, led by the Christian kingdoms of Aragon and Castile (united in 1479) and Portugal. The reconquest was finally accomplished in 1492 with the fall of Granada, the last Muslim kingdom. That very same year, Spain started its colonial empire in Central and South America. In 1516, the throne passed to the Habsburgs. In 1700, the death of the childless Charles II led to the war of the Spanish Succession (1700–1713), which ended with the Peace of Utrecht and the accession to the throne of the Bourbons. Following the invasion of Spain in 1808 by Napoleon (who named his own brother King of Spain), an independence movement developed in the South American colonies. The last colonies in Central America were lost by the end of the nineteenth century in the Spanish-American war (1898). Spain became a republic in 1931, but a military rising headed by general Francisco Franco unleashed a bloody civil war that took place between 1936 and 1939. As a result, Franco ruled the country as a dictator until his death in 1975. The Monarchy was then restored with the ascension to the throne of Juan Carlos I, and, with the adoption of a new Constitution in 1978, the country became a parliamentary monarchy.

Spain occupies an area of 506,000 sq km and has a population of 40,847,371 (2001).

The economy of the country is based on services, industries, and agriculture. Spain is one the world's major producers of wine and olive oil. Tourism is also a major industry, with more than 50 million foreign tourists visiting the country each year. The GDP per person is 16,000 Euros (2001 est.).

Spain has no minority racial groups but is composed by several regional minorities. The major ethnic groups are: Andalusians, Aragonese, Asturians, Basques, Catalans, Galicians, Navarrese, and Valencians. Spain was traditionally an emigration country, but this tendency was reversed in the 1990s, when the migratory balance became positive. In December 2001, there were 1,109,060 foreign residents in Spain, the majority of whom (21%) came from Morocco. It must also be mentioned that Spain has an important gypsy community, estimated by the Union Romani (Union of the Gypsy People) at 500,000 to 600,000 people.

In 2000, 83% of the Spaniards defined themselves as Catholics (although 43% of them declared they never or rarely attended mass); two percent said they belonged to other religions (Protestant, Jewish, and Muslim); and 14% declared themselves agnostics or atheists. Moreover, according to a 1998 survey, 95% of the Spaniards received a Catholic education. Catholicism was the official religion of the State until the Constitution of 1978, which guarantees complete religious freedom.

According to the Constitution, Spanish (*Castilian*) is the official language for the whole country; in addition, there are co-official languages in some Autonomous Communities. That is the case of the Basque (*Euskera*) in the Basque Country, the Galician in Galicia, the Catalan in Catalonia and the Balearic Islands, and the Valencian in the Community of Valencia.

Contextual Features

Spain is a parliamentary monarchy formed by 50 provinces integrated in 17 Autonomous Communities, as well as two autonomous cities (Ceuta and Melilla). The King is the Head of State and the symbol of its unity and permanence. There is a bicameral legislature called the *Cortes Generales* that includes a lower house, the Congress of Deputies, and an upper chamber, the Senate. The Government is headed by a Prime Minister, called the President of the Government, who is appointed by the King following his investiture by the Congress of Deputies. The judicial system is independent and headed by the Supreme Court, which is the country's highest tribunal, except for constitutional questions, for which there is a Constitutional Court. The General Council of the Judiciary governs the judicial power. The Public Prosecutor (*Fiscal del Estado*) —

appointed by the King upon nomination by the Government after consultation with the General Council of the Judiciary—is responsible for promoting the action of Justice in defense of the legitimate rights of the citizens and of the public interest.

The country has a civil law system, typical of European continental countries. In the field of criminal justice, the present Penal Code, adopted in 1995, is heavily influenced by the German penal doctrine. The procedure is governed by the legality principle. An instruction judge carries out the investigative stage of the criminal process, and, at the end of that stage, the case passes to a criminal court. Finally, there is a special judge (*Juez de vigilancia penitenciaria*) responsible for the execution of the sentences eventually imposed by the courts.

The State has exclusive authority over penitentiary legislation, but the Autonomous Communities can assume the execution of that legislation. However, only Catalonia has exercised this right, and it has its own Penitentiary Administration who is responsible for 11 penal institutions. The other 66 penal institutions are under the responsibility of the General Direction of Penitentiary Institutions.

As stated by the *Council of Europe Annual Penal Statistics* (SPACE), on September 1, 2002, there were 50,994 prisoners aged 18 or more, of whom a little bit less than 23% were pre-trial detainees. Thus, the prison population rate was 126 prisoners per 100,000 inhabitants. As penal institutions had capacity for 45,320 prisoners, the prison density was 112.5 prisoners per 100 places. Eight percent of the prisoners were females, and 25 percent foreigners. It should be mentioned that on September 1, 1983, there were only 14,659 prisoners in Spain, which means a prison population rate of 37 prisoners per 100,000 inhabitants. According to the indicators used by SPACE, the growth of the prison population is due to a simultaneous increase of the number of persons sent to prison and of the length of the sentences imposed.

The following table presents the offenses registered by the Spanish security forces and corps between 1995 and 2000.

Notes:

- Statistics do not include offenses recorded by the Autonomic Police of Catalonia.
- Between 1995 and 1997, statistics include offenses recorded by the National Police Corps and the Civil Guard. Since 1998, they also include offenses recorded by the Autonomic Police of the Basque Country. These represent a little bit less than five percent of the total offenses recorded. Thus, the Autonomic Police of the Basque Country registered 48,521 out of the 965,835 offenses recorded in 1998 (4.99%); 43,734 out of 961,787 in 1999 (4.55%); and 414,92 out of 923,270 in 2000 (4.49%).
- Since 1997, domestic violence is included in assault and is the main explanatory factor of the increase registered in this offense. There were 3,492 domestic violence offenses recorded in 1997; 6,135 in 1998; 7,238 in 1999; and 7,122 in 2000.

Police Profile

Background

Like most European countries, Spain did not have bodies with police functions until the beginning of the nineteenth century. During the Middle Ages, the region of Castile had some brotherhoods that were in charge of keeping the public order. Then the army took charge of these functions. Nevertheless, during the eighteenth century some cities developed bodies that assumed police tasks. It seems that the first one was Valls, a town near Tarragona (in the present Autonomous Community of Catalonia), whose Major founded a body with such characteristics in 1721. This model was later adopted by the then Principality of Catalonia, who introduced it in other cities. In the Basque country, the first bodies that fulfilled police tasks arose during the Carlista War (1833–1840). These precedents were then invoked by the respective Autonomous Communities to justify the creation of their own police forces.

In 1824, the King Ferdinand VII signed a Real Certificate (*Real Cédula*) creating the General Police of the Kingdom, placed under the orders of a Magistrate with the title of General Superintendent. According to the first police regulations that followed, each province was divided in sub-delegations established in the main cities and localities. There were 126 sub-delegations that constituted the forerunner of the present structure of Provincial and Local Police stations.

From its creation, the aims of the police were twofold: on the one hand, to guarantee the exercise of the citizens' rights by putting in the hands of Justice "in a maximum term of eight days" (according to Article XVI) those who violated them; and, on the other hand, to guarantee welfare and public security. Taken into account these two aims, the police structured itself historically in two branches that remained until the

Constitution of 1978: one of a civil nature, responsible for investigations (the General Police Corps), and another of a military nature, responsible for keeping the public order (the Armed Police). These two forces merged in 1986 into the CNP.

The Civil Guard was established in 1844, taking as a model the National Gendarmerie of France. It started with 3,250 members and was organized by the Duke of Ahumada. It was defined as a "public security body of a military nature" and placed under the orders of the Ministry of the Interior in matters relating to its tasks and under the Ministry of War in matters relating to its organization, discipline, personnel, material, and salaries. This double affiliation to civil and military authorities (in case of war or a serious threat to the public order, the Civil Guard had to be put under the orders of the Army) was a source of conflict since the very moment of the creation of the Force. During the short Spanish Second Republic (1931–1936), the Civil Guard was separated from the Ministry of the War, but, after the Civil War (1936–1939), its military nature was reinforced during Franco's dictatorship (1939–1975).

Since its creation, the mission of the Civil Guard was to protect "people and properties inside and outside the populations" and to keep the public order. As time went by, it assumed functions of judicial, military, and fiscal police as well as public charity and, from 1876, of keeping the public order in the countryside.

The Civil Guard is known in Spain as the "Meritorious One" (*La Benemérita*), an informal name made official by a General Order of 1929. Its members wear a green uniform and a hat with three peaks (*tricornio*). Until the 1970s, it was also compulsory to wear a moustache.

Since the creation of the two State Security Forces in the nineteenth century and up until the Constitution of 1978, although administratively the Spanish State was divided in regions, provinces, and municipalities, there were in fact only two levels of responsibility for security forces: state and municipal. It is true that, as we have already mentioned, there were some provincial police forces in Catalonia, Navarra, and the Basque Country, but their functions were very limited. At the municipal level, the existing forces were characterized by their heterogeneity and, with very few exceptions, by their few professional qualifications.

The situation changed with the Constitution of 1978, which mentioned the existing security forces andtheir tasks, and respected the existence of municipal police forces, but which also introduced as an innovation the possibility of developing autonomic police forces whenever the existence of these forces was included in the Autonomy Statutes of each community. As a consequence, the Law of Police Forces 55/1978, promulgated only a few days before the approval of the Constitution, became almost obsolete.

A law according to the new political organization of the State was not promulgated until 1986 (Statutory Law of Security Forces and Corps

Offences known to the Spanish security forces and corps (1995–2000)

Type of offence	1995	1996	1997	1998	1999	2000
Criminal offences						
Total	908,264	930,780	924,393	965,835	961,787	923,270
Of which: Traffic offences (defined as criminal)	***	***	29,905	31,162	32,461	30,375
Intentional homicide						
Total	958	945	927	1,064	1,102	1,192
Of which: Completed	411	394	370	429	416	460
Assault	***	***	12,956	18,048	18,337	17,286
Rape	1,723	***	1,237	1,468	1,292	1,402
Robbery	87,254	99,282	104,008	104,475	100,716	93,504
Theft						
Total	618,237	637,545	627,888	650,058	654,559	636,664
Of which: Theft of a motor vehicle	98,847	113,916	133,330	138,075	138,961	134,584
Of which: Burglary						
Total	223,177	235,531	229,790	244,262	239,896	224,725
Of which: Domestic burglary	***	***	84,430	86,513	88,570	***
Drug trafficking	15,118	15,307	14,274	13,769	12,389	11,032

Source: European Sourcebook of Crime and Criminal Justice Statistics (Home Office, University of Lausanne, WODC: in press)

2/1986, known as LOFCS). This gave enough time to some Autonomous Communities to approve their Autonomy Statutes and to start developing their own police forces. In fact, one of the aims of the LOFCS, evident in the parliamentary debates that led to its approval, was to avoid the proliferation of autonomic police forces. But, by the time of the approval of the LOFCS, the Basque Country, Catalonia, and Navarre had already developed their own police forces. Indeed, the Basque Country had more than 2,000 agents working.

Demographics

At the beginning of 2003, it was estimated that the CNP had 47,000 members and the Civil Guard 71,500. At the autonomic level, the Autonomic Police Force of the Basque Country (*Ertzaintza*) had 7,500 agents, the Autonomic Police Force of Catalonia (*Mossos d'Esquadra*) had 8,000, and the Autonomic Police Force of Navarre (*Policía Foral*) had 750 agents. Finally, at the municipal level, the 1,800 local police forces had around 55,000 agents. Thus, the rate of police density (number of police per 1,000 inhabitants) is 4.6, and this constitutes the second highest ratio of the European Union, only surpassed by Italy.

It must be mentioned that this data refer only to members in active duty and students in education and training courses in the different police academies. It does not include reservists. It can be estimated that including the reservists, the total number of members of the two State Forces would increase the total by 25 to 30%.

The female participation is still very low and is estimated at around 3% in the State forces, 10% in the autonomic police forces, and 7% in the local police forces.

Organizational Description and Functions

The political organization of Spain, based in three levels (state, autonomic, and municipal) is reflected in the organization of its police forces. Thus, the country has two state forces, three autonomic forces, and around 1,800 municipal forces.

At the state level, there are two police forces: The National Police Corps (*Cuerpo Nacional de Policia*, designated in the rest of this article as CNP), and the Civil Guard (*Guardia Civil*). The CNP is responsible for the urban centers, and the Civil Guard is responsible for the countryside. The CNP has a civil nature while the Civil Guard has a military nature. Thus, in Spain, one usually does not talk about Police Forces but of Security Forces

and Corps, although in this article we will speak generally of security forces. Furthermore, one usually use the word *agents* instead of *officers,* as the Civil Guard uses a military scale that divides its members in officers and sub-officers.

At the autonomic level, the distribution of functions is made on the basis of the respective Autonomy Statutes and, secondarily, according to the 1986 Statutory Law of Security Forces and Corps (LOFCS: *Ley orgánica de fuerzas y cuerpos de seguridad*). At the present time, there are three autonomic police forces. Those of the Basque Country (*Ertzaintza*) and Catalonia (*Mossos d'Esquadra*), have tasks of security, judicial, administrative, assistance, and traffic police, leaving to the State forces the rest of the tasks. In the Autonomous Community of Navarre, the autonomic police force (*Policía Foral*) is in charge, basically, of tasks of administrative police, traffic, and transports.

Finally, at the municipal level, police forces are called Local Police (*Policía Local*), and they assume functions of administrative police, traffic, and assistance within their respective municipalities.

Criminal offenses that are mentioned in the Penal Code are treated by both State forces and by the autonomic police forces. Local police are responsible for traffic offenses and must transfer to the responsible State or autonomic force all other cases in which they get involved while accomplishing their duty.

In the territorial distribution defined by the LOFCS, the capitals of provinces and the municipalities or other population centers determined by the Government are attributed to the CNP; as a rule of thumb, the CNP dealt with cities with more than 20,000 inhabitants. The Civil Guard is responsible for the rest of the national territory and the territorial sea. As a result, the latter created the Marine Service or Civil Guard of the Sea.

The distribution of tasks between these two forces is done according to two big groups: common tasks of both forces and specific tasks of each force. The common tasks are those that are typical of most police force worldwide: security police, judicial police, traffic police, administrative police, and assistance police. These tasks are exerted in the whole country with the exceptions of the Autonomous Community of the Basque Country and a great part of the Autonomous Community of Catalonia, where the development of an autonomic police force for the whole territory is not yet achieved. The case of the Autonomous Community of Navarre is a special one, since it has a very low number of autonomic police agents.

The CNP is responsible for:

- Expedition of the national document of identity and of passports;

- Control of entries and exits of the Spanish territory;
- The tasks included in the laws regarding foreigners, refugees and asylum, extradition, expulsion, emigration, and immigration;
- Monitoring the fulfillment of gambling laws;
- Investigation and pursuit of drug-related offenses;
- Collaboration with and assistance to foreign police forces; and
- Control of private security agencies and services.

The Civil Guard is responsible for:

- The tasks included in the law of arms and explosives;
- Taxes and contraband;
- Traffic, transit, and transport in the in-terurban public routes;
- Safekeeping of ground communication routes, coasts, borders, ports, airports, and other facilities of this kind;
- Monitoring the fulfillment of the laws protecting all natural resources as well as the environment; and
- The interurban transportation of prisoners.

The LOFCS distinguishes three types of Autonomous Communities: (a) those whose Autonomy Statutes forecast the creation of autonomic police forces and decide to create them; (b) those whose Autonomy Statutes forecast the creation of autonomic police forces but have decided not to create them yet; and (c) the rest of the Autonomous Communities. In 2003, the first group included: the Basque Country, Catalonia, and Navarre; the second group: Andalusia, the Canary Islands, Galicia, and the Valencian Community; the third group: the other ten Autonomous Communities that can sign agreements of specific cooperation with the State.

In the Basque Country and Catalonia, the Autonomy Statutes were approved in 1979, and their dispositions regarding police forces are very similar. In fact, they assign some tasks, denoted extra-communitarian or supra-communitarian, to the Central Administration (i.e., to the State security forces), and keep the rest. The tasks attributed to the State security forces are: the monitoring of ports, airports, coasts and borders; customs; control of entries and exits of the national territory; general regime of foreigners; extradition and expulsion; emigration and immigration; expedition of passports and the national document of identity; arms and explosives; fiscal defense of the State; contraband; and fiscal fraud to the State.

Andalusia, Galicia, the Valencian Community, and the Canary Islands have not created their own police forces yet. The CNP lends some units to Autonomous Communities that act almost as an autonomic police. The tasks of these units are set by the LOFCS and by special agreements of collaboration between the two parts. The laws provide, for example, that this assignment can only concern units and not individuals, and that these units must remain under the authority of their natural chiefs, and depend functionally of the autonomic authorities but administratively of the Ministry of the Interior. In practice, the communities asked for 500 officers, but for the moment there are more or less 300 in Galicia, 300 in Valencia, and 250 in Andalusia. On the other hand, and although the Autonomous Communities were supposed to finance 50 percent of the costs of the units, for the moment the main financial cost is assumed by the Ministry of the Interior.

The rest of the Autonomous Communities have assumed the task of coordinating their local (municipal) police forces by promulgating the corresponding laws of coordination. This is also the case for the cities of Ceuta and Melilla, after the approval of their Autonomy Statutes in 1995.

According to the LOFCS, the municipalities with more than 5,000 inhabitants can have local police forces. These forces can act only in the territory of their own municipality and assume the following tasks:

- To protect the authorities of the local corporations and their buildings and facilities;
- Traffic police in the territory of the municipality (in case of accident, they begin the procedure but must transmit it to the competent State or autonomic police force);
- Administrative Police concerning the fulfillment of municipal decrees, regulations, or other dispositions;
- To collaborate in the field of judicial police;
- To help the population in case of accident, catastrophe, or public calamity, participating, according to the laws, in the execution of the plans of civil defense;
- To take measures in order to avoid the commission of criminal acts (in which case they must inform the competent State or autonomic police force);
- To protect public spaces and to collaborate with the State or autonomic police forces in case of demonstrations or large human gatherings whenever they are required for it; and
- To cooperate in the resolution of private conflicts whenever they are required for it.

The Constitution of 1978 indicated that the judicial police force was placed under the supervision of the courts and the prosecution authorities, but did not define which security force was responsible for it. The Basque and Catalan Autonomy Statutes of 1979 did not clarify the situation. Then, in 1985, the Statutory Law of the Judicial Power (6/1985), indicated that it was a task that should be carried out by all members of the security forces, whether they belonged to the State, the Autonomous Community, or the Municipality, within the scope of respective jurisdictions.

In 1986, the LOFCS introduced a more restrictive scope, indicating that the tasks of judicial police should be carried out by the State security forces (CNP and Civil Guard) and that the other police forces—autonomic and local—should collaborate with them. In 1987, a Royal Decree regulating the judicial police completed this law. Although for the general tasks of judicial police the Decree includes all the security forces, for the judicial police in a strict sense it refers to the judicial police units mentioned in the LOFCS that are integrated only by members of the CNP and the Civil Guard.

Nevertheless, in practice, the autonomic police forces of the Basque Country and Catalonia are acting as judicial police, and the plan for the development of the police of Navarre goes in the same direction. At the same time, the courts, invoking the principle of their independence, continue to ask for information from any security force.

The cooperation between the CNP and the Civil Guard is compulsory. Thus, both forces receive documents directed to either one of them. Periodically, the mass media and some political parties predict an eventual fusion of these forces, but the Government has always denied this possibility.

According to the LOFCS, the cooperation between the State security forces and the autonomic police forces was supposed to be coordinated at the national level by the Council of Security Policy (which was never created), and at the autonomic level by a series of Security Boards in each Autonomous Community. These Security Boards have produced mixed results, probably because, with the exception of the one of Navarre, police professionals are underrepresented in them.

In the municipalities with local police forces, there are Local Security Boards that are responsible for the collaboration between those forces and all other police forces. There are also a series of Commissions of Coordination of Local Police Forces, that should help in coordinating their work and unifying the education and training courses by creating Training Schools.

Finally, the LOFCS introduced a series of Commissions (at the national and provincial level, but not at the autonomic level) of Coordination of Judicial Police. At the beginning, this Commissions only had representatives from the State forces, but, little by little, representatives of the autonomic forces are being integrated.

Training

The admission to the security forces is done through a system called opposition, which is a sort of public concourse. The conditions to join any security force are quite similar. As an example, these are the requirements to joint the CNP at the basic scale (for the executive scale there are higher requirements):

- To be Spanish;
- To be at least 18 years of age and less than 30;
- To have a minimum height of 1.70 meters for men, and 1.65 meters for women;
- To be in possession of the title of Graduated in Secondary Education;
- To be in possession of a driver's license;
- To sign a commitment to carry arms and, eventually, to use them;
- Not to have been sentenced by a criminal court for an intentional offense and not to have been the object of an administrative sentence implying the interdiction of working as a public servant.

The entrance process includes a series of tests (psycho-technical, of knowledge, of physical aptitude as well as an optional test of knowledge of English), a medical examination, and a personal interview. In a second phase, there is a course of education, accompanied by a period of practical formation.

Police Use of Firearms

All members of the Spanish security forces are armed whenever they are on duty. According to the LOFCS, security force members will only use their guns in situations where it is rational to think that there is a risk for their life, the life of other people, or in circumstances that may represent a serious risk for the security of the citizens. They should act with the necessary resolution and without delay to avoid a serious, immediate, and irreparable damage, governing themselves by the principles of congruence, opportunity, and proportionality in the use of the means at their disposition. In practice, the use of guns is very rare.

It must also be mentioned that the security forces cannot apply sanctions. Thus, the reprimand or cautioning, a typical sanction applied by police forces of England and Wales, does not exist in Spain.

Complaints and Discipline

Each Security Force has its own disciplinary regime. In the case of the Civil Guard, and because of its military nature, the regime is very similar to the one used in the Army, with sanctions that include deprivation of freedom. This severe regime has been questioned several times, but it still remains. In other police forces, the actual trend is to use a system of sanctions similar to the one used for the rest of the public servants.

All police educational programs have sessions dedicated to the respect of the human rights, and the violation of these rights is severely punished. Of course, this does not mean that there have been no complaints against members of the security forces. These complaints usually refer to the treatment of immigrants, especially during expulsion procedures.

Terrorism

At the beginning of the twenty-first century, one can consider that the only terrorist group that exists in Spain is ETA (*Euzkadi Ta Askatasuna*, or "Basque Fatherland and Liberty" in the Basque language). During the so-called transition years after the death of dictator Francisco Franco, there was another group called GRAPO (meaning "First of October Antifascist Resistance Group"), but it had been practically dismantled. Although ETA defines itself as a movement of strictly Basque character, its eventual connections with other terrorist groups of international scope cannot be disregarded. In order deal with that type of crime, which belongs to the Jurisdiction of the National Hearing (*Audiencia Nacional*), the State forces have special groups. The same is true for the Autonomic Police of the Basque Country and, to a lesser extent, for the Autonomic Police of Catalonia.

International Cooperation

Spain is part of the international organization of police INTERPOL and has representatives in the Main Headquarters of that organization and a national office in Madrid. As a member of the European Union, Spain participates in the EUROPOL network. There is a particular collaboration with the police forces of countries included in the Schengen's Space.

Police Education, Research, and Publications

Each Spanish Security Force has its own centers for the education and training of their members. At the State level, the CNP has academies in Avila for both basic and executive members, while the Civil Guard has academies in Aranjuez (Madrid) for officials and in Baeza (Jaén) for sergeant majors, corporals, and guards. There are also Promotion Centers held by the CNP in Madrid and the Civil Guard in El Escorial. In addition, both forces have specialization centers.

At the autonomic level, all the communities have academies for the education and training of their police agents. For those that have their own police force, the academies are in Arkaute (Vitoria) for the Basque Country, in Mollet del Vallés (Barcelona) for Catalonia,and in Pamplona for Navarre. The rest of the Autonomous Communities concentrate their efforts on the education as the Central Administration or the Autonomous Communities.

At the State level, there are:

- an Institute of Police Studies (*Instituto de Estudios de Policía*); and
- a Center for Analysis and Prospects of the Civil Guard and University Institute "Duke of Ahumada" of Security Studies (*Centro de Análisis y Prospectiva de la Guardia Civil e Instituto Universitario "Duque de Ahumada" de Estudios de Seguridad*).

Main Journals

- *Policía*Published by: Instituto de Estudios de Policía -Redacción y Administración- C/Rafael Calvo 33- 28010 Madrid – Spain –Tel.: (++34) 91 322 33 29 – Fax: (++34) 91 576 32 77
- *Ciencia policial* Published by: Instituto de Estudios de Policía -Redacción y Administración- C/Rafael Calvo 33- 28010 Madrid – Spain –Tel.: (++34) 91 322 33 29 – Fax: (++34) 91 576 32 77
- *Interpol* Spanish Edition of the Interpol JournalContact: Instituto de Estudios de Policía -Redacción y Administración -C/Rafael Calvo 33- 28010 Madrid – Spain –Tel.: (++34) 91 322 33 29 – Fax: (++34) 91 576 32 77
- *Policía Hoy: Revista Digital del Cuerpo Nacional de Policía www.policia.es/policiahoy/*
- *Guardia Civil* Official journal of the Civil Guard. Available on-line *http://www.guardiacivil.org/00revista/index.asp*

- *Cuadernos de la Guardia Civil: Revista de Seguridad Pública* Published by: Centro de Análisis y Prospectiva de la Guardia Civil e Instituto Universitario "Duque de Ahumada" de Estudios de Seguridad –C/Madrid, 126-128 – 28903 GETAFE (Madrid) – Tel. (++34) 91 624 93 62 – Fax (++34) 91 624 93 89 - E-mail: iahumada@pa.uc3m.es

MARCELO F. AEBI AND
GONZALO JAR-COUSELO

Websites

- Civil Guard (*Guardia Civil*): *www.guardiacivil. org/*
- National Police Corps (*Cuerpo Nacional de Policía*): *www.mir.es/policia/*
- Autonomic Police of Catalonia (*Mossos d'Esquadra*): *www.gencat.es/mossos/*
- Autonomic Police of the Basque Country (*Ertzaintza*): *www.ertzaintza.net*

Bibliography

Amoedo Souto, Carlos Alberto, *Policía Autonómica e Seguridade Pública* (*Autonomic Police and Public Security*), Santiago de Compostela: Xunta de Galicia, 1994.

Barcelona Llop, Javier, *Policía y Constitución (Police and Constitution)*, Madrid: Tecnos, 1997.

Blázquez González, Félix, *La Policía Judicial (The Judiciary Police)*, Madrid: Tecnos, 1998.

Gil Márquez, Tomás, *Modelo policial y forma de Estado en España (Police Model and State in Spain)*, Barcelona: Atelier, 1999.

Hernández Lores, Mario, "La victimación en España" (Victimization in Spain), *Ciencia Policial* 44 (1998): 7-56.

Izu Belloso, Miguel J., *La Policía Foral en Navarra (The Autonomic Police in Navarra)*, Pamplona: Gobierno de Navarra, 1991.

Jar Couselo, Gonzalo. *Modelo Policial Español y Policías Autónomas (Spanish Police Model and Autonomic Police Forces)*, Madrid: Dykinson, 1995.

———. *Modelos comparados de policía (Comparative Police Models)*, Madrid: Dykinson-Ministerio del Interior, 2000.

Jar Couselo, Gonzalo & Pérez Martin, Juan Luis, *Legislación sobre Cuerpos de Policía: Ámbito Estatal, Autonómico y Municipal (Legislation on Police Corps: State, Autonomic and Municipal Levels)*, 2nd ed., Madrid: Dykinson, 2001.

Lazúen Alcón, Mª Piedad, *Cuerpos de Policía y Seguridad Ciudadana: Situación actual y perspectivas de futuro (Police Corps and Citizen Security: Present situation and perspectives for the future)*, Madrid: Ministerio del Interior, 1999.

López-Nieto Y Mallo, Francisco, *La Policía Municipal (The Municipal Police)*, 2nd ed., Madrid: Abella, 1998.

Loubet del Bayle, J.L., *La Policía (The Police)*, Madrid: Acento, 1998.

Martín, Manuel.

———. *La profesión de policía (The Profession of Police Agent)*, Madrid: CIS-S. XXI, 1991.

———. *Mujeres Policías (Policewomen)*, Madrid: CIS-S. XXI, 1994.

Martínez Pérez, Roberto, *Policía Judicial y Constitución (Judiciary Police and Constitution)*, Navarra: Aranzadi, 2001.

Recasens I Brunet, Amadeu, "The Control of Police Powers", *European Journal on Criminal Policy and Research* 8/3 (2000): 247-269.

Torrente, Diego, *La Sociedad Policial: Poder, Trabajo y Cultura en una Organización Local de policía (The Police Society: Power, work and culture in a local organisation of police)*, Madrid: CIS, 1997.

Valriberas Sanz, Ángel, *Cuerpo Nacional de Policía y Sistema Policial Español (The National Police Corps and the Spanish Police System)*, Madrid: Marcial Pons-Ministerio del Interior, 1999.

Villagómez, Alfonso J., *Las Fuerzas y Cuerpos de Seguridad: del orden público a la seguridad ciudadana (Security Forces and Corps: From Public Order to Citizen Security)*, A Coruña: Ara Solís, 1997.

SRI LANKA

Background Material

Sri Lanka, referred to as Ceylon until 1971, is an island located at the southeastern tip of India in the Indian Ocean, with Colombo as its capital. Its total land area is 65,610 sq km, and it has a population nearing 20 million, with one of the lowest rates of annual population growth, 0.85%, in South Asia. Sri Lanka is divided into nine provinces, each consisting of districts, subdistricts, and villages. The literacy rate is over 90%, and the life expectancy at birth is about 72 years of age. The population is 74% Sinhalese, 18% Tamil, seven percent Moors (of Arab descent), and one percent others, including Burghers (of Dutch origin), Malayans, and Veddas (the original people of the land). Close to 70% of the population are Theravada Buddhists (mainly Sinhalese), 15% Tamil Hindus, 7% Muslims, and 8% Christians. The main languages spoken are Sinhalese and Tamil, with English used as the medium in government and largely in the public sphere.

Most people of Sri Lanka trace their descent from the Indian subcontinent. Some arrived from Northern India, who came to be known as Sinhalese, and some from Southern India, the Tamil speaking people, as early as the fifth century BC, and established their kingdoms on the land of the Veddas. From that time on, frictions and wars developed between the Sinhalese and Tamils, and their relationship over time was further strained by frequent invasions from the South Indian Tamil kings. One of those lines of kings, Cholas, ruled Sri Lanka from 973 to 1070 AD. By the fifteenth century, the Sinhalese established full control of the country, to be later partially controlled by the Portuguese (1505–1658). From 1640, the Dutch ruled the land, to be gradually taken over by the British. The British controlled the nation from 1802 to 1948, when Sri Lanka attained independence.

The Constitution recognizes all religions and ethnic groups, and allows individuals to pursue their customs and beliefs. However, the Constitution is very much influenced by the needs of the Sinhalese Buddhist majority, and so is the administration of the country. This has engendered animosity and sometimes violence toward Hindus, Muslims, and Christians. Christians are allowed to pursue their faith, but foreign missionary activities are under government regulation. Overall, the people of the land got along well during much of Sri Lanka's history, but after independence the ethnic rifts, more than the religious differences, began to surface between the Sinhalese and Tamils, resulting in a big divide and prolonged violence, continuing even today.

Sri Lanka has changed in recent decades from a primarily agricultural to a more industrial and service-oriented economy. The export of garments and textiles has increased beyond the export of plantation commercial crops (tea, rubber, coconut) to 63% of the exports in 1996. For the year 2000, the Sri Lankan GDP was estimated at about $16.6 billion USD, and the per capital GDP was $856 USD. The GDP consists of about 21% from agriculture, 27% from industry, and 52% from service areas. The Gross Domestic Product growth rate was good, 5.3%, between 1997 and 2000, but it began to fall below one percent in 2001, due to droughts, energy shortages, financial crises, and ethnic strife. Since independence, the Sri Lankan economy has greatly progressed, and the quality of life has improved by following a socialistic and welfare state model of development. However, some 15 to 20% of the people live in poverty.

Contextual Features

After independence, the Sinhalese nationalist movement began to gain momentum under the primary leadership of the Sri Lankan Freedom Party and the United National Party, the two main political parties of the country. Sinhalese nationalism, led mainly by Buddhists, neither helped to curb violence against the Tamils nor did it help the efforts of people, organizations, and government officials sympathetic and accommodating to Tamil interests. Various Sinhalese organizations, prominent among them the Leftist Janatha Vimukthi Peramuna party (JVP), wanted Tamils to be ousted from the country, and they instigated hate and violence. The Tamils organized themselves to defend their identity, safety, and well-being, and they began to demand equal treatment, rights, and justice. Fearing continued ill treatment and danger, some Tamils wanted a separate homeland state in the northern region and the eastern coast, which was denied. This led to the formation of Tamil organizations, the most militant being the Liberation Tigers of Tamil Eelam (LTTE), which formed around 1972. This organization followed terrorist strategies and adopted guerrilla tactics. The LTTE committed atrocities against all, particularly Sinhalese and Tamils who did not share its demands and agenda.

Many reasons are given to explain why the Sinhalese and the Tamils succumbed to divisive, hateful relationships. These include the memory of historical wars between the Sinhalese and the Tamil kings, complicated by the invasion of the Tamil kings, and the current fear that Tamils could get military support from India. The Sinhalese also believe they are racially superior, due to their Aryan origin, to the Tamils, who are of Dravidian origin, even though studies indicate there are no distinguishable racial differences between them. Additionally, during British rule, Tamils held important positions in the government, military, and police, as well as in education, business, and banking. After independence, the Sinhalese deliberately set out to undermine Tamil importance, advancement, and power. This resulted in the government championing Sinhalese interests through actively recruiting mainly Sinhalese into positions of importance, especially in the military and police forces.

During the early years of independence, only a small number of persons were employed in the military, and they were recruited on a voluntary basis to primarily help the police. However, given this ethnic strife, the military and police forces grew tremendously. The 1971 major uprising, instigated by the People's Liberation Front (JVP) against the Tamils, and similar violence in 1983, when thousands of Tamils were killed, led to the development of a strong Tamil militant movement, spearheaded by the LTTE, which shook up governmental abilities to control and establish order. A series of terrorist activities led to the arming of the police with firearms for the first time in 1982. These events of large-scale violence resulted in the enlargement military forces through a national draft system introduced in 1985, and led to the government augmenting their forces with foreign military and police forces to maintain domestic order. Before the Indian Peace-Keeping Force (IPKF) arrived as part of the Indo-Sri Lankan Accord, Pakistani, Israeli, and British military officers provided counsel to the Sri Lankan security and police forces.

Currently, Sri Lanka has a parliamentary form of democratic government in which the Prime Minister is chosen from elected representatives. The President, however, is elected by popular vote. The two main political parties are the Sri Lankan Freedom Party (SLFP) and the United National Party (UNP). The other political parties are: the Marxist Party, the Lanka Sama Samaja Party (LSSP), the Communist Party of Sri Lanka (CPSL), the People's United Front, the Tamil United Liberation Front, and others.

Published crime statistics presented in Table 1 indicate that the volume and rates of violent crimes are taking a declining trend, even though some newspaper reports mention they are increasing. Property crimes show an increase, which correlates with the ailing economy. Additionally, rape and sex-related offenses also show an increasing trend, which can be construed as the ill effects of the ongoing domestic war.

The population of Sri Lanka was estimated at 18.66 million in 1998, and 19.3 million in 2002.

The present Sri Lankan criminal law procedure is mainly founded on British Common Law, with some influence from Dutch and Portuguese Civil Law systems, and the customary legal practices of Sinhalese, Tamils, Muslims, and other groups. The Penal Code of 1883, introduced by the British, is an important basis for criminal and procedural law as they exist today, even though this has been periodically modified, such as by the Code of Criminal Procedure of 1979. Similarly, the criminal justice system is also founded on the criminal justice organizations that the British developed in India and introduced in Sri Lanka as well. Subsequent to independence, confronted with emerging communal riots and modernization trends, some changes in law and criminal justice organizations were made. As per the Constitution of 1978, there are four levels of courts: the Supreme Court, the Court of Appeals, and High Courts, and Magistrate Courts at local levels, with original jurisdiction. The majority of criminal cases are settled in the Magistrate Courts, and serious criminal cases are processed by the High Court. In these trial courts, the accused have various rights: the right to legal counsel, the right to cross-examine witnesses, and the right to privacy, unless search and seizure occurs by consent or with a warrant. The law provides for a jury trial only in the High Court, and trials in both these courts are generally public trials. Decisions from the Magistrate and High Courts can be appealed to the Court of Appeals, where three judges decide on the case by providing due process rights to the offenders. The Supreme Court is the court of last resort, where a chief justice and six to ten justices at a sitting decide on cases referred to them. The Constitution, apart from providing rights to citizens and the accused, also contains provisions to abridge those rights when there is large-scale communal violence, at which time the Parliament or the President may impose emergency regulations. This provision was frequently used with the introduction of the Prevention of Terrorism Act of 1979, and with various emergency acts and administrative government orders thereafter. The police detained suspects and terrorists, mainly Tamils, for extended periods of time, placed many under preventive detention, and searched premises and seized evidence without warrants.

Sentences given by the courts range from the death penalty for such crimes as murders and serious crimes against the state, to 20 years of maximum imprisonment or minimum incarceration for less than three months. The total number of prisoners in 1996 was 89,083 (83,290 males and 5,793 females), and this increased by 2002 to 107,210 (102,295 males and 4,915 females). The incarceration rate for 2002 was around 555 per 100,000 population. Punishment can include imprisonment with or without labor, whipping, fines, confiscation of property, and placement in rehabilitation programs; and, for juveniles, training and reform schools. Juveniles who are below

Selected grave crimes by type of crime in Sri Lanka, 1998 and 2002 (per 100,000 population)

Type of Crime	1998	rate for 1998	2002	rate for 2002
Grievious hurt	2,043	10.9	1,848	9.6
Hurt by knife	6,641	35.6	4,784	24.8
Homicide/Abetment to commit suicide	1,919	10.3	1,347	7.0
Attempted homicide	564	3.0	504	2.6
Rape/Incest	1,076	5.8	1,247	6.5
Unnatural offencses/Grave sexual abuse	131	0.7	303	1.6
Riots	99	0.5	317	1.6
Robberies	4,778	25.6	5,663	29.3
Burglary	12,506	67.0	14,476	75.0
Counterfeiting currency	29	0.2	166	0.9

Twenty-two grave crimes are recognized in the police crime report. The total of all these offenses for 1998 is 56,767 (with the rate of 304.2); and for 2002, it is 48,978 (with the rate of 253.8).

Source: Sri Lankan Police Department and Statistical Abstract 2003, Department of Census and Statistics, Sri Lanka, www.statistics.gov.lk/abstract/social_conditions/tab2015.pdf

17 years of age and pregnant women are exempt from the death penalty. Even though the death penalty was a debated topic and has not been implemented since 1976, there is a recent attempt to reactivate it, in the wake of assassinations of judges and political leaders.

Police Profile

Background

Traditional, colonial, and modern forces, as well as political events, have shaped the Sri Lankan police. In remote villages, locally elected headmen have traditionally carried out police roles, and many continue to do so today. The appointment of Sir Richard Aluvihare as the first Sri Lankan Inspector General of Police in 1947 led to some reforms. Both reactive and proactive approaches to crime control were followed. From 1952, women were incorporated into police service, and policing transformed from a purely crime control focus to a public service orientation. Shortly after independence, the police were moved from the Home Ministry to the Defense Ministry, which later paved the way for police-military cooperation in confronting social turmoil.

Demographics

The police strength increased tremendously, from 11,300 in 1969, to 21,000 in 1987, to 38,472 in 2002. In 1973, there were 9.7 police for every 100,000 people, which increased to 254 by 2002.

Organizational Description

In 1963, the national police system was divided into Northern, Central, and Southern ranges. Each range is divided into divisions, districts, and stations. Colombo has a separate Division of Police.

Beginning in 1985, the Sri Lankan police began to function under the umbrella of Joint Operations Command, which includes the army, navy, and air force, and the National Intelligence Bureau. The council that makes security decisions consists of the President, the Prime Minister, the Minister of Internal Security, the Three Military Service Commanders, the Inspector General of Police, the Director of the National Intelligence Bureau, and the General Officer heading the Joint Operations. Consequently, a strong connection was developed between the military forces and the police to deal with the insurgent and terrorist activities, and with communal violence, especially in the context of the Tamils seeking a separate state or homeland for themselves.

As a part of the national police operations or as adjunct organizations, Commando Squads of the Colombo police and the Special Task Force were created to control the insurgent activities of the LTTE and JVP. The Special Task Force was developed through the help of the British in 1984 for the main purpose of controlling Tamil insurgents. Upon the creation of the Indo-Sri Lankan Accord, this special force was reassigned to control the JVP anti-Tamil and anti-government activities in the Southern Province, while the Indian military forces controlled the Northern Tamil areas.

At the top level in the police hierarchy is the Inspector General of Police, and below that rank are Senior and Deputy Inspector Generals for the three ranges. At the district level are different ranks of Superintendents of Police, who direct and supervise activities of police personnel in some 2,600 police stations. At the police station level are Inspectors and Sub-Inspectors of Police. Under them are Police Sergeants and Constables engaged in regular police work—patrol, criminal investigation, traffic, and services to the community, as well as presenting cases in courts, maintaining public order, maintaining jails, and maintaining records.

Direct recruitment of police occurs for Probationary Assistant Superintendent of Police, Probationary Sub-Inspector of Police, Police Constable, Police Women Constable, and Police Constable Drivers. Promotions are given based on experience, education, and achievements. Except for the rank of Probationary Assistant Superintendent of Police, which requires a university graduate degree, all other lower positions require the General Qualifications Certificate of Education (similar to a high school education). At the recruitment level, the men and women are expected to be 18 to 25 years of age, physically fit, unmarried, and not divorced. Recruits receive training in criminal investigation, traffic control, fingerprinting, firearms use, narcotics control, escort security, communication, driving, auto mechanics, information technology, police band music, terrorism control, medical help, life-saving, police kennel division, legal matters, and help and assistance services for victims of crime, especially women and children.

Training

The police are trained in the Police College in Katukurunda, in the Western Province. The Special Task Force Police are trained in Kalutara, about 100 miles from Colombo; these police are primarily devoted to counter-insurgency control, and are sometimes trained with British, Indian, French, and Swedish cooperation. There are also training programs for higher ranks of police officers, beginning from the Sub-Inspector of Police. Some select few are sent abroad for special training and education.

War and the Police

With Sinhalese nationalism becoming intense in the 1980s, many government-sponsored Sinhalese settlers moved into Tamil areas. The LTTE fought against this vigorously. In order to help protect the settlers, Home Guards, local small-scale defense groups, developed and expanded. Many of them were armed and untrained, and they killed many Tamils. After the Indian forces came in 1987 to help Sri Lanka maintain peace, the activities of these groups declined in the Tamil areas. Out of this idea of Home Guards later developed many small forces, including militias created for the protection of United National Party legislators, some of whom were threatened or killed by Sinhalese militants while trying to implement the Indian-Sri Lankan Accord.

The involvement of India in Sri Lankan affairs from 1987 led to resentment, as the JVP felt that the sovereignty of the nation was threatened by foreign intervention, and the LTTE felt the Indian Government was making unacceptable agreements, thwarting their desire for a separate homeland. In 1991, an LTTE suicide bomber assassinated Rajiv Gandhi, the Prime Minister of India.

In relation to the increasing incidents of confrontations and violence between the Sinhalese and Tamils, the police force steadily increased, as noted above, while Tamil participation decreased. Between 1969 and 1974, police increased by 42%. At the dawn of independence, Tamil participation in the police and military forces was over 30%, but this was sharply reduced to 5% by 1983. In 1988, the combined number of persons in the armed forces and the police was 69,000, which increased to 193,522 by 2002. The armed forces expenditures also increased from US$408 million in 1988 to US$719 million by 2002. Radical and anti-Tamil persons were selected for police and military work, and were placed in Tamil areas. National Emergency Acts were introduced, which reduced the Constitutional freedoms of citizens and increased the police and military forces. These forces worked together and treated the Tamils violently, and the LTTE reacted violently as well. The military and police tortured, maimed, and killed many Tamils, including innocent men, women, and children, and they raped women and some children, under the pretext of maintaining peace and order, and retaliating against Tamil insurgents. Examples of incidents abound. In 1996, soldiers and policemen killed a school girl and her mother, brother, and a neighbor in Jaffna, and were found guilty. They were also found guilty of raping the school girl, for which the culprits were given the death penalty. By responding to events like this, the LTTE became stronger and more fierce. For instance, the LTTE attacked Colombo International Airport, destroyed planes, and killed people. Some estimated 60,000 people, mostly Tamils, have died because of the communal wars. The formation of the Sri Lankan security forces, predominantly Sinhalese, through the government initiatives has made peace-making impossible to this day.

Many police brutality and human rights violations have been lodged against the police and security forces, which were not for the most part fairly investigated or dealt with. The National Police Commission mandated by the Constitution to inquire into abuses and excesses of the police has come under severe criticism in recent years for covering up police violence and crimes of lower and higher level officers, and for corrupting the whole police organization. The Asian Human Rights Commission (AHRC), located in Hong Kong, blamed the Sri Lankan National Police Commission (NPC) for developing connections with criminals and the criminal underworld by finding support from some politicians. In 2004, the AHRC wanted the head of the NPC to resign for ignoring police torture, or pouring of hot, burning water on an individual, who was arrested without adequate cause. In light of these abuses, the Sri Lankan Inter Ministerial Human Rights Working Group recently established the Sri Lanka Police Human Rights Division, not only to attend to abuses, but also to promote human rights awareness among the police.

The nationalist movement continues to cause problems for the Tamils through support of some local and foreign-residing Sinhalese. The pro-Sinhalese Society for Peace, Unity, and Human Rights (SPUR), based in Australia, blames the Sri Lankan government for trying to accommodate the Tamil Tigers by almost granting them a separate state, and for ignoring Tamil protests against the military forces, while at the same time seriously curtailing nationalist protests against these government initiatives.

Many citizens and politicians who are tired of the 20-year internal war seek peace in the interest of promoting general safety and economic improvement. Some are leaving the military forces. Poverty and unemployment are forcing many into criminal activities, and into joining the growing number of criminal gangs and the narcotics trade. Under these conditions, because of their long exposure to violence, many are desensitized to violence, which is also said to increase the nation's violent crime.

Peace is desperately sought without clear directions to accommodate differences and pursue justice. The Norwegian initiative to create peace, beginning in 2001, seemed to work, but again this was disturbed by sporadic events of violence on both sides, such as when a suicide bomber destroyed a government building in Colombo. Some Western news reporters recently hoped that the humane concerns that the tsunami experience generated in Sri Lanka would promote soul-searching and help the Sinhalese and Tamils to develop understanding and peaceful relationships.

S. GEORGE VINCENTNATHAN

Bibliography

AllRefer.com. "Sri Lanka: National Police and Paramilitary Forces." Reference, Country Study and Country Guide. http://reference.allrefer.com/country-guide-study/sri-lanka/sri-lanka175.html, 2005.

Asian Human Right Commission. "Sri Lanka: Chairman of Sri Lankan Police Commission Urged to Protect Torture Victims or Resign." www.ahrchk.net/state ments/mainfile.php/2004statement/180/, 2004.

Asian Tribune. "Sri Lankan NPC Probe of Top Police Officials: A Test of Its Credibility." December 22. www.asiantribune.com/show_news.php?id=12596, 2004.

Bell-Fialkoff, Andrew. Ethnic Cleansing. New York: St. Martin's Griffin, 1999.

Burger, Angela. "Ethnicity and the Security Forces of the State: The South Asian Experience." In Ethnicity and the State. Political and Legal Anthropology, Volume 9. Judith D. Toland (ed.). 79-102. New Brunswick, NJ: Transaction Publishers, 1993.

de Silva, K. M. A History of Sri Lanka. London: C. Hurst, 1981.

Dias, Wije. "Sri Lankan President Moves to Reinstate the Death Penalty." World Socialist Web Site. November 26. www.wsws.org/articles/2004/nov2004/sri-n26.shtml, 2004.

Human Rights Watch. "Sri Lanka: Human Rights Developments." World Report 1999. www.hrw.org/worldreport99/asia/srilanka.html, 1999.

LonelyPlanet. "Sri Lanka: History." WorldGuide. www.lonelyplanet.com/destinations/indian_subcontinent/sri_lanka/history.htm, 2005.

Norton, James H. India and South Asia. Fifth Edition. Global Studies Series. Guilford, CT: McGraw-Hill/Dushkin, 2001.

Nubin, Walter. Sri Lanka: Current Issues and Historical Background. New York: Nova Science Publishers, 2002.

Peebles, Patrick. The Plantation Tamils of Ceylon. London: Leicester University Press, 2001.

Phrase Base. "Sri Lanka Information: Detailed Facts and Statistics about Sri Lanka: Sri Lankan Political Facts." www.phrasebase.com/countries/Sri%20Lanka.html, 2005.

Ross, Russell R., and Andrea Matles Savada. Sri Lanka, A Country Study. Washington, D.C.: Federal Research Division, United States Government, 1990.

Society for Peach, Unity, and Human Rights. "SriLanka Police Action to Remand Democratic Protesters is a Clear Violation of Human Rights." Press release, November 4. www.spur.asn.au/SPUR_20031104_Human_Rights_Violations_by_Police.htm, 2003.

Sri Lanka Information. 2005.

Sri Lanka Police Service. "Crime Trends." www.police.lk/divisions/crime.html, 2005.

———. "History." www.police.lk/divisions/history.html, 2005.

————. "Organizational Structure." www.police.lk/divi-sions/organize_chart.html, 2005.

————. "Recruitment/Training." www.police.lk/divi sions/recruitment.html, 2005.

————. "Human Rights Division." www.police.lk/divi-sions/human_rights.html, 2005.

Tambiah, Stanley J. *Sri Lanka: Ethnic Fratricide and the Dismantling of Democracy*. Chicago: University of Chicago Press, 1986.

U. S. State Department, Bureau of Consular Affairs. "Sri Lanka." Consular Information Sheet. http://travel.state.gov/travel/cis_pa_tw/cis/cis_1025.html, 2005.

SUDAN

Background Material

On November 19, 2004, the government of Sudan and the Sudan People's Liberation Movement/Army signed a declaration committing themselves to conclude a final comprehensive peace agreement by December 31, 2004, in the context of a special session of the United Nations Security Council in Nairobi; Kenya; it was only the fourth time the Council has met outside of New York since its founding. At this session, the UNSC unanimously adopted Resolution 1574, which welcomed the commitment of the government and the SPLM/A to achieve agreement by the end of 2004, and underscored the international community's intention to assist the Sudanese people and support implementation of the comprehensive peace agreement. It also demanded that the Government of Sudan and the SLA/M and JEM halt all violence in Darfur.

In keeping with their commitment to the Security Council, the government of Sudan and the Sudan People's Liberation Movement/Army initialed the final elements of the comprehensive agreement on December 31, 2004. The two parties formally signed the Comprehensive Peace Agreement (CPA) on January 9, 2005. The United States and the international community have welcomed this decisive step forward for peace in Sudan.

The civil war had displaced more than four million southerners. Some fled into southern cities, such as Juba; others trekked as far north as Khartoum and even into Ethiopia, Kenya, Uganda, Egypt, and other neighboring countries. These people were unable to grow food or earn money to feed themselves, and malnutrition and starvation became widespread. The lack of investment in the south resulted as well in what international humanitarian organizations call a "lost generation" who lack educational opportunities and access to basic health care services, and who have little prospect for productive employment in the small and weak economies of the south or the north.

As Sudan became the world's largest debtor to the World Bank and International Monetary Fund by 1993, its relationship with the international financial institutions soured in the mid-1990s and has yet to be fully rehabilitated. The government fell out of compliance with an IMF standby program and accumulated substantial arrearages on repurchase obligations.

In 2000–2001, Sudan's current account entered surplus for the first time since independence. In 1993, currency controls were imposed, making it illegal to possess foreign exchange without approval. In 1999, liberalization of foreign exchange markets ameliorated this constraint somewhat. Exports other than oil are largely stagnant. However, the small industrial sector remainsdepressed, spending for the war continues to preempt other social investments, and Sudan's inadequate and declining infrastructure inhibits economic growth.

In Sudan's 1993 census, the population was calculated at 26 million. No comprehensive census has been carried out since that time, due to the continuation of the civil war. Current estimates range to 32 million. The population of metropolitan Khartoum (including Khartoum, Omdurman, and Khartoum North) is growing rapidly and ranges from six to million, including around two million displaced persons from the southern war zone as well as western and eastern drought-affected areas. Sudan has two distinct major cultures—Arab and black African—with hundreds of ethnic and tribal divisions and language groups, which makes effective collaboration among them a major problem.

The northern states cover most of the Sudan and include most of the urban centers. Most of the 22 million Sudanese who live in this region are Arabic-speaking Muslims, though the majority also use a traditional non-Arabic mother tongue, such as Nubian, Beja, Fur, Nuban, and Ingessana. Among these are several distinct tribal groups: the Kababish of northern Kordofan, a camel-raising people; the Ja'alin and Shaigiyya groups of settled tribes along the rivers; the semi-nomadic Baggara of Kordofan and Darfur; the Hamitic Beja in the Red Sea area; Nubians of the northern Nile areas, some of whom have been resettled on the Atbara River; and the Negroid Nuba of southern Kordofan and Fur in the western reaches of the country.

The southern region has a population of around six million and a predominantly rural, subsistence economy. This region has been negatively affected by war for all but 10 years since independence in 1956, resulting in serious neglect, lack of infrastructure development, and major destruction and displacement. More than two million people have died, and more than four million are internally displaced or have become refugees as a result of the civil war and war-related impacts. The Sudanese practice mainly indigenous traditional beliefs, although Christian missionaries have converted some. The south also contains many tribal groups, and many more languages are used than in the north. The Dinka—whose population is estimated at more than one million—is the largest of the many black African tribes of the Sudan. Along with the Shilluk and the Nuer, they are among the Nilotic tribes. The Azande, Bor, and Jo Luo are "Sudanic" tribes in the west; and the Acholi and Lotuhu live in the extreme south, extending into Uganda.

Contextual Features

Sudan has an authoritarian government in which all effective political power is in the hands of President Omar Hassan al-Bashir. Bashir and his party have controlled the government since he led the military coup on June 30, 1989. The government is a military dictatorship with a pro-government Parliament.

The Sudanese criminal code embodies elements of British law, the penal code of British colonial India, and the Egyptian civil code. In 1977, a committee dominated by the Muslim Brotherhood revised the legal code according to the *sharia* (Islamic law). In September 1983, the Nimeiri government introduced a version of the *sharia* prescribing harsh corporal punishments for such crimes as murder, theft, drinking alcohol, prostitution, and adultery. These "September Laws," sometimes known as *hudud,* provided for execution, flogging, amputation, and stoning as modes of punishment for both Muslims and non-Muslims. During the final 20 months of Nimeiri's rule, at least 90 persons convicted of theft had their hands amputated. The military and civil governments succeeding Nimeiri between 1985 and 1989 suspended the September Laws. Progress on a new Islamic penal code to replace the September Laws was delayed by the legislature, pending a Constitutional Assembly that would include the SPLA. Although flogging, consisting normally of 40 lashes, was limited to offenses involving sex or alcohol, it was often inflicted summarily. In 1989, the RCC-NS extended flogging as a punishment for a much wider range of offenses. Extreme *hudud* sentences, such as amputations, were not handed down, however, and many *hudud* sentences imposed under the Sadiq al Mahdi government were converted to jail terms and fines.

In the regular criminal court system, extensive guarantees of due process were prescribed for accused persons. These courts consisted of a panel of three judges. The judicial process involved a police or magistrate's investigation and an arrest warrant preceding the arrest. Trials were held in public, except when the accused requested a closed trial. The accused had to be brought before a court within 48 hours of arrest, informed of the charges, and provided with access to an attorney of his or her choice. There were legal aid services for the poor, but, because resources were limited, legal aid was apportioned to those facing serious charges and those most in need. Bail was permitted, except in some capital cases. Defendants had the right to speak, to present evidence on their own behalf, and to appeal judgments through a series of courts from the magistrate level to the High Court of Appeal.

Under the state of emergency imposed by the Sadiq al Mahdi regime in 1987, the government had wide powers in areas declared to be emergency zones to arrest and preventively detain for an indefinite period anyone suspected of contravening emergency regulations. Military personnel could not be arrested by civilian authorities, nor was there provision for judicial review of actions by the armed forces. The Sadiq al Mahdi government declared emergency zones in the southern and western areas of the country and used the detention powers on people suspected of sympathy with the rebellion.

On seizing power in 1989, the RCC-NS declared a state of emergency for the whole of Sudan and granted itself broad powers. The government initially detained more than 300 people without warrants, including many prominent political and academic figures, journalists, alleged leftists, and trade unionists. About 60 judges who petitioned against the government's action were also detained. Many of the original detainees were released within several months, but they were replaced by others. There were an estimated 300 to 500 detainees at the close of 1990; some reports claimed as many as 1,000 detainees.

After the 1989 coup, the regular civilian courts continued to handle ordinary criminal offenses, including theft and some capital crimes, although the court system was seriously backlogged, and the judiciary was less independent of the executive than previously. After experimenting with various forms of special courts, the RCC-NS established special security courts in November, 1989. These courts were formed by the military governors of the regions and the commissioner of the national capital. The courts had three-member panels of both military and civilian judges. They tried persons accused of violating constitutional decrees, emergency regulations, and some portions of the criminal code, notably drug crimes and currency violations. The new security courts did not extend normal protections to the accused. Attorneys were permitted to sit with defendants but were not permitted to address the courts. Sentences imposed by the courts were to be carried out immediately, with the exception that death penalties were to be reviewed by the Chief Justice and the Head of State. The special security courts gained a reputation for harsh sentences. Two defendants convicted of illegal possession of foreign currency and another convicted of drug smuggling were executed, and others were sentenced to death for similar crimes, although the sentences were not carried out.

In areas of the south affected by the war, normal judicial procedures could not be applied, and civil authorities were made redundant by the application of the state of emergency. Units of the armed forces and militias ruled by force of arms, and in many cases the accused were summarily tried and punished, especially for offenses against public order. In war-torn southern Kurdufan, the government authorized a system of justice administered by village elders, and a similar system was reportedly in effect in areas controlled by the SPLA.

The Comprehensive Peace Agreement signed on January 9, 2005 provides for a new Constitution, and new arrangements for power sharing, wealth sharing, and security applicable throughout the country. New institutions will be created, and a new government of national unity will be installed, once the Constitution is ratified during the six-month pre-interim period. Once it is ratified, SPLM Chairman John Garang will become the First Vice President of Sudan, and the new Government of Southern Sudan will be established.

Almost every northern state has a prison, and they vary in capacity. There are four federal prisons, 26 government prisons, and three open prisons. There are four juvenile centers and also one female prison in Omdurman. Prisons are dilapidated, with no new prisons having been built in the last 50 years. The infrastructure is in need of a complete overhaul. Similarly, existing juvenile reformatories are poorly maintained.

Overcrowding is a huge problem. The official prison population is estimated at 14,000 with a prison capacity of only 4,300. There is neither registration nor classification of prisoners in order to separate first-time offenders and those who have committed minor offenses from serious criminals. This problem is further compounded by the fact that juveniles share premises with adult prisoners and can be subject to abuse by older and stronger prisoners, or lured by the need for extra food. The food budget is usually not sufficient, and families and NGOs have to provide supplements. Access to legal aid is not easily available, as most of those arrested and detained are usually from the poorer part of the society and cannot afford the legal fees. A number of NGOs, a committee of the Bar Association, and the Legal Aid Department of the Ministry of Justice provide legal aid, although this does not adequately cover the needs.

Furthermore, the police keep a number of pretrial prisoners in their custody, in deplorable conditions, in addition to reports of abuses that are allegedly committed with impunity under the National Security Forces Act. There are no alternatives to imprisonment, except flogging in some cases. The death penalty is still in place; Muslim women are sometimes executed for adultery. Before executions can be carried out, the sanction of the Chief Justice is necessary, as well as that of the President.

The total prison staff is estimated at 7,500, all of whom are from the police force, including about 400 senior police officers. All correction officers have to undergo training at the police college and the police academy, while prison wardens receive only limited training.

Women prisoners are one of the vulnerable groups of prisoners in need of special attention. Estimated at about two percent of the prison population, their main crimes are brewing of alcohol, prostitution, and petty theft. Most of these women are displaced from the South and the only bread-winners of the family, lacking any income-generating activities. Most of these women do not know the procedure in the courts, and they lack both the language skills and legal counselling necessary to defend their cases. In addition, a number of women bring their children with them to the prison, which, in turn, lacks any budget to provide for the needs of these children.

Another area of concern is that of children. Many imprisoned children appear to be street children, displaced by the war. The detention of street children is known as *kasha,* meaning mass arrest based on public order priorities. Reportedly, children are arrested without proper warrants and usually remain in detention for lengthy periods, lacking access to interpreters or legal counselling. The problem of street children and their arbitrary detention is a serious one that will require investment in education and social service, as well as a number of measures to upgrade the Sudanese juvenile justice system. At present, there are still serious incompatibilities between domestic legislation, policies, procedures, the quality of institutional facilities and international standards, such as:

- Children under 18 are at the same risk as adults of being arrested and detained.
- Children are often detained pre-trial with adults.
- There is no legislative statement governing the right to legal representation after conviction.
- Children may be sentenced to lengthy prison sentences for certain crimes.
- Children may be sentenced to a maximum of 10 lashes.

While there is a criminalization of vagrant children, staff of penitentiary and correction institutions are generally not qualified to handle juveniles. Although the new Child Law of 2004 reflects a commitment to international standards, lack of resources and/or political will may hamper actual implementation.

The prison system in southern Sudan is in an equally dire state. There are some 55 prisons, but many are not operational, or only partially functioning. Conditions are dire and inconsistent with international human rights standards. Prisoners lack food, health services, water, and electricity. Often they are let out on day release to search for food to survive. Only a few prisons keep a record of their prisoners, causing confusion and unnecessarily lengthy pre-trial detention problems.

In addition to constructing new facilities and rehabilitating current premises, reform of the prison system should revolve around clear definitions of deterrence; prison reform and rehabilitation; treatment based on minimum standards and the protection of human rights; and, execution of orders based solely on judicial decrees. The prison service is well aware of its shortcomings, and it is keen to provide an accountable, humanitarian, and reform-based system. However, this will require considerable support for plans to recruit and train staff, create and rehabilitate facilities, and provide a prison service that meets the needs of southern Sudan.

There are presently only about 800 prison officers and other ranks in South Sudan's five regions, and the withdrawal of prison officers from the government controlled areas during the Interim Period will create an additional void. As with the police service, many of the wardens are former military officers, and, due to their background, they conduct duties as soldiers rather than in a manner consistent with international police standards. None of the wardens has received any training.

Police Profile

In addition to the regular police and the Sudan People's Armed Forces, the Government maintains an external security force, an internal security force, a militia known as the Popular Defense Forces (PDF), and a number of police forces, including the Public Order Police (POP), whose mission includes enforcing proper social behavior, including restrictions on alcohol and "immodest dress." In addition to the group of regular police forces, there is the Popular Police Force, which is made up of nominees from neighborhood popular committees for surveillance and services, and which acts with police powers for political and social ends.

Under the CPA, major responsibilities to promote the welfare of the people of Sudan and protect human rights rest with the police force. The police force is also expected to absorb a large number of demobilized individuals, who have no previous training in policing. It is also likely that crime and violence will increase in the immediate period after the CPA, resulting from population movements and disputes over property and land.

These challenges should be viewed against the realities of post-peace-agreement Sudan. The war and military culture have contributed to the erosion of the fundamental objective of the civil police force to protect the citizens of Sudan. Military and security have been the principal agents of "law and order," often at the cost of basic human rights. It will, therefore, be essential to promote an understanding of the police as service providers of the society and communities.

An alteration of attitudes must focus on the police as an integral part of a wider justice system and civil society in general. Mechanisms like the Joint Military Commission (JMC) in the Nuba Mountains and the Verification and Monitoring Team (VMT) could play an important role in providing a reasonably secure environment, and could be used as models for building a police force in the South and improving the existing one in the North. Given the almost endemic violence against women and the difficulties faced to report SGBV, it will be imperative to ensure that training entail a strong gender component and that women be recruited into the police force. Moreover, a special unit should be established to deal with cases of SGBV.

Northern Sudan

In the North, the Sudanese Police Force (SPF) is a traditionally structured police force—paramilitary in formation and with 13 levels of command in the hierarchy, based on military ranks and designations. Out of a total 30,000 law-enforcement force, approximately 10,000 are officers and 20,000 other ranks. At officer level, education is good, with diplomas from the Rabat National University (Police Academy). However, the training is largely academic and does not necessarily prepare the cadets for a police role. In contrast, lower-rank training is mainly paramilitary, tilted towards outdoor field training at the expense of theoretical and policing skills oriented training. Many of the lower rank recruits (gundi in Arabic) are often illiterate. Generally, training appears to be poor and outdated, and mainly lecture-based, addressing hundreds of students at a time.

Southern Sudan

In the South, it is estimated that there are approximately 5,000 police officers—many lacking adequate training, operational equipment, and transport. Of these, about 4,000 have been transferred from the SPLA to the police, and thus have a military rather than a policing background. The police, therefore, tend to conduct their duties based on their military experience—often in a manner inconsistent with their professional mandate. In addition to training and trust building, it will be essential to provide operational equipment, transport, and communication, since Southern Sudan is largely characterized by inaccessible terrain in the absence of paved roads.

Working under the Secretariat of the Interior, all Southern Sudan enforcement agencies will need skills training and assistance with equipment, rehabilitation, and refurbishment of their infrastructure. In many locations, there are no buildings left in serviceable condition, and thus there is an immediate need for communication, transport, and buildings that will allow them to function at even the most basic level of service delivery. Initially, law enforcement agencies have proposed that they initially share such facilities, until they can establish separate premises. This approach is a reasonable, economic, and pragmatic shared solution to their immediate problems.

There are proposals to develop the experience of senior police officers through courses in management, study tours, and residential training in Uganda. A unified training centre (UTC) is being planned to provide basic and officer cadet training for all Southern Sudan enforcement agencies, thereby ensuring a cost-effective solution to an immediate and substantial training demand common to all agencies. Training of trainers is a priority to allow large-scale training to commence both at the UTC, and by deploying 40 trained trainers in each agency across the 10 states of Southern Sudan.

In order to develop a viable relationship with statutory structures, and to enable communities to enjoy protection and access to justice within the conventional structure, it will be important to strengthen community policing. In this regard, the entire police force in Southern Sudan, from inspector-general to village (Boma) police, will need training to ensure that the community-based policing model is well understood and to develop appropriate southern policing practices.

Another area of importance, particularly in the South, is the need to strengthen the capacity of law-enforcement to carry out its duties for the protection of wildlife from poachers and the population from attacks by wild animals. Southern Sudan has six National Parks, six game reserves, and a number of areas on the Nile and on lakes, which are important for fisheries. All these areas contain sustainable natural resources with enormous potential for development.

There is currently no fire brigade or facility to tackle any emergency typically handled by such agencies elsewhere. It will, therefore, be necessary to start with fire coverage at Rumbek's earth airstrip. At the moment, flights (bringing in aid and international workers, land at already busy airstrips, where refuelling of aircraft takes place by hand pumping aviation fuel from barrels without fire cover. There are often several aircraft in close proximity, many people loading and unloading goods, vehicles driving around the aircrafts, and passengers, officials, and spectators wandering around. As air traffic increases, and the strip is extended to take larger aircraft, the risks will increase proportionally; it is an urgent priority to provide fire cover at this location. There is a pressing need for an effective fire brigade to be trained, equipped, and deployed throughout Southern Sudan.

Government forces have been responsible for extrajudicial killings and disappearances. Government security forces regularly tortured, beat, harassed, arbitrarily arrested and detained, and detained *incommunicado* opponents or suspected opponents of the Government with impunity. Security forces beat refugees, raped women, and reportedly harassed and detained persons on the basis of their religion. Authorities do not ensure due process, and the military forces summarily tried and punished citizens.

MINTIE DAS

Bibliography

Central Intelligence Agency. "Country Report." 2005. www.cia.gov/cia/publications/factbook.

Library of Congress. "Country Reports." 1991. www.lcweb2.loc.gov/rfd/cs.

Swedish Embassy. "Sudan Police." (Paper presented at the Government of Sudan Power sharing Meeting Paper) May 2004, Navesha, Kenya.

United States Department of Justice. "Background Note." www.travel.state.gove/travel, 2005.

SURINAME

Background Material

Suriname is a small country, with a population of approximately 440,000 inhabitants. In 1667, it became a colony of The Netherlands, when the English wanted to exchange Suriname for New Amsterdam. The Dutch colonists turned Suriname into a plantation economy, based on slave labor. After slave labor was made illegal in 1863, large-scale immigration took place from contract laborers from British-India (mostly Hindustani) and Dutch-Indonesia (mostly Javanese). This explains why the composition of the population is ethnically diverse. The largest ethnical groups are the Creoles (32%), Hindustani (35%), Javanese (16%), and Marrons (descendants from African slaves) (10%). There are also Chinese (2%) and the original inhabitants, the Indians (2%). The Dutch and Lebanese are few in number, but economically important. According to the Surinameese police, a group of about 40,000 Brazilians live in Suriname, most of whom are not legally resident. Hence, Suriname is far from culturally homogenous, and ethnic tensions are detrimental for politics and leadership.

Suriname has been a prominent exporter of bauxite since 1920. A Royal Statute in 1954 made Suriname part of the Royal Kingdom of The Netherlands, and it acquired autonomy with the exception of defense and foreign matters. On 25 November 1975, Suriname became an independent republic. It was agreed that The Netherlands would pay the country 3.5 billion guilders in support finance. Moreover, the independence of Suriname caused a large exodus to The Netherlands: around 50,000 Surinameese people had migrated there before or in 1975. Another 25,000 to 30,000 people emigrated to The Netherlands in 1979 and 1980 (Buddingh, 1999).

Contextual Features

One of the most traumatic events in the history of Suriname is the military coup that took place on February 25, 1980, and which was led by Desi Bouterse. This reached its climax in December 1982, when 15 opponents of the repressive military regime were executed. After a pact with the old democratic parties, a new Constitution was adopted in 1987. The "*Front voor Democratie en Ontwikkeling*" won the open elections on November 25, 1987, but the Shankar-government was brought down on Christmas Eve in 1990, after a telephone coup by Bouterse. The police service has been severely traumatized by the militarization period; in particular, the killing of Police Inspector Gooding in 1990 left a scar.

The elections were again won on May 24, 1991 by the Front, and Ronald Venetiaan became President. This government ensured that the military were submitted to civilian authority. The relationship with The Netherlands cooled down severely after Wijdenbosch, who allegedly had close links with Desi Bouterse, won the elections in 1996 (Buddingh, 1999). Venetiaan was, however, re-appointed as President after the latest elections in 2000, and the relationship with The Netherlands was fully restored. This government intended to introduce various reforms in the public administration and focused on the fight against corruption, adjudication of human rights offenses, anti-drugs trafficking, encouraging administrative transparency, optimalisation of law enforcement, the strengthening of the police apparatus, improvement of prison conditions, crime prevention, and raising the effectiveness of law enforcement interventions.

The Republic of Suriname now has a mature parliamentary-presidential system, with executive power for the President, who is both head of government and head of state. The National Assembly elects him or her with a two-thirds majority. Moreover, the country has a mixed system of majority and (10) districts (*www.NRC.nl*; Dossier Surinamee 2004). There is also a State Council (*Staatsraad*) which can initiate legislative proposals and refer back laws that have already been approved by the Assembly.

Suriname has 16 different Ministries. The supreme judicial authority of Suriname is the Court of Justice (*Hof van Justitie*). The independent judges and the procurator-general are appointed for life by the government after recommendation of the Court itself.

Suriname has significant problems with crime and security. First, international organized crime groups exploit the country as transfer or final destination for their drug-trafficking activities. Second, crime is becoming more serious in general, and there are some persistent problems with fire-arms crime and juvenile crime. At the same time, however, the statistics do not show a rise in crime (Dienst Criminele Informatie Voorziening, Korps Politie Surinamee). The total number of registered criminal offenses was 23,885 in 2003, which resembles statistics of the previous years. Most of these offenses are committed in the most densely populated part of Suriname, namely its capital Paramaribo. Compared with other Caribbean countries, Suriname has five murders per 100,000 inhabitants; Guyana averages 22; Trinidad 19; and Jamaica 37. Nevertheless, the relative number of murders is much higher than the Netherlands (less than one

per 100,000). In the United States, the number went down from 10 to 4 per 100,000 inhabitants during the last decade. It can thus be concluded that the Caribbean countries have a rather high murder ratio (*www.iaca.net*, International Association of Crime Analysts 2004).

The Surinameese population perceives crime and insecurity to be on the rise: respondents in Paramaribo claimed that 50% had been the victim of a criminal offense during the previous 12 months. Thirty-six percent of all the people who had notified the police were dissatisfied about the way in which the police handled their complaint (NIKOS onderzoek 1998). The Marrons are allegedly over-represented in the population of criminal offenders (Schalkwijk 2004).

The concern about the penetration of international organized crime, in particular drug trafficking (mainly cocaine from Colombia and Brazil) and money laundering, is considerable, as it corrupts the civil apparatus and undermines the rule of law. The majority of the Suriname drug barons are of Hindustani origin (Kwattakartel). In addition, the legal service (Justitiële Dienst) claims that criminals from Eastern Europe, Turkey, Lebanon, and China have found a safe investment climate for illegally obtained profits. Organized crime is evident in various activities, including: establishing casinos, exchange bureaus (cambios), estate property, tourist attractions, security services, illegal exploitation of mines and forests, and the sponsoring of political parties.

Police Profile

Background

In the protocol of Bonaire, which was signed in 1991 between The Netherlands and Suriname, a joint commitment was agreed to consolidate and strengthen the rule of law in Suriname. This was translated in a financial support program that had been approved by the Dutch Minister of Development. The objectives of the program included raising the level of trust of the population in police and justice organizations, and also included the immediate approval of the working conditions, the material means, the means of support, and the management of the elements of the police organization. The program was evaluated at the end of 1994, and many improvements were noted. However, the report was less positive about the steps that had been made towards further democratization and the establishment of a Rule of Law. One of the factors, the report said, was that many qualified people had left the country.

In June 2001, Suriname and The Netherlands defined safety and the rule of law as one of the sub-sectors where support from the Netherlands had to be mobilized. Moreover, several regional Dutch police forces (e.g., Rotterdam-Rijnmond, Amsterdam-Amstelland, Utrecht en Haaglanden) have been active in the support of the Surinameese police (*Korps Politie Surinamee*: KPS). The KPS has been severely damaged by the military dictatorship in Suriname (Berenschot 1992: 52; see also COWOS report, Lo Fo Sang).

Prior to the military coup in 1973, the police force had already been transformed from an armed police force (*Korps Gewapende Politie*) to a civilian force (*Korps Politie Surinamee [KPS]*). Anchored in a police charter (Karsowidjojo 1971), its structure and regulatory status are incomparable with other police forces in the Caribbean, because it was completely based on the Dutch model due to Suriname's colonial history. Until 1984, all Surinameese police officers had to undergo training at the Police Academy of the Netherlands (*Nederlandse Politie Academie*) in Apeldoorn (The Netherlands). The new force was submitted to the authority of the Chief Constable (*korpschef*), who is accountable to the Minister of Police and Justice, and who is responsible for the management of the police. The Chief Constable was appointed or dismissed by the Governor, and subsequently, after the independence in 1975, by the President (Kwie 1995). The state autonomy has had little or no effect on the functioning of the police.

Demographics

The KPS Annual Report of 2002 reveals that in there were 1,134 executive police officials and another 313 employees in administrative-technical functions. This means that there is one police officer per 428 inhabitants (2.3 per 1000 inhabitants), not taking into account the administrative-technical staff. In 2004, the total number of executive police officers went down to about 1,000.

The recruitment and training of police officers are rather difficult processes, as the police organization is suffering from a negative image and because police officers earn low wages. Moreover, there is a natural exit (e.g., police officers reaching the age of retirement), but there are also reports that police officers are recruited by private security firms (the total number of employees in the private security sector in Suriname is 5,000). Eight percent of those in executive police functions are women. Seen from an ethnic perspective, the KPS has historically been dominated by the Creoles. Despite the recruitment of more Hindustani police officers, the most senior position of Chief Constable has been held by a Creole. The ethnic diversity of the force has become a political matter. Interestingly, most senior positions in the legal institutions have been held by Hindustani, which is by some regarded as the consequence of a political conspiracy.

Organizational Description and Functions

The KPS is a national police force that is subdivided in regions, the borders of which coincide with the 10 districts. This local police service resides under the responsibility of the *Hoofdstedelijke Dienst* (city commander) and *Gewestendienst* (commander of the other nine districts).

Every region has one or more jurisdictions with one or more police posts. The regions have a regional commander, the jurisdictions a jurisdictional commander. The executive police officers of KPS have powers that can be used in the whole territory (and waters) of the Republic of Suriname. The current formal organizational structure have been established in a decree by the Minister of Justice and Police (*Besch.nr.1341/1991*).

According to the Police Charter and article 178 of the Constitutional Law, the tasks of the police include maintaining the public order and the internal security, the prevention of infringements thereof and protection of persons and goods, detection of criminal offenses, and supervision of obedience to the law, infringement of which is unlawful. Article 6 of the Police Charter determines that other tasks have been granted to the police service, including: aliens service, transport and guarding of prisoners, serving judicial writs in criminal proceedings, maintenance of the order in legal proceedings and public meetings, fire service in regions where such service is absent, other activities referred to the service in relation to the maintenance of the public order, the rendering of assistance in cases where it can

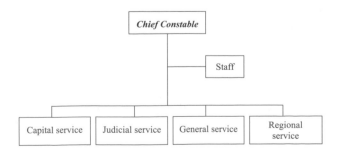

be reasonably expected; and emergency assistance to the needy.

Article 7 of the Police Charter determines that the general authority over the police resides with the Minister of Justice and Police. The general opinion is that the function of Chief Constable is politicized, as he or she is expected to belong to the same political affiliation as the Minister of Justice and the Police. The KPS depends on the influence the Minister, and can exercise influence within the Ministerial Council when it concerns budgets (for whom the Minister of Finance is responsible). The whole Ministerial Council has to agree on significant police expenditures.

When it concerns democratic control on the police, it should be noted that the National Assembly has a committee for Justice and Police, but it is said that the KPS is not structurally accountable to this committee and that the committee does not actively initiate any inquiries into the functioning of KPS. Nor has the Committee any influence on the establishment of a policy plan for the Surinamese police.

According to Article 8 of the Police Charter, the Procurator General is responsible for the judicial police service. He has the authority to issue instructions for the prevention and investigation of criminal offenses, and he monitors the professionalism of the police. He is also authorized to collect information and to make proposals to the police which he considers useful for maintaining the quality if the police service. The division of labor between the public prosecutors is based on region and on forms of crime. There is little or no contact between the prosecutors and the regional police commanders. Public prosecutors are generally dissatisfied with the quality of police work and the criminal records.

Article 9 of the Police Charter determines that the district commander is in charge of the public order in his district. This mandate should not undermine the authority of the Procurator General. District commanders are neither involved in the establishment of district policy plans, nor is there any structural contact between the regional and the district commander. The Chief Constable thus has extensive informal powers in the districts, based on Article 9-2 of the Police Charter.

A new Policy Plan was recently adopted for 2002-2005 (*Beleidsadviesgroep* K.P.S. 2002:1.3), which included the contribution to a safe, democratic society; integrity; and openness. As for the internal functioning of the KPS, it was recommended that

there should be geographical de-concentration, a general tasking, a spreading of responsibilities by general management, a flat organization, policy participation, an open work attitude, professionalism, and effectiveness. The core tasks of the police that have been mentioned in the Policy Plan 2002–2005 include service support, preventive care, and repressive police care. More than two thirds of all police officers in Suriname work in the first category of service support. One can only assume that this is the case, as there is no registration of working hours and the way in which professional time is used. The lack of a proper internal administration is subject of criticism in the Strategic Business Plan 1999–2003 (Rampersad 1999:40–42). Moreover, the KPS has a structural lack of employees, and there is a structural deficit of the most elementary means and instruments.

The KPS is still involved in a reform process but does not clearly model itself on any blueprint. The military coup of 1980 has left significant scars within the organization, and this undermines mutual trust, integrity, and professionalism. Moreover, as the KPS is directed by one Ministry, and as the Chief Constable belongs to the same political party as the Minister, the system of checks and balances is still rather deficient. This shortcoming cannot be compensated for by the National Assembly, and there is no police complaints board or ombudsman who could respond to citizens' concerns. The large private security sector remains unaccountable to public authorities, which could undermine the state of Suriname.

MONICA DEN BOER AND MARTIN SITALSING

Bibliography

Beleidsadviesgroep KPS. *Beleidsplan 2002–2005 KPS.* Paramaribo, KPS, 2002.
Berenschot. *Rapport Onderzoek: Wetgeving rechtspleging, Politie en Gevangeniswezen in de Republiek Surinamee.* Utrecht, Berenschot B.V., 1992.
Buddingh', H. *Geschiedenis van Surinamee.* Utrecht, Uitgeverij Het Spectrum B.V., 1999.
Karsowidjojo, F.R. *Gouvernementsblad van Surinamee nr.70, Landsverordening van 17 april 1971, houdende regelen omtrent de politie in Surinamee; Politiehandvest.* Paramaribo, 1971.
Lie A Kwie, C.J., Esajas, H.G. & Loor, A. (red.) "100 jaar Surinaamse politie". In: *Suralco Magazine* juni 1995, Para District, Suralco Public Relations Department, 1995.
NIKOS onderzoek. *Eindrapport Sociologisch onderzoek te Pontbuiten en Sophia's Lust 1997.* Paramaribo, NIKOS, 1998.
Rampersad, H. *K.P.S. 2000, Strategisch Businessplan 1999-2003.* Korps Politie Surinamee, Paramaribo, 1999.
Schalkwijk, M. *Anti-Criminaliteitsplan Surinamee, Een leefbare omgeving voor alle Surinameers.* Paramaribo, DOE, 2004.

SWAZILAND

Background Material

Swaziland is a country of approximately 1.2 million people made up of 97% Africans and three percent Europeans. The official languages of the country are siSwati and English. The major religious denominations are Zionist (a blend of African traditional religion and Christianity), 40%; Roman Catholic, 20%; Muslim, 10%; and others, 30%. The GDP per capita was estimated at $4,900 in 2003. The major economic activity is subsistence farming and livestock grazing, involving about 80% of the population. Mining has declined in importance, with only coal and quarry mines remaining active. The country exports some manufactured soft drinks, coal, sugar, and textiles mainly to South Africa, and receives worker remittances from its citizens working in South Africa. Foreign aid is about one third of the amount of external debts owed by the country, and about one third of the population is HIV positive.

Swaziland is blessed with fertile soil and rich mineral resources, and the hilly landscape is picturesque. The people speak the Bantu language of *Nguni*. Swaziland is ruled by a Prime Minister and by a constitutional dual monarchy led by the King (*Ngwenyama* or lion) and the Queen Mother (*Ndlovukazi* or cow-elephant), hence the police force is known as the Royal Swazi Police with the lion as the mascot on the coat of arms. According to historians, the Swazi were part of the Nguni expansion from east-central Africa. Their leader, Dlamini, led them across the Limpopo River, and they settled in the southern part Tsongaland (present-day Mozambique) in the fifteenth century. Their fellow *Nguni* speakers, the Xhosa and the Zulu, continued their migration further south and later came into conflict with the Swazi during the Zulu northward expansion under Shaka.

The Swazi pride themselves with being a warlike people who defended their territory and conquered weaker groups or negotiated with them diplomatically to expand their kingdom. This militaristic era in the history of the kingdom laid the foundation for militaristic policing because the army was essentially the only police force, often camped in hostile territory for the purpose of acquiring surplus cattle, captives, and extending suzerainty. Much of the centralization of military authority in the Kingdom was accomplished by King Mswathi in the nineteenth century. Prior to his reign, local chiefs took it upon themselves to mobilize an army of volunteers to defend the kingdom; but Mswati was influenced by his mother, Thandile laZwide, to adopt the *Ndwandwe* or age-regiment military institution nationwide, requiring the conscription of Swazi youth into a military service that emphasized loyalty to the King rather than to local war lords. This centralized authority placed the Swazi in a good maneuvering position between the British and the Boers, resulting in the 1879 accord in which the Swazi assisted British colonization conquests in return for a pledge by the British to defend Swazi autonomy forever. The British also exploited its rich natural resources through royal mining concessions that eventually dispossessed the peasantry of their land and turned many into wage laborers.

In September 1968, Swaziland became politically independent under King Sobhuza II, who ruled the kingdom for more than 60 years and up to the early 1980s. Independence came after the 1964 Constitution that retained all mineral rights in the colonial government under the British Queen's commissioner. Soon afterwards, King Sobhuza formed the Imbokodvo National Movement (INM) to mobilize the peasantry and ensure that that the popularity of the monarchy was maximized under the constitutional dispensation. INM joined with the European settler political party, United Swaziland Association (USA) to write the new Constitution of 1965 without the involvement of any opposition party members from the Ngwane National Liberation Council (NNLC). That new Constitution vested all mineral rights in the King, and the INM gradually split from its alliance with the United States as the power and influence of the King became solidified. Soon, King Sobhuza was installed as the constitutional monarch in 1967, and the next year, he heralded the kingdom into independence with the monarchy's power being strengthened, unlike the diminished powers of most African monarchs following colonialism.

Contextual Features

The legal system in Swaziland is based on traditional Swazi law for most cases. This involves chiefs and elders in restorative justice in which the guilty are often fined as punishment. Even the King can be fined when he contravenes traditional law, as was once the case when the King took an under-aged bride, and the women on the country rallied to demand that he pay a fine of a cow as punishment. The traditional law allows the King to seize any beautiful girl he likes during the annual reed dance, and the girl would become one of his wives. The middle-class mother of one of the girls seized by the king to become his twelfth wife alleged that the conduct of the King was criminal because her daughter was still a minor under her parental authority. However, the King is immune from prosecution under statutory law, and so the only recourse available to the aggrieved parent was to complain that the King breached traditional law, which required the representatives of the palace to discuss the wedding with parents of the potential bride and reach an agreement before the wedding. That was how the father of the King married his 99 wives during his own reign, but the current young king appears to be abducting the girls with his apparent absolute powers. The fact that women are able to sanction the King under traditional law suggests that the King is not completely an absolute monarch, despite his immunity under statutory law. Yet, it is rare to find any family or group of women opposing the King's choice of a wife because such a choice was seen as a way to redistribute the royal wealth and influence to the region of the wife's origin by, for example, building a multi-million dollar palace for the new wife. This also suggests that some conflicts between statutory law and native law would be resolved in favor of the latter, which is frequently proclaimed by royal decree with wide support from the local chiefs and loyalist politicians.

While the traditional legal system remains popular among the majority of the citizens who remain peasant farmers, increasingly there are statutory offenses that require adjudication in courts under the Roman-Dutch system of law also found in South Africa, where it is characterized by a blending of Common Law and Civil Law principles. This formally places the statutory law under the Civil Law tradition that operates in continental Europe, but the close links between the country and Britain mean that aspects of the common law would also be found in Swaziland as in South Africa. In reality, even those African countries that follow the British Common Law tradition are more like Civil Law countries in practice because they rely on statutes and do not have jury systems, although they still cite precedents in court as is done in Britain and America. However, even in Britain and America, the use of the jury system only takes place in a minority of cases (about 7%), and many Civil Law jurisdictions now allow precedent to be used as part of the interpretation of statutory law. Thus, Swaziland reflects the reality that the differences between Civil Law and Common Law traditions are increasingly blurred. The major uniqueness of the country is that, like most African countries, native law operates side by side with statutory law and, unlike many African countries, Swaziland has not accepted the jurisdiction of the International Court of Justice.

Crimes reported to the police declined by eight percent from 55,881 to 51,303 cases between 2002 and 2003. Among these were drunken drivers, who made up 1,131 of the cases, and jaywalkers, who made up 2,182 of the cases in 2003. The crimes that increased during the same year include armed robbery, which increased by 0.01%; rape increased by 1.99%; car hijacking by 0.14%; and housebreaking and theft by 1.13%. In 2002, there were 3,245 prisoners in Swaziland, giving an imprisonment rate of approximately 324 per 100,000 or 10 times the rate in Nigeria. The proportion of prisoners who were female was 4.6%; juveniles made up 1.8%, and foreigners made up 1.2%. There are 12 correctional establishments in the country, with a combined capacity of 3,130. The Swaziland Correctional Services are under the administration of the Ministry of Justice and Correctional Development. The proportion of prisoners who were pre-trial detainees or remand prisoners was approximately 50% of the prison population.

To understand why the prison population is made up of such a high proportion of pre-trial detainees, it is important to look at the history of public order in the country briefly. The newly independent nation was beset by crises that ranged from attempts to control labor unionism to attempts to intimidate opposition politicians with heavy reliance on the police. During the 1967 elections, for instance, the opposition NNLC won 20% of the popular vote but failed to win any seat, due to the way the constituencies were drawn. In the 1972 election, the opposition finally won four out of the 24 seats in the Parliament. The government reacted by deporting one of the victorious opposition politicians to South Africa as an "undesirable" person. He appealed to the High Court, which set aside his deportation order, but when he came to be sworn in, INM members boycotted that session of Parliament, and so he could not be sworn in without a quorum. The Parliament passed an amendment to the Immigration Act, making the Prime Minister the final arbiter in disputed citizenship cases, a power that resided with the High Court previously. The opposition went to the Swaziland Court of Appeal, which declared the Immigration Amendment Act unconstitutional. Two weeks later, the King suspended the British-imposed Constitution that he disliked greatly, dismissed Parliament, and announced that he would rule only by decree. The first decree he issued was to authorize a 60-day detention without trial, and the first people to be detained under the decree were the elected opposition politicians.

During the decade of rule by royal decree, 1973–1983, social tensions remained, even after the King managed to co-opt some of the opposition leaders. Strikes by workers were often broken by force with the help of the Royal Swazi Police. For instance, in 1975, railroad workers attempted to march to the royal residence but were beaten back by the police who tear-gassed them. The same tactic was used in combination with mass arrests and detention without trial when striking sugar workers set cane fields on fire in 1978. The highlights of popular protests were the 1977 teacher boycotts and student uprisings. This was after the government failed to intimidate the 3,000-strong teachers' union from demanding improved wages and conditions. The government tried to woo the teachers over with a salaries commission in 1975 that recommended a pay increase in 1976, but the anger of teachers boiled over due to the small amount of increase recommended and the government's reluctance to address other recommended reforms. The government promptly banned the Teachers' Association, but the students declared their solidarity with the teachers and burned cars, stoned ministers, and destroyed property on a large scale. The Royal Police were given the order to shoot, and two students were wounded before the teachers and students gradually returned to classes.

It was not only in political activism that the state of emergency declared by the King failed to produce the public order he had promised. During the decade, ritual murders of the very young or the very old for "powerful medicine" called *muti* and prepared by *tinyanga* ritual medicine practitioners reached an epidemic proportion. Wage earners and school dropouts, as well as businessmen, were the ones who were suspected of needing such powerful medicine to improve their luck in love, business, and dangerous employment, or to cure acute illnesses. Since the reintroduction of non-partisan parliamentary elections, Swazi newspapers link increases in such ritual killings with times of political contest and allege that politicians are probably involved in hiring the professional killers. Worries about such killings became more urgent because of the high rate of HIV-AIDS infection in the country and the belief by some that *muti* could be used to render people invulnerable to infection or even to cure them. In 2003, David Simelane was arrested, and he confessed that over three years, he had personally kidnapped and killed 60 women and children in order to "harvest" their organs for a fee, but it was not yet clear who hired him. The government punished such ritual murderers with capital punishment, but few people had ever been convicted of the crime.

Police Profile

Background

The government of Swaziland's web page (*http://www.gov.sz/home.asp?pid = 2858*) dates the origin of the Royal Swazi Police to the reign of King Sobhuza I, who used the traditional regiments to police the kingdom, a practice that was continued by his son, King Mswati I. A formal police force emerged in 1895, but it was withdrawn soon afterwards, due to the Anglo-Boer war. In 1902, Britain established control over the kingdom and sent a force of 150 South African constabulary made up of Europeans and Africans with a new headquarters in Mbabanen and reporting to the South African constabulary headquarters in Caroline, Transval. In 1907, the British High Commissioner for South Africa, Lord Selborn, signed the Swaziland Administration Proclamation with provisions for the Swaziland Police Force made up mainly of Zulu officers. A 1957 Police Act defined the powers and functions of the police force, and in 1968, after independence, the King changed the name of the force to the Royal Swaziland Police and assigned to himself the role of the Commander in Chief of the police force.

Demographics

The personnel of the police force has been documented as follows: one Police Commissioner, one Deputy Commissioner, Five Assistant Commissioners, 15 Senior Superintendents, 34 Superintendents, 52 Assistant Superintendents, 115 Inspectors, 416 Sub-Inspectors/Sergeants, 10 Cadets, 2,130 Constables, for a total of 2,774 officers. In addition, there are 223 civilian employees working with the police to make for a grand total of 2,997 in the year 2003. In 2002, 25 officers retired, seven resigned, four were dismissed, and 46 died. The high death rate probably reflects the problem of the AIDS epidemic.

The police emphasize "visibility policing" as a strategy to deter crime through strong police presence throughout the country. However, such a strategy would need more officers on the beat than they could possibly afford, and so they have relied on partnership with people in the community to augment the numerical strengths of the officers while pressing the government to approve more hiring for the police force. Nevertheless, the police-population ratio for Swaziland is comparable to that of many industrialized countries at 1:433, compared to Germany with 1:315, Ireland with 1:326, and New Zealand with 1:337. The ratio also compares well with that of its neighbor, Botswana, with 1:270, whereas Lesotho has a double ratio at 1:897, and Tanzania has a triple ratio of 1:1,289. The lower technological development of Swaziland and its neighboring countries is obviously why they seek to increase the number of police officers, given that more industrialized countries with relatively smaller landmass, better communication equipments, and better systems of transportation could rely on their current ratios more effectively than a less-industrialized country. It might also be the case that the development of advanced democratic values in governance could lead to less reliance on police numbers as citizens become more consenting to legitimate authority, whereas a police state with a lot of police officers could still fail to maintain order as the people struggle for social justice.

Organizational Description and Functions

There is an Operational Support Service Unit, formerly known as the Police Mobile Unit, that is equipped "with competence and professional skills" to respond to public disorder, bomb disposal, VIP protection, and vehicle or aircraft rescue operations. Apart from the King as Commander in Chief of the Police Force, the ranks of Swaziland police officers are similar to those of the British: Commissioner of Police, Deputy Commissioner of Police, Assistant Commissioner of Police - Directors, Senior Superintendent, Superintendent, Assistant Superintendent, Inspectors, Sergeants, and Constables. The rank of sub-Inspectors was abolished, and officers on that rank would continue until retirement, promotion, or death.

There are four regional police divisions in the country with different numbers of police posts as follows:

HHOHHO: Mbabane, Piggs Peak, Lobamba, Mbabane City Post, Bulembu, Horo, Buhleni, Ngwenya, Bulembu Matsamo;

MANZINI: Manzini, Malkerns, Bhunya Sidvokodvo, Mankayane, Matsapha, Mliba, Mafutseni Mhlambanyatsi Mahlangatsha Lushikishini Matsapha Airport Lundzi Sandlane;

LUBOMBO: Siteki Tshaneni Lomahasha Lubuli Simunye Siphofaneni Big Bend Mpaka Tikhuba Shewula Sithobelweni St. Phillips Mlawula Ngomane Mhlumeni Mananga, Lomahasha ;

SHISELWENI: Nhlangano, Hlathikulu, Hluthi, Lavumisa Ka-Phunga, Gege, Mahlalini, Dumako, Debedebe Sigwe, Matimatima, Mahamba, Nsalitje, Lavumisa, Sicunusa, Gege.

Training

The country has a police college for the training of officers. The first police training school was established by the British colonial administration in 1927 in Mbabane. A more modern facility for training was established in Matsapha in 1965 with an administrative block, lecture blocks, dormitories, a kitchen, and quarters for college staff. The college ran basic courses for recruits, offered refresher courses, advanced courses and promotion courses. In 1989, a Command Wing was added to the college with a dining hall, a computer room, a library, conference room, and offices for the administrators. The Command Wing offers courses to senior officers in their role as managers and supervisors of the rank and file. There are a Command Course Part I for line managers, a Command Course Part II for middle managers, and a Command Course Part III for senior managers. In addition, occasional seminars and workshops are offered.

Complaints and Discipline

Swaziland has been under some kind of emergency rule since the early 1970s, when the previous King suspended the Constitution and assumed rule by royal decree. Recently, his successor, King Mswati III, told a conference of church leaders on "The disadvantages of multi-party democracy" that "democracy is not good for us because God gave us our own way of doing things." In response, one of the clerics present agreed with the King by observing that when people are given the option of choosing their leaders they always choose evil. This is the familiar idea of the divine right of Kings that the Enlightenment challenged in Europe successfully to bring forth representative democracy. Citizens of Swaziland protest against royal authoritarianism and clamor for democratic rule in the country with increasing international support. On the other hand, about 70 chiefs in former apartheid homelands along the Swazi boarder with South Africa demand that the border should be shifted to exclude them from a democratic South Africa and include them with about one million South African citizens within the kingdom of Swaziland.

The Coalition of Concerned Civil Organizations (under the leadership of the Swaziland Chamber of Commerce and Industry and involving the Federation of Swaziland Employers, the Association of Swaziland Business Community, the Swaziland Law Society, the Swaziland National Association of Teachers and religious groups like the Swaziland Council of Churches) issued a manifesto in 2003 calling for greater democratization because repressive government policies were not only hurting the lives of ordinary citizens, they were also damaging business interests. According to the manifesto that was published in the unusual source of the *Swazi Observer* that is owned by the royal family, 'The coalition believes that governance is a collective responsibility of society, and hence civic society has both a right and a moral duty to ensure that the country is assisted to resolve its problems." The demands of this bourgeois grouping that calls itself the civil society is simply that the "government immediately recognize the independence of the judiciary, and desist from making threats against judicial officers."

This was a reference to the fact that the Court of Appeal had ruled against a royal decree that gave unlimited powers to the police and gave the King the power to appoint all judges. The Prime Minister decided to ignore the ruling, and six judges of the Court of Appeal resigned in protest. The demand for the rule of law is a major demand of the militant Swaziland Federation of Trade Unions and the Swaziland Federation of Labour. In 2002, Amnesty International published a report on the Kingdom of Swaziland in which it stated that during the year:

The rights to freedom of association, peaceful assembly and expression remained restricted. Government actions threatened the independence of the judiciary and undermined court rulings. There were reports of torture and ill-treatment. Government opponents were subjected to arbitrary detention and politically motivated trial proceedings. The king commuted four death sentences; no executions were carried out. Violations of women's rights remained systematic.

The specific threats to the rule of law reported by Amnesty International included the fact that on June 22, 2002, the King proclaimed Decree No. 2

to further restrict fundamental human rights in the kingdom. The decree reversed a judgment by the Court of Appeal that said that it was unlawful to ban newspapers. The decree also reversed a ruling by the Court of Appeal saying that it was illegal for the police to remove rural community members from their homes at gunpoint just because they were protesting against the imposition of a chief on their community. The decree also stated that no court had the jurisdiction to hear cases related to these matters and gave the king the sole authority to appoint judges.

One month later, due to massive internal and international criticism, the King repealed the decree and replaced it with Decree No. 3 on July 24. This new decree stated that any action taken by ministers prior to the decree was valid and that they were not open to challenge in any court. The new decree also reinstated a 1993 decree, called the Non-Bailable Offences Order No. 14, which states that people accused of certain crimes must be denied bail by the courts. The Court of Appeal had earlier ruled that such a law was "draconian" and that it violated the presumption of innocence under the law. About 1,000 people were in detention under that law, and some of them had been awaiting trial for more than two years.

Police were empowered to disrupt public meetings that they considered to be political, given that opposition political parties were banned when the Constitution was suspended in 1973. In 2002, several journalists were harassed for doing their job, a number of newspapers were banned, and the government threatened to reintroduce a Media Council Bill to further restrict freedom of expression. On October 19, 2002, police officers broke up a news conference organized by the Swaziland Democratic Alliance to protest against the indefinite detention of an opposition leader, Mario Masuku, and to complain against the continuing lack of democratic accountability in the country. Armed police officers blocked the entrance to the news conference and claimed that it was an illegal news conference. When the organizers relocated to another venue, the police called for more heavily armed paramilitary police to help them push the organizers and journalists out of the building. A reporter for *The Times*, Thulasizwe Mkhabela, was allegedly assaulted by a senior police officer, and he was forced to make a formal complaint against the officer at the police station under the officer's command. In August, the High Court ruled that the banning of the *Guardian* newspaper was unlawful, but the government prevented the re-opening of the paper by immediately filing an appeal.

Political trials also continued in the kingdom. On October 4, 2002, Mario Masuku, President of the People's United Democratic Movement, was re-arrested. He had earlier been detained under the charge of sedition in November 2000. The condition for his bail was that he should report to the Police Commissioner every day to seek permission to address a public gathering or to the High Court for permission to travel abroad. He stopped going after some time to seek such permissions that he did not need on a daily basis, and so he was re-arrested and detained to face trial for the initial charge of sedition. His health suffered from the harsh conditions in prison, and he needed treatment for diabetes and hypertension.

On September 24, 2002, six trade unionists who had participated in a strike action were charged with contempt of court but the Magistrates Court acquitted them, citing "contradictory" evidence presented by police witnesses during the trial. The government immediately appealed the acquittal.

There have also been reports of torture and death in custody, forcing the Prime Minister to order a rare public inquiry in 2002. One of the cases involved two youths who were arrested as they slept; they were said to be suspected of being involved in some criminal activity. Hours later, they were dead, and the police claimed that they committed suicide by swallowing poison. Public protest over their death forced the government to grant an inquest under the Chief Magistrate. Although the inquiry was held in an open court, the police obstructed the investigation of the independent forensic pathologists representing the bereaved families and refused to provide reports of the toxicology tests to the magistrate. This made it impossible for the inquest court to deliver a verdict by the end of 2002.

The demand for democratic governance by the masses of the people has attracted some support from the international community. The Congress of South African Trade Unions would often support strikes by transport workers in Swaziland by ensuring that the boarder services in South Africa were also closed. The US secretary of State, Colin Powell, was reported as telling the Swazi authorities that if the country did not improve governance, it would not continue to benefit from the African Growth and Opportunity Act (AGOA). Observers say that the palace appears to be yielding to international pressure in order to be seen as relaxing the repression of political dissent. Since the banning of opposition to the King in the 1970s, there had been no Constitution, but the palace appointed one of the princes to write a new Constitution that was not released, after seven years in the making. The palace still believed that the opposition leaders were in the minority and that the king remained popular with the majority of the people. Consequently, the opposition called for a Constitutional Convention to draft the new Constitution and a referendum on the rule of the King, but the palace was not yielding to such demands. It was reported that no such referendum was planned and that, although the new Constitution was authored by the palace, ordinary Swazi citizens were said to have had input into it and that such a Constitution would serve as a referendum on the political system in the country.

The next parliamentary elections were scheduled for October 2004, but no political parties were allowed. Instead, candidates seeking votes from the 55 national constituencies, known as Tinkhundla, would present their individual promises to create jobs, build new clinics, construct roads, and the like. The new Parliament might have more legitimacy, given the ruling by the Court of Appeal that the King should not bypass Parliament to decree laws, but the fact that the Prime Minister rejected the ruling of the court is indicative of more struggles to come. It can be expected that as African countries deepen their unity through the African Union and through programs like the New Partnership for African Development, the African people as a whole will seek new paths to development that would emphasize the role of the people and eliminate oppressive rule.

BIKO AGOZINO

Bibliography

Amnesty International. *Swaziland*, AI, 2002.

Bonner, P.L. "Classes, the Mode of production and the State in Pre-Colonial Swaziland," in A. Atmore and S. Marks, eds, *Economy and Society in Pre-Industrial South Africa*, London, Longman, 1980.

Booth, A.R. *Swaziland: Tradition and Change in a Southern African Kingdom*, Boulder, Co, Westview Press, 1983.

Feminist Daily News Wire. "Swaziland: Mother Challenges King for Abducting her Daughter," Feminist Majority Foundation, October 28, 2002.

Gastrow, P. "The SADC Region, A Common Market for Criminals?" in *African Security Review*, 10 (4) 1–3, 2001.

Gastrow, P. *Organised Crime in the SADC Region, Police Perceptions*, Institute for Security Studies, Monograph 60, 2001.

Hall, J. "Swaziland: Reform is in the Air" in *New African*, February, Issue 415, 2003.

Heinecken, L. "Living in Terror: The Looming Security Threat to Southern Africa," *African Security Review*, 10(4) 1–9, 2001.

Institute for Security Studies. "The Southern African Police Chiefs Co-Operation Organization," *Monograph Building Security in Southern Africa*, 43: 1–6, 1999.

IRINNews.Org. "Swaziland: Strikers Beaten by Police," UN Office for the Coordination of Humanitarian Affairs, 2003.

Klipin, Judith, and KirstenHarrison *The Future for Policing and Crime Prevention in SADC*, Montreal, International Crime Prevention Centre, February, 2003.

Kuper, H. *An African Aristocracy: Rank Among the Swazi.* London, Oxford University Press, 1980.

Marks, M. "Organising the Blues: Police Labour Relations in Southern Africa," African Security Review 11(2) 1–8, 2002.

Matsebula, J.S.M. *A History of Swaziland*, London, Longman, 1972.

Moamu, L and D.M. *Crime in Southern Africa: Towards the Year 2000, Summary Proceeding of a Regional Training Workshop*, Gaborone, Botswana, 1996.

The Economist "Celebrating 30 Oppressive Years" Vol. 367, Isssue 8324, 2003.

United Nations. *Criminology in Africa*, Rome, United Nations Interregional Crime and Justice Research Institute, Publication, No. 47, 1993.

Van der Spuy, E. "Regionalism in Policing: From Lessons in Europe to Developments in Southern Africa," African Security review 6(6) 1–9, 1997.

World Almanac and Book of Facts. *Swaziland*, Academic Search Premier, EBSCO HOST, 2004.

SWEDEN

Background Material

Sweden is a relatively large country in terms of area. In Europe, only France, Spain, Russia, and Ukraine are larger. It extends 1,600 km from north to south. In the north, winters are long, cold, and snowbound. In the south, winters are considerably milder, and summers are longer.

Sweden has a small population, about nine million (8.9 million in 2003). Some 85% of its inhabitants live in the southern half of Sweden, in three major urban centers in particular: the capital city of Stockholm on the east coast (1.7 million including suburbs), Gothenburg on the west coast (800,000) and Malmö in the south (500,000).

Ethnic minorities are the Sami, Tornedal Finns, and Roma. The official language is Swedish, and the primary religion is Christianity (Evangelical Lutheran).

The average taxable earned income per capita is US$23,900 (2004 est.).

The capital of Sweden is Stockholm.

Sweden has a constitutional monarchy, while also operating as a parliamentary democracy.

Contextual Features

Sweden is a parliamentary democracy. The Swedish parliament, the *Riksdag*, is a unicameral assembly with 349 seats. General elections are held every fourth year, and the minimum voting age is 18. Seats are distributed proportionately between those parties that poll at least 4% of the national vote or at least 12% in any one constituency.

The Swedish monarchy is purely constitutional. In all essentials, the duties of the monarch as Head of State are of a representative, ceremonial nature.

The Government rules Sweden and is the driving force in the process by which laws are changed. The Government is accountable to the Swedish *Riksdag* and must have its support to be able to implement policies. In the business of governing Sweden, the Government is assisted by the Government Offices, consisting of a number of Ministries and a substantial number of Government authorities.

In Sweden, there are about 300 central committees, agencies, authorities, and state-owned companies accountable to the Government and organized under the various ministries. The National Police Board is an example of such an authority. Its task is to implement the decisions adopted by the *Riksdag* and the Government.

Government authorities are autonomous. This means that they act on their own responsibility, albeit in accordance with the guidelines set out by the Government in the budget bill and the appropriation directions. Cabinet Ministers also maintain regular contact with the respective head of authority. However, neither the Government nor an individual Cabinet Minister may exert influence on an authority in an individual decision. That is "ministerial control" and is prohibited under Swedish law.

Sweden is divided into 21 counties, each with a county administrative board. The County Administrative Board is the government body in the county with a County Governor appointed by the Government as its head. The County Administrative Board is responsible, *inter alia*, for some social welfare issues and regional community planning.

Sweden also has 18 county councils, as well as the regions Västra Götaland and Skåne and the municipality of Gotland, which carry out the same tasks as the county councils. Each county council consists of an elected assembly, the County Council Assembly, which functions as a regional parliament. County Council Assemblies take decisions on matters that are too extensive or costly for the municipalities included in the county council to be responsible for, such as health and medical care, and public transport.

Sweden is divided into 290 municipalities. Each municipality has an elected assembly, the Municipal Council, which takes decisions on the municipality's own affairs: compulsory school and upper secondary school, pre-school activities, care of the elderly, roads, water and sewage, and energy. Municipal elections take place at the same time as parliamentary elections, every four years. The Municipal Council in its turn appoints the municipal government, which is the Municipal Executive Board.

To secure a functioning judicial system, it is important that the courts be independent and autonomous in relation to Parliament, the Government, and other public agencies. This is guaranteed, *inter alia*, through the provisions of Article 6 of the Convention for the Protection of Human Rights and Fundamental Freedoms and through provisions in the Swedish Instrument of Government on the independence of the courts and the employment conditions of judges. The Instrument of Government is one of the four fundamental laws that make up the Swedish Constitution.

The provisions on public access to official information in the Instrument of Government and the Freedom of the Press Act serve to guarantee that the public have an insight into the administration of justice. This principle, which is fundamental regarding statutory rights, means that the public have access to negotiations and other meetings of the court, and that they have the right to access documents pertaining to a specific case or matter. To protect individuals and public interests in certain cases, this right of access may be restricted by secrecy regulations. Such restrictions must be clearly set out in an act of law.

A central point of departure for assessing crime development in Sweden is the issue of statistics on crimes reported to the police. Since all crimes are not reported to the police, this source does not give an exhaustive picture of the actual level of crime. On the other hand, it provides a good basis for assessing changes in the level of crime and in the composition of crime. Crimes reported to the police in Sweden increased steadily from about 200,000 reported crimes in 1950 to some 1,200,000 crimes reported in 1990. After 1990, the level of crime evened out, and it has since remained around the same level. Comparisons with data from polls on the general public's exposure to crime indicate that developments in crimes reported to the police reflect the actual crime trend relatively well.

However, since 1990, there have been certain changes in the composition of crime. Reported crimes of violence, including assault, sexual crimes, and unlawful threat, have continued to increase since 1990. During this period, offenses involving the infliction of damage have also increased. On the other hand, the large category of crimes of unlawful appropriation, including the very common vehicle-related offenses, has decreased since 1990. Crimes of unlawful appropriation currently constitute about 55% of all reported crimes. Fraud is another category of crime that has decreased in the statistics during the corresponding period, although in this case it is less certain that there has been an actual decrease. A difference in Sweden compared with many other western countries is that the proportion of petty crimes is relatively high, for example bicycle thefts alone make up six percent of all reported crimes.

The Prosecutor-General is the head of the public prosecution service and supervises the work of the public prosecution authorities. He is the only prosecutor who is entitled to institute proceedings in the Supreme Court.

The public prosecution service in its entirety employs a staff of approximately 1,000, of whom about 700 are prosecutors. Sweden is divided into six prosecutor districts, each with one regional public prosecution authority. In turn, each district is divided into local public prosecution offices. There are 41 local offices, which are led by chief district prosecutors.

A special prosecution agency, the Swedish National Economic Crimes Bureau, deals with economic crime.

Sweden has two parallel types of courts: general courts, which deal with criminal and civil cases; and general administrative courts, which deal with cases relating to public administration. The hierarchy of general courts of jurisdiction comprises three levels: District Courts, Courts of Appeal, and the Supreme Court. The administrative courts are also a three-tier system: County Administrative Courts, Administrative Courts of Appeal, and the Supreme Administrative Court. In addition, a number of special courts and tribunals have been established to hear specific types of cases and matters.

The National Courts Administration is a special central agency for the courts and is accountable to the Government. It is in charge of certain central and joint issues pertaining to the courts.

Every district court, court of appeal, county administrative court, and administrative court of appeal has, besides the legally qualified judges, also a number of lay judges. The latter are appointed by the Municipal and County Councils in each respective court district. They are chosen for a term of four years. The lay judges take part in the adjudication of both specific concrete cases and matters of law, and each has the right to one vote.

The district court is the court of first instance. There are 68 district courts across the country. They vary in size, the largest having several hundred employees and the smallest about ten.

The next level is the court of appeal. There are six courts of appeal. In general, a party is free to lodge an appeal against a district court decision with the court of appeal, although leave to appeal is required in minor cases.

The Supreme Court is the highest instance. The primary responsibility of the Supreme Court is to try cases that may be of interest from the point of view of legislative development (i.e., to create precedents). Before a case is taken up for examination, leave to appeal is normally required. A condition for the granting of leave is either that it is of importance for the judicial process that the case be examined, or that a grave procedural error occurred in the course of the proceedings at the court of first instance. If leave to appeal is granted, the case is normally heard by five justices.

The county administrative court is the court of first instance. There is at least one county administrative court in each county. The administrative courts of appeal are courts of second instance. There are four administrative courts of appeal. For most categories of case, leave to appeal is required for a complete trial by an administrative court of appeal. The Supreme Administrative Court is the court of final instance. It consists of at least 17 justices. As in the case of the Supreme Court, the primary task of the Supreme Administrative Court is to create precedents. Leave to appeal is required for most categories of cases. Cases that have been granted leave to appeal are normally heard by five Justices of the Supreme Administrative Court.

The most common sanctions are fines (summary fines, or fines determined on the basis of the defendant's daily income, and day fines). For more serious crimes or in the case of relapses into crime, the sanction prescribed may be imprisonment. Instead of imprisonment, the court may also prescribe a conditional sentence if the convicted person has no previous record; or probation, for example, if the individual has a drug problem and needs supervision. The court can also commit a person to special care. Individuals who are mentally ill can receive forensic psychiatric care, while young offenders may be committed to care by the social welfare services.

The Swedish Prison and Probation Service oversees the National Prison and Probation Administration, with headquarters and five regional offices, 35 local prison and probation services, and the Transport Service. The National Prison and Probation Administration is the central administrative agency for the Swedish Prison and Probation Service. The local prison and probation services include remand prisons, non-institutional care, and prisons.

There are 28 remand prisons in Sweden with a total of some 1,700 places. Remand prisons are intended for those who are detained, apprehended, and arrested, as well as aliens taken into custody, pending the enforcement of an expulsion order. Every day, some 1,700 people are remanded into custody. A special act of law covers the treatment of those held in detention or under arrest. To make their situation easier and to try to limit their isolation during the period of detention, the act contains a number of regulations about curative and social support. As far as possible, detainees should be offered some form of work or occupation during their time in remand.

On average, approximately 4,800 people are held in custody every day. There are 55 prisons throughout the country. They include both open and closed institutions. The closed institutions are more secure and are designed to prevent inmates from escaping. The open institutions are not actually designed to obstruct escapes. Two institutions have especially high security levels. Certain institutions have special resources for the treatment of different categories of convicted persons, for example, drug abusers or sex offenders.

Police Profile

Background

Up to 1965, the police service was largely a municipal matter. In 1965, the police became a national matter and to some extent centralized in order to create a uniform and effective police organization throughout the country. At the same time, the National Police Board was established as a central administrative agency.

A gradual reform of the police system was carried out during the 1980s to improve police efficiency by less-detailed control and greater local self-determination.

During the 1990s, rationalizations were made, resulting in a reduction in the number of police authorities in the kingdom from 117 to the 21 there are today, with areas of responsibility corresponding to the country's division into counties.

During the same period, initiatives were taken to establish a new police organization, a Community Police Service, with officers who are acquainted with the area in which they operate and who work in partnership with the local community. The cornerstones of community policing are visibility in the community and crime prevention. Each community police station is responsible for a specific geographic area within the district, a community police area. Activities are dealt with in a problem-oriented manner, with a focus on the more direct causes of crime and public disturbances.

Community police officers maintain a regular exchange of information with other public agencies in their area, such as schools and social services.

Demographics

The Swedish Police Force has 23,062 employees, of whom 16,292 are police officers, which is equivalent to 1.81 police officers per 1,000 inhabitants. Almost one third of the total number of employees are women (8,000). Among the actual police officers, one fifth (3,159) are women. The majority of the civilian employees are women: 4,849 out of 6,770.

The majority of employees (21,652) work at the local level; 1,410 work at the central level.

The number of employees at each of the 21 police authorities varies. The Stockholm police authority is the largest, with 5,800 employees, approximately 4,500 of whom are police officers. Gotland is the smallest police authority, with 135 employees, approximately 100 of whom are police officers. The average number of employees at Swedish police authorities is about 500, of whom 300 are police officers.

Organizational Description

The Swedish Police Service is organized under the Ministry of Justice. It consists of the National Police Board, the National Laboratory of Forensic Science, and 21 police authorities, each of which is responsible for policing in the county in which it is based.

The police officers that the public comes in contact with in the community are normally stationed at one of Sweden's 21 police authorities. In each county, the police authority is responsible for local police operations, including responses to emergency calls, investigations, and crime prevention measures.

Each police authority is headed by a Chief Commissioner. Chief Commissioners are appointed by the Government and are usually lawyers with special police management training or with basic training in policing in combination with a law degree. However, since 1999, neither a law degree nor police training is an absolute requirement for the position of Chief Commissioner or head of a police authority.

Police authorities have a board responsible for their management, appointed by the Government. Police authorities decide on their own organization, the division of the police district into police areas, and also the distribution of staff at the departments within the authority.

In addition to a Chief Commissioner and Deputy Chief Commissioner who constitute the management at county level, each police authority normally has: a Staff Department, a County Police Department, and a Public Order and Safety Department.

- The Staff Department is responsible for common administrative functions, such as economy, personnel, information, IT, and office service.
- County Police Departments are divided into different sections/divisions. There are usually four divisions: Investigation Squad, Drugs Squad, Economic Crimes Division, and Technical Division.
- The Public Order and Safety Department may be divided into different police areas or smaller community police areas. It is in these community police areas that daily contact with the general public takes place. The community police areas have their own police stations and force. Traffic police and, in relevant cases, border police may be organized under the Public Order and Safety Department. Departments with police dogs are also common. The three largest police authorities in Stockholm, Gothenburg, and Malmö have police horses, in all about 70.

The National Police Board (NPB) is the central administrative and supervisory authority of the police service. Its activities are headed by the National Police Commissioner, who is appointed by the Government.

The main duties of the NPB are to supervise the police and to ensure co-ordination and the rational use of resources in the police service. The NPB may also be instructed by the Government to direct police work aimed at the prevention and detection crimes against the safety of the realm.

The National Security Service (NSS) is part of the National Police Board. As the NSS's areas of responsibility are counter-espionage, anti-terrorist activities, protection of the constitution, and protection of sensitive objects (including royal and diplomatic protection), it is to be expected that its work is often surrounded by a great deal of confidentiality. In recent years, however, there has been a development towards greater openness.

It is the duty of the NSS to detect and take measures against crimes against national security, and in many cases, the NSS also handles the investigations of such crimes. Sometimes, however, regular police units carry out such investigations, while the NSS provides the necessary intelligence.

The National Criminal Investigation Department (NCID) is chiefly active in international police work, the fight against aggravated organized crime, and specialised tasks requiring peak competence. The role of the NCID in the police service is to coordinate, support, and direct police work. The NCID is also increasingly active in various international police partnerships and is an important link between the local, national, and international levels of the police service.

The NCID also has a Police Helicopter Service with six police helicopters

The National Police Academy is the competence development centre for the Swedish police service. Its primary function is to provide basic police training, but the Academy also provides a wide range of advanced training courses.

The National Laboratory of Forensic Science performs laboratory analyses of samples deriving from various types of suspected crimes. The laboratory has expertise in most science disciplines, and it uses advanced technology to find and preserve trace evidence and to establish links between people, places, and objects.

Ranks and hierarchy within the Swedish Police are as follows:

Head of the National Police: National Police Commissioner (*Rikspolischef*);

Head of the National Criminal Investigation Department: Head of National Criminal Investigation Department (*Rikskriminalchef*);

Head of County Police Department: County Police Commissioner (*Länspolismästare*);

Deputy Head of County Police Department: Deputy County Police Commissioner (*Biträdande länspolismästare*);

Head of a Police district within a County Police Department: District Police Commissioner, or Deputy Police Commissioner (*Polismästare*, or *Polisöverintendent*).

Other ranks:

- Chief Superintendent (*Polisintendent*);
- Superintendent/Chief Inspector (*Kommissarie*);
- Inspector/Sergeant (*Inspektör*);
- Constable (*Polisassistent*).

The normal training for Superintendent/Chief Inspector, Inspector/Sergeant, and Constable is the Swedish Police Academy. As for the other titles, they reflect different kinds of chiefs of police, who traditionally have degrees in law, although other educations may be possible nowadays.

Functions

Under the Swedish Police Act (1999) the main duties of the police are to:

- prevent crime and other disturbances of public order or safety;
- maintain public order and safety, prevent disturbances of the same, and take action when such disturbances occur;
- carry out investigations and surveillance in connection with indictable crimes;
- provide the public with protection, information, and other kinds of assistance whenever such assistance is best given by the police; and
- perform the duties as are incumbent on the police pursuant to special regulations.

Police work may be divided into three branches: crime prevention, investigation and institution of legal proceedings, and other duties (for example, in the form of service to the public). The major spheres of operation are public order and safety, crimes of violence, crimes of unlawful appropriation and damage, and administrative duties of the police authority such as issue of passports and permits.

The crime prevention work consists of planned and concrete measures to prevent crime. Examples of crime prevention work are:

- Cooperation with local actors, businesses, municipal authorities;
- Formulation of crime prevention strategies;
- Follow-up of types of crime committed; and
- Contact with the victims of crime.

In the crime prevention area, the police authorities carry out different projects around the country, relating, for example, to drugs, youth crime, and violence against women. In 2003, some 194,700 cases were reported by the police to the public prosecutor. On-the-spot fines were issued in 249,600 occasions in 2003. The average time that elapsed from reporting a crime to the police to its being handed over to the public prosecutor was 37 days that same year.

The number of administrative matters in 2003 was 1.6 million. Investments are currently being made by the police in improved service to the public through telephone and Internet.

In addition to these three branches, the police force carries out international peace support and conflict prevention work, and is part of this country's civil defense.

The police have an obligation under law to support the victims of crime. It may be a question of providing information about rights, facilitating contacts with other support agencies, and making assessments of threat and risk scenarios that may lead to measures for personal protection. Several agencies and organizations collaborate in assisting the victims of crime, including the police.

Training

Police education is offered at three institutions in the country: at The Swedish Police Academy in Solna outside Stockholm, at the University of Umeå, and at Växjö University.

The general requirements to become a policeman are a particular blend of personal characteristics. In addition, the applicant must have reached the age of at least 20 during the year of application, hold a driver's licence for a motor vehicle, be able to swim, and be a Swedish citizen. Regarding the physical prerequisites, the applicant must fulfil certain general health requirements, be in sound mental health, have approved visual acuity, normal color vision, and full hearing.

The educational requirements are mainly that the applicant is qualified for acceptance to higher education; has special qualifications in Swedish, his-tory, and social studies; and has taken the national university aptitude test. An applicant with at least 20 credits from a university college or a university need not present the results of a national university aptitude test. Academic studies, additional languages, and work experience are extra merits.

Police Use of Firearms

A Swedish policeman has the right to exercise self-defense against an ongoing or imminent criminal attack on a person or property, against a person who by violence or threat of violence or in some other way prevents the return of property after having been caught in the very act of stealing it, against anyone unlawfully entering or attempting to enter a room, building, walled or fenced space or vessel, or against anyone refusing to leave a dwelling after being told to do so. In these cases, the police may use their firearms to avert serious violence against the police themselves or against other persons. If immediate action is necessary, a policeman may also use his/her firearms in order to:

- arrest a person suspected on reasonable grounds of serious crimes, for example murder, abduction, spreading poison or a contagious substance, and high treason;
- prevent a prisoner from escaping or to apprehend someone who has escaped if he/she has been detained, arrested, or apprehended for crimes in accordance with the preceding paragraph;
- take into custody a person who, due to serious mental disturbance or possession of a weapon it is feared may be misused or for some other reason, is obviously a danger to other people's lives or health.

Before a policeman uses his firearm, he must take into consideration the risk that an outsider may be injured. Before a shot is fired, the policeman must give clear warning by shouting or firing a warning shot. When a policeman aims at a person, he should attempt merely to temporarily injure that person.

When firearms are used, a written report of the event must be submitted as soon as possible to the National Police Board.

The number of shootings while on duty has long been on average about 30 a year for the police force as a whole. Thus, during their entire professional lives, the majority of Swedish policemen have never fired their weapon, apart from at the shooting range.

All weapons are owned by the police authorities.

Complaints and Discipline

Anyone may file complaints against the police by applying to the Parliamentary Ombudsman. The Parliamentary Ombudsman investigates the matter and takes a decision on the complaint.

When a policeman commits a crime, it is dealt with in the normal legal system. In addition, there are special systems of rules on investigation and penalties.

There are internal investigation departments within the police, which look into suspected crime or other misconduct on the part of a member of police staff. If a crime has been committed, the public prosecutor institutes court proceedings. Before the court decides what punishment the policeman is to be sentenced to, the Staff Disciplinary Board, PAN (*Personalansvarsnämnden vid Rikspolisstyrelsen*) is consulted as to whether the policeman will be dismissed if he is found guilty. If the reply from PAN is "yes," the policeman will be given a lesser punishment than would otherwise have been the case.

If a crime has not been committed but there has been a breach of duty, the matter is usually forwarded to PAN because the police authority wants disciplinary punishment to be imposed on the member of staff. Disciplinary punishments include a warning or salary deduction.

Police Academy basic training includes lectures on human rights, both general lectures on the relevant statutes and lectures focusing on police documents drawn up by the Council of Europe and the United Nations.

During 2003, the police focused on human rights skills enhancement throughout the police organization. Training courses for human rights supervisors will be organized, and they in their turn will hold training courses for local supervisors, who can organize courses for their personnel.

Terrorism

The National Security Service is responsible for leading and carrying out police operations with regard to fighting terrorism.

The National Counter Terrorist Unit is organized under the National Police Board, and it is the country's ultimate response in exceptional situations such as terrorist attacks, the taking of hostages, or when there is a clear risk to human lives.

In Sweden, there are no Swedish organizations that can be considered terrorist organizations in the full sense of the word. However, sometimes terrorist organizations use Swedish territory for planning and implementing acts of terror in other countries.

International Cooperation

The Swedish Police's operative international cooperation is chiefly related to crime investigation and border police operations and primarily takes place through Interpol, Europol, Schengen, and Baltic Sea cooperation, as well as Nordic police and customs cooperation. In addition, there is bilateral cooperation with other countries, particularly in the adjacent area.

Non-operative cooperation principally follows from Sweden's international undertakings, for example in the EU. The police also take part in a considerable number of international specialist networks and working groups, and also carry on international development cooperation. Like its operative cooperation, Nordic non-operative police cooperation is advanced.

Swedish police take part in efforts carried on within the framework of the UN and the Council of Europe to fight organized crime, and drug trafficking, and to strengthen the protection of human rights.

The National Police Board coordinates and carries out development efforts in Central and Eastern Europe, Central America, and Africa, particularly South Africa.

The Police Academy carries on international cooperation within the framework of its operations, above all through the European Police College (CEPOL) and the Association of European Police Colleges (AEPC). In basic training, experts from other countries are not consulted; however, they are consulted in connection with the development of further training.

The National Laboratory of Forensic Science also carries on international cooperation by participating in research and development projects, primarily within the framework of the European Network of Forensic Science Institutes (ENFSI).

The Swedish police are open to exchange appointments in other countries. Among other things, there is an international agreement promoting this through the Government Offices. There are also agreements between the Nordic countries on cooperation and opportunities for exchange appointments.

Police Education, Research, and Publications

Institutions for Higher Education of the Police

The Swedish Police Academy offers further education for police officers. Some Swedish police officers also go abroad for further education, for example to the United States FBI.

Leading Researchers/Authors/Reporters/Columnists

Professor Janne Flyghed
Department of Criminology
Stockholm University
SE-106 91 Stockholm;
Professor Johannes Knutsson
Swedish Police Academy
Research unit
SE-170 82 Solna;
Professor Leif GW Persson
The Swedish National Police Board
PO Box 122 56
SE-102 26 Stockholm
Sweden;
Professor Jerzy Sarnecki
Department of Criminology
Stockholm University
SE-106 91 Stockholm;
Associate professor Marie Torstensson
  Levander
Vaxjo University
Department of Sociology
SE-351 95 Vaxjo;
The National Council for Crime Prevention,
  BRÅ
Box 1386
SE-111 93 Stockholm
www.bra.se.

The National Council for Crime Prevention (*Brottsförebyggande rådet, BRÅ*) is an agency under the Swedish Ministry of Justice. The Council's principal task is to encourage crime prevention measures through evaluation, research, development, and information activities within the field of criminal policy. The Council is also responsible for the official Swedish judicial statistics.

The National Council for Crime Prevention (Brotts-förebyggande rådet, BRÅ) has a responsibility for police research within the system of criminal justice. A restricted part of the Council's total budget of 42 million SEK (2003) is used for police-related research.

Police research at universities can be funded by The Swedish Research Council and by independent foundations.

Leading Police Journals, Magazines, Newsletters

The newspaper *Svensk Polis*, issued by the National Police Board.

- Language: Swedish only.
- Address: Svensk Polis, Box 12256, SE-102 26 Stockholm Internet: *www.polisen.se*

Polistidningen, issued by the Swedish Policemen's Union (the police trade union organisation)

- Language: Swedish only
- Address: Svenska Polisförbundet, Box 5583, SE-114 85 Stockholm Internet: *www.polisfor bundet.se.*

Major Police Publications

- National Police Board. *Police Service, Annual report 2001, Annual report 2002 and Annual report 2003* (in Swedish). Can be ordered from the National Police Board (see address in section References and Further reading below). Also available as a file on *www.polisen.se.*
- Swedish Security Service. *Annual report 2001, Annual report 2002* and *Annual report 2003* (both in Swedish and English). Available as a file on *www.sakerhetspolisen.se* (language on the website is Swedish). Can be ordered from the National Police Board (see address in section References and Further reading below).

Police-Related Websites

- The Swedish Police Service's Official Website: www.polisen.se (contains information in English);
- The National Security Service: *www.sakerhet spolisen.se* (in Swedish only);
- Swedish Policemen's Union: *www.polisfor bun-det.se* (in Swedish only).

The Swedish Article is compiled by the Ministry of Justice. All information, statistics etc are gathered from the Ministry's own information material or from the Government authorities' information services.

ANDREAS EGERYD

SWITZERLAND

Background Material

The history of Switzerland started in 1291, when the three cantons of Uri, Schwyz, and Unterwalden signed a contract *(Bundesbrief)* in which they agreed on helping each other against foreign authorities. Switzerland as we know it today was founded in 1848, when the cantons—the original States—joined together to form the Confederation, to which they ceded part of their sovereignty. Today, Switzerland consists of 26 cantons (20 cantons and 6 half-cantons). The division of three cantons into 6 half-cantons has historical reasons.

The population of Switzerland is 7,258,500; 20.1% are foreigners. There are four languages in Switzerland: German, French, Italian, and Rumansh. Every citizen has the right to communicate with the authorities in one of these languages. Federal law is published in German, French, and Italian.

Everyone in Switzerland is free to choose his religion (Federal Constitution Art. 15); 87% of the Swiss people are Christians; 0.26% are Jews; and 2.2% are members of an Islamic community.

In 1999, the per capita income amounted to SFr. 46,620. The economy consists of: 4.8% farming; 25.9% industry; and 69.3% service.

Contextual Features

According to the Federal Constitution of the Swiss Confederation, the Swiss people are sovereign and ultimately the supreme political authority. The concept includes all Swiss citizens (male and female; minimum age 18) who are eligible to vote.

Switzerland has a federal structure with three different political levels: the Confederation, the cantons, and the communes. The Confederation has authority in all areas in which it is empowered by the Federal Constitution, such as in foreign and security policy, customs and monetary affairs, nationally applicable legislation, and certain other areas. Tasks which do not expressly fall within the domain of the Confederation are matters of the cantons.

The people elect directly the members of the two Chambers of the Federal Assembly (Parliament): the National Council, with 200 members; and the Council of States, with 46 members (two for each canton and one for each half-canton). Together, the National Council and the Council of States form the United Federal Assembly and constitute the Legislative authority.

Swiss citizens can also cast their vote in popular ballots. A vote must be held for all amendments to the Constitution and for membership to some international organizations. A double majority is required for adoption: a majority of the popular vote and a majority of the cantons (cantons in which a majority of voters adopted the proposal).

Amended or new Federal laws, generally binding decisions of the Confederation, and international treaties of indefinite duration are only put to the vote if an optional referendum is sought by at least 50,000 citizens. In such a case, a popular ballot must be held. The referendum is similar to a veto and has the effect of delaying the political process by blocking amendments adopted by Parliament or the Government.

Citizens may also seek a decision on an amendment they want to make to the Constitution (People's Initiative). For such an initiative to take place, the signature of 100,000 voters must be collected within 18 months. People's Initiatives do not originate from Parliament or Government, but from the people. They are the driving force behind direct democracy.

The Swiss Government (Executive) consists of the seven members of the Federal Council, who are elected by the United Federal Assembly for a four-year term. The President of the Confederation is elected for just one year and is regarded as *Primus inter pares*, or first among equals during that term. He chairs the sessions of the Federal Council and undertakes special ceremonial duties.

The United Federal Assembly also elects the Federal Chancellor (chairperson of the Federal Chancellery, the central staff office of the Federal Council) and the judges of the Supreme Court.

In Switzerland, legislative, executive, and judicial powers may not be exercised by the same persons (separation of powers).

Each canton and half-canton has its own constitution, parliament, government, courts, Code of Criminal Procedure, Code of Civil Procedure, and its own State Police. At the cantonal level, people elect—

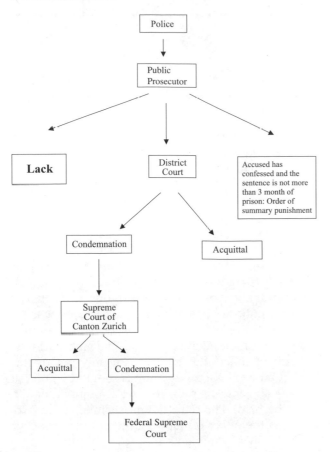

according to the cantonal law—the cantonal parliament (Legislative authority), the cantonal government, and the members of the cantonal courts. There are also votes at the cantonal level, especially concerning cantonal law or the cantonal constitution.

All the cantons are divided into communes, of which there are currently 2,873 in Switzerland. Around one fifth of these communes have their own parliament; in the other four fifths, decisions are taken by a process of direct democracy in the local assembly. In addition to the tasks entrusted to them by the Confederation or the cantons, the communes have their own responsibilities in the areas of education and social affairs, road building, and taxation. The degree of autonomy granted to the communes is determined by the individual cantons and therefore varies considerably.

As Switzerland is divided in 20 cantons and 6 half-cantons, there are 26 different criminal justice systems. Besides these criminal justice systems of the cantons there is also the federal criminal justice system. Criminal law (the Swiss Criminal Code and other federal law comprising sanctions) is, in principle, federal law, but the rules of procedure are based on cantonal law. So every canton has its own Code of Criminal Procedure.

The Code of Criminal Procedure (*Strafprozessordnung; StPO*) of the canton Zurich dates from May 4, 1919.

According to §25 StPO, every investigation concerning a crime (threat of penalty: prison or penitentiary) is led by the public prosecutor, of which there are presently 59 in the canton of Zurich. The police make the inquiries (collect proofs, question suspects) and then hand the file over to the public prosecutor. The public prosecutor questions the suspect and the witnesses, and collects further proof. When the criminal investigation is complete, the public prosecutor hands the file over to the district court or, the case of a serious crime, directly to the Supreme Court of the canton Zurich. If the accused is condemned by the district court, he can appeal to the Supreme Court of the canton Zurich. A verdict of the cantonal Supreme Court can be appealed to the Federal Supreme Court in Lausanne.

Criminal justice system of the canton Zurich:

275,591 criminal offences were registered in Switzerland during 2001. See the table (below) for the most common crimes.

As each canton has its own Code of Criminal and Civil Procedure, each canton has its own structure of courts (Art. 122 und Art. 123 of the Federal Constitution). In the canton Zurich, the district courts and the cantonal Supreme Court have jurisdiction for all cases of criminal or civil nature. If somebody is charged with a serious crime (such as murder), the Supreme Court is the court of first instance. A few cases must be judged by a jury, but only if the accused has not confessed: murder, killing, manslaughter, robbery (when a weapon was used or there was more than one perpetrator). A jury consists of 12 jurors and 3 judges. The jurors and the judges consult together about the question, whether the accused is guilty or not. For a verdict of guilty, it needs 8 votes out of 15.

In all other cases, the court is composed of three judges. Minor cases (the prosecutor seeks a verdict of less than six months of prison) are judged by a

Criminal offence	Number	Trend
Theft	178,667	Rising
Theft of vehicles	64,241	Rising
Fraud	10,447	Rising
Bodily injuries	5,768	Rising
Threat	4,869	Rising
Robbery	2,256	Falling
Killings (incl. murder)	175	Falling

single judge. A verdict of the district court can be appealed to the Supreme Court as the appellate court; a verdict of the Supreme Court can be appealed to the Federal Supreme Court.

Almost every district in the canton Zurich has its district correctional center. These correctional centers are primarily for people in detention while awaiting trial. Men and women are separated. The prisoners are placed in these correctional centers irrespective of the local jurisdiction of the district courts. For example, a person under the jurisdiction of the district court or the prosecutor in the district of Zurich can be placed in the district correctional center of the district of Winterthur. Convicted persons are sent to prisons, which can also be located in another canton. For example, there is only one prison for women in the German-speaking part of Switzerland. The prisoners must work, so they can earn some money for after their release. They can also learn a profession. After the time in prison, each prisoner should be able to live as a normal member of the society.

As the majority of the long-term prisoners are not Swiss citizens, these prisoners are sent back to their native countries after having served their time in prison.

Police Profile

Background

According to the federalistic structure of the Swiss Confederation, every canton has its own cantonal police force (State Police). The bigger cities and communities often have their own City Police. The size of each cantonal police force depends on the size and number of citizens of each canton. The size, the structures, the ranks, the uniforms, the schooling, and the arming are different in each canton.

Each of Switzerland's 26 police forces has its own history. Because it is impossible to describe each Swiss police force, The State Police Zurich will serve as an example. The State Police Zurich was founded on June 19, 1804 and consisted then of 63 police officers. Before that time, there were many different (and very small) city and village police forces, so-called "*Stadt- und Landharschiere.*" In 1832, the State Police Zurich was composed of 118 police officers (population: about 180,000 citizens in the Canton Zurich). In 1897, the first law concerning the State Police Zurich was enacted. In the beginning, the State Police Zurich investigated criminal cases and was responsible for public security. In 1929, the Traffic Police was founded and added as a new department to the State Police Zurich. In 2001, the State Police Zurich took over one part of the Criminal Investigation Department of the City Police Zur-

ich. In 2001, in the Canton Zurich a vote was held about the question, whether there should be only one police force in the Canton Zurich instead of the State Police Zurich, the City Police Zurich, the City Police Winterthur, and 37 other city and communal police forces. The citizens voted against this reorganization of the Zurich police forces. In the canton Zug and the canton Schaffhausen, the different police forces have been combined, so that nowadays these cantons have only one Cantonal Police Force each, and no longer any other city or local police forces.

Demographics

Switzerland has about 14,800 police officers. The State Police Zurich consists of 1,510 male police officers and 90 female police officers (5.6%); 449 employees of the Airport Security Police; and 355 civilian employees. Everyone who wants to join the State Police Zurich as a police officer or as a member of the Airport Security Police must be a Swiss citizen. In some State Police forces in Switzerland, Swiss citizenship is not a prerequisite.

The employees of the Traffic Police (220 police officers) and the employees of the Airport Security Police work in uniform. All the other police officers do their daily work non-uniformed.

In the Canton Zurich, there are the State Police Zurich, the City Police Zurich (1,173 police officers), the City Police *Winterthur* (192 police officers), and 37 communal police forces. That makes a total of about 3,500 police officers in the Canton Zurich.

Organizational Description

As there are 26 different State Police forces in Switzerland, it is impossible to describe the organization of each of these police forces. The organization of the State Police Zurich will be discussed. In 2002, 1,206,858 citizens lived in the Canton Zurich. That means one police officer per 350 citizens. In the whole country, the relation is one police officer per 500 citizens. Although the crime rate is not that high in Switzerland, the actual number of police officers is very low.

In the Canton Zurich, the State Police Zurich is part of the Department of Security and Social Affairs. So the State Police Zurich is controlled by this Department and the Cantonal Council (legislative), because the Cantonal Council has to determine the number of police officers working at the State Police Zurich. If a member of the State Police Zurich or any other police force commits a crime or an offense, this person is prosecuted as any other delinquent. The crime or offense is investigated directly by a public prosecutor or a member of another police force.

Ranks and hierarchy in the State Police Zurich can be compared with military ranks. After one year of schooling, the young police officers are sworn in. The ranks are the following: Private, Private First Class, Corporal, Constable, Sergeant, and Adjutant. Officers with command authority are: Lieutenant, First Lieutenant, Captain, Major, Colonel, and Police Chief. There are 41 officers with command authority at the State Police Zurich; in 2002, two of them were women (both in the rank of First Lieutenant).

Every other year, all members of the State Police Zurich, are evaluated by their superiors. To become a Private First Class, a police officer needs at least three years of service; to become a Corporal, six years of service; and to become a Constable, nine years of service. Until the rank of Adjutant, a qualification "good" is needed to get into a higher rank. For promotion to the higher ranks, the qualification "very good" or "excellent" is required. Each month, every available job is advertised, and every member of the State Police Zurich can apply for these jobs. The best-qualified person will be chosen. Half of the officers made their way through all the ranks; half of the officers are academics (lawyers or scientists) who automatically became officers. The State Police Zurich is divided in six departments:

- Headquarters;
- Criminal Investigation Department;
- Public Security Department;
- Traffic Police Department;
- Airport Police Department;
- District Police Department.

Each of these departments is divided in different units. The Criminal Investigation Department for example is divided into eight different units:

- Organized Crime;
- Business Delinquency (fraud, computer-crime, money-laundering);
- Serious crimes against individuals (murder, rape, protection of children and young people);
- Theft / Burglary;
- Drugs / Arson / Explosion;
- Search / Surveillance;
- Archives / Wanted persons, objects, vehicles;

Forensic Investigation (photographic unit, fingerprints).

The special response unit is part of the Public Security Department. The so-called "grenadiers" are brought to action in dangerous situations, for example if somebody has taken hostages or a dangerous killer has to be arrested. A special bomb squad is part of the Airport Police Department (the so-called "Barbara-Team"; named after Saint Barbara, the saint for all miners and people who work with explosives).

Functions

The State Police Zurich handles primarily criminal law, but some units are administrative. All units of Headquarters do administrative work: the Personnel Department, the Training Department, the Police Psychologist, Logistics (accounting, construction, canteen), EDP Equipment Department and Technical Department (vehicles, radio). The Weapons/Explosives Unit, as part of the Public Security Department, also does administrative work, because this unit has to grant people the permissions for carrying a gun.

Training

If somebody wants to join the State Police Zurich, he/she must have the following qualifications:

- Swiss Citizen;
- At least 20 years of age, but not older than 30;
- Men: fit for military service;
- Completed apprenticeship in any profession;
- Men: height more than 170cm; Women: height more than 160cm;
- Perfect reputation;
- Perfect school reports and references;
- Driver's license.

In other Swiss police forces the prerequisites are similar.

The Federal Office of Police works with its international and cantonal partners as a center for information, coordination, and analysis in matters concerning the internal security of Switzerland. Its activities include preventive measures in the field of national security, and the protection of people and sites considered to be at risk.

The Federal Office of Police also assumes tasks connected with criminal prosecution, particularly in connection with the fight against organized crime. Besides coordinating investigation procedures, this office makes its own investigations into the drug trade, including its financing, and counterfeiting. It also manages the Money Laundering Reporting Office Switzerland.

Since 2002, The Federal Office of Police has carried out its own investigations under the direction of the Attorney General of Switzerland in cases of extremely serious crimes involving organized crime, money laundering and corruption.

The Federal Criminal Police (FCP) makes preliminary investigations and carries out criminal police proceedings in those areas in which the Confederation has jurisdiction. The FCP functions as the judicial police of the Swiss Attorney General. It also coordinates inter-cantonal and international investigations, and ensures a smooth exchange of police information with Interpol. The FCP has the following divisions:

- *Preliminary Investigation Division*: This division is involved in the fight against organized crime, money laundering, and the prosecution of breaches of national security.
- *Money Laundering Investigation Division*: This division investigates suspected money-laundering cases with an international or inter-cantonal connection.
- *Economic Crime Investigation Division*: Under the direction of the Attorney General, this division investigates suspected cases of economic crime as well as the counterfeiting and the financing of drug trafficking.
- *Organized Crime Investigation Division (OC)*: This division is involved in the fight against serious crimes in the complex web of organized crime internationally and on the inter-cantonal level (Article 340bis of the Swiss Criminal Code). Such crimes include particularly the participation in a criminal organization, the support of such an organization under Article 260ter of the Swiss Criminal Code and crimes that are committed as a result of such participation or support. International trade in illegal drugs and trafficking people is of primary interest.
- *Division for investigations into national security/ special affairs*: This division, under the direction of the Attorney General's office, investigates suspected crimes related to national security including crimes against the state, crimes involving explosives and the contravention of legislation controlling war materials, nuclear materials and dual-use-goods, corruption (bribery counter to the interests of the Confederation or by administration officials), and genocide.
- *Coordination Division*: Inter-cantonal and international investigations that are not conducted by the Confederation are coordinated by the FCP in its own center. This center also manages the police liaison offices abroad, which are responsible for gathering and exchanging information concerning the investigation in question. The Coordination Division functions as a center for the exchange of information with Interpol offices outside the country.
- *Special Operations Division*: This division includes the following units: Undercover Investigation Unit, Surveillance Unit, Mobile Equipment Unit, and Fugitive Investigation Unit. These units support both federal teams involved in preliminary and full investigations, as well as cantonal or foreign criminal prosecution authorities. The department for special police units conducts targeted operations and specific investigations against wanted individuals.
- *Operations and Planning Division*: This division supports the operations of the Federal Criminal Police and administers its various information systems.

The investigating officers are responsible for the coordination and management of proceedings involving more than one division. They are the contacts for the Attorney General's office and, through that office, can order the opening of investigations.

Police Public Projects

Traffic control (speed control, alcohol, red lights) is part of the duties of each Swiss police force (except the federal police forces). At the State Police Zurich, traffic controls are implemented by the Traffic Police Department. Police officers of a specialized unit ("Traffic education") go to schools and kindergartens, to teach the children how to act on the sidewalks, how to cross streets correctly, and how to ride a bike correctly in the road traffic.

Crime prevention is also part of the duties of the police forces. The State Police Zurich distributes, for example, leaflets to the citizens ("Protection Against Burglary," "Dangerous Dogs"). There are also campaigns to prevent accidents on the streets and highways (for example placards and leaflets).

Police Use of Firearms

The general legal regulation about the use of firearms can be found in the Swiss Criminal Code (Art. 32: "An action demanded by law or duty ... is no crime or offence"; Art. 33: self-defence). In the canton Zurich, the police use of firearms is regulated in the "Regulation for the State Police Zurich" (*Dienstreglement für das Polizeikorps des Kantons Zürich*). The use of firearms is allowed:

- in self-defense;
- to help another person in danger;

- to stop an escaping person who has committed a crime; and
- to free hostages.

The use of firearms is always the *"ultima ratio."* If there is another possibility to stop or arrest a suspect, the use of firearms is not allowed. Every time a police officer uses a firearm, there will be an investigation, to determine whether the action was necessary and correct.

In 2002, members of the State Police Zurich made use of firearms in two cases. On an average, there have been eight instances per year with the State Police Zurich since 1978.

The ownership of firearms (guns, revolvers, pistols) is regulated in the "Federal Firearm Code" (*Waffengesetz*). Everybody who wants to buy a firearm or carry a firearm in public needs a permit. The following individuals will not be granted this permit:

- individuals under the age of 18;
- individuals put under tutelage;
- individuals who could endanger themselves or others by possessing a firearm;
- individuals with a criminal background.

To get the permit to carry a firearm in public one:

- has to have the qualification to get the allowance to buy a firearm;
- has to prove that he or she needs a firearm to protect himself / herself, other persons, or things against a real danger;
- has to pass an examination (handling of the firearm and knowledge of the law).

The permit to carry a firearm is valid for five years.

Complaints and Discipline

The State Police Zurich—as well as all other Swiss police forces—distinguishes complaints against a police officer from criminal activities committed by a police officer. If a police officer commits a crime or an offence as a private person, he or she will be treated as any other private person.

If a member of the State Police Zurich commits a crime as a police officer, two different proceedings will take place at the same time: the criminal investigation and the disciplinary investigation. If a police officer is accused of misconduct in office there is an agreement between the State Police Zurich and the City Police Zurich: the State Police Zurich investigates against a member of the City Police Zurich and *vice versa*.

If somebody complains about the behavior (not an unlawful action) of a police officer, the complaint will be passed on to the Police Chief of the State Police Zurich. The supervising officer of the police officer in question has to find out all the facts concerning the complaint. If misbehavior can be proven, there are different possibilities (depending on the seriousness of the misbehavior): admonition, rebuke, degradation, suspension, formal abrogation, dismissal without notice.

In the State Police Zurich, the young police officers are taught in psychology (39 lessons), social competence (100 lessons), ethics (15 lessons), and human rights (two lessons). All these subjects are taught by a police psychologist, except the lessons concerning human rights, which are taught by members of the *"Association pour la prévention de la torture"* (Association to prevent torture). This guarantees that all police officers are aware of human rights and that they respect them. They know that all their actions must be based on a legal foundation and must be proportionally (always chose the appropriate method; do not go further than absolutely necessary). If a member of the police should violate human rights — which are protected either by the Federal Constitution, by federal criminal law, or by the European Human Rights Convention—this violation would be investigated as any other breach of law.

The work of the State Police Zurich (and any other police force in Switzerland) is critically observed by different organizations (for example, Amnesty International) and the media. The awareness of this external observation and the strict investigation (criminal or disciplinary) of any incorrect behavior help ensure that every police officer does his / her work according to the law.

Terrorism

In Switzerland, there are no known terrorist organizations. There may be some sympathizers of foreign terrorist groups in Switzerland—even members of such groups—but they didn't appear criminally in Switzerland.

International Cooperation

Switzerland made treaties with all surrounding countries concerning international cooperation with the different police forces. These treaties help the local authorities to cooperate directly (without involving federal authorities), which helps in sharing information without delay.

Switzerland works closely with Germany concerning advanced vocational training in specialized subjects. This means that Swiss police officers can attend classes at the *Bundeskriminalamt* in Wiesbaden, for example concerning subjects like "corruption" or "Environmental Delinquency."

Police Education, Research, and Publications

Every cantonal police force trains its members by itself. But there is some cooperation between the cantons. For example, the young members of the cantonal polices of Glarus and Appenzell are schooled at the State Police Zurich. Cantons also cooperate on the political level.

The Swiss Police Institute in Neuchâtel offers several courses for members of the cantonal police forces concerning various subjects (for example, economic crimes and corruption). Members of the Swiss police forces also have the opportunity to do some courses at the *Bundeskriminalamt* in Wiesbaden/Germany, or other police institutes in Germany.

Each cantonal police force and some local police forces have their magazines, most of them published monthly. At the State Police Zurich it's the *Nachrichtenblatt* (News magazine). In these police magazines, legal questions of interest are discussed, and other matters concerning the police force in question are published.

KARIN KELLER

Bibliography

Federal Constitution of the Swiss Confederation of April 18, 1999.

Schubiger H., and Rinderknecht, R. *Das Kriminalmuseum* (The criminal Museum of Zurich); Verbrechen – Sühne – Polizei im Wandel der Zeit, Zürich, 1980.

Semarek, Arved. *Die Polizeien in Westeuropa* (The Police Forces of Western Europe), Stuttgart, 1989.

Staatskalender des Kantons Zürich 2002/2003.

Statistisches Jahrbuch der Schweiz 2002 (Statistical yearbook of Switzerland 2002).

The Swiss Confederation 2002, a brief guide; Swiss Federal Chancellery, 24th edition, February 2002.

www.admin.ch (website of the Federal Administration; link to the Federal Constitution of the Swiss Confederation, the Swiss Criminal Code etc; website also available in English).

www.fedpol.admin.ch (website of the Federal Office of Police; website also available in English).

www.kapo.zh.ch (website of the State Police Zurich).

www.polizei.ch (contains links to all cantonal police forces and some local police forces).

www.stzh.ch (website of the City Police Zurich).

SYRIA

Background Material

In the aftermath of September 11, 2001, the Syrian government began limited cooperation with U.S. in the global war against terrorism. However, Syria opposed the Iraq war in March, 2003, and bilateral relations with the United States swiftly deteriorated. In December 2003, President Bush signed into law the Syria Accountability and Lebanese Sovereignty Restoration Act of 2003, which provided for the imposition of a series of sanctions against Syria if Syria did not end its support for Palestinian terrorist groups, end its military and security presence in Lebanon, cease its pursuit of weapons of mass destruction, and meet its obligations under United Nations Security Council resolutions regarding the stabilization and reconstruction of Iraq. In May, 2004, the President determined that Syria had not met these conditions and implemented sanctions that prohibit the export to Syria of items on the U.S. Munitions List and Commerce Control List, the export to Syria of U.S. products except for food and medicine, and the taking off from or landing in the United States of Syrian government-owned aircraft. At the same time, the U.S. Department of the Treasury announced its intention to order U.S. financial institutions to sever correspondent accounts with the Commercial Bank of Syria, based on money-laundering concerns, pursuant to Section 311 of the Patriot Act. Acting under the International Emergency Economic Powers Act (IEEPA), the President also authorized the Secretary of the Treasury, in consultation with the Secretary of State, to freeze assets belonging to certain Syrian individuals and government entities.

Syria's economy has been growing, on average, more slowly than its 2.4% annual population growth rate, causing a persistent decline in per capita GDP. Recent legislation allows private banks to operate in Syria, although a private banking sector will take years and further government cooperation to develop. External factors such as the international war on terrorism, the Israeli-Palestinian conflict, and the war between the US-led coalition and Iraq probably will drive real annual GDP growth levels back below their 3.5% spike in 2002. A long-run economic constraint is the pressure on water supplies, caused by rapid population growth, industrial expansion, and increased water pollution.

Syria has a young and rapidly growing population, reaching approximately 17,585,540. Most of the people are of Arab descent and speak Arabic, the country's official language. French and English are understood by many; and Kurdish, Armenian, Aramaic, and Circassian are spoken in some areas. The chief minority is the Kurds; others include the Armenians, Turkomans (Turks), Circassians, and Assyrians. About 75 percent of the country's inhabitants are Sunni Muslims. There are also significant numbers of Shiite Muslims, especially the Alawites, who live in the Jabal al-Nusayriyah; *Druze*, who live in the south, principally in the Jabal al-Duruz; and smaller Muslim sects; all of these groups comprise about 16 percent of Syria's population. The largest Christian groups are the Greek Orthodox, the Armenian Orthodox, and the Syrian Orthodox, together comprising about 10 percent of the population. Before 1992, Syria had a Jewish community of more than 4,000; all but a few hundred left the country after emigration restrictions were lifted in that year.

Contextual Features

Officially, Syria is a republic. In reality, however, it is an authoritarian regime that exhibits only the forms of a democratic system. Although citizens ostensibly vote for the President and members of Parliament, they do not have the right to change their government. The late President Hafiz Al-Asad was confirmed by unopposed referenda five times. His son, Bashar Al-Asad, also was confirmed by an unopposed referendum in July, 2000. The President and his senior aides, particularly those in the military and security services, ultimately make most basic decisions in political and economic life, with a very limited degree of public accountability. Political opposition to the President is not tolerated. Syria has been under a state of emergency since 1963. Syrian governments have justified martial law by the state of war, which continues to exist with Israel, and by continuing threats posed by terrorist groups.

The Asad regime (little has changed since Bashar Al-Asad succeeded his father) has held power longer than any other government since independence; its survival is due partly to a strong desire for stability and the regime's success in giving groups such as religious minorities and peasant farmers a stake in society. The expansion of the government bureaucracy has also created a large class loyal to the regime. The President's continuing strength is due also to the army's continued loyalty and the effectiveness of Syria's large internal security apparatus, both comprised largely of members of Asad's own Alawi sect. The several main branches of the security services operate independently of each other and outside of the legal system. Each continues to be responsible for human rights violations.

All three branches of government are guided by the views of the Ba'ath Party, whose primacy in state institutions is assured by the Constitution. The Ba'ath platform is proclaimed succinctly in the party's slogan: "Unity, freedom, and socialism." The party is both socialist, advocating state ownership of the means of industrial production and the redistribution of agricultural land, and revolutionary, dedicated to carrying a socialist revolution to every part of the Arab world. Founded by Michel 'Aflaq, a Syrian Christian, and Salah al-Din Al-Bitar, a Syrian Sunni, the Ba'ath Party embraces secularism and has attracted supporters of all faiths in many Arab countries, especially Iraq, Jordan, and Lebanon. Since August, 1990, however, the party has tended to de-emphasize socialism and to stress pan-Arab unity.

Six smaller political parties are permitted to exist and, along with the Ba'ath Party, make up the National Progressive Front (NPF), a grouping of parties that represents the sole framework of legal political party participation for citizens. While created ostensibly to give the appearance of a multi-party system, the NPF is dominated by the Ba'ath Party and does not change the essentially one-party character of the political system. Non-Ba'ath Party members of the NPF exist as political parties largely in name only and conform strictly to Ba'ath Party and government policies. There were reports in 2000 that the government was considering legislation to expand the NPF to include new parties and several parties previously banned; these changes have not taken place.

The Ba'ath Party dominates the Parliament, which is known as the People's Council. Elected every four years, the Council has no independent authority. Although parliamentarians may criticize policies and modify draft laws, they cannot initiate laws, and the executive branch retains ultimate control over the legislative process. During 2002, two independent members of Parliament who had advocated political reforms were stripped of their parliamentary immunity and tried and convicted of charges of "attempting to illegally change the constitution." The government has allowed independent non-NPF candidates to run for a limited allotment of seats in the 250-member People's Council. The current allotment of non-NPF deputies is 83, ensuring a permanent absolute majority for the Ba'ath Party-dominated NPF. Elections for the 250 seats in the People's Council last took place in 2003.

There was a surge of interest in political reform after Bashar al-Asad assumed power in 2000. Human rights activists and other civil society advocates, as well as some Parliamentarians, became more outspoken during a period referred to as "Damascus Spring" (July 2000–February 2001). Asad also made a series of appointments of reform-minded advisors to formal and less formal positions, and included a number of similarly oriented individuals in his Cabinet. The arrest and long-term detention of two reformist Parliamentarians, Ma'mun al-Humsy and Riad Seif, in August and September 2001, respectively, and the apparent marginalizing of some of the reformist advisors in the past four years, indicate that the pace of any political reform in Syria is likely to be much slower than the short-lived Damascus Spring promised.

In 1986, petty offenses were tried in magistrate courts, also called peace courts, found in all population centers. Courts of the first instance, located in 24 major urban areas, tried more serious crimes and acted as courts of appeal from the magistrate courts. The courts of appeal heard appeals from both lower courts. Juveniles, defined as those between the ages of seven and 18, were tried in separate juvenile courts.

The Court of Cassation acted as Syria's supreme court. Located in Damascus, it reviewed appeal cases to determine if the lower courts had applied the law correctly. If an error were found, the case was sent back for retrial to the court of original jurisdiction.

The judicial system and constitutional rights to some extent were abrogated and superseded by martial law imposed when the National Revolutionary Command Council invoked Syria's State of Emergency Law on March 8, 1963. By early 1987, Assad had not repealed this condition. The State of Emergency Law provided for the selection by the President of a Martial Law Governor (the Prime Minister) and a Deputy Martial Law Governor (the Minister of the Interior). Article 4 of the State of Emergency Law empowered the Martial Law Governor or his Deputy to issue written orders to impose restrictions on freedom of individuals with respect to meetings, residence, and travel. It sanctioned preventive arrest, censorship, withdrawal of licenses for firearms, evacuation or isolation of areas, and the requisitioning or sequestration of movable property, real estate, and companies, with compensation to be deferred indefinitely.

Article 6 of the State of Emergency Law defined as violations of martial law "offenses against the security of the state and public order, or public authority, and actions which disturb public confidence, or constitute a general danger." More specifically, Article 6 prohibited "actions considered incompatible with the implementation of the socialist order in the state" and opposition to the unification of the Arab states or any of the aims of the revolution. Furthermore, it enjoined communicating with or benefiting from any organization or foreign state for the purpose of undertaking any action, verbal or physical, hostile to the aims of the revolution. Article 6 also proscribed attacks on places of worship, command centers, military establishments, or other government institutions. Finally, hoarding of or profiteering in foodstuffs, and currency regulation violations, fell under martial law.

Because the 1963 martial law directives gave blanket authority to the Martial Law Governor, in 1979 Assad vowed to "apply firmly the sovereignty of law" and to "strengthen the authority of the judiciary." He issued orders limiting the jurisdiction of the State Security Courts and annulled martial law in cases not actually affecting state security. Moreover, the written orders implementing extraordinary measures were subject to review by the Administrative Court of Justice (*Majlis ad Dawlah*), which had ruled in several instances that the Martial Law Governor's powers did not exceed the limits specified in Article 4. In such cases, the administrative court could rule the Martial Law Governor's actions illegal and invalid, and award compensation to the injured party.

Martial law offenses were tried at State Security Courts, whose presiding members were appointed by presidential decree. The verdicts of State Security Courts were not subject to appeal, but were ratified by the President, who could suspend or vacate the verdict, order a retrial, or reduce the penalty. The decision of the President was irreversible.

In 1987, criminal and judicial procedures continued to be modeled after those of France. Following an arrest, the police presented their evidence to a public prosecutor, who conducted his own investigation. If the prosecutor decided to proceed, he referred the case to the appropriate court. Decisions were made by a majority of the three judges of the court, who ruled on questions of law and fact. There was no trial by jury. In the mid-1980s about 90 percent of all criminal court cases resulted in a conviction. Although the legal code provides for due process, it is not always followed. For example, in its Human Rights Report to the United States Congress of 1985, the United States Department of State stated that "under the state of emergency in force since 1963 ... an individual may be held indefinitely without charge or trial, especially in political and security cases." Penalties were severe. They included loss of civil rights, fines, imprisonment for up to life, forced labor, exile, and death by hanging or firing squad. Public hangings in Damascus Square of convicted thieves, murderers, assassins, and spies continued to be a common occurrence in 1987. Amnesty International reported that 15 "officially confirmed executions" took place in 1985.

Observers have asserted that the Syrian penal system was geared toward punishment rather than rehabilitation. In a 1986 report, the United States Department of State provided little detailed information about prison conditions, but reported that those charged with or convicted of criminal offenses have been detained in isolation from those charged with political and security offenses. Health care, food, and access by family to persons held in ordinary prisons were reported to be adequate, while conditions at prisons where political and security prisoners were held were reported to be more severe, with family visits prohibited. In its 1985 human rights report, the Department of State also noted that "there have been numerous credible reports of torture, primarily during arrest and interrogation," and (referring to the 1985 Amnesty International Report) added that "use of torture by the Syrian security forces is routine."

Prison conditions vary but generally are poor and do not meet minimum international standards for health and sanitation. Facilities for political or national security prisoners generally are worse than those for common criminals. The prison in Palmyra, where many political and national security prisoners have been kept, is widely considered to have the worst conditions. At some prisons, authorities allow visitation rights, but in other cases, security officials demand bribes from family members who wish to visit incarcerated relatives. Overcrowding and the denial of sufficient nourishment occur at several prisons. Some former detainees have reported that the Government prohibits reading materials, even the Koran, for political prisoners. The Government does not permit independent monitoring of prison or detention center conditions.

Arbitrary arrest and detention are problems. The Emergency Law, which authorizes the Government to conduct preventive arrests, overrides Penal Code provisions against arbitrary arrest and detention, including the need to obtain warrants. Officials contend that the Emergency Law is applied only in narrowly defined cases. Nonetheless, in cases involving political or national security offenses, arrests generally are carried out in secret, and suspects may be detained *incommunicado* for prolonged periods without charge or trial, and are denied the right to a judicial determination for the pretrial detention. Some of these practices are prohibited by the State of Emergency, but the authorities are not held to these strictures. The Government apparently continues to detain relatives of detainees or of fugitives in order to obtain confessions or the fugitive's surrender.

Defendants in civil and criminal trials have the right to bail hearings and the possible release from detention on their own recognizance. There is no bail option for those accused of national security offenses. Unlike defendants in regular criminal and civil cases, security detainees do not have access to lawyers prior to or during questioning.

Detainees have no legal redress for false arrest. Security forces often do not provide detainees' families with information on their welfare or location while in detention. Consequently, many persons who have disappeared in past years are believed to be in long-term detention without charge or possibly to have died in detention. It appears that the number of such disappearances has declined in recent years, although this circumstance may be due to the Government's success in deterring opposition political activity rather than a loosening of the criteria for detention. Many detainees brought to trial have been held incommunicado for years, and their trials often have been unfair.

Pretrial detention may be lengthy, even in cases not involving political or national security offenses. The criminal justice system is backlogged. Many criminal suspects are held in pretrial detention for months and may have their trials extended for additional months. Lengthy pretrial detention and drawn-out court proceedings are caused by a shortage of available courts and the absence of legal provisions for a speedy trial or plea bargaining.

Although laws provide for freedom from arbitrary interference, the Emergency Law authorizes the security services to enter homes and conduct searches with warrants if security matters, very broadly defined, are involved. The security services selectively monitor telephone conversations and facsimile transmissions. The Government opens mail destined for both citizens and foreign residents. It also prevents the delivery of human rights materials. In August, authorities repealed a five-year ban on entry of Jordanian newspapers. The Government continues its practice of threatening or detaining the relatives of detainees or fugitives in order to obtain confessions or the fugitive's surrender.

Security checkpoints continue to exist, although primarily in military and other restricted areas. There are few police checkpoints on main roads and in populated areas. Generally, the security services set up checkpoints to search for smuggled goods, weapons, narcotics, and subversive literature. The searches take place without warrants. The Government and the Ba'ath Party have monitored and tried to restrict some citizens' visits to foreign embassies and cultural centers.

Police Profile

Background

Since independence, Syria's police and internal security apparatus have undergone repeated reorganization and personnel changes, reflecting the security demands of each succeeding regime. During the relative political stability of the 1970s and 1980s, police and security services were credited with having grown and become professional.

Organizational Description

The largest intelligence-gathering and internal security organization is the National Security Directorate, employing about 25,000 personnel. Other security organizations are under the supervision of the Ministry of Interior. These organizations included a national police force, responsible for routine police duties. It incorporated the 8,000-man Gendarmerie, which had originally been organized by the French Mandate authorities to police rural areas. During the 1960s, the civil police forces were believed to have been used extensively to combat internal security threats to the government, but during the 1970s and 1980s these forces assumed a more conventional civil police role; this change in role coincided with increased professionalization and the parallel development of an effective and pervasive internal security apparatus. Nevertheless, the police continued to receive training in such functions as crowd and riot control.

In 1987, the internal security apparatus consisted of myriad organizations with overlapping missions to gather intelligence concerning internal security and to engage in activities (largely covert) to apprehend and neutralize opponents of the regime. According to Amnesty International, there were several security force networks in Syria. Each had its own branches, detention cells, and interrogation centers, located throughout the country, and each also had its own intelligence service. Each organization was directly responsible to the President and his closest advisers. The organizations operated independently, with no clear boundaries to their areas of jurisdiction and no coordination among them. For example, although the civilian security police dealt with internal security matters, the responsibilities of Military Intelligence, headed by General Ali Duba, were not limited to matters affecting the armed forces, but also included internal security. In the mid-1980s, Western sources reported that the power and pervasiveness of Syria's internal security apparatus inspired fear among the Syrian population.

Complaints and Discipline

Despite the existence of constitutional prohibitions and several Penal Code penalties for abusers, there was credible evidence that security forces continued to use torture. Former prisoners and detainees report that torture methods include electrical shocks; pulling out fingernails; the insertion of objects into the rectum; beatings, sometimes while the victim is suspended from the ceiling; hyperextension of the spine; and the use of a chair that bends backwards to asphyxiate the victim or fracture the spine. Although torture may occur in prisons, torture is most likely while detainees are being held at one of the many detention centers run by the various security services throughout the country, and particularly while the authorities are trying to extract a confession or information about an alleged crime or alleged accomplices.

The government continues to deny the use of torture and claims that it would prosecute anyone believed guilty of using excessive force or physical abuse. Past victims of torture have identified the officials who beat them, up to the level of Brigadier General. If allegations of excessive force or physical abuse are to be made in court, the plaintiff is required to initiate his own civil suit against the alleged abuser.

Courts do not order medical examinations for defendants who claim that they were tortured. There are credible reports of military corruption and mismanagement. There were reports of the corporal punishment of army recruits that led to injury or death.

MINTIE DAS

Bibliography

Central Intelligence Agency. "Country Report." 2005. www.cia.gov/cia/publications/factbook.

Library of Congress. "Country Reports." 1987. www. lcweb2.loc.gov/rfd/cs.
United States Department of Justice. 2005. "Background Note." www.travel.state.gove/travel.

T

TAIWAN, REPUBLIC OF CHINA (ROC)

Background Material

Taiwan encompasses 36,000 square kilometers, with a population of 23 million. The capital is Taipei City. Languages spoken include Mandarin, Taiwanese, and Hakka. Buddhism, Taoism, and Christianity are the main religions.

Taiwan lics on the southeastern part of mainland Asia, in between the Taiwan Straits and mainland China, one of the solitary islands on the western coast of the Pacific Ocean. To the north lies Japan and Okinawa, to the south is the Philippines. Many airlines fly to Taiwan; this convenience makes it the perfect travel destination.

Taiwan and mainland China have always been inseparable, both geographically and historically. They share the same prehistoric heritage and culture, and during the Yuan, Ming, and Qing dynasties, both were part of Chinese territory. However, because of its location at the far end of the Asian continent, Taiwan was easily neglected in the past, and time and time again faced invasion by foreign powers. In chronological order, the Portuguese, Dutch, Spanish, French, and Japanese invaded; the latter occupied Taiwan for fifty years and thus had a large impact on life in Taiwan. Only in 1945, after World War II, was Taiwan returned to China. In 1949, the Nationalists fled from China, and Taipei became the location of their new government.

Mandarin, the national language of both the Republic of China and the People's Republic of China, is based on the Beijing dialect. Formerly referred to as Official Speech, the Beijing dialect has had approximately 1,000 years of history as the common language of politics and commerce in China, particularly in the north. The official language of Taiwan is Mandarin Chinese, but because many Taiwanese are of southern Fijian descent, Min-nan (the Southern Min dialect, or Holo) is also widely spoken. The smaller groups of Hakka people and aborigines have also preserved their own languages. Many elderly people can also speak some Japanese, as they were subjected to Japanese education before Taiwan was returned to the Chinese in 1945 after the Japanese occupation.

The success with which the Republic of China has pursued economic development over the last five decades has led many to refer to Taiwan's developmental experience as an "economic miracle." The ROC has been listed as the fourteenth largest exporter (2001), sixteenth largest importer, and third largest holder of foreign exchange reserves in the world, with over US$140 billion. In general, export-related sectors such as manufacturing and the information technology industry have performed extremely well.

The ROC's GNP topped US$286.8 billion in 2001, with per capita annual GNP reaching US $12,876. That same year, the ROC's GDP amounted to US$281.2 billion. Agriculture's contribution to the economy continued to shrink, accounting for only 1.9% of the GDP. Industry's contribution also dropped, going from 32.4% of GDP in 2000 to 31.1% in 2001. The service sector, on the other hand, continued to increase in importance, accounting for 67.0% of GDP for 2001. With its accession to the World Trade Organization (WTO) in January 2002, Taiwan is poised to make significant contributions to the global trading system and economic prosperity (*www.stat.gov.tw/bs8/ stat/english1.htm*).

Contextual Features

The Republic of China was founded by Dr. Sun Yat-sen in 1912, and is a sovereign state, described in the Constitution as "a democratic republic of the people, by the people, and for the people."

The ROC Constitution is based on Dr. Sun Yat-sen's "three principles of the people: nationalism, democracy, and people's livelihood." The principle of nationalism includes not only equal treatment and sovereign international status for China, but also equality for all Chinese ethnic groups within the nation. The principle of democracy assures every individual the right to political and civil liberties. The principle of people's livelihood states that the powers granted to the government must ultimately serve the welfare of the people by building a strong and prosperous economy and a fair and just society.

There are three distinct levels of government in the ROC. The central level consists of the presidency, the five Yuan (executive, legislative, judicial, examination, and control), and the National Assembly. The provincial/special municipality level in the Taiwan area consists of the Taiwan and Fujian provincial governments and the governments and councils of the special municipalities of Taipei and Kaohsiung. The local level consists of five provincial municipalities and sixteen county governments, along with the governments of their subordinate cities. The constitutional amendment of July 23, 1997, reduced the three levels of government to two. The downsized administrations of Taiwan and Fujian provinces are now under the central government, with councils nominated by the premier and appointed by the president (*www.gio.gov.tw/*).

Shortly after his inauguration as president in the first-ever transfer of political power, Chen Shui-bian proposed the goal of "building of a human rights state." This not only represented the announcement of the goal and guiding principle of the new administration, but also declared the central political values of the country as it entered the new century.

The Ministry of Justice (MOJ) is organized into numerous units, such as the Department of Legal Affairs, Department of Prosecutorial Affairs, Department of Corrections, Department of Judicial Protection, and Department of Government Ethics. There are also a number of committees. Other units include the Secretariat, Department of General Affairs, Department of Personnel, Department of Accounting, Department of Statistics, and Department of Computer Information. Furthermore, to handle specific tasks, ad hoc task commissions have been established.

The functions of each unit of MOJ follow:

Laws and Regulations Committee: Drafting annual legislative plans, conducting research on statutory bills and participating in the drafting, enactment, and revision of statutes by the executive Yuan and agencies thereof.

Department of Legal Affairs: Revising and drafting the civil code and other civil regulations; directing and supervising matters concerning state compensation, commercial arbitration, mediation and conciliation by village or town arbitration commissions; and providing legal services to the agencies of the executive Yuan.

Department of Prosecutorial Affairs: Planning reform of the prosecutorial system, supervising prosecutorial affairs, revising the penal code, drafting other criminal laws and regulations, and supervising the administrative affairs of bar associations.

Department of Corrections: Drafting plans for the correctional system and correctional facilities, directing and supervising correctional institutions, and handling matters related to rehabilitation, security in prisons and detention houses, vocational training of inmates, and rehabilitation and parole.

Department of Judicial Protection: Supervising and directing matters concerning adult probation and post-release projects, researching causes of crime and related subjects, propagating knowledge of the law, and preventing crimes.

Department of Government Ethics: Supervising matters concerning government ethics at

Crime volume, 1991 to 2001

Year	Offenses Known to the Police (cases)	Index 1995yr.=100	Offenses Cleared (cases)	Offenders (persons)	Cleared Rate (%)	Offender Rate Per 100,000 Population
1991	304,141	71	191,492	145,442	62.96	1,486.89
1992	289,052	67	208,298	172,551	72.06	1,399.45
1993	319,179	74	214,409	176,748	67.18	1,530.96
1994	323,459	75	209,177	153,097	64.67	1,537.73
1995	429,233	100	230,513	155,613	53.70	2,023.25
1996	456,117	106	265,471	173,047	58.20	2,132.60
1997	426,425	99	242,392	172,540	56.84	1,971.08
1998	434,513	101	251,638	158,923	57.91	1,989.92
1999	386,241	90	253,299	179,597	65.58	1,754.80
2000	437,390	102	259,645	181,614	59.21	1,976.69
2001	490,736	114	271,128	180,527	55.25	2,196.56

large, enforcing the prevention and elimination of corruption, and maintaining the security of confidential documents and government offices.

Criminal investigation is crucial to national security, social stability, and the people's rights and interests. This heavy burden falls on the shoulders of the MOJ Investigation Bureau. According to Article 2 of the Bureau's organic statute, it is responsible for investigating cases that may endanger national security and interests and for protecting national secrets.

Currently, the investigations are still based on the principle of "ensuring national security, protecting national interests, maintaining social stability, and safeguarding people's rights and interests." There are six priority tasks for fulfillment in accordance with the law: "carry out national status survey," "counteract enemy infiltration," "tighten secret-protection measures," "ferret out corruption and dereliction of duty," "prevent and control heinous crimes," and "improve scientific examination and determination."

Crime levels and comparisons among the various crimes and time periods are summarized in the two following tables. The first table shows that between 1991 and 2001, the crime rate increased a bit, and the cleared rate goes down from time to time. The second table compares crimes in the Taiwan and Fuchien Area between 2001 and 2002, and shows similar patterns and trends.

Police Profile

Background

Taiwan has a centralized police system. The highest authority of the police system of this nation is the National Police Administration (NPA) operating under the Ministry of the Interior, headed by the general commissioner.

In 1912, after the Republic of China was founded, the central government set up the National Police Department (NPD) under the Ministry of the Interior, to supervise national police affairs. Under the NPD, there were the Police Headquarters in the capital, the Provincial Police Administration in each province, and the Police Department in each special municipality, and the Police Bureau in each county. In 1946, the NPD was upgraded as National Police Service (NPS). However, following the relocation of the central government of the ROC to Taiwan in May 1949, the NPS was downsized as National Police Department (NPD). In 1972, the NPD was reorganized as the National Police Administration (NPA).

In 1945, when Japanese occupation ended, the Taiwan Provincial Police Administration (TPPA) was established under the Taiwan Provincial Administration Office. Under the TPPA, there were the City Police Department in the cities of Taipei, Keelung, Kaohsiung, Taichung, Tainan, Hsinchu, Chiayi, Changhwa, and Pingtung, the County Police Department in each county of Hsinchu, Taichung, Tainan, and Kaohsiung, and the Police Station at seaports Hualien, Taitung, and Penghu.

On May 15, 1947, following the establishment of the Taiwan provincial government, the Taiwan Provincial Police Administration (TPPA) took charge of Taiwan provincial police affairs according to the Administrative Regulations of Taiwan provincial government. On July 1, 1999, the Taiwan Provincial Police Administration was taken over by the National Police Administration due to the downsizing of the provincial government. So, at this time, the NPA took charge of the entire police system.

Offenses cleared, cleared rate known to the police in Taiwan and Fuchien area, 2001 and 2002

Item	Offenses Known to the Police (cases)				Offenses Cleared (cases)				Cleared Rate (%)		
	January–August 2002 (cases)	January–August 2001 (cases)	Compared to last period (cases)	Compared to last period (cases)	January–August 2002 (cases)	January–August 2001 (cases)	Compared to last period (cases)	Compared to last period (%)	January–August 2002 (%)	January–August 2001 (%)	Compared to last period
Crime volume	339,510	321,402	18,108	5.63	199,167	182,672	16,495	9.03	58.66	56.84	1.83
Violent crime	9,782	9,258	524	5.66	6,683	5,747	936	16.29	68.32	62.08	6.24
Murder and non-negligence	715	740	−25	−3.38	655	666	−11	−1.65	91.61	90.00	1.61
Kidnapping	56	44	12	27.27	47	41	6	14.63	83.93	93.18	−9.25
Robbery	2,314	2,070	244	11.79	2,003	1,680	323	19.23	86.56	81.16	5.40
Forceful taking	5,143	4,919	224	4.55	2,546	2,001	545	27.24	49.50	40.68	8.83
Serious injury	40	40	0	0.00	38	32	6	18.75	95.00	80.00	15.00
Intimidation	63	21	42	200.00	65	17	48	282.35	103.17	80.95	22.22
Forcible rape	1,451	1,424	27	1.90	1,329	1,310	19	1.45	91.59	91.99	−0.40
Larceny theft and automobile theft	230,532	220,306	10,226	4.64	119,341	104,138	15,203	14.60	51.77	47.27	4.50
Serious theft	421	429	−8	−1.86	248	285	−37	−12.98	58.91	66.43	−7.53
Common theft	68,047	62,208	5,839	9.39	21,987	16,337	5,650	34.58	32.31	26.26	6.05
Automobile theft	34,192	33,125	1,067	3.22	24,264	21,874	2,390	10.93	70.96	66.03	4.93
Motorcycle theft	127,872	124,544	3,328	2.67	72,842	65,642	7,200	10.97	56.96	52.71	4.26

Demographics

Police force numbers total around 67,000 sworn officers, and 5,000 civilians. But the police department, fire department, and coast guard may be amalgamated into a single department due to the reinventing of government in the near future. And if this reorganization movement succeeds, then the population and efficiency of this new security department may increase.

Organizational Description

The National Police Administration has twenty-three staff divisions, and directly commands nine bureaus, eight corps (Peace Preservation Police, and so on), five specialized departments, and Taiwan Police College. The Administration directly commands and supervises the county, city, and municipal police departments all over the nation, and indirectly supervises the Central Police University. At the local level, there are twenty-five county and municipal police departments. Under the departments are 129 police precincts/stations. The next rungs down are comprised of 1,591 police sub-stations, and 18,386 police beats (or *koban* system).

The administrative police, known as the uniformed police as well, are the main force in the police administrations, and include duty officers, and officers tasked with guarding, patrolling, household visits, and raiding; removing administrative perils, and maintaining administrative safety and benefits.

The criminal investigation and prevention police—or the detectives, also known as plainclothes police—mainly enforce the Social Order Maintenance Law; prevent crime; assist public procurators to investigate crime; and execute searches, and detentions and arrests in accordance with laws.

Crime prevention aims at carrying out crime precautions, coordinating relevant agencies to cooperate with each other, and propagating crime prevention strategy, that is, the police and community working together to fight crime.

The main duties of traffic police, one of the specialized police forces, are to keep traffic in order, maintain road safety, prevent traffic accidents, and improve traffic flow. The Traffic Division of the NPA takes charge of planning and supervising traffic safety protection. The Highway Police Bureau under the NPA, the Traffic Police Corps under the Taipei/Kaohsiung Municipal Police Department, and each city/county police station take charge of handling traffic accidents, ticketing drivers against traffic regulations, towing parked vehicles without permits, and directing, guiding and controlling traffic, and propagating for traffic safety.

Foreign affairs police are responsible for protecting foreigners, and dealing with crime involving foreigners. Their goals are to protect foreigners, while simultaneously ensuring national sovereignty, enhancing international cooperation, and promoting international friendship.

The Border Police are responsible for the security of departure and arrival points and guarding borders according to the fifth provision of the Police Law. However, the duties of the Border Police are carried out by the Bureau of Immigration, the Aviation Police Bureau, the Harbor Police Bureaus, the City/County Police Stations along the seacoast, and the Third Peace Preservation Police Corps. The NPA is responsible for mapping out and supervising the approach for security checks. With the establishment of the Coastguard Administration in February 2000, the responsibilities of the Border Police for inspections were partially transferred to the Coastguard Administration.

The Airborne Police are responsible for observing and reporting the traffic, assisting in air surveying, pursuing, and capturing criminals, and providing rescue and back-up in all kinds of disasters (fires, mountain disasters, and perils of the sea, air crashes, and other emergencies). Currently, a total of twelve AS-365 medium helicopters are on duty.

The Specialized Police are responsible for policing state-run railways, highways, aviation, forests, and harbors. Therefore, they are deployed to the Railway Police Bureau, the Highway Police Bureau, the Aviation Police Bureau, the National Park Police Corps, and the Harbor Police Bureau.

Peace Preservation Police are in charge of protecting the central government, establishing contingency plans to guard national security, and assisting local police in keeping social order and tranquility. The first, second, third, fourth, fifth, and sixth Peace Preservation Police Corps are classified as the Peace Preservation Police Forces.

Functions

Police missions in the ROC are outlined in the second provision of the Implemental Regulation of the Police Law. They are divided into two parts. The main missions are by operation of law to maintain public order, maintain social security, and protect the public from all hazards. The subsidiary mission is by operation of law to promote the welfare of the public. The four tasks derived from these missions follow: prevent and investigate crime, maintain traffic order, preserve good customs, and establish good relationships and partnerships with the community.

The duties of the police are specialized according to their particular mission; for instance, detectives are responsible for crime prevention and investigation, foreign affairs police are responsible for foreigners' protection and crime involving foreigners. Police operations can be classified into six patterns: household visits, patrolling, raids, guarding, counter service, and reserves. Therefore, there is a command and control center setup in the NPA, with all municipal police departments/stations and city/county police station/precincts operating twenty-four hours a day to collect updated intelligence about social order and commanding the operation of each police unit.

Police Education, Research, and Publications

The police education system has three different programs in Taiwan: basic education, in-service training, and advanced (or graduate) education (NPA, *www.npa.gov.tw*).

New recruits attend the Central Police University (CPA) and Taiwan Police College for basic education. The CPA is a four-year university; new recruits graduate as police lieutenants. On the other hand, Taiwan Police College provides a two-year junior college–level education for patrol officers.

In-service training is conducted in the above two schools for specialized and promotional training. Also, each police agency executes its own routine basic in-service training. The advanced programs include graduate studies at CPU and some exchange programs overseas.

The Central Police University is the most advanced police school in Taiwan, operating under the Ministry of the Interior, with supervision by the Ministry of Education. The curricula provided by this school must meet university education requirements and the special demands of cadet education as well.

On September 1, 1936, the Central Police College was established with the idea of uniting police education systems all over the nation (while in Mainland China). In 1957, it was expanded to a four-year college (in Taiwan). In 1970, a graduate school offering a master's degree in police administration was established. In 1994, a doctoral program in the Department of Crime Prevention and Corrections was created. In December 1995, the name of this college changed to Central Police University.

Up to the present, the basic education for the middle-rank officer, police lieutenant, at this university includes thirteen departments of four-year undergraduates for the new recruits from senior high school graduates. These departments include Police Administration, Foreign Affairs, Border Police, Administrative Management, and Information Management (these five departments may be integrated as the College of Policing). The departments of Criminal Investigation, Forensic Science, Law, and Crime Prevention and Corrections may be integrated as the College of Criminal Justice. The departments of Public Security, Fire Service, Traffic Service, and Maritime Police may be integrated as the College of Public Safety in the near future. Additionally, there is also a two-year supplementary technical program for officers who graduated from the two-year junior college program at Taiwan Police College. The student population totals about 1,600. The students who graduate from this university can be appointed as police lieutenants and assigned to any county or city in the country.

Advanced education includes twelve graduate-level programs and two doctoral. The twelve are in the same departments described above, except for the Department of Border Police. The Department of Criminal Investigation, and Department of Crime Prevention and Correction have doctoral programs. Any officers can take the entrance examination of the graduate school after serving in the field for at least two or three years. Upon completing graduate school, students obtain more credits for promotion. Any citizen can take this entrance exam, but non-police officers pay their own tuition, and receive a master's degree when completing the program. Further, if these students wish to join the force, they must pass a police qualifying examination.

In-service education programs of the university offer one to four months specialization or promotional classes for the middle- or high-ranking police officers. Specialization classes include supervisor management, criminal investigation, forensic science, personnel management, and so on. Anyone who completes these classes can be appointed to the related new police job. The promotional classes are specific to the lieutenant, chief, and commander ranks. Anyone with seniority as a police sergeant and cannot pass the entrance exam of two-year supplementary technical program of this university can join the four-month lieutenant class exam. Similarly, anyone who wants to be promoted as a chief in a precinct (or branch), or a commander in a county or city, needs to take the entry examination (written and interview) to these classes and complete the courses. Also, an extension education project offers one- to three-month classes for officers who wish to get graduate credits. Furthermore, for services to citizens and society, the extension classes also include fire safety, private security, and neighborhood watch courses for citizens.

Faculty members include ninety-two people with Ph.D. degrees, and sixty-seven people with master's degree. These faculty members account of nearly 90% of the total. Faculty by rank include forty-five professors, sixty-one associate professors, eight assistant professors, thirty-five lecturers, and twenty-five instructors (teachers with police rank). The student population in 2002 totaled 30 doctoral fellows, 244 graduate students, 897 undergraduate students, and 461 technical program students (*www.cpu.edu.tw*, *2002*).

The Taiwan Provincial Police Training Institute, the predecessor of Taiwan Police College, was established on October 27, 1945. On April 1, 1948, it was charged with the responsibility of police basic education for police officers, reorganized, and entitled "Taiwan Provincial Police Academy."

On July 1, 1986, the Taiwan Provincial Police Academy became the Taiwan Police Academy, which was subordinated to the NPA, Ministry of Interior. It was then charged with the responsibility of providing police basic education for police officers throughout the country.

On April 16, 1988, the Act of "the Organizational Regulations of Taiwan Police College" was passed; the president announced its initiative thirteen days later. Therefore, the Taiwan Police College was executed on June 15, 1988.

The education system of this College includes:

1. The basic two-year program, which consists of junior college classes for new rank-and-file officer recruits, and a one-year nondegree program for new rank-and-file officers. Departments include Police Administration, Criminal Investigation, Fire Safety Science, Traffic Management, and Maritime Police.
2. Short-term in-service training designed to promote professional skills and increase working efficiency for rank-and-file officers.
3. One year of advanced supplementary classes at junior college level for regular graduated police officers. These advanced classes are designed for officers with seniority for the purpose of improving their knowledge and skills to fit into their new job as a police sergeant.

Central Police University has an International Academic Exchange Center. The committee of the Center is responsible for promoting exchange programs with the overseas universities or research facilities. As of this writing, the CPU has formal relationships with John Marshall Law School in Chicago, Pittsburgh State University in Kansas, and Sam Houston State University in Texas (all in the United States), University of Ulster of North Ireland, and Beppu University of Japan. The CPU has exchange programs for undergraduate and graduate students, as well as exchange programs for faculty members in the capacity of visiting professors or scholars (*www.cpu.edu.tw, 2002*). In addition, the National Science Council Committee provides funding to support doctoral fellows or faculty members of our University to study overseas. Typically, the CPU will hold an international conference on policing on the average of about once a year. The University also urges faculty members to partake in international symposiums overseas.

Taiwan Police College, on the other hand, also has some international associations, such as Oklahoma City University, Oklahoma State University, and Shenandoah University (Winchester, Virginia) have established some exchange projects for their faculty members (Taiwan Police College 2001).

The NPA of Taiwan believes that the development of international police fellowship has great influence on dealing with transnational crime via mutual support, intelligence and experience exchange, and cooperation. Therefore, the ROC police do their best to strengthen international fellowship, such as frequent visits or exchanging experiences and information with police institutions and organizations from other nations, enthusiastic participation in international police conferences and seminars, as well as striving to host the international conferences or activities in Taiwan (*www.npa.gov.tw, 2002*). Further, at present the NPA also selects officers to go abroad for short-term study. The institutions for this study are the John Marshall Law School in Chicago or the Federal Bureau of Investigation in the United States.

MARK MING-CHWANG CHEN

Websites

Central Police University: *www.cpu.edu.tw*
Taiwan Police College: *www.tpa.edu.tw*
National Police Administration: *www.npa.gov.tw*
Officer.com: *www.officer.com*
ROC statistics: *www.stat.gov.tw/bs8/stat/english1.htm*
Government Information Office, ROC: *www.gio.gov.tw*
Tourism Bureau, ROC: *www.tbroc.gov.tw*

Bibliography

Central Police University. *Introduction to Central Police University*. Taipei: Central Police University, October 2002.

National Police Administration. *The Police of the Republic of China*. Taipei: National Police Administration, 2002.

Swanson, Charles R., Leonard Territo, and Robert W. Taylor. *Police Administration—Structures, Processes, and Behavior*, 4th ed. Upper Saddle River, NJ: Prentice Hall, 1998.

TAJIKISTAN

Background Material

The Republic of Tajikistan (RT) has a population of 7,011,556 (2004 estimate). Tajik is the official language, although Russian is widely used in government and business matters. Uzbek is also spoken. The major religion is the Sunni branch of Islam, practiced by 85% of the population, with 5% of the population adhering to the Shi'a branch of Islam. The nation's ethnic composition follows: Tajik 64.9%, Uzbek 25%, Russian 3.5% (declining because of emigration), and other 6.6%.

The RT has the lowest annual per capita GDP among the fifteen former Soviet republics. Less than 6% of the land area is arable, and cotton is the most important crop. Mineral resources include silver, gold, uranium, and tungsten. Industry consists of the production of aluminum, hydroelectric power, zinc, lead, chemicals and fertilizers, cement, vegetable oil, metal-cutting machine tools, refrigerators and freezers, and food processing. The Civil War, which lasted from 1992 to 1997, severely damaged the already weak economic infrastructure and caused a sharp decline in industrial and agricultural production. This war resulted from the collapse of the Soviet Union, leading to a power struggle between the former communists, who dominated in the southern area of Tajikistan, and the United Tajik Opposition (UTO), a coalition of parties representing the eastern and southeastern regions. In 1992, the UTO took control of the capital city, Dushanbe, and fighting broke out in the south. Emomali Rakhmonov was elected president in October 1992, and two months later government forces took control of central Tajikistan, paving the way to a peace agreement on June 27, 1997 between the UTO and the National Democratic Party. The current government is led by the National Democratic Party, and the opposition is led by the UTO. The power is shared between these parties under conditions set by the peace agreement.

Even though 60% of its people continue to live in poverty, with purchasing power parity at $1,000 per year (2003 estimate), Tajikistan has experienced steady economic growth since 1997, reaching GDP growth of 10% in 2003 and in the first half of 2004. Continued privatization of medium and large state-owned enterprises will further increase productivity. Tajikistan's economic situation, however, remains fragile due to uneven implementation of structural reforms, weak governance, widespread unemployment, and a large external debt.

Contextual Features

Along with Dushanbe, Tajikistan has four administrative divisions: Sughd Oblast, Khatlon Oblast, and Mountainous Badakhshan Autonomous Oblast (MBAO), and Regions of Republican Subordination (RRS). The legal system is based on civil law, without judicial review. The judicial branch is headed by the Supreme Court, with judges appointed by the president. The most common crimes from 1990 to 2002 are summarized in the following table.

Political instability, economic collapse, and social unrest contributed to the sharp increase in criminal activity in the RT following the collapse of the Soviet Union. The sharp decline in criminal activity in 1994, as the table shows, was due in part to the government's consolidation of territorial control in 1993. But theft continues to be the most common crime, which is overall much higher in urban than rural areas. In 1991, 78% of crimes were thefts, and the percentage has never fallen below 55%. Crime rates peaked in 1999, with unemployment and poverty still causing mounting theft and drug crimes. The table demonstrates the alarming growth of drug-related crimes in the RT. Unemployment and poverty have resulted in an increasing number of people involved in drug traf-

Most common crimes

Type of Crime	1990	1991	1992	1993	1994	1995	1997	1998	1999	2000	2001	2002
Theft	2,274	3,398	4,657	4,343	1,111	6,676	5,283	4,555	5,845	5,401	5,127	4,755
Drug crimes	63	69	47	157	139	265	658	979	1,646	1,922	1,922	1,087
Robbery	35	28	432	649	142	530	300	248	268	304	286	287
Swindles	119	111	77	151	84	57	480	748	706	603	236	240
Hooliganism	406	190	150	161	108	532	351	451	435	475	490	653
Premeditated murder	54	45	223	500	207	148	498	491	357	283	233	180
Premeditated severe bodily injury	123	85	108	106	55	260	198	204	181	127	123	108
Rape and violation	34	85	43	50	31	103	71	61	60	65	83	74
Bribery	24	19	6	7	8	39	27	39	50	64	63	31
Total	3,435	4,350	6,011	6,299	2,021	8,813	8,396	8,245	9,952	9,648	8,889	7,817
% Theft crimes	66	78	77	69	55	76	63	55	59	56	58	61
% Drug crimes	2	2	1	2	7	3	8	12	17	20	22	14

Source: State Statistical Agency.

ficking from Afghanistan to Russia and Europe through Tajikistan. Drug-related crimes have grown sharply from 8% in 1997 of total crimes to 22% in 2001. But the downward trend in crime since 1999, two years after the peace settlement, is a sign of restored stability and normalization of law and order in the country. The percentage breakdown of crime in 1999 was as follows: murder 5%, reckless driving causing traffic accident 4%, hooliganism 4%, swindles 7%, robbery 3%, drug-related 17%, theft 59%; and other 1%.

About 90% of criminals are men. Fifty percent of the criminals are over thirty years old (1997), and the number of crimes committed by this age group grew steadily to 56% in 2002. The number of employed persons committing crimes fell from 22% of total crimes in 1997 to 6% in 2002. The number of crimes committed by persons with just primary or secondary education has steadily grown from 64% of total crimes in 1997 to 75% in 2002.

The RT Constitution created three branches of power: legislative, executive, and judicial. The RT president heads the executive branch and the legislature is comprised of the Majlisi Milli (Upper Parliament) and the Majlisi Namoyandagon (Lower Parliament). The Supreme Court heads and monitors the judicial branch, which is also comprised of the Constitutional Court, Supreme Economic Court, Martial Court, Court of the MBAO, and regional, city, and district courts. The martial and economic courts have two instances, and civil courts have three instances. The role of the Constitutional Court, which has seven members, is to settle disputes among government organizations and determine the constitutionality of laws and other legal acts. Creation of emergency courts is forbidden.

Judges serve five-year terms, and are all appointed and dismissed by the president upon nomination by the Council of Justice. Judges are independent, and intervention in their actions is illegal. Nonprofessional judges—public assessors who have the same rights as judges—also take part in court procedures. This practice, which underscores the courts' popular nature, was widespread in the Soviet court system. The constitution gives the president the power to introduce to the Parliament the candidates of chairmen, their deputies and judges of the Constitutional, Supreme, and Supreme Economic Courts for both election and recall. Such power makes the judiciary dependent on the executive branch, but the creation of the Judicial Council and Constitutional Court has lessened that dependence.

The Procurator Office, independent of all other state bodies, supervises execution of laws, and has both executive and judicial functions. The general procurator heads the centralized system of bodies of Offices of Public Procurators, and is accountable to the Majlisi Milli and to the president. The general procurator is appointed for five years and is responsible for appointing and dismissing the public procurators, who also have five-year terms.

As a rule, cases are considered in three versions: by essence, that is, by fact; by appeal; and by control or inspection. Currently, contrary to the principle of precessional independence of courts, the Supreme Court and mid-level courts share responsibilities. Recent judicial reforms, such as training of regional judges by the Justice Ministry, have helped the courts gradually becoming more independent. But independence remains stifled because court personnel are chosen by the Minister of Justice; the number of lawyers has declined and they are less qualified; and because of ongoing interference between the work of investigative offices, the Attorney General's office, and the courts. In addition, lawyers and court staff are financially and materially dependent on the local government administrations that evaluate their work.

The RT's prison system is comprised of nine labor correctional colonies for men, one for women, and one educational labor colony for juveniles. The prison system was under the supervision of the Directorate for Prisons of the Ministry of Internal Affairs (MIA) until 2003, when it was transferred to the Ministry of Justice.

There are five types of labor correctional colonies for men, distinguished by their regime: open type of relatively free regime, closed type with common regime, closed type with intensified tight regime, closed type with severe regime, and closed type with a specific regime for the most dangerous recidivist criminals. Both the women's labor correctional colony and the juvenile educational labor colony have mixed regimes. Both have prisoners who committed misdemeanors as well as serious crimes. Both colonies separate inmates on the basis of the regime required. In addition to the correctional colonies, there are also local facilities for the isolation and incarceration of criminal suspects and those arrested and awaiting trial.

Police Profile

Background

The birth of the Tajik police dates back to the meeting of the Revolutionary Committee of Tajik Autonomous Soviet Socialist Republic (Tajik ASSR) on February 6, 1925, when the National Committee of Internal Affairs presented its Report on Creation of the Police of Tajikistan. Due to the importance and necessity of forming a government police force, the National Committee of Internal Affairs immediately began formation of the Tajik Police—first, the Dushanbe Police, and then the Oblast Police.

The structure of the RT police has changed little since the collapse of the Soviet Union. However, since the police forces suffer from lack of funding, qualified personnel, and professionalism, the government and international community must collaborate to develop needed long-term reforms.

Demographics

Although reliable statistics are not available, most police personnel are men, and women do not enjoy the same level of respect within the agency as men do. During the Soviet era, the ethnic representation of the police was mixed. But with most ethnic Russians emigrating, most of the police are now Tajik. Since the Civil War broke out, the police forces were mainly drawn from the same ethnic population as President Rakhmonov, who is from the Khatlon region of southern Tajikistan. After the 1997 Peace Agreement, however, the government has successfully integrated former opposition fighters and their private armies into the police.

Organizational Description

Police powers are divided between the forces of the MIA and the Ministry of Security. Other institutions with security roles are the Ministry of Emergency Situations, Border Guards, and the Presidential Guard. The MIA remains the most powerful military institution, which the International Crisis Group (ICG) estimates, in its 2002 report "Central Asia: The Politics of Police Reform," has 28,000 personnel.

The Procurator's Office is responsible for oversight of activities by the MIA and other security forces. Dushanbe city procurators and *oblast* procurators are responsible for oversight of Dushanbe police and *oblast* police, respectively. Organizational structure, number of personnel, salaries, and location of police forces are decided by the national government. Police subdivisions are organized and funded by local municipalities along with a variety of enterprises, institutions, and organizations, but the amount of funding is approved by the MIA.

The management of the police forces is carried out by the minister of internal affairs, who is appointed and dismissed by the president upon the order of the full parliament. In the regions, cities, and districts, the management of the police is carried out by the chair of the Internal Affairs Unit (IAU). Appointment and dismissal of the IAU chairmen of MBAO, regions, Dushanbe, districts, railway and airport police are carried out by the minister of internal affairs upon approval of the president.

The headquarters of the MIA, in Dushanbe, consists primarily of three main sectors. The largest in terms of personnel is the Department of Interior Army, and the second is the RT Militsia [Police] Academy. The third is comprised of ten civil departments: ecological crime, anti-terrorism, organized crime combat, public crime, illegal drug crime, criminal investigation, state auto inspection, public order, investigation, and human resources and management.

Internal affairs are monitored by the internal affairs departments of Dushanbe City and of each of the country's four districts: RRS, Khatlon, Sughd, and MBAO. Each department supervises all internal affairs units of its respective region as well as each the internal affairs subdepartments in the region's various districts.

Functions

The police have nine main functions:

- Protection of life, health, rights, and freedoms of citizens from illegal actions
- Prevention of crime and other illegal activities
- Protection of state and public interests
- Provision of public order and safety
- Investigation and resolution of crimes through powers such as searches
- Protection of property from criminal encroachments
- Implementation of the law and legal propaganda among citizens, authorities, enterprises, institutions, and organizations regardless of the form of property
- Provision of traffic safety
- Application and execution of administrative punishments

Police activities are based on the following eight principles: legality; equality of the systems of police organs and centralization of its management; respect and insurance of rights and freedoms of the person and of citizens; social justice and humanism; secrecy; equality for all; social connection with the population, including incorporation of public opinion in the fight against crime; and nonaffiliation with political parties. It is forbidden to involve the police in resolving any problem that has not been assigned to it by law, in addition, and only those bodies and officials directly authorized by the law have the right to interfere in police activity.

Training

Since 1998, the Supreme School of Militsian Forces (SSMF) has been changed to a two-level education system. Experts of mid-level vocational education are trained on the first level, and experts of high-level vocational training on the second level. The third level is for long-term planning and education for leaders of law enforcement bodies. The Militsia Academy is an institution for vocational education of MIA employees and high-ranking officers.

Admission into the police forces is voluntary, but has the following requirements:

Citizens of Tajikistan between the ages twenty and thirty-five—regardless of place of residence, gender, nationality, race/ethnicity, language, religion, political affiliation, wealth status, education, physical readiness, and health status—capable of carrying out duties of a police worker after carrying out the duties of military service (except those in mid-level and high-level educational institutions of the MIA).

Once admitted, candidates are required to pass mandatory state fingerprint registration.

Previously detained persons may not be admitted into the police forces. This is regardless of the term of detention, with the exception of those freed upon rehabilitation motives, or those rehabilitated by amnesty order of the court.

Vacancies in the police forces are filled based on competitive selection, and on a contract base defined by the law.

The probation period for the newly hired is three to six months.

The employee must take an oath, and must provide written notification in accordance with Article 8 of the Law on Corruption.

Military personnel, including students of special educational institutions of MIA, are exempt from the military monitoring system.

Police Use of Firearms

Regulations on firearm use by the police are clearly defined in Law 41, "On Militsia," which was adopted on May 17, 2004. In all cases when it is impossible to avoid the use of firearms, the officer should strive to avoid moral, property, and physical harm as much as possible. The police officer must give a warning about firearm use, provide first aid to anyone who is wounded, and report any death to his immediate supervisor for subsequent notification of the public procurator.

The police officer can use firearms for preventing crimes and other illegal activities, for arresting criminals, for weakening the defense mechanisms of the opposing side, for self-defense—and all of the above only when other non-firearm means are not applicable. The following is the list of cases when the use of firearms is legally permissible:

Protection of citizens from attack, and release of hostages

Against group or armed attack on police workers or other people, and carrying out their duty to fight crime and to protect public order

Against group or armed attack on private homes, strategically important objects, public buildings, private enterprises, institutions and organizations regardless of their affiliation, and MIA military and civilian installations

Arrest of persons using firearms during the commission of a crime, of escaping criminals, and of armed persons refusing to lay down their own firearms

Against persons forcefully attempting to seize police firearms

Stopping vehicles by damaging them in cases where the driver has put the life and health of the people in danger and refuses to comply with demands of police officers

Killing an animal threatening people's lives or health

Giving out warning signal and signal calling for help.

In all cases, the police officer must ensure the safety of surrounding citizens, provide first aid, and inform relatives and respective authorities. The police officer is obliged to present a report regarding the use of firearms within twenty-four hours of the incident. It is unlawful to use firearms against women, disabled persons, and underage persons, with the exception of cases of their attack, defense using firearms, commitment of group or armed crimes, and gathering of crowds of people who endanger the lives or health of other citizens. The law places legal responsibility on any officer who uses firearms while abusing their power.

Complaints and Discipline

Complaints are received by the secretariat of the MIA. Upon review, the complaints are sent to the appropriate departments of the MIA for further investigation. Additionally, people can file a complaint in city, regional, and municipal units of the MIA by dialing 02, the emergency telephone number.

By law, the police must protect the rights and freedoms of each person irrespective of citizenship, residence, nationality, race/ethnicity, gender, language, religion, political convictions, education, and social and property status. In cases of arrest or detention, the police must protect the due process rights of all persons whom they detain or guard, explain the basis and reason for the arrest or detention, and minimize the infringement of the rights and freedom of the citizen, foreigner, and person without citizenship. The police have no right to collect, store, use, and distribute information on the private life of persons without their consent, except in cases stipulated by the law.

Functioning as head of the armed forces during the Civil War, the MIA enjoyed little scrutiny from society, the courts, and other state organs. Management of the police by the procurators' offices remains ineffective as a result, which has led to human rights abuses. Another human rights legacy of the Civil War has been a pattern of police abuse, even against those who have served in the security sector. Human rights activists and international organizations report regular complaints of police brutality, with up to fifty cases of complaints against police brutality brought to the procurators' offices every year. Human Rights Watch gives a very low ranking to Tajikistan and asserts that torture by police and security forces is endemic. Although occasionally the procurator brings cases against the police, the police officers remain armed and police abuse against the populace remains common. The following are a few of the many causes of police brutality:

Most harmful is the lack of professionalism among police. Most police officers have little knowledge and awareness of laws protecting individual human rights. The law stipulates that detainees are innocent, until proved guilty, but in practice officials widely apply an assumption of "guilty until proved innocent."

The police system emphasizes gaining confessions rather than gathering evidence. People are afraid to step forward to provide evidence to the police since they fear being arrested themselves.

The RT's weak court system ensures that confessions obtained by torture are almost always accepted without question.

Lack of investigative capacity is another factor. Officers do not have the necessary materials, funding, or technical training to conduct proper criminal investigations.

Lack of oversight from other institutions, primarily the procurator's office.

The quota system for arrests and crime detentions, where clear-up rates are the main basis for assessment, puts extraordinary pressure on police to make detentions at any cost.

Statistics systems also contribute to the brutality and imprisonment of many people, especially women and minor drug users. To maintain "impressive" high rates of arrests in drug-related crimes, the police tend to arrest women and minor traffickers, whose load is insignificant compared to major drug traffickers.

The above obstacles will be difficult to overcome, but change could begin by police training that focuses on the psychology of the police officer, accompanied by provision of adequate technical means to document crimes and conduct investigations. The quota and statistical systems should be changed and reformed to help the police to produce qualitative rather than quantitative work.

The international community recognizes the need to train MIA police officers in international human rights practices. In March 2001, the delegation of the International Committee of the Red Cross (ICRC) in RT gave a five-day course on human rights and international humanitarian rights for employees of the MIA in Dushanbe. MIA officers also took several courses geared toward putting work skills, knowledge, and human rights in practice. To help meet this goal, the ICRC has invited the high-ranking officer of police of Netherlands, Dick Dable, who led a course for officers of the MIA's Higher School of Militsia and for students of the Ministry of Defense in 2000. In December 2004, in addition, a manual for MIA Academy students was introduced, covering the following topics, among others: human rights, the police and human rights, detention and arrest, investigation, special police operations, cooperation of police with society, the police and vulnerable sectors of the population, and emergency situations. Such courses will help bring change to the police officers' views of human rights. To bring about sustainable improvement in human rights practices, though, the international community must also get involved in reforming police structure.

The Forced Migration Projects urged the establishment of an Independent Center for Human Rights, in according with recommendations made by the June 1997 mission of the UN Office of the High Commissioner for Human Rights. The needs for legislative reform, institutional development in the rule of law, human rights education, and monitoring of civil and political rights are vast and urgent. Only one independent human rights nongovernmental organization, Human Rights Watch, has had a permanent representative in Tajikistan.

Terrorism

On November 15, 1988, during the final years of the Soviet Union, the MIA established the Department of the Fight Against Social Crimes. The department's mandate was to fight against organized crime, terrorism, corruption, and other dangerous crimes. Law 845 of 1999 on the Fight Against Terrorism defines all policies related to terrorism, terrorist activities, and the legal bases of antiterrorist actions. The following state organs are directly involved in the fight against terrorism:

1. The Ministry of Security, which is responsible for development and presentation of state programs and policies on terrorism; coordinating activities of the bodies fighting terrorism; collecting, analyzing, and processing information on terrorism, including information coming into the interagency data bank and from all other agencies involved. The Security Ministry is also responsible for proposing changes in the legal framework of anti-terrorism policy, and for the identification, warning, and prevention of international terrorist activities and of crimes of terrorist character based on political, national, racial, and extremist religious goals. It also provides safety to RT offices abroad, including their employees and their families.

2. The Ministry of Internal Affairs, responsible for identification, warning, and prevention of crimes of a terrorist nature.

3. The Ministry of Defense, which provides antiterrorist safety to air space and assistance to the organs of state security in their preparation and execution of antiterrorist operations.

4. The Ministry of Emergency Situations, which, together with other security bodies, provides antiterrorist safety to areas of rescue missions and rehabilitation operations during the ending and aftermath of emergency situations.

5. The Committee on the Protection of State Border, which has four roles: identification, warning and prevention of attempts by terrorists to cross the RT's borders; prevention of illegal border traffic of guns, firearms, explosives, poisons, radioactive chemicals, and other materials that can be used for terrorist actions; assistance to the security organs in the fight against international terrorism; and participation in preparation and execution of antiterrorist operations.

6. The Presidential Guard, which participates in provision antiterrorist safety of protected persons and facilities, as well as in

preparation and execution of antiterrorist operations.

7. The Ministry of Justice monitors the activities of registered public organizations and political parties.

8. The Ministry of Foreign Affairs conducts dialogue and negotiations with foreign nations regarding the identification, warning and prevention of international terrorist actions.

9. The Customs Committee prevents illegal traffic of guns, firearms, explosives, poisons, radioactive chemicals, and other objects that can be used for terrorist acts; and assists the security organs in the fight against international terrorism.

10. The procurator offices and courts participate in the fight with terrorism on conditions and regulations defined by the constitution, laws, and other civil and criminal regulations.

During the 1992–1997 Civil War, there were several terrorist acts involving the taking of foreign nationals as hostages. The hostage takers demanded political changes, but were liquidated by military operations. Although the government's ability to protect its territory from terrorist actions has improved considerably since 1997, there is continuing threat of terrorist acts from Afghanistan. In addition, the Central Asian region is vulnerable to terrorist activities of Islamic extremist nature. Until 2001, the Islamic Movement of Uzbekistan (IMU) used this area to carry out armed incursions into the national territory of Uzbekistan and Kyrgyzstan in the Ferghana Valley, which all three countries border. The IMU had its main training bases in Afghanistan, and has suffered heavy losses—including death of its leader, Juma Namangani. Following these losses, the IMU diminished substantially, and is now virtually absent from the terrorist front.

Another organization is Hisb ut Tahrir al Islami (Islamic Party of Liberation), an outlawed extremist Islamic party with a history of activity in the Middle East dating back to the 1950s. In Central Asia, its activities coincided with the collapse of the Soviet Union. The party's goal is to unite the Muslim nations of Central Asia and to reestablish an Islamic caliphate in the region. Thus far, the party has not been involved in terrorist activities and claims to achieve its goals by nonviolent means, but the United States continues to monitor its activities. Despite its nonviolent history, the party's fundamentalist radical ideology presents a major threat to the region, particularly since it promotes jihad (holy war against infidels). To curb fundamentalist radical propaganda, the MIA's Organized Crime Combat Department—along with joint efforts of the Ministry of Security and other security organizations—continuously monitors the activities of Hisb ut Tahrir al Islami within Tajikistan. Because the activities of Hisb ut Tahrir al Islami have intensified throughout the region over the past six years, numerous arrests have been carried out in neighboring countries.

The need for maintaining regional stability and security has also pushed the region's governments to create regional cooperation organizations. In 2004, the six-member Shanghai Co-operation Organization (SCO)—comprised of China, Russia, Kazakhstan, Kyrgyzstan, Tajikistan, and Uzbekistan—established a secretariat, which is expected to play a vital role in coordinating activities of the group by prioritizing common security and economic progress in the region. The group has been devoted to building confidence along their border areas, reducing the number of border troops in the region and making joint efforts to fight international terrorism, separatism, and extremism in Central Asia.

International Cooperation

The international community has expressed very little interest in improving the Tajik police forces. International cooperation is mainly focused on the struggle against drug smuggling from Afghanistan and on the integration of former fighters into government forces or into civilian life. The distrust of international organizations of the police is mutual: Police officials often complain that international organizations have kept few of their promises to provide them with training and technical assistance. Nevertheless, international involvement has started, conducted primarily by four organizations. The United Nations provides technical assistance, mainly with the goal to improve human rights. The Organization for Security and Cooperation in Europe conducts trainings in human rights for law enforcement agencies. The Open Society Institute (OSI) conducts small programs with law enforcement agencies, including provision of computer equipment for investigators, and trainings on human rights. The UN Office for Drug Control and Crime Prevention and the Drug Control Agency concentrate on creating an environment in which drug trafficking eventually can be combated effectively.

Nevertheless, the international community must get more involved in raising awareness and punishing police officers involved in crime and rights abuse. In addition, it has to provide training, financial, and technical support to local and international media and human rights groups and to nongovernmental organizations working closely with security forces.

Police Education, Research, and Publications

Police training is provided by the MIA Academy, as well as abroad at the Academy of Police of Russian Federation.

Listed below are writers and publications who regularly make contributions in police-related matters.

Khabibulo Ashurov, deputy chairman of the Court of Sino District of Dushanbe writes articles for the *Crime-Info* newspaper.

Major Jamshed Sadriddinov, chairman of the Press Center of Internal Affairs Unit of Dushanbe, writes articles in *Crime-Info*.

Shahloi Najmiddin, journalist for *Crime-Info*.

Roza Shaposhnik, journalist for *Asia Plus* newspaper.

Turko Dikaev, Olga Tutubalina, and Parvina Khamidova of *Asia Plus*.

General Mirzo Chonov , "The Tajik Militsia."

MIA Press Center Informs, TV program, by Chaloliddin Nozimov in Tajik and Russian languages.

Websites

There are no websites that specifically contain information about the police. However, the following websites periodically publish articles regarding police forces:

www.eurasianet.org, Eurasia Online
www.times.kg, The Times of Central Asia
www.tol.cz, Transitions Online
www.asiaplus.tajik.net, Asia Plus Information Agency
http://news.somoni.com, Somoni News, the Latest News from Tajikistan

SITORA GULOMOVA ZARIFOVNA AND
LOLA GULOMOVA ZARIFOVNA

TANZANIA

Background Material

Tanzania consists of Tanganyika, on the African mainland, and the islands of Zanzibar, Mafia, and Pemba, a few miles off the coast of East Africa. Beginning in the sixteenth century, the region was occupied by Portugal. In 1884, however, the Germans claimed Tanganyika, but about six years later, English hegemony became strong via their control of the sultanate on the island of Zanzibar. After World War I, Great Britain was granted a mandate over Tanganyika by the League of Nations.

The independence movement gained force in the 1950s, led by Julius Nyerere and his organization, the Tanganyika African National Union (TANU), founded in 1954. Tanganyika became independent in 1961, and the first elections in the new country were held a year later, with TANU as the over-whelming victor. Zanzibar was granted independence in 1963, and in 1964 merged with Tanganyika to form the United Republic of Tanzania. The union has not been harmonious, and Zanzibar retains a semiautonomous status.

Tanzania was founded as a socialist nation, with a socialist economic model and a one-party government led by TANU. However, in the mid-1980s under President Ali Hassan Mwinyi, a number of political and economic reforms were carried out, and in 1992 the constitution was changed to allow multiple political parties. The year 1995 saw Tanzania's first multiparty elections. Benjamin Mkapa of the ruling CCM (Chama cha Mapinduzi, or Revolutionary) party, was elected president and was reelected in 2000 despite reports of voting irregularities, political violence on Pemba Island, and a legislative boycott by sixteen members of the National Assembly in protest of the election results on Zanzibar. However, a reconciliation agreement was signed in October 2001, and the elections in 2003 to fill empty legislative seats were observed to have progressed peacefully and equitably. As of this writing, Mkapa was scheduled for elections in October 2005.

Tanzania's population is estimated at 36,588,225. AIDS has had a significant effect on the country, causing lower growth rates and altering the distribution of age and sex from the typical ratios. The capital is Dar Es Salaam, whose population is estimated at 3 million.

Tanzania covers a land area of approximately 886,037 square kilometers. With bodies of water included (the country has significant shares of Lake Victoria on the Kenyan/Ugandan border, Lake Tanganyika on the border with Burundi, the Democratic Republic of the Congo, and Zambia, and Lake Nyasa on the Malawi/Mozambique border), the area comes to 945,087 square kilometers. On the mainland, the ethnic composition is 99% native African, of which 95% come from more than 130 Bantu tribes; the other 1% are Asian, European, and Arab. Zanzibar consists mostly of Arabs and native Africans, as well as people of mixed races. Although most people's first language is one of a wide variety of local languages, Swahili (Kiswahili) and English are the official languages, and Arabic is widely spoken in Zanzibar. Religious distribution on the mainland is split almost evenly among Christians (30%), Muslims (35%), and indigenous beliefs (35%). On Zanzibar, however, more than 99% of the population is Muslim. The GDP per capita per annum is US$600 (2003 estimate).

Contextual Features

Tanzania's legal system is based on English common law. Legislative acts are not subject to judicial challenges; review is limited strictly to matters of interpretation. The judiciary consists of an official ombudsman, called the Permanent Commission of Enquiry; a Court of Appeal comprised of a chief justice and four judges; a High Court, consisting of thirty members appointed by the president, which holds regular sessions in all regions; as well as District Courts; Primary Courts. District Courts and Primary Courts have limited jurisdiction; appeals may be made to higher courts. The justices of the Court of Appeal and High Court are appointed by the president; all others are appointed by the Chief Justice of the president's cabinet. Zanzibar has a separate court system structured identically to the nation's as a whole, and all cases originating in Zanzibar can be appealed in the union with the exception of constitutional and Islamic law cases.

The president is both the chief of state and head of government. The president and vice president (currently Ali Mohammed Shein) are elected on the same ballot every five years. The president appoints the cabinet from the members of the National Assembly, discussed below. It should be noted that Zanzibar elects a separate president, currently Amani Abeid Karume, who is responsible for Zanzibar's internal affairs.

The legislative branch of government consists of the unicameral National Assembly (Bunge), which contains 274 seats. Of these, 232 are elected by popular vote, 37 are reserved for women nominated by the president, and 5 to members of the Zanzibar House of Representatives. The National Assembly is responsible for matters concerning the entire country; however, it may also enact laws that apply only to the mainland. Zanzibar's House of Representatives has fifty members, all of whom are directly elected. Members of both bodies serve five-year terms.

Although Tanzania was for three decades a one-party government, several political parties are at work today, including the Chama Cha Demokrasia na Maendeleo (Party of Democracy and Development) or CHADEMA; Chama Cha Mapinduzi or CCM (Revolutionary Party); Civic United Front or CUF; the unregistered Democratic Party; Tanzania Labor Party or TLP; and the United Democratic Party or UDP.

Police Profile

The Tanzania Police Force is a national police force, supervised by the inspector general of police, who is assisted by commissioners in the departments of Administration and Finance, Operations and Training, Criminal Investigation, and a fourth branch devoted to police affairs in Zanzibar. The inspector general appoints a regional police commander to supervise policing in each of Tanzania's twenty-five regions. Police stations and posts serve as centers for the initial reporting of crimes and processing of crime reports. The ratio of police to population is one police officer for every 1,200 inhabitants, and the police budget is low, preventing the hiring and training of more officers as well as the mobility of extant officers.

For the 1996–2000 period, about half a million crimes were reported each year. However, studies concluded that while certain crimes were frequently reported (83% of car thefts, for example), violent crimes frequently were not (only 47% of robbery victims and 45% of assault victims made a police report). In some cases, this was due to the distance that a victim in a rural area would have to travel to report the crime. In others, victims did not believe that the police would investigate the crime, believed the police to be corrupt, or feared retaliation by the perpetrator. Surveys have reported a general belief among the population that crime has increased.

Criminal prosecutions are the responsibility of the director of public prosecutions, who is appointed by the president. As there are very few attorneys in the country, all police officers of assistant inspector rank or above are considered public prosecutors; officers in other fields (labor, health, postal, and so on) are also considered prosecutors for cases related to their respective fields.

Bibliography

Central Intelligence Agency. *The World Factbook*, "Tanzania." Available at: www.cia.gov/cia/publications/fact book/geos/tz.html.
Mutahunwa Tibasana, Laurean. "Effective Administration of the Police and Prosecution in Criminal Justice: The Practice and Experience of the United Republic of Tanzania." In *Annual Report for 2001*. Tokyo: Asia and Far East Institute for the Prevention of Crime and the Treatment of Offenders, 2001. Available at: www.unafei.or.jp/english/pdf/PDF_rms/no60/toc.pdf.

THAILAND

Background Material

The Kingdom of Thailand, covering an area of 514,000 sq km, lies in the heart of Southeast Asia, roughly equidistant between India and China. It shares borders with Myanmar to the west and north, Lao PDR to the north and northeast, Cambodia to the east and Malaysia to the south. Thailand is divided into four distinct areas: the mountainous North, the fertile Central Plains, the semi-arid plateau of the Northeast, and the South peninsula, distinguished by its many beautiful tropical beaches and offshore islands. Thailand lies within the humid tropics and remains hot throughout the year. Average temperatures are about 29°C, ranging in Bangkok from 35°C in April to 17°C in December. There are three seasons: the cool season (November to February), the hot season (April to May), and the rainy season (June to October), although downpours rarely last more than a couple of hours.

Thailand has a population of about 60 million. Ethnic Thais form the majority, though the area has historically been a migratory crossroads, and thus strains of Mon, Khmer, Burmese, Lao, Malay, Indian, and most strongly, Chinese stock produce a degree of ethnic diversity. Integration is such, however, that culturally and socially there is enormous unity.

Thailand is one of the most strongly Buddhist countries in the world. The national religion is Theravada Buddhism, a branch of Hinayana Buddhism, practiced by more than 90% of all Thais.

The remainder of the population adheres to Islam, Christianity, Hinduism, and other faiths, all of which are allowed full freedom of expression. Buddhism continues to exert a strong influence on daily life. Senior monks are highly revered. Thus, in towns and villages, the temple (*wat*) is the heart of social and religious life.

Thailand means "land of the free," and throughout its 800-year history Thailand can boast the distinction of being the only country in Southeast Asia never to have been colonized. Its history is divided into five major periods:

Nanchao Period (650–1250 CE). The Thai people founded their kingdom in the southern part of China, which is Yunnan, Kwangsi, and Canton today.

Sukhothai Period (1238–1378 CE). Thais began to emerge as a dominant force in the region in the thirteenth century, gradually asserting independence from existing Khmer and Mon kingdoms.

Ayutthaya Period (1350–1767 CE) The Ayutthaya kings adopted Khmer cultural influences from the very beginning.

Thon Buri Period (1767–1772 CE). General Taksin, as he is popularly known, decided to transfer the capital from Ayutthaya to a site nearer the sea, which would facilitate foreign trade, ensure the procurement of arms, and make defense and withdrawal easier in case of a renewed Burmese attack. He established his new capital at Thon Buri on the west bank of the Chao Phraya River.

Rattanakosin Period (1782–the present). After Taksin's death, General Chakri became the first king of the Chakri Dynasty, Rama I, ruling from 1782 to 1809. His first action as king was to transfer the royal capital across the river from Thon Buri to Bangkok and build the Grand Palace.

During the reign of King Prajadhipok (1925–1935), Thailand changed from an absolute monarchy to a constitutional monarchy. The king abdicated in 1933 and was succeeded by his nephew, King Ananda Mahidol (1935–1946). The country's name was changed from Siam to Thailand with the advent of a democratic government in 1939.

The present monarch, Bhumibol Adulyadej, is King Rama IX of the Chakri Dynasty.

Police Profile

Background

The Thai police, as it could be traced in the Ayuthaya Period, came into existence in the reign of King Pra Brom Triloganat in 1375 or over 600 years ago with improvement and growth, gradual and unceasing through the passage of time.

In the third reign of Ratanakosin period, the police organization and administration were Westernized through the help of foreign experts in police affairs, a police force to maintain peace and order in the Bangkok metropolis in the Western style was first established.

In the fifth reign of the period, there arose a growing need to have a police unit in the provincial area. In the light of such necessity, a program was conceived and implemented later by the setting up, with some support from the army, of a police force know as the Provincial Police. In those days, the two forces, the Metropolitan Police and the Provincial Police, worked under the separate command. Later, on October 13, 1915, the two units were combined, and the newly integrated body came to be known as the Police Department under the direction of the director-general of police. The date therefore becomes Police Day for annual celebration.

In 1898, the Provincial Police Cadet School came into being. In 1907, the Metropolitan School was established to provide training for the recruited policemen afterward, the new school for police cadets was set up to train those who will be appointed commissioned officers after graduation. In following years, modernized and scientific methods in crime detection were introduced and practiced, such as the examination of fingerprints, firearms, and others. In modern days, the department has undergone a number of changes to keep the organization abreast of the time. In its status, the department is a national police force.

Organizational Description

The Royal Thai Police is headed by the director-general of police who is under the supervision of the prime minister. At present, after the director-general, there are three deputies and six assistants.

Police officials are civilian employees whose ranks are classified in accordance with position holding. Commissioned police officer holds the ranks ranging from police general down to police sublieutenant whereas noncommissioned police officers are from police senior sergeant major to police constable.

The director-general of police holds the rank of police general. He is the supreme commander of the police force with the power to direct, control, and supervise police activities throughout the kingdom. He exercises his power through various police bureaus and divisions down to police stations at the local level.

There are three deputy director-generals and six assistant director-generals under the director-general of police. They are selected from among most senior police lieutenant generals and are responsible respectively for crime suppression, administration and special activities.

At the bureau level, a police bureau is headed by a commissioner of police, holding the rank of police lieutenant general. The commissioner of police has senior police major generals under him as his deputies and assistants. The number of deputy commissioners and assistant commissioners attached to each bureau varies according to the bureau's workload and responsibility.

Each police bureau controls a number of police divisions. Each police division has a commander, who holds the rank of police major general, as its head. Under a commander, there are deputy commanders with the rank of police (special) colonel, and superintendents with the rank of police colonel in charge of the subdivision. Under the superintendent, there are deputy superintendents selected from among senior police lieutenant colonels.

There are two categories of police subdivisions. The first category comprises those subdivisions in the central administration level, each consisting of several sections whose chiefs are called inspectors, holding the rank of police lieutenant colonel or police major. The second category comprises subdivisions in the provincial level, including the Bangkok metropolitan area. Each provincial and metropolitan subdivision controls police stations within its area. The chief of a police station is the chief inspector, holding the rank of police lieutenant colonel or police major. Under the chief inspector, there are inspectors, with the rank of police lieutenant colonel or police major, in charge, respectively, of investigation, administration and crime control, and traffic.

Under the inspector, both in the case of the police station and in the case of section, there are subinspectors holding ranks ranging from police captain to police sublieutenant. Below the subinspector, there are noncommissioned officers ranging from police senior sergeant major to police constable.

Administration Service

Office of the Secretariat: Responsible for supervising and performing secretariat works, correspondence, filing, meetings, public relations, and intelligence. It is also in charge of receiving complaints lodged by the people with other matters governing laws, regulations, orders, and policy as assigned, and works of the computer center to furnish urgent information.

Personnel Division: Supervises personnel administration in accordance with laws and regulations, to carry out the policies and assignments entrusted and to participate in any meeting concerning police personnel administration matters.

Welfare Divisions: Provide welfare and housing for police personnel of all levels, promote vocational training sporting activities, funeral rites, control of construction, cooperatives, welfare for wounded or crippled personnel and educational allowances for their children.

Legal Affairs Division: Examines investigation files submitted to the division by inquiry officials or public prosecutors in accordance with the Criminal Procedure Code, and to handle cases relating to criminal liability and

discipline of police officers. Besides, the division will act as plaintiff or defendant for the Police Department when legal disputes arise.

Technical Service Division: Maintains metropolitan and provincial libraries, publishes and disseminates textbooks, examines legal drafts, and gives recommendations on legal matters. Moreover, the division continuously conducts research and reviews the scope of police studies, as well as promotes the personnel to further their education in the major institutions of the country with a view to providing qualified personnel to the department.

Research and Planning Division: Compiles statistically all reports, both of a criminal and noncriminal nature, and to conduct research with a view to finding effective measures to reduce crimes.

Office of Police General Staff: Responsible for coordinating with police units in the department in accordance with the director-general's policy and any assignment that might require determination and consideration. The outcome will be reported to the director-general for final decision making, and implementation, and the order will be received from alternate advisors.

Office of Police Internal Auditing: Established to audit the use of office supplies and unit expenditures that are relevant to setting the budget. Suggestions are directly received from the director-general who supervises all unit workloads.

Operation Service

Central Investigation Bureau: Responsible for maintaining law and order and assisting other police units in suppression of serious crimes throughout the Kingdom. The ten divisions under this Bureau are described below.

- General Staff Division is responsible for the screening, planning, and processing of matters as well as submitting recommendations.
- Crime Suppression Division is in charge of investigating all criminal offenses throughout the Kingdom, that is, forgery and commercial crimes, offences against public peace and security, liberty, and offences against life and body and property as well as narcotics trafficking and smuggling.
- Criminal Records Division is responsible for the compilation of records, methods of opera-

tion of crime and statistics of criminals, ex-convicts, hoodlums, and robbers. It keeps records of wanted persons, including dead and missing persons, and circulates information to all units concerned. This Division also collects fingerprints of civil servants, municipal officials, and persons dying unnatural deaths. It also helps to identify persons upon request.

- Scientific Crime Detection Division helps officers throughout the country in searching for clues and establishing facts concerning criminal offences by scientific crime detection, and technical operation with the aid of photography at crime scenes.
- Registration Division is responsible for the registration of vehicles and firearms; granting of licenses to pawnshops, hotels and secondhand goods dealers; public subscriptions; and the censorship of both Thai and imported films and theatrical performances.
- Railway Police Division is responsible for combating crime, and constantly patrols in order to be able to suppress harmful incidents, and provide safe conduct to citizens within railyard areas and on trains, and also to look after the properties of the state-owned railway. It has the authority to carry out crime investigation in the areas under its jurisdiction. .
- Marine Police Division is in charge of safeguarding coasts and rivers. It is responsible for combating crime against customs, fishery, immigration, and navigation laws, and supervising transport and harbor activities as well as providing sea rescue services.
- Highway Police Division supervises, controls, and inspects vehicles on the nation's highways and of traffic beyond municipal limits, protects public safety and properties, and combats and investigates offenders on the highway.
- Forestry Police Division is responsible for the prevention, suppression, and investigation of violations of the Forestry Act and other laws pertaining to forest lands, such as the cutting of trees without a proper license or in restricted areas.
- Special Branch's functions are mainly concerned with national security. The Office of Displaced Persons is attached to this division.
- Metropolitan Police Bureau is responsible for crime prevention and suppression in Bangkok Metropolis, which comprises 5,986 square kilometers in area with approximately 5.1 million inhabitants. There are six divisions and one subdivision attached to the Metropolitan Police Bureau. The General Staff Division is responsible for screening, planning, and processing, as well as making recommendations to the Metropolitan Patrol commissioner. Special Operation Division is responsible for crime prevention and suppression in patrol systems by patrolling with various vehicles including the canine police and mounted police. It is responsible for guarding important places and providing protection for H.M. the King and the Royal Family as well as VIPs. It controls and suppresses disturbances, and supports the work of the local police and other branches. Its area of responsibility covers those within the Metropolitan Police jurisdiction, and any other areas as ordered by the authorized superior. The Traffic Police Division is responsible for road safety in the metropolitan area, not only to control and tackle traffic problems on day-to-day basis, but also for traffic planning, control and investigation of traffic accidents, and compiling traffic accident statistics and research. The Northern Bangkok Metropolitan Division is responsible for maintaining peace and order within the northern area of Bangkok. There are seven subdivisions controlling twenty-six police stations under the responsibility of this division. The Southern Bangkok Metropolitan Division is responsible for maintaining peace and order within the Southern area of Bangkok. It has altogether five subdivisions controlling sixteen police stations under the responsibility of this division. The Dhonburi Metropolitan Division's areas of responsibility are similar to the other two Bangkok Metropolitan Divisions. Its jurisdiction covers the Dhonburi area, with seven subdivisions responsible for twenty-seven police stations. The Juvenile Aid Subdivision is responsible for handling matters relating to juvenile delinquency and welfare.
- There are nine Provincial Police Bureaus, each responsible for maintaining peace and order in its area of jurisdiction and areas along the borders as well. Each Provincial Police Bureau works jointly with the Border Patrol Police in fighting crime, disorder, and infiltration and subversion of communist terrorists.
- Border Patrol Police General Headquarters, composed of many units ranging from headquarters division, subdivision, company, platoon, and operation base. The basic task is to maintain peace, security and order along the

border areas of the Kingdom. These officers collaborate with the Armed Forces and governmental organizations concerned with preserving national sovereignty, and preventing and suppressing subversion as well as insurgency. Their secondary mission is to support crime prevention efforts and narcotics control in border areas. These responsibilities are discharged in close cooperation with the local police and the Narcotics Control Board of the Prime Minister's Office.

In addition the abovementioned activities, the Border Patrol Police is also engaged in the rural development programs to offer help to hill tribes and inhabitants in remote areas, in support of the work under royal patronage, and the training of scouts, which contributes to national security.

The Border Patrol Police General Headquarters is divided into the following units:

Border Patrol Police General Staff: Responsible for directing and supervising the matters concerning personnel, intelligence, strategic training, and budgeting as well as logistics and civil affairs.

Border Patrol Police General Support Staff Headquarters: Responsible for controlling and instructing in matters of accommodation, welfare, communication network, quartermasters, ordinance, transportation, finance, medical service, and personnel health.

Special Training Division: Responsible for directing and supervising as well as developing special training courses. There are nine subdivisions acting as training centers throughout the country in each region.

Border Patrol Police Regional Headquarters 1: Responsible for operations in the central part of the country, controlling provinces especially in the western and eastern part.

Border Patrol Police Regional Headquarters 11: Responsible for operations in the northeastern part of the country.

Border Patrol Police Regional Headquarters 111: Responsible for operations in the northern part of the country.

Border Patrol Police Regional Headquarters IV: Responsible for operations in the southern part of the country.

Border Patrol Police Aerial Reinforcement Headquarters: Responsible for operations of unconditional warfare psychological operations, aerial reinforcement for air support as well as nationwide air rescue, and generally for reinforcement to the department.

Border Patrol Police General Headquarters was established with three special characteristics to perform duties as follows:

As an armed force unit to any condition of battle
As a prevention and suppression unit to fight against crime similar to local police units
As a development unit to engage in the rural development, offering help to people in remote areas, which contributes much to national security in parallel with civil employees' responsibility.

Auxiliary and Special Service

The Police Education Bureau is responsible for police education and improvement of the efficiency of police personnel through training. The units of the Bureau are described below.

- Education Planning Division: In-service training programs and various courses established under authorization of the Police Educational Bureau.
- Headquarters Company: The Company is responsible for maintaining peace and order within the Police Education Bureau and protecting property of the Bureau and other public property as assigned.
- Institute of Police Development: The unit has been established to promote police efficiency in various fields of knowledge and methodology through training. Courses are assigned based on the level of an officer's responsibility; the courses are Criminal Investigation and Detective Training, Police Inspector Training, Police General Staff, Superintendent Training Course, and Advanced Course in Police Administration.
- Police Noncommissioned Officer Training School: The institute is for those who are admitted to the school on account of their terms and performance in the service. After the completion of the course, certificates are awarded.
- Metropolitan Police Training School: The Metropolitan Police Training School was established to provide academic and military training for recruits and volunteers in Bangkok. It handles matters concerning the violation of rules of discipline and other regulations of recruits and providing emergency forces.
- Provincial Police Training School: Nine provincial police training schools were established throughout the Kingdom to provide academic and military training for recruits in the pro-

vinces. These schools, each of which is divided into six companies, handle matters concerning the violation of rules and discipline and other regulations affecting recruits and provide emergency forces.

Responsibilities of the Office of the Inspector-General follow:

- Supervise all policemen attached to the Office.
- Inspect activities and works of the Metropolitan Police, Provincial Police, Technical Service, and welfare and other police units of the Royal Thai Police Department. The inspector-general has the authority to assign police officers attached to the office or regional police officers to make an inspection at any police unit within their respective regions and report their findings to the inspector-general.
- Inspect and give advice to police officers and other police units concerning discipline and operations in accordance with the rules, regulations, orders, and notices of the Police Department and the Ministry of Interior.
- Carry out special assignments occasionally given by the director-general of police.
- To propose recommendation to the director-general for the benefit of the Police Department.

Responsibilities of the Surgeon-General Office include providing medical services to patients in general, offering medical preventive plans for policemen, performing forensic science work, and providing medical supplies for all police units and mobile medical units in the field when necessary. It also operates a Police Nursing College, and offers first-aid training courses for police personnel. The Surgeon-General Office includes the General Staff Division, Police General Hospital, Police Nursing College, and Institute of Forensic Medicine.

Responsibilities of the Finance Division include financial affairs and accounting of the Police Department, auditing the financial activities of all police units, and performing administrative matters for the division.

Next, the Quartermasters Division procures, constructs, repairs, and provides materials, uniforms, transportation equipment, offices, and houses for police personnel. In addition, it is responsible for transporting food supplies and other necessary equipment to police units in need.

The Communications Division cooperates with all units in the Police Department in crime suppression efforts by making available to them an ef-

ficient system of communications, as well as providing them with technical services.

The Police Aviation Division provides transportation service and air support to requesting police units and other government agencies engaged in crime and communist suppression. It also gives air support to other government units whose work is related to economic development, welfare, and safety of the people.

The Foreign Affairs Division is responsible for all foreign affairs of the Police Department as well as promoting and maintaining close cooperation with other police forces all over the world through the Interpol network. It handles matters relating to overseas studies or observation tours of police officials. Its responsibilities also include making necessary arrangements for foreign visitors of the Police Department and promoting close relationship with other police forces.

The Immigration Bureau checks persons and conveyances coming into and going out of the Kingdom in accordance with immigration law. Its responsibilities include prevention, investigation, and suppression of acts violating the immigration law, control of immigrants and alien quotas, granting and issue of entry and exit permits, and keeping of records and statistics of all aliens and immigrants.

The Alien Registration and Taxation Division, a central registry of all aliens domiciling in Thailand, coordinates activities with regional and provincial registration officers. It is also responsible for the prevention and suppression of acts violating tax regulations, including revenue, excise, and customs.

The Fire Brigade Division handles arson cases and prevents accidental fires in accordance with the Fire Prevention and Fire Fighting Act B.E. 2495 and other related laws. The division also provides training to volunteers who may be either boy scouts or government officials or ordinary citizens to help the police fire fighters when needed. In addition, it provides rescue services in times of natural disaster.

The Royal Court Police Office is responsible for providing maximum security and safeguards to the king and queen and members of the royal family during their stay in the royal palace or royal ceremonies, as the director-general of police gives his loyalty to the throne on their behalf.

Functions

The Royal Thai Police Department is responsible for crime prevention and suppression, alleviation of public grievances, and maintenance of public peace and order. Duties of the police can be divided up as prevention and suppression of crime, public service, and protection of national security.

It is always understood by the Department that crime prevention and the protection of life and property of the people is a traditional duty of utmost importance. All performance must be carried out on a continued basis with full preparedness and vigilance.

To carry out such responsibility, manpower, weapons, communications devices, vehicles, and other equipment must be acquired to meet the need and necessity in each area of operation. Special patrol units are on beats, such as foot patrols and they work in all types of terrain, in particular at night. All units can contact one another through the radio network, enabling them to arrive at the scene of crime and deal with the offense immediately. Apart from operational activities, the Department has a technical unit to collect all data and figures to establish crime trends and their socioeconomic implications.

The master plan to protect the life and property of the people is formulated for all operational units, but with some modification and training, depending on special features of geographical setting and the degree of violence. Places such as banks, gold shops, department stores, gambling dens, prostitution dens, dwellings of well-to-do families, slum areas, or poorly lit streets may induce petty offenses or offenses against property, while in the provincial areas cattle theft may by frequent. The Department follows the Thai saying "Prevention is better than cure."

Crime Suppression

The Department has sufficient strength to deal with all types of crimes, including incidents in the wake of social unrest, and menaces and threats caused by communist insurgents, terrorists, and secessionists. Suppressive operations are well planned and sometimes carried out in coordination with the army and other administrative departments concerned.

In the metropolis, the lead agency in crime control is the Metropolitan Police Bureau. In the provincial areas, the responsible agencies are the Provincial Police Bureaus.

Since crime control is an assignment of paramount importance, the central body in support of the said responsibility is set up within the Department. The Central Investigation Bureau is composed of the Crime Suppression Division, Special Branch Division, Scientific Crime Detection Division, Criminal Records Division, Highway Police Division, Railway Police Division, Forestry Police Division, and Marine Police Division.

Sometimes in the campaign against crime, a special plan is formulated to cope with the roaring incident of crime in certain areas, such as illegal cutting down of trees and teaks, smuggling of goods, and so on. A special unit task force in support of government policy is set up. At the moment, there is a suppressive squad on economic offenses to protect the interest of the consumers that works with various agencies concerned.

Training

The Police Cadet Academy is an undergraduate institution of academic and military training provided only for matriculated students. Successful graduates become sublieutenants in the force.

Anyone wishing to join the police force as a constable must undergo a one-year police training course offered at Metropolitan Police Training School in Bangkok and Provincial Police Training Schools located across the country. Due to the fact the police training schools now available are incapable of accommodating all people who wish to attend, potential students must take a competitive examination to establish their eligibility. Major qualifications follow:

- Thai citizenship
- High school completion
- Not obligated by the Conscription Law at the time of filing application
- Age between twenty and twenty-seven

In practice, there are four ways to join the Thai police force as police commissioned officers:

- High school graduates can undergo police training at the Police Cadet Academy for four years before being commissioned as police sublieutenants.
- Graduates with a bachelor's degree in law or political science from a domestic educational institution are eligible to take a competitive examination provided by the Police Department. Successful candidates will then be required to undergo a six-month police officer training course before being commissioned as police sub-lieutenants.
- Certain divisions need personnel with knowledge in specific fields. For instance, the Surgeon-General Office needs nurses and physicians, and the Finance Division prefers persons with certificates or degrees in accounting and commerce. In these cases, competitive examinations will be arranged if necessary.

- On a case-by-case basis, some applicants may file applications at the division that they wish to work for. Their applications will then be reviewed and considered by the division commander. If the division commander approves of the applications, they will be forwarded to the Police Personnel Division for further processing.

For people who work in the police service, it is required that they develop themselves with diverse police tactics and techniques, together with the knowledge of law and regulations as guidelines in the execution of entrusted assignments. Major subjects for police training courses are political science, law, physical and mental health testing, fingerprint identification techniques, traffic control, forensic sciences, and ballistics and firearms.

Police schools in the central and provincial areas educate and train the police so that they will be fully qualified at given ranks. Special schools and courses are also provided with technical knowledge and modern techniques such as in the Criminal Investigation and Detective Training School, the School for Inspectors and Superintendents, and the Special Staff Courses. For the non-commissioned officers, there is also a training course in criminal investigation.

For personnel in auxiliary units, special courses are also arranged to increase their specialization in the given fields. Refresher courses for police practice and conduct, special assignment, and operation are also requirements for many units. This is arranged by the Technical Service Division with contributions from visiting lecturers and experts from other government bodies.

The Royal Thai Police Department offers a variety of in-service training courses for police commissioned and noncommissioned officers. The Police Noncommissioned Officer Training School offers a three-month detective training course. Those attending the course must be holding the rank of police lance corporal up to police sergeant.

The unit responsible for organizing training courses for police commissioned officer is the Institute for Police Development. Courses offered by the Institute are described below.

- Criminal Investigation and Detective Training Course. The course is designed to provide police officers with techniques and relevant knowledge that good investigators should possess. The duration of the course is four months. The training course is offered at least once a year or three times a year at the most. All trainees must be police commissioned officers, and local administration officials and civilian officials from other agencies may be sent in on selective basis.

- Police Inspection Training Course. The course is designed for officers with the rank of police captain or higher holding a position of at least subinspector or an equivalent of inspector. Their educational qualification must be at least a bachelor's degree. Frequency of training is not specific. Duration of the course is six months.

- Police General Staff Course. This course aims to prepare police personnel in screening, planning, and processing of information or matters, as well as submitting recommendations to supervisors for further decision making. The course is for subinspectors up to deputy superintendent, from police captain to police lieutenant colonel. Course duration is six months.

- Superintendent Training Course. It offers training for those who are deputy superintendents at the time the course is offered. Frequency of training is not fixed. Duration of the course is eight months.

- Advanced Course in Police Administration. This eight-month course offers methodologies and techniques in police administration for officers of the special police colonel rank serving as deputy commanders in any division.

Entrants to the academy must have successfully entered and completed the two-year course at the Royal Thai Armed Forces Academy (RTAFA). Instruction at the Academy is according to the visiting lecturer method. During the school term, the Academy's regular training staff is augmented by approximately 250 visiting lecturers and technicians who have been selected because of their particular qualifications in the fields of police science and administration or allied sciences. Many are veteran police officers, some are outstanding professors from the universities in Bangkok, and others are judges or public prosecutors who lecture in law.

After final examinations, the first, second, and third companies are required to train in various techniques of warfare for thirty days in training camps. The fourth company is required to train in practical police methods at metropolitan police stations for a month.

Besides technical education and physical training inside the campus as specified in the curricula, each class of cadets is required to undergo special training, which is carried out shortly after the second academic semester examination.

After graduation, a cadet is awarded a bachelor's degree in public administration, and the Ministry of Interior will consider appointing the cadet as a police sublieutenant. Then the Police Department will assign the cadet to a subinspector attached to various bureaus, including the Metropolitan Police Bureau, Bureau of Provincial Police Regions 1, 2, 3, and 4, Border Patrol Police Bureau, and Central Investigation Bureau.

Police Public Projects

Police–community relations, especially in a democratic society, are unavoidable for public service, which is obviously a means for police to reach their goals of good relations, better understanding, and mutual cooperation in crime prevention. Continuous service that the police give to the public around the clock, therefore, has been found necessary to implement community service to the public, which aims at the following:

Invoking a feeling of mutual cooperation
Seeking people's participation in controlling crimes
Creating consciousness among people to pay due respect to the law, regulations, and rule and order of the society

Thus, a better image of the department itself will emerge.

Additionally, the Department is aware the importance of public relations, which help people to understand police burdens and workloads to fight against crime, and in return people will be more interested in cooperating. Public relations indirectly or directly assist in developing the progress of the Department, society, and nation. The Department has established the Police Public Relations Center with a view to receiving complaints of any mischief caused by police officers, as well as any public suggestions for the improvement of the Department.

At the police station level, there are information desks for police to answer questions and to look after people who come by to lodge a complaint or request for help that might be beyond daily police duty.

Besides the regular duties of police, the unit is to offer help and services in connection with natural disasters and accidents that may occur at any time. Examples are dangers from natural disasters such as flooding and strong winds, damage and loss in various types of accidents, automobile collisions, people in elevators, incidents connected with high buildings, industrial accidents with workers trapped in the tunnels or in places with suffocation potential. The police are ready in these situations to provide help at a moment's notice. In the absence of other demands, police provide the extra service of supplying water to places in need where shortages occur.

The unit in charge of disaster relief and fire control is operational and auxiliary in itself. It has personnel and supporting equipment and apparatus for fighting fires in all situations on land and waterways.

Additionally, special training for the public is arranged for prevention and immediate response to events or to be of help to the authorities. Many from all parts of the country have been trained. In certain circumstances, the unit with its equipment and apparatus can act as a supporting element in the event of rioting and unrest.

Tourism is a major source of national income. All government agencies try to promote and support this kind of industry. Every year a great number of tourists come to Thailand to visit places of interest, but there are also things that obstruct the flow of tourism, such as burglary and violence. Many tourists have been robbed or assaulted, and this leads to negative images of the country and tourists concerned about personal safety. The Department, in close cooperation with the Tourism Authority of Thailand, has set up the Tourist Police Unit to offer services to visitors. The unit is in the Crime Suppression Division, Central Investigation Bureau, with sufficient personnel, weapons, and communications apparatus. Police officers in this unit are screened on personal appearance and foreign language ability. The Tourist Police work closely with the authorities of immigration, customs, local police, and hotel management. Service to tourists is around the clock.

WISOOTRUJIRA CHATSIRI

Bibliography

Royal Thai Police Department. *War Veterans Organization of Thailand under Royal Patronage*, 2000.
Royal Thai Police Department, *Police Cadet Academy*, 1987.

TOGO

Background Material

The Republic of Togo is a small developing country situated in West Africa between Ghana to the west, Benin to the east, and Burkina Faso to the north. The capital of Lomé is the largest city of the country.

The Togolese population of 5.5 million people consists of 21 ethnic groups. The two major groups are the Ewe and the Kabye. The Ewe, who dominate the civil service and flourish in commerce, represent about 21% of the population, and are situated in the south where colonial administrators concentrated infrastructure. The Kabye, situated in the north and representing 12% of the population, reside on subsistence land and habitually migrate to the south for employment. They tend to dominate the military and the security forces.

The official languages are French, Kabye, Ewe, and Mina. English is also taught in some secondary schools that share boundaries with Ghana. As a result, many Togolese people are bilingual in both English and French.

About 51% of the population follows indigenous animistic beliefs, including participation in voodoo cults. Twenty-nine percent of the population is Christian, mainly Roman Catholic, and 20% are Muslim. The government does not interfere with religious practice.

Togo was originally the eastern section of the former German Protectorate of Togoland. After World War I, it was partitioned into British and French zones by a League of Nations mandate and, on April 27, 1960, under the leadership of the Ewe, Sylvanus Olympio,gained independence from the trusteeship of the United Nations administered by France. In 1963, President Olympio was killed in a coup and was replaced by Nicolas Grunitzky. He in turn was ousted in 1967 by the northerner, Major General Gnassingbe Eyadema, who remained president until his death in 2005. Despite a democratic constitution, Eyadema relied on military rule to maintain control. After his death, the army installed Eyadema's son as president.

Togo stretches longitudinally through six geographic regions, so there are a variety of soils, and the climate ranges from tropical humidity in the south and coastal areas to semi-aridity in the north. This allows Togo to grow a wide range of crops. Despite insufficient rainfall in some regions, there is self-sufficiency in food crops, such as corn, cassava, yams, sorghum, millet, palm kernels, and peanuts. The economy is heavily dependent on commercial and subsistence agriculture, which generates employment for about 65% of the labor force. Cocoa, coffee, and particularly cotton, account for 40% of export earnings. In addition, cattle, sheep, and pigs are raised in the plateau district and the northern part of Togo.

Togo also produces marble and limestone, and is the fourth largest producer of phosphate in the world. There is also potential for commercial mining of gold, diamonds, and base metals. The annual GDP is US$8 billion, which is equivalent to US$1,500 per capita. Thirty-two percent of the population lives below the poverty line.

Encouraged by an economic boom in the mid-1970s Togo borrowed heavily to invest in infrastructure and industrial development. A subsequent economic downturn resulted in large deficits and economic collapse. The International Monetary Fund, World Bank, and Paris Club provided aid, but Togo had to adopt austerity measures. Much international aid is frozen because of its poor human rights record.

Togo is one of sixteen members of the Economic Community of West African States (ECOWAS), a subregional group that has its development fund located in Lomé. It also belongs to the West African Economic and Monetary Union (UEMOA), and is a member of the West African Development Bank (BOAD), which is associated with UEMOA. Togo's role as the regional banking center eroded because of political instability and fiscal decline in the early 1990s.

Contextual Features

Under the 1992 Constitution, executive power is vested in the president, who is directly elected by universal adult suffrage for five years. The members of the unicameral National Assembly are also elected by universal suffrage and serve for a term of five years. The president appoints a prime minister from among the majority party in the legislature. In consultation with the president, the prime minister nominates other ministers. For administrative governance, the country is divided into five regions, which are further divided into thirty prefectures and subprefectures. Despite democratic trappings, Togo is criticized by international organizations for its human rights abuses, and suffers from political unrest. Togolese dissidents in Ghana and Burkina Faso have tried to overthrow the government without success.

The legal system is based on the French Napoleonic Code, although traditional law is also recognized. The constitution prohibits arbitrary interference with privacy and provides for an independent judiciary. Trials are public, and defendants have the right to counsel and to appeal cases from lower courts.

The Constitutional Court has nine members and is responsible for constitutional matters, and preserving the basic rights and freedom of the people. The Supreme Court, established in 1961, consists of judicial, administrative, and auditing chambers, the Court of Sessions, and the Appeals Courts. There is a labor tribunal and a tribunal for children's rights. In the countryside, village chiefs or councils of elders try minor civil and criminal cases. There is also a military tribunal, and a special state security court which holds closed hearings on crimes against the internal and external security of the state.

Despite constitutional guarantees, arbitrary detention is common. It is reported that both civilians and military personnel can be detained without charge or trial, and members of the political opposition can be held in custody for minor crimes or on suspicion of participating in revolutionary activities.

Prison conditions are reported to be harsh. There is overcrowding, poor sanitation, and unsafe food. The Central Prison in Lomé is designed for 350 prisoners, but is said to hold 1,285 inmates, including 39 women. Women are held separately from men and often have their children with them. Juvenile prisoners are accommodated separately from adult prisoners, but pretrial detainees are not separated from convicted offenders.

Amnesty International has reported that medical facilities are poor, that drug use and diseases are common, and guards have exacted payment from inmates for the use of showers and lavatories. At least one political prisoner is reported to have died from lack of medical attention.

Street crime in Togo has been growing in recent years. There is pick-pocketing and theft in the mar-ket and beach areas of Lomé, while residential burglary and carjacking are not uncommon. There is some family violence and, although genital mutilation is illegal, the law is not generally enforced. Togo is also a source, passage, and target country for human trafficking, in which girls are generally the victims. Traffickers are of Togolese, Beninese, and Nigerian nationality. The government of Togo has cooperated with neighboring countries to extradite human traffickers.

There is little threat of international terrorism in Togo, but domestically there is political dissent, some ethnic conflict, and periodic skirmishes with the neighboring country of Ghana, primarily because of Togolese politicians who have taken refuge there.

Police Profile

Organizational Description and Functions

Policing is based on the French system. There is a National Gendarmerie, which is part of the armed forces and directed by the Minister of Defense, a National Police under the authority of the Ministry of the Interior, Security, and Decentralization, and the City Police of Lomé, responsible for policing the metropolitan area of the capital. There are reports that the Togolese police are corrupt and ineffective.

The Gendarmerie is a paramilitary police force structured on a detachment model. It is responsible for order throughout the country. It consists of five brigades: Air, Criminal Investigation, Harbor, Traffic, and Territorial Policing. It also maintains the Central Criminal Archives, performs domestic intelligence duties, and trains the Presidential Guard. The presidential guard is primarily responsible for protecting the presidency.

The National Police is commanded by an inspector general. It is responsible for the regulatory and administrative aspects of policing and has a number of divisions, including Intelligence (Special Service), Harbor, Railway, Fire Service, and the Judicial Police. The National Police is also officially responsible for Togolese security and monitoring potential sources of subversion against the state. Because its activities are distrusted by the president, some of its functions have been duplicated by the creation of similar brigades attached directly to the presidency.

The judicial police are responsible for criminal investigation. While they are under the authority of the Ministry of the Interior, Security and Decentralization organizationally, when they conduct investigations they come under the jurisdiction of the courts and are supervised by the chief prosecutor. During an investigation they establish that an offence has been committed, collect evidence, and search for offenders. Once a charge is laid, they have delegated judicial powers to hold preliminary inquiries, to receive complaints and charges, to search, to detain and to process a suspect's testimony. It has been noted that the system is vulnerable to human rights abuse.

Work conditions are being improved to raise the effectiveness of the judicial police. Police buildings are being renovated and temporary detention facilities properly outfitted, computerization introduced, and office materials and stationery supplied. Officer ranks are being trained in a school for judicial police, modern scientific methods introduced, and a minimum entrance qualification of a high school graduation certificate set for judicial police agents.

Training

Education in Togo is modeled on the French system. The University of Lomé, established in 1970, provides educational and research opportunities in arts and science, humanities, and science and technology. France has been traditionally the chief and largest aid donor to Togo. In 1992, it provided a grant of FF3.5 million for the training of Togolese police and security services. Japan has also provided aid.

The National Police School is responsible for the training of the Togolese police. The presidential guards have received training from North Korean security academies. Entry into the police service is by means of competitive examinations.

IHEKWOABA D. ONWUDIWE

Bibliography

Africa, South of the Sahara. "Togo." 2004. Available at: www.sul.stanford.edu/depts/ssrg/africa/togo.html. Accessed May 29, 2004.

Amnesty International Library. "Togo: Rule of Terror," 1999. Available at: http://web.amnesty.org/library/print/ENGAFR570011999. Accessed May 25, 2004.

Assensoh, A. B., and Alex-Assensoh, Yvette M. *African Military History and Politics: 1900–Present*. New York: Palgrave of St. Martin's Press, 2001.

Banks, S. Arthur, and Muller, Thomas C. *Political Handbook of the World: Governments and Intergovernmental Organizations*. New York: CSA Publications, 1998.

Central Intelligence Agency. *World Factbook, 2004*. "Togo: Country Facts Sheet." Available at: www.4freephonebill analysis.com /worldfactbook /togo php. Accessed November 28, 2004.

Constitution of Togo. Available at: www.idlo.int/texts/leg5588.pdf. Accessed May 29, 2004.

Curkeet, A. A. *Togo: Portrait of a West African Francophone Republic in the 1980s*. Jefferson, NC: Mcfarland and Company, 1993.

Decaldo, Samuel. *Historical Dictionary of Togo*. Metuchen, NJ and London: Scarecrow Press, 1987.

Europa World. *The Europa World Yearbook*. London: Europa Publications, 1999.

Kurian, George Thomas. *World Encyclopedia of Police Forces and Penal Systems*. New York: Facts on File, 1989.

Legun, Colin. *Africa: Contemporary Record*. New York and London: African Publishing Company, 1992–1994.

Mars-Proietti, Laura. *Nations of the World: A Political, Economic and Business Handbook*. Millerton, NY: Grey House Publishing, 2004.

Onwudiwe, Ihekwoaba D. *The Globalization of Terrorism*. Aldershot: Ashgate Publishers, 2001.

U.S. Department of State. "Togo: Country Reports on Human Rights Practices," 2003. Available at: www.state.gov/g/drl/rls/hrrpt/2003/27757pf.htm. Accessed May 24, 2004.

TONGA

Background Material

The first Polynesian settlers are believed to have settled Tonga about 500 BCE. Captain Cook named Tonga the "Friendly Islands," but inter-island fighting among chiefs had characterised centuries of history. Tonga is the only nation in the Pacific not to have been colonised by a Western power. A Polynesian kingdom was created from disparate islands of the South Pacific archipelago in 1845. It became a hereditary constitutional monarchy in 1875 and then a British protectorate in 1900. Tongan forces saw some service during World War II. Regaining its independence on

June 4, 1970, Tonga remains a monarchy, although there is increasing pressure for constitutional reform to curb the power of the wealthy aristocracy and monarchy. The king, who has held power for nearly forty years, holds the predominant place in Tongan politics and life, and makes hereditary appointments to the token parliament. The prime minister and deputy prime minister are appointed for life, which also applies for the minister of police. The king also appoints the cabinet. The nobility-dominated parliamentary system ensures that voters can only choose a minority of members of the Legislative Assembly. The nine elected commoners constitute a powerless minority in the parliament. Universal suffrage applies to citizens twenty-one and older. The U.S. ambassador to Tonga has indicated that changes towards democracy "should happen at a pace appropriate for the society concerned" (Radio New Zealand, February 20, 2003). Tonga has never been invaded or colonised, but its political system is run by an extravagant monarchy.

Economic poverty is the major challenge for Tonga. The country remains dependent on external aid and remittances from exiled Tongan communities (mainly in New Zealand, Australia, and the United States) in order to offset its trade deficit. More nationals live outside the country than inside. Diplomatic sources indicate that the Kingdom of Tonga is nearing ruin after disastrous royal decisions, including investing AUD$35 million (approximately 40% of the government's revenue) with the king's court jester's Arizona re-investment scheme. The nation has a somewhat notorious reputation for "get-rich-quick" schemes. Due to economic stagnation, Tonga requires extensive economic and public sector reform. Programs are in place to improve fiscal policies, develop a more equitable taxation system, promote private sector growth, and create a streamlined public service. Environmentally, deforestation is a growing concern.

Politically, progress toward democracy has been slow and hazardous. Tonga's aristocratic hierarchy is fighting to maintain its autocratic rule in the midst of democratic challenges. In February 2003, the government declared the *Times of Tonga* newspaper (printed in Auckland with a circulation of 20,000) a prohibited import, and made it a criminal offence to possess any copies of it. Its editor has challenged the ban in the Tongan Supreme Court. The Crown Law Office has charged an entire television show panel, including the station manager, with contempt of court for daring to discuss the banning of the *Times of Tonga*. Hardliner Police Minister Clive Edwards informed the court that the ban was imposed because the paper was saying "that the leaders of this country are sodomites and poofters." He apparently was referring to a cartoon in the paper (*Australian*, April 5, 2003). On 10 March 2003, a pro-democracy march advocating freedom of speech took place in the main street of Nuku'aloofa. The march was reported as peaceful, the police helpful, and hundreds of people applauded the marchers. A second Order in Council placed a second ban on the paper, after a Supreme Court ruling that the earlier royal ban was unlawful. The paper has reappeared on Tongan streets. In October 2003, an estimated 8,000 people marched through the capital of Nuku'alofa to the Legislative Assembly in protest at the King's plan to change the Constitution so that he can control newspapers and limit the rights of the courts to review his decisions (*Wellington Post*, October 20, 2003).

The population is 110,237 (July 2004 estimate). Tonga comprises 171 islands, of which 45 are inhabited. Most people live on the main island, Tongatapu. Languages spoken are Tongan (a Polynesian language) and English. The Free Wesleyan Church is the single largest denomination, with a congregation of approximately 30,000 adherents. Annual GDP per capita is $US2,200 (2002 estimate). The Kingdom of Tonga is close to financial ruin, reportedly in debt of $AUD43 million (*Sun-Herald*, March 12, 2003).

Tonga is one of the most fertile nations in the Pacific. Tonga's economy is small but open, with active export markets in squash, bananas, vanilla, coconuts, and a lucrative squash pumpkin market in Japan. Nevertheless, much of its food is imported from New Zealand. Agriculture accounts for approximately 40% of GDP, and agricultural and fish products account for almost all of Tonga's total export earnings. Tourism is a major source of foreign currency. Tonga remains dependent on foreign aid to support its trade deficit.

Contextual Features

Tonga has a written constitution. The king and Privy Council can make ordinances, but none have been made since independence. Some English statutory law remains in force in Tonga. The remaining body of written law consists of acts and regulations produced by the Legislative Assembly with the king's assent. Common law applies as far as local circumstances and legislation allow.

The total number of reported crimes in 1990 in Tonga was 1,434. Of these, 50.4% were theft offences, and 30.2% assaults (UN Survey of Crime Trends, cited in Newton 2000:11).

The court structure of Tonga is based on the standard model of inferior court, superior court, and court of appeal. The Privy Council is the body appointed by the king to assist him, rather than a court. The Privy Council has jurisdiction to hear appeals from the Land Court in relation to hereditary estates and titles.

The Court of Appeal has all the powers of the Supreme Court, and exclusive jurisdiction to determine criminal and civil appeals from the Supreme Court.

Any person who has been convicted on trial in the Supreme Court may appeal to the Court of Appeal. It has jurisdiction to hear appeals from the Land Court, except in matters relating to the determination of hereditary estates and titles, where appeals pertain to the Privy Council. Judges of the Court of Appeal are empowered to give opinions on important or difficult matters when requested so to do by the king, the cabinet, or Legislative Assembly.

The Supreme Court has all the powers of the magistrate's courts and appellate jurisdiction in relation to decisions of the magistrate's courts. The Supreme Court is empowered to try all indictable offences and has criminal jurisdiction in relation to all offences that carry a maximum penalty of a fine that is more that AUD $500 or a period of imprisonment exceeding two years. Judges in Tonga determine that where there is a lack of definition in legislation, the English common law meaning is applied (Findlay 1996:18).

A magistrate's court, constituted by the chief police magistrate, has jurisdiction throughout Tonga. Other magistrates may exercise jurisdiction within the district to which they are assigned. Every magistrate has the general powers and jurisdiction in civil cases in order to make orders for maintenance, issue subpoenas for witnesses, enforce payments, exercise powers set down by law, and make temporary orders where prompt action is required. All magistrates have jurisdiction with regard to hearing and determining criminal matters in which the prescribed punishment does not exceed a fine of $1,000 or a period of three years' imprisonment. In addition, the chief police magistrate has jurisdiction to hear cases in which the fine provided by law is no more than $2,000.

Land Courts apply the Land Act of 1927, and address all questions of title affecting land or any interest in land (Care et al. 1999).

As of June 2002, Tonga had six prisons holding some 113 prisoners. The total prison capacity of Tonga is 139. The main penal institution is at Hu'a-tolitoli, near Nuku'lofa. Prisoners are often required to undertake public works or work on government copra plantations (*www.kcl.ac.uk/depsta/rel/icps/worldbrief/oceania_records.php?code=18*).

Police Profile

Background

The Tonga Police Force is a national agency with jurisdiction throughout the Kingdom. There are no separate local or municipal police agencies.

Demographics

King Taufa'ahau Tupou IV joined the Kingdom to the U.S. coalition engaged in war in Iraq, but Tonga has only a 430-man defence force that has rarely left the Kingdom and functions mainly as a palace guard. The army forms largely a ceremonial role and has not been involved in any affairs of state.

Tonga is a heavily policed country, with 418 officers for a ratio of one officer for every 226 inhabitants (1998 research questionnaire distributed to chief officers of police, cited in Newton 2000:5). The same survey revealed a male-dominated force (82%).

Organisational Description

The Tonga Police Force is commanded by a commissioner of police. The force is deployed in three territorial districts: Tongatapu, Haapai, and Vava'u island groups. Many remote small islands lack any police presence, so law and order is dependent on the authority of local chiefs.

Functions

The legally prescribed function of the Royal Tongan Police Force states: "The Force shall be employed in and throughout the Kingdom for the maintenance of law and order, the preservation of the peace, the protection of life and property, the prevention and detection of crime and the enforcement of all laws and regulations with which it is directly charged, and the serving and execution of such process as they are required by law to serve and execute" (Police Act, Tonga, 1988). The regular police also issue fishing licences, register bicycles, apprehend school truants, and enforce Tongan custom and tradition.

Training

Physical training for police recruits is estimated to comprise approximately 80% of the six-month initial training period conducted at the Police Training School in Tonga (Newton 1998:352).

Police Use of Firearms

Section 7 of Tonga's Police Act states: "All members of the Force shall with the approval of the Prime Minister carry arms for the performance of their duties." Under what circumstances, the Prime Minister has granted such approval is unknown. Batons are held in reserve and issued when required.

Terrorism

Tonga has expressed its opposition to all forms of terrorism. The *Washington Post* reported in early January 2003 that Bin Laden's terrorist network was transporting operatives on a shipping fleet flagged in Tonga (Tonga International Registry of Ships). Noble Fielakepa, chair of a cabinet committee stated: "Internationalism terrorism and an increase in people smuggling and asylum seekers were clearly key factors. Even our own region has felt the impact of these problems" (*Sydney Morning Herald*, January 3, 2003). Tonga, keen to pursue global money-making enterprises destined for the Middle East, has been criticised by the United States for offering "flags of convenience" through an open shipping register. The U.S. Central Intelligence Agency has suspected that al-Qaeda has used as many as sixty-two Tongan-registered "flag ships" to carry arms for terrorist purposes (*Four Corners*, ABC TV, July 29, 2003).

The conference of the thirtieth South Pacific Chiefs of Police Conference (SPCPC) (of which the Tongan Police Force is a member) in October 2001 stressed the need to combat terrorism and to prevent its initiation in the South Pacific. The SPCPC resolved to urge commissioners to seek legislative changes to:

- Ban proscribed terrorist groups
- Freeze and seek the early forfeiture of assets of proscribed terrorists and their associates
- Facilitate the extradition of known terrorists and their associates

The Nasinoi Declaration of 2002 recommitted Pacific nations to fight terrorism, money laundering, drug trafficking, people smuggling, and people trafficking.

International Cooperation

The Tongan police force belongs to two central cooperative policing organisations:

South Pacific Chiefs of Police Conference
South Pacific Islands Criminal Intelligence
  Network (SPICIN)

Tonga was one of seven founding members when the South Pacific Chiefs of Police Conference began in 1970 in Fiji, and determined the need for regional cooperation in law enforcement as a priority for its future endeavour. The annual conference provides a forum for Pacific Island police to "exchange information, experience, and technology in law enforcement, the opportunity to plan and implement cooperation projects and to facilitate efforts to combat inter-jurisdictional crime through policy discussion, strategy and common issues." The SPCPC is a leading component of law enforcement in the Pacific region, especially with increased international travel, technological advances, the spread of transnational crime, and terrorist threats. Murder, serious assaults, drugs, money laundering, fraud, paedophilia, electronic crimes, people smuggling, weapons control, and official corruption are central concerns for Pacific police leaders.

In October 1987, SPICIN was created by the seventeen executives of SPCPC at the sixteenth annual conference. SPICIN coordinates and disseminates the exchange of criminal information to combat narcotics trafficking, white collar crime, organised crime, mobile criminals, money laundering, terrorism, and other international crime. SPICIN also instigates training and instruction to assist island nation law enforcement personnel in recognizing and combating major criminal activity.

Tonga belongs to the Pacific Islands Forum (PIF), an annual conference of the heads of states of sixteen Pacific nations. The Forum has been central to the development of a number of initiatives related to police work. Tonga is one of the Pacific regional members of Interpol, the global police organisation that facilitates cooperation among police forces at the international level. Tonga sent police to the Solomon Islands to assist the implementation of the Townsville Peace Agreement in October 2000.

In November 2002, Tonga hosted a transnational crime seminar, sponsored by the Australian Federal Police's Law Enforcement Cooperation Programme (LECP). LECP funds training programmes, workshops, and conferences, and provides short-term attachments and exchanges between countries for operational law enforcers. The Tongan conference discussed transnational crimes such as people smuggling, illicit drug trafficking, and money laundering, as well as terrorism (BBC Monitoring Asia-Pacific, December 2, 2002).

DAVID BAKER

Websites

Pacific Islands Development Program. *Pacific Islands Report* with archives from 1997–2001. Available at: *http://pidp.ewc.hawaii.edu/pireport.*

Central Intelligence Agency. *The World Factbook, 2005.* "Tonga." Available at: *www.odci.gov/cia/publications/factbook/geos/tn.html.*

Bibliography

Care, J., Newton, T., and Paterson, D. *Introduction to South Pacific Law.* London: Cavendish Publishing, 1999.

Findlay, M. *Criminal Laws of the South Pacific.* Suva: University of the South Pacific, 1996.

Newton, T. *Policing in the South Pacific Region.* Occasional Paper No. 1. Suva: School of Law, University of the South Pacific.

Newton, T. Policing in the South Pacific Islands. *Police Journal* 71 (1998):349–352.

TRINIDAD AND TOBAGO

Background Material

The islands of Trinidad and Tobago came under British control in the nineteenth century, and became independent in 1962. The country is one of the most prosperous in the Caribbean, thanks to its petroleum and natural gas industries, and tourism is a growing source of income.

Trinidad and Tobago are located in the Caribbean. The islands lie between the Caribbean Sea and the North Atlantic Ocean, northeast of Venezuela. Their total area is 5,128 square kilometers. The population is 1,096,585 (2004 estimate). Over 40% of the population identifies as East Indian, which is a local term referring to immigrants from northern India. Ethnically, the rest of the population breaks down as follows: black 39.5%, mixed 18.4%, white 0.6%, Chinese and other 1.2%. In terms of religious practice, the population breaks down as follows: Roman Catholic 29.4%; Hindu 23.8%; Anglican 10.9%; Muslim 5.8%; Presbyterian 3.4%; and other 26.7%.

English is the official language. Hindi, French, Spanish, and Chinese are also spoken. The capital is Port-of-Spain.

Trinidad and Tobago are the leading Caribbean producers of oil and gas. The country has earned a reputation as an excellent investment site for foreign businesses. Tourism is a growing sector, although not proportionately as important as in many other Caribbean islands. The economy benefits from low inflation and a growing trade surplus. Annual GDP per capita is US$9,500 (2003 estimate).

Contextual Features

The Republic of Trinidad and Tobago is a parliamentary democracy. The president is the chief of state, while the prime minister acts as the head of the government. The cabinet is appointed from among members of Parliament. The bicameral Parliament consists of the Senate and the House of Representatives. The Senate has thirty-one seats, and the House of Representatives has thirty-six seats.

The Supreme Court of Judicature is comprised of the High Court of Justice and the Court of Appeals. The chief justice is appointed by the president after consultation with the prime minister and the leader of the opposition. Other justices are appointed by the president on the advice of the Judicial and Legal Service Commission. Other courts include the High Court of Justice and the Court of Appeals. The highest court of appeal is the Privy Council in London.

The legal system is based on English common law. The Supreme Court carries out judicial reviews of legislative acts.

The constitution provides for an independent judiciary, and the government has generally respected this provision in practice. The judiciary provides citizens with a fair judicial process.

The judiciary is represented by the Supreme Court of Judicature and the Magistracy. The Supreme Court is composed of the Court of Appeal and the High Court. The Magistracy is composed of summary courts and the petty civil courts.

All criminal cases start with the filing of a complaint in the summary court. Minor offenses are tried before the magistrate. For more serious offenses, the magistrate holds a preliminary inquiry. If there is sufficient evidence, the accused goes to trial before a judge and jury of the High Court.

The constitution explicitly provides for the right to a fair trial, and an independent judiciary vigorously enforces this right. All criminal defendants have the right to an attorney.

Trial delays continue to be a problem. Adults prosecuted for serious offenses have been committed for trial or discharged in two to three years in capital cases or within five years in noncapital cases; and minors have been tried or discharged within one year. The High Court has showed improvement in reducing trial backlogs, but backlogs remain significant at the magistrate court level.

Prison conditions at two of the three largest men's prisons generally meet international standards. However, conditions were worse at the Frederick Street Prison in Port-of-Spain, which dates from the 1830s, in 2002. It was designed for 250 inmates, but housed approximately 800 prisoners in December. Diseases such as chicken pox, tuberculosis, HIV/AIDS, and viruses spread easily, and prisoners had to purchase their own medication. The Commissioner of Prisons reported that the prison system held 4,090 inmates at year's end. Overcrowding was a problem in four of eight facilities where 2,290 inmates were housed in prisons built for 980 inmates. A new maximum security prison, opened in late 1998, has a capacity of 2,450. However, at year's end, it was not fully operational, held approximately 800 inmates, and had done little to relieve overcrowding in the detention system.

Police Profile

Organizational Description

The Ministry of National Security oversees the police. An independent body, the Police Service Commission, makes personnel decisions in the Police Service.

The Minister of National Security may authorize preventive detention in order to prevent actions prejudicial to public safety, public order, or national defense, and the Minister must state the grounds for the detention. There were no reports that the authorities abused this procedure.

Functions

In February 2002, the government launched Operation Anaconda, a police action that promised to address the problem of crime through a new zero-tolerance policy. Press reports indicated the program had led to the arrests of more than 500 people by June.

Complaints and Discipline

There have been credible reports that police and prison guards have committed some human rights abuses. Poor prison conditions and significant violence against women remain problems. There have been credible reports of police and prison personnel abusing prisoners in incidents that involved beating, pushing, and verbal insults. The commissioner of police has admitted that there were frequent citizen allegations of police brutality, but he asserted that such claims often were "counterclaims" by citizens who had been arrested for crimes.

Police corruption continues to be a problem. An independent body, the Police Complaints Authority, receives complaints about the conduct of police officers, monitors the investigation of complaints, and determines disciplinary measures where appropriate, including dismissal. However, Public Service Commission restrictions limit oversight authority to impose final discipline through dismissals.

Bibliography

Central Intelligence Agency. *The World Factbook*. "Trinidad and Tobago." Available at: www.cia.gov/cia/publications/factbook/geos/td.html.

U.S. Department of State. *Country Reports on Human Rights Practices, 2002*. "Trinidad and Tobago." Released by the Bureau of Democracy, Human Rights, and Labor, March 31, 2003. Available at: www.state.gov/g/drl/rls/hrrpt/2002/18346.htm.

TUNISIA

Background Material

Tunisia is a moderate Muslim country that has enjoyed peace and political stability since gaining its independence from France in 1956. Despite the heightened tensions in the region since the September 11, 2001 terrorist attacks in the United States and the war in Iraq, the security situation in Tunisia has remained calm. The government of Tunisia continues to promote moderation and encourage engagement in the Middle East peace process.

The French colonial rule of Tunisia ended in 1956. For three decades thereafter, the nation was led by Habib Bourguiba. He advanced secular ideas and increased his own powers to the point of becoming, essentially, a dictator. Bourguiba was removed from power in 1987, ostensibly on the grounds of senility. He was replaced by Zine El Abidine Ben Ali.

Ben Ali has continued Bourguiba's anti-Islamic fundamentalism stance. Like Bourguiba, he has made efforts to increase his own power and solidify his position. Despite an early move toward introducing some press freedom, today media censorship is commonplace.

In 1999, Ben Ali won the elections by 99.44% of the vote, a figure that is disputed. Bourguiba died in April 2000, which inspired widespread antigovernment dissent. However, the Ben Ali regime remains in power.

The African nation of Tunisia has a population of 9.9 million (2004 estimate). Its capital is Tunis. The nation comprises a total area of 164,150 square kilometers (63,378 square miles). Arabic is the official language, and French is also spoken. The major religion is Islam.

Tunisia's main exports include agricultural products, textiles, and oil. The annual GDP per capita is US$6,900 (2003 estimate).

Contextual Features

Tunisia has an increasing crime rate. Criminals have targeted tourists and business travelers for theft, pick-pocketing, and scams. Theft from vehicles is also common. Items high in value like luggage, cameras, laptop computers, or briefcases are often stolen from cars. Although vehicle break-ins occur with frequency, theft of vehicles is rare.

Pickpockets, purse snatchers, and snatch-and-run cell phone thieves are common, and particularly adept in high-traffic tourist areas such as the Tunis medina and the central market, as well as other large cities nationwide. Thieves, usually single males, will target Western women walking alone and then rob their victim (day or night) once the opportunity (no bystanders or passing vehicles) presents itself. Young men on motor scooters will pass women on the street and snatch a handbag or cell phone from the victim as the motor scooter speeds by. Burglaries are occurring with more frequency. Residential break-ins occur as frequently during the day, when homes are often unoccupied, as at night. Burglars, while assumed to be prepared for confrontation, are generally not predisposed to it. For the most part, crimes of stealth are usually committed by a thief who is unarmed, or armed with nonlethal weapons. Although criminals are prepared to be confrontational, most generally avoid gratuitous violence.

Tunisia's dependence on tourism as a source of convertible currency has contributed, in part, to the continued expansion of the internal security services over the past decade. Security services are highly visible, and ensure that the country's image remains one of tranquil stability. The focus on security and a growing economy (average annual GDP growth has been approximately 5% for the last few years, and inflation has remained under 3% since 1996) have helped Tunisia avoid many of the problems faced by other nations in the region.

Police Profile

Reliable and accurate information on the police in Tunisia is virtually inaccessible.

The Tunisian police are relatively well trained and professional. Many senior officials have received advanced training in France, Italy, or the United States. The police are generally responsive to visitors in need of assistance, and they ensure that their presence is particularly high in tourist and other areas frequented by foreigners. By law, Tunisian police officers can and do conduct random traffic stops, and drivers are required to show their Tunisian identity card or residence permit and vehicle registration. Visitors who are briefly detained by the police are encouraged to remain cooperative and professional, traits that the police appreciate and that may assist in expediting a quick resolution to an arbitrary police stop. The national police provide security in major urban areas, while the paramilitary National Guard is responsible for other areas, including the nation's roadways. Police and National Guard personnel are generally responsive to the needs of visitors.

Although Tunisia has introduced some press freedoms and has freed a number of political prisoners, human rights groups say the authorities, including the police, tolerate no dissent, harassing government critics as well as rights activists.

Bibliography

BBC World News. "Country Profile: Tunisia." Available at: http://news.bbc.co.uk/1/hi/world/middle_east/country_profiles/791969.stm. 2004.

Overseas Security Advisory Council. "Tunis, Tunisia: 2005 Crime and Safety Report." Overseas Security Advisory Council, U.S. Department of State. Available at: www.ds-osac.org/Reports/report.cfm?contentID=24376.

TURKEY

Background Material

Turkey was founded in 1923, after the collapse of the Ottoman Empire. Its official name is the Republic of Turkey, and the capital city is Ankara. Following a period of one-party system, it became a multiparty system and a democratic republic in the 1950s. The Republic of Turkey, which is a long-standing associate member of the European Union (since 1963), faces separatist terrorism and high inflation as two major problems. The area of Turkey is 814,578 square kilometers. The population is 62,610,252. Languages spoken include Turkish (official, 90%) and Kurdish. The major religion is Islam. The per capita annual income is approximately US $2,500. Major economic activities are agriculture, energy production, manufacturing industry, textile, mining, trade, construction, transportation, and tourism.

Contextual Features

The Republic of Turkey is a democratic republic. It is a multiparty system with a unicameral parliament. The power to legislate is vested in the parliament, which has 550 members who are elected for five-year terms.

For administrative purposes, Turkey is divided into eighty-one provinces (*vilayet*) and subdivided into districts (*ilce*). Each province has a governor, appointed by the central government, and a council elected by the local community.

The head of state is the president of the Republic, elected by Parliament for a nonrenewable term of seven years. The president appoints the head of government, the prime minister, who presides over the council of ministers and who must have confidence of the Parliament. The administration is centralised in the capital, Ankara.

The Turkish legal system is based on several European legal systems. The legislative body is the parliament, and the judicial power is exercised by independent courts. Judges are independent in discharging their duties, and rule on the basis of the provisions of the constitution, the laws, jurisprudence, and their personal convictions.

The legislative and executive organs and the administration must comply with court rulings, and they may not change or delay the application of these rulings. The constitution also stipulates that as a general rule, court hearings are open to the public.

In Turkey, the power of the judiciary is exercised by judicial, administrative, and military courts. These courts render their verdicts in the first instance, and the superior courts examine the verdict for the last and final ruling. The structure of these courts and their powers are as follows (Payaslıoglu 1993:80).

Judicial courts are divided into two groups as criminal law courts, and civil law courts. There are also state security courts for offences against the democratic republic. Decisions of these courts are reviewed at the higher-level Court of Appeal. Turkey also recognises the right of individual petition to the European Court of Human Rights.

Administrative Courts deal with the administrative law cases, and are named as Regional Administrative Courts, Administrative Courts, and Tax Courts. The higher-level administrative court is the Council of State.

Military courts are another group of courts and are named as Military Criminal Courts, Military Court of Appeal, and Supreme Military Administrative Court.

The Court of Conflict solves jurisdictional problems among all courts (judicial, military, and administrative) explained above.

The Constitutional Court, apart from reviewing the constitutionality of law, tries the president of the Republic, members of the Council of Ministers, and some other officials indicated in the constitution. It also considers the constitutional existence of political parties.

Crimes are mainly defined in the Turkish Criminal Act, and they may be committed by physical or verbal acts. The examples of the crimes committed by physical acts are; murder, arson, rape, theft, armed robbery, and so on. The examples of crimes committed by verbal act may be listed as; defamation, libel, slander, perjury, false testimony, and so on. These are also categorised as felonies and misdemeanours.

According to criminal statistics released by the General Directorate of the Turkish National Police, major crimes generally recorded by the Turkish police are murder, violence against person, robbery, burglary, theft, smuggling, criminal damage, and crimes involving motor vehicles. These groups of crime contain a considerable variety of offences, in terms of both context and seriousness.

For every crime indicated above, there is a punishment stated in the Turkish Criminal Act. The punishments differ according to different crimes. The punishments for felonies may be listed as death, heavy imprisonment, imprisonment, heavy fine, and disqualification from holding public office. The punishments for misdemeanours may be listed as light imprisonment, light fine, and disqualification from practising a profession or trade.

Police Profile

Background

The first policing service in Turkish history was formed in the eighth century, but little is known about the police before the foundation of the Ottoman Empire in 1299. Because the Republic of Turkey was only founded in 1923, it is a relatively new state that inherited the Ottoman policing system. During the time before the establishment of the "professional" police in 1845, which is considered as the "old policing period," policing in the empire was carried out by various kinds of military commanders, along with their other duties.

The event that made necessary the establishment of professional and civil police in Turkey was the replacement of independent military organisations with a new professional army during the 1830s. The Janissaries, the largest military force that was also responsible for policing, was abolished, although the new army had no policing responsibilities. The empire was declining at the beginning of the nineteenth century, and the Janissaries who had been involved in demonstrations demanding social and economic rights, were blamed by the sultan, the head of the empire, for this decline. When the Janissaries were abolished, there was a gap in maintaining public order, and a new civil police force was required to fill that gap.

On April 10, 1845, the first Police Regulation was introduced. With this regulation, the police remained within the framework of the military force, but were slowly becoming a nonmilitary force. As the police began to fulfil more policing functions than military functions, the police organisation underwent administrative and structural change.

When the Ottoman Empire collapsed after World War I, the old police commanders disappeared or changed their uniforms and functions so that they were no longer recognisable. New personnel appeared, performing the police functions in different ways but with a similar organisation and approach to their responsibilities.

Just after the foundation of the new republic in 1923, the name of the national police organisation became the General Directorate of Security, and the organisation of the gendarmerie was reorganised again and attached to the Ministry of the Interior for their policing functions. (The gendarmerie are also responsible to the Ministry of Defence for their military functions.) A further reorganisation of the gendarmerie took place in 1930, and of the national police in 1932 that divided the police into two branches: uniformed and plainclothes detectives. The last form of the police regulations affecting general organisational structures took effect in 1937 with the Police Organisation Act. This Act still controls the Turkish national police force, despite some small changes that have been made from time to time.

No significant organisational changes were made in the Turkish police from 1937 to the 1960 military coup. After 1960, there have been only two major changes. The first one was the formation of a public order police force, the Riot Police (Toplum Polisi), within the central and provincial police departments in 1965. These changes were either preemptive or responsive to public disturbances and political violence following the introduction of the new constitution in 1961. These police units were replaced by the Rapid Action (Cevik Kuvvet) units in 1982. On the other hand, the number of public order police forces, namely the rapid Action Police, is also increasing. There are such units in almost all provinces. The total number of police personnel employed in these units by the end of 2002 was about 25,000. The second change was the creation of special response units, the Special Operation Teams (Ozel Harekat Timleri), and the Anti-Terror Police Units, within the central and provincial police departments and within the gendarmerie organisation in 1986.

Demographics

As a result of an effort to make policing more efficient against growth in the population and crime rate, the number of police officers and expenditures have grown in Turkey, especially during the postwar period.

The most rapid increase in the number of police personnel was seen after the military coup in 1980. Before that time, it was difficult to find recruits for the police force because of widespread terrorism. By the middle of the 1980s, the number of personnel working in the Turkish national police force (including police officers, civilians and night watchmen, and excluding the gendarmes and special police officers) had doubled to about 100,000.

According to figures released at the beginning of 2000, the total number of personnel working in the Turkish police organisation was about 200,000 (including the civilian personnel). But the regulations require even more personnel to bring the organisation up to full strength. About 10% of police personnel are women, and almost 30% of the police are plainclothes.

Considering the total number of the national police and Turkey's population (62 million), there is one police officer for approximately every 310 citizens. However, this number needs to be doubled since the number of the military police forces is almost the same.

Organizational Description

In terms of police organisational structures in Turkey, the "public police" consists of three separate national and centralised forces: the civil police and two military police forces (gendarmerie and coastal security guards). Centralisation has been a traditional feature of the political and administrative system in Turkish history generally. Turkey's long tradition of civil disorder is one of the factors that has produced a public order police force through a highly centralised system. Especially by the end of the nineteenth century when the collapse of the Ottoman Empire began, and by the beginning of the twentieth century when the Republic of Turkey was founded, a high priority was given to public order policing functions. Despite the highly centralised organisational structure of the Turkish police, however, there is not a national public order policy or a national public order training policy, but it is applied locally, by local police training centres (Moore and Cerrah 1996–1997:108).

The three national organisations in charge of policing are constitutionally a part of the executive. The body generally responsible for policing in Turkey is the Ministry of Interior, which carries out policing functions through police that constitute a national and armed civil force, and the gendarmerie and coastal security guards, which are also national and armed military police forces.

The organisations of all three forces (General Directorate of the Police, General Command of the Gendarmerie, and Command of Coastal Security) have duplicate structures and facilities, such as separate budgets, central headquarters in Ankara, provincial units, training schools and communications systems. The highest officials of the organisations are attached to the Ministry of the Interior with respect to their policing functions, and at the local level, the forces are under the highest civil authority with respect to their administrative functions and under the public prosecutor with respect to their judicial functions.

The territorial organisation of the Turkish national police force corresponds to administrative subdivisions. There are three kinds of units or departments within the central organisation or headquarters: principal, support, and advisory units.

Below the large central organisation (headquarters), there are police departments in eighty-one provinces as subdivisions of the central organisation. Each provincial police organisation also has subdivisions in districts or small towns. At the final level of the national police are local police stations attached to the district police commands. Despite this wide territorial distribution, a vast majority of police personnel are clustered in the larger cities such as Istanbul, Ankara, and Izmir (Kurian 1989:385).

In terms of ranks, the police manpower may be divided into two groups: ordinary police personnel and police officers. The ranks of police officers, in order from the bottom to the top, are as follows: assistant commissar, commissar, chief commissar, police commander, police director. Police directors are also divided into four levels. As will be explained below, the students who complete a two-year course at any of the police professional high schools of the Police Academy become ordinary police, while those who complete a four-year course at the Police Academy, Faculty of Security Sciences, become assistant commissars. Promotion to other ranks is subject to working for three or four years, certain examinations, and sometimes courses for each rank.

Functions

All functions performed by the police and other military forces are the same, but normally the police are responsible for policing within the municipal boundaries of cities and towns, the gendarmerie work in rural areas, villages, and small towns, and the coastal security guards are responsible for the security of coasts and territorial waters.

The issue of police powers and functions in Turkey is complex. Historically, the major threat to public order and the security of the state in Turkey has been derived from mass popular movements, rather than occasional riots. This is perhaps why especially the stop and search powers of the police are too extensive and not well defined.

Since the military intervention of 1980, the Turkish police have been given increased powers to combat terrorist movements. A new edict apparently extended the authority and powers of the police and the military forces still further to deal with political militants. Since 1990, further laws have been introduced giving to the police more extended powers.

According to the Police Functions and Powers Act, police powers can be summarised as, taking fingerprints of suspects, making decision on opening or closing down of a public area after an investigation, search and seizure, arrest and interrogation, checking identification of suspicious people, and using certain types of force and firearms as identified by the related laws.

Street-level discretionary powers for the Turkish police are not individual but collective, and occur according to decisions of the officer in charge of the team. Article 1 of the Police Functions and Powers Act stipulates that in situations that are not clearly identified by laws or regulations, the officer on duty has to ask for a decision from the commander in charge and act according to the order given.

Police Public Projects

The Turkish police are not encouraged and are not subject to any law that requires them to establish a system of community consultation, and there are no legal consultative bodies. There is a little encouragement from internal regulations, but this is only for improving community relations. For example, all police stations are requested to meet, at least once a month, those members of the community who wish to come to the station, to discuss policing matters in their areas, including crime prevention, traffic control, and terrorism, to hear complaints against the police and to listen to community ideas on policing issues.

These meetings are types of community consultation meetings. The aim of these meetings was to establish coordination between the police and the public. Also, it was aimed at establishing a channel for people to express their ideas about general policing issues in order to help the police.

As a result of this effort, most local police stations began to arrange public meetings, but it would be true to say that it is still not enough and does not work efficiently. The people still have no share in police duties, or any involvement with the police. However, such an effort can be a channel toward a real police community consultation procedure and better police–public relations.

Police Use of Firearms

Considering the issue of using fire-arms, it has to be indicated that almost all police are given at least a pistol and a personal radio. Also, the old pistols are replaced with new and more powerful ones and the antiterrorism, special operational, and rapid action teams are given additional weapons and armoured vehicles. The police are trained periodically in order to develop their shooting skills.

Coercive policing in Turkey is currently increasing in the form of establishing heavily armed police forces or units, and increasing the number of weapons and armoured vehicles available to the police. In other words, policing is becoming even more coercive by heavily arming all police officers, and having many "military-style" police units or departments. One reason why the police are becoming even more armed and militarised is that the Turkish community requires such a police force. The general idea here is that the police should be armed more heavily than the terrorists in order to suppress terrorism and violence.

Complaints and Discipline

It can be argued that the Turkish police sometimes go beyond the limits of lawful power of using force or firearms. Four factors associated with excessive use of force can be identified. These are personal, situational, organisational, and environmental characteristics (Durna 2002:121–124).

Accountability of the Turkish police is not a well-researched issue. Because of the complexity of policing laws, it is not well defined who or which part of the police has which powers and responsibilities, or who is accountable to whom for their actions and use of discretionary powers. What is clear is that the Turkish police are fully responsible to the Minister of the Interior for all police activities including judicial (criminal) and political (state security) branches, as well as the general or administrative police.

Formally, the Turkish Interior Minister is given the responsibility and political power concerning policing is accountable through the doctrine of ministerial responsibility to Parliament, and through Parliament to the electorate.

It is clear that the Turkish police are accountable only to the law and to internal disciplinary procedures. There is no accountability to the community or any democratically elected body such as local police authority or local government. In other words, the Turkish police organisation itself formally controls police accountability. The internal command staff potentially have considerable powers of internal accountability. Its disciplinary procedure contains many formal sections of a highly centralised military organisation.

Police officers, like everyone else, are subject to the law of the land, but they are also subject to internal discipline codes and regulations. There is already in place a coherent and formal complaints system. It is a constitutional right that people can complain against any official or organisation including the police by using any means, such as letter, statement, the press, and so on.

Complaints against the police are made to the director-general and are then forwarded to the Department of Personnel and the Police Inspection Board. After that, in the central or provincial organisations, police inspectors who are actually the higher rank police officers begin to investigate. After the investigation, the inspector submits a report to the chairman of the Board. It is then forwarded to the appropriate Discipline Board for a decision. If the officer is found guilty of a criminal offence, as well as a disciplinary offence, one copy of the report is also sent to the general or local public prosecutor.

A major reason for complaints against the police has been the violations of human rights. Treatment of offenders by the police has been the subject of many Amnesty International reports. As a result of intensive scrutiny and accusations from Western countries concerning police actions violating political, civil, and human rights, the Turkish government initiated some changes during 1980s and 1990s. For example, a commission was set up consisting of representatives from the Ministries of Interior, Foreign Affairs, and Justice, and representatives of lawyers and police officers. In addition, since the mid-1980s, courses on human rights have been taught at police educational institutions. In 1994, the Parliamentary Commission on Human Rights, the Human Rights Consultation Board, and the Ministry of Human Rights were established.

Most human rights violations are seen in combating terrorism. Terrorism, as a worldwide challenge and threat to the state, has been a major internal issue for the Turkish police. During the 1960s, Turkey first experienced widespread terrorist actions. Student demonstrations in larger cities initiated major clashes between the police and demonstrators. In other words, the first activist groups in Turkish society influenced by Marxism were students and workers. As part of a worldwide movement in the 1960s, the radical student movement with organisations such as DEV-GENC (Revolutionary Youth) protested against the U.S. presence in Turkey. As the demonstrations subsided, terrorist groups such as THKO (Turkish People's Liberation Army) began a series of bombings, kidnappings, and assassinations throughout the country, and the police began to find ways of dealing with this problem. An extremist rightwing movement, the Ulkuculer (Idealists) also appeared to oppose the Left.

Terrorism

The terrorist organisations that have been active in Turkey may be divided into three types: leftwing, rightwing, and separatist organisations. The main extreme leftwing terrorist organisations, apart from those indicated above, are the Turkish People's Liberation Party-Front (THKP-C), Revolutionary Left (DEV-SOL), Revolutionary Path (DEV-YOL), and Turkish Workers and Peasants Freedom Army (TIKKO). The most important separatist terrorist organisation is the Kurdistan Workers' Party (PKK), or KADEK. In 1990s, an Islamic separatist organisation called Hezbollah also became active in Turkey. Major rightwing organisations that have been involved in terrorist actions are the Idealists organisation Ulkucu Seriat Komandoları (USK) and a radical Islamic organisation IBDA-C.

New antiterrorism departments and special response teams with extended powers were established by legislation during the 1970s and 1980s to fight against domestic terrorism. In 1993, the Special Operation Unit attached to the Antiterror Department was reorganised and extended as an independent department. This department has provincial subunits. The personnel work in the Antiterrorism and Special Operation Departments, and their subunits are fully armed and equipped with military equipment, and their primary duty is to fight against terrorism.

International Cooperation

Terrorism is one of the major reasons why Turkey establishes cooperation with other countries. The Turkish police organisation cooperates with European countries, neighbouring countries, and international police organisations in order to be successful in combating terrorism, as well as to improve policing in Turkey. Many Asian and Middle Eastern countries wish to establish similar cooperative contacts with Turkey in order to improve their own policing systems.

The Turkish police organisation has cooperated with most of European countries in terms of information and technology exchange, training facilities, and working tactics and techniques that will help to develop more democratic and lawful, as well as effective and efficient policing. Apart from cooperation in terms of educational facilities and information exchange, there are many agreements and protocols between Turkey and other countries, encouraging cooperation to combat domestic and international terrorism, drug smuggling, and organised crime. The main signatories to current agreements with Turkey are the United States, Germany, Italy, and neighbouring countries such as Bulgaria and Romania. One reason for such coordination, particularly with neighbouring countries, is that most terrorist and smuggling organisations also operate in neighbouring countries. Turkey would like to extend the scope of these agreements, since the Turkish police need outside assistance to combat problems that pose a serious threat to the stability of Turkish society. This international relationship does not only offer financial and other material assistance, but also the exchange of information, cooperation, and division of labour.

Turkey has been a member of Interpol since 1930, and the Turkish police have a limited relationship with Europol. There are attempts in Turkey to bring the policing system in line with European standards, in order to be accepted by the European Union for full membership. To do this, it needs to reorganise and reshape its own police organisation, making it less coercive with more democratic powers and introducing Western-style police strategies, but there is still a long way to go. Turkey's human rights record has stood in the way of its application for membership.

Turkey has been concerned with establishing relationships with the new independent Balkan countries and Central Asian republics, in terms of different policing issues such as information exchange and educational facilities. For example, Turkey and Macedonia signed a Security Cooperation Protocol in 1993, and Turkey has agreed to a protocol with Uzbek police to offer educational facilities such as the establishment of training centres similar to those in Turkey or offering training in Turkey. The Turkish Police Academy accepts students every year from Azerbaijan, Uzbekistan, Turkmenistan, Kyrgyzstan, and many other Central Asian and Balkan countries.

Police Education, Research, and Publications

The way to become a police officer is to graduate from one of the police training institutions—the Police College or Police Academy.

The Police College is located in Ankara. Graduates of the College, after a four-year course, are the main source of students for the Faculty of Security Sciences that is part of the Police Academy.

The Police Academy based in Ankara consists of the Police Professional High Schools, the Faculty of Security Sciences, and the Institute of Security Sciences. Ordinary police personnel are generally graduated from the Police Professional High Schools. In order to educate police candidates, there are twenty of these schools all around the country, although they are administered by the Police Academy in Ankara, where the main campus is based.

These schools follow: A. S. Mermerci (Istanbul), A. G. Okkan (Diyarbakır), Aksaray, Aydin, Balikesir, Z. Agar (Elazıg), Erzincan, Erzurum, Gaziantep, Kastamonu, Kayseri, K. Serhatlı (Adana), Malatya, Nazilli, Nigde, R. Unsal (Izmir), 19 Mayıs (Samsun), S. Balcı (Istanbul), Trabzon, and Yozgat. The people who complete a high school (*lyce*) level enter these schools for a two-year special policing course, and then they become ordinary police personnel.

The Faculty of Security Sciences, which gives university degrees after a four-year course, is based in Ankara as part of the Police Academy at the main campus. The main source of students for the Faculty is the Police College, but sometimes, if necessary, the students who graduated from any civilian high schools (*lyce*) may also be accepted. Students who complete a four-year course at the Faculty become assistant commissars, which is the first rank of police officers. They can be promoted to other ranks, including higher ranks.

The main purpose of the Institute of Security Sciences, founded in 2001 as part of the Police Academy, is to provide master's and doctoral degrees in policing, criminology, and criminal justice.

Apart from these police education institutions, there are also some local police training centres in some major cities and towns for in-service training. These are Afyon, Bayburt, Bursa, Bornova (Izmir), Etiler (Istanbul), K. Eröge (Istanbul), and Eskişehir Police Training Centres. They provide all kinds of in-service training, while the Eskişehir Police Training Centre is specialised in traffic.

The leading researchers who publish books and articles both in English and Turkish on policing are F. Yenisey of Bahçeşehir University (Istanbul); A. H. Aydin of Kahramanmaras S. University; A. Safak, T. G. Icli, I. Cerrah, H. I. Bahar, and M. Karakaya of Police Academy (Ankara); K. Mutlu and Y. Z. Ozcan of the Middle East Technical University (Ankara); and A. Caglar of Hacettepe University (Ankara). They are usually funded by their own universities since the sources of funding for police research are very limited in Turkey.

Apart from those included in the bibliography below, some books published by some of these researchers (all originally in Turkish) are *Criminology* (T. G. Icli, Ankara, Bizim Büro Basımevi, 2001); *Police Law* (A. Safak and V. Bicak, Ankara, Liberte, 6. Edition, 2000); *Preliminary Investigation* (A. H. Aydin and H. Yalçinkaya, Van, Sakarya Matbaacılık, 2000); and *Crime and Policing in Turkey* (I. Cerrah and E. Semiz, eds., Ankara, Güner

Matbaacılık, 2001). Two major books published in English are *Police Organisation and Legitimacy* (A. H. Aydın, Aldershot, Avebury/Ashgate, 1997), and *Crowds and Public Order Policing* (I. Cerrah, Aldersot, Dartmouth/Ashgate, 1998).

The notable regular journal publishing articles on policing in Turkey is *The Turkish Journal of Police Studies* (Polis Bilimleri Dergisi). This journal, which is edited by Professor T. Icli, is published by the Turkish Police Academy. It publishes papers in both English and Turkish (Polis Akademisi, Necatibey Cad. Anittepe, Ankara, Turkey).

Police-related websites follow: Ministry of Interior (*www.icisleri.gov.tr*), Turkish National Police Organisation (*www.egm.gov.tr*), and Police Academy (*www.pa.edu.tr*).

AHMET HAMDI AYDIN

Bibliography

Arslan, Feyzullah. "Turk Emniyet Orgutunde Surekli Eğitim" (Regular Training in the Turkish Police Organisation). *Turkish Journal of Police Studies* 4, nos. 3–4 (2002): 49–64.

Aydın, A. Hamdi. *Polis Meslek Hukuku* (Police Professional Law). Ankara: Doğuş Matbaası, 1996.

———. *Police Organisation and Legitimacy*. Aldershot: Ashgate-Avebury, 1997.

Bahar, H. Ibrahim. *Demokratik Polislik* (Democratic Policing). Ankara: Maset Matbaacılık, 1998.

Barchard, D. "The Intellectual Background to Radical Protest in Turkey in the 1960s." In *Aspects of Modern Turkey*, edited by W. M. Hale, 21–37. London: Bowker, 1976.

Bicak, Vahit. *Improperly Obtained Evidence*. Ankara: Yardımcı Ofset, 1996.

Bright, M. "Turkey: From Empire to Modern State." *The Guardian Education* 12 April (1994): 9–11.

Cerrah, Ibrahim. "Policing Demonstrations in Turkey." *Turkish Yearbook of Human Rights* 17–18 (1995/1996): 69–87.

———. *Crowds and Public Order Policing*. Aldershot: Ashgate-Dartmouth, 1998.

Criminal Justice Act. 1929. No. 1412.

Durna, Tuncay. "The Effects of Training and Education on Police Use of Excessive Force." *Turkish Journal of Police Studies* 4, nos. 3–4 (2002): 119–140.

Gulmez, Mesut. "Polis Orgutunun Ilk Kurulus Belgesi ve Kaynagi" (The Founding Document and Source of the Police Organisation). *Amme Idaresi Dergisi* 16 (1993): 3–15.

Kurian, G. T. *World Encyclopedia of Police Forces and Penal Systems*. New York: Facts on File, 1989.

Moore, Tony, and Cerrah, Ibrahim. "Public Order Policing in Turkey." *Turkish Public Administration Annual* 22–23 (1996/1997): 107–117.

Payaslıoglu, Arif. *An Introduction to Law and the Turkish Legal System*. Ankara: YOK Matbaasi, 1993.

Police Organisation Act. 1937. No. 3201.

Police Functions and Powers Act. 1934. No. 2559.

Turkish Criminal Act. 1926. No. 765.

TURKMENISTAN

Background Material

From the 1930s, Moscow kept Turkmenistan under firm control. The Communist Party of the Soviet Union (CPSU) fostered the development of a native political elite and promoted Russification. Slavs in Moscow and Turkmenistan closely supervised the national cadre of government officials and bureaucrats; generally, the Turkmen leadership staunchly supported Soviet policies. Moscow initiated nearly all political activity in the Republic, and, except for a corruption scandal in the mid-1980s, Turkmenistan remained a quiet Soviet republic.

When other constituent republics of the Soviet Union advanced claims to sovereignty in 1988 and 1989, Turkmenistan's leadership also began to criticize Moscow's economic and political policies as exploitative and detrimental. Turkmenistan declared its sovereignty in August 1990. Turkmenistan's independence from the Soviet Union was formally declared, and the Republic of Turkmenistan was established on October 27, 1991.

The capital of Turkmenistan is Ashgabat. The population is 4,863,169 (2004 estimate). Turkmenistan covers an area of approximately 488,100 square kilometers. The ethnic composition of the nation is Turkmen 85%, Uzbek 5%, Russian 4%, and other 6% (2003). Turkmen, the official national language, is spoken by about 75% of the population. Russian (replaced as the official language by the 1992 Constitution) is still much used in official communications despite campaigning to limit its influence. In 1993, English was named the second official language. Approximately 87% of the population identifies as Muslim (mainly Sunni), although many who profess Islam are not active adherents. Eleven percent of the population adheres to Russian Orthodoxy.

Annual GDP per capita is US$5,800 (2003 estimate). Turkmenistan is a member of the United Nations, International Monetary Fund, World Bank, Economic Cooperation Organization, Organization for Security and Cooperation in Europe, and the Islamic Development Bank.

Contextual Features

The chief of state and head of the executive branch of the government is the president, who also acts as chair of the cabinet of ministers. The president is both chief of state and head of government. The members of the cabinet of ministers are appointed by the president.

The 1992 Constitution created two parliamentary bodies. The unicameral People's Council or Halk Maslahaty is the supreme legislative body. It has up to 2,500 delegates, some of whom are elected by popular vote, and some of whom are appointed. There is also a unicameral Parliament or Mejlis, with fifty seats.

In late 2003, a new law was adopted, reducing the powers of the Mejlis and making the Halk Maslahaty the supreme legislative organ; the Halk Maslahaty can now legally dissolve the Mejlis, and the president is now able to participate in the Mejlis as its supreme leader; the Mejlis can no longer adopt or amend the constitution, or announce referenda or its elections. Since the president is both the "chairman for life" of the Halk Maslahaty and the supreme leader of the Mejlis, the 2003 law has the effect of making him the sole authority of both the executive and legislative branches of government.

The judicial branch consists of the Supreme Court; its members are appointed by the president. The Supreme Court upholds the constitution and the Supreme Law, as the national codex of civil and criminal law is called. The Ministry of Justice oversees the judicial system, while the Office of the Procurator General is responsible for ensuring that investigative agencies and court proceedings are in compliance with the constitution and the Supreme Law. The president appoints the Republic's procurator general and the procurators in each province, and the procurator general appoints those for the smallest political jurisdictions, the districts and cities.

The court system comprises three levels. At the highest level is the Supreme Court. The Supreme Court hears only cases of national importance; it does not hear appeals. At the next level, appellate courts function as courts of appeal. Trial courts have jurisdiction over civil, criminal, and administrative matters. Separate from these levels, military courts decide cases involving military discipline and crimes committed by and against military personnel. Also, the Supreme Economic Court performs the same function as the state arbitration court of the Soviet period, arbitrating disputes between enterprises and state agencies. The constitution stipulates that all judges at all levels are appointed by the president to terms of five years, and they may be reappointed indefinitely. Enjoying immunity from criminal and civil liability for their judicial actions, judges can be removed only for cause.

In 1996, thirteen crimes were punishable by death, but few executions were known to have been carried out. Prison riots in 1996 revealed that the prison administration is corrupt and that conditions are poor, with overcrowding being a problem.

Observers of several trends in the administration of justice in the court system have concluded that rudimentary elements of legal culture are absent in the implementation of legal proceedings in Turkmenistan. First, the judiciary is subservient to the Ministry of Justice, and it is especially deferential to the wishes of the president. Second, because the Office of the Procurator General fills the roles of grand jury, criminal investigator, and public prosecutor, it dominates the judicial process, especially criminal proceedings. Third, disregard for due process occurs frequently when higher officials apply pressure on judges concerned about reappointment, a practice known as "telephone justice." Fourth, the legal system disregards the role of lawyers in civil and criminal proceedings, and the Ministry of Justice has not permitted an organized bar. Finally, the Republic's citizenry remains largely ignorant of the procedures and issues involved in the nation's legal system.

Turkmenistan has a low rate of violent crime, but ordinary street crime is common.

Police Profile

The criminal justice system of Turkmenistan is grounded in Soviet-era institutions and practices. Turkmenistan's Committee for National Security, for example, retains basically the same duties and personnel of the KGB. As it did in the Soviet period, the Ministry of Internal Affairs continues to direct the operations of police departments and to work closely with the Committee for National Security on matters of national security.

The national police force, estimated to include 25,000 personnel, is under the jurisdiction of the Ministry of Internal Affairs. The force is located in cities and settlements throughout the country, with garrisons in Ashgabat, Gyzylarbat, and Dashhowuz.

Police departments do not have an investigative function in Turkmenistan. The police focus on maintaining public order and administrative tasks such as controlling the internal passport regime, issuing visas for foreign travel, and registering foreign guests.

At the national level, the primary security concerns are drug trafficking and organized crime. In December 1994, Turkmenistan's Committee for National Security and the Russian Federation's Foreign Intelligence signed a five-year agreement for cooperation in state security and mutual protection of the political, economic, and technological interests of the two governments.

Bibliography

Central Intelligence Agency. *The World Factbook*, "Turkmenistan." Available at: www.cia.gov/publications/factbook/geos/tx.html. 2005.

Library of Congress. Country Studies. "Turkmenistan." Available at: http://lcweb2.loc.gov/frd/cs/. 2005.

TUVALU

Background Material

"Tuvalu" means "group of eight," referring to the eight traditionally inhabited coral atolls in the South Pacific Ocean. (The southern-most island is not permanently inhabited.) From the 1820s to the 1870s, the islands were visited by whalers and beachcombers. During that period, about 400 islanders were forcibly removed from the islands by "blackbirders" to work the mines of Peru. After early European forays into the islands, modern Tuvalu (also known as the Ellice Islands) was annexed by Britain in 1892. It was placed in the same crown colony as the nearby Gilbert Islands. By the 1970s, however, ethnic tensions between the Polynesian people of the Ellice Islands and the Micronesians of the Gilbert Islands had become sufficiently serious to merit the separation of the two groups in 1974. The Ellice Islands became the separate British colony of Tuvalu in 1975, and independence followed in October 1978. In 1986, the people of Tuvalu rewrote their 1978 Constitution to reinforce their concerns for Tuvaluan traditions and values.

One of the lowest-lying countries in the world, Tuvalu's highest point is a mere five metres above sea level. Rising sea levels pose a threat to the very territorial survival of Tuvalu. It is one of the smallest and most remote sovereign states on the planet, with a land surface of only twenty-six square kilometres. As there are no streams or rivers, supplying water is a perennial problem. Tuvalu has no notable mineral resources. In 1997, three cyclones hit the islands. Tuvaluans are beset by fears about global increases in greenhouse gas emissions and their effects on rising sea levels that threaten the country's underground water table. Rising sea levels could even make evacuation necessary (*www.odci. gov/cia/publications/factbook/geos/tv.html*).

The population is 11,146 (July 2002 estimate), with a growth rate of 1.4%. Almost a third of the population is under fifteen years of age and only 5% are over sixty-five.

Languages spoken are Tuvaluan (Polynesian language close to Samoan), English, Samoan, and Kiribati (on the island of Nui). Religions are the Church of Tuvalu (Congregationalist) 97%; Seventh-Day Adventist 1.4%; and Baha'i 1%. The annual GDP per capita is US$1,556 (2000).

Tuvalu is a small, scattered country of eight inhabited islands with poor soil. There are no known mineral resources and few exports. Its mixed-market economy consists of subsistence farming and fishing as the primary economic activities. Tuvalu receives less than a thousand tourists per year. The nation's economic growth is constrained by its isolation, small dispersed land area, and limited infrastructure.

One of the main sources of income is the granting of fishing licenses to foreign vessels (Japan, South Korea, Taiwan) operating in Tuvalu's exclusive economic zone. Government revenue is mainly from the sale of stamps and coins and remittances from overseas workers, a position common to a number of "microstates." About a thousand Tuvaluans worked in Nauru's declining phosphate industry, but Nauru has begun repatriating Tuvaluans as phosphate resources decline. Tuvalu's other major source of foreign currency comes from the sale of internet domain names. Tuvalu is fortunate to have the domain name ending "TV," of considerable value to media companies. Tuvalu has effectively managed its economy. It has no foreign debt and the government annually produces a balanced budget.

Substantial income is received from an international trust fund established in 1987 by Australia, New Zealand, and the United Kingdom, supported also by Japan and South Korea. In order to reduce its dependence on foreign aid, the government is pursuing public sector reforms, including personnel cuts. Australia's bilateral aid to Tuvalu was AUD$2.8 million in 2002–2003.

Contextual Features

Tuvalu has a constitution, enacted in 1986, which creates the framework for a broader body of law that includes acts of Parliament, ordinances, and regulations. In addition, a considerable body of law was inherited in the form of English acts. English common law also operates in Tuvalu, except where it is inconsistent with the constitution and customary law. The latter governs mainly property rights and land use, and is abrogated when inconsistent with the constitution.

The court hierarchy is laid down in Section 119 of the constitution. In addition to the standard model court hierarchy, there are additional courts to deal with land matters and local disputes. Unlike neighbouring island countries, these are separate bodies (Care et al. 1999).

The Privy Council is part of the judicial system in Tuvalu. It has jurisdiction to hear appeals from the decisions of the Court of Appeal with leave of the Court of Appeal, in the following matters:

- Final decision on a question as to interpretation or application of the constitution
- Final decision in proceedings for the enforcement of the fundamental rights provisions in Part II of the constitution
- Final or interlocutory decision in any case which the Court of Appeal considers involving a question of great general or public importance or which ought to be submitted to the Privy Council
- Any civil case involving US$2,000 or more
- Proceedings for dissolution or annulment of marriage

The Court of Appeal has jurisdiction to hear civil appeals as of right from the High Court exercising any type of jurisdiction, except where an order was made by consent or relates to costs only, and where an order or judgment is interlocutory, except in a case prescribed by rules of court.

A chief justice visits twice a year to preside over sessions. These rulings can be appealed to the Court of Appeal in Fiji. The High Court has unlimited original jurisdiction in civil and criminal cases; jurisdiction to hear appeals as of right from all decisions of the senior magistrate's court, other than orders made ex parte, by consent, or as to costs only; and a supervisory jurisdiction over inferior courts.

Magistrates' courts have jurisdiction to hear civil cases involving up to US$10,000; may hear appeals from island courts exercising divorce jurisdiction or jurisdiction in any civil matter where the amount involved exceeds US$10; and have power to review any civil or criminal island court case, either on the petition of a party or of its own motion.

Island courts have limited jurisdiction. Island courts have jurisdiction within the boundaries of the island on which they are established and over inland and adjacent waters. Within that area they have summary jurisdiction to deal with the following civil matters: petitions for divorce or associated proceedings under the Native Divorce Ordinance, provided both parties are domiciled in Tuvalu; claims in contract and tort where the amount involved does not exceed US$60; and applications under the Custody of Children Ordinance (Care et al. 1999).

Tuvalu, befitting its small size, had a prison population of six, as of mid-2000. No further information is currently available.

Police Profile

Background

The Tuvalu Police Force is the modern form of the former Gilbert and Ellice Islands Colony Constabulary, which was responsible for the maintenance of law and order in the former British colony. At independence, the police were split into two forces: the Kirabati Police and the Tuvalu Police. At that time, the Tuvalu Police consisted of ten officers, half of whom were women.

Demographics

Officers must be at least eighteen years of age. In 1991, the police force totaled approximately thirty, with a ratio of about one police officer per 300 inhabitants (Newton 2000:5).

Organizational Description

The Police Ordinance and Regulations of Tuvalu (henceforth, Ordinance) governs the organisational structure of the Tuvaluan police force. The force has a chief of police and four subordinate ranks: inspectors, sergeants, corporals, and constables. The chief of police has broad authority to appoint, promote, discipline, and dismiss officers in the force. Promotion is based on qualifications, experience, and merit.

Functions

Section 6 of the Ordinance states: "The Force shall be employed in and throughout Tuvalu for the maintenance of law and order, the preservation of the peace, the protection of life and property, the prevention and detection of crime and the enforcement of all laws and regulations with which it is directly charged." The police force is also required to control traffic, although there is only 19.5 km of unpaved highway.

The Tuvalu Police Force is legally empowered to act as a paramilitary body (Tuvalu has no standing military), but to date it has never used these powers. The national police force includes the Maritime Surveillance Unit for search and rescue missions and surveillance operations.

Training

New recruits are considered to be on probation for two years from initial recruitment. No details on training programs are currently available.

Police Use of Firearms

Police have legal authority to use firearms (Section 6 of the Ordinance).

Complaints and Discipline

Offences relating to mutiny and sedition within the force, desertion, and violently hindering a superior officer in the execution of his duty are punishable in criminal courts with a fine of AU $100 and/or twelve months' imprisonment.

Complaints against senior police officers (inspectors and chief of police) are handled in accordance with Public Service Commission regulations. Junior ranks in the force can be admonished, reprimanded, fined, or confined to quarters by inspectors; the chief of police can severely reprimand, interdict from service, demote or dismiss offenders. A substantial list of misdemeanours against discipline is included in the Ordinance.

Terrorism

The 30th South Pacific Chiefs of Police Conference (SPCPC) in October 2001 stressed the need to combat terrorism and to prevent its initiation in the South Pacific. The SPCPC, of which Tuvalu is a member, resolved to urge commissioners to seek legislative changes to:

Ban proscribed terrorist groups
Freeze and seek the early forfeiture of assets of proscribed terrorists and their associates
Facilitate the extradition of known terrorists and their associates

The Nasinoi Declaration of 2002 recommitted Pacific nations to fight terrorism, money laundering, drug trafficking, people smuggling, and people trafficking.

Anxiety has been expressed about the vulnerability of small Pacific states such as Tuvalu to function autonomously in the light of terrorist and organised crime activities in the region. The Australian government has even voiced the possibility of such small states binding together for security and policing needs. Tuvalu has been criticised by the United States for offering "flags of convenience" through an open shipping register. The Australian Federal Police in April 2003 on the high seas boarded the 4000-tonne North Korean freighter, "Pong Su," and seized 125 kilograms of high-grade heroine valued at US$146 million. The freighter was registered in Tuvalu in order to avoid close inspection.

International Cooperation

The Tuvaluan police force belongs to two central cooperative policing organisations: the South Pacific Chiefs of Police Conference (SPCPC), and the South Pacific Islands Criminal Intelligence Network (SPICIN).

Tuvalu was one of seven founding members when the South Pacific Chiefs of Police Conference began in 1970 in Fiji and determined the need for regional cooperation in law enforcement as a priority for its future endeavours. The annual conference provides a forum for Pacific Island police to exchange information, experience, and technology in law enforcement, the opportunity to plan and implement cooperation projects, and to facilitate efforts to combat interjurisdictional crime through policy discussion, strategy, and common issues. SPCPC is a leading law enforcement organisation in the Pacific region, especially with increased international travel, technological advances, the spread of transnational crime, and terrorist threats. Murder, serious assaults, drugs, money laundering, fraud, paedophilia, electronic crimes, people smuggling, weapons control, and official corruption are central concerns for Pacific police leaders.

In October 1987, the SPICIN was created. SPICIN coordinates and disseminates the exchange of criminal information to combat narcotics trafficking, white-collar crime, organised crime, mobile criminals, money laundering, terrorism, and other international crime. SPICIN also organizes training and instruction to assist island-nation law enforcement personnel in recognizing and combating major criminal activity.

Tuvalu belongs to the Pacific Islands Forum (PIF), an annual conference of the heads of states of sixteen Pacific nations.

DAVID BAKER

Websites
Central Intelligence Agency's *The World Factbook*: *www. odci.gov/cia/publications/factbook/geos/tn.html*.
Pacific Islands Report, with 1997–2003 archives. Available at: *http://pidp.ewc.hawaii.edu/pireport*.

Bibliography
Care, J., Newton, T., and Paterson, D. *Introduction to South Pacific Law*. London: Cavendish Publishing, 1999.
Newton, T. *Policing in the South Pacific Region*. Occasional Paper 1, School of Law, University of the South Pacific, Suva, 1997.

U

UGANDA

Background Material

The Republic of Uganda achieved independence from the United Kingdom in 1962. The dictatorial regime of Idi Amin, which lasted from 1971 to 1979, was responsible for the deaths of some 300,000 people. Guerrilla war and human rights abuses under Milton Obote, who held power from 1980 to 1985, claimed at least another 100,000 lives.

Uganda is located in eastern Africa, west of Kenya, comprising a total area of 236,040 square kilometers, with a population of 26,404,543 (2004 estimate). The ethnic composition of the population is as follows: Baganda 17%, Ankole 8%, Basoga 8%, Iteso 8%, Bakiga 7%, Langi 6%, Rwanda 6%, Bagisu 5%, Acholi 4%, Lugbara 4%, Batoro 3%, Bunyoro 3%, Alur 2%, Bagwere 2%, Bakonjo 2%, Jopodhola 2%, Karamojong 2%, Rundi 2%, non-African (European, Asian, Arab) 1%, and other 8%. The religious composition of the population is as follows: Roman Catholic 33%, Protestant 33%, Muslim 16%, and indigenous beliefs 18%.

English is the official national language. Ganda or Luganda are the most widely used of the Niger-Congo languages. Other Niger-Congo languages in use include Nilo-Saharan languages, Swahili, and Arabic.

The annual GDP per capita is US$1,400 (2003 estimate).

Contextual Features

In the early 1990s, Uganda was still trying to recover from two decades of instability and civil war. In 1995, the government restored the legal system to one based on English common law and customary law.

The president is both chief of state and head of government. The prime minister assists the president in supervising the cabinet, the members of which are appointed by the president from among elected legislators. The unicameral National Assembly has 303 members, 214 of whom are directly elected by popular vote, and 81 of whom are nominated by legally established special interest groups.

The Court of Appeal has judges appointed by the president and approved by the legislature. In the High Court, judges are appointed by the president.

When Britain first assumed control of Uganda in the nineteenth century, the judicial system consisted of a number of local authorities, tribal chiefs, and kin group elders, who worked primarily to enforce local customary law. During the twentieth century, British jurisprudence was gradually imposed. At independence, the resulting legal system consisted of the High Court, which heard cases involving murder, rape, treason, and other crimes punishable by death or life imprisonment; and subordinate magistrates' courts, which tried cases for crimes punishable by shorter terms of imprisonment, fines, or whipping. Magistrates' court decisions could be appealed to the High Court.

After independence, the director of public prosecutions (DPP), appointed by the president, prosecuted criminal cases.

The legal system was essentially nonoperative during the 1970s, as Idi Amin undermined the judicial system when it attempted to oppose him. Amin granted the security forces the right to "search and arrest." The military took this as an incentive to harass political opponents. The courts were then blocked from rendering verdicts against security agents through a second decree, which granted government officials immunity from prosecution. Therefore, soldiers and police could act freely, without any threat of legal accountability.

The end of Amin's regime brought no significant improvement in the criminal justice system. In June 1984, the government prohibited the army from arresting civilians suspected of opposition to the government, and it allowed prisoners, for the first time in over a decade, to appeal to the government for their release from prison. The army ignored the 1984 law, however, and continued to perpetrate crimes against the civilian population.

When Museveni became president in 1986, he pledged to end the army's tyranny and reform the country's criminal justice system. He succeeded in granting greater autonomy to the courts, but several thousand suspected opponents were arrested during counterinsurgency operations in northern and eastern Uganda. In late 1988, a constitutional amendment was passed that gave the president the power to declare any region of the country to be in a "state of insurgency." Subsequent legislation allowed the government to establish separate courts in these areas, authorized the military to arrest insurgents, permitted magistrates to suspend the rules of evidence to allow hearsay and uncorroborated evidence in the courtroom, and shifted the burden of proof from the accuser to the accused.

During colonial times, the principal penal facility was Luzira Prison near Kampala, although jails were common in larger towns. The government also maintained smaller prisons for local convicts in Buganda, Bunyoro, Toro, and Ankole. Terms of less than six months were generally served in smaller jails located in each district.

In 1964, the Prison Service operated thirty prisons, many of which were actually industrial or agricultural facilities, intended to rehabilitate prisoners. By mid-1968, the Prison Service had a force of about 3,000 under the command of the commissioner of prisons.

During the 1970s, civilian and military prison conditions deteriorated, and prisoner abuse became common. Prison conditions in the early 1980s were also dismal. According to Amnesty International, the Obote regime imprisoned civilians without charge or for political crimes. Many were held in police stations, military barracks, and detention centers. Almost all penal facilities were overcrowded, sometimes housing ten times the number of inmates intended. Other reports, however, indicated that members of the Uganda Prison Service sometimes treated inmates relatively humanely, allowing them to read, exercise, and attend religious services.

When Museveni seized power, he promised to improve the country's prison system, but this proved to be a difficult task, in part because so many people had been incarcerated. In late 1986, the Uganda Human Rights Activists (UHRA) charged that the authorities had imprisoned as many as 10,000 people at the Murchison Bay Prison in western Uganda, a facility with an 800-inmate capacity. Moreover, the UHRA and Amnesty International claimed that prisoners lived in abominable conditions, which caused a number of deaths from disease.

In 1987, Museveni allowed the International Committee of the Red Cross (ICRC) to survey conditions in Uganda's civilian prisons. Although some reports suggested that prison conditions improved as a result, there had in fact been little change. In late 1990, for example, Chief Justice Samuel Wako Wambuzi condemned overcrowding in the Masaka Central Prison.

During the colonial period, most arrests were for murder, rape, robbery, and, on occasion, treason. People were also imprisoned for failing to pay taxes. After Uganda gained independence, crime patterns shifted to more violent crimes. In the 1970s, political crimes were dominant. Many arrests and executions were not recorded, and statistics are generally unavailable for this time period.

Uganda's parliament tried to stop the rise of organized violent crime in 1968, amending the 1930 Penal Code to mandate the death penalty for those convicted of armed robbery. A few months later, the government passed the Public Order and Security Act, authorizing the president, or a delegated minister, to detain indefinitely anyone whose actions were judged prejudicial to national defense or security. After 1970, the government increased its reliance on this act to detain political opponents.

Following the overthrow of the second Obote regime in 1985, the government freed about 1,200 prisoners held under the Public Order and Security

Act. Some abuses continued to be reported in 1990, despite government promises to end abuse by police and prison officials and to respect individual rights before the law.

Police Profile

Ugandan police history began in 1900 when Special Commissioner Sir Harry Johnston established the Armed Constabulary, with 1,450 Africans under the command of British officers. In 1906, the Protectorate Police replaced the constabulary, and the colonial government appointed an inspector general as the commanding officer of all police detachments.

Although created as a civilian force, the police frequently carried out military duties. To support this expanded role, colonial authorities enlarged the Protectorate Police. By 1912, the police operated fifteen stations and possessed a small criminal investigation division. The police continued their paramilitary functions, patrolling border areas between Uganda and German East Africa (later Tanzania) during World War I, and patrolling Karamoja District to suppress cattle raiding and border skirmishes.

After 1918, the police became a more traditional internal security force. Most of their work involved homicide investigations; traffic control; and supervision of vehicle, bicycle, and trade licenses. Worldwide economic depression caused the colonial government to reduce the size of the police force from its 1926 level of 33 officers and inspectors with 1,368 regular police, to 37 officers and inspectors with 1,087 regular police.

At the outbreak of World War II, the police again undertook military duties. In 1939, the protectorate police dispatched a garrison to Lokitaung, Kenya; arrested German nationals in Uganda; and provided security at key installations. In addition, the police assumed responsibility for operating and guarding camps for detained aliens. Many members of the police force also served in British army units in East Africa and in overseas operations. After World War II, the colonial authorities expanded the police force, and in July 1954, the Legislative Council established new police stations and posts throughout Uganda. The government also formed a specially recruited Internal Security Unit that subsequently became the Special Force Units. By the mid-1960s, there were eighteen Special Force Units, each comprising fifty police trained in commando tactics, normally assigned to crowd control duties and border patrols.

Uganda's independence constitution in 1962 reaffirmed the British policy of allowing the kingdoms of Buganda, Bunyoro, Toro, and Ankole to maintain local police forces, which were nominally accountable to Uganda's inspector general of police. When the 1967 Constitution abolished the federal states and Buganda's special status, the local police forces merged into the Uganda Police Force or became local constabularies.

During the 1960s, the Uganda Police Force comprised a Uniform Branch, which was assigned mainly to urban duties, and Special Branch and Criminal Investigation Department (CID), Special Constabulary, Special Force Units, Signals Branch, Railway Police, Police Air Wing, Police Tracker Force, Police Band, and Canine Section. Four regional commanders directed police operations and assisted the inspector general. The Police Council—composed of the inspector general, the permanent secretary of the Ministry of Internal Affairs, and four other members appointed by the minister—recommended policies regarding recruitment and conditions of service. The Public Service Commission, in consultation with the inspector general, appointed senior police officers.

By 1968, the Uganda Police Force was a multiethnic, nonpolitical, armed constabulary of between 7,000 and 8,000 officers and constables. In addition to regular urban police activities, it undertook extensive paramilitary duties, provided honor guard detachments for visiting dignitaries, and performed most of the public prosecution in the criminal courts.

During the late 1960s, the government increased its use of the police to eliminate political dissent. President Obote also created the General Service Department (GSD) outside the police organization to monitor the political climate and report disloyalty. Some GSD agents infiltrated other organizations to observe and to record discussions.

During the 1970s, the police force was practically moribund, but President Amin, like his predecessor, used a number of agencies to root out political dissent. More arrests were made for political crimes than for street crimes or corruption. Amin's government relied on the Military Police, the Public Safety Unit (PSU), and the State Research Bureau (SRB) to detect and eliminate political disloyalty. In 1971, Amin created the SRB as a military intelligence unit directly under the president's control. Its agents, who numbered about 3,000, reportedly kidnapped, tortured, and murdered suspects in their headquarters in Nakasero.

During the early years of the Amin regime, the PSU and the Military Police also acquired reputations as terrorist squads operating against their compatriots. Amin ordered PSU agents to shoot robbers on sight, but in practice, he exerted almost no control over them, and PSU agents became known among many Ugandans as roving death squads.

Another internal security agency, the National Security Agency (NSA), was formed in 1979. Many of its first recruits were former GSD members. NSA agents testified before human rights investigators later in the 1980s that although they did not wear uniforms, they carried arms, and many believed themselves to be above the law. Their testimony also related instances of torture and murder, as well as frequent robbery and looting.

Museveni inherited a force of 8,000 when he came to power. A screening exercise revealed that out of the 8,000 personnel, only 3,000 qualified to be retained as police officers. The government augmented this force by contracting 2,000 retired police officers. However, at 5,000 this force was too small to maintain law and order. Museveni therefore ordered the National Resistance Army (NRA) to assume responsibility for internal security.

In December 1989, President Museveni announced that the police, then numbering almost 30,000, and other internal security organs eventually would assume responsibility for law and order in all districts except Lira, Apac, Gulu, Kitgum, Moroto, Kotido, Soroti, and Kumi, where antigovernment rebels remained active.

During the 1980s, Britain, France, North Korea, Egypt, and Germany provided assistance to the Uganda Police Force. British instructors taught courses on criminal investigations and police administration, and they trained future police instructors. In 1989 French police officials provided three-month training courses in riot control and suppression techniques. Museveni also accepted North Korean offers of equipment and training assistance.

By May 1991, the police force numbered about 20,000. Despite British, French, and North Korean training, the government admitted that the police still needed specialized training programs to improve its investigative capabilities.

Bibliography

Central Intelligence Agency. *The World Factbook, yr.* Uganda. Available at: www.cia.gov/cia/publications/factbook/geos/ug.html. 2005.

Library of Congress. "Uganda." Country Studies. Available at: http://lcweb2.loc.gov/frd/cs/. 2005.

UKRAINE

Background Material

In the late ninth century, modern Kyiv was one of the centres of the Kievian Rus state. By the end of the fourteenth century, the lands had been divided among Poland, Lithuania, Hungary, and Moldavia. Russia annexed lands to the east of the river Dnepr in 1667, and the right-bank territories in 1793. Western Ukraine remained part of the Austro-Hungarian Empire until 1920. Following World War I and the collapse of tsarist authority, Ukraine finally had a chance to gain independence, but none of the array of factions could win decisive support. After prolonged fighting involving Russia, Poland, and various Ukrainian political and ethnic factions, Poland retained parts of western Ukraine and the Soviets held the rest. In December 1922, the Union of Soviet Socialist Republics was created, with Ukraine becoming a part of it. In 1991, Ukraine acquired its independence after the collapse of the Soviet Union.

Political divisions and various historical developments of eastern and western parts of contemporary Ukraine largely explain the complicated political problems that Ukrainian society faces today. The major challenges are the weakness of the emerging Ukrainian state, factionalism and fragmentation within the government and parliament, economic crisis, high unemployment and impoverishment of the majority of the population, and growth in corruption and the shadow economy.

The population of Ukraine is 49,153,027 (2000 estimate), made up of Ukrainians (73%), Russians (22%), Jews (1%), and others (4%). Languages spoken are Ukrainian, Russian, Romanian, Polish, and Hungarian. The major religions are Ukrainian Orthodox, Ukrainian Autocephalous Orthodox, Ukrainian Catholic (Uniate), Protestant, Jewish, and Muslim.

The per capita annual income is US$750 (1999). Major economic activities include agriculture, heavy industry particularly ferrous metals and machine building, electric power, chemicals, food industries, and mining and extractive industries.

Contextual Features

The legislative body in Ukraine is the unicameral Parliament (Verkhovna Rada), which consists of 450 deputies: 225 seats are allocated on a proportional basis to those parties who gain at least 4% of the national electoral vote. The other 225 members are elected by popular vote in single-mandate constituencies. All deputies serve a four-year term. The president is elected by popular vote for a five-year term and has very broad powers, including control over the government. The cabinet of ministers is appointed by the president and approved by Parliament.

The Ukrainian Constitution was adopted in 1996. It is the country's fundamental law, followed by various codes (Civil Code, Criminal Code, Labour Code, Land Code, etc.), followed by laws of a general nature and laws of a special nature. Normative Legal Acts embrace not only laws proper (*zakon*), but also various normative acts of competent state bodies issued on the basis of laws. The Parliament has the exclusive right to adopt laws. Other state authority bodies are entitled to issue normative acts on issues under their jurisdiction. The president has the authority to issue edicts and orders, and the cabinet of ministers has the power to adopt resolutions, and issue orders and instructions on implementing the legislative acts of the cabinet of ministers and other branches of government. Local state administrations and local self-government bodies issue resolutions, orders, and decisions to ensure the observance of laws and freedoms of citizens, and the implementation of development programmes and regional budgets.

Between 1990 and 1995, recorded crime increased from 369,809 to 641,860, which was followed by a decrease over the following six years, from 641,860 in 1995 to 503,700 in 2001 (Foglesong and Solomon 2001; Ministry of Internal Affairs 2002). Although the reliability of official crime statistics in Ukraine is highly questionable, there are reasons to believe that there was an increase in property crimes between 1990 and 1995.

The most common recorded crimes are economic crimes, bank fraud, illegal migration, drug trafficking, unlawful possession, production and selling of firearms, theft of private and state property, hooliganism, robbery, and crimes committed within families. One of the most serious problems is a constant increase in the number of offences related to drug trafficking: in 2001, 42,831 such crimes were recorded, representing 8.5% of all recorded crime. Rates of organised crime are also increasing rapidly: In 2001, some 770 criminal groups were identified and 6,703 crimes committed by their members were recorded (Dzhuzha et al. 2001).

According to official statistics, clearance rates are constantly increasing, up from 46.5% in 1992 to 79.5% in 2002, although these figures are notoriously unreliable due to very low levels of crime recording and reporting. It is estimated that about 40% of criminal offences and 95% of economic and occupational crimes are not recorded. The main reasons put forward for an increase in the number of crimes not recorded by the police is the greater incidence of nonreporting by citizens due to lack of confidence and trust in the efficacy of the criminal justice system, and the crime recording practices adopted by the police.

The Ukrainian Constitution provides for an independent judiciary; however, in practice the judiciary is subject to considerable political interference from the executive branch and also suffers from corruption and inefficiency. Ukraine has a unified system of courts consisting of a Constitutional Court (which is responsible for issues involving the constitution, such as interpreting the constitution and reviewing the constitutionality of legislation), and a system of courts of general jurisdiction. General jurisdiction courts are organised on several levels: local courts, appellate courts and the Appellate Court of Ukraine, the Cassation Court of Ukraine, specialised high courts, and the Supreme Court. Specialised courts include commercial and administrative, among others. The Supreme Court is the highest judicial body in the system of courts of general jurisdiction and may review their judgments. Regional courts, including the Supreme Court of Crimea, and the Kyiv and Sevastopol city courts, are appellate courts for lower-level courts. They may examine evidence independently in a case, call for additional witnesses or evidence, and render a decision that supersedes the judgment of a lower court.

The Constitutional Court consists of eighteen judges, appointed for nine-year terms in equal numbers by the president, Parliament, and Congress of Judges. The Constitutional Court is the ultimate interpreter of legislation and the Constitution, and it determines the constitutionality of legislation, presidential edicts, cabinet acts, and acts of the Crimean Autonomous Republic. The president, at least forty-five members of Parliament, the Supreme Court, the Ombudsman, and the Crimean legislature may request that the Constitutional Court hear a case. Citizens may apply to the Constitutional Court through the Ombudsman. In some limited cases, the Constitutional Court can interpret law for individual citizens when the applying citizen provides compelling evidence that a constitutional provision is violated, or that it is interpreted differently by different government bodies.

Under the existing court system, cases are decided by judges who sit singly, occasionally with two public assessors (lay judges or professional jurors with some legal training), or in groups of three for more serious cases. The constitution provides for public, adversarial trials, including a judge, public assessors, state prosecutor, defence, and jury (when required by law). With some qualifications, these requirements are respected in practice. Observers believe that a jury system will not function until a comprehensive judicial reform is completed and additional funding is provided for the judicial system.

A presidential edict issued in 1998 called for the creation of a department for the execution of punishments in place of the former Directorate for the Execution of Punishments of the Ministry of Internal Affairs (MIA). Beginning in 1999, this department no longer came under the competence of the MIA. In 2001, a new Criminal Code was adopted and the death penalty was abolished.

There are 180 institutions in the Department for the Execution of Punishments, 131 of which are prison camps; 12 are for women; 11 for juveniles; and 33 are investigatory isolation units. There are also five enforced treatment clinics and about twenty hospitals. As of August 2002, there were 202,000 people in prison in Ukraine, including 147,500 in penal institutions and 41,000 on remand. At the end of 2001, 20,000 were in prison for murder, 19,200 for grievous bodily harm, 19,720 for robbery and aggravated robbery, and 900 for other violent behavior. In 2001, 88,000 people were released from prison, including 29,000 who were given amnesty. Of those released from prison, 72% were given registration permits, and 34% were placed in jobs.

A total of 45,000 people work in the correctional system. Since 1992, the number of people held in penal institutions has almost doubled, leading to an acute shortage of space for prisoners. Other problems within the penal system include very poor conditions for those serving life sentences, and no opportunities for the re-education and re-socialisation of prisoners to prepare them for their release. In 2003, it was estimated that about 13,000 prisoners (6.4%) have serious illnesses, such as tuberculosis, HIV, and AIDS.

A criminal-executive inspectorate has been established within the department to manage alternatives to custodial sentences. Around 139,600 convicts were registered with the inspectorate as of early 2003.

Police Profile

Background

Before 1917, the police force was a specialised body responsible for law enforcement in the Russian Empire of which Ukraine was part. Between 1917 and 1919, there were attempts to establish a people's militia in Ukraine subordinated to local governments. In March 1919, the People's Commissariat of Internal Affairs issued an instruction about the organisation of a Soviet militia. According to a decree from the Soviet of People's Commissars of the Ukrainian Soviet Socialist Republic on 29 December 1930, the militia was removed from the control of local governments and subordinated directly to the State Political Department of the Soviet Union. In 1931, the National Regulations on Worker-Peasant Militia were adopted, which regulated all aspects of the militia's activity: organisational structure, duties and rights, service regulations, and provisions and privileges for militia workers and their families. It specified that the main task of the militia was to protect revolutionary order and public safety, necessary for socialist construction.

In the Soviet period, the militia underwent a number of organisational transformations and changes to its functions and practices. It changed from the militarised institution it was under Stalin (1926–1953) into an institution focusing primarily on crime control and maintaining public order, while retaining diverse functions. In 1991, following the collapse of the Soviet Union, police power in Ukraine was transferred to the Ministry of Internal Affairs of the newly independent Ukrainian state. Current reforms of the bodies of internal affairs are considered part of the process of building a democratic state based on the rule of law, and, in particular, are aimed at building cooperative relationships and developing partnerships between the militia and the public (Ministry of Internal Affairs 1999). However, recent policy reviews recognise that steps undertaken in this direction have as yet been insufficient and ineffective.

Demographics

According to existing law, the overall number of employees of the Ministry of Internal Affairs (MIA) should be 386,600 people, including 284,400 who have special militia ranks, from private to general. As of mid-2003, the Ukrainian militia was understaffed by around 12%. The most understaffed units were the patrol services, beat officer services, and criminal investigation departments. Women represent around 11% of the militia; they mainly work in the passport service, forensics, and in the scientific and educational institutions of the MIA system.

Organizational Description

The militia consists of the following subdivisions:

- Criminal militia
- Militia for public safety
- Transport militia
- State motor vehicle inspection
- Guard militia
- Special militia units

The militia is subordinated to and governed by the MIA. The MIA system in Ukraine is centralised and regulated by a single set of laws covering the whole country. Each body of internal affairs covers a territory: a settlement, city district, city, province district, province, or autonomous republic (Crimea). The MIA heads the system and governs it through the main directorates, directorates of branch services, city directorates of the MIA, directorates of the MIA in twenty-four provinces, directorates for the cities of Kyiv and Sevastopol, and the autonomous republic of Crimea, and MIA directorates for transport.

The main directorates consist of Headquarters, Directorate for Combating Organised Crime, Directorate for Criminal Investigation, Economic Crime Directorate, Administrative Service Directorate, Directorate of State Motor Vehicle Inspection, Investigation Directorate, and Personnel Directorate. A typical city or district directorate consists of a number of departments, including criminal militia, public order, investigation, illegal trade in narcotics, juvenile offenders, economic crime, forensics, and motor vehicle inspection.

Heads of the main directorates, directorates in the provinces, and the cities of Kyiv, Sevastopol are appointed and dismissed by the MIA. The head of the main directorate of the MIA of Ukraine in Crimea is an MIA deputy, and is appointed and dismissed by the cabinet of ministers.

Militia employees are given the following special ranks: private, junior sergeant, sergeant, senior sergeant, sergeant-major, warrant officer, senior warrant officer, junior lieutenant, lieutenant, senior lieutenant, captain, major, lieutenant-colonel, colonel, general-major, general-lieutenant, and general-colonel.

On 22 January 2001, the president issued an edict entitled "On the setting up of the local militia," which aimed to increase the efficiency of the MIA and develop partnerships with the public. According to the edict, local militia consisting of road and general patrol services, and beat officers are to be set up by local government bodies. At this moment in time it is not clear what progress has been made in this area.

Functions

According to the law, the main tasks of the militia are providing personal safety for citizens, protecting their rights, freedoms, and lawful interests; crime prevention; protecting and maintaining public order; detecting and solving crime, and arresting offenders; providing road traffic safety; protecting property from criminal encroachments; execution of criminal punishments and administrative punishments; participating in providing social and legal aid to citizens; and helping government bodies, enterprises, and organisations in performing their duties according to the law.

Militia employees are given certain rights and powers to enable them to perform their duties. In particular, they have a right to apply force including physical force, or other special means (handcuffs, rubber batons, tear gas, light and sound devices, water cannon, armoured cars, dogs), as well as firearms to stop crimes being conducted; to detain suspects and offenders for a period of up to three days; to perform undercover operations, check documents, and search the personal belongings and luggage of citizens.

The Criminal Militia is aimed at preventing, interrupting, and solving crimes; searching for persons who are trying to escape investigation and trial; and searching for missing persons and other persons who may be relevant to cases under investigation. The Criminal Militia performs the following specific tasks: fighting illegal drug trafficking; solving crimes involving arms and explosives, and crimes connected with thefts of vehicles; solving economic crimes, and crimes related to privatisation, foreign trade, fuel and the energy sector; and working with underage offenders.

The Militia for Public Safety is tasked with ensuring the personal safety of citizens, the protection of public order and public safety, preventing and interrupting crime and administrative violations, solving crime, and providing help to citizens, enterprises, and organisations. Its preventative functions consist of preventing crime and administrative violations such as hooliganism, burglaries, and domestic violence. Their criminal procedural function is to consider reports and information about crimes, and conduct investigations into crimes that do not represent a serious threat to society.

The State Motor Vehicle Inspectorate is responsible for road patrols, and preventing and responding to traffic accidents (including investigations); road safety campaigns; observance of traffic laws; control over the design and construction of roads; establishing minimum requirements for the design of vehicles (including environmental impact); and the registration of vehicles and drivers (including testing).

The Guard Militia is a centralised system of departments providing contract guard services for public and private properties, and personal protection services for individuals. These include installation and monitoring of alarms and responding to activations; carrying out security surveys of government buildings and making recommendations to the cabinet of ministers and other governmental departments; and monitoring private security companies, including those producing alarm equipment and those providing guard services.

Special Units of the Militia include the "Berkut," a rapid-response unit created in 1992 to help deal with unusual circumstances, such as large public order incidents, or serious crimes involving weapons. Officers working in this unit must have a minimum of two years service and are given specialist training. These units have been involved in dealing with organised crime and terrorist incidents (including hostage release). The Titan special militia unit was created in January 1993, and provides specialist guard services (including the delivery of money, valuable freight, and so on) and personal protection. Individuals or organisations who require specialist protection services can hire this unit. There are also special rapid-response units called Sokol that are part of the Department for Fighting Organised Crime. Their tasks include conducting antiterrorist and organised crime operations, release of hostages, confiscation of weapons, and armed support for criminal investigations.

Training

Ukrainian citizens are recruited to the militia on a contractual basis from the age of eighteen. Candidates are expected to be educated to at least the secondary school level, and to be physically and mentally fit and healthy. The selection of candidates consists of several consecutive stages of examination: social, medical, and psychological tests. The background of candidates is also checked (whether s/he has prior convictions) together with recommendations from former employers or educational institutions. Some services (such as drivers and applicants for the Berkut and Sokol special units) have special requirements, including speed of reactions, emotional stability, and strength of character. For candidates to higher educational institutions of the MIA

there are special tests and examinations (such as knowledge of the law, Ukrainian language and literature, history, and physical fitness).

Those accepted to work in the militia receive a special rank of militia private and undergo a six-month training course. This provides basic knowledge in the theory of law, criminal law and forensic science, crime detection, and training to develop physical skills necessary for work in the police force (shooting, driving, and physical training). After graduating from the course, a person is given a rank of militia junior sergeant and begins working (usually in the patrol service).

Militia employees with secondary education can be promoted to new ranks in the course of their service, up to senior warrant officer. To be promoted further and receive an officer rank (junior lieutenant or higher) they have to complete a programme of higher education in one of the institutions of the MIA.

Another type of police training and education is special militia education (2 years of college). Individuals with secondary education and those who have completed the two years of national army service are eligible. Students receive knowledge in all basic law disciplines, and upon completion, graduates receive a rank of lieutenant or warrant officer, enabling them to work as a beat officer or transport police officer. Serving officers may also take short courses—usually six months—aimed at retraining and improving their qualifications.

Police Public Projects

In the Soviet period, public involvement in policing was centrally initiated and controlled. There were a number of forms of public involvement in the protection of public order in Ukraine in that period. There were semimilitary "detachments" of citizens as well as citizens' patrols. The detachments operated during the 1920s and 1930s and then after World War II during the 1950s and 1960s, while the citizens' patrols existed until the end of the 1980s. There were also groups focused on crime prevention and the "reeducation" of citizens. These included supervisory committees (1950s to 1980s); committees for fighting alcohol abuse (1960s to 1980s); housing and neighbourhood committees (1980s); guardianship councils (1950s to 1970s), prevention councils (1970s to 1980s); councils for studying the causes of crime (1980s); groups for assisting prosecution (1930s); groups for crime prevention (1970s to 1980s); comrades' trials (1930s to 1980s), and youth and children's organisations for assisting the militia (1970s to 1980s). Finally, there were individual assistants to the militia, or militia workers not on permanent staff.

After the collapse of the Soviet Union, most of the "Soviet" forms of public involvement in policing disappeared, but by the mid-1990s there was a revival of some of the old forms (such as public patrols) and the emergence of new forms of public involvement in policing such as services that passed information from the public to the militia (usually through local radio networks), committees for protecting blocks of flats and their entrances, and groups helping to maintain public order.

Police Use of Firearms

The Ukrainian militia is fully armed. Article 15 of the Ukrainian law stipulates that firearms may be used in the following cases: to protect citizens from life-threatening assaults; to release hostages; to resist an armed attack on a militia employee or members of his family or other attack if there is a threat to their lives or health; to resist attacks on guarded objects, convoys, private residences, offices of state and public organisations, as well as to release them from illegal seizure; to detain a person who has committed a serious crime and is trying to escape; to detain a person who demonstrates armed resistance or is trying to escape from custody; against an armed person who threatens to use weapons and other objects that threaten the lives and health of a militia officer; and to stop a vehicle in cases where the driver creates a life-threatening situation to a militia officer.

Complaints and Discipline

Included in the training of militia officers is a basic course in human rights, which includes the International Bill on Human Rights, the Declaration on the Police of the Parliamentary Assembly of the Council of Europe (1979), and the UN Code of Conduct for Law Enforcement Official (1979). However, there are regular reports in the mass media of militia officers abusing the rights of ordinary citizens and those suspected of committing an offence. Rudeness, excessive use of physical force, bureaucratic delays in investigating complaints from citizens, refusals to open criminal cases, and unreasonable arrests and fines are some of the most common incidents reported. According to the MIA, approximately 4,000 complaints from citizens are received annually about unlawful militia activities, although this is bound to be a serious underestimate. Problems of endemic corruption continue to plague the Ukrainian police despite recent interventions by the Ukrainian government (such as the Law on the Fight Against Corrup-

tion in 1995). Some sources suggest that as much as 60% of government officials' incomes come from bribes, with militia officers being the most prominent in this group (26% of those convicted were from the militia). Many argue that until the levels of pay and service conditions are improved, corruption will continue to be a major problem, while others suggest that it is far more of a systemic problem requiring major social and political change.

Terrorism

Terrorism in Ukraine is not seen as a particularly serious problem. No terrorist organisations are recognised by law enforcement bodies as being currently active in the country.

International Cooperation

The MIA currently maintains close links with police organisations and training and research institutions in Austria, Belgium, China, Czech Republic, France, Germany, Hungary, Israel, Italy, the Netherlands, the Newly Independent States, Poland, Romania, Slovakia, Spain, Switzerland, Turkey, United Kingdom, United States, and Vietnam.

The types of collaboration include student, teaching staff, and practitioner exchange programmes and training courses; the sharing of training materials and literature; joint research projects; and seminars, conferences, and symposiums.

Since 1994, Ukraine has taken part in United Nations and Organisation for Security and Cooperation in Europe civilian police peacekeeping missions. About 500 officers from Ukraine have taken part in peacekeeping operations in Bosnia and Herzegovina, Eastern Timor, Kosovo, Macedonia, the Republic of Congo, and Yugoslavia.

Police Education, Research, and Publications

Institutions of Higher Education

There are three types of higher education establishments: institute/college, university, and academy. Currently there are fourteen such establishments in Ukraine. Secondary school graduates, special secondary and higher school graduates and those who completed their military service can apply. After graduation they receive the title of militia lieutenant and a diploma.

The major institutions of higher education in the Ukrainian police are the National Academy of Internal Affairs (Kyiv); the National University of Internal Affairs (Kharkiv); the Lviv Institute of Internal Affairs; and the Zaporozhskii Law Institute of Internal Affairs.

In addition to the higher education institutions, there are also scientific establishments within the MIA, such as the Scientific Research Institute, which is part of the National Academy of Internal Affairs, and scientific laboratories within the National University of Internal Affairs.

Leading Researchers/Authors/Reporters

Leading researchers in the area of policing are Y. Kondratiev (police management, detective and investigative activity, legal psychology); P. Mikhailenko (criminal law, criminology); A. Dzhuzha (criminology, penology, criminal executive law); A. Bandourka (management theory, legal psychology); M. Kostitsky (legal psychology); and A. Zakalyuk (criminology, crime prevention).

Sources of Funding for Police Research

There are few sources of funding within the MIA for supporting research work. Researchers mainly rely on applying for funding from private foundations and other funding bodies inside and outside the country. Areas of recent research include police management; administrative activities of the police and administrative law; criminal law and criminal procedure; context-driven community policing; and legal psychology.

Leading Police Journals/Magazines/Newsletters

Militsia Ukrainy (Militia of Ukraine), monthly journal (since 1997). Chief editor V. Nizhnik. Website: *www.galaxy.com.ua/svit/milicia_ua/*

Weekly bulletin of the MIA of Ukraine *Imenem zakonu* (In the Name of Law) (since 1955). Chief editor N. Vavirovski. Website: *www.police-weekly.kiev.ua*

KROK, newspaper of the Co-ordination Council on Fighting Corruption and Organised Crime in the President's Office (published once or twice a month). Chief editor Y. Boitchenko. Website: *http://mndc.naiau.kiev.ua/krok/krok2001.htm*

Borot'ba z Organizovanoyu Zlochynnistyu i Koruptsieyu (Fighting Organised Crime and Corruption), biannual scientific practice journal. Chief editor Y. Kondratiev. Website: *http://mndc.naiau.kiev.ua/Gurnal/gurn_main.htm*

Naukovyj Visnyk Natsional'noj Akademii Vnutrishnych Sprav (Academic Newsletter of the National Academy of Internal Affairs), quarterly. Chief editor O. Logvinenko. Website: *www.naiau.kiev.ua/tslc/pages/biblio/visnik/1_fset.html*

Pravo i Bezpeka (Law and Safety Journal), National University of Internal Affairs. Chief editor A. Bandourka. E-mail: Zozulja@adm.univd.kharkov.ua

Visnyk Natsional'nogo Universiteta Vnutrishnych Sprav (Newsletter of the National University of Internal Affairs). Chief editor A. Bandourka

Major Recent Publications

In Ukrainian/Russian:

Bandourka, A. *Operativno-rozshukova diyalnyst': pydruchnik dlya vischich zakladov osvyti* (Operative-investigative activity: A handbook for higher education institutions). Kharkiv: National University of Internal Affairs, 2002.

Bandourka, A. *Psichologiya upravleniya organami vnutrennich del* (Psychology of managing organizations in the Ministry of Internal Affairs). Kharkiv: University of Internal Affairs, 2000.

Danshin, I., and Obolentsev, V. *Latentna zlochinnist': ponyattya, prichini, negativny naslydki* (Latent crime: Concept, causes, and negative consequences). Kharkiv: University of Internal Affairs, 2000.

Dzhuzha, A., Kondratiev, J., and Kulik, A., eds. *Kriminologiya*. Kyiv: Yurinkom-Inter, 2002.

Ischenko, A. *Metodologitcheskie problemy kriminalistitcheskich issledovanii* (Methodological problems of forensic science). Kyiv: National Academy of Internal Affairs, 2003.

Kuzmitchev, V. *Kriminalistitcheskii analis rassledovaniya prestuplenii* (Forensic analysis of investigating crimes). Kyiv: National Academy of Internal Affairs, 2000.

Panov, M. *Ugolovnoe pravo Ukrainy* (Criminal law of Ukraine). Kyiv: Yurinkom-Inter, 2001.

Rushchenko, I. *Sotsiologiya zlochinnosty* (Sociology of crime). Kharkiv: National University of Internal Affairs, 2001.

In English:

Foglesong, S., and Solomon, P. *Crime, Criminal Justice and Criminology in Post-Soviet Ukraine*. Washington, DC: National Institute of Justice, Office of Justice Programs, 2001.

Police-Related Websites

www.naiau.kiev.ua (National Academy of Internal Affairs)

www.univd.edu.ua (National University of Internal Affairs) www.galaxy.com.ua (Lviv Institute of Internal Affairs)

www.zli.boom.ru (Zaporozhskii Law Institute of the Ministry of Internal Affairs)

www.centrmia.gov.ua/ (Ministry of Internal Affairs)

ADRIAN BECK, YULIA CHISTYAKOVA, AND VADYM BARKO

Bibliography

Dzhuzha, O., and Mikhailenko, P. *Kurs krominologii: pydruchnik* (Criminology handbook). Kyiv, 2001.

Foglesong, S., and Solomon, P. *Crime, Criminal Justice and Criminology in Post-Soviet Ukraine*. Washington, DC: National Institute of Justice, Office of Justice Programs, 2001.

Ministry of Internal Affairs, Ukraine. *Programa Rozvitku Partnerskich Vidnosin Mizh Militsieyu I Naselennyem* (Programme of Development of Partnerships Between Militia and Population). Kyiv: Ministry of Internal Affairs, 1999.

Ministry of Internal Affairs, Ukraine. *Kriminogenna situatsiya v Ukraine: otsenka, tendentsii, prognoz, 2001* (Crime in Ukraine: Evaluation, Trends, and Forecasts, 2001) Kyiv: Ministry of Internal Affairs, 2002.

Shelley, L. *Policing Soviet Society*. London: Routledge, 1996.

Sobolev, V. "Ugolovno-pravovaya statistika v Ukraine: problema pervichnogo ucheta prestuplenii (Criminal law statistics in Ukraine: the problem of initial recording of crimes)." In *Doverie militsii i latentnaya prestupnost': vzglyad ukrainskich I rossiiskich issledovaletei* (Trust in the police and latent crime as viewed by Ukrainian and Russian academics), edited by Svezhentseva, Y., Sobolev, V., Rushchenko, I., Tonkov, E., and Didenko, V., Kharkiv: Finart.

UNITED ARAB EMIRATES

Background Material

In 1971, the states of Abu Zaby, 'Ajman, Al Fujayrah, Ash Shariqah, Dubayy, and Umm al Qaywayn merged to form the United Arab Emirates (UAE). They were joined in 1972 by a seventh state, Ra's al Khaymah.

The UAE is located in the Middle East, bordering the Gulf of Oman and the Persian Gulf, between Oman and Saudi Arabia. It comprises a total area of 82,880 square kilometers, and it has a population of 2,523,915 (2004 estimate). The ethnic composition of the population is as follows: Emirati 19%; other Arab and Iranian 23%; South Asian 50%; and other expatriates (includes Westerners and East Asians) 8%. The population is 96% Muslim (Shi'a 16%), although there are Christian and Hindu communities as well. Arabic is the official language. Persian, English, Hindi, and Urdu are also spoken.

The capital of the UAE is Abu Dhabi. The UAE has an open economy with a high per capita income and a sizable annual trade surplus. Its wealth is based on oil and gas output (about 33% of GDP), and the fortunes of the economy fluctuate with the prices of those commodities. Since 1973, the UAE has undergone a profound transformation from an impoverished region of small desert principalities to a modern state with a high standard of living. At present levels of production, oil and gas reserves should last for more than 100 years. The government has increased spending on job creation and infrastructure expansion, and is opening up its utilities to greater private sector involvement.

The UAE has annual GDP purchasing power parity of $23,200 (2003 estimate).

Contextual Features

The UAE is a federation, with specified powers delegated to the UAE federal government and other powers reserved to member emirates.

The UAE has a president and a vice president, as well as a prime minister. The president appoints the members of the Council of Ministers. The UAE has a unicameral Federal National Council (FNC) or Majlis al-Ittihad al-Watani. The FNC has forty seats. Members appointed by the rulers of the constituent states to two-year terms.

A federal court system was introduced in 1971. It applies to all emirates except Dubayy (Dubai) and Ra's al Khaymah, which are not fully integrated into the federal system. All emirates have secular courts to adjudicate criminal, civil, and commercial matters, and Islamic courts to review family and religious disputes.

In the past, dynastic rivalries were often sources of tension. A lack of clearly established rules of succession contributed to this situation. In an attempt to quell this problem, heirs apparent have usually been designated in more recent times. Usually the eldest son of the amir is named the heir.

Threats and tension stemming from the presence of resident Iranians and native Shi'a seem to be less acute in the UAE than in other Gulf states. Dubayy and Sharjah have traditionally maintained good relations with Iran, and enjoyed profits from maritime trade, particularly the transshipment of items officially banned in Iran to conserve foreign exchange. The UAE is not a target of Iranian terrorist attacks.

Criminal cases are tried by Sharia courts within each emirate, or by civil courts of the federal system. Due process is honored under both systems. Defendants are entitled to legal counsel. No formal public defender system exists. However, each judge has the responsibility of looking out for the best interests of any person being tried without representation by counsel. The accused has the right to defense counseling cases involving sentences of death or life imprisonment. The government must provide legal representation if necessary in these cases. There are no trials by jury. According to U.S. Department of State human rights reports, the criminal court system is generally regarded as fair.

The attorney general must be notified of any detentions of persons within forty-eight hours. Then, within twenty-four hours after notification, the attorney general must decide whether to charge the individual, release him or her, or return him or her to detention. Most persons receive timely trials.

Police Profile

The provisional constitution authorizes the creation of a federal police force and a security guard force, both of which are subordinate to the Ministry of Interior. The strength of the police force has not been reported but is estimated as relatively large and vigilant in exercising control over political activities. Individual shaykhs had their own police forces before independence. After unification, they kept these forces active for the most part. Both the federal government and the emirate of Dubayy retain independent internal security organizations. The police forces of the other emirates are also involved in antinarcotic and antiterrorist activities.

Each emirate maintains its own independent police force. While all emirate internal security organs are branches of one federal organization, in practice they operate quite independently. There were no reports that security forces committed human rights abuses.

Bibliography

Central Intelligence Agency. *The World Factbook*. "United Arab Emirates." Available at: www.cia.gov/cia/publications/factbook/geos/ae.html. 2005.

Library of Congress. "United Arab Emirates." Country Studies. Available at: http://lcweb2.loc.gov/frd/cs/. 2005.

UNITED KINGDOM

Background Material

The United Kingdom encompasses four territories: Wales, Scotland, Northern Ireland, and England, with distinct policing, criminal justice, and legal arrangements, reflecting their particular historical, social, and political development. While the four exist within a single state, each has some degree of devolved political power that makes it impossible to provide a simple overview of the policing arrangements as they apply across the whole territory, although what follows will demonstrate that there are broad similarities among them.

"United Kingdom" refers to the four nations of England, Wales, Scotland, and Northern Ireland. "Great Britain" refers only to England, Wales, and Scotland. Wherever possible, this contribution refers to the United Kingdom as a whole, but not all relevant information is available on this basis, and so at times only Great Britain is discussed.

UK population, 2001

England	49,138,831
Northern Ireland	1,685,267
Scotland	5,062,011
Wales	2,903,085
Total	58,789,194

Source: Office for National Statistics.

The 2001 census found the overall population of the UK to be 58,789,194, spread across the four nations as seen in the following table. The English population accounts for 83.6% of the UK total.

The ethnic composition of Great Britain is shown in the next table, which indicates that the majority of the population—some 92.3%%—is white, and that of minority ethnic groups, the largest (50% of all minority population) is Asian. It is important to show these figures in some detail since the extent of ethnic diversity is markedly different by region. While the minority ethnic population amounts to almost one-third of the population of London (28.5%), and one-tenth in the West Midlands (10.9%) this figure is very much smaller in Wales and Scotland (2.1% and 1.8%, respectively).

Even within these regions, the size of minority ethnic communities varies considerably; in general terms, most conurbations have a visible minority ethnic presence while more rural communities are likely to remain overwhelmingly white.

While the size of Britain's minority ethnic communities varies considerably in geographical terms, Britain has a long history as a multicultural society, which

can be traced back at least as far as the third century CE when African soldiers were part of the Roman army present in the north of England. More recent patterns of migration, however, have reflected later imperial adventures and have stemmed from Britain's former colonies on the Indian subcontinent and in Africa and the Caribbean. From the latter two areas, recent migration was in response to a labour shortage in the late 1940s and 1950s, while most of the Asian community are of Indian, Pakistani, or Bangladeshi heritage, who came to Britain in the 1960s and 1970s. It is important to note that the majority of the minority ethnic population were born in and are citizens of the United Kingdom. As will be detailed later in this contribution, much recent public controversy relating to policing has centred on relations with minority ethnic groups, which is why brief details of the composition of the population are important background information.

Contextual Features

The extent of crime in Britain is most accurately gauged by the British Crime Survey (BCS) conducted every year along similar lines to victimisation studies elsewhere. The BCS published in 2001 was based on a survey of nearly 9,000 respondents who were asked about their experiences of crimes committed against themselves and their households. By asking members of the public directly about their experiences of crime, the BCS avoids the main pitfall associated with reporting rates and recording practices associated with official crime figures. On this

Resident population by ethnic group, 2001–2002

		Total Population (thousands)	White Population (%)	Minority Ethnic Population (%)	Ethnic Breakdown (%)				
					Mixed	Asian or Asian British	Black or Black British	Chinese	Other
Great Britain		57,458	92.3	7.7	12	50	28	4	6
	North East	2,534	97.9	2.1	..	73	..	..	..
	North West	6,801	94.9	5.1	15	60	16	5	4
	Yorkshire and the Humber	4,996	93.8	6.2	12	67	14	3	4
	East Midlands	4,172	94.3	5.7	8	65	19	6	..
	West Midlands	5,265	89.1	10.9	9	66	20	2	3
	East	5,436	95.9	4.1	19	51	19	5	6
	London	7,370	71.5	28.5	9	42	38	3	8
	South East	8,022	95.8	4.2	21	48	16	6	9
	South West	4,920	97.7	2.3	31	27	26	..	12
England		49,517	91.3	8.7	11	50	28	4	6
Wales		2,909	97.9	2.1	32	37	20	..	..
Scotland		5,031	98.2	1.8	13	51	12	12	13

Source: Labour Force Survey.

basis, the BCS estimated that 12,899,000 offences were committed in 2000, a decrease of 12% from the previous year, and some 21% lower than in 1997, the peak year in the BCS estimate.

The BCS data suggest that crime in 2000 was categorised as follows: burglary, 8%; all vehicle thefts, 20%; vehicle vandalism, 12%; home vandalism, 9%; common assaults, 15%; wounding, 3%; mugging, 2%; and other thefts, 31%.

In addition to estimating the true level of crime in Britain, the BCS also makes it possible to assess what proportion of offences are reported to the police, and, of these, how many the police actually record. Of the 12,899,000 offences recorded by the BCS, 9,879,000 fell into categories comparable to those used by the police in officially recorded figures. The next table shows how the statistics generated by the BCS compare to those compiled by the police.

The table indicates that 45% of crimes identified by the BCS were reported to the police, but that only 25% of offences go through the various stages before being recorded as in the official crime figures. The remaining 75% of offences constitute what is usually called the "dark figures" of crime, but the table also shows that this proportion varies considerably across the various categories of offences, with some 90% of common assaults not being recorded but incidents involving wounding were much more likely to be recorded, at 47%. The BCS (Kershaw et al. 2001:10) found that the main reasons given for not reporting offences was that incidents were too trivial, or that the police were unlikely to be able to do anything in response.

The BCS was first conducted in 1981, and analysis of trends in its findings over the intervening period suggests that different categories of offences have changed in distinct ways. While most crimes have increased fairly significantly between 1981 and 2000, vandalism and wounding offences declined. Changes in crime by selected BCS category over the period follow: vandalism, –4; burglary, +42%; all vehicle thefts, +50%; bicycle thefts, +74%; other household thefts, +6%; theft from persons, +45%; common assault, +35%; wounding, –18%; and robbery, +68%. The 2001 BCS report showed that all BCS-reported crime fell by 33% between 1995 and 2000 (Kershaw et al. 2001:45).

In the British criminal justice system, two types of court exist, with very different sentencing remits and types of personnel.

The magistrates court is known as the lower court, where magistrates (justices of the peace, JPs) who try summary offences carry out sentencing. These magistrates are not professionals or legally trained, and are assisted by legally qualified clerks in court. However, in some magistrates courts, principally in metropolitan areas, stipendiary magistrates also sit. They are legally trained and sit on their own. Magistrates courts' sentencing powers are restricted to the imposition of up to six months imprisonment and/or a £5000 fine for each offence. Magistrates courts are crucial to the sentencing process, as at least 95% of all criminal cases are dealt with in these courts (Uglow 1995). If they wish, defendants sent for trial to a magistrates court can select to appear before a Crown court, where their case is considered before a jury of their peers.

Organisationally, the Crown court is a single court located at various sites across the country. Professionally trained judges who sit alone, and hear cases involving indictable offences and the more serious either-way offences control these. In the Crown court, a jury determines the guilt or inno-

Crimes estimated by the BCS and recorded by the police, 2000

	Police (000s)	BCS (000s)	% BCS Reported	% Recorded of Reported	% Recorded of all BCS
Vandalism	481	2608	34	54	18
All comparable property crime	1553	4689	51	65	33
Burglary	409	1063	66	59	38
All vehicle thefts	938	2619	49	73	36
Bicycle theft	119	377	54	58	31
Theft from person	88	629	35	40	14
All comparable violence	466	2582	45	40	18
Wounding	195	417	68	69	47
Robbery	78	276	54	52	28
Common assault	193	1890	39	26	10
All comparable crime	2501	9879	45	56	25

Source: Kershaw et al. 2001.

cence of the defendant (unless the defendant enters a guilty plea), and the judge then passes sentence.

It has been observed that the English system of justice is unique in conferring sentencing powers on two different sets of individuals who contrast in the extent of their powers, their legal knowledge, and personal characteristics (Cavadino and Dignan 1997: 84). Domestically, the ultimate appeal court is the House of Lords.

The prison system in Britain has long been based on the dictum that offenders are sent to prison "as punishment, not for punishment" (Paterson, quoted by Tumim 1996:18). For this reason, prisoners are entitled to have their human rights respected and to expect certain minimum conditions in terms of standards of accommodation, food, health care, and so on. There is much less agreement, however, on the extent to which the prison system is able to rehabilitate and reform offenders. The mission statement of the prison service reads as follows: "Her Majesty's Prison Service serves the public by keeping in custody those committed by the courts. Our duty is to look after them with humanity and help them lead law-abiding and useful lives in custody and after release."

Throughout much of the 1990s and into the twenty-first century, there has been an increase in prison numbers. On 11 October, the prison population was 72,700, up 4,800 (7%) than a year earlier and the highest ever recorded. A number of private prisons have been established, following the privatization of the Wolds Remand Prison near Hull in 1992.

Police Profile

Background and Organisational Description

Precise arrangements for policing across the United Kingdom vary somewhat from area to area. Within England and Wales, there are forty-three police services, in Scotland another eight, and in Northern Ireland the Royal Ulster Constabulary was restructured and renamed as the Police Service of Northern Ireland in 2001. Details of the process of policing reform in Northern Ireland are outlined below. In addition to these local constabularies, there are a number of other police organisations such as the British Transport Police, the Royal Parks Police (responsible for the policing of seventeen parks and public spaces owned by the Crown), the Ministry of Defence Police, and various other specialist agencies. While there is no national police service in the United Kingdom, agencies such as the National Crime Squad—which targets "high-level" organised crime—and the National Criminal Intelligence Service—which operates as a quasi-clearing-house for information supplied by local police services—do have a countrywide brief.

Historians of policing in the United Kingdom have often noted that important features of contemporary policing have a very long pedigree. The local basis of each police service, for example, is often seen as a continuance of community involvement in the provision of policing that can be traced back as far as the thirteenth-century Statute of Winchester, which established the "watch and ward" system, and required public involvement in the apprehension of criminals. This Statute provided the major framework for policing prior to the 1832 Metropolitan Police Act that established the first recognisably modern professional police service in London. This emphasis on provision of a service to local communities was reflected in the rhetoric of the first commissioners of the Metropolitan Police who described the police as servants of the community rather than of the central state, although this may have been to manufacture public consent in the face of considerable opposition from many sections of society (Emsley 1996). That the police have often had difficulty in establishing their legitimacy among certain sections of the community is also a long-standing feature of the United Kingdom experience, this has been a particularly intractable problem in relation to police relations with minority ethnic communities in many urban areas of England and Wales, and also with regard to sections of the Catholic/Nationalist community in Northern Ireland.

By the middle of the nineteenth century, constabularies were established across the country. Bunyan (1978:15) points out that by 1860, there were 259 police forces of varying sizes throughout England and Wales. Each force was locally controlled by a Watch Committee, which meant there were disparities in policing from one area to another, and limited interforce cooperation. From this time until the middle of the twentieth century was a period of amalgamation of police forces, whereby central government attempted, sometimes in the face of opposition from police forces themselves, to remove some of the smaller forces. This process of reorganisation inevitably involved increasing powers of the central government, in the form of the Home Secretary, in relation to local authorities. By 1960, the number of police forces had been reduced to 125. The 1964 Police Act established a further process of amalgamation that saw the number of police services in England and Wales reduced to the current forty-three by the mid-1970s.

Contemporary police governance in England and Wales continues to be premised on the provisions of the 1964 Police Act, which established the tripartite system of accountability whereby responsibilities are shared among the local police authority, Home Office, and chief constable. The local police authority, in each of the forty-three police services in England and Wales, is responsible for setting priorities and targets for the police, establishing a budget and raising revenue via local taxation, appointing senior officers, and monitoring complaints made against the police. The Home Office also provides resources to each police service, approves the appointment of senior officers, and establishes national priorities for policing. Via instruments such as Home Office Circulars, it is able to provide direct and detailed "advice" to chief constables. Under the tripartite arrangements, chief constables retain operational independence for the implementation of policing in their area. Collectively, chief constables and deputy and assistant constables comprise the Association of Chief Police Officers (ACPO), which contributes to the development of policing policy and offers recommendation and guidance to local police forces. While not formally an arm of central government, the ACPO is partly funded by the Home Office. Another means by which central government exercises power and influence over locally based police services is via Her Majesty's Inspectorate of Constabulary (HMIC). First established in 1856, the role of HMIC was outlined in the 1996 Police Act to "promote the efficiency and effectiveness" of police services in England and Wales by ensuring that agreed objectives are achieved, that good practice is spread, and that performance is improved. This is achieved through a process of annual inspection, now carried out at Basic Command Unit level (see below), and through "thematic" inspections based on generic issues of interest, such as training, community relations, and so on.

The arrangements for police governance in Scotland have been broadly similar to those for England and Wales, although Walker (2000) argues that this is largely explained by the relatively peripheral nature of Scottish legal and constitutional arrangements within the UK political and parliamentary system. The principles of the tripartite process outlined above apply with only minor differences in Scotland: Most notably that the Scottish Parliament replaces the role played by the Home Office and the local police authorities consist of elected local councillors. For six of the eight forces, the police authorities are "joint boards" consisting of members from several local government areas, since the police services themselves cut across political boundaries. Only in the case of Dumfries and Galloway and Fife constabularies is there a unitary police authority. The HMIC plays a similar role in Scotland to that in England and Wales.

Policing of Northern Ireland has undergone considerable change in the wake of the ongoing peace process in the province. The Royal Ulster Constabulary (RUC), which was established with the province in 1922, had been widely regarded as sectarian and had under-recruited Catholics. From the first development of the contemporary "troubles" in 1969 until 2001, a total of 302 RUC officers were killed and Sinn Fein had long demanded that it be disbanded. Against this background, the 1998 Good Friday Agreement, which provided the framework for a political solution to the long-standing sectarian divisions between the nationalist and unionist communities, contained explicit recognition that policing structures needed to be addressed. The Agreement established a Commission on Policing for Northern Ireland, which was chaired by Chris Pattern, former governor of Hong Kong. The Pattern Report made 175 recommendations for reform, including renaming the police service and changing recruitment procedures to boost the number of Catholics employed. On this basis, the Police Service of Northern Ireland (PSNI) was established in November 2001, with a new uniform and a recruitment policy based on a 50:50 ratio between Catholics and Protestants. The PSNI is overseen by the Northern Ireland Policing Board, which comprises of members of the public and representatives of the main political parties.

Following the reelection of the Labour government in 2001, a further process of police reform in England and Wales commenced, culminating in the 2002 Police Reform Act, the most significant legislation on policing since the 1984 Police and Criminal Evidence Act. The legislation contained a wide range of provisions, including the following:

Establishing an independent element to the police complaints system

Increasing the powers of the Home Secretary and police authorities to require senior officers to resign

Creating a new position of Community Support Officer

Increased powers for civilian employees, for example, to escort prisoners

Enabling chief constables to accredit local authority community safety schemes

Changing regulations on taking samples from suspected drunk drivers

Of the myriad of measures outlined in the Act, the most hotly contested were those that critics argued greatly increased the powers of the Home Secretary at the expense of chief officers. An article on these reforms in *Police Review* magazine expressed these concerns in the following terms (Pickover 2002): "The supervision of police forces is well established and has long been effected by Her Majesty's Inspectorate of Constabulary with little or no scope, at least under statutory authority, for direct political control, direction, or influence. Such days are now gone..."

While the power of the Home Secretary vis-à-vis the two other strands of the tripartite system established by the 1964 Act had been strengthened by various statutory and other methods in the intervening decades, the 2002 legislation contains a number of measures that will provide for more centralised power. Among these is section 2 of the 2002 Act, which allows the Home Secretary to issue statutory Codes of Practice outlining how chief officers will discharge their duties. Section 4 enables the Home Secretary to issue directions to a police authority found to be in some way ineffective or inefficient by an HMIC inspection. Section 5 allows the Home Secretary to require action plans to be established to address issues raised by HMIC. Section 6 gives the Home Secretary power to stipulate the standard of equipment to be used by police forces.

Demographics

As of March 31, 2002, there were 129,603 police officers in England and Wales, an increase of 3.1% over the previous year. Of these, 127,267 were employed in the forty-three constabularies, the rest being employed in centralised services such as the National Crime Squad. The largest force is the Metropolitan Police Service, which accounts for 21% of all officers. Between them, the eight metropolitan forces (Greater Manchester, City of London, Merseyside, Metropolitan Police, Northumbria, South Yorkshire, West Midlands, and West Yorkshire) accounted for 46% of all officers. In contrast, the eight smallest forces (Bedfordshire, 1,069 officers; Cumbria, 1,100 officers; Dyfed Powys, 1,132 officers; Gloucestershire, 1183

officers; Lincolnshire, 1,198 officers; Suffolk, 1,203 officers; Warwickshire, 969 officers; and Wiltshire, 1,157 officers) accounted for 7% of all officers. In England and Wales, there were 240.4 officers per 100,000 population, which amounts to one officer for every 408 people. Proportions by gender and minority ethnic origin are shown in the following table.

In addition to these officers the police service employed some 58,909 civilian staff and 11,598 special constables, who are unpaid volunteers with some of the powers of a constable.

Training

Discussion of training in the British police needs to distinguish between that run for probationary constables when first recruited, specialist training in particular subject areas, and tasks and that offered at a higher level as officers are promoted in the rank hierarchy.

Applicants to the police service must be at least eighteen years of age and a British, Irish, or Commonwealth citizen. There is no upper age on joining the force, although in practice few forces will accept those over the age of fifty. There are no specific educational qualifications that applicants must possess, but candidates should have achieved a good educational standard. However, regardless of educational attainment, there is a Police Initial Recruitment Test that is taken by all candidates, and they must undergo health tests and the national job-related fitness test. For the first two years of their service, new recruits remain on probation, and are subject to continuous training—much of which is carried out in the workplace. The initial training programme typically consists of a week with whichever constabulary is involved followed by a longer period at a district training centre. Once that is completed, the trainee returns to force and works under the supervision and guidance of a tutor constable.

Police officer strength in 43 police force areas in England and Wales, by rank, gender, and minority ethnic origin, March 31, 2002

| Rank | Male | | Male Minority Ethnic | | Female | | Female Minority Ethnic | | Total |
	N	%	N	%	N	%	N	%	N
Chief constable	47	89	1	2	6	11	0	0	53
Assistant chief constable	141	93	2	1	10	7	0	0	151
Superintendent	1,173	93	22	2	83	7	1	<0.05	1,256
Chief inspector	1,433	92	23	1	117	8	1	0.06	1,550
Inspector	5,717	92	89	1	479	8	10	0.1	6,195
Sergeant	16,621	89	338	2	1,953	11	34	0.2	18,574
Constable	79,351	80	2,234	2	20,137	20	631	0.1	99,487
All ranks	104,483	82	2,629	2	22,784	18	677	0.5	127,267

Source: Home Office 2002.

While there is no system of direct entry for officers—in other words, all recruits commence as constables—the High Potential Development scheme is designed to identify future senior leaders in the service. Through provision of intensive training and education, these officers are "fast tracked" through to the rank of chief inspector within approximately seven years after joining.

In addition to this training, the police service provides numerous programmes on a wide range of subject areas of specialist interest. As with much else in policing in the United Kingdom, the arrangements for training on topics such as community relations, informant handling, use of information communication technology, and many other topics vary enormously. Most forces have an in-house training department that may provide programmes directly or that will help the force to determine training needs and contract these out to private consultants or to universities. While there is no reliable indicator of how much specialist training is provided for the police, the resource implications of officers being diverted from frontline duties to attend training programmes (known as "abstractions") are apparent. Given that a recent HMIC (1999:35) report suggested that the cost of delivering a one-day training programme across the entire police service in Britain is between £11.2 and £27.7 million, it is clear that the human and financial resources invested are considerable. A Home Office (Langmead Jones 1999) study argued that the police service ought to improve the evaluation of training, and seek more imaginative methods of delivery in order to maintain a balance between the costs and benefits of training.

Higher-level police training has traditionally been centred on the work carried out by the Police Staff College at Bramshill in Hampshire, an organisation now known as Centrex. Programmes for those seeking more senior positions include the junior command course, strategic command course, and international commander's course. Centrex also provides a wide range of specialist courses.

Police Use of Firearms

While the UK police are widely renowned for being unarmed, there are a significant number of occasions in which firearms are deployed, but not necessarily discharged, during operations. The next figure provides an overview of incidents in which firearms were deployed in England and Wales in the 1996–2000 period. Firearms were deployed in slightly more than 10,000 operations in 1999–2000, after declining every year in the period. In addition, a smaller number of operations had utilised armed response vehicles (ARVs), and there were some 6,262 authorised firearms officers, most of whom would not be routinely armed but who could be deployed in response to particular incidents.

It should be noted that the number of operations referred to above relates to incidents in which firearms were issued, not in which they were discharged. Any incident in which a member of the public is shot by the police is referred to the Police Complaints Authority (see below), which reported that in 2000–2001 four fatalities were caused by police use of firearms. In contrast, during the same period, forty-four members of the public were killed by police vehicles engaged in pursuits.

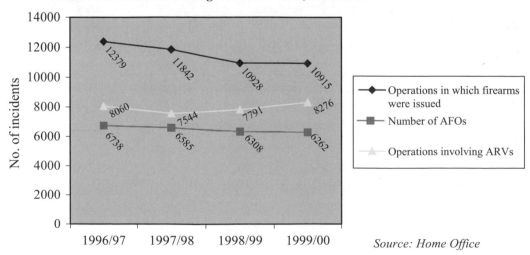

Police use of firearms in England and Wales, 1996–2000.

Survey data suggest that police officers do not wish to carry firearms as a matter of routine. In 1995, the Police Federation conducted a survey asking officers for their views on firearms and policing. More than 73,000 members (60%) responded.

By an overwhelming majority (four to one), police officers stated that they did not wish to be routinely armed on duty. However, a large proportion (62%) called for more police officers to be trained to use firearms, and said that they should be issued to trained officers as and when required. By 2003, this opposition to carrying firearms as a matter of routine remained high. While 43% of officers polled by the Police Federation felt that their lives had been seriously threatened by a member of the public during the previous two years, and 30% reported that they had been threatened with a knife, a substantial majority of 78% were opposed to officers being routinely armed. However, 47% of officers favoured the mandatory wearing of body armour for all operational duties and 80% believed there should be more officers trained and issued with firearms.

Complaints and Discipline

The system for dealing with serious complaints against the police in England and Wales was established by the 1984 Police and Criminal Evidence Act, which established the Police Complaints Authority (PCA). The PCA consists of no fewer than nine members (there were actually eighteen at the end of 2002), none of whom can ever have been a member of the police service. The PCA's role is to oversee investigations of complaints, which are carried out by members of a force other than that which is the subject of the complaint. As well as dealing with complaints from the public, the police service itself voluntarily refers certain incidents to the PCA for investigation, typically when an individual dies in custody, when a police vehicle is involved in a fatal road traffic accident, or when a police officer discharges a firearm. In 2001–2002, the PCA supervised investigations into 622 complaints against the police. The Police Reform Act 2002 contains provisions to replace the PCA with the Independent Police Complaints Commission.

In Northern Ireland, complaints are dealt with by the Police Ombudsman established by the Police (Northern Ireland) Act of 1998 and 2000, and in Scotland by the Deputy Crown Agent.

A countervailing tendency to the process of centralisation that has been described above has been a process whereby responsibility for policing has been devolved down the traditional hierarchical system. While it remains the case that England and Wales are organised around forty-three constabularies, the development of policing plans that establish the priorities for each area and control over budgets and other resources has been devolved to smaller scale Basic Command Units (BCUs). There are 318 Basic Command Units in England and Wales serving an average population of 166,000, and typically commanded by a superintendent or a chief superintendent. Over the past few years, around half of all police forces have reorganised their BCUs so that they are coterminous with the boundaries of one or more local authorities. Devolving powers in this way is designed to improve relations between the service and local communities, and more closely integrating the police with other local authorities is consistent with the 1998 Crime and Disorder Act requirements for multiagency responses to crime that are built on partnerships. However, some tension seems apparent between these efforts and increasing requirements to meet central government targets and comply with performance standards determined by the Home Office. Since January 2001, crime statistics have been published at the BCU level, and HMIC has been carrying out inspections at this level, rather than the force level, since April of the same year.

Police Education, Research, and Publications

There are numerous organisations and individuals conducting research into policing in the UK. The Home Office has a Research Development Statistics (RDS) directorate, which covers the wider remit of the Home Office, not just policing. The budget of the RDS in 2001–2002 was in excess of £41 million. The website of the RDS is www.homeoffice.gov/uk/rds/index.htm. In terms of the work that the Home Office RDS does on policing, the following was established as its scope in 2001–2002: a continuing programme of policing research across a range of topics including efficiency, police leadership, forensic science, community relations, vehicle crime research, evaluation of the crime and disorder partnerships, and organised crime. In addition, some research on tools for tackling crime and high-tech crime is also planned.

In addition to carrying out in-house research, the Home Office commissions studies from public and private sector organisations. Many, if not all, of the police services in UK employ their own teams of researchers, engaged, for example, in community safety and crime reduction audits with local authorities. As with so much else to do with policing in the UK, the size and scope of this research work vary considerably from force to force.

Academics are engaged in research of policing in several of the leading universities. Among those with criminology, law, and related departments that are active in police research are the universities of Cambridge, Keele, Leicester, Manchester, Oxford, and Portsmouth, among others.

Major journals based in the UK follow:

British Journal of Criminology (*http://bjc. oupjournals.org/*)

Policing & Society (*www.tandf.co.uk/journals/ titles/10439463.html*)

Police Practice and Research (*www.tandf.co.uk/ journals/titles/15614263.html*)

In addition to the major publishers, there are a number of smaller independent companies working in this field. Among these are:

Perpetuity Press (*www.perpetuitypress.com/*)

Waterside Press (*www.watersidepress.co.uk/ acatalog/frameset.htm*)

Willan Publishing (*www.willanpublishing.co.uk/*)

Among the most significant texts on policing in the UK that have been published in recent years are:

Emsley, C. *The English Police: A Political and Social History.* London: Longman, 1996.
Johnston, L. *Policing Britain: Risk, Security and Governance.* Harlow: Longman, 2000.

Newburn, T., ed. *A Handbook of Policing.* Cullompton: Willan Publishing, 2003.
Waddington, P. A. J. *Policing Citizens.* London: UCL Press, 1999.

MIKE ROWE

Bibliography

Bunyan, T. *The History and Practice of the Political Police in Britain.* London: Unwin Hyman, 1978.
Cavadino, M., and Dignan, J. *The Penal System: An Introduction.* London: Sage, 1997.
Emsley, C. *The English Police: A Political and Social History.* London: Longman, 1996.
Her Majesty's Inspectorate of Constabulary (HMIC). *Managing Learning: A Study of Police Training.* London: Home Office, 1999.
Home Office. *Police Service Strength, England and Wales, 2002.* London: Home Office, 2002.
Kershaw, C., Chivite-Matthews, N., Thomas, C., and Aust, R. *The 2001 British Crime Survey, First Results England and Wales.* Home Office Statistical Bulletin 18/01. London: Home Office, 2001.
Langmead Jones, P. *On a Course: Reducing the Impact of Police Training on Availability for Ordinary Duty.* Police Research Series Paper 111. London: Home Office, 1999.
Pickover, D. "Police Reform 2002." *Police Review*, 110, no. 5702 (2002).
Tumim, S. "The State of Our Prisons." In *Prisons 2000: An International Perspective*, edited by R. Matthews and P. Francis. Basingstoke: Macmillan, 1996.
Uglow, S. *Criminal Justice.* London: Sweet and Maxwell, 1995.
Walker, N. *Policing in a Changing Constiutional Order.* London: Sweet and Maxwell, 2000.

UNITED STATES

Background Material

The United States of America is one of the world's largest countries with 3,537,438 square miles (9,161,959 sq km). The forty-eight states located in North America comprise the country's main land body. The two exterior states of Alaska and Hawaii, the commonwealth island of Puerto Rico, and small islands in the Caribbean and Pacific Ocean comprise the rest of the land area of the country. The physiographic regions of the United States consist of mountains, lowlands, and plains. The climate of the United States varies from tropical in Hawaii and Puerto Rico to arctic in northern Alaska. Rainfall varies from 226.75 inches (5,759.45 mm) in Little Port Walter, Alaska, to 2.38 inches (60.45 mm) in Death Valley and the Mojave Desert in the state of California (western United States). Snow occurs in the northeast, upper midwest, and western mountains, but rarely in the southern part of the country. The country has areas that are comprised of forests, grassland, and desert.

There are numerous natural resources in the United States. These natural resources include metals, minerals, energy sources, water, rich soil, and timberlands. Specific metals found in the country are iron, copper, lead, zinc, phosphates for fertilizers, and limestone for cement. Energy sources found in America include coal, petroleum, and natural gas.

The United States has a population of approximately 281,421,906. The density of the population is approximately 79.6 persons per square mile. The country has a gender distribution of 50.9% female to 49.1% male. The age distribution of the population can be divided as follows: 21.4% under age 15; 13.9% are 15 to 24; 30.2% are 25 to 44; 18.2% are 45 to 59; 10.3% are 60 to 74; and 5.9% are 75 years and older. The life expectancy of the average person in the United States is 77.4 years.

The major race/ethnic groups of the United States are Caucasian 75.1%; African-American 12.3%; Hispanic 12.5%; Asian and Pacific Islanders 3.6%; and American Indian and Eskimo slightly less than 1%. The United States has neither an official language nor an official religion. However, English is the primary language spoken by the majority, and almost all written documentation is written in English. Although the United States does not have an official religion, the religious affiliations of the population are 76.5% Christian—(52% Protestant, 24.5% Roman Catholic); 1.3% Jewish; 0.5% Muslim; 0.5% Buddhist; 14.1% none; and 7.1% other. Over 88.9% of the residents of the United States are native-born; most foreign-born residents come from Mexico, Germany, Philippines, Canada, United Kingdom, Cuba, South Korea, Italy, Vietnam, China, India, Japan, Poland, and Russia.

The United States is a product of the Industrial Revolution of the nineteenth century. Because of this, the United States, according to sociologists, has a class system based on economics (money), position (job), and education. The class system in the United States is divided into lower, middle, and upper classes. The upper classes have the most power and financial resources, and are those at the top levels of corporate America. In the United States, the upper class tends to be an exclusive club that socializes and marries within. Members of the upper class hold key positions in the boardrooms of corporations and businesses and may be involved directly and indirectly in politics. The middle class, the largest of the three classes, comprises the vast majority of Americans. Attorneys, medical doctors, college professors, and other educated people comprise this class. Police officers, firefighters, postal employees, and school teachers are also in the middle class, although with somewhat less status than their better-educated middle-class counterparts. The lower class usually is characterized as having limited formal education and few marketable skills. The lower class is affected dis-

proportionately by physical and mental health problems. Almost any loss of income, such as loss of employment or severe medical illness, could place a middle-class person in the lower class. The lower class may live in, at, or near poverty. Approximately 12.4% of the United States population lives in poverty. These figures have remained relatively steady for a number of years. The government updates the poverty threshold on an annual basis. Social class mobility exists; the lower class can move to the middle class and, in some situations, move to the upper class. The opposite also holds true, as upper- and middle-class people can move downward to the lower classes.

Contextual Features

The United States is a constitutional republic in which the citizens of the country do not actually pass the laws or enforce them, but elect representatives who pass legislation and enforce the laws. In 1787, America adopted the first written constitution that established the governmental structure of the country, which still exists in the twenty-first century. The U.S. Constitution divided government powers between the central or national government and the states. Currently, there are fifty states that have legal authority to pass legislation and enforce laws specifically for their states. These laws include driver's licenses, property, and income and sales taxes. The powers that the federal (central) government does not possess are reserved for the states. The Ninth and Tenth Amendments of the U.S. Constitution protect the powers and authority of the fifty state governments.

The constitution has built into it separation of powers and a check-and-balance system. The national government is divided into three branches, which were intentionally put into place by the framers of the Constitution. The three branches divided the powers of the central governments and each branch operated as a check on the other two. The goal was to balance the power of the three branches, while no one branch would become dominant over the other two.

The branches of the federal government are executive, legislative, and judiciary. The executive branch enforces the laws. The president oversees the executive branch and is the chief executive officer and commander-in-chief of the military. The legislative branch passes federal laws and approves the federal budget and appropriations. The legislative branch is divided into the Senate, which approves all presidential appointees, and the House of Representatives, which approves appropriations. Both the president and members of the House and Senate are installed via direct popular elections. The judiciary branch consists of the Supreme Court with one chief justice and eight associate justices who have the authority for judicial review; and the Court of Appeals whose primary assignment is judicial review of the federal trial courts known as District Courts. All federal judges are appointed by the president with the approval of the Senate and serve for life. Federal judges are given lifetime appointments to remove them from the influence of partisan politics.

When the U.S. Constitution was adopted in 1787 it lacked a Bill of Rights. In order to get the Constitution adopted, the founders promised that a Bill of Rights would be adopted once the constitution was approved. In 1789, the Bill of Rights was adopted, which guarantees freedom of speech, freedom of religion, freedom of the press; and the right of the people to assemble and to petition the government for a redress of grievances. Also, the Bill of Rights guarantees due process of law, the right to an attorney and to cross-examine witnesses, the right to a speedy and public trial, and search and seizure protection from the government.

The term criminal justice can be defined as "the structure, functions, and decision processes of those agencies that deal with the management of crime—the police, the courts, and corrections" (Inciardi 1996). Since the United States has a federal form of government, there are two criminal justice processes—that of the federal government and that of the states. There are federal law enforcement agencies and state law enforcement agencies, federal correctional institutions and state correctional institutions, and a federal court system and a state court system. There are federal laws passed by the Congress of the United States and state laws passed by fifty state legislatures. The federal legal system deals with federal laws, while the state legal system deals with state laws.

Under the U.S. legal system, a crime can only exist when the legislative branch of government defines a specific act as a crime. Only when an act has been declared illegal by the legislative branch can the criminal justice components—police, courts and corrections—step in and take legal action. Legal action includes arrest, trial or hearing, conviction, sentencing, and punishment. A convicted offender generally receives, depending on the seriousness of the offense, probation (sent back to the community with specific restrictions and supervision) or a prison term.

The most serious (violent) crimes in the United States are homicide, assault, rape, robbery, theft,

burglary, and arson. Generally, the following crimes considered less serious (i.e., less violent or nonviolent): criminal trespass, shoplifting, embezzlement, fraud, forgery, and automobile theft. Beginning in the early twentieth century, the U.S. government has considered the illegal use and selling of drugs a major offense. In the last decades of the twentieth century, drug arrests were major efforts by both federal and state law enforcement agencies. These drug arrests led to a substantial increase in the prison population in the United States.

Police Profile

Background

The structure of American law enforcement has its roots in England. The English law enforcement structure located order maintenance at the local level, giving the responsibility to counties, cities, and villages. Thus, since colonial times to the present, the United States has had a decentralized policing system.

The structure of American policing can be divided into three categories: federal, state, and local. The U.S. Constitution allows the federal government to pass laws to protect the central government and to establish law enforcement agencies to protect the central government and to establish law enforcement agencies to enforce federal laws. The Tenth Amendment of the Constitution reserves for the states, or for the people, those powers not provided to the federal government. State governments do not have the right to pass laws that violate the federal constitution. Local police agencies are divided into cities, towns, and villages dependent on state laws or county police departments and the sheriff's department.

Demographics

In the twenty-first century, there are an estimated 18,000 local police departments in the United States. Municipal (city, towns, and villages) governments account for 99% of the total number of local police departments, while county police account for less than 1%. The vast majority of police departments are small. Approximately 50% of police agencies employ ten or fewer police officers. Ninety-four percent of local police departments employ fifty or fewer officers, and 90% of the police departments serve a population of less than 25,000. Three out of four police departments in the United States serve a population of less than 10,000. This can be contrasted with less than 2% of local police departments serving a population of 100,000 or more, and less than 1% of local police departments serving a population of 250,000. Cities with a population of 1 million average about 5,000 police officers, while communities with a population of less than 2,500 average three police officers. Although small communities comprise the majority of police agencies in the United States, the vast majority of police officers are employed in communities with a population of 100,000 or more.

Organizational Description

Local government in the United States includes any level of government that clearly cannot be defined as either federal or state. A local law enforcement officer can be defined as "an employee of a local government agency who is an officer sworn to carry out law enforcement duties" (U.S. Department of Justice 1981:127). Examples of local law enforcement officers include sheriffs, deputy sheriffs, chiefs of police, sworn police officers, and special police officers, which include state colleges and university police. A local police officer should not be confused with either a federal law enforcement officer or a state law enforcement officer. These officers are employees of either the federal or state government. Although there are local police agencies that employ part-time police officers for their departments, most local police departments are staffed by permanent, full-time police officers. Part-time officers are usually employed in rural communities with small populations.

Responsibility for policing lies primarily with local government in the United States, with most police agencies operated by small police agencies controlling crime in small communities.

The office of sheriff was brought to the United States by the early English colonists. The county sheriff is unique in policing since the sheriff is elected by the people of the county usually for a term of four years. In many instances, the sheriff has prior law enforcement experience as a state patrol officer or city police officer. The sheriff's duties vary from count to county and from state to state; however, these duties often include being a tax collector, coroner, assessor, and/or oversight of county highway maintenance. Normally, the sheriff's office has charge of a detention facility. Most prisoners await trial, but at times, prisoners serve their sentences in the county jail rather than in a state prison. Sheriff's departments usually have the task of executing criminal warrants and serving papers. Another function of sheriff's departments is the security of the county courthouse; many function like a municipal police agency, performing routine police tasks and criminal

investigations. Sheriff's deputies perform routine police work in unincorporated areas where city police lack jurisdiction.

Generally, the state constitution provides that the sheriff is the chief law enforcement officer of a county. Services rendered by the sheriff's office vary from county to county and from state to state. In some cases, the sheriff has practically no responsibilities at all, or may provide a full range of law enforcement services. The variety of functions provided by the sheriff can include providing traditional police services in unincorporated areas of the county or being present at the meeting of a county board of supervisors for the purpose of maintaining order and serving notices and subpoenas.

The full-service sheriff's department provides patrols, courts, and correctional services. As a model of the full-service sheriff's office, the Los Angeles Sheriff's Office is the largest sheriff's office in the United States, providing policing service for the unincorporated areas of Los Angeles County and contracting police services for incorporated cities within the county. The Department has a police academy, crime laboratory, investigation unit, air patrol, marine patrol, and communication systems to assist in the performance of its police services. The Los Angeles Sheriff's Department also operates the largest jail in the country.

There are approximately 3,100 sheriff's departments at the local level and about 1,500 special police operating at the local government level. Ninety-eight percent of the sheriff's departments perform court-related work, 97% function as law enforcement officers, and 80% are involved in jail-related activities. Generally, sheriff's departments are small, with approximately one-third employing fewer than ten officers, and two-thirds employing fewer than twenty-five sworn officers. Approximately one-half of the sheriff's departments serve counties with populations of less than 250,000. Sheriff's departments that serve counties with populations over 250,000 employ about one-half of all deputy sheriffs. Sheriff's departments that serve counties with populations of 1 million or more employ over one-fifth of all sheriff's deputies. Although two-thirds of the departments employ fewer than twenty-five deputies, the departments serving counties with populations over 250,000 employ the vast majority of deputies.

During the nineteenth century, only two states in the United States had established police agencies—Massachusetts and Texas. Generally, the states delegated policing to local government. Prior to Texan independence in 1836, an unofficial militia, known as the Rangers, protected settlers from raids. At independence, the Rangers became an appendage of the government, and their duties took on the characteristics of more general police work. In 1865, Massachusetts created a state police force to handle liquor law enforcement; however, the force was disbanded in 1875. Now all states, except Hawaii, have some form of state police agency.

Ultimately, the violence between labor and management in the first decades of the twentieth century led to the formation of the first modern police agency. Because of labor disputes in coal and iron companies and the violence occurring as a result of labor disputes, the governor of Pennsylvania saw the need for creating a state police agency to maintain order, because he felt that the Coal and Iron Police, the companies' private police force, could not be impartial when dealing with coal and iron workers. The Pennsylvania governor believed that an impartial state police agency should be established to oversee disagreements between labor and industry. The Pennsylvania State Police were created in 1905 with a complement of 228 men.

The Pennsylvania State Police became a model for other states creating their own state police agencies. Typically, the state police developed in response to the following needs:

- Necessity of coordinating state and local law enforcement agencies
- Need for a uniformity of law enforcement practices
- Lack of police protections and services in rural areas
- Inability of local law enforcement agencies to cope with crime problems
- Hesitancy of local law enforcement to enforce laws that were unpopular
- Lack of coordination in controlling crimes involving mobility
- Need to counteract political pressures on local law enforcement
- Mismanagement, corruption, and inefficiency characterizing many local departments
- Increase in volume of automobile and traffic accidents

In the 1920s, a number of states began to establish another form of state police known as the "highway patrol," who had as their primarily responsibility the enforcing of traffic laws on state highways and state laws in areas adjacent to state highway property. States with highway patrols are Kansas, Georgia, Ohio, California, and Florida. These states have created general investigative agencies to investigate crimes occurring in rural areas or to assist local police agencies that lack the manpower to investigate sophisticated crimes. States that have created elite

investigative agencies are Kansas (the Kansas Bureau of Investigation) and Georgia (Georgia Bureau of Investigation). Many of these agencies, the Georgia Bureau of Investigation, for example, maintain a crime laboratory, Automatic Fingerprint Identification System (AFIS), and criminal history database, and perform undercover drug investigations.

Prior to the twentieth century, the federal government had a restricted role in law enforcement. The emphasis of federal law enforcement was on safeguarding the country's revenues and protecting the mail. Postal inspectors protected the mails, while Secret Service agents protected the country's currency. It was not until the early part of the twentieth century that the federal government began to increase its role in law enforcement.

In 1908, the Attorney General created the Bureau of Investigation—the present-day Federal Bureau of Investigation (FBI)—to investigate corruption and violations of business law. The Harrison Act of 1914 was designed to regulate the import, manufacture, and dispensing of drugs. Since regulation was achieved through taxation, the law was enforced by the Treasury Department, Bureau of Internal Revenue.

Until the 1960s, the federal government had emphasized that federal law enforcement agencies should concentrate on enforcing federal laws. However, with the passage of the Omnibus Crime Control and Safe Streets Act of 1968, the U.S. Congress provided financial resources to local police agencies for equipment, training, and staff. In the 1970s, the Justice Department initiated "Strike" programs among various federal law enforcement agencies aimed at combating organized crime. Currently, local police officers are incorporated into federal task forces for the Drug Enforcement Agency (DEA) and the FBI. For example, in Wichita, Kansas, police officers from the police department and the county sheriff's department are members of the FBI Task Force investigating commercial robberies.

There are approximately fifty federal law enforcement agencies, and to discuss each individually would be too cumbersome. Most federal police agencies have limited powers and their investigative powers are narrow in scope. Federal law enforcement agencies can be found in the Departments of Justice, Treasury, State, Agriculture, Transportation, Interior, Transportation, and Education, and the U.S. Post Office.

There are approximately 69,000 full-time federal law enforcement personnel who are authorized to make arrests and carry firearms.

Functions

Police officers are assigned a wide variety of functions, usually without any degree of government planning. The priorities or objectives of police functions are not specified. The police fulfill a rather broad mission with broad functions, often responding to the influence of local, state, and federal governments. Factors that influence the police function include "broad legislative mandates to the police; the authority to use force lawfully; the investigative ability of the police; the twenty-four-hour availability of the police; and community pressure on the police" (American Bar Association 1973: 47). Police are assigned a variety of miscellaneous functions to which no other government agencies are normally assigned. For example, police are often asked to report burned-out streetlights that they observe or to report potholes that they discover while on patrol.

Studies of police activities show that most police tasks revolve around noncriminal activity. Approximately 80% to 90% of police functions involve handling family disturbances, dealing with traffic accidents, finding missing persons, directing traffic, and dealing with a myriad of hazards and dangers. Since the advent of telephones and radios in patrol cars in the 1930s, the police have provided a reactive approach to policing. Police officers respond to calls for service or to incidents. For example, a citizen telephones the police to report an automobile accident or disturbance, and the police dispatcher assigns a patrol unit to handle the call.

One misconception about U.S. police is that they are concerned with all types of crime. The police are concerned primarily with predatory crimes like murder, rape, and theft. Generally, the police have no authority regarding enforcement of economic, civil rights violations, or labor laws.

Police work deals with specific situations that involve behavior prohibited by either state or local law. When a law has been violated, the police have the option of arresting and prosecuting or informally handling specific incidents. The total police function includes the objectives of the police and the methods that they employ. When citizens call the police, they want action and they want it immediately. Citizens consider their problems important, and they want the police to handle these situations right away. Occasionally, an officer on a murder call may encounter a citizen who feels that his own complaint about a noise pollution problem is more important. Usually, a citizen assumes that the police have the authority to handle any situation that concerns them. In order to intervene effectively, a police officer can take various actions depending on the circumstances. These actions may include conducting an investigation, issuing an order to leave or desist, or move on.

Training

Basic police training covers law, criminal justice, patrol, investigation, police proficiency (that is, first aid, firearms, and self-defense), and administration. The most common number of hours for police training in the United States is 400. The number of hours that police officers spend in training varies from six weeks to about one and a half years. For example, all officers in the state of Kansas are required to receive 320 hours of basic police training. However, within the same state, the City of Wichita requires twenty-six weeks of basic police training for all police officers. Basic police training varies from state to state and city to city. Generally, large urban areas require more hours for basic police training than less populated rural areas. The norm for firearms training as part of basic training is forty hours. Some basic training programs may have eighty hours of firearms training. The Wichita Police Department requires eighty-four hours of firearms training for a basic police training class. Usually, police trainees must qualify with their service firearm before they are allowed to work as a police officer, and may be dismissed if they are unable to qualify. Also, most police departments require that all police officers qualify with their service firearms at least once a year.

Upon completion of basic police training, most of the fifty states. All sworn police officer are usually required to obtain forty to forty-five hours of police-related training yearly. The subject can vary from criminal law to multiculturalism to criminal investigations. This continuous training is usually in addition to firearms training.

Complaints and Discipline

Most police departments in the United States provide for a complaint procedure that allows citizens to make legitimate complaints regarding police employees, and often police departments have policies that allow citizens to file complaints in person, by telephone, or by mail.

Ideally, every complaint, regardless of its nature, should impartially be investigated. Generally, complaints are handled by the lowest appropriate level of the organization. For example, sergeants will handle complaints against officers; lieutenants will handle complaints against sergeants. Minor violations of departmental policies and procedures are normally handled by the supervisor of the accused officer, while serious accusations are normally turned over to the internal affairs unit. The head of the internal affairs units reports directly, to the police chief or police commissioner, to the chief executive officer of the police department. In any formal investigation, all witnesses will be interviewed, all relevant physical evidence will be examined, and all information pertinent to the complaint will be obtained. Internal affairs units are responsible for investigating police misconduct. These include corruption and the excessive use of physical force by police officers, including deadly force.

In addition to the internal affairs unit of a police department, the legal system of each state holds police officers accountable for misconduct that violates the laws of their specific state or of the federal government. The legal system expects the police to follow guidelines established by the legislative branch and appellate court decisions. It also examines the manner in which the police enforce the law. The police are expected to impartially enforce state laws and federal laws and to protect the constitutional rights of all citizens, and when they do not, they are informed of such by the courts.

Since the 1970s, the Supreme Court has applied Title 42 US Code Section 1983 to check police misconduct. Essentially, this federal law forbids agents (police officers are agents) of the government to use any state law, ordinance, regulation, or custom as a method of denying citizens their constitutional rights.

Human Rights

In the United States, human rights are referred to as civil rights. Police receive civil rights training at all levels of government in the United States. These government divisions include the federal, state, and municipal level. In fact, the concept of civil rights means that police officers are guardians of citizens' civil rights. These rights are contained within the first ten amendments of the U.S. Constitution known as the Bill of Rights. Within the Bill of Rights are a vast number of civil rights protections. Training in civil rights includes the following constitutional rights: probable cause for arrest, constitutional rights advised, search and seizure, and police use of excessive force.

Under the Bill of Rights, police must have probable cause to arrest someone. Probable cause means a set of facts and circumstances that would lead the average person to believe that a particular person has committed a particular crime. Generally, police must witness a crime, or have a valid warrant from a judge to make a legal arrest. Additionally, the Bill of Rights protects people from unlawful search and seizures; protects people from having to incriminate themselves, and guarantees the right to a speedy trial by jury.

The length of recruit training varies according to state law. The mission of training facilities is to provide police recruits a working knowledge of the civil rights of citizens.

Generally, police in the United States have the public's support. However, police officers have violated the civil rights of citizens, and there are several approaches to hold the police accountable for civil rights violations. Large police departments include an internal affairs unit that monitors citizens' complaints and investigates alleged police violations. In small rural police agencies, the chief of police may fill this position.

The second means of preventing/controlling the violation of civil rights by police is civilian review boards. Civilian review boards are made up of members of the community and have oversight on incidents pertaining to police misconduct. A third tool for dealing with civil rights violations is the legal system. The legal system holds police accountable not only for enforcing the law, but also for how they enforce it.

The fourth tool for dealing with civil rights violations is found in federal law under Title 42 Section 1983, which allows citizens to sue police agencies and personnel for personal damages due to civil rights violations.

Terrorism

Resulting in part on the attacks of September 11, 2001, on March 1, 2003, the Department of Homeland Security was formed. The Department of Homeland Security encompasses over 180,000 government employees. The responsibility of Homeland Security is centered on increasing the security of the United States from terrorist attacks. To accomplish this mission, Homeland Security efforts include: strengthening border and transportation security, protecting communications systems and power grids, and guarding against chemical and biological threats. As of this writing, the federal government had allocated $13 billion to Homeland Security to equip and train first responders to handle situations caused by terrorism. Due to open borders, land mass size, and individual rights and freedoms, democracies such as the United States are vulnerable to terrorist activity. Terrorist organizations that operate within the United States are both foreign and domestic in origin. Some terrorist organizations strive to achieve goals that are political in nature, while others have religious goals.

Police Education, Research, and Publication

Police Education

The impetus for police officers obtaining baccalaureate degrees in the United States can be traced to the President's Commission on Law Enforcement and Administration of Justice. In 1965, President Lyndon Johnson appointed a Crime Commission to study crime and violence in the United States. The President's Commission, which made its report in 1967, recommended that all police officers with law enforcement powers have baccalaureate degrees. The 1960s was a period of social disruption and violence. The police lacked the ability to cope with ghetto riots, and appeared to be helpless in controlling the spiraling crime rate. Both liberal and conservative politicians in the United States believed that higher education for police officers was desirable. The federal government from the late 1960s to the late 1970s provided funds for the education of persons employed in or preparing for a career in law enforcement. Because of the availability of federal funding, universities and colleges established academic programs for the formal education of law enforcement personnel. There are approximately 1,000 universities and colleges that offer academic programs for current or potential law enforcement personnel. In the twenty-first century, law enforcement personnel can obtain undergraduate and graduate degrees in criminal justice (law enforcement). There currently are more police managers and line personnel in the field of law enforcement than ever before in American law enforcement. This trend of better-educated police personnel is expected to continue in the twenty-first century.

Researchers

To name all criminal justice researchers would be cumbersome and require more space than this sections allows. However, the following is a representative list of researchers on policing in the United States: August Vollmer, Herman Goldstein, George Kelling, James Q. Wilson, Jerome Skolneck, David Bayley, Peter Manning, and O.W. Wilson.

Publications

The following list provides a small sample of the many publications available.

Conti, P. M. *The Pennsylvania State Police: A History of Service to the Commonwealth, 1905 to the Present.* Harrisburg, PA: Stackpole,1977.

Felkens, G. T. *The Criminal Justice System: Its Functions and Personnel.* Englewood Cliffs, NJ: Prentice-Hall, 1973.

Gladwin, I. *The Sheriff: The Man and His Office.* London: Victor Gollancez, 1974.

Goldstein, H. *Policing a Free Society.* Cambridge, MA: Ballinger, 1977.

Inciardi, J. A. *Criminal Justice*, 5th ed. New York: Harcourt Press, 1996.

Johnson, D. R. *American Law Enforcement: A History.* St. Louis: Forum, 1981.

Extent of Funding for Research

The National Institute of Justice is the research, development, and evaluation branch of the U.S. Department of Justice. The mission of the National Institute of Justice is to maintain advanced scientific research, development, and evaluation to enhance the administration of justice and public safety. Recent publications include *Police in Large Cities 1990–2000, Police Use of Force, Prevalence of Imprisonment in the U.S Population, 1974–2001,* and *Local Police Departments, 2000,* to name a few. The Department of Justice provides applications for the funding of continued research within the field of criminal justice.

Leading Journals

American Journal of Police, Anderson Publishing Company Cincinnati, OH

Criminal Justice Studies, Taylor & Francis, Champlain, NY

FBI Law Enforcement Bulletin, U.S. Department of Justice, Federal Bureau of Investigation, Washington, DC

Journal of Criminal Justice, International Chiefs of Police, published by Elsevier Inc., New York, NY

Journal of Police Science & Administration, Arlington, VA

Journal of Crime & Justice, Anderson Publishing Company, Cincinnati, OH

Law and Order, Hendon Inc., Wilmette, IL

Police Quarterly, Police Executive Research Forum, Washington, DC

Policing, MCB University Press, Cambridge, MA

Police Chief, International Association of Chiefs of Police, Gaithersburg, MD

Police-Related Websites

Federal Bureau of Investigation, *www.fbi.gov*

Department of Justice, *www.usdoj.gov*

National Institute of Justice, *www.ojp.usdoj.gov/nij*

Drug Enforcement Administration, *www.usdoj.gov/dea*

International Association of Chiefs of Police, *www.theiacp.org*

Police Foundation, *www.policefoundation.org*

Department of Homeland Security, *www.dhs.gov/dhspublic*

Bureau of Justice Statistics,
  www.ojp.usdoj.gov/bjs
National Criminal Justice Reference Service,
  www.ncjrs.org/statwww.html
U.S. Border Control, *www.usbc.org*

PAUL A. IBBETSON AND MICHAEL J. PALMIOTTO

Bibliography

American Bar Association. *The Urban Police Function.* New York: American Bar Association, 1973.

Felkens, George T. *The Criminal Justice System: Its Functions and Personnel.* Englewood Cliffs, NJ: Prentice-Hall, 1973.
Iniciardi, James A. *Criminal Justice*, 5th ed. New York: Harcourt Press, 1996.
Johnson, David R. *American Law Enforcement: A History.* St. Louis: Forum, 1981.
Reaves, Brian A. *State and Local Police Departments, 2002.* Washington, DC: U.S. Department of Justice, Office of Programs, Bureau of Statistics, 2002.
U.S. Department of Justice. *Dictionary of Criminal Justice Data Technology*, 2nd ed. Washington, DC: U.S. Department of Justice, Bureau of Justice Statistics, 1981.

URUGUAY

Background Material

The Spaniards arrived in the territory of present-day Uruguay in 1516. Uruguayan territory was defined in 1777. An independence movement led by José Artigas emerged in 1810. After years of struggle, the Portuguese invaded the county in 1817, defeating Artigas. The Portuguese and Brazilians left the country, and the Oriental Republic of Uruguay became independent in 1830, with the establishment of its first constitution. The first president of the Republic was General José Fructuoso Rivera, whose administration was characterized by civil unrest.

The first half of the twentieth century saw strong growth in state institutions. The country had education levels, health, and per capita income superior to the rest of the countries of the region. At the end of the 1950s, however, economic decline set in. Social unrest led to the growth of an urban guerrilla movement, the National Liberation Movement (also known as the Tupamaros). The guerrillas were defeated in 1973, and a military government was set up. In 1985, the democratic system was restored.

The official language of Uruguay is Spanish, and the predominant religion is Roman Catholicism. Uruguay's total population is 3,399,237 (July 2004 estimate); its capital is Montevideo. GDP per capita (purchasing power parity) is US$12,800 (2003 estimate).

The most important economic activity in the country is livestock raising. The three most important export items, accounting for 68% of the total exports (according to the Ministry of Economy and Finance) are wool, leather, and meat. Another important source of economic development is tourism.

Contextual Features

Uruguay is a democratic republic. The political structure is organized around a strong presidency, subject to legislative and judicial checks. The country is divided into nineteen administrative subdivisions, overseen by nineteen departments. Each department is headed by a governor who is responsible for local administration.

The Supreme Court of Justice judges offenders against the constitution, who commit crimes that violate treaties, pacts, and conventions with other states. It also has the ability to grant parole. The lower courts, in descending order, are the appellate courts on criminal matters, the courts of first instance, and lawyer courts of first instance. There are also courts for misdemeanor offenses.

From the structural point of view, the penal process is always continued in the same form, drawn from Books I and II of the Penal Process Code. An individual charged with a crime is processed, a defense attorney is named, the charge is formulated against him or her, and a sentence is dictated that can be based on punishment or acquittal.

Under Uruguayan law, "offenses" includes three categories: crimes, felonies, and misdemeanors. Misdemeanors are the less serious offences, while crimes are more severe and will generally receive harsher punishments. Felonies include crimes, and generally only the most severe crimes are designated felonies.

The Uruguayan judicial branch focuses exclusively on the judgment of criminal cases. It is comprised of the Supreme Court of Justice (the highest organ of the judicial branch), and the lower courts. The Supreme Court of Justice consists of five members. The law allows the creation of as many appellate courts as are deemed necessary. Each one of them is composed of three members. Penal Courts judge on criminal matters, and Work Tribunals judge on labor-related matters.

Police Profile

Demographics

The police force in Uruguay is composed of approximately 27,800 officials, of which 23,650 belong to the executive division. A more exact demographic breakdown follows:

- 21,302, members of the security force, 1,878 officials (1,772 men and 106 women), 19,424 subordinate personnel (17,994 men and 1,430 women)
- 1,048 firemen, 83 officials (79 men and 4 women), 965 subordinate personnel (965 men and 0 women)
- 1,300 penitentiary police, 67 officials, (53 men and 14 women), 1, 233 subordinate personnel (1, 111 men and 122 women)

Organizational Description

National, regional, and local structures are as follows:

The National Department of Information and Intelligence has national jurisdiction, with direct dependence on the Ministry of the Interior.

The National Department of Technical Police also has national jurisdiction. For this reason, it has the management and general supervision of all technical offices of the country, being guided specifically and fundamentally toward the study, examination, and systematic analysis of the material indications of crime and delinquency, with the purpose of collaborating in police and judicial tasks.

The Inspection of Schools and Courses Department is charged with overseeing the implementation of educational doctrine among the Institutes of Police Teaching.

The National Department of Fire Fighters is in charge of fire fighter police in the whole national territory.

The National Department of Traffic Police has to systematize and control all traffic-related procedures, and develop means of reducing the total number of traffic accidents. It also assists traffic accident victims.

The National Department of Police Social Assistance is integrated with the routine services related to retirement, pensions, and housing for police personnel and their families.

The National Department of Police Health is concerned with the certification of police personnel health requirements, and preventive health and medical care of police personnel and family members (both active duty and retired).

The National Department of Civil Identification administers the nation's identification service.

The National Department of Social Prevention of the Crime is responsible for proposing, execution, coordination, and evaluation prevention policies pertinent to violent crime and/or the protection of specially vulnerable social groups.

General Department of Penal Institutes

Department of Migration

The Planning and Advisory Organs plan and to coordinate all police services throughout the country, and provide relevant guidelines and technical services.

Police careers can begin via entry as a cadet to the National Police School, as well as through transfers from other government departments or ancillary positions within the police force.

The police force consists of executive police (police field agents/officers), administrators, professional technicians, and specialists. Officer and enlisted titles follow: general inspector, principal inspector, major inspector, commissar inspector or commissar major or captain, (subcommissar or first lieutenant, principal officer or second lieutenant, assistant officer or second lieutenant, officer subadjutant, major subofficer, first sergeant, agent, (cuirassier, and first- and second-class guard or firefighter.

The police force is organized hierarchically, according to rank. To rank equality, they will deprive the date of obtaining of the rank successively, the antiquity in the Police Institute and the age.

Promotions are awarded according to formulas of vacancies in the structure, and officer seniority and qualifications (meeting qualifications, selection by superior officers, merit-based competition).

Functions

The police are responsible for defending and protecting citizens' lives and property, maintaining law and order, tranquility, and security.

Training

The National Police School is in charge of the formation and training of police officers for the entire country, and, through the School of Advanced Police Studies, the continuing education and training of officers through the ranks. The National Police School also supervises municipal training efforts.

Recent seminars for police officers at all levels follow: integration with the community and improvement of the institutional image; violence, citizen security, and democratic governability; and interdisciplinary focuses on domestic violence.

Police Public Projects

Under a broader program focused on "citizen security," the Ministry of the Interior carried out a police–community partnership project. This project included participants in public and private sectors who analyzed and debated proposals for policing reforms.

Police Use of Firearms

Firearms and ammunition are provided to all police officers, who receive training before entering the force, and throughout their careers.

Human Rights

The police were accused of human rights violations during the military dictatorship. Since then, the police have exercised their activities in strict adherence to laws protecting human rights.

Terrorism

One of the duties of the National Department of Information and Intelligence is to investigate and prevent terrorism. In this regard, there are a few antecedents of extradition orders for residents with presumed links to terrorism.

International Cooperation

European Community nations (mainly Spain and England) have provided scholarships for police training and equipment donations. U.S. providers recently collaborated in a course on community policing at the National Police School.

Uruguay has provided scholarships for specialization courses to police officers from Argentina, Brazil, Bolivia, Honduras, Panama, and Paraguay.

FIORELLA ESPINOSA RIBEIRO

Bibliography

National Statistics Institute: www.ine.gub.uy.

UZBEKISTAN

Background Material

Uzbekistan as a landlocked country in Central Asia, with Kazakhstan on the north, Turkmenistan on the south, and Tajikistan, Afghanistan, and Kyrgyzstan on the east. Most of the terrain consists of desert (MSN Maps Web Site 2004), which has long shaped the country's culture, politics, and agriculture. As a result, its capital city, Tashkent, was founded centuries ago close to rivers and water resources. During the Soviet era, Uzbekistan intensively produced cotton and grain, which led to such overuse of agricultural chemicals and depletion of water supplies that the country poisoned much of its soil and lost half of the water of its rivers and the Aral Sea. Since gaining independence in 1991, therefore, the Uzbek government has sought to decrease dependency on agriculture by focusing on its large gold, natural gas, and petroleum reserves. But the country still struggles to overcome economic problems.

Uzbekistan has a very young population. Of the country's total population of approximately 26.5 million, according to 2004 estimates, 30% are under the age of fourteen. Uzbeks comprise 80% of the population, with the rest made up of ethnicities such as Russian (5.5%), Tajik (5%), Kazakh (3%), Karakalpak (2.5%), and Tatar (1.5%) (1996 estimate). Likewise, Uzbek is the most used language in the country (74.3%), along with other languages such as Russian (14.2%) and Tajik (4.4%). Uzbekistan's largest religion is Islam, mostly Sunni, accounting for 88% of the population, and Eastern

Orthodoxy is the second largest religion, covering 9% of the population. The literacy rate is high, at 99.3% for people over the age of fifteen (Central Intelligence Agency 2004).

Contextual Features

Politically and administratively, Uzbekistan is officially a republic, with a government, prime minister, cabinet of ministers, and a parliament, the Supreme Assembly. But it is not a democracy, since the country is under authoritarian presidential rule, with the president having the power to appoint the prime minister and cabinet ministers. Although these appointments must be confirmed by the Supreme Assembly, indicating a measure of legislative power, in reality, all parties in the Supreme Assembly support the president. President Islam Karimov won the country's first presidential election, and extended his term through a 1995 plebiscite. He then won a five-year term in 2000 in an election that the Organization for Security and Cooperation in Europe (OSCE) asserted was not a fair one.

Similarly, the Supreme Court is the most important institution in the judicial system of the country, but all its judges are nominated by the president. Uzbekistan not only lacks an independent judicial system, but any of its own laws, as the entire system is based on Soviet civil law (Central Intelligence Agency 2004).

Police Profile

Demographics

The police force of Uzbekistan is comprised of approximately 25,000 individuals.

Functions

Uzbekistan has a significant drug production and trafficking problem. An estimated 2,000 to 3,000 hectares of domestic opium poppy are grown annually. Narcotics are also transported across the border from Afghanistan (often by way of Tajikistan). Since independence, border security with Afghanistan and among the former Soviet Central Asian republics has become more negligent, intensifying the problem of drug trafficking.

The National Security Service, the Ministry of Internal Affairs, and the State Customs Committee share jurisdiction in the area of drug trafficking and drug control. However, the specific duties of each organization are somewhat ill defined. In 1995, Uzbekistan established a National Commission on Drug Control to improve coordination among professionals and to increase public awareness of the problem. The government's eradication program, which targeted only small areas of cultivation in the early 1990s, expanded significantly in 1995, and drug-related arrests more than doubled over a single year.

Interaction also has been expanded with the National Security Service, the chief intelligence agency, which still is mainly staffed by former KGB personnel. About 8,000 paramilitary troops are believed available to the National Security Service.

International Cooperation

In 1992, the U.S. government began urging all five Central Asian nations to make drug production and trafficking control a top policy priority. The United States has channeled most of its aid through the UN Drug Control Program, whose programs for drug-control intelligence centers and canine narcotics detection squads began to be adopted in Uzbekistan in 1996. In 1995, Uzbekistan signed a bilateral counternarcotics cooperation agreement with Turkey, and acceded to the 1988 UN Convention Against Illicit Traffic in Narcotic Drugs and Psychotropic Substances.

Training

Uzbekistani police are trained according to Soviet standards. The U.S. Department of Justice has begun a program that trains the police in Western techniques.

Complaints and Discipline

The police in Uzbekistan are beset by corruption and the influence of organized crime. In a society facing upheaval, tremendous economic shortages, and tight political control from the top down, the government and criminal world have become intertwined. Citizens routinely have been required to pay bribes for all common services. These bribes often involve enormous sums of money.

The police are widely viewed in Uzbekistan as supporting and taking part in drug and weapons trafficking.

OSMAN DOLU

Bibliography

MSN. "Uzbekistan, Asia." 2005. Available at: www.maps. msn.com/(1lciit55vtrwp2bn0mppy445)/map.aspx?C=41.7 7202%2c63.14602&L=WLD&A=5000&PN=1010688172 &S=800%2c740&P=|f7|&TI=Uzbekistan%2c+Asia. Accessed November 1, 2004.

Central Intelligence Agency. "Uzbekistan." *The World Factbook.* 2004. Available at: www.odci.gov/cia/publi cations/ factbook/geos/uz.html. Accessed September 5, 2004.

Library of Congress. "Uzbekistan." Country Studies. Available at: http://lcweb2.loc.gov/frd/cs/.

V

VANUATU

Background Material

Vanuatu has had a unique colonial history. After being settled by both French and English settlers in the late nineteenth century, the two colonial powers in 1906 agreed to treat it as a "condominium," that is, as a territory administered jointly by France and England. The condominium provided for two resident commissioners (French and English), two public services, two courts, and two police forces. This condominium continued until 1980, when Vanuatu regained independence. Under the Vanuatu Constitution, the unicameral parliament consists of 52 members elected by universal suffrage. A Council of Chiefs advises the government on matters of customs, land tenure, and the preservation of traditions.

Vanuatu is prone to both volcanic/tectonic disasters and to tropical storms. Its economy is small and largely agricultural and is currently shrinking at approximately 2.5% per annum.

Increasing unemployment and underemployment are major problems confronting Vanuatu, a country racked by political instability. Unemployment has aggravated economic and social inequities, which in turn have exacerbated disoder in Vanuatu. Its infrastructure is weak and unstable, especially outside the capital of Port Vila. Inter-island shipping can be unreliable; flights are expensive and road networks limited. Beyond the urban areas, electricity, water, sanitation, health care, education, and telecommunications are limited (Jowitt 2002). In terms of human development, Vanuatu in 1997 was ranked in the bottom third of United Nations medium-developed countries. Deforestation is a pressing environmental concern.

Local divisions survive from the colonial past. The road to independence was marred by bitter conflict between the pro-French parties and the nationalist Anglophone parties. Politically, Vanuatu is prone to great volatility with six changes of government since 1995. There is a growing indigenous movement whose leaders describe themselves as national "freedom fighters." Many of the members are former veterans of the 1970s struggles for independence from the colonial powers. There is considerable suspicion of the country's most powerful neighbor, Australia. There have been allegations of Australian police spies (even by Vanuatu's deputy Prime Minister). There is distrust of both the Australian Federal Police involvement and Australian government intervention in internal Vanuatuan affairs (SBS *Dateline*, October 2, 2002).

The population is estimated at 196,178 persons (July 2002). Vanuatu has the third most rapid population growth rate in the South Pacific. However, it suffers from a high infant mortality rate (34 per 1000 births).

English, French, Bislama (the local pidgin language that is most commonly spoken), and about 100 indigenous languages are spoken. The inherited language complexities, originating from the dual French and English language and education system, combined with customary law, restrict legal reform.

The population's religion makeup is: Presbyterian (36.7%), Anglican (15%), Roman Catholic (15%), indigenous beliefs (7.6%), Seventh-Day Adventist (6.2%), Church of Christ (3.8%), and other (15.7%).

The GDP per capita is US$1300 (1999 est.).

Vanuatu is an archipelagic nation of 83 islands, whose population live predominantly in rural villages. The country is in transition from subsistence agriculture to a cash economy. The 1999 census indicated that 67 percent of the workers in the labor force were subsistence farmers, although many also cultivated a garden for a small cash economy. Fishing, financial services, and tourism are the other major economic activities.

Economic development is hindered by the scarcity of commodity exports, vulnerability to natural disasters (January 2002 earthquake in capital), long distances from markets and between islands, and periods of political instability. The only significant exports are copra, cocoa, beef, and timber. The agricultural crops are prone to natural disasters such as cyclones and droughts. There is considerable dependence on imported goods, and this has created a steadily increasing balance of trade deficit. The recurring budget and trade deficits are funded by overseas aid, mainly from Australia, France, the European Union, New Zealand, and Japan. Tourism, especially from Australia and New Zealand, is an important economic contributor.

Vanuatu is regarded as the prime tax haven in the Pacific. A Port Vila offshore finance centre, established in the 1970s, has been used as a tax haven by international bankers and overseas trust companies.

Contextual Features

The only recent and original penal code in the South Pacific region is the Vanuatu *Penal Code* enacted in 1981. Vanuatu, as a result of its complex colonial past, has a complex system of law. Largely based on English practice, it nevertheless includes some French law. The Constitution is the predominant law. Also in force are: Acts of the Vanuatu Parliament, Regulations made by the joint English and French colonial administrators, some English Acts of Parliament, some King's regulations, and some French codes and statutes. There is also a body of subordinate legislation. English common law applies in Vanuatu where it is consistent with Vanuatu law; customary law also applies where consistent with the Constitution.

The people of Vanuatu, afflicted by unemployment and underemployment, perceive that their country is in a rising crime spiral. Given the country's economic stagnation, it is not surprising that the law and order problem has been fuelled by the rising rural unemployment and inequity, and the subsequent increasing urban migration.

There are no reliable statistics of reported crimes in Vanuatu; nor are there any studies of unreported crime. The Criminal Record Office (CRO) of the Vanuatu Police Force collates the only statistics on crime, but many rural police stations fail to submit figures. The gathered statistics are dubious; there are inconsistencies in data collection.

However, the CRO figures do provide some indication of the types of crimes detected. The majority relate to crimes against property, including unlawful entry and theft (52% fall in this category from 1997 to 2000). The second largest category constitutes crimes against the person, such as homicides, assaults, and threats (29%). Other crimes are categorized in a uniquely Vanuatu way: these are crimes against morality, including rape and indecent assault (5%). Also listed are crimes against public order such as drunkenness, unlawful assembly, and obstruction (14%) (Jowita 2002). In Vanuatu, there have been public campaigns to raise awareness of women's rights and the illegality of wife beating.

Vanuatu has been cited by the Australian Federal Police as a transit point for drug trafficking (*Asia Pacific News*, March 20, 2003). The Organisation for Economic Cooperation and Development has identified the South Pacific as a center for international money laundering and has threatened to exclude Vanuatu from international financial systems. In March 2001, the U.S. money laundering report named Vanuatu, which hosts 55 offshore banks, as a state of concern.

The court structure of Vanuatu is based on the standard model of inferior court, superior court, and appeal court. Separate courts administer customary law and local customary land disputes.

The Court of Appeal hears civil and criminal appeals from the Supreme Court and has the same power, authority, and jurisdiction as that Court. The Chief Justice of the Supreme Court is appointed by the President after consultation with the Prime Minister and the leader of the opposition. This Court has jurisdiction to hear and determine: civil and criminal proceedings, questions concerning elections and similar matters, civil and criminal appeals from a magistrate's court, and appeals from island courts as to ownership of land.

The Island Courts deal with civil or criminal matters in which the defendant is ordinarily resident within their territorial jurisdiction, or in which the cause of action is within their boundaries. These courts are empowered to administer the customary law prevailing within their territorial jurisdiction to the extent that it is not in conflict with any written law and is not contrary to justice, morality, and good order. The Island Courts do not function regularly on account of a lack of resources (Care et al. 1999). The newly introduced Village Courts are entrusted to resolve customary land disputes. The court's function is to identify the true customary landowner in each village based on the history of each tribe. Men who have settled in their wives' villages, who can no longer claim customary ownership of land in those villages, have refused to support the concept (*Radio NZ*, April 4, 2003).

Vanuatu reportedly has four prisons and one rehabilitation centre. Vanuatu is reported to have held 46 prisoners in mid-1999, indicating that the Vanuatu prison system is small and simply organized.

Amnesty International has recently found the Vanuatu prison system to be grossly inadequate. The authorities have moved to rectify the failures identified by Amnesty International. Escapes are a problem. Captain John Taleo, who was head of Correctional Services when six prisoners escaped in 2003, argues that Vanuatu needs "a prison built out of town" with appropriate rehabilitation programs (*Vanuatu Daily Post*, October 16, 2003).

Police Profile

Background

The Vanuatu Police Force evolved from the combination of the former French and British police forces of the Anglo-French Condominium of New Hebrides. Vanuatu has no regular military forces, but the Vanuatu Police Force (VPF) includes a paramilitary wing, the Vanuatu Mobile Force (VMF), which acts independently. In 1996, the VMF (prior to incorporation into the VPF) kidnapped the President in protest over non-payment of allowances owing to them (Newton 2000).

Demographics

There is a paucity of reliable and comprehensive data on crime and policing in Vanuatu. 1998 information provided by the public relations officer for the VPF revealed that there were 680 police officers, with a police to population ratio of 1:222. This figure indicates that Vanuatu is heavily policed, even over-policed, especially in the urban areas. There remains resistance to police authority in some isolated rural districts, where police may still rely on the permission of village chiefs to investigate certain crimes (Newton 2000). Ongoing tensions in the Vanuatu Police Force (VPF) are presently one of the major challenges for the nation. The law and order problems have had negative impacts on the amount of direct foreign investment in Vanuatu.

Organizational Description

The ranks of the force, in order of seniority, are:

Senior Officers

- Commissioner;
- Deputy Commissioner;
- Assistant Commissioner;
- Superintendent;
- Chief Inspector;
- Senior Inspector;
- Inspector.

Subordinate Officers

- Senior Sergeant;
- Sergeant;
- Corporal;
- Constable.

Functions

The formal functions of the Vanuatu Police Force (as stated in the Vanuatu *Police Act* Cap 105, available online at the University of the South Pacific's webpage) are:

1. "To maintain an unceasing vigilance for the prevention and suppression of crime";
2. a. to preserve peace and order;
   b. to protect life and property;
   c. to enforce the law;
   d. to prevent and detect offenses and produce offenders before the courts.

The Vanuatu Police Force can also be used as a defense force. At times, the VPF has not been able to adequately cope with internal disorder, such as the January 1998 riots (Newton 2000). In January 2001, a crisis was averted when a Thai company provided Police Commissioner Peter Bong with a

US$42,000 check so that outstanding allowances could be paid. In order to combat Vanuatu's spiralling crime and disorder problems, more "customary" ways of policing and providing social stability are being explored.

Land ownership squabbles remain a central feature of Vanuatu life and policing. For instance, men from outside the Eratap Village in Efate, who were protesting against the ruling of the local village court, attacked a primary school, forcing it to close and causing serious injuries to one man. A village chief appealed to police for assistance. In March, 2003, 10 people were injured in an ongoing dispute over land. Tensions were high on the island due to the absence of police intervention (*Radio NZ*, March 6 and April 4, 2003).

The VPF is poorly placed to deal with any serious breakdown of law and order, while the Vanuatu Mobile Force "is showing signs of discontent and indiscipline." Tribal loyalties still derail the concept of nationhood, and the government has failed to provide a satisfactory and regular level of goods and services, including police pay (Ranmuthugala 2002).

Training

Vanuatu has no facilities for general police training, although trainees are sometimes sent to police education classes in Fiji. Training of Pacific Island police officers usually needs to be conducted in Australia, New Zealand, or the United States, as the island countries lack policing experience, knowledge, and resources. The South Pacific Chiefs of Police Conference conducts training initiatives, sometimes in partnership with the Forum Islands' secretariat and Customs' agencies, on topics such as community policing, fraud, operational intelligence analysis, and management. In August 2003, 23 members of the VPF went to New Caledonia for special commando training; some have been selected to form part of the Solomon Islands policing contingent.

Police Use of Firearms

Police are "entitled" to use firearms in the course of duty, but are prohibited from doing so unless they act in accordance with the instructions of the Commissioner and the guidelines of the relevant parliamentary Minister.

Complaints and Discipline

The Police Services Commission (whose three members are appointed by the Chief Justice, the Minister, and the Public Service Commission) hears most disciplinary offenses by senior officers. Hearings are generally akin to those of a fully constituted court. However, the courts hear serious offenses such as mutiny, desertion, and failing to suppress a riot. The Ombudsman, first appointed in 1995, has power to investigate complaints and other evidence of police and government department malfeasance, and to recommend appropriate action.

Disciplinary breaches by subordinate officers are dealt with within the Force and can be punished by a fine of not more than eight days' pay, confinement to barracks, or a reprimand. The Commissioner may review these cases and impose a more serious penalty, including dismissal, demotion, or a fine of up to 15 days' pay. Subordinate officers may appeal, initially to the Commissioner and then to the Police Service Commission.

The performance of Vanuatu's Police Commissioner, Robert Diniro, was under review in late 2003, despite the fact that he had only been in office for six months. According to the British High Commissioner, there was no intention to appoint a foreign police commissioner as has occurred in Fiji and the Solomons (Radio New Zealand International, August 21, 2003).

Terrorism

The 30th South Pacific Chiefs of Police Conference (SPCPC) conference in October, 2001 stressed the need to combat terrorism and to prevent its initiation in the South Pacific. The SPCPC resolved to urge Commissioners to seek legislative changes to:

- Ban proscribed terrorist groups;
- Freeze and seek the early forfeiture of assets of proscribed terrorists and their associates;
- Facilitate the extradition of known terrorists and their associates.

The Nasinoi Declaration of 2002 recommitted Pacific nations to fight terrorism, money laundering, drug trafficking, people smuggling, and people trafficking. Vanuatu has expressed its opposition to all forms of terrorism. Its Prime Minister refused to endorse the war in Iraq without UN authorization.

International Cooperation

The Vanuatu Police Force belongs to two central cooperative policing organizations:

- South Pacific Chiefs of Police Conference;
- South Pacific Islands Criminal Intelligence Network (SPICIN).

Vanuatu was one of seven founding members when the South Pacific Chiefs of Police Conference began in 1970 in Fiji and determined the need for regional cooperation in law enforcement as a priority for its future endeavour. The conference was held in Vanuatu in 1997. The annual conference provides a forum for Pacific Island police to exchange information, experience, and technology in law enforcement; it also provides the opportunity to plan and implement cooperation projects and to facilitate efforts to combat inter-jurisdictional crime through policy discussion, strategy and common issues.

In October 1987, the South Pacific Islands Criminal Intelligence Network (SPICIN) was created by the 17 executives of SPCPC at the sixteenth annual conference. The then-Commissioner of the Vanuatu Police Force, David Willie Saul, presented a paper, "Regional Drug Intelligence Unit," that became the catalyst for the creation of a regional criminal intelligence system. Commissioner Saul declared:

> Experience has shown that the Pacific Island territories are used as transiting points for drug running to our larger neighbours of New Zealand and Australia ... the time is fast approaching when there should be established a regional crime, drugs, intelligence unit to coordinate and disseminate information for unified action to combat what I see as increasing problems.

Respective governments approved such a proposal, and assistance was attained from the larger neighbors. The Australian Federal Police maintains a liaison officer in Port Vila.

Vanuatu belongs to the Pacific Islands Forum (PIF), an annual conference of the heads of states of 16 Pacific nations. The Forum has been central to the development of a number of initiatives related to police work. After the Townsville Peace Agreement in October 2000, Vanuatu sent police to the Solomon Islands to help quell the ethnic violence.

In July 2003, Australia and Vanuatu signed a Memorandum of Understanding aimed at improving the operational capacity of the Vanuatu Police Force. Three Australian advisers are providing support to the project's initial phase, including the refurbishment of the capital's police station. More exchange programs are being negotiated between the VPF and its neighboring French counterpart in New Caledonia.

Police Education, Research, and Publications

Vanuatu does not have any institutions for police education. The nation is not home to any major police research or publications.

DAVID BAKER

Bibliography

Care, Jennifer, Tess Newton, and Don Paterson. *Introduction to South Pacific Law*, Cavendish Publishing, London, 1999.

Jowitt, Anita. "Migration, Employment and Crime in Vanuatu" (Occasional Paper No. 9, University of the South Pacific, School of Law, 2002).

Mark Davis report, SBS TV: *Dateline*, October 2, 2002.

Newton, Tess. "Policing in the South Pacific Region" (Occasional Paper No.1, University of the South Pacific, School of Law, 2000).

Newton, Tess. "Policing in the South Pacific Islands" *Police Journal*, vol. LXX1/4 (1998): 349–352.

Ranmuthugala, Douglas. "Security in the South Pacific — the law enforcement dimension" *Platypus Magazine*, vol. 77, December 2002: 10–17.

Website: http://pidp.ewc.hawaii.edu/pireport (Pacific Islands Report with archives from 1997–2001). www.odci.gov/cia/publications/factbook/geos/tn.html.

VENEZUELA

Background Material

Venezuela stretches from the Caribbean coast in the north, across mountain ranges and the Orinoco river basin to the northern rim of the Amazon River system in the south. Indigenous peoples, mainly Caribe and Arawak, occupied this territory before it was discovered by Columbus in 1498 and subsequently colonized by the Spanish crown. Venezuela attained formal independence from

Spain in 1830 and was largely ruled by autocrats until 1958, when democratic government was instated. Two unsuccessful military coups in 1992 highlighted growing dissatisfaction with the ruling parties and were the precursor to the 1999 Constitution that marked the transition from the Fourth to the Fifth Republic, that is, from a "party-dominated" regime to a "popular" democracy.

According to the 2001 Census, Venezuela had 23,054,210 inhabitants, of whom 87% lived in settlements of more than 2,500 population, mostly in the north of the country. Caracas, the capital city, had approximately 2.3 million inhabitants, although the entire metropolitan area probably includes four million inhabitants. Venezuelans are a mix of indigenous, African, and European peoples and proudly point to the absence of overt racism in their country. One indicator of this is that neither the census nor other population surveys ask about racial or ethnic affiliation. The official language is Spanish, and the majority of Venezuelans profess the Catholic religion.

Prior to the twentieth century, Venezuela's economy was overwhelmingly agrarian, relying principally on exports of cocoa and coffee. The discovery and exploitation, starting in 1907, of rich petroleum reserves marked the transition to an oil-based economy, and Venezuela is currently the world's fifth largest oil producer. Although there are other important natural resources (agricultural, hydrological, iron ore, aluminum and gold), the economy is still largely sustained by oil revenues, which currently account for about one third of the GDP, 80% of export earnings, and more than half of governmental revenues. Oil has made Venezuela one of the wealthier Latin American nations, and per capita annual income in 2002 was 4,090 dollars.

Contextual Features

Since 1958, Venezuela has been a federal democratic republic. The most recent Constitution, enacted in 1999, provides for the hierarchical organization of government. At the lowest level are the municipalities, with elected mayors and municipal councils. The municipalities oversee urban planning, local commerce and industry, and sanitation. Some of the larger municipalities also have their own police forces. At the intermediate level is state government. The country is divided into 23 states, each with an elected governor, legislative council, and a state government that includes a uniformed police force. This level of government also includes the Capital District (centered on Caracas) and a federal dependency of 11 island groups. Finally, there is the national government, which is based in Caracas.

The national government is divided into five branches: legislative, executive, judicial, citizen, and electoral. Legislative power is vested in a single-chamber National Assembly with 165 representatives. Executive power is exercised by the President, Vice-President, and Council of Ministers. The Judiciary, including judges and public defenders, is headed by the Supreme Court. The Citizens' branch is defined as the "moral power" of government and comprises the Ombudsman, the Attorney General, and the Comptroller. Two important functions of this moral power are the defense of human rights and investigations into governmental corruption. The major institutions of criminal justice belong to the national government. States and municipalities can create their own uniformed police forces, but there are proposals to merge these into a single national force. Many state governments have also been granted limited responsibilities for prisons located within their jurisdictions, although they have not yet taken significant action on prison matters. Finally, municipalities can also name Justices of the Peace, a relatively new program that has still to be put into practice in most of the country.

Venezuela's legal system was historically influenced by the European civil law tradition and places much emphasis on the use of legislation to prescribe ideals rather than to codify and regulate current practices. Idealism fosters impracticality, and is often accompanied by formalism, which leads to slow and cumbersome legal procedures. The primary legislation defining crimes is the Criminal Code, first enacted in 1926 and subjected to minor reforms in 1964 and 2000. This code is based on nineteenth century classical European criminal codes, with imprisonment as the main sanction, and concedes little discretion to judges at sentencing. Over the 75 years since the enactment of the code, changing social mores have made some crimes (such as adultery) obsolete, while economic activities and criminal organization have produced new forms of crime (such as drug and computer crimes) that need to be defined and sanctioned. These new crimes have been the subject of separate laws, such as the 1982 Anti-Corruption Law, the 1984 Drug Law, the 1992 Environmental Crimes Law, and the 1998 Law on Violence Against Women and the Family. The passage of time has also made certain provisions of the Criminal Code anachronistic. For example, inflation (particularly pronounced in the late 1980s and early 1990s) has reduced to absurdly low real values the monetary amounts used to classify certain property crimes and to set fines. Since 2000, there have been several proposals for a comprehensive reform of the Criminal Code.

Until 1999, criminal procedure was similarly based on continental European models, being inquisitorial, written, and slow. However, a new Criminal Procedure Code, which came into effect that year, marked the change to a common law model, with provisions for oral proceedings, the right to trial by jury, pre-trial diversion, and plea bargaining. This radical reform of criminal procedure also placed heavy restrictions on police arrests and made preventive detention the exception rather than the rule. Criticisms of the new legislation from police groups, elected officials, and the public, at a time when serious crime rates were rising rapidly, forced two reforms to the Criminal Procedure Code (in 2000 and 2001), relaxing the restrictions on preventive detention and reducing access to alternatives to imprisonment.

Table 1 shows crimes reported to the judicial police between 1986 and 2003. While the figures for homicide and vehicle robbery have a high measure of validity, those for battery, theft, and robbery are affected by a large unreported figure (70% to 85%, depending upon the type of offense) and the fact that between 20% and 30% of less serious crime reports are directed to agencies other than the judicial police. Homicide rates increased fivefold between 1986 and 2003, reflecting a wave of interpersonal violence that has overtaken the country. Similarly, vehicle robberies more than doubled

between 1990 and 2003. While the rates for other crimes have generally declined, this trend may reflect an increasing unwillingness to report to the police, rather than a real decrease in victimization.

Starting in 1999, the criminal courts were reorganized to implement the new Criminal Procedure Code. "Control" (pretrial) judges oversee cases up to the preliminary hearing in which the suspect is formally charged. Trial judges oversee the trial procedure, with or without the presence of a jury, and set the sentences for convicted offenders. "Execution" (supervisory) judges oversee the sentence and grant or revoke sentence remissions together with alternatives to imprisonment, such as probation and parole. Jurisdiction in criminal matters is generally organized by state, such that each state has its own judicial circuit, with pretrial, trial, and supervisory judges, together with prosecutors and public defenders. Despite national laws and guidelines, local variations in criminal justice procedures and outcomes are frequently observable.

The new system of adversarial justice emphasizes the roles of both prosecutors and ordinary citizens. The former must not only direct the police in criminal investigation, but also prepare and conduct the case in court. The latter appear in criminal cases as both victims and witnesses, as lay judges accompanying the trial judge (moderately serious offenses), and as jurors (serious offenses). While prosecutors have willingly accepted their new role, the public has been far less willing to participate in trials, based partly on a fear of reprisals from offenders

Reported crimes (per 100,000), Venezuela, 1986–2003

Year	All Crimes	Homicide	Battery	Theft	Robbery	Vehicle Robbery
1986	988	08	134	409	155	NA
1987	1,110	08	143	535	135	NA
1988	1,158	09	154	427	139	NA
1989	1,272	13	116	450	179	NA
1990	1,255	13	152	398	132	51
1991	1,184	13	167	391	114	41
1992	1,210	16	174	323	117	47
1993	1,276	21	163	326	154	69
1994	1,270	22	152	358	175	82
1995	1,153	21	141	357	161	85
1996	1,173	22	138	384	166	99
1997	1,040	19	137	316	141	70
1998	1,030	20	138	291	133	69
1999	1,041	25	132	268	144	105
2000	977	33	105	212	145	124
2001	783	32	107	179	132	96
2002	1,047	38	121	196	161	121
2003	831	43	108	209	147	127

and partly on a general distrust of legal proceedings. Restitution agreements between victim and offender (a form of pretrial diversion) have been particularly common, leading to reforms restricting their use and increasing the sanctions for noncompliance by the offender.

Unwillingness to confront offenders directly is also the keynote of informal social control, which relies heavily on target hardening, decreased exposure to strangers, and surveillance personnel (ranging from private security guards to traditional watchmen). Although public opinion generally tolerates violence against presumed offenders, mob actions ("lynchings" as they are locally known) are relatively infrequent (less than 30 per year).

Official sanctions for convicted offenders primarily involve imprisonment in one of the country's approximately 30 prison facilities. Although prison legislation distinguishes between penitentiaries (most serious offenders), prisons (less serious offenders), and judicial internment centers (preventive detention), this distinction has long since disappeared in practice as overcrowding and inmate violence have led to numerous transfers between facilities. The implementation of the 1999 Criminal Procedure Code led to a considerable reduction in the prison population, as prisoners in preventive detention were released, and the use of preventive detention was greatly restricted. From 23,597 in 1999, the prison population fell to 16,642 in 2001 (56.3% convicted offenders, the rest in preventive detention). However, the prison population has been increasing again, and by 2003 it was 19,362.

Conditions in most of the prisons are deplorable and have been the subject of frequent criticism by national and international human rights organizations. The physical infrastructure is dilapidated and unsanitary; food is frequently in short supply; and educational and vocational programs reach only a small number of prisoners. At many facilities, prison authorities have lost control over the inmates, who organize themselves. Violence is a primary mechanism of control, whether exercised by the prisoners or by the National Guard when called in to restore order. During 2003, 253 prisoners were killed, and 1,1519 were injured in prison violence.

Since 1980, alternatives to imprisonment have become increasingly important. Convicted offenders can apply for probation (immediately after sentencing), work release (after completing a quarter of the sentence), open prison (after one third of the sentence), or parole (after two thirds of the sentence), all of which place them under the supervision of probation officers. In mid-2001, approximately 10,500 offenders (52.9% of all convicted offenders) were in alternatives to imprisonment. However, the 2001 reform of the Criminal Procedure Code placed greater restrictions on access to these alternatives and may decrease their importance in the future.

Police Profile

Background

The structure of modern policing in Venezuela was largely set in 1938, with the passage of the Law on the National Security Service, which established two different types of police. The first was the National Guard (founded in 1937), attached to the Ministries of the Interior and Defense, which had Rural, Highway, Sanitary, Urban, and Frontier Divisions and has remained largely unchanged until the present. The second was the Investigative Branch, attached to the Ministry of the Interior, which was designed to serve both as a judicial police force and an urban patrol group. The former function was consolidated in the Criminological Department, which, following the overthrow of the last dictator (Marcos Pérez Jiménez) in 1958, became the Judicial Police and was renamed in 2000 as the National Directorate of Criminal Investigation (known locally as the CICPC). The urban patrol group became the Political-Social Section (i.e., political police), becoming the General Police Directorate in 1959 and the Directorate of Intelligence and Prevention Services in 1969 (known as the DISIP).

Meanwhile, state police forces were consolidated under their respective governors, with strong links to the National Guard. The latter provided training and top level commanders, and even today many state police commanders are drawn from the National Guard. Not surprisingly, state police forces had something of a military flavor, with daily drilling in the central patio and a rigid disciplinary system. However, since the mid-1980s, state police forces have moved increasingly toward a civilian institutional environment.

Demographics

Internal functional specialization is directly related to the size of the force: the national forces tend to have the largest number of special units, the municipal forces the smallest. One example is the judicial police (CICPC), whose national headquarters houses divisions assigned to vehicles, banks, robbery, homicide, kidnapping, drugs, organized crime, and special responses. Another are the state police forces, which—apart from ordinary patrol officers—typically have an anti-riot squad, cycle, tourist and canine brigades, and a criminal investigation department. No comprehensive figures are available on the proportion of civilian personnel or females in the police, but the Caracas Metropolitan Police may serve as an example. This force has 11,000 employees, of whom 9,500 are involved in police work (700, or 7.4%, are women). The remaining 1,500 employees have administrative and service responsibilities. Of the 9,500 police officers, about 8,000 are uniformed and the rest civilian (including 400 officers who work in criminal investigation). There are 650 supervisory officers, 40 (6.2%) of whom are women.

Apart from the National Guard, which uses military ranks, police forces use a hierarchical structure comprising inspectors and commissioners. Each level has three ranks (e.g., junior inspector, inspector, chief inspector), and officers normally spend four years at each level. The traffic police and state police also include a separate lower tier with four ranks (agent, special agent, corporal, and sergeant) that make up the majority of their personnel. Once again, officers typically spend four years at each rank, but cannot be promoted from sergeant to junior inspector. Promotion at any level is based mainly on years of service, but may also require a short in-service training course. Officers are eligible for retirement after completing 25 years of service.

Organizational Description

Currently, police forces exist at the national, state, and municipal levels. Each is founded on legislation that defines its mission, structure, and responsibilities. At the national level, there are four police forces, with largely separate functions. The CICPC is the principal judicial police force, charged with investigating crimes, collecting evidence, and arresting and interrogating suspects. These functions, which can occasionally be carried out by other police forces, are under the direction of the Public Prosecutor. The CICPC is part of the Ministry of the Interior and Justice, with its national headquarters in Caracas, an office in each state capital, and additional offices in some other cities. Its structure and functioning are defined in Executive Decree No. 48 (1958) and the Investigative Police Law (1998). The CICPC currently has about 6,000 officers and civilian personnel.

The DISIP is a political police force that is also attached to the Ministry of the Interior and Justice, with headquarters in Caracas and an office in each state capital. The DISIP is primarily concerned with national security and terrorism, and is a much smaller force than the CICPC, with approximately 2,500 officers. Its structure and functioning are defined by Presidential Decree No. 15 (1969).

The National Guard is part of the armed forces and is attached to the Ministry of Defense. Apart from military duties, this force is responsible for policing frontiers, checkpoints, and ports (especially for contraband); for providing perimeter security at prisons; for policing environmental crimes; and for providing auxiliary service as judicial police, or in the restoration of public order. Policing responsibilities are overseen by the Ministry of the Interior and Justice. The national headquarters are in Caracas, with local headquarters in each state and numerous other offices and checkpoints relating to specific duties. Structure and functions are defined by Executive Decree, August 4, 1937, and the Organic Law of the Armed Forces (1983). The force comprises approximately 35,000 members.

Finally, the National Traffic Police, attached to the Ministry of Infrastructure, is responsible for surveillance, preliminary investigation, and occasional arrests in traffic offenses that involve violations of the criminal law. Its structure and functions are defined by the Traffic Law (1996) and Traffic Regulations (1998). There are about 4,000 traffic officers.

Twenty-two of the 23 states and the Caracas Metropolitan Area have a uniformed police force. (Only Vargas State, just north of Caracas, has no state police force. It is served by a municipal police force.) The state police are responsible for patrol work and public order, for arrests (when offenders are found at or near the scene of the crime), and for community service. The uniformed police are a branch of state government, with the state Governor as Commander in Chief (in Caracas, the Metropolitan Police are under the Capital District Mayor's office). Each force is regulated by a local Police Code. State police forces are also coordinated by an office in the Ministry of the Interior and Justice that compiles selected statistics and sets guidelines for internal procedures. There are approximately 40,000 state police officers in the country.

Finally, beginning in 1990, wealthier municipalities in the country's largest cities began to set up municipal police forces. Currently, there are 77 municipal forces attached to mayors' offices and regulated by state Police Codes and municipal ordinances.

Given this multiplicity of forces, since at least 1977 there have been diverse proposals to create a unified national police force. The most recent is the National Police Law, currently under consideration in the National Assembly, which would join all uniformed police forces (state, Capital District, municipal), together with the traffic police, into one national force.

Training

Typical entry requirements include age (17 to 22 years), education (high school certificate), and Venezuelan nationality. The CICPC, the National Guard, and the Traffic Police also specify a minimum height. New recruits to the CICPC normally undertake a three-year training course at its Police University Institute in Caracas, from which they graduate with a technical qualification in Police Science, Forensics, or Criminal Casework. The last three months of training are spent on placements. Successful candidates then begin work as detectives. Detectives are required to undertake a further two years of schooling while at work, in order to complete a degree in Police Science. Recently, the CICPC has also instituted six-month training courses for university graduates who wish to enter the force. Graduate qualifications are necessary for promotion to the most senior ranks.

Until 1999, national guardsmen received 18 months of training in one of three national training centers, but starting in 2000, training was extended to three years, leading to a technical degree in one of the Guard's special areas of competence: environmental protection, security, or drugs. Supervisory officers attend a five-year university program at the National Guard's training school in Caracas. Traffic Police receive approximately one year of initial training. The Traffic Police School, in the state of Aragua, was closed for several years, but in 2000 the Aragua State Police assumed training of traffic police until the school can be reopened.

State police forces directly recruit and train some lower-tier officers (agents). Courses usually last six months. Other prospective lower tier-officers attend one of six regional police training schools, where training lasts for either 6 or 12 months. Two of these training schools (located in the cities of Maracaibo and Maracay) also provide an 18-month training program for upper-tier (supervisory) officers. There is also a four-year university program for upper-tier officers at the Metropolitan Police University Institute in Caracas. Municipal police forces provide their own initial training (four to five months) for new recruits.

Police Use of Firearms

Norms on the use of force provide only general and superficial guidelines for its use and do not figure prominently in either initial or in-service training. Rules applicable to all police forces are found in the Constitution and the Criminal Code, but specific guidelines on the use of force are only found, and with varying levels of detail, in state and municipal police forces.

Articles 55 and 68 of the Constitution call for the protection of dignity and human rights by the government, at the same time limiting the use of firearms and toxic substances by the police. The Criminal Code, in Article 65, provides for the legitimate exercise of authority, including the lawful use of firearms by the police, and also for self-defense, provided that the means used are proportional to the threat and that there has been no prior provocation by the person who acts in self-defense. Article 282 of the Criminal Code restricts the use of firearms by the police to self-defense or the maintenance of public order.

As an example of departmental rules on the use of force, the Caracas Metropolitan Police's General Regulations specify (in Article 67) that police officers must use non-violent means for the purposes of maintaining order and keeping the peace. Article 68, referring specifically to the use of firearms, is a copy of Point 9 of the United Nations Basic Principles on the Use of Force or Firearms by Law Enforcement Officials. Nothing is indicated in the General Regulations about the use of non-lethal force, although the Operations Manual of the Metropolitan Police (a kind of "pocket guide" for procedures on the street) outlines a number of situations in which "physical arrest" may be made. For example, "persuasion" is recommended if there is failure to comply, while the "incorrect" use of the baton is to be avoided. However, none of these terms is defined operationally.

Prohibitions on the use of force are found in the Disciplinary Regulations of the Metropolitan Police. According to Article 64, officers will be terminated if they "cause injury to others by shooting, or otherwise using firearms or other weapons, in an improper, imprudent or negligent manner." Unauthorized carrying of a service firearm while off duty leads to a written warning, as does carelessness or negligence in the use of equipment, including batons (Article 63). But these disciplinary regulations, like those in other departments, do little to indicate specific behaviors or situations that are to be avoided.

Rules for the use of force, techniques for physical control, self-defense, and weapons handling are included in initial training, but not thereafter. Nor is periodic firearms practice mandatory. Thus, some officers may go for years without discharging a gun, and a 2003 survey of municipal police officers found that 70% wanted more firearms practice. Frequency of firearms use is impossible to determine because there are almost no administrative controls, such as forms for reporting discharges. Weak administrative controls may also foster the misuse of weapons, as in the "shootouts" in which the police kill one or more civilians, usually alleged criminals, who had supposedly fired on them first. The nongovernmental human rights group PROVEA (Venezuelan Program for Education and Action in Human Rights) estimates that between October 2002 and September 2003, 130 people were killed by the police, mainly in alleged "shoot-outs."

Of additional concern are the "extermination groups" (death squads), which are thought to be made up of off-duty state police officers and national guardsmen who engage in "social cleansing." A report by the government's Human Rights Ombudsman indicates that two such groups killed 105 civilians in the state of Portuguesa during 2001 and 2002, and similar groups are thought to exist in seven other states. Extermination groups apparently receive support from local storekeepers, which reflects punitive public attitudes to rising crime rates, but may also be a compensatory mechanism for the police's loss of arrest and punishment powers under the 1999 Criminal Procedure Code.

Complaints and Discipline

Complaints against the police may be lodged with a wide variety of institutions and individuals; for example, with neighborhood associations, Prefects, Ombudsmen, the media, or human rights groups. Prominent among the latter are PROVEA and Human Rights Watch, both of which produce annual reports detailing police abuses. However, complaints are only subject to formal processing when they are presented, or redirected, to either of the following: the police (leading to internal review of police behavior), or prosecutors (representing external review). These review procedures are separate, although each may set off inquiry in the other domain. For the National Guard, the procedures are slightly more varied.

Complaints against state and municipal police may be presented to the Police Inspector's office (or its equivalent), an internal agency that investigates complaints or police misconduct and recommends disciplinary measures when considered necessary. Most police forces use the Disciplinary Rules drafted by the Ministry of the Interior in 1981. These rules define disciplinary actions, ranging from verbal and written warnings through "simple" and "strict" arrest to termination of employment, and specify the authority of each rank to impose such measures. The Disciplinary Rules also define and enumerate three levels of infraction (minor, serious, and very serious) that mainly reflect a concern with institutional discipline and order rather than acceptable interaction with citizens.

Complaints against all police may also be presented to the prosecutor's office in each jurisdiction. In these cases, the prosecutor must examine the alleged actions of the police in terms of Article 65 of the Penal Code, which exonerates public employees from criminal responsibility, provided they act within the legal limits established for their agency, or they act in self-defense. If the prosecutor finds sufficient grounds for establishing criminal responsibility, the case is processed under criminal law in the same manner as others handled by prosecutors.

Complaints against national guardsmen may be presented to their immediate superiors, leading to an administrative inquiry and possible disciplinary measures under the military's disciplinary rules. Alternatively, complaints may be presented to prosecutors. In either case, if the infraction constitutes a crime, Article 261 of the Constitution provides separate jurisdictions for adjudication and sentencing, depending on the circumstances. Military crimes (e.g., treason, espionage, rebellion, mutiny) should be processed through the military justice system; common crimes and human rights violations should be processed through the criminal justice system. In practice, many common crimes allegedly committed by national guardsmen are still processed through the military justice system.

Terrorism

Venezuela has no clearly identified domestic terrorist organizations, although there were a small number of politically motivated bombings (with no fatalities) in Caracas during 2003. The western frontier has long been permeable for Colombian guerrilla and paramilitary groups, considered by many governments to be terrorist organizations. However, primary terrorist activities, such as bombings and assassinations, are not practiced in Venezuela by these groups, which appear to confine themselves to secondary activities such as kidnapping (for fund raising), in which they have a complex relationship with domestic criminal groups. The National Guard, the political police, and the judicial police deal with kidnappings, while the political police have a special anti-bomb squad.

International Cooperation

International cooperation is most frequent in criminal investigatio,n and Venezuela's CICPC is a member of INTERPOL. Beyond that, cooperation involves occasional visits by foreign experts or missions to Venezuela (such as the widely publicized visits by William Bratton to Caracas in 2000-2002), and visits by Venezuelan police officers to other forces abroad (such as the FBI in the United States and the Gendarmerie in France).

Police Education, Research, and Publications

Institutions for Higher Education of the Police:

- Instituto Universitario de la Policía Científica (judicial police), Caracas. (*http://www.cicpc. gov.ve*);
- Escuela de Formación de Oficiales de la Guardia Nacional (National Guard), Caracas. (*http://www.guardia.mil.ve/efofac.htm*);
- Instituto Universitario de la Policía Metropolitana (Metropolitan and state police), Caracas. (*http://www.iupm.tec.ve/*);
- Escuela de Criminología, Universidad de Los Andes, Mérida.

Leading Researchers and Authors

- Luis Gerardo Gabaldón, Universidad Católica Andrés Bello, Universidad Central de Venezuela, Caracas. (Research) (lgabaldo@ ucab.edu.ve);
- Christopher Birkbeck, Universidad de Los Andes, Mérida. (Research) (birkbeck@ula.ve).

Extent and Sources of Funding for Police Research

National funding for police research is primarily available through university research allocation committees (providing up to US$15,000 per research project), and the Ministry of Science and Technology (providing up to US$40,000 per project). International sources of funding do not include funds specifically and permanently dedicated to police research and have not been used

in police research. As of 2003, the major area of research relates to the use of force by the police, through a project started in 1994 at the Universidad de Los Andes in Mérida. The Universidad de Los Andes was also the site of the first meeting of the international project on "Normative Frameworks for Use of Force by the Police" (see *http:// www.policeuseofforce.org*), which is examining justifications for the use of force developed by police officers in nine countries.

Police Journals/Magazines/Newsletters

There are no academic journals specializing in police research. Two criminology journals include academic articles (in Spanish) on the police: *Capítulo Criminológico*, published by the Universidad del Zulia (editorial contact: jparraga@iamnet. com); and *Revista Cenipec*, published by the Universidad de Los Andes (http://www.saber.ula.ve/ revistacenipec).

There are no widely available police magazines. The judicial police publish an annual magazine (called *CICPC*) to mark its founding date (November, 24), but this is only distributed within the force. The judicial police also produce an internal newssheet (called *El Cangrejo*—literally meaning "The Crab," the slang name for difficult cases) with articles and letters from members. This is published irregularly and is only distributed to some members of the force.

Recent Publications

The most recent publication on the police is *Policía y Fuerza Física en Perspectiva Intercultural* (Police and Physical Force in Intercultural Perspective), edited by Luis Gabaldón and Christopher Birkbeck; Caracas: Nueva Sociedad, 2003. This book includes material from the first international meeting on "Normative Frameworks for the Use of Force by the Police," with case studies of Venezuela and four other countries.

CHRISTOPHER H. BIRKBECK

Bibliography

Birkbeck, C., and L.G. Gabaldón. "Avoiding Complaints: Venezuelan Police Officers' Situational Criteria for the Use of Force Against Citizens." *Policing and Society* 6, 1996: 113–129.
———. "The Effect of Citizens' Status and Behavior on Venezuelan Police Officers' Decisions to Use Force." *Policing and Society* 8 (1998): 315–338.
Birkbek, C., L.G. Gabaldón, and G. LaFree. "The Decision to Call the Police: A Comparative Study of the United

States and Venezuela." *International Criminal Justice Review* 3 (1993): 25–43.

———. "Venezuela." World Factbook of Criminal Justice Systems. 2003. www.ojp.usdoj.gov/bjs/pub/ascii/wfcjsvz.txt.

Gabaldón, L. "Police Violence and Uncertainty in Latin America: Linking the Macro- and Micro-Levels of Analysis." *International Criminal Justice Review* 3 (1993): 44–59.

Gabaldón, L. and Christopher Birkbeck, eds. *Policía y Fuerza Física en Perspectiva Intercultural*. Caracas: Editorial Nueva Sociedad, 2003.

Gabaldón, L., Yoana Monsalve Briceño, and Carmelo Boada Tomé. "La Policía Judicial en Venezuela: Organización y Desempeño en la Averiguación Penal." In *Justicia en la Calle. Ensayos sobre la Policía en América Latina*, edited by Peter Waldmann. Medellín, Colombia: Biblioteca Jurídica Diké, 1996.

VIETNAM

Background Material

Vietnam covers an area of 331,689 sq km, which is about the same size as Malaysia (330,000 sq km), slightly larger than the Philippines (300,000 sq km), and smaller than Thailand (514,000 sq km). Vietnam has 3,260 kilometers of coastline. It is bordered by the Pacific Ocean to the east and the south, by Cambodia and Laos to the west, and by China to the north. The population of Vietnam is 80 million.

The Vietnamese language is written in Roman letters, as a result of the French influence. The major religions of the Vietnamese are Buddhism and Catholicism.

Vietnam is divided into 57 provinces and four cities: Hanoi, Haiphong, Danang, and Ho Chi Minh City. Hanoi is the capital of Vietnam. Vietnam has a central government that administers the affairs of the whole country. Local governments are responsible for the affairs of their regions. Cities and provinces are divided into districts. Districts are divided into communes.

Vietnam's economy is primarily socialist in nature, although free market tendencies are apparent.

The Communist Party of Vietnam has undertaken significant renovation projects in recent years, making improvements in the fields of construction, development, the economy, industrialization, and modernization. Vietnam has adapted itself to the demands of the international economy.

In the aftermath of the Vietnam War, numerous social problems developed, as did a black market economy. These factors, combined with the stresses of modernization, play a role in the Vietnamese crime situation.

Contextual Features

In 1945, after independence from France was achieved, Vietnam implemented a Constitution, incorporating principles of the rule of law and representative government. This Constitution provided for the separation of powers and the protection of civil liberties. Criminal justice was administered according to law as enacted by the national legislature.

The criminal justice system in Vietnam is composed of three segments: police, procuratorate, and court. Each has a distinct structure and function.

In Vietnam, the Police Agencies include the Ministry of Public Security (MPS). The Police force is charged with the functions of protecting the rights and the freedoms of the individuals and with maintaining public peace and order of the country.

The Police Law was enacted in 1962 and was amended in 1989. The Police Force of Vietnam is headed by the Vice-Minister of Public Security, Director General of the Police General Department. Today, the Vietnamese Police Force is composed of of 80,000 officers, of whom about 15 percent are women. The Force Headquarters is made up of 17 departments.

The Police Law (Article 5) stipulates the duties of the Police as "prevention, suppression, and detection of crime and apprehension of suspects." Of these functions, those which most directly relate to criminal justice are crime detection and the apprehension of suspects.

Crime detection is one of the primary duties of the Police prescribed by the Police Law. This is the duty of all police officers. Every police agency, however, be it a National Police Headquarters or a local quarter police, has officers and units specializing in crime detection. The Criminal Procedure Code of Vietnam was created to control the procedures of criminal investigation, including arrests of suspects.

In Vietnam, procuratorates form an independent system, and they are established at three levels. At the Central level is the Supreme Procuratorate, which supervises 61 city, provincial, and military procuratorates. The Procurator-General of the Supreme Procuratorate is elected by the National Assembly of Vietnam.

The functions of the Procuratorates at all levels are defined as follows in the Organic Law of the Procuratorates of the Socialist Republic of Vietnam:

- Review cases investigated by Police and National Security organs and determine whether or not to arrest, prosecute, or exempt from prosecution;
- Conduct investigation in criminal cases they handle directly;
- Initiate public prosecutions of criminal cases, support such prosecutions, and exercise supervision over the judicial activities of the Court to determine whether they conform to the laws;
- Exercise supervision over the execution of judgments and orders in criminal cases and over the activities of prisons and detention houses to determine whether such activities conform to the laws.

Corresponding to the procuratorates are three levels of courts. At the Central level is the Supreme Court, which supervises 61 courts at the cities and provincial level and also the military courts. The Supreme Court handles major criminal cases of national consequence. The district courts handle all cases, except for those that fall within the jurisdiction of the Supreme Court and the Provincial Court.

The process of appointing presidents, vice presidents, and judges is the same as for the appointment of procuratorates.

In Vietnam, the collective term "penal institutions" denotes prisons, juvenile prisons, and detention houses. Both prisons and juvenile prisons mainly accommodate convicted prisoners and conduct correctional treatment. Detention houses are mainly for those who are awaiting trials. The Correction Police Agency is charged with the responsibility of administering rehabilitation programs for drug addicts and prostitutes. In Vietnam, all penal institutions are under the jurisdiction of the Correction Police Department of the Ministry of Public Security of Vietnam. The Correction Police Department has direct control over all correctional facilities throughout Vietnam.

Police Profile

Background and Organizational Description

In Vietnam, the People's Police are commanded and managed by the Ministry of Public Security. The police are considered one of the armed forces of the Socialist Republic of Vietnam. The police agencies include the Ministry of Public Security at the central level, the local public security bureau at various levels, and public security forces for railways, highways, navigation, air transport, and other fields.

The Ministry of Public Security is the highest police agency in the country. Local public security agencies are responsible for public security in their respective localities under the dual leadership of local government and higher public security agencies. The People's Police are a part of the armed forces of Vietnam.

The Ministry of Public Security of Vietnam consists of six General Departments and other dependent units, including the People's Police General Department.

The People's Police General Department as made up of 17 following units:

- The People's Police Staff Department;
- Department of Police managing the Administration of Social Order;
- Criminal Intelligence Police Department;
- Economic Police Department;
- Criminal Investigation Police Department;
- Anti-Narcotics Police Department;
- Institute for Forensic Science;
- Department for Security Guard Police;
- Fire Police Department;
- Department of Traffic Highway and- Railway Police;
- Department of Traffic Navigation Police;
- Department of Provision of Information and Data;
- People's Police Politics Department;
- People's Police Logistics Department;
- The Vietnam National Bureau of Interpol;
- Professional Dog Training Center; and
- The Standing Office on Drugs Control of Vietnam (namely the Office of Vietnam National Drugs Control Committee).

Moreover, there also are:

- Correctional Police Department;
- People's Police Academy; and

- People's Police Secondary School, placed directly under the Ministry of Public security.

In the localities, provinces, and cities, there are corresponding police services. The lowest basic level of the Vietnam People's Police is the Quarter Police.

As of December, 2003, the forces of the People's Police of Vietnam consisted of 80,000 officers and policemen serving 80 million inhabitants. In comparison with the police to population ratio in other countries, this 1:1,000 ratio is still very low.

The Police Law stipulates that the fulfillment of the responsibilities of the police (i.e., "protecting the life and property of people" and "maintaining public peace and order") be assigned to the Provincial Police, who are responsible for the enforcement of various police duties. The Police Law also prescribes that the national government set up a central police organization to control and supervise the Provincial Police, to the extent of the specific national concerns. At both the national and provincial levels, The People's Police General Department has been established as the administrative institution of the police. It is a national police organization that operates under the supervision of the Ministry of Public Security of Vietnam (MPS).

The head of the People's Police General Department is the Commissioner General, who is appointed or dismissed by the Prime Minister of Vietnam. Under control of the Ministry of Public Security, the Commissioner General administers the operation of the General Department, appoints and dismisses General Department employees, and controls and supervises Provincial Police regarding matters under the jurisdiction of the General Department.

Under control of the Ministry of Public Security, the People's Police General Department performs the following duties:

- Planning and research of various systems relating to the police;
- National budget related to the police;
- Command of police forces in case of incidents affecting the public peace and order on a national scale, such as large-scale disasters and disturbances;
- Formulation and implementation of the plans to cope with emergency situations;
- Traffic control on trunk highways across the country;
- International criminal investigation assistance;
- International emergency aid activities ;
- Maintenance and management of police edu-

cational institutions and other matters pertaining to police education;
- Maintenance and management of police communication facilities and other matters pertaining to police communications;
- Maintenance and management of criminal identification facilities and other matters pertaining to criminal identification;
- Criminal statistics;
- Police Equipment;
- Standards pertaining to recruitment, duties, and activities of police personnel;
- Coordination pertaining to police administration; and
- Inspection of matters concerning the responsibilities of the People's Police General Department.

To summarize the above, the People's Police General Department is responsible for the following:

- Planning of laws concerning the police, the standards of police activities, and various police systems;
- Support of Provincial Police activities in both "hardware" and "software" aspects;
- Coordination of the Provincial Police activities;

To perform part of the functions of the People's Police General Department, Regional Police Bureaus have been established as the Agency's regional organizations. Outside of Hanoi and Ho Chi Minh City, there are two Regional Police Bureaus throughout the country in South country and in Central country. Hanoi has no Regional Police Bureau because of the long establishment of the Metropolitan Police Department, which shares the same location with the People's Police General Department. Ho Chi Minh City also has no Regional Police Bureau because the Ho Chi Minh City Police Headquarters has the whole region under its jurisdiction.

The Director General of each Regional Police Bureau is responsible for the matters under the Bureau's jurisdiction and for the supervision of the Bureau personnel. As well, The Director General controls and supervises the Provincial Police in matters under the Bureau's jurisdiction, acting as ordered by the Commissioner General of the People's Police General Department.

The Police Law stipulates that each provincial and district government, the local governmental entity, shall have its own Provincial and district Police force, which shall carry out all police duties within the borders of the provinces and districts.

The Provincial and district Police Headquarters are provincial- and district-level police organizations.

The Provincial Police divide their territories into districts, each of which comes under the jurisdiction of the police station or police Commune. Under the direction and supervision of the Chief, as the case may be, the Chief of Police Station or Police Commune is responsible for policing the district and for directing the personnel of the Police Station or Police Commune. As a front-line operational unit of the District Police, a Police Station or Police Commune fulfils the vital duties of performing police work, keeping close relationships with local residents in day-to-day affairs.

Each Police Station or Police Commune has police boxes and residential police boxes as its subordinate organizational units. They are the bases of local police work in the sub-divisions of the jurisdiction of a police station or police Commune, and they function as a point of contact between the police and community residents.

As a basic rule, the Provincial Police perform their duties within their provincial borders. However, the Provincial Police may, for the sake of efficient execution of duties, exercise their authority beyond territorial jurisdiction to such an extent that is necessary for the suppression or investigation of criminal acts or the arrest of suspects. Accordingly, the Provincial Police are allowed to carry out, outside territorial jurisdiction, the investigation of a crime relating to one perpetrated within their own territory, or relating to a suspect arrested within their own territory for possible involvement in other crimes.

Neighboring Provincial Police are also allowed, according to a pre-arranged mutual agreement, to exercise their authority beyond their territorial jurisdiction in order to handle a case occurring near the provincial boundary.

Furthermore, in the event of a large-scale incident that is difficult for a single Provincial Police force to deal with, the relevant Provincial Police Headquarters may request assistance from the People's Police General Department or other Provincial Police forces by notifying the General Department. Police officers thus dispatched from the General Department or other Provincial Police forces may exercise their authority within the territorial jurisdiction of the relevant Provincial Police. They are, however, under supervision of the Provincial Police Headquarter requesting such assistance.

According to the Article 26 the People's Police Forces' Law of Vietnam, for purposes of efficient administration, supervision, and control, the rank classification of the members of the Police of Vietnam shall be as follows:

1-General Army	8-Major	15-Corporal
2-Colonel General	9-Captain	
3-Lieutenant-General	10-First Lieutenant	16-Policeman of 1st class
4-Major General	11-Lieutenant	
5-Colonel	12-Second Lieutenant	
6-Senior-Lieutenant-Colonel	13-Sergeant Major	17-Policeman of 2nd class
7-Lieutenant-Colonel	14-Sergeant	

Demographics

The personnel of the Police of Vietnam consist of police officers and civilian employees such as clerical workers and technicians. All these employees function as a unified whole in the execution of police duties.

There are approximately 12,000 female police officers throughout the country; some female employees also work as traffic patrol personnel or juvenile guidance personnel, performing duties similar to those of police officers.

Functions

The Police of Vietnam shall have the following powers and functions:

(1) The Police Law sets forth the duties of the police in Vietnam as "protecting the life and property of people, preventing, suppressing and investigating crimes, controlling traffic and also maintaining public safety and order," for which various police activities are undertaken.

(2) For control of crime, the Code of Criminal Procedure stipulates that "when a judicial police officer judges that an offence has been committed, he shall investigate to determine the offender and gather evidence," according to which the police officers have the right to investigate all kinds of offenses. Thus, the police have authority regarding all violations punishable under all laws, including, of course, criminal offenses.

As a rule, the cases investigated by the police are handed over to the procuratorators' office, where decisions are made as to whether the case is to be prosecuted.

Procuratorators, as well as the police, also have the right of investigation. However, the primary duty of public procuratorators is to pursue the prosecution of cases, and their investigations are usually supplementary.

As for other authorities of investigation, the Code of Criminal Procedure provides that "officials who should perform duties as judicial police officers to investigate special cases and the scope of their activities are provided by other laws." Such officials include Maritime Police officers and the Narcotics Control officers, who have the right of investigation concerning special cases provided by law, although the number of cases they handle is extremely small.

In addition to the control of crime, the police are engaged in various activities to maintain public peace and order. The major responsibilities of the police under their legal jurisdiction include the following:

The police perform administrative duties covering all areas of road traffic. These duties include the issue of driver's licenses, cancellation of the license of traffic offenders, regulation of traffic by setting up road signs and traffic signals, issue of permits for use of roads such as for parades, implementation of traffic education, and supervision of driving schools.

The police issue business licenses to entertainment establishments, including bars and nightclubs, as well as receive the reports on the opening of establishments such as strip-show theaters. They also conduct on-the-spot inspections of the businesses that might affect the public morals.

Besides having the authority to make arrests for illegal acts, the police are also authorized to take punitive administrative action, such as a suspension of business operation.

The police are empowered to authorize security companies that offer the protective services of guards and security facilities. The police provide guidance on the training and control of guards, and also offer guidance to these companies by implementing on-the-spot inspections and other regulatory measures.

In the event of offenses, the police can order a suspension of business operation.

(3) The police can detain an arrested person for a period not beyond what is prescribed by law, informing the person so detained of all his rights under the Constitution.

(4) The police issue licenses for the possession of firearms and explosives in accordance with law.

(5) The police are responsible for the prevention and suppression of all destructive fires on buildings, houses and other structures, forests, land transportation vehicles and equipment, ships or vessels docked at piers or wharves or anchored in major seaports, petroleum industry installations, plane crashes and other similar incidents, as well as the enforcement of the Fire Code and other related laws.

(6) Police provide both adult and juvenile correctional services. The police supervise penal institutions, which are composed of prisons, juvenile prisons, and detention houses. The police also supervise juvenile correctional institutions, which are composed of training schools.

(7) The police have the authority to license pawnbroking businesses, as well as to oversee their business operations, including the keeping of accounts. The police have the right to make on-the-spot inspection of pawnshops, and in the event of an offense, may order a suspension of business operation or the cancellation of the business license.

The police enforce similar regulations on second-hand goods dealers.

(8) The police undertake extensive activities that are closely connected with everyday life of the community people. These activities include various kinds of crime-prevention work, keeping and returning of lost-and-found articles, guidance of juveniles, assistance of the victims of disasters and accidents, protection of lost children and runaways home, and consulting services to help citizens solve a variety of problems.

(9) The police also guard against ideologies that can endanger the society and country.

(10) Police carry out other special tasks in accordance with certain state regulations.

Training

Police organizations in Vietnam consist of the People's Police General Department as a national body and the Provincial Police as the local entity. Accordingly, recruitment for the Agency differs from that for the Provincial Police.

Applicants for the Police Forces must first pass the National Category I Examination (applicants for senior official positions) or the Category II Examination (applicants for mid-level positions) at the Police Personnel Agency. From applicants who have passed one of these tests, personnel are selected by the Police Forces through the interview process. The Police Personnel Agency also recruits personnel from the Provincial Police forces, selecting officers based on experience, outstanding job performance, and excellence of working record from those recommended by Provincial Police Headquarters. Police officers thus recruited are assigned either to the duties within the Agency or to essential posts within the Provincial Police.

Applicants for the Provincial Police must first take an examination conducted by the Provincial Police Personnel Agency. Those who pass this test are then interviewed, with personnel selected based on ability and adaptability to the rigors of police duty. Officers thus recruited by the Provincial Police are assigned principally to positions within the respective Provincial Police.

In 2003, approximately 20,000 applicants took examinations conducted by the Provincial Police; of these, about 10,000 passed. Provincial Police throughout the country hold separate examinations for university graduates and senior high school graduates. Currently, about 56 percent of the successful applicants are university graduates.

The People's Police Academy provides education and training needed by senior police officers, and carries out academic research concerning police matters. The Academy's departments include: Community Safety Affairs Education, Criminal Affairs Education, and Traffic Affairs Education. Experts in each of these areas serve as instructors or researchers. The Academy also has the Highest Training Institute for Investigation Leaders, the International Research and Training Institute for Criminal Investigation, the Police Science Research Center. These institutions train specialists in criminal investigation and police communications, and conduct research on police communications.

The training program for police officers immediately after recruitment consists of a pre-service training course, on-the-job training (OIT) course, and a pre-service comprehensive training course.

Police officers recruited by the Provincial Police enroll in the 10-month pre-service training course at their respective Provincial Police Schools. During this course, recruits live communally in dormitories and receive an education to acquire the basic attitude toward readiness and alertness required for police duties. In addition, they receive basic knowledge and skills that a community police officer must have.

Upon completion of this course, recruits are assigned to front-line police stations, where they receive eight-months of OIT at police boxes. During this course, recruits gain experience in the execution of actual duties as a community police officer under the man-to-man personal supervision of senior police officers.

Upon completion of the OIT course, recruits enroll in a three-month comprehensive training course. In this last course of initial education, the recruits receive further training to build character, acquire professional legal knowledge, and other knowledge and skills essential for community police activities. This training also enhances their physical and mental fitness, all of which is aimed at helping them become full-fledged community police officers.

The method for promotion of a police officer differs according to his rank. Promotions up to the rank of Major are determined by examination, in principle. However, promotions are also made by recommendation for those having a special skill, specialist knowledge and experience in a specific area, or a good working record over a period of many years.

Promotion to the rank of Major General or higher is in principle determined by recommendation, according to an individual's ability to perform the duties of position, experience, and working record.

Traditionally, policemen holding the rank of Second Lieutenant or Corporal have accounted for 80% of all police officers in Vietnam. However, in order to cope with the increasingly sophisticated and difficult nature of police duties, it is planned to increase the number of officers above the rank of Second Lieutenant to approximately 40% of total officers.

Upon each occasion of promotion, a police officer must complete the education and training necessary for the new rank.

Police officers who pass the examination for promotion to Police Sergeant are enrolled in the Police Sergeant Appointment Course at the Secondary Police School. There they are given an education that allows them to acquire the knowledge and skills required of the "core" officers of a police station. This course takes four weeks.

Police officers who pass the examination for promotion to Second Lieutenant are enrolled in the Second Lieutenant Police Appointment Course at the Secondary Police School. They are given two years of education pertaining to the knowledge and skills required of the section Chiefs of a Police Station or a Police Commune.

Police officers who pass the examination for promotion to Police Major are enrolled in the Police Major Appointment Course at the People's Police Academy, where they are given education pertaining to supervisory and commanding skills, and professional training required for the Division Chiefs. This requires two months, and is the final educational course associated with promotion.

The People's Police Academy provides a supervisor's educational course to police officers who hold the rank of Major and are soon to be appointed to a higher position, such as Division Chief of a Provincial Police Headquarters or Chief of a Police District or a Police station or Commune. This constitutes the highest level of educational course for a police officer.

Additional educational courses for high-ranking police officers include the training given at the

People's Police Academy. Provided to the police officers holding the rank of Police Inspector or above, this course aims to train high-ranking investigative officers in the command and supervision of crime investigation, and also focuses on the sophisticated special technology available to criminal investigations.

As an institution to train the police officers engaged in international investigations, the Research and Training Institute for International Criminal Investigation has been established at the People's Police Academy. This institute provides, to the trainees including those dispatched from overseas, training pertaining to the professional techniques of international crime investigation and foreign language skills.

The People's Police Academy of Vietnam has offered the training courses for post-graduates since 1993 and on doctors of law since 1995.

International Cooperation

International cooperative actions are focused on the prevention of crime and on combating crime. In 1993, the Vietnam National Central Bureau of Interpol was set up and placed directly under the command of the Head of the People's Police General Department, who assumed the duties for collaborating with Interpol and the National Central Bureau in Interpol of various countries in the prevention of and fight against international crimes.

Vietnam has signed agreements and treaties of cooperation in criminal justice and in preventing and combating crime with the Ministry of Interior or Ministry of Justice of Russia, Germany, China, Laos, Ukraine, Cuba, Poland, Thailand, Cambodia, and Myanma.

Since 1991, Vietnam has been an official member of the International Criminal Police Organization (Interpol).

Taking part in the ASEAN countries' association in 1995, the Government of Vietnam has also set up close relations with the United Nations and with governments in the region concerning the control and prevention of drug trafficking.

In general, international law enforcement cooperation between Vietnamese and foreign law enforcement agencies falls under the following two channels:

- Mutual legal assistance through diplomatic channels;
- Law enforcement cooperation through Interpol channels.

The cooperative crime prevention agreements signed by the Ministry of Public Security of Vietnam and other countries are focused on the common prevention of and fight against the following crimes:

- Unlawful trade and transportation of various kinds of weapons, munitions explosive matters, inflammable matters, toxic matters, and radio-active matters;
- Illicit traffic in narcotics and psychotropic substances;
- Women and children trafficking;
- Organized crime;
- Terrorism;
- Hijacking;
- Piracy;
- Transnational smuggling;
- Illicit manufacture and consumption of false papers, currency, and checks;
- International economic crime; and
- Stealing of art works and antiquities.

The Police Force of Vietnam also enjoys close and productive relations with the following overseas law enforcement agencies: Australian Federal Police, Federal Bureau of Investigation of USA, Royal Thai Police, Korean Police, Hong Kong Police, Royal Canadian Mounted Police, Ministry of Public Security of P.R. of China, Russian Police, German Police, Japanese Police, and the Taiwanese Police.

Through the Vietnam National Central Bureau of Interpol, the Vietnamese Police have been in cooperation with the police of several countries in exchanging information concerning criminals, arresting offenders, collecting evidence, and extraditing offenders.

All extradition in Vietnam takes place between sovereign governments. All requests must ultimately come through a diplomatic channel and an Interpol channel. The People's Police General Department acts on behalf of the Vietnam government on all extradition matters. From 1993 to 2002, there were 20 extradition requests received from other countries, and the Vietnamese government had made 80 extradition requests to Thailand, Australia, Germany, Russia, and Ukraine From 1993 to 2003, the Vietnamese government surrendered 12 fugitives. Out of nine extraditions, six were drug-related criminals.

During recent years, especially after taking part in Interpol (1991) and becoming an official member of ASEAN, the Government and Ministry of Interior of Vietnam adopted the beliefs of "DOI MOI" (Renovation) and "Vietnam wants to become the friend of all countries." Vietnam highly appreciates international cooperation in the fight against crime, especially between the Police of Vietnam and other countries, while at the some time respecting mutually the sovereignty, independence, and integrity of foreign territories.

In recent years, the international cooperation on criminal prevention and suppression of the People's Police of Vietnam has been developed and expanded, thus making contributions to the implementation of external policy of the party and government, improving effectiveness of the work of criminal prevention and suppression, and creating favorable conditions for the cause of national socio-economic development.

International crime related to Vietnam continues to show complex development and is on the rise with new dangerous and sophisticated *modus operandi*. Organized crime, drug-related offenses, fraud, smuggling, economic fraud, money laundering, and trafficking in women and children all have increased and caused serious consequences for the country's society and economy. The international cooperation in the fight against crime through Interpol and ASEANAPOL is one of the activities directly serving the struggling missions of the People's Police of Vietnam.

Every year, the police of Vietnam receive a great amount of information on international crimes from the General Secretariat of Interpol and from the police of other countries. The received information has been concentrated on such matters as: criminals with international wanted warrants, offenses relating to the trafficking in and transportation of drugs, international fraud, economic frauds, smuggling of women and children, child sexual abuse, smuggling of weapons, theft of vehicles and the import or export of stolen automobiles spare parts, money laundering, international terrorism, production of counterfeit currency and forged travel documents, illegal immigration, smuggling of humans, and trans-national organized crime.

Based on information provided by police forces of Interpol member countries, the Police of Vietnam have apprehended several wanted criminals and completed necessary procedures to extradite them to concerned countries for investigation and conviction. At the same time, police forces of other countries, upon the request from Vietnam, have also arrested several dangerous fugitive criminals who have committed offenses in Vietnam. Moreover, the police of Vietnam have received crucial information relating to persons suspected of involvement in trans-national criminal organizations, organized crime, or in the trafficking in and transport of drugs; they then initiated investigations into these cases to discover and prevent dangerous crime from occurring in Vietnam.

In order to improve effectiveness and build a legal framework favorable for the cooperation on criminal prevention and suppression (particularly drug trafficking) , the Government of Vietnam and Ministry of Public Security have concluded 13 bilateral agreements and MOU with China, Russian Federation, The People's Democratic Republic of Laos, Cambodia, Cuba, the People's Democratic of Korea, Ukraine, Hungary, France, Germany, Myanmar, and Thailand.

The conclusion and implementation of the above-mentioned agreements have demonstrated the active participation of Vietnam in international cooperation in the areas of criminal prevention and suppression. In the process of implementation of cooperative agreements with neighboring countries (namely Laos, China, Cambodia), the police forces of border provinces and districts have coordinated and exchanged information and discussed concerted measures to fight crime.

Up to now, the People's Police General Department of Vietnam has welcomed many police delegations to visit Vietnam to exchange experiences, to discuss measures to expand international cooperation on the fight against crime, criminal justice, and experiences in making legislation related to criminal prevention and suppression. Delegations have come from: The Philippines, Thailand, Australia, Japan, United States, Cambodia, France, Germany, Republic of Korea, Laos, and China. At the same time, many Vietnamese police delegations have been sent to take part in seminars and international conferences on drugs, trans-national crimes, and organized crime.

It is through such discussions that the understanding between Vietnamese police and police of foreign countries has been strengthened, and experiences in criminal prevention and suppression have been exchanged. In addition, there has been the appointment of liaison police officers between Vietnam and some countries. Vietnam has also successfully organized several conferences on criminal prevention and suppression, such as the ASOD Conference in 1996; the Meeting of Senior Officers of regional countries (MOU) on drug control, which included China, Myanmar, Thailand, Laos, Cambodia, and Vietnam; and the UNDCP in Hanoi in May, 1998. In May, 2003, the ASEAN Conference on the prevention of drug abuse among youth was held, as part of the joint declaration on a drug-free ASEAN.

Furthermore, the Vietnam Police have organized the implementation of projects on enhancing the capacity of drug law enforcement and drug control, fire prevention, genetic identification, criminal ill system, and the training on drug investigative techniques with the support of German Police and the DEA. The installation of a computerized communication system, the connection between X400 with Interpol Headquarters, has been completed, and the ASEANAPOL's ADS is now preparing for operation.

The international cooperation in the fight against trans-national crime has recorded encouraging achievement and brought about practical results, serving the cause of maintaining national security and social order, making contributions to the cause of national development, and raising the position of Vietnam Police in the international arena. This also demonstrates Vietnam's capacity and determination to integrate into the common fight against international crime for a peaceful international community, which is the common desire of countries all over the world. Similar to other fields, the expansion and promotion of international cooperation on criminal prevention and suppression by police forces have been characterized by the external policies of openness, diversification, and multi-lateralization aimed at building a prosperous people, strong country, and an equal and civilized society.

Since the mid-1970s, ASEAN member countries have tried to promote cooperation on fighting against trans-national crimes because their growth and development had negative effects in the region and within ASEAN countries. Initially, ASEAN countries' concern focused on drug trafficking and abuse. However, with the expansion and diversity of trans-national crimes, including terrorism, arms smuggling, money laundering, and illegal immigration, together with increased organization, ASEAN countries have been, step by step, joining together and pooling their resources to fight these crimes.

In the process of developing cooperation, ASEAN countries have made some policies, and implemented mechanisms, activities, and programs to combat trans-national crimes. This is shown through related decisions of the annual ASEAN Summits. The main objective of ASEAN as expressed in Bangkok Declaration on August 8, 1967 is to "rapidly promote economic development, social progress and culture development through joint efforts to strengthen the expansion of the foundation for a peaceful and prosperous ASEAN community" and to "improve people's living standards." By setting up this development target, ASEAN understood that effects of trans-national crimes possibly destroy and cause great harm to the economic, social, and political structures of any member of ASEAN.

Recognizing the danger of trans-national crimes, the meeting of Heads of Governments, or ASEAN Summit, reiterated the necessity for member countries to cooperate with each other and to closely cooperate with other international organizations related to the fight against trans-national crimes. The decision to fight against drug trafficking crimes (the most common trans-national crime) of the Heads of ASEAN States was expressed in the declaration of ASEAN Concord on February 24, 1976, which reads: "To expand cooperation among country members as well as with international organizations related to the prevention and combat of drug abuse and drug traffickers."

At all the Summits, ASEAN countries' leaders paid attention to and were worried about the situation of drug abuse and trafficking in the region. At the sixth ASEAN Summit held in December, 1998 in Hanoi, leaders of the countries adopted the decision: "ASEAN will promote and strengthen the joint cooperative relations among institutions of ASEAN in the fight against drug abuse and trafficking in order to eliminate drug processing, production, trafficking and abuse by 2015." They further promised to "enhance joint and separate efforts to struggle with trans-national crimes such as drug trafficking, money laundering, terrorism, piracy, trafficking in arms and people."

In addition to traditional activities, transnational crimes expand their operations to other fields and are better organized. That is why the ASEAN leaders suggest that it is necessary to study and basically coordinate efforts in the fight against these trans-national crimes at local levels. At the unofficial Summit in November, 1996 in Jakarta-Indonesia, leaders of ASEAN countries directed that: "ASEAN related agencies study the possibility to cooperate in the region on fighting against crimes including criminal extradition."

Beside the decisions made at Summits, the issue of cooperation on crime prevention and combat is also expressed in the decisions of ASEAN Ministerial Meeting.

Confronted by the increase of trans-national crime activities in the region of ASEAN, ASEAN countries' Foreign Ministers suggested closer cooperation and coordinated of activities among ASEAN countries in the fight against this kind of crime. At the Jakarta meeting in July, 1996, ASEAN countries' Foreign Ministers adopted a resolution, which stated: "Considering the need to focus attention to drug crimes, economic crimes including money laundering, environment crimes, and illegal immigration which are trans-border crimes and have negative effects on people's lives in the region, it is agreed at the Meeting that: A method to manage the issues of trans-national crimes is urgently needed so that these crimes can not affect the sustainability of ASEAN as well as of every member country."

After that, at the 30th Foreign Ministers Meeting, ASEAN countries' Foreign Ministers once again emphasized the necessity of cooperation in combating trans-national crimes, including: the fight against terrorism; against trafficking in people, drugs, and arms; and against piracy.

Fighting against trans-national crimes is not only the responsibility of one department or a specific country; ASEAN has these mechanisms in place: the Conference of Chiefs of National Police of ASEAN countries (ASEANAPOL); Meeting of anti-drug senior officials of ASEAN countries (ASOD) and Meeting of ASEAN countries' Finance Ministers (AFMM). ASEANAPOL is related to the field of cooperation on prevention and law enforcement against trans-national crimes. ASOD also has similar functions but mainly focuses on drug crimes. AFMM has a duty to consider national issues in the fields of customs and finance, such as the control of the illegal trafficking in drugs and psychotropic substances, and it seeks to design policies, procedures, and regulations to combat trans-national crimes.

The admission of Vietnam to INTERPOL, ASEANAPOL, and ASOD expresses the determination of the Vietnamese Government and Vietnam Police Forces in the fight against trans-national crimes. In the past, the Vietnamese Police have acted upon and implemented some resolutions of ASEANAPOL, INTERPOL, and ASOD in various ways: in the fight against trans-national crimes such as the establishment of data bases and the assignment of officers to monitor the trans-national crime situation in the world that is related to Vietnam; in the study and making of policies and laws related to the task of combating trans-national crimes; in crime studies and crime situation forecasts; and in setting up step-by-step cooperation plans and effective cooperation mechanisms in some specific fields such as drug crimes, women and children trafficking for prostitution.

YEM XUAN NGUYEN

W

WALES

See **United Kingdom**

Y

YEMEN

Background Material

The Republic of Yemen is an Arab Islamic country of mountains, plains and deserts covering 203,849 square miles (527,970 sq km). Yemen is derived from the Arabic word, *alyomen*, which means good and blessing or Happy Arabia (National Information Center 2004). Now Yemen is named Republic of Yemen. Yemen's territory includes 112 islands. Yemen is located on the southwestern part of Asia and in the south of the Arabian peninsula. It is bordered on the north by Saudi Arabia, on the south by the Arab Sea and Aden Gulf, on the east by Oman, and on the west by the Red Sea. Yemen has many islands along its coasts on the Red Sea and Arab Sea (CultureGrams 2003).

People have inhabited settled communities in present-day Yemen for thousands of years. The kingdom of Sheba, established around 1000 BC, prospered from the frankincense trade route through the Arabian Peninsula. During the fourth century A.D., Christianity spread throughout Europe, and the demand for frankincense diminished. The Himyarite Dynasty followed the reign of Sheba. During the fourth and fifth centuries, Jewish and Christian religions influenced and converted many Yemen people. Nonetheless, the governor of Yemen accepted Islam as the official religion in 628 (CultureGrams 2003).

Ottoman Turks took control of most of the east coast of Yemen by 1548. In the late 1800s, the British gained control over Yemen's independent southern port of Aden. This led to an agreement between the Turks and British to form a border between the two territories, forming North and South Yemen. North Yemen ultimately became an independent country after World War I. South Yemen, through many years of violent struggle, eventually gained independence from Britain in 1967 and became the first Marxist state on the Arabian Peninsula. When communism collapsed in the Soviet Union and after 300 years of separation, North and South Yemen united as the Republic of Yemen on May 22, 1990 (*Encarta* 2004; CultureGrams 2003).

Yemen's Parliament in May, 1993 elected the first President of the Republic of Yemen. Integrating two different governments proved difficult; and divided loyalties, among other problems, eventually led to a 65-day civil war in 1994. The civil war produced major infrastructural damage throughout the country, resulting in rampant inflation and devaluation of the Yemen *Rial* (currency). Since the civil war, there has been conflict between the more secular south and the conservative north, as well as border skirmishes with Saudi Arabia (*Encarta* 2004).

In September of 1999, Ali Abdullah Saleh was re-elected President in the country's first direct Presidential elections. In 2000, Yemen and Saudi Arabia agreed to end their 66-year border dispute. In October of 2000, Yemen made world headline news when the terrorist bombing of a U.S. navel vessel in Aden harbor killed 17 sailors and injured 37 others (CultureGrams 2003).

There are a number of major challenges facing a country that has been unified within the recent past, and that still faces a number of political dissenters. Nonetheless, it is a country determined to make progress. The current challenges of Yemen range from natural resource issues and illiteracy, to the carjacking and kidnappings of foreign tourists.

The rate of illiteracy (those 15 and over who cannot read and write) reaches 50.2%. There has been increased emphasis on the enrollment of all school-aged children, particularly girls (*The World Factbook* 2004; *Encarta* 2004). Yemen's expenditures on education increase annually, and there is the ongoing establishment of educational institutions at different levels (National Information Center 2004). Respective to education, the current President of Yemen, Ali Abdullah Saleh, stated that the country should emphasize scientific research because he believes it is the key to growth in Yemen (National Information Center 2004).

For many Yemen people, the scarcity of natural fresh water resources is a daily challenge. There are inadequate supplies of potable water, despite the fact that the country is surrounded on two sides by bodies of water (*The World Factbook* 2004).

For a struggling economy looking toward tourism as a possible source of income, carjackings and the kidnapping of foreign tourists, especially Americans, pose major challenges. State departments are routinely advising travelers that carjackings are the most serious foreign tourist problem. In addition, in recent years, kidnapping of foreigners has been a regular event; more than 200 foreigners have been kidnapped and traded for money, jobs, and cars, usually with unqualified success to the kidnappers. While most of those taken were subsequently released unharmed, not all were (Bureau of Consular Affairs 2005; CultureGrams 2003).

Northern Yemen, particularly the town of Saada and further north towards the Saudi border, has faced the challenge of armed insurgency since late June, 2004. Though the government is reported to be gaining the upper hand against the rebels, the fighting is described as intense (Bureau of Consular Affairs 2005).

One of the most recently reported challenges for Yemen is the problem of child trafficking. While the prevalence of the issue is somewhat uncertain, one study reports the figure of children trafficked across the Saudi boarder as around 50,000. Poverty has been labeled the root cause of the problem, while the lack of education and unemployment may also contribute to the problem (IRIN 2005).

The population of Yemen as of 2004 was 20,024,867 (*The World Factbook*, 2004). Males comprise 50.1% of the total population, and females 49.9% (National Information Center, 2004). People between the age ranges of 0–14 constitute 46.6% of the total population. People whose age ranges between 15–64 constitute 50.6%, and those over 65 constitute 2.8% of the total population. The median age is 16.5 years (National Information Center 2004; *The World Factbook* 2004). The infant mortality rate is 63.26 deaths per 1,000 live births, and the life expectancy at birth is 54 years (National Information Center 2004; The *World Factbook* 2004; nationbynation 2003). The average size of a Yemeni family is 7.4 members.

With respect to ethnicity, 90% of the citizens are Arab, with two thirds being Sunni Muslins and the rest Shiite Muslims. The remaining 10% are of African, Indian, or Pakistani descent. A few small Jewish communities are active in the northern highlands (CultureGrams 2003; *The World Factbook* 2004).

The official language of Yemen is Arabic. Arabic has 28 characters and is read from right to left. A growing number of educated people also speak English because they recognize the need for more international interaction. Those who speak English can primarily be found in the larger cities (CultureGrams 2003).

The official religion of Yemen is Islam. The Muslim religion includes the Shaf'i (Sunni) and Zaydi (Shi'a). Islam teaches that life on earth is a period of testing that prepares one for life after death (CultureGrams 2003). There are also a small number of Jewish, Christian, and Hindu followers residing in Yemen (*The World Factbook* 2004).

Yemen has been considered one of the poorest Arab countries in the world. However, strong growth has been reported since the mid-1990s with the onset of oil production. Yemen benefits from current high oil prices. Yemen has established the beginnings of a modernized and streamlined economy, which has led to substantial foreign debt relief, international financial support, and inflation reduction. A distinctly high population growth rate and internal political dissension complicate the government's task of economic improvement. Improvement plans include diversification of the economy, encouragement of tourism, and more efficient use of scarce water resources (*The World Factbook* 2004).

The Yemen per capita income in 2003 is reported to be $520 (Geohive 2005). The official currency is the *Rial* (YER). In 2003, the average currency rate was 183.45 *Rial* per $1 (National Information Center 2004).

Natural resources of Yemen include petroleum; fish; rock salt; marble; small deposits of coal, gold, lead, nickel, and copper; and fertile soil in the west (Geohive 2005; *The World Factbook* 2004). Oil and natural gas are the country's most valuable natural resources (CultureGrams 2003).

Contextual Features

Yemen is a republic which is a representative multiparty democracy in which the people's elected representatives, not the people themselves, vote on legislation. The Constitution was adopted in 1990, ratified in 1991, and again in 2001.

As of 1990, an elected President of Yemen serves as the Chief of State and head of the executive branch of government. The President is elected by direct, popular vote for a seven-year term, with the next Presidential election scheduled for 2006. The President then has the authority to appoint the Vice President.

The head of government for the executive branch is the Prime Minister. Like the Vice President, the Prime Minister is appointed by the President. Also included in the executive branch of government is the Cabinet or Council of Ministers. The Cabinet members are labeled Deputy Prime Ministers and are appointed by the President on the advice of the Prime Minister (*The World Factbook* 2004; *Encarta* 2004).

The legislative branch of government recently undertook a modification. According to a Constitutional amendment ratified in February of 2001, the legislature is now bicameral. The Shura Council consists of 111 seats, and its members are appointed by the President. The House of Representatives consists of 301 seats, and its members are elected by popular vote to serve six-year terms (*The World Factbook* 2004).

The judicial branch, according to the Constitution, includes an independent judiciary. The former northern and southern legal codes have been unified. The legal system includes separate district courts, appeals courts, and a Supreme Court based in Sana'a. In 1994, the legislators approved a new Constitution that established *shari'a* (Islamic law) as the source of all legislation.

The government is also separated into administrative divisions that consist of 18 governorates subdivided into districts. Sana'a is the capital of the Republic of Yemen and serves as an additional separate administrative division. Each village, town, and city is governed by a sheik (tribal leader) who has ultimate authority to make decisions, resolve disputes between villagers, and keep peace (CultureGrams 2003).

The Yemen system of law is based primarily on Islamic law, but influenced by Turkish law, English common law, and local tribal customary law. (*The World Factbook* 2004). Yemen's law, according to the Constitution, emphasizes equality under the law, and respect of basic human rights. Islamic procedural law tends to consist of a combination of adversarial and inquisitorial aspects. In addition, Yemen has not accepted compulsory International Court of Justice (ICJ) jurisdiction (*The World Factbook* 2004). Traditional Islamic law of Yemen recognizes no distinction between a legal system and other controls on a person's behavior. Islam is said to provide all the answers to questions about appropriate behavior in any sphere of life. Islamic law is the divinely ordained system of Allah's (God's) commands; to deny that would be to renounce the Islam religion (Reichel 2005).

Islamic law is called the *Shari'a*, the path to follow. It consists of writings from the Qur'an (the holy book of Islam) and the Sunna (the statements and deeds of the Prophet Muhammad). The Qur'an and the Sunna have been supplemented with analogical reasoning (*qiyas*) and consensus by Islamic legal scholars (*ijma*). While the law is Allah-given, its application fell to humans, thus Muslims rely upon the system of witnesses and oath taking (Reichel 2005). The system of witnesses and oath taking, a tradition of Islamic law, is to seek truth through statements made by reliable people.

The *Shari'a* does not distinguish between private (civil torts) and public (crimes) law. If there is an accusation of a violation of the Qur'an or Sunna, the accuser is responsible for initiating the court action and bringing a complaint against the offender. The accuser is responsible for showing the truthfulness of his complaint, thus shouldering the burden of proof. This may be accomplished by presenting witnesses on behalf of the accuser (plaintiff) and/or by taking appropriate oaths. If there are adequate numbers of qualified witnesses as determined by the judge (*qadi*), ruling will be made in favor of the accuser. This is done without cross-examination or even presentation of evidence for the defendant. The number of qualified witnesses needed for certain crimes is outlined by the *Shari'a* (Reichel 2005).

Upon incomplete evidence, the tradition of oath taking may be utilized. Witnesses are not sworn before testifying, nor is there any punishment for perjury. In Islamic courtrooms, witnesses speak freely, while judges inquire throughout the discussion. If neither side can present adequate support for its claim, the challenge to take an oath in support of the court-made assertions may be called. The *qadi* decides which party will first challenge the other to take an oath. If the opponent accepts the oath challenge, that party automatically wins. The oath works under *Shari'a* because of the intense Muslim beliefs that false swearers will suffer the consequences on judgment day (Reichel 2005).

With respect to the court system, the above-mentioned procedures may somewhat vary among the various types of Yemeni courts. The Supreme Judicial Council is the administrative authority of the Yemen judiciary. The Council reviews policies regarding the structure and function of the judiciary, and it supervises appointment, promotion, discharge, and transfer of judges (Brown 2004).

The Yemen judicial system is organized in a three-tiered court structure with no jury trials. At the base are the courts of first instance that have jurisdiction over personal status, civil, criminal, and commercial matters. A single judge may hear a case in these courts. Appeals can be made to the courts of appeal in each of the 18 administrative provinces and one in the capital with civil, criminal, matrimonial, and commercial divisions. Each division is composed of three judges (United Nations Development Programme 2004; Bureau of Democracy, Human Rights & Labor 2001).

The Supreme Court is the highest court of appeal of Yemen and sits in Sana'a. The Supreme Court has authority to determine the constitutionality of laws and regulations, settle jurisdictional disputes between different courts, hear cases brought against high government officials, and serve as the final court of appeal for all lower court decisions. There are eight separate divisions of the Supreme Court: constitutional, appeals, scrutiny, criminal, military, civil, family, commercial, and administrative (Yemen 2004; Brown 2004).

There are also a number of specialized courts at the higher court levels that handle issues concerning military, juvenile, tax, customs, and labor matters. These courts and tribunals function as courts of first instance, and decisions made in them may be appealed to the courts of appeals (United Nations Development Programme 2004).

The crime rate overall is low in Islamic countries. Muslim goals are to obtain a peaceful afterlife with Allah, which is partially dictated by their actions on earth. Thus, crime is not a major issue of the country. The total crime rate for Yemen in 2000 was 1.24 crimes per 1000 people. Of the major crimes, assault has the highest rate, with 0.05 offenses per 1000 people. Assault being the highest crime is of no surprise since there still appears to be some dissention since the unification of North and South Yemen (Nationmaster 2004).

Islamic law embraces the idea of individualization, thus wrongs are actions against the individual rather than against the government. This sets the stage for a very victim-oriented legal system and system of corrections. Formal punishment in Yemen ranges from fines to the death penalty. However, the Qur'an condones at least two types of responses that do not involve the court system and may never result in a police record being made: retaliation (retribution) and compensation (restitution) (Reichel 2005).

Islamic law allows for retaliation by a victim's family in the case of murder. However, the Qur'an clearly tempers retaliation by encouraging forgiveness. Therefore, when retaliation is not the victim's response, it is typically replaced by *diyya*—money paid to the harmed or victim's family in compensation for the injuries (restitution).

When the formal correctional system is imposed, punishment is dictated by the *Shari'a* and varies by offense. Corporal punishment may be imposed, but only after strict legal criteria of guilt have been met. Corporal punishment of flogging is allowed for such crimes as premarital sexual relations and consumption of alcohol (Human Rights Watch 2004).

Imprisonment is a sentencing option that is currently imposed upon approximately 14,000 prisoners. This equates to 83 prisoners per 100,000 Yemenis (Nationmaster 2004). The U.S. Depart-

Yemen crimes and rates table

Crime	Number (source year)	Rate per 1000 people
Assaults	1,015 (2000)	0.05
Burglaries	110 (1999)	0.00
Car thefts	812 (2000)	0.04
Frauds	658 (2000)	0.03
Manslaughters	129 (2000)	0.00
Murders	697 (2000)	0.03
Rapes	80 (2000)	0.00
Robberies	175 (1999)	0.00
Total Crime	24,066 (2000)	1.24

Source: Nationmaster.com, *2004.*

ment of State recently reported that Yemen prison conditions are poor and do not meet internationally recognized minimum standards. Prisons are characterized by overcrowding, unsanitary conditions, and inadequate food and health care. Inmates are said to depend on relatives for food and medicine. Many inmates lack mattresses or bedding. In women's prisons, children are likely to be incarcerated along with their mothers. It has also been found that juveniles are incarcerated with adults (Bureau of Democracy, Human Rights & Labor 2001; Human Rights 2001). The Yemengovernment has recently issued directives intended to remedy many of the poor prison conditions and to house juveniles separate from adults (Bureau of Democracy, Human Rights & Labor 2001).

Capital punishment is the ultimate sentencing option for grave crimes, including murder, adultery, apostasy, and kidnapping. Yemen is one of six countries that will execute people for acts committed before the age of 18. The others are Iran, Nigeria, Pakistan, Saudi Arabia, and the United States (Human Rights Watch 1998 via Reichel 2005). The death penalty and corporal punishments are often carried out in public (Human Rights Watch 2004).

Police Profile

Background

Prior to the unification of North and South Yemen, policing was a centralized entity operating under the existing government. Policing consisted of two branches: a civil branch and an armed branch. The civil branch, which was unarmed, had general police functions such as patrolling the streets and enforcing the local law. The armed police branch included police officers trained along military lines, and they were armed generally with rifles. They were housed in military barracks near the major cities. Their duties, among others, included crowd control, riot control, and dispersing labor demonstrations (Willis 1999).

Since unification in 1990, police forces from both the north and the south have struggled with some of the inefficiencies of the centralized police structure under the Ministry of Interior. There is wide recognition of the need to strengthen police capacity to enforce laws and provide security. However, the "public administration suffers from poor institutional capabilities, inefficient personnel, under-paid and poorly motivated civil servants, inadequate training and cumbersome procedures and management systems" (United Nations Development Programme 2003).

There appears to be to some degree a large discretionary application of laws and regulations administered by various Yemen police.

Demographics

The size of the civil service in Yemen, which includes police officers, increased from 95,000 in 1990 to 200,000 in 1992, and to 500,000 in 2003 (United Nations Development Programme 2003). The overall number of policewomen in the police service had reached 1,476 by the end of 1999 (Duais, 2000). The Ministry of Interior plans to recruit 500 policewomen in an effort to boost women's public role. The first large group of 450 policewomen graduated from the Yemen police training program in 2001. There appears to be a growing demand for female staff in many government institutions and installations (*Observer* 2004).

The first policewomen graduated from Aden Police Academy in the early 1980s and are now represented throughout the ranks, except that of brigadier. Policewomen work in various branches of the Interior Ministry, generally beginning their duties at the Ministry's headquarters before proceeding to specialized areas of police work (Duais, 2000).

Organizational Description

The primary state security agency of Yemen is the Political Security Organization (PSO), an independent agency that reports directly to the President. The Criminal Investigative Department (CID) of the police conducts most criminal investigations, makes most arrests, and reports to the Ministry of Interior. The Central Security Organization (CSO), which is also a part of the Ministry of Interior, maintains a paramilitary force used as a form of national guard (Bureau of Democracy, Human Rights, & Labor 2001). There are then civilian police authorities who perform the general service law enforcement responsibilities. The focus of this discussion is upon the general service law enforcement.

The organizational structure is quasi-military, but considered a civilian entity. The Yemen police possess military characteristics, such as the hierarchical structure, uniforms, and rank structure. Within the organizational structure of the civilian police agencies there are specialized units. These units include prisons, juvenile centers, homicide divisions, Interpol, civil registration, immigration and passport control, general and central security, civil defense, guarding installations, and communications and tourism police. Police officers may also

927

be assigned to the police training school or to work directly for the Ministry of Interior.

Functions

According to the Yemen Constitution, the police force's "function is to serve the people and guarantee their safety, security, and peace. The police force shall be entrusted with guaranteeing public order and security and public manners" (Republic of Yemen, Article 25). Therefore, police handle most of the daily law enforcement functions in the country. Police are generally divided into regular police officers and specialized investigative police officers (Reichel 2005). General police officers work at various posts, including airports, police stations, and prisons (*Observer* 2004).

Women police officers are needed to perform special functions in accordance with Yemeni customs and traditions. The inspection of women in airports, harbors, and land routes are made by policewomen. Women police are also needed for the interrogation of women, arresting prostitutes, special investigations into juvenile or female cases, and the civil registration of women (Duais 2000).

In addition to specific functions and because of strong affiliation with Islamic traditions, Yemen police do not often engage in the same police practices as other popular countries. The lack of any formal community policing programs is such an example (Reichel 2005).

Training

There is little information reported on the extent or content of Yemen police officer training. However, there have been a number of reports that contend there is insufficient training among Yemen law enforcers (United Nations Development Programme 2003). Nonetheless, the duration of police training is documented as six months. The primary police training school is located in Aden.

As a means of improving its law enforcement training, Yemen has reached outside its borders by requesting assistance from the Pakistan government in training their police personnel and coastguards. Yemen wanted to take advantage of Pakistan's experience in tackling the issues in tribal areas of the country. Yemen has also shown interest in importing anti-riot equipment from Pakistan (*Dawn* 2004).

Policing Needs

Similar to other functions of government, Yemeni police are in need of the basic equipment and in need of improving their existing equipment, including firearms (United Nations Development Programme 2003). There is also a need for knowledge of professional methods of gathering evidence, which alienates the public from police officers and the justice system as a whole (United Nations Development Programme 2003).

Yemen police are falling behind technology with respect to the types of weapons on the streets. Many Yemenis consider a gun a basic part of their dress, no different than traditional dagger that many wear in their belts (Hutchinson 2004). However, recently Yemen has established a weapons ban that slowly may change civilians' opportunity of gun ownership.

Complaints and Discipline

The Yemen Constitution in Article 25 states that "The law shall regulate the work of the police force under the judicial power, and the manner this force shall implement the orders of the judicial power without prejudice to the proper conduct of justice. It shall also carry out all duties entrusted to it by laws and statutes, in the manner specified by the law" (Republic of Yemen 2004). Despite a constitutional mandate, corrupt officials are said to be among the security and judicial sectors. There is little evidence that complaints to authorities are seriously considered (Oudah 2005). For instance, two police officers were charged with the torture and ill-treatment of five men arrested and detained at a Shiban police station. Those same men were later released without charges (Amnesty International 2003).

There have been a documented number of complaints about lack of Yemen police protection for property, particularly in rural areas. Enforcement of the law is irregular and in some cases nonexistent (Bureau of Democracy, Human Rights & Labor 2001). Other complaints include lack of respect by law enforcers, particularly of women citizens, arbitrary torture, abuse of detained citizens, and failure to observe due process procedures when arresting and detaining suspects (United Nations Development Programme 2003; Bureau of Democracy, Human Rights & Labor 2001).

Despite the documented number of complaints regarding Yemen police corruption, deviance, and miss-use of authority, there is little evidence to date of police accountability or the mechanisms of accountability.

Terrorism

Since Yemen has become a unified country, international relationships have improved dramatically. One means of improved international relations comes in wake of the fight against terrorism. Yemen's position toward terrorism is to partner with the United States and other countries to fight terrorism (Yemen Embassy 2004). Since the September 11, 2001 attacks on the United States, Yemen authorities have cracked down on militants and rounded up hundreds of suspected members of the al-Qaeda network (Deutsche Press 2004). As a reward for Yemen efforts in the fight against terrorism, the United States lifted a ten-year embargo on arms sales to Yemen (Deutsche Press 2004).

Police Education, Research, and Publications

Yemen is a relatively newly unified country that has been handling numerous political, governmental, economic, and terrorism issues. Research in all areas of Yemen justice has been nearly obsolete. Therefore, to date there is no recent research in the area of Yemen policing. It is a country ripe for examination. The current President understands the need for research if the country wishes to be progressive, and he has placed emphasis and resources on all forms of scientific research in Yemen.

Police Related Websites

Customs Authority – *www.yemencustoms.gov.ye*
Ministry of Human Rights – *www.mhryemen.org*
Yemen Parliament – *www.parliament.gov.ye*
Ministry of Interior – *www.yemen.gov.ye/egov/ interior-english/*
Ministry of Information – *www.yemeninfo.gov.ye*
BETSY WRIGHT KREISEL

Bibliography

Amnesty International. *Yemen, Republic of.* Amnesty International. 2003. web.amnesty.org/report2003/Yem-summary-eng. (30 September 2004).

Brown, Nathan. *Arab Judicial Structures. United Nations Development Programme.* www.undp.org.ye/justice.htm (30 September 2004).

Bureau of Consular Affairs. "Yemen." *Consular Information Sheet.* U.S. Department of State. 10 January 2005. http//travel.state.gov/travel/cis_pa_tw/cis_1061.html (10 January 2005).

Bureau of Democracy, Human Rights, and Labor. *Yemen: Country Reports on Human Rights Practices.* U.S. Department of State. 23 February 2001, www.state.gov/g/drl/rls/hrrpt/2000/nea/826.htm (10 October 2004).

CIA. *The World Factbook.* "The Republic of Yemen." 16 December 2004. www.cia.gov/cia/publications/factbook/geos/ym.html (30 December 2004).

CultureGrams. "Republic of Yemen." *CultureGrams Standard Edition 2002.* New York: Oxford University Press. 2003.

Deutsche Presse. "U.S. Lifts Ban on Arms Sales to Yemen." Arab News. 2 September 2004. www.aljazeerah.info/news%20archives/2004%20News%archives/September (30 September 2004).

Duais, Saleh Al. *Yemeni Women Police Force.* May 2000. www.hdii.de/y-women.html (30 September 2004).

Encarta. *Republic of Yemen.* 2004. http://encarta.msn.com/encyclopedia_761578405.Yemen.html (15 October, 2004).

Geohive. *Global Statistics.* http://www.geohive.com/global. (10 January 2005).

Human Rights Watch. "Yemen: Human Rights Developments." *Human Rights Watch World Report 2001.* http://hrw.org/wr2llmideast/yemen/html (15 October 2004).

Hutchinson, White. "Travel in Sana'a, Yemen." *White Hutchinson Leisure & Learning Group.* www.whitehutchinson.com/leisure/sanatravel.shtml. (30 September 2004).

IRIN. "Yemen: Authorities Attempt to Tackle Child Trafficking." *Reuters AlertNet* Foundation. 12 Jan. 2005. www.alertnet.org/printable.htm?URL=/thenews/newsdesk/IRIN/ (12 January 2005).

National Information Center. *Republic of Yemen.* http://www.nic.gov.ye/English%20site/index.htm (30 September 2004).

NationbyNation. *Yemen: Country Reports on Human Rights Practices – 2002.* 31 March 2003. http://www.nationbynation.com/Yemen/Human.html (15 October 2004).

NationMaster. *Seventh United Nations Survey of Crime Trends and Operations of Criminal Justice Systems: 1998–2000.* www.nationmaster.com/country/ym/crime (30 September 2004).

Observer Staff. "More Women to Join Yemen's Police Force." *Yemen Observer.* 4 December 2004. www.yobserver.com/cgi-bin/exec/view.cgi/1/3038/printer (10 January 2005).

Ouda, Abdul-Aziz. "What Comes After Judicial Reforms." *Yemen Observer.* 8, January 2005. www.yobserver.com/news/printer_3448.html (10 January 2005).

Reichel, Philip. L. *Comparative Criminal Justice Systems: A Topical Approach,* 4th ed. Upper Saddle River, NJ: Prentice Hall. 2005.

Republic of Yemen Constitution, Article 25. www.oefre.unibe.ch/law/icl/ym00000_.html (30 September 2004).

Staff Reporter. "Pakistan to Train Yemeni Security Personnel." *DAWN the Internet Edition.* 8 December 2004. www.dawn.com/2004/12/08/nat16.htm (10 January 2005).

United Nations Development Programme. Public Administration. 14 January 2003. www.undp.org.ye/justice.htm (30 September 2004).

United Nations Development Programme. *Yemen: Judiciary.* (30 September 2004).

Willis, John Matthew. "Aden Police During Colonial Times." *Yemen Times.* 4 January 1999. www.yementimes.com/99/iss01/culure/htm. (15 October 2004).

Yemen, Republic of. www.law.emory.edu/IFL/legal/yemen.htm (30 September 2004).

Yemen Embassy. *Yemeni is a Partner in the Fight Against Terrorism.* Yemen Embassy in USA. http://www.yemenembassy.org/. (30 September 2004).

Z

ZAMBIA

Background Material

Zambia is located in southern Africa, east of Angola. It has a total area of 752,614 sq km and a population of 10,462,436 (2004 est.). The capital is Lusaka. The predominant religion is a combination of traditional beliefs and Christianity, but Christianity is the official national religion.

The Republic of Zambia is governed by a President and a unicameral national assembly. Formerly, this area was the territory of Northern Rhodesia, and it was administered by the South Africa Company from 1891 before British control in 1923. Zambia became an independent country on October 24, 1964. Bordering a large neighbor such as the Democratic Republic of Congo (Zaire), Zambia is about the area of the state of Texas in the United States of America. The majority of the inhabitants derive their origins from the Bantu language heritage. Some ethnic groups are small, and most of them claim either Luba or Lunda origins, primarily from the southern Democratic Republic of the Congo and northern Angola. Some have East African roots; the Ngoni, for example, migrated from South Africa in the nineteenth century.

Generally, most of the people in Zambia practice subsistence farming, leading to the production of crops like corn, sorghum, rice, groundonuts, sunflower seeds, vegetables, soybeans, and sugarcane. It has been reported that over 70% of the population live below the poverty line and experience dismal, economic conditions. Historically, the Zambian economy has been based on the copper mining industry. Copper has been both "a blessing and a curse" on Zambian economic well being. Indeed, copper exports in the 1970s accounted for about 95% of Zambia's foreign exchange earnings. Due to lack of investment and a pro-longed policy that was rooted in command economic principles, production of copper had declined to a low of 228,000 metric tons in 1998. However, in 2002, because of a change in government policy, such as privatization of the industry, copper output increased to 337,000 metric tons. Currently, the Zambian administration is trying to reduce the country's reliance on a one-crop economy by engaging in various economic diversification programs that will improve the quality of life of its population. These include economic strategies to promote agriculture, tourism, gemstone mining, and hydro power. Zambia also has appreciable cobalt, coal, emeralds, amethyst deposits; and potential wealth in gold, oil, and uranium deposits. Arguably, the country's economic future may come from aggressive investments in the spheres of agricultural exports such as cotton, sugar, tobacco, and coffee.

Contextual Features

Zambia's Constitution of 1964 specifically named Kenneth Kaunda as its first indisputable President of the country. Indeed, the foremost figure in Zambian politics from 1964 to 1991 was Kenneth Kaunda, who represented the struggle that "Zambia shall be free" from Great Britain. Kaunda was the leader of the United National Independence Party (UNIP), which was founded in 1954 until its demise in 1991. In December, 1973, the government promulgated a new Constitution that banned all political parties and laid the foundation for a one-party participatory democracy. The 1973 Constitution provided for an executive President and a unicameral national assembly. In 1990, President Kaunda endorsed a law that ended his party's monopoly on power. Subsequently, in 1991, due to tumultuous riots and attempted coups, Zambia enacted a new Constitution that allowed other political parties and their candidates to participate in presidential elections. Frederick Chiluba, under the banner of Movement for Multiparty Democracy (MMD), won the presidential race in a landslide.

In 2001, Levy Mwanawasa was the elected President of Zambia. His administration is steadfast in stamping out corruption in Zambia by prosecuting, not only former President Frederick Chiluba, but all members of his administrative cadre charged with corruption. In addition, President Mwanawasa established a Task Force in 2002 to aggressively investigate corrupt officials of the government. He has also encouraged Zambian courts to hear cases of abuse of the Chiluba's regime.

The Zambian legal system is based on the English common law and customary law. The Court of Appeal, also known as the Supreme Court, is the highest court in the country as well as Zambia's final appellate court under the supervision of a Chief Justice. There is a High Court, which is also presided over by the Chief Justice. Below these courts are the Magistrates' Courts and other local courts. The Chief Justice, Justices of the Appeal Court and the High Court are all appointed by the President. The Constitution provides for an independent judiciary, and the government has generally not interfered with judicial proceedings. Allegedly, the judiciary was weakened because of inadequate resources, inefficiency, and reports of possible corruption.

Based on the principles of Zambian law, the source of criminal law is the Penal Code, which is separated into two areas: General Provisions and Crimes. Criminals and children have rights under the Constitution. But, prison conditions were reported to be harsh and life threatening. Based on the available statistics, prisons designed to hold 5,500 inmates kept more than 13,200 prisoners, for which over 5,000 were pre-trial detainees. The Lusaka Central Prison, constructed with a capacity of 400 prisoners, was reported to have warehoused 1,396 offenders. Allegedly, Zambian prisons are characterized by poor sanitation, overcrowding, inadequate medical facilities, malnutrition, and lack of clean water. Reportedly, between January and September 2004, about 149 offenders and 107 detainees died in prison or custody due to tuberculosis, malaria, and other poor hygienic conditions. However, in order to correct these anomalies, the government is determined to improve prison sanitation and provision of portable water for prison inmates. It has been reported that the government plans to spend about $120,000 (600 million *kwacha*) on prison management and construction. The Constitution prohibits torture of its citizens and has permitted visits of its prisons by both domestic and civil society organizations, as well as diplomats from foreign countries.

Police Profile

Background

Like most of its African neighbors, the Zambian police emerged from the crucible of colonial administration. Prior to political independence in 1964, the native authorities were primarily vested with police powers to maintain law and order in local jurisdictions. The forces were unarmed, generally served as messengers, and were inadequately equipped to carry out police duties. In matters of serious infractions, the native authorities summoned the help of the Northern Rhodesia Police through the auspices of the district commissioners. Established in 1912 by a merger of the North-Eastern Rhodesia Constabury and the Barotse Native Police, its membership at that time consisted of 27 British officers and 750 Africans. Unlike the native authorities, the Northern Rhodesia Police was better equipped with rifles and machine guns. At independence, the Northern Rhodesia Police force had about 6,000 officers, and members were responsible for both civil and military functions.

In 1932, the administration of Northern Rhodesia separated the civil and military entities of the police, and in 1933 the military component became the Northern Rhodesia Regiment. In 1937, a British-appointed commissioner completely revamped the police force. Before independence in 1964, senior officers of the force were British expatriates. In 1964, senior African officers were trained and incorporated into the Northern Rhodesia Police force, and the force was renamed the Zambia Police Force (ZPF). Subsequently, expatriates began leaving the force in great numbers; however, some Europeans and Asian officers stayed with the force, which permitted an orderly reassignment of police functions to the natives.

Converted from the old Northern Rhodesia Police, the ZPF was established by the first Zambian Constitution at independence as one of the national public (civil) services. The first commissioner of police, a Zambia police officer, was appointed by the President on November 1, 1965.

Demographics

The force is made up of about 12,000 police officers, including an additional 2,000 officers from the Zambia Police Reserve.

Organizational Description

The 1973 Constitution mandated the separation of the police and prison services from the command of the Public Service Commission, and instituted the Police and Civil Service Commission with about six members and a Chairperson. Additionally, in 1979, the government combined both the Police and Prison Service Commission with three other commissions under the heading of Civil Service. The Minister of State, housed in the Office of the Prime Minister, was given the supervisory power over Civil Service matters. The Inspector General of Police is at the apex of the hierarchical structure of the ZPF, and the staff consists of a Commissioner, a Deputy Commissioner, and a Senior Assistant Commissioner. Like in other bureaucratic institutions, authority flows from the top of the organization to other units of the police command. The police operate under the leadership of the Ministry of Home Affairs.

The ZPF has national jurisdiction over police matters. The force is headquartered in Lusaka, the capital of Zambia. The ZPF has six functional divisions: administration, staff, criminal investigation, communications, training, and traffic (signals). The force is also divided into nine territorial divisions and maintains four special units: the Mobile Unit, located in Kamfinsa; the paramilitary battalion with headquarters at Lilayi; the Police Training School in Lilayi; and the Tazara Police, which is located in Lusaka. The Tazara Police serves as a security force with the functional authority to protect the Tanzania-Zambia Railway. These divisions are commanded by either a Senior or Assistant Commissioner or a Senior Police Superintendent.

Within the ZPF are also other subsidiary police units like divisional police, district police, and local police formations located in towns and villages. Individuals may enter the police force at the level of constable, sub-inspector, or assistant superintendent. Assistant superintendent candidates are required to have college or university degrees. Grade structures are determined by rank and conform to the British standards.

The Mobile Unit or the Paramilitary Battalion and their platoons are occasionally summoned during major turbulence in the country. The country also has a Mounted Police unit, which has the responsibility of guiding the President, participating in ceremonial activities, and preventing cattle rustling. Additionally, the Marine Service operates as a counter-smuggling patrol along the lakes in the northeastern section of the country. Indeed, Zambia has a unique feature of its police, known as the Prosecution Branch. This unit prosecutes criminal cases in Magistrate Courts under the supervision of public prosecutions.

Police Use of Firearms

The ZPF are vested with the power to carry weapons with some explicit restrictions on the use of deadly force.

Complaints and Discipline

According to published reports, the Zambian police force is notoriously low paid, and its officers are widely accused of corruption and participation in drug trade.

According to published reports, lack of professionalism, investigative skills, and internal discipline in the police force posed a serious problem. Allegedly, the police have been accused of releasing prisoners in exchange for bribes.

Terrorism

The government of Zambia rejects international terrorism, and has condemned strongly the tragedy of September 11, 2001, which was perpetrated against the United States. The government of Zambia has pledged its support and cooperation to help the United States fight the war against terrorism.

International Cooperation

The United States and Zambia maintain fine international relations. The United States is determined to help Zambia beat HIV/AIDS, fight corruption, and strengthen Zambia's nascent democracy. Aside from its good relations with the United States, Zambia is also a member of the Non-Aligned Movement (NAM), the African Union, the Southern African Development Community, and the Common Market for Eastern and Southern Africa, which is located in Lusaka.

Police Education, Research, and Publications

The Police Training School is situated in Lilayi, and it provides primary instructions for fresh police personnel. It offers promotion courses, traffic courses, instructor training for constables, sergeants, superintendents, and other ranks, refresher training, and motor vehicle and motor cycle instructions. The training school is directed by a senior police administrator. Usually, new recruits (between 18 and 25 years old) receive their education for a period of 26 weeks. Police officers who act as public prosecutors receive training in criminal law, criminal procedures, and rules of evidence.

IHEKWOABA D. ONWUDIWE

Bibliography

Banks, S. Arthur, Thomas C. and Muller. *Political Handbook of the World: Governments and Intergovernmental Organizations*. CSA Publications: New York, 1998.

Grotpeter, John J., Brian V. Siegel, and James R. Pletcher. *Historical Dictionary of Zambia*. The Scarecrow Press, Inc.: Lanham: Maryland, 1998.

Ingleton, D. Roy. *Police of the World*. Charles Scribner's Sons: New York, 1979.

Kurian, George Thomas. *World Encyclopedia of Police Forces and Penal Systems*. Facts on File: New York, 1989.

Legun, Colin. *Africa: Contemporary Record*. African Publishing Company: New York and London, 1992–1994.

Mars-Proietti, Laura. *Nations of the World: A Political, Economic and Business Handbook*. Grey House Publishing: Millerton, New York, 2004.

Onwudiwe, Ihekwoaba D. *The Globalization of Terrorism*. Ashgate Publishers: Aldershot, 2001.

Ramsay, Jeffress. 1993. *Global Studies: Africa*. An Annual edition's Publications. Connecticut: The Dushkin Publishing Group.

The Europa World Year Book. Europa Publications Limited: London, 1999.

U.S. Department of State. "Background Note: Zambia." 2005. www.state.gov/r/pa/ei/bgn/2359.htm (23 January, 2005).

U.S. Department of State. "Zambia: Country Reports on Human Rights Practices – 2003. www.state.gov/g/drl/rls/hrrpt/2003/27759.htm (23 January, 2005).

The World Fact Book. "Zambia: Country Facts Sheet." 2004. www.cia.gov/cia/publications/factbook/geos/za.html (23 January, 2005).

ZIMBABWE

Background Material

Zimbabwe's original rulers were the Shona and Ndebele tribes. The area had seen Portuguese traders and Catholic missionaries, but the first substantial European presence came with Cecil Rhodes's establishment of the British South Africa Company (BSAC) (and the commencement of the diamond trade) in 1880. Rhodes defeated the Shona in 1890 and established what he called Rhodesia. Great Britain gave BSAC political control of the area, which it ruled until the UK reclaimed the area and white settlers established their own government in 1923.

Independence came in 1965 under Ian Smith's government; however, this was not born of a native independence movement as in Tanganyika (now Tanzania), but rather continued white rule of the country, only without the auspices of England. The native African population (the vast majority of the population) was denied suffrage. The indigenous population began a struggle for independence, based mostly on guerrilla warfare, until 1979. A settlement was negotiated, and Robert Mugabe, one of the leaders of the indigenous movement, was elected Prime Minister in the country's first universal elections that same year. Officially titled President since 1987, Mugabe has been in power ever since, carrying out an increasingly autocratic regime involving badly planned land redistribution (causing the flight of white farmers and shortages in basic goods), inequitable presidential elections in 2002 (ensuring Mugabe's continuation in office), and repression of dissent. Zimbabwe was also involved from 1998 to 2002 in the war in the Democratic Republic of the Congo, which depleted its economic resources even further.

Zimbabwe's population is estimated at 12,671,860. In contrast to most regions of the world, Zimbabwe's population has fallen in the past several years (it was estimated at 12,890,000 in 2003). Zimbabwe has been drastically affected by HIV/AIDS, with which 34 percent of the population is estimated to be infected.

Zimbabwe's capital is Harare, whose population is estimated at 1.6 million. The country's land area is 386,670 sq km. Ethnically, Zimbabwe is 98% native African (82% Shona, 14% Ndebele, and 2% other), 1% Asian and multiracial, and less than 1% white. Fifty percent of the population practices syncretic forms of Christian and indigenous beliefs; 25% are solely Christian; 24% solely practice indigenous religions; and Islam and other religions comprise the remaining 1% of the population. English is the official language; Shona and Sindebele (the language of the Ndebele, sometimes referred to as Ndebele) are also widely spoken; and a wide variety of tribal dialects are spoken, though none in great numbers.

Zimbabwe has faced a number of economic problems in the late twentieth and early twenty-first centuries. The DRC war, as mentioned above, caused great economic hardship, as have the AIDS crisis and the effects of Mugabe's land reform program. The commercial farming sector, which was most disrupted by the land reform, was the country's largest source of exports and strongest sector for foreign exchange; it also provided 400,000 jobs in Zimbabwe. Inflation rose from 32% to 383% between 1998 and 2003, and the GDP (currently $1900 per capita) has a negative growth rate of -13.6%. The industrial production growth rate is also negative (14.7%). The public debt totals 41.3% of Zimbabwe's GDP.

In 1996, the labor force, totaling 4.7 million people, was divided between agriculture (66%), industry (10%), and services (24%). The land itself is resource rich, with agricultural products that include corn, cotton, wheat, coffee, sugarcane, and peanuts; and industrial products including mining (coal, gold, copper, nickel, tin, clay, numerous metallic and nonmetallic ores), steel, wood products, cement, chemicals, fertilizer, and clothing and footwear. However, between the land reform, the DRC war, and the unemployment rate (70% in 2002), it is likely that this distribution has changed considerably. The country receives $178 million in economic aid, including humanitarian food aid from the United States and European Union. IMF support, however, has been suspended due to Zimbabwe's failure to meet budget goals.

Contextual Features

The executive branch effectively dominates all other branches of government in Zimbabwe. The President is both the Chief of State and the Head of Government. The last election was held in March 2002, and the next will be in March 2008. The Vice President, currently Joyce Mujuru, is appointed by the President, as is the Cabinet. Since coming into office in 1980, Mugabe has used a series of constitutional amendments to provide himself with broader powers. In 2002, legislation was passed that made it illegal to criticize him.

Legally, elections are democratic; however, in practice, Mugabe has restricted the funds available to political parties other than his own, and has also used the police and military to intimidate his opponents. As the media are largely state controlled, Mugabe has been able to limit his opponents' access. He has also been accused of ballot-stuffing and voter intimidation, and international observers reported widespread inequities in the 2002 elections.

Zimbabwe's legal system is a mixture of Roman-Dutch and English common law. The judiciary consists of a Supreme Court, appointed by the President, and a High Court. President Mugabe has traditionally appointed political allies to the Supreme Court. Though legally independent of the executive branch, the judiciary has in practice only a limited ability to curtail the President's activities.

The legislative branch of government consists of the unicameral House of Assembly, which contains 150 seats: 120 of these are elected by popular vote to five-year terms; 12 are nominated by the President; 10 seats are occupied by tribal chiefs, who are chosen by their peers; and eight seats are occupied by provincial governors, who are appointed by the President. The Assembly has been accused of serving merely as a rubber-stamp for Mugabe.

Technically, Zimbabwe is a multi-party democracy. In practice, Mugabe's Zimbabwe African National Union (ZANU) party has dominated the nation's politics. However, the Movement for Democratic Change (MDC) party, founded in 1999, has gained strong support in urban areas and among young voters, and in 2000 won 57 seats in the National Assembly. Despite these successes, MDC supporters still face severe repression, and hundreds have been beaten and killed.

Reliable information on the penal and criminal justice systems in Zimbabwe is difficult to locate.

The prisons are overcrowded by about 20 percent; while severe compared to the Gambia, where prisons are at less than their official capacity, or to Nigeria, where overcrowding is at about seven percent, it is not as dire as in Kenya (128%), Tanzania (116%), Botswana (100%), or Mauritius (153%). A community service program for nonviolent offenders has been instituted in order to relieve the crowding.

Police Profile

The national police force of Zimbabwe is called the Zimbabwe Republic Police. This includes a Police Support Unit as well as Paramilitary Police. Reliable and easily accessible statistics regarding the history of the force, the number of officers, the organization of the force, and the functions of the police are not available. The Zimbabwean police have, however, been accused of wide-ranging human rights abuses in support of the Mugabe regime, including violence against opposition party members, threats towards white farm owners and workers, and threats towards black Zimbabweans living on communal land. The police force has also been used to suppress demonstrations against the Mugabe government.

Bibliography

CIA World Factbook: "Zimbabwe." www.cia.gov/cia/publications/factbook/geos/zi.html, 2005.

Eric Kibuka. "Prisons in Africa." *World Prison Population: Facts, Trends, and Solutions*. Vienna, Austria: United Nations Programme Network Institutes Technical Assistance Workshop, May 2001. www.unicri.it/pdf/un_workshop/kibuka.pdf.

Marshall, Monty G., and Keith Jaggers. "Polity IV Country Report 2003: Zimbabwe." *Polity IV Country Reports 2003*. College Park, MD: Center for International Development and Conflict Management, 2003.

Peter Takirambudde. "HRW Letter to the Southern African Development Community." Human Rights Watch, Africa Division; November 22, 2001. www.hrw.org/press/2001/11/zimlet1122.htm.

INDEX

A

B

Ba'athist Party
  Iraq, 399
    Syria, 816, 817, 819
Babovic, Budimir, 575, 733
Babovic, Milo, 575
Bacanovik, Oliver, 521
Badoglio, Pietro, 418
Baetolinga, Joe, 757
Bagaza, Jean-Baptiste, 142
Bagirov, Hasan, 63
Bahamas, The, 65, 66
Bahar, H.I., 861
Bahrain, 66–68
Bail
  Azerbaijan, 61
  Canada, 157
  Kuwait, 468
  Lesotho, 490
  Nepal, 593
  Swaziland, 799
Bajagic, Mladen, 733
Bakic Tomic, Ljubica, 216
Balague, Joaquin, 247
Balan, Oleg, 566
Bali bombing, 41, 44, 48
Balkan countries
  European Union relations, 282
  international cooperation
    Bosnia and Herzegovina, 118
    Greece, training assistance to, 336
    with Turkey, 860
Balkan émigrés, criminal operations in Czech Republic, 226
Balkan route, smuggling, 215, 226
Baltic Sea regional cooperation
  Denmark, 240
  Finland, 294
  Norway, 633
  Sweden, 807
Banda, Hastings Kamuzu, 524
Banditry
  Madagascar, 522
  Mali, 533, 534
  Somalia, 764
Bandourka, A., 876
Bangladesh, 68–73
  Congolese police force training, 195
  geography, society, demography, economy, 68, 69
  police system, 70–72
  political and legal system, 69, 70
Bank guard corps, Dominican Republic, 248
Banking sector, see Money laundering; Tax havens
Banks, Cyndi, 655
Banzer Suarez, Hugo, 104, 105, 107
Baranja, 34
Barbados, 73, 74
  international cooperation
    Caribbean Regional Security System, 704
    with Guyana, 354
    with St. Vincent and The Grenadines, 709
Barbuda, see Antigua and Barbuda
Bardales, Ernesto, 367
Barents Region, 633

Barrientes Ortuno, Rene, 107
Barros, L., 181
Bashir, Omar Hassan al-, 787
Basque country, 677, 773–779
Basque separatists (ETA)
  France, 299
  Portugal, 677
  Spain, 779
Batis, R., 755
Battuta, Ibn, 529
Bavig, Flemming, 241
Bayidikila, Alice Bienvenu, 202
Bayley, David, 983
Bazhanov, O.L., 78
Beare, Margaret, 161
Beheading, 642
Belarus, 74–78
Bele, Ivan, 754
Belgian law enforcement model, Congo (DRC), 192, 193
Belgium, 78–84; see also European Union
  colonial regimes
    Burundi, 142
    Congo, Democratic Republic of, 190, 191
    Rwanda, 697, 698
    Rwanda-Kigali, 142
  European Union, 279
  geography, society, demography, economy, 78, 79
  international cooperation
    with Cameroon, 155
    Congolese police force training, 194
    with France, 301
    with Russia, 695
    Schengen Information System (SIS), 323
    Somalia intervention (Operation Restore Hope), 764
    with Ukraine, 875
  Netherlands border area cooperation, 603
  police system, 79–84
    education, research, and publications, 82
    functions, 80
    international cooperation, 80–82
    organization of, 79, 80
    public projects, 80
    training, 80
    weapons/use of force, 80, 81
  political and legal system, 79
Belize, 84–92
  geography, society, demography, economy, 84, 85
  police system, 86–92
    crime statistics, 92
    functions, 89
    gun amnesty/cash for information program, 90, 91
    historical development, 86, 87
    organization of, 87–91
    public projects, 89, 90
    training, 89
    weapons/use of force, 91, 92
  political and legal system, 86
Bemba, Jean-Pierre, 192
Ben Ali, Zine El Abaidine, 854
Benelux treaties, Luxembourg, 514
Benin, 93–96
  early slave trade, 717
  human traffickers from, 847
  training at Cameroon National Police College, 154
Bertrand Gobela, Sosthène, 202

D

INDEX

L

V